INTERNATIONAL CRIMINAL LAW

INTERNATIONAL CRIMINAL LAW

KRIANGSAK KITTICHAISAREE

Honorary Visiting Fellow,
University of New South Wales School of Law

OXFORD
UNIVERSITY PRESS

OXFORD

UNIVERSITY PRESS

Great Clarendon Street, Oxford OX2 6DP

Oxford University Press is a department of the University of Oxford.
It furthers the University's objective of excellence in research, scholarship,
and education by publishing worldwide in

Oxford New York

Athens Auckland Bangkok Bogotá Buenos Aires Cape Town
Chennai Dar es Salaam Delhi Florence Hong Kong Istanbul Karachi
Kolkata Kuala Lumpur Madrid Melbourne Mexico City Mumbai Nairobi
Paris São Paulo Shanghai Singapore Taipei Tokyo Toronto Warsaw

with associated companies in Berlin Ibadan

Oxford is a registered trade mark of Oxford University Press
in the UK and in certain other countries

Published in the United States
by Oxford University Press Inc., New York

A catalogue record for this book is available from the British Library

Library of Congress Cataloging in Publication Data
Data available
ISBN 0–19–876577–0

Typeset by RefineCatch Limited, Bungay, Suffolk
Printed in Great Britain
on acid-free paper by
T.J. International Ltd., Padstow, Cornwall

PREFACE

A textbook on international criminal law is clearly needed in response to the increasingly considerable international interest in the subject. The Statute of the International Criminal Court has been adopted by the United Nations Conference of Plenipotentiaries on the Establishment of an International Criminal Court, held in Rome between 15 June and 17 July 1998. The Elements of Crimes and the Rules of Procedure and Evidence of the International Criminal Court have been adopted by the Preparatory Commission for the International Criminal Court since 30 June 2000. The International Criminal Tribunal for the Former Yugoslavia and that for Rwanda have delivered a series of judgments to elucidate their respective substantive laws, starting from July 1997. The worldwide publicity surrounding General Augusto Pinochet and his 'international crimes' has brought further attention to the relevance of international criminal law in our era. These developments seriously challenge or even disprove many premises and assumptions in the literature on the subject published before the last few months of 1998.

This book will endeavour to analyse systematically the current state of international criminal law. The book's objectives are: to make readers understand international criminal law; to develop readers' knowledge of international criminal law through critical assessment of the jurisprudence underpinning such law; and to develop readers' discipline in the advocacy of international criminal law. It will also fill the gaps in the existing literature by complementing the most recent publications that focus mainly on the legislative history of the Rome Statute or on certain issues pertaining to the initiation, function, jurisdiction, and viability of the International Criminal Court. Thus, it is hoped that students and practitioners of public international law, international human rights law, international humanitarian law, and international criminal law, as well as diplomats whose work touches on these fields, will find the book reasonably comprehensive in fulfilling their needs.

Part I introduces readers to the legal foundations of international criminal law. Part II analyses the substantive law of international crimes. Part III shows how various modes of perpetration of international crimes are criminalized, and the extent to which a person can invoke grounds (or 'defences') to exclude criminal responsibility. Part IV illustrates practical procedural and other issues and problems involved in the implementation of international criminal justice before international criminal tribunals. As there is usually no separate chapter on 'conclusions' in a textbook, a brief epilogue is offered instead. The four appendices should be useful sources of reference, and their contents will be reproduced elsewhere in the textbook only where they add something useful to the discussion.

Finally, this book is dedicated to the persons who appreciate the value of international criminal law and who also happen to be the world's most endangered species: rational and humane *Homo sapiens*.

K.K.

Sydney/Bangkok/New York
January 5, 2001

CONTENTS

PART III MODES OF PARTICIPATION AND GROUNDS FOR EXCLUDING CRIMINAL RESPONSIBILITY

PART IV PROCEDURAL AND OTHER ASPECTS

10 INITIATION OF PROCEEDINGS AND INTERNATIONAL COOPERATION

11 RIGHTS OF PARTIES

TABLE OF CASES

TABLE OF CONVENTIONS

ABBREVIATIONS

AJIL	*American Journal of International Law*
ALL ER	All England Law Reports
Ann. Dig.	*Annual Digest and Reports of Public International Law Cases,* vols. 1–16 (1932–55)
AP I	Protocol Additional to the Geneva Conventions of 12 August 1949, and Relating to the Protection of Victims of International Armed Conflicts, Geneva, 12 December 1977
AP II	Protocol Additional to the Geneva Conventions of 12 August 1949, and Relating to the Protection of Victims of Non-International Armed Conflicts, Geneva, 12 December 1977
App. Ch.	Appeals Chamber
Bevans	*Treaties and Other International Agreements of the United States of America, 1776–1949* (ed. C. F. Bevans, 1970), 13 vols.
BYBIL	*British Yearbook of International Law*
CMR	*Court-Martial Reports* (United States)
F. 2d	Federal Reporter, Second Series (United States)
F. Supp.	*Federal Supplement* (United States)
GC I	Geneva Convention for the Amelioration of the Condition of the Wounded and Sick in Armed Forces in the Field, 12 August 1949
GC II	Geneva Convention for the Amelioration of the Condition of Wounded, Sick and Shipwrecked Members of Armed Forces at Sea, 12 August 1949
GC III	Geneva Convention Relative to the Treatment of Prisoners of War, 12 August 1949
GC IV	Geneva Convention Relative to the Protection of Civilian Persons in Time of War
Hague Convention IV	The 1907 Hague Convention IV Respecting the Laws and Customs of War on Land, 18 October 1907
Hague Recueil	*Recueil des cours de l'Académie de droit international de la Haye*
Hague Regulations (1907)	Regulations Respecting the Laws and Customs of War on Land, 18 October 1907, annexed to the 1907 Hague Convention IV Respecting the Laws and Customs of War on Land
ICC	International Criminal Court

ICC Statute	Statute of the International Criminal Court, adopted at the Rome Conference on 17 July 1998
ICJ	International Court of Justice
ICJ Rep.	International Court of Justice Reports: Judgments, Advisory Opinions and Orders
ICRC	International Committee of the Red Cross
ICTR	International Criminal Tribunal for the Prosecution of Persons Responsible for Genocide and Other Serious Violations of International Humanitarian Law Committed in the Territory of Rwanda and Rwandan Citizens Responsible for Genocide and other such Violations Committed in the Territory of Neighbouring States, between 1 January 1994 and 31 December 1994
ICTR Statute	Statute of the ICTR
ICTY	International Tribunal for the Prosecution of Persons Responsible for Serious Violations of International Humanitarian Law Committed in the Territory of the Former Yugoslavia since 1991
ICTY Statute	Statute of the ICTY
ILC	International Law Commission
ILM	*International Legal Materials*
ILR	*International Law Reports*, vol. 17– (1956–) [Previously published as *Ann. Dig.*]
Nuremberg Charter	Charter of the Military Tribunal at Nuremberg annexed to the Agreement for the Prosecution and Punishment of Major War Criminals of the European Axis, London, 8 August 1945
Nuremberg Proceedings	*The Trials of German Major War Criminals: Proceedings of the International Military Tribunal Sitting at Nuremberg, Germany*, Part 22 (H. M. Stationery Office, 1950), Judgment, 411 ff.
Nuremberg Tribunal	The International Military Tribunal Sitting at Nuremberg, Germany
PCIJ	Permanent Court of International Justice
PCNICC	Preparatory Commission for the International Criminal Court, 1999–
Rome Conference	United Nations Diplomatic Conference of Plenipotentiaries on the Establishment of an International Criminal Court (15 June–17 July 1998)
Stat.	*United States Statutes at Large*
Tadic Appeals Judgment	*Prosecutor v. Dusko Tadic*, Case No. IT-94-1-A, Appeals Chamber of the ICTY, 15 July 1999

Tadic Judgment	*Prosecutor v. Dusko Tadic*, Case No. IT-94-1-T, Trial Chamber II of the ICTY, 7 May 1997
Tadic Jurisdiction Decision	*Prosecutor v. Dusko Tadic*, Case No. IT-94-1-AR72, Appeals Chamber of the ICTY, Decision on the Defence Motion for Interlocutory Appeal on Jurisdiction, 2 October 1995
Tadic Sentencing Judgment	*Prosecutor v. Dusko Tadic*, Case No. IT-94-l-A and IT-94-1-A*bis*, Appeals Chamber of the ICTY, 26 January 2000
T. Ch.	Trial Chamber
Tokyo Charter	Charter of the International Military Tribunal for the Far East, approved by the Supreme Commander of the Allied Powers on 19 January 1946, and amended by General Order No. 20 of the Supreme Commander, General Headquarters, APO 500, 26 April 1946
Tokyo Tribunal	The International Military Tribunal for the Far East Sitting at Tokyo, Japan
TWC	Trials of War Criminals before the Nürnberg Military Tribunals under Control Council Law No. 10, Nürnberg, October 1946–April 1949, 15 vols. (US Govt. Printing Office, 1949–53)
UN GAOR	UN General Assembly Official Records
UNTS	*UN Treaty Series*
UNWCC *Law Reports*	United Nations War Crimes Commission: *Law Reports of Trials of War Criminals*, 15 vols. (H. M. Stationery Office, 1947–49)
US	Reports of the Supreme Court of the United States
USC	*United States Code*

PART I

LEGAL FOUNDATIONS

1

REVIEW OF RELEVANT CONCEPTS

1.1 INTERNATIONAL CRIMINAL LAW

What is an international crime, and why has the international community succeeded in adopting the Statute of the International Criminal Court (hereinafter the 'ICC Statute') only recently—in July 1998?

In *re List and Others*, the US Military Tribunal at Nuremberg defined an 'international crime' as follows:

'An international crime is such act universally recognized as criminal, which is considered a grave matter of international concern and for some valid reason cannot be left within the exclusive jurisdiction of the State that would have control over it under ordinary circumstances . . .'[1]   *defⁿ*

It is the international community of nations that determines which crimes fall within this definition in light of the latest developments in law, morality, and the sense of criminal justice at the relevant time. Apartheid, for example, was not recognized as an international crime until quite recently. It is correct to contend that what acts should be characterized as international crimes depends on the machinery by which such acts are to be dealt with.[2] As generally understood, since the UN Conference of Plenipotentiaries for the Establishment of an International Criminal Court in June and July 1998, international crimes are those prosecuted before an international criminal tribunal, whether *ad hoc* or permanent.

International criminal law is the law that governs international crimes. It may be said that this discipline of law is where the penal aspects of international law, including that body of law protecting victims of armed conflict known as international humanitarian law and the international aspects of national criminal law converge.[3]

International criminal law is distinguishable from international human rights law

---

[1] *Hostages Trial*, US Military Tribunal at Nuremberg, 19 Feb. 1948 (1953) **15** *Ann. Dig.* 632 at 636.

[2] M. M. Whiteman, *Digest of International Law*, xi (US Dept. of State, 1968), 835.

[3] J. J. Paust, M. Cherif Bassiouni, S. A. Williams, M. Scharf, J. Gurulé, and B. Zagaris (eds.), *International Criminal Law: Cases and Materials* (Carolina Academic Press, 1996), 3–19. However, in view of the latest developments that culminated in the adoption of the Rome Statute of the International Criminal Court, the elaboration of the meaning and content of international criminal law as appeared in ibid., 3–19, may not be all valid.

in general as well as from national criminal law.[4] The International Criminal Court to be set up under the ICC Statute, for example, is to punish 'the most serious crimes of concern to the international community as a whole',[5] not mere violations of human rights law, although the application and interpretation of the law of the ICC Statute must be consistent with 'internationally recognized human rights', as required by Article 21(3) of the Statute itself.

Compared to other branches of law, international criminal law has been slow in crystallization as a viable legal system. Foremost among the reasons hindering its development is the shield of State sovereignty and its attendant ramifications.

1.2 SOVEREIGNTY

The concept of sovereignty has been asserted vigorously in three different phases in the history of the international legal order.

The first phase came in 1648. Until then, the concept of 'natural law' had been widely accepted as a law higher than all laws enacted by rulers and one which all rulers must obey.[6]

The doctrine of sovereignty was first enunciated explicitly in 1576 by Jean Bodin in his treatise *De Republica* based on his observations of political facts in France at that time. Bodin defined the essence of statehood as the unity of its government under '*majesta*' (sovereignty) from which a State's law proceeded. The essential manifestation of sovereignty was the power to make laws and as the sovereign made laws he was not bound by the laws made by him but was bound only by the divine law of nature or reason.[7] In the Middle Ages, the Holy Roman Emperor and the Pope were the absolute power in Europe under the Holy Roman Empire. The Thirty-Year's War among several European powers from 1618–48 ended with the Peace of Westphalia of 1648 which broke up the Holy Roman Empire and led to the emergence of sovereign States in Europe.[8]

The doctrine of State sovereignty was asserted by sovereign monarchs to be free from the authority of the Pope. At first, it was an assertion of the divine right to rule,

---

[4] This view was propounded by the Delegations of Sweden, the United Arab Emirates, and Bahrain, among others, at the 5th Sess. of the Preparatory Commission for the International Criminal Court, held in June 2000.

[5] Fourth preambular paragraph of the ICC Statute.

[6] E-I. Daes, *Status of Individual and Contemporary International Law: Promotion, Protection and Restoration of Human Rights at National, Regional, and International Levels* (United Nations, 1992), 15–17.

[7] J. L. Brierly, *The Law of Nations: An Introduction to the International Law of Peace*, 6th ed. C. H. M. Waldock (Clarendon Press, 1963), 7–10.

[8] The Holy Roman Empire was replaced in July 1806 by the Confederation of the Rhine under the control of Napoleon. It was formally dissolved on 6 Aug. 1806 by the Habsburg Emperor Francis. See L. S. Sunga, *The Emergence of a System of International Criminal Law: Development in Codification and Implementation* (Kluwer, 1997), 335–8. Cf. L. Gross, 'The Peace of Westphalia, 1648–1948' (1948) **42** *AJIL* 20.

and, subsequently, of the absolute power of the State to rule. The transition was from the supremacy of God to the supremacy of the State; that is, from the supremacy of natural law to positivism in international law. The law binding on the international community was now the law which all nations, or at least the majority of them, agreed upon through the usages or practices followed in their international intercourse.

From 1648 to 1815, international law was concerned with rules of non-interference in other States' affairs. The Congress of Vienna of 1815, which was held after the defeat of Napoleon, aimed to achieve an international law based on international co-operation to maintain the balance of power. States jointly prohibited slave-trading and piracy on the high seas, and undertook to prosecute offenders under their respective criminal law.

In essence, State sovereignty as traditionally understood had three legal implications. Firstly, the ruler of a particular State had the sole and exclusive authority and autonomy over his territory. Secondly, States were treated as legally equal to one another in terms of rights, obligations, and autonomy. Thirdly, as a consequence of these two implications, States were subject to no higher law except the law created by their consent through treaties, customs, and general principles recognized by them.[9]

Almost three centuries later, in 1927, the Permanent Court of International Justice stated in the *Lotus Case (France v. Turkey)* that:

'International law governs relations between independent States. The rules of law binding upon States therefore emanate from their own free will as expressed in conventions or by usages generally accepted as expressing principles of law and established in order to regulate the relations between these co-existing communities or with a view to the achievement of common aims. Restrictions upon independence of States cannot therefore be presumed. Now the first and foremost restriction imposed by international law upon a State is that— failing the existence of a permissive rule to the contrary—it may not exercise its power in any form in the territory of another State. In this sense jurisdiction is certainly territorial; it cannot be exercised by a State outside its territory except by virtue of a permissive rule derived from international custom or from a convention. It does not, however, follow that international law prohibits a State from exercising jurisdiction in its own territory, in respect of any case which relates to acts which have taken place abroad, and in which it cannot rely on some permissive rule of international law. Far from laying down a general prohibition to the effect that States may not extend the application of their laws and the jurisdiction of their courts to persons, property and acts outside their territory, [international law] leaves them in this respect a wide measure of discretion which is only limited in certain cases by prohibitive rules . . .'[10]

The second phase of the resurgence of the concept of sovereignty came with the adoption of the United Nations Charter after WWII. Article 2(1) of the Charter provides that the United Nations (UN) 'is based on the principle of sovereign equality

---

[9] Brierly, *Law of Nations*, 7–16, 51–2; A. C. Arend and R. J. Beck, *International Law and the Use of Force: Beyond the UN Charter Paradigm* (Routledge, 1993), 16.

[10] (1927) PCIJ Rep., Series A, No. 10, at 18–19.

leadership / predominance

of all its members'. The rationale behind this is to pre-empt assertion of hegemony by one State over another, as Germany and Japan did during WWII. Furthermore, Article 2(7) of the Charter proscribes intervention 'in matters which are essentially within the domestic jurisdiction of any State'. The Charter does not provide for compulsory settlement of disputes. Only in the extreme case of threats to the peace, breaches of the peace, and acts of aggression could the UN Security Council resort to enforcement measures pursuant to Chapter VII of the Charter to compel compliance by deviant States.

C.

The third phase of the reassertion of the importance of State sovereignty came with the advent of de-colonization in the 1950s and the 1960s. Newly independent African and Asian States decried interference in any forms with their domestic affairs. The advent of de-colonization has further entrenched the doctrine of State sovereignty. It is interesting to note that UN General Assembly Resolution 49/186 of 1994, sponsored by a coalition of Third World States and rejected by the West by the vote of 110 in favour, 35 against, and 24 abstaining, emphasized 'respect for the independence, sovereignty and territorial integrity of each State . . . with a view to solving international economic, social and humanitarian problems; . . .'

Although the strength of sovereignty in an interdependent world may be on the wane, with political decisions taken by the international community to intervene, for example, in South Africa to end the apartheid regime there,[11] international law is slow to negate the international 'legal' concept of sovereignty *in toto*. As late as 1986, the International Court of Justice held in *Military and Paramilitary Activities in and against Nicaragua (Nicaragua v. US)* (Merits) that '[a] State's domestic policy falls within its exclusive jurisdiction, provided of course that it does not violate any obligation of international law . . .'[12] As will be seen shortly, obligations of international law are, in turn, formed by the consent of sovereign States themselves.

Ramifications of the entrenchment of the concept of State sovereignty in terms of international criminal law include the following. There shall be no interference in domestic affairs of another sovereign State, and this also leads to the doctrine of sovereign or State immunity and the act of State doctrine that shields foreign States from legal action in the court of another State. Territoriality is the primary basis for criminal jurisdiction.[13] In these circumstances, how could the international community of States forge an international criminal legal regime to prosecute and punish atrocities committed within the territory of a sovereign State? Such atrocities are frequently ordered or condoned by the people in control of national power who are immune *de facto* and/or *de jure* from criminal prosecution and punishment under their domestic legal system.

NB! ✗ The question

---

[11] See H. J. Steiner and P. Alston, *International Human Rights in Context: Law, Politics, Morals* (Clarendon Press, 1996), 364–73, on the waning obstacle of domestic jurisdiction, with case studies of apartheid in South Africa and martial law in Poland.

[12] ICJ Rep. 1986, 14 at 131.

[13] Cf. I. Brownlie, *Principles of Public International Law*, 5th ed. (Oxford University Press, 1998), 289–90.

1.3 SUBJECTS OF INTERNATIONAL LAW

As a corollary, since the State is a collective entity that includes individuals within that State, it is the State that acts on the international plane. According to the ninth edition of the classic treatise *Oppenheim's International Law*, published in 1992, the State, not the individual within a State, is responsible for international wrongs or for conduct in breach of international obligations. This is because '[s]uch responsibility attaches to a State by virtue of its position as an international person'.[14]

In 1976, the International Law Commission (ILC) adopted the concept of international crimes of States in Article 19 of its Draft Articles on State Responsibility. This proposal has generated much controversy. Article 19 of the Draft stipulates:

'1. An act of a State which constitutes a breach of an international obligation is an internationally wrongful act, regardless of the subject-matter of the obligation breached.

2. An internationally wrongful act which results from the breach by a State of an international obligation so essential for the protection of fundamental interests of the international community that its breach is recognized as a crime by the community as a whole constitutes an international crime.

3. Subject to paragraph 2, and on the basis of the rules of international law in force, an international crime may result, *inter alia*, from:

   (a) a serious breach of an international obligation of essential importance for the maintenance of international peace and security, such as that prohibiting aggression;

   (b) a serious breach of an international obligation of essential importance for safeguarding the right of self-determination of peoples, such as that prohibiting the establishment and maintenance by force of colonial domination;

   (c) a serious breach on a widespread scale of an international obligation of essential importance for safeguarding the human being, such as those prohibiting slavery, genocide, and apartheid;

   (d) a serious breach of an international obligation of essential importance for the safeguarding and preservation of the human environment, such as those prohibiting massive pollution of the atmosphere or of the seas.

4. Any internationally wrongful act which is not an international crime in accordance with paragraph 2 constitutes an international delict.'

The idea behind this provision in the Draft Articles originated from Garcia Amador, the ILC's first special *rapporteur* on State Responsibility. In his opinion expressed in 1956, crimes under international law committed by individuals who are organs of the

---

[14] Sir Robert Jennings and Sir Arthur Watts (eds.), *Oppenheim's International Law*, 9th ed., i, Peace: Introduction and Part I (Longman, 1992), 501.

State and are acting as such are 'punishable' in the sense that the individuals could be pursued and punished by States other than the State of which they are organs. However, this idea was not supported by the other members of the ILC because it would not be appropriate to deal with the issue of punishment of State organs in the context of codification of the law on State responsibility.[15] The idea was revived in 1976 by another special *rapporteur*, Professor Roberto Ago, who drew the ILC's attention to the development of international law since the end of WWII that recognized criminal responsibility for breaches of certain particularly important obligations, such as the obligation not to commit genocide or to wage a war of aggression. He suggested that the ILC reflect this development in its work. His view attained the immediate support of almost all the ILC members; hence, Article 19 of the Draft Articles on State Responsibility.[16] It should be noted, however, that it is the State that would bear responsibility for a crime attributable to it by acts of individuals acting as its organ.[17] Such responsibility would include non-recognition of the situation created by such a crime and not giving aid or assistance to the maintenance of the situation created by such a crime.[18]

The ILC proceeded along this route because it had suspended its work on the Draft Code of Offences against the Peace and Security of Mankind since 1954. The Draft Code would incorporate the concept of individual criminal responsibility pronounced by the International Military Tribunal at Nuremberg and the International Military Tribunal for the Far East right after WWII—a matter discussed in the next chapter. However, without an acceptable definition of 'aggression' in international law, the ILC could not proceed on the Draft Code any further. 'Aggression' was defined in 1974 by UN General Assembly Resolution 3314. Not until 1981 did the UN General Assembly, in its Resolution 36/106, invite the ILC to resume its work on the Draft Code, taking into account developments in international law since 1954. The ILC decided in 1984 to resume its work on the Draft Code by focusing on the responsibility of individuals, postponing to a later stage a decision on whether to contain rules on State responsibility for international crimes in the Draft Code as well.[19]

The long-entrenched concept of sovereignty stood in the way of efforts to realize the responsibility of the individual on the international plane. In November 1989, the UN Centre for Human Rights Special *Rapporteur* Erica-Irene Daes concluded her

---

[15] (1956) ii *Yearbook of the ILC* 105, 182–3, 211–3; ibid., i, 219–20, 228, 231, 237–42, 246. Also cited in M. Spinedi, 'Crimes of State: The Legislative History', in J. H. H. Weiler, A. Cassese, and M. Spinedi (eds.), *International Crimes of State: A Critical Analysis of the ILC's Draft Article 19 on State Responsibility* (Walter de Gruyter, 1989), 7 at 11–12.

[16] (1976) i *Yearbook of the ILC* 8 ff; ibid., ii, 24–54. Also cited in Spinedi, 'Crimes of State', 21–3.

[17] (1976) i *Yearbook of the ILC* 253.

[18] Art. 14 of the Draft Articles on State Responsibility submitted by the Special *Rapporteur*, Prof. Riphagen, in 1984. Fifth Rep. of the Special *Rapporteur* (*Doc. A/ CN. 4/ 380*), at 4–9.

[19] Rep. of the ILC on the Work of its Thirty-Sixth Sess., *Doc. A/ 39/ 10*, chap. II, para. 32. Cited in Spinedi, 'Crimes of State', 110–2.

report on the Status of the Individual and Contemporary International Law. The report was based on a comparative study of the major legal systems, theories, and State practice related to the subject, as evident from, *inter alia*, replies to her questionnaires by Governments, specialized agencies of the UN, regional organizations, nongovernmental organizations, and the writings of recognized scholars on the subject. The report concludes:

'The subjectivity of the individual in contemporary international law still remains controversial; it seems still difficult to formulate one doctrine which reflects both a general consensus between scholars, lawyers of different legal systems, and conformity with State practice in the world community.

. . .

Though international law aims at regulating human relations and originated in the necessity of intercourse between human beings, nevertheless, as a rule under classical international law, its main purpose was the regulation of the relations between States, which were considered the exclusive subject of international law and individuals only its objects.'[20]

State responsibility and individual criminal responsibility under international law are not the same thing. For instance, for an individual to be held criminally liable for an act of genocide under international law, he would have to be prosecuted and punished by an international criminal tribunal applying an international criminal statute.[21] In the case of State responsibility, contemporary international law only permits one State to demand that the State committing genocide cease and desist from committing genocide against nationals of the victim State; wipe out the consequences of genocide and restore the situations existing before the genocide; and provide to the victim State, in its own right and as *parens patriae* for its citizens, compensation for the damage and losses caused by another State committing genocide against the nationals of the victim State.[22]

---

[20] Daes, *Status of Individual*, 56. It should be noted, however, that Daes treats the post-WWII prosecution of individuals before the Nuremberg Tribunal for war crimes, crimes against humanity, and aggression, as well as their prosecution in national courts for piracy, as signifying that the individuals were 'subjects of international duties' (ibid., 40–4). This conclusion is rather unorthodox . As will be seen, such prosecution has been generally considered under the notion 'individual criminal responsibility' on the international plane; that is, individuals can also be 'subjects of international law'.

[21] If a perpetrator of genocide is tried in the domestic court of his State or another State to which he is extradited, either of these courts will be applying its own domestic law. Individual criminal responsibility under domestic law is not controversial. It has been recognized by the international community from time immemorial.

[22] See, e.g. *Case Concerning Application of the Convention on the Prevention and Punishment of the Crime of Genocide (Bosnia-Herzegovina v. Yugoslavia)*, (Preliminary Objections), ICJ Judgment of 11 July 1996, paras. 13–14. The same type of remedy is being sought by Croatia against Yugoslavia for the latter's alleged violation of the Genocide Convention.

1.4 FORMULATION AND OPERATION OF INTERNATIONAL LAW

CONSENT IN THE FORMULATION OF INTERNATIONAL LAW

An authoritative reference to sources of international law can be found in Article 38(1) of the Statute of the International Court of Justice (ICJ). By virtue of that provision, the ICJ shall apply: (a) international conventions establishing rules *expressly recognized* by the contesting States; (b) international customs, as evidenced of a general practice *accepted as law*; (c) the general principles of law *recognized* by civilized nations; and (d) judicial decisions and teachings of the most highly qualified publicists of the various nations, as 'subsidiary' means for the determination of rules of law.

The requirement of consent of sovereign States permeates the 'primary', as opposed to 'subsidiary', sources of international law. The case of treaties is obvious, they bind States that consent to be bound thereby. As for international customs, they crystallize through extensive and virtually uniform State practice, including that of a State whose interests are specially affected, in such a way as to show a general recognition that a rule of law or legal obligation is involved.[23]

As late as 1986 and 1996, the ICJ affirmed the classic pronouncement in the *Lotus* Case that sovereign States are bound only by rules of international law which they have consented to. In the *Nicaragua* Case, it was held that 'in international law there are no rules . . . whereby the level of armaments of a sovereign State can be limited'.[24] This was also referred to by the ICJ in its Advisory Opinion on *Legality of the Threat or Use of Nuclear Weapons* of 8 July 1996. According to the ICJ, State practice shows that the illegality of the use of certain weapons, such as nuclear weapons, must be formulated in terms of prohibition, but at the current stage of development in international law States have not been able to conclude a treaty of general prohibition of nuclear weapons. Hence, there is in neither customary nor conventional law any specific authorization or any comprehensive and universal prohibition of the threat or use of nuclear weapons as such.[25]

Therefore, in order to prosecute an individual before an international criminal tribunal, sovereign States must consent to this kind of action. They have been unwilling, at least until recently, to let this happen as it would undermine the notion of sovereignty that includes the sovereign power to prosecute perpetrators of crimes committed within their respective territories.

---

[23] *North Sea Continental Shelf Cases*, ICJ Rep. 1969, 3 at paras. 71 ff. On the question of the right of States to 'opt out' of being bound by customary international law, see J. I. Charney, 'The Persistent Objector Rule and the Development of Customary International Law' (1985) **85** *BYBIL* 1; C. Tomuschat, 'Obligations arising from States without or against their will', *Hague Recueil* 241 (1993-IV), 195 at 283 ff; Brierly, *Law of Nations*, 51–6.

[24] ICJ Rep. 1986, at 135.

[25] ICJ Advisory Opinion of 8 July 1996, paras. 21, 52 ff.

LEGAL STANDING TO TAKE ACTION *ACTIO POPULARIS*

Generally, the right residing in any member of a community to take legal action in vindication of a public interest (*actio popularis*) on the international plane is hollow in practice.

Once, there was a high hope that such right would be realistically enforceable since the ICJ referred to it in *Barcelona Traction (Second Phase)*. In that case, Belgium brought a claim before the ICJ against Spain as a result of the adjudication in bankruptcy in Spain of Barcelona Traction, a company incorporated in Canada. Belgium sought reparation for damage alleged by Belgium to have been sustained by Belgian nationals, shareholders in the company, as a consequence of acts said to violate international law committed towards the company by organs of the Spanish State. The ICJ found that Belgium lacked legal standing (*jus standi*) to exercise diplomatic protection of shareholders in a Canadian company because international law only recognizes such legal standing of the State of nationality of the aggrieved party to assert diplomatic protection or a claim *vis-à-vis* another State. The ICJ then went on to distinguish between inter-State obligations on the one hand, and obligations towards the international community as a whole, on the other. It said:

'. . . [A]n essential distinction should be drawn between the *obligations of a State towards the international community as a whole*, and those arising *vis-à-vis* another State . . . By their very nature, the former are the *concern of all States. In view of the importance of the rights involved, all States can be held to have a legal interest in their protection*; they are obligations *erga omnes*. Such obligations derive, for example, in contemporary international law, from the outlawing of acts of aggression, and of genocide, as also from the principles and rules concerning the basic rights of human persons, including protection from slavery and racial discrimination. Some of the corresponding rights of protection have entered into the body of general international law . . . ; others are conferred by international instruments of a universal or quasi-universal character.'[26]

Thus, while it is generally necessary for a State to establish its right to bring a claim in respect of the breach of an obligation the performance of which is the subject of diplomatic protection, every State has a legal interest in the observance of obligations *erga omnes*.

This pronouncement by the ICJ might be an apology for and a departure from its negative posture in *South West Africa Cases (Second Phase)*, decided a few years earlier, by the ICJ President's casting vote, the votes being equally divided (seven-seven). Then, the ICJ had ruled that neither Liberia nor Ethiopia had legal standing to challenge the policy of apartheid implemented by South Africa in South West Africa (Namibia) in disregard of the League of Nations Mandate entrusted to South Africa to promote the material and moral well-being and the social progress of the inhabitants of that territory. The ICJ rejected the principle of 'sacred trust of civilization' cited by

---

[26] *Case Concerning the Barcelona Traction, Light and Power Company, Limited (Second Phase)*, ICJ Rep. 1970, 3 at 32. Emphasis added.

Liberia and Ethiopia as a basis of their legal right or interest in the conduct of the Mandate by South Africa. According to the ICJ in that case, the principle of 'sacred trust' was no more than a moral or humanitarian ideal, without residual judicial content that would operate in itself to give rise to legal rights and obligations. In its view, international law as it stood at that time did not know 'an *actio populanis*, or right resident in any member of the international community in vindication of a public interest'.[27] The ICJ's pronouncement in *Barcelona Traction* is therefore a welcome development.[28]

A relevant issue is the category of acts that can be characterized as being subject to obligations *erga omnes*. The ICJ in *Barcelona Traction* cited some examples, all of which could be classified as *jus cogens* or 'peremptory norm of international law'. Article 53 of the Vienna Convention on the Law of Treaties of 1969[29] stipulates that a treaty is void if, at the time of its conclusion, it conflicts with a peremptory norm of general international law. The Article defines a peremptory norm as 'a norm accepted and recognized by the international community of States as a whole as a norm from which no derogation is permitted and which can be modified only by a subsequent norm of general international law having the same character'. Article 64 of the 1969 Convention calls this norm *jus cogens* and stipulates that if a new peremptory norm of international law emerges, any existing treaty in conflict with this norm becomes void and terminates. There is no criteria to define how and when a norm becomes a *jus cogens*, however. It seems that one has to look for the answer in pronouncements of international tribunals and from State practice for further indication.

Optimism regarding the implication of obligations *erga omnes* has been shattered by the ICJ Judgment in *Case Concerning East Timor (Portugal v. Australia)* instituted by Portugal against Australia. Portugal contended, *inter alia*, that Australia's conclusion of an agreement with Indonesia with respect to maritime areas lying between Australia and East Timor, then occupied by Indonesia, failed to observe the right of the people of East Timor to self-determination and the related rights. The case was dismissed because Indonesia did not consent to the ICJ's jurisdiction. ICJ reasoned that it had no jurisdiction over a third party to a dispute unless that third party submitted to the ICJ's jurisdiction in that particular case. The ICJ rejected Portugal's argument that the rights which Australia had allegedly breached were rights *erga omnes* and as such permitted Portugal to sue Australia individually, regardless of whether or not another State had conducted itself in a similarly unlawful manner. While the ICJ fully shared the assertion of Portugal that the right of peoples to self-determination had an *erga omnes* character, the ICJ considered that the *erga omnes* character of a norm and the principle of consent to the ICJ's jurisdiction were two

---

[27] ICJ Rep. 1966, 6, esp. at 47.

[28] See further A. de Hoogh, *Obligations* Erga Omnes *and International Crimes: A Theoretical Inquiry into the Implementation and Enforcement of the International Responsibility of States* (Kluwer, 1996), chap. 2; M. Byers, 'Conceptualizing the Relationship between *Jus Cogens* and *Erga Omnes* Rules' (1997) **66** *Nordic J. Int'l L.* 211.

[29] (1969) **8** *ILM* 679.

different things. Whatever the nature of the obligations invoked, the ICJ could not rule on the lawfulness of the conduct of a State when its judgment would imply an evaluation of the lawfulness of the conduct of another State not a party to the case. Where this is so, the ICJ cannot act, even if the right in question is a right *erga omnes*.[30]

Therefore, the international community still faces an impediment to its assertion of *actio popularis*. Even if one State has legal standing because of the *erga omnes* nature of the rights being violated, it cannot take the offending State to the ICJ if the latter State does not consent to the ICJ's jurisdiction in that case! Only those States honestly convinced that their conduct does not fall foul of international law would be willing to subject themselves to action of this kind before the ICJ.

In sum, State consent has once again prevented the use of international legal standing to prevent or punish violations of fundamental human rights that the international community would characterize as 'international crimes'.

1.5 PRINCIPLE OF LEGALITY

The notion of State sovereignty and its attendant ramifications was also linked to another entrenched principle that once impeded developments of international criminal law—the principle of legality. This principle is peculiar to criminal justice.

The Permanent Court of International Justice, the forerunner of the ICJ, gave an Advisory Opinion on the *Consistency of Certain Danzig Legislative Decrees with the Constitution of the Free City, 4 December 1935* that touched on the principle of legality as follows:

'The problem of the repression of crime may be approached from two different standpoints, that of the individual and that of the community. From the former standpoint, the object is to protect the individual against the State: this object finds its expression in the maxim *Nulla poena sine lege*. From the second standpoint, the object is to protect the community against the criminal, the basic principle being the notion *Nullum crimen sine poena*. . . . It must be possible for the individual to know, beforehand, whether his acts are lawful or liable to punishment.'[31]

This principle has lasted till the present day. Its modern version is enshrined in Article 11(2) of the Universal Declaration of Human Rights:[32]

'No one shall be held guilty of any penal offence on account of any act or omission which did not constitute a penal offence, under national or international law, at the time when it

---

[30] ICJ Rep. 1995, 90 at 102. See also A. J. J. de Hoogh, 'Australia and East Timor: Rights *Erga Omnes*, Complicity and Non-Recognition' (1999) *Australia Int'l L. J.* 63.

[31] (1935) PCIJ Rep., Series A/B, No. 65, 3 at 514.

[32] Adopted 10 Dec. 1948, UN GA Res. 217A (III), *UN Doc. A/ 810 (1948)*, at 47.

was committed. Nor shall a heavier penalty be imposed than the one that was applicable at the time the penal offence was committed.'

In order not to offend this principle of legality, prosecution of individuals before an international criminal tribunal applying international criminal law would require proof of the pre-existence of at least two things. First, there would have to be international recognition or precedents that an individual, as opposed to a State, could be subject to criminal punishment by an international tribunal. Secondly, the conduct for which the individual could be guilty would have to be proscribed by the international community of States as a crime subject to international sanction, with a clear set of penalties.[33] These conditions are difficult to fulfil as long as an international criminal code does not exist.

Prior to the judgment of the International Military Tribunal set up to prosecute major Nazi war criminals after WWII, attempts were made to find such precedents, international recognition, or international proscription, but to no avail.

One oft-cited precedent is the trial and execution of Sir Peter von Hagenbach in Breisach, Austria, in 1474.[34] He was tried for atrocities committed against civilians in Breisach in an attempt to force them to submit to the rule of Duke Charles of Burgundy. After the deliberation of the town by Austria and its allies (Berne, France, and the towns and knights of the Upper Rhine), he was arraigned before a tribunal of twenty-eight judges from the allied States and constituted specially for his trial. The tribunal convicted him of murder, rape, perjury, and other crimes against the 'laws of God and man', stripped him of knighthood, and sentenced him to death. Commentators find some caveats about treating this case as a precedent for international criminal sanction against individuals. The twenty-eight judges were drawn from the confederate entities of the Holy Roman Empire, thus depriving the tribunal of its 'international' character, and the law applied was, therefore, not 'international' law.[35]

Another classic example cited by commentators is piracy under international law (*jure gentium*). As stated by Judge Moore in the *Lotus* Case before the Permanent Court of International Justice, any nation may, in the interest of all, exercise jurisdiction to capture and punish piracy by law of nations, and a pirate is subject to a universal jurisdiction of every State which may try and punish him if he comes within its jurisdiction.[36] In fact, any State may assert jurisdiction over piracy although the elements of the offence of piracy under their respective national laws may vary. Some States may simply wish to exert criminal jurisdiction over certain acts considered by them to deserve punishment although such acts are not piracy as defined by international law. The modern definition of piracy *jure gentium* appears in Article 101(a)

---

[33] For a detailed analysis of the principle of legality, see M. C. Bassiouni and P. Manikas, *The Law of the International Criminal Tribunal for the Former Yugoslavia* (Transnational Publishers, 1996), 265–91.

[34] Discussed in T. L. H. McCormack, 'From Sun Tzu to the Sixth Committee: The Evolution of an International Criminal Regime', in T. L. H. McCormack and G. J. Simpson, *The Law of War Crimes: National and International Approaches* (Kluwer, 1997), 31 at 37–9.

[35] Ibid., 38–9; R. K. Woetzel, *The Nuremberg Trials in International Law* (Stevens & Sons, 1962), 19–22.

[36] (1927) PCIJ Rep. Series A, No. 10, at 70.

of the UN Convention on the Law of the Sea of 1982.[37] It is 'any illegal acts of violence or detention, or any act of depredation, committed for private ends by the crew or the passengers of a private ship or a private aircraft, and directed: (i) on the high seas, against another ship or aircraft, or against persons or property on board such ship or aircraft; (ii) against a ship, aircraft, persons or property in a place outside the jurisdiction of any State'. The main rationale behind this 'universal jurisdiction' is the *lacuna* in the jurisdiction on the high seas and a place outside jurisdiction of any State (for example, no man's land or *terra nullius*), and the fact that pirates deserve to be treated as enemies of all mankind (*hostis humani generis*).[38] However, pirates are tried by municipal courts and punishable under municipal law, not international law. International law merely concedes that every State has universal jurisdiction to try and punish pirates when they come within their respective jurisdiction.

These 'precedents' were not accepted as sufficient to fulfil the principle of legality when attempts were being made to set up international tribunals before the end of WWII.

In 1919, at the end of WWI, a Commission on the Responsibility of the Authors of the War and on Enforcement of Penalties listed at least thirty-two categories of violations of the laws and customs of war committed by the government and armed forces of Germany, Italy, and their allies during WWI. The Commission proposed that the envisaged peace treaties confer criminal jurisdiction over the persons involved in the violations, particularly the German Emperor Kaiser Wilhelm II. The applicable law would be 'the principles of the law of nations as they result from the usages established among civilized peoples, from the laws of humanity and from the dictates of public conscience'. The proposal failed after being opposed by the US, contending that war crimes should be punished by domestic courts, not by an *ad hoc* international tribunal, otherwise it would violate the principle of legality. According to the US, the laws of humanity would amount to *ex post facto* laws since they had not been in existence before. The matter came to an end when the Netherlands refused to extradite the Kaiser on the grounds that the offence of the supreme offence against international morality and the sanctity of treaties he was charged with was political in nature and not punishable according to Dutch law.[39]

The same principle of legality impeded prosecution of Turkey's leaders for their attempted extermination of the Armenian people in 1915.[40] It was alleged that Turkey had undertaken systematic deportation of Armenians from their homeland to the desert of Northern Syria, together with extensive killings to further a Turkish nationalistic goal. The Joint Declaration by Russia, France, and Britain of May 1915 warned the Turkish Government that: 'In view of these crimes of Turkey against humanity and civilization, the Allied governments announce publicly to the Sublime Porte that

---

[37] (1982) **21** *ILM* 1261.

[38] *per* Viscount Sankey L.C., *In re Piracy Jure Gentium* [1934] AC 586 (Privy Council), citing Hugo Grotius (1583–1645), *De Jure Belli ac Pacis*, ii, cap. 20, Sect. 40.

[39] McCormack, 'From Sun Tzu to the Sixth Committee', 44–8.

[40] Ibid., 44–5.

they will hold personally responsible [for] these crimes all members of the Ottoman Government and those of their agents who are implicated in such massacres'. The crimes continued nevertheless. The threat was not carried out due to the lack of consensus on the international legal status of this category of crimes. Unlike war crimes for which a military tribunal could be instituted to punish war criminals in the territory of the defeated State or in the national territory of the tribunal, no tribunal could be instituted in the territory of another State to punish crimes against humanity without a war between the States concerned.

The establishment of a permanent international criminal court was discussed, for example, by the Advisory Committee of Jurists appointed by the Council of the League of Nations to draft a constituent statute for the Permanent Court of International Justice (PCIJ). The Committee recommended in 1921 that the League consider setting up a High Court of International Justice alongside the PCIJ to try a category of international crimes that had already existed. Unfortunately, two objections were raised even among some members of the Committees. Firstly, individuals were not subjects of international law; hence not being subject to trial before an international tribunal applying international law. Secondly, while war crimes had been well established, the same could not be said of crimes committed in times of peace.[41]

The Convention for the Creation of an International Criminal Court was adopted by the League of Nations in 1937. States Parties would have primary jurisdiction to try offenders; but each State could choose first whether to become a State Party to the Convention and then whether to submit particular cases to the jurisdiction of the Court. The idea was connected to punishment of terrorism. However, the Convention did not have a sufficient number of States parties and was forgotten when WWII broke out.[42]

It was the International Military Tribunal at Nuremberg that proceeded with international criminal prosecution in violation of the principle of legality. By violating this principle for the first time, the Nuremberg Tribunal set precedents for future criminal prosecution of individuals before an international tribunal applying international criminal law.

[41] Ibid., 51–4.   [42] Ibid., 54–5.

2

AD HOC INTERNATIONAL TRIBUNALS AND THE INTERNATIONAL CRIMINAL COURT

Four *ad hoc* international criminal tribunals were set up in the course of the twentieth century; namely, the international military tribunal at Nuremberg and the Tokyo Tribunal, the international criminal tribunal for the former Yugoslavia, and that for Rwanda.[1] On 17 July 1998, the UN Conference of Plenipotentiaries on the Establishment of an International Criminal Court (the 'Rome Conference') adopted the Rome Statute of the International Criminal Court (hereinafter the 'ICC Statute')[2] to establish the permanent International Criminal Court (ICC).[3]

The notion of sovereignty has been sidelined by the four *ad hoc* tribunals because of the unconditional military surrender of Germany and Japan, and the exercise by the UN Security Council of the enforcement power under Chapter VII of the UN Charter in the case of the former Yugoslavia and that of Rwanda.

2.1 THE NUREMBERG AND TOKYO TRIBUNALS[4]

The International Military Tribunal at Nuremberg ('Nuremberg Tribunal') was an occupation court for Germany set up after WWII by four victorious Powers to whom Germany had surrendered unconditionally—Great Britain, France, the Soviet Union, and the US acting in the interests of all nations—which was subsequently endorsed by

[1] For a general introduction to the subject, see H. Ball, *Prosecuting War Crimes and Genocide: The Twentieth-Century Experience* (University Press of Kansas, 1999).

[2] *UN Doc. A/ CONF. 183/9 (1998).*

[3] For a succinct history of these tribunals and a comprehensive reference to legal literature and documents on the subject, see M. C. Bassiouni, 'Historical Survey: 1919–1998', in M. C. Bassiouni (ed.), *ICC Ratification and National Implementing Legislation* (Association Internationale de Droit Pénal, 1999), 1–44.

[4] For historic events leading to the creation of these two Tribunals, see: M. M. Whiteman, *Digest of International Law*, xi (US Dept. of State, 1968), 874–97, 965–73; M. P. Scharf, *Balkan Justice: The Story behind the First International War Crimes Trial since Nuremberg* (Carolina Academic Press, 1997), chap. 1.

nineteen other States.[5] It had four judges appointed by each of the Powers. The prosecutors also came from the four Powers. The Nuremberg Tribunal considered its Charter a product of 'the exercise of the sovereign legislative power by the countries to which the German Reich unconditionally surrendered', and it affirmed 'the undoubted right of these countries to legislate for the occupied territories [as] recognized by the civilized world'.[6]

The Tribunal tried twenty-four 'major Nazi war criminals', leaving prosecution of minor Nazi war criminals to the States where they committed their crimes. One defendant committed suicide, and another was declared unfit to stand trial. In the Tribunal's judgment of 1 October 1946, three were acquitted, twelve sentenced to death, three sentenced to life imprisonment, and four sentenced to prison terms. One of the twelve defendants sentenced to death was Martin Bormann, Head of the Nazi Party Chancellery, who was tried *in absentia*.

Article 6 of the Nuremberg Charter[7] demanded individual responsibility for crimes against peace, violations of the laws or customs of war, and crimes against humanity. The Nuremberg Tribunal considered its task to be one of interpretation and application of the law laid down in the Nuremberg Charter, stating that the law of the Charter was 'decisive and binding upon the Tribunal'.[8] The Nuremberg Tribunal brushed aside the argument that it was violating the principle of legality in the following statement made in the context of crimes against peace:

'In the first place, it is to be observed that the maxim *nullum crimen sine lege* is not a limitation of sovereignty, but is in general a principle of justice. To assert that it is unjust to punish those who in defiance of treaties and assurances have attacked neighbouring States without warning is obviously untrue, for in such circumstances the attacker must know that he is doing wrong, and so far from it being unjust to punish him, it would be unjust if his wrong were allowed to go unpunished . . .'[9]

The Nuremberg Tribunal also rejected the doctrine of State sovereignty in favour of that of individual criminal responsibility. According to the Tribunal, '[c]rimes against international law are committed by men, not by abstract entities, and only by punishing individuals who commit such crimes can the provisions of international law be enforced'.[10]

As for the offences of war crimes, the Tribunals applied, *inter alia*, the norms of the 1929 Geneva Conventions relating to protection of victims of armed conflict and the

   [5] Australia, Belgium, Czechoslovakia, Denmark, Ethiopia, Greece, Haiti, Honduras, India, Luxemburg, the Netherlands, New Zealand, Norway, Panama, Paraguay, Poland, Uruguay, Venezuela, and Yugoslavia.

   [6] *Trials of German Major War Criminals*, Proceedings of the International Military Tribunal Sitting at Nuremberg, Germany, Part 22 (H. M. Stationery Office, 1950) (hereinafter '*Nuremberg Proceedings*'), 411 at 443; International Military Tribunal (Nuremberg), Judgment and Sentences, (1947) **41** *AJIL* 172 at 216.

   [7] Agreement for the Prosecution and Punishment of Major War Criminals of the European Axis, 8 Aug. 1945, **8** *UNTS* 279.

   [8] *Nuremberg Proceedings*, 443–4.

   [9] (1947) **41** *AJIL* 217–8.

   [10] Ibid., 222.

1907 Hague Convention Respecting the Laws and Customs of War on Land although these instruments contained no reference to the possibility of their criminal sanction. Crimes against humanity were novel. Atrocities committed during WWII by Germans against Germans, or against nationals of Germany's occupied territories like Austria and nationals of Germany's allies like Hungary and Romania, although not in violation of the laws of war as those laws applied only between belligerents, were crimes against humanity. The Nuremberg Charter linked the prosecution of this genus of crimes to the 'execution of or in connection with any crime within the jurisdiction of the Tribunal'. In effect, the crimes had to be committed in execution of or in connection with war crimes or the crime against peace.

On 20 December 1945, the four Allied Powers in Berlin proclaimed Control Council Law No. 10, authorizing the Allies to apprehend 'war criminals and other similar offenders, other than those dealt with by the [Nuremberg] Tribunal', and to set up appropriate tribunals to try them.[11]

The International Military Tribunal for the Far East ('Tokyo Tribunal') was set up by the United States Supreme Commander-in-Chief in Japan, who also appointed the eleven judges of the Tribunal, including judges appointed from the names submitted by the signatories of the Japanese terms of surrender (the US, Australia, Canada, China, France, Great Britain, the Netherlands, New Zealand, and the Soviet Union) and by India and the Philippines.[12] The Tokyo Tribunal followed the reasoning of the Nuremberg Tribunal in applying its own Charter,[13] proclaimed in January 1946 and modelled on the Nuremberg Charter. The Tokyo Tribunal first convened on 3 May 1946 and did not pronounce its judgment until November 1948. Japanese war crimes suspects were classified as 'A', 'B', or 'C' suspects. The 'A' suspects were charged with crimes against peace; the 'B' suspects with conventional war crimes; and the 'C' suspects with atrocities known as crimes against humanity. The Tokyo Tribunal prosecuted only the 'A' suspects, comprising former Prime Minister Hideki Tojo and twenty-four other perpetrators,[14] leaving the 'B' and 'C' suspects to be tried before military courts in various States.

The oft-repeated criticisms of the Nuremberg Tribunal and the Tokyo Tribunal are that it dispensed victor's justice and violated the principle of legality. In terms of victor's justice, for example, Japan was not permitted to accuse the US before the Tokyo Tribunal of the US atomic bombings of Hiroshima and Nagasaki, or to accuse the Soviet Union of its violation of the neutrality agreement of 13 April 1941.[15] With

---

[11] 36 *ILR* 31. Such tribunals implementing Control Council Law No. 10 are usually referred to as 'Military Tribunals' of various nations (e.g., the 'US Military Tribunal' sitting at Nuremberg), as opposed to the 'International Military Tribunal' at Nuremberg (or the 'Nuremberg Tribunal'), which had tried major war criminals.

[12] For a concise account of the establishment and proceedings of the Tokyo Tribunal, see B. V. A. Röling and C. F. Rüter (eds.), *The Tokyo Judgment* (APA—University Press Amsterdam, 1977), chap. 1.

[13] (1970) 4 *Bevans* 20.

[14] Two other defendants had died during the trial, and another defendant was declared mentally unfit to stand trial.

[15] See, e.g. Y. Onuma, 'The Tokyo Trial: Between Law and Politics', in C. Hosoya, N. Ando, Y. Onuma, and R. Minear (eds.), *The Tokyo War Crimes Trial: An International Symposium* (Kodansha, 1986), 45 ff.

respect to the principle of legality, crimes against humanity and individual criminal responsibility for crimes against peace were not concepts accepted in international law at that time.[16] Indeed, Justice Pal, the Indian Judge of the Tokyo Tribunal, would have acquitted all the defendants on the ground that there had been no individual criminal responsibility under international law.

On the other hand, it has been contended that international law is not a body of codes or statutes, but it evolves like the Common Law of the Anglo-American tradition to reflect the moral judgments of the community of nations. The two Tribunals were set up to render justice that would have been elusive if the pre-existence of the law of the Charters had not been proved. The choice was between, on the one hand, having a fair trial to deter future generations, and, on the other, a summary execution of those who deserved to be avenged for their roles in the unprecedented atrocities committed by one human-being against another.[17]

What counts is the *ex post facto* endorsement of the 'principles of international law recognized by the Charter of the Nuremberg Tribunal and the Judgment of the Tribunal', unanimously adopted by the UN General Assembly Resolution 95(1) on 11 December 1946. The said principles were subsequently formulated by the International Law Commission (ILC) and accepted by the UN General Assembly on 12 December 1950.[18] The principles are as follows:

'*Principle I.* Any person who commits or is an accomplice in the commission of an act which constitutes a crime under international law is responsible therefor and liable for punishment.

Principle II. The fact that domestic law does not punish an act which is an international crime does not free the perpetrator of such crime from responsibility under international law.

Principle III. The fact that a person who committed an international crime acted as Head of State or public official does not free him from responsibility under international law or mitigate punishment.

Principle IV. The fact that a person acted pursuant to order of his government or of a superior does not free him from responsibility under international law. It may, however, be considered in mitigation of punishment, if justice so requires.

Principle V. Any person charged with a crime under international law has the right to a fair trial on the facts and law.

Principle VI. The crimes hereafter set out are punishable as crimes under international law:

---

[16] Ibid. This is also the conclusion of Prof. Woetzel in relation to crimes against peace (R. K. Woetzel, *The Nuremberg Trials in International Law* (Stevens & Sons, 1962), 153–4,165). Cf. R. S. Clark, 'Nuremberg and Tokyo in Contemporary Perspectives', in T. H. L. McCormack and G. J. Simpson (eds.), *The Law of War Crimes: National and International Approaches* (Kluwer, 1997), 171; A. J. Kochavi, *Prelude to Nuremberg: Allied War Crimes Policy and the Question of Punishment* (University of North Carolina Press, 1998).

[17] US Secretary of State Henry L. Stimson, '"The Nuremberg Trial": Landmark and Law', *Foreign Affairs* (Jan. 1947), cited by the US Military Tribunal, Nuremberg, in *Trial of Josef Altstötter & Others* (the '*Justice*' Trial), 4 Dec. 1947, excerpted in G. K. McDonald and O. Swaak-Goldman (eds.), *Substantive and Procedural Aspects of International Criminal Law*, ii (Kluwer, 2000), 1843 at 1879. See also *Trial of Ernst von Weizsaecker et al.* (the '*Ministries*' Trial), US Military Tribunal, Nuremberg, 6 Apr. 1949, excerpted in ibid., 2145 at 2146.

[18] (1950) ii *Yearbook of the ILC* 374–5.

a. *Crimes against Peace*:

   (1) Planning, preparation, initiation or waging of a war of aggression, or a war in violation of international treaties, agreements or assurances;

   (2) Participation in a common plan or conspiracy for the accomplishment of any of the acts mentioned under (1).

b. *War Crimes*: namely, violations of the laws or customs of war. Such violations shall include, but not limited to, murder, ill-treatment or deportation to slave labour or for any other purpose of civilian population of or in occupied territory, murder or ill-treatment of prisoners of war or persons on the seas, killing of hostages, plunder of public or private property, wanton destruction of cities, towns or villages, or devastation not justified by military necessity.

c. *Crimes against Humanity*: namely, murder, extermination, enslavement, deportation, and other inhuman acts done against a civilian population, or persecutions on political, racial or religious grounds, when such acts are done or such persecutions are carried out in execution of or in connection with any crime against peace or any war crime.

Principle VII. Complicity in the commission of a crime against peace, a war crime or a crime against humanity, as set forth in Principle VI, is a crime under international law.'[19]

At about the same time, attempts were made in the ILC to have a permanent international criminal court established. Mr. Donnedieu de Vabres, the French Judge of the Nuremberg Tribunal, raised this question in the ILC on 13 May 1947. He was concerned with the criticism raised against the Nuremberg Tribunal that it was composed only of representatives of victor States and did not represent the international community. He recommended setting up a criminal chamber as part of the International Court of Justice (ICJ) to be composed of fifteen judges elected under the same conditions as the other members of the ICJ. The chamber would deal with indictments against a State or its rulers for crimes against peace or crimes against humanity. In addition, a special international court of justice might be set up to deal with all international offences capable of being committed in time of peace, war crimes, and all offences *communis juris* connected with crimes against humanity committed by the rulers of a State. The jurisdiction of this special court would be optional in that the State having custody of the offender might prosecute him in its own court, extradite him, or surrender him to the special court. The ILC referred this matter to the UN General Assembly.[20]

A potential debate in the General Assembly on the establishment of an international criminal tribunal was overtaken by the drafting of a convention on genocide. The draft convention, as prepared by the UN Secretariat, provided two alternatives regarding an international court to punish genocide alongside national jurisdictions. The first alternative was to have an international court having jurisdiction in all

[19] (1950) ii *Yearbook of the ILC* 374–8.
[20] UN Secretary-General, *Historical Survey of the Question of International Criminal Jurisdiction* (United Nations, 1949), 25–30.

matters connected with international crimes. The second was to set up a special international court either as a permanent court or an *ad hoc* court, with jurisdiction limited specifically to the crime of genocide. Representatives of several States opposed the creation of such an international criminal tribunal. According to the representatives of the Dominican Republic, India, Poland, and the Soviet Union, it would constitute a violation of national sovereignty of States, an important aspect of which was the right to try all crimes within their territory. On 10 November 1948, the Sixth (Legal) Committee of the UN General Assembly decided by a vote of twenty-three in favour, nineteen against, with three abstentions, to delete any reference in the draft convention to the international criminal tribunal. Several delegations voting in favour of the deletion clarified their position, in that they did not oppose the principle of international criminal jurisdiction, but were unable to support a provision which did not express a reality but only a hope. At the insistence of the US delegation, the Committee reconsidered the matter and found that it could go along with a toned-down provision. The compromise that was adopted was that persons charged with genocide shall be tried by a competent national tribunal of the State in whose territory an act of genocide is committed, or 'by a competent international penal tribunal subject to the acceptance at a later date by the contracting party concerned of its jurisdiction'. State responsibility for genocide is a matter to be adjudicated before the ICJ.[21]

2.2 THE ICTY AND THE ICTR

The International Criminal Tribunal for the Former Yugoslavia (ICTY) was set up by the UN Security Council in 1993, pursuant to Resolution 808 of 22 February 1993 and Resolution 827 of 25 May 1993.[22] The widespread violations of international humanitarian law within the territory of the former Yugoslavia, including the practice of 'ethnic cleansing', were considered by the Security Council as a threat to international peace and security. The Security Council therefore exercised its powers under Chapter VII of the UN Charter to set up the ICTY as its subsidiary organ in order to contribute to the restoration and maintenance of peace in the former Yugoslavia.[23]

The ICTY Statute was adopted by the Security Council following the submission of a report by the UN Secretary-General on 3 May 1993.[24] The ICTY is based in The Hague, the Netherlands. It is composed of sixteen permanent independent judges and

---

[21] Ibid., 30–46. See Arts. VI and IX of the Convention on the Prevention and Punishment of the Crime of Genocide of 1948, 78 *UNTS* 277.

[22] *UN Doc. S/RES/808 (1993); UN Doc. S/RES/827 (1993).*

[23] For detailed accounts relating to the creation of the ICTY see: Sharf, *Balkan Justice*, chaps. 2–5; M. C. Bassiouni and P. Manikas, *The Law of the International Criminal Tribunal for the Former Yugoslavia* (Transnational Publishers, 1996), chaps. I–III; A. Fatíc, *Reconciliation via the War Crimes Tribunal?* (Ashgate, 2000).

[24] Report of the Secretary-General pursuant to para. 2 of Security Council Res. 808 (1993) and Annex thereto, *UN Doc. S/25704.*

a maximum at any one time of nine *ad litem* independent judges, elected by the General Assembly from a list of nominations received from States submitted by the Security Council, taking due account of the adequate representation of the principal legal systems of the world. There are a total of twenty-seven *ad litem* judges, elected for a term of four years, who serve in the ICTY Trial Chambers for one or more trials, for a cumulative period of up to three years. The Appeals Chamber is composed of seven judges. For each appeal, the Appeals Chamber shall be composed of five of its members.[25] The ICTY proceedings are governed by the ICTY Statute and by Rules of Procedure and Evidence adopted by the judges. The ICTY is not subject to any national laws and has concurrent jurisdiction alongside, as well as primacy over, national courts to prosecute persons for serious violations of international humanitarian law committed in the territory of the former Yugoslavia since 1991.[26] Its subject-matter jurisdiction consists of the power to prosecute natural persons responsible for grave breaches of the Geneva Conventions of 1949 relating to the protection of victims of international armed conflicts, violations of the laws or customs of war, genocide, and crimes against humanity when committed in armed conflict, which are beyond any doubt part of customary international law.[27] The requirement that the ICTY is to apply customary international law is in order to avoid violating the principle of legality in the event that a party to the conflict is not bound by a specific treaty at the time of the alleged offences.[28]

The Prosecutor, who is an independent organ of the ICTY, is responsible for the investigation and prosecution of persons responsible for these offences. The Prosecutor is appointed by consensus of the UN Security Council on nomination by the UN Secretary-General. The exercise of the Prosecutor's power is checked by a judge of a Trial Chamber who reviews and confirms an indictment submitted by the Prosecutor.[29] There is no trial *in absentia*.[30] Penalties imposed by the ICTY are limited to imprisonment.[31] Imprisonment is enforced in a State designated by the ICTY from a list of States which have indicated to the UN Security Council their willingness to accept convicted persons. Such imprisonment is to be in accordance with the law of the State concerned, subject to the ICTY's supervision.[32]

---

[25] Arts. 11–14, ICTY Statute, as amended by UN Security Council Resolution 1329 (2000) of 30 Nov. 2000 (*UN Doc. S/RES/1329 (2000)*, Annex I).

[26] Arts. 8–9, ICTY Statute.

[27] Arts. 2–5, ICTY Statute.

[28] *Prosecutor v. Dusko Tadic*, Case No. IT-94–1-T, ICTY T. Ch. II, 10 Aug. 1995, Decision on the Defence Motion on Jurisdiction, para. 143.

[29] Arts. 16, 18–19, ICTY Statute.

[30] Art. 21(4)(d) of the ICTY Statute and Art. 20(4)(d) of the ICTR Statute state that the rights of the accused include the right 'to be tried in his presence'. However, the ICTY Appeals Chamber has held that *in absentia* proceedings may be permitted exceptionally in cases of contempt of the ICTY, where the person charged fails to appear in court and thereby obstructs the administration of justice. *Prosecutor v. Tihomir Blaskic*, Case No. IT-95–14-AR 108 *bis*, Decision on Subpoena, ICTY App. Ch., 29 Oct. 1997, para. 59.

[31] Art. 24, ICC Statute.

[32] Art. 27, ICTY Statute.

The legality of the establishment of the ICTY by the Security Council, the ICTY's primacy jurisdiction over national courts, and the subject-matter jurisdiction of the ICTY have been upheld by the Appeals Chamber of the ICTY itself.[33] In its view, the UN Security Council was justified in exercising its authority under Chapter VII of the UN Charter to set up the ICTY as a response to the threat to the peace in the former Yugoslavia, and all UN Members must observe the measures adopted by the Security Council under Chapter VII.

The ICTY considers itself the first truly international tribunal to be established by the United Nations to determine individual criminal responsibility under international humanitarian law, while the Nuremberg and Tokyo Tribunals were considered 'multinational in nature, representing only part of the world community'.[34]

The International Criminal Tribunal for Rwanda (ICTR) was set up by UN Security Council Resolution 955 of 8 November 1994, in response to genocide and other systematic, widespread, and flagrant violations of international humanitarian law that had been committed in Rwanda.[35] Based in Arusha, Tanzania, it has jurisdiction over genocide, crimes against humanity, and violations of Article 3 common to the Geneva Conventions of 12 August 1949 for the protection of war victims, and of Additional Protocol II thereto of 8 June 1977, committed in the territory of Rwanda, and over Rwandan citizens responsible for such violations committed in the territory of neighbouring States, between 1 January and 31 December 1994 when members of the Tutsi ethnic group and their Hutu sympathizers were massacred or attacked by members of the Hutu ethnic group. Like the ICTY, the ICTR exercises jurisdiction over natural persons. The ICTY Prosecutor also serves as the ICTR Prosecutor. The provisions in the ICTR Statute regarding organization of the Tribunal, investigation and preparation of indictment, review of indictment, rights of the accused, penalties, appellate proceedings, and cooperation and judicial assistance, mirror the corresponding provisions in the ICTY Statute. However, whereas the ICTY Statute provides that the ICTY shall have its seat at The Hague, the ICTR Statute omits to mention the seat of the ICTR due to the sensitivity involved in choosing Arusha over Kigali, the capital of Rwanda, as proposed by Rwanda itself. The provisions on the composition of the Chambers, election of judges, and officers and members of the Chambers under the ICTR Statute now differ from those under the ICTY Statute as a result of the amendment made by UN Security Council Resolution 1329 (2000) of 30 November 2000.[36]

---

[33] *Prosecutor v. Dusko Tadic*, Case No. IT-94-1-AR72, ICTY App. Ch., Decision on the Defence Motion for Interlocutory Appeal on Jurisdiction, 2 Oct. 1995.

[34] *Prosecutor v. Dusko Tadic*, Case No. IT-94-1-T, ICTY T. Ch. II, 7 May 1997 (hereinafter '*Tadic* Judgment'), para. 1.

[35] For background and materials, see J. Oppenheim and W. van der Wolf (eds.), *Global War Crimes Tribunal Collection*, i (Global Law Association, 1997); J. Tebbs, *Rwanda, War and Peace?!* (Global Law Association, 1999); C. Scheltema and W. van der Wolf (eds.), *The International Tribunal for Rwanda: Facts, Cases, Documents* (Global Law Association, 1999).

[36] *UN Doc. S/RES/1329 (2000)*, Annexes I and II.

Essentially, the ICTR does not have a pool of *ad litem* judges to assist in its work as in the case of the ICTY.[37]

The legality of the creation of the ICTR has been upheld in *Kanyabashi*.[38] The Trial Chamber of the ICTR in that case followed the reasoning of the ICTY Appeals Chamber on this matter very closely. It noted, first of all, that since Rwanda itself had requested the establishment of the ICTR, and other States were bound by the UN Charter obligations, it could not be contended that the establishment of the ICTR violated the sovereignty of Rwanda and the other States. Secondly, as the internal conflict in Rwanda was a threat to international peace and security, the UN Security Council was justified to invoke its competence under Chapter VII of the UN Charter and set up the ICTR. The Trial Chamber also rejected the contention that its creation violated the principle of *jus de non evocando*—a principle under constitutional law in Civil Law systems that prohibits the creation of a special or extraordinary court designed to prosecute political offences in times of social unrest without a fair trial. The Chamber reasoned that Chapter VII of the UN Charter was the legitimate source of its creation, and that the right to a fair trial was guaranteed adequately by the ICTR Statute and the ICTR's Rules of Procedure and Evidence. The Chamber conceded, however, that the Security Council's extension of international obligations and criminal responsibilities directly to individuals in situations of internal armed conflict was 'an important innovation of international law' which was justified only by the seriousness, magnitude, and gravity of that conflict.[39]

One unique characteristic of the ICTY and the ICTR is the co-existence of both the concurrent jurisdiction and primacy jurisdiction each of them has *vis-à-vis* national courts. Neither the ICTY nor the ICTR has exclusive jurisdiction over crimes included in its mandate. Article 8(1) of the ICTR Statute, for example, recognizes the complementary nature of the ICTR's jurisdiction and the jurisdiction of national courts. However, Article 8(2) of the ICTR Statute confers on the ICTR primacy over the national courts of all States, and at any stage in the procedure, the ICTR may formally request any national jurisdiction to defer investigations or on-going proceedings. Thus, the ICTR has held that once proceedings are instituted before the ICTR against a person, the ICTR has primacy over any other national court and the question of concurrent jurisdiction cannot be invoked in support of a request for withdrawal of an indictment or deferral to a national court.[40] This is despite the fact that the ICTR encourages all States to exercise universal jurisdiction over international crimes.[41] This primacy is further recognized by Article 9 of the ICTR Statute which provides that no person shall be tried by a national court for acts for which he has already been

---

[37] Arts. 12–14 of the ICTY Statute, as amended, and Arts. 11–13 of the ICTR Statute, as amended. See Appendices 1 and 2 below.

[38] *Prosecutor v. Kanyabashi*, Case No. ICTR-96–15-T, ICTR T. Ch., Decision on Jurisdiction, 18 June 1997.

[39] Ibid., paras. 30–2. Also summarized by V. Morris (1998) 92 *AJIL* 66.

[40] *Prosecutor v. Bernard Ntuyahaga*, Case No. ICTR-98–40-T, ICTR T. Ch. I, Decision on the Prosecutor's Motion to Withdraw the Indictment, 18 Mar. 1999, para. 1.

[41] Ibid.

tried by the ICTR, but that a person who has been tried before a national court may be tried subsequently by the ICTR if the act for which he was tried was characterized as an ordinary crime, or the national court proceedings were not impartial or independent, were designed to shield the accused from international criminal responsibility, or the case was not prosecuted diligently. Article 9 and Article 10 of the ICTY Statute are identical to Article 8 and Article 9, respectively, of the ICTR Statute.

Tadic is illustrative of the ICTY's primacy jurisdiction under Article 9 of the ICTY Statute. The prosecution of Dusko Tadic by the German authorities for crimes allegedly committed by him and his alleged co-perpetrators in the former Yugoslavia in June 1992 had to be deferred to the ICTY after the ICTY issued a formal request for deferral addressed to the Federal Republic of Germany. In the ICTY's opinion, it would not be acting in the proper interests of justice if some of the alleged co-perpetrators of the same set of serious violations of international humanitarian law were to be judged in national courts and others by the ICTY. The surrender of Tadic to the ICTY by Germany was made possible only after Germany enacted the necessary implementing legislation to permit his surrender.[42]

The following is a summarized comparison and contrast between the ICTY and the ICTR.

SIMILARITIES

(1) Both are set up by the UN Security Council exercising its enforcement power under Chapter VII of the UN Charter to maintain international peace and security. All UN Members are obligated to cooperate with the ICTY and the ICTR.

(2) Both are subsidiary organs of the UN Security Council.

(3) Both are bound to apply rules of international law that are beyond doubt part of customary international law.

(4) Both have almost identical Rules of Procedure and Evidence. Unlike the Nuremberg Tribunal, the ICTY and the ICTR do not allow trials *in absentia*.

(5) Both have the same Prosecutor. Moreover, Article 13(4) of the ICTR Statute stipulates that the judges of the Appeals Chamber of the ICTY also serve as the judges of the Appeals Chamber of the ICTR. Two judges of the ICTR are assigned to be members of the Appeals Chamber of the ICTY. This is to ensure consistency in the application of the law. Thus, the President of the Appeals Chamber of the ICTY is also the President of the Appeals Chamber of the ICTR.

---

[42] *Tadic* Judgment, paras. 6–9. See also B. S. Brown, 'Primacy or Complementarity: Reconciling the Jurisdiction of National Courts and International Criminal Tribunals' (1998) 23 *Yale J. Int'l L.* 383.

DIFFERENCES

(1) The ICTY has jurisdiction over crimes committed in both international armed conflict (hence, the 'grave breach' regime under Article 2 of the ICTY Statute) and internal armed conflict. The ICTR has jurisdiction over crimes committed in internal armed conflict only (hence, the absence of the 'grave breach' regime under the ICTR Statute).

(2) The ICTY has jurisdiction over crimes against humanity only if they are 'committed in an armed conflict'.[43] The ICTR has jurisdiction over crimes against humanity only if they are committed 'on national, political, ethnic, racial, or other religious grounds';[44] that is, when committed with discriminatory intent. As will be seen, both of these requirements depart from rules of customary international law on crimes against humanity.

(3) The ICTY has jurisdiction over crimes under the ICTY Statute committed in the territory of the former Yugoslavia since 1991.[45] The ICTR has jurisdiction over crimes under the ICTR Statute committed in Rwanda and Rwandan neighbouring States between 1 January 1994 and 31 December 1994.[46]

(4) Unlike the ICTY, the ICTR does not have a pool of *ad litem* judges to assist in its work.

2.3 THE INTERNATIONAL CRIMINAL COURT

Aspirations to establish a permanent international criminal court were revived in the 1980's with a proposal before the UN General Assembly by Latin American States, led by Trinidad and Tobago, who envisaged such a standing court as their last resort to prosecute international drug-traffickers.[47] The matter was referred by the General Assembly to the ILC.[48] In 1993, the ILC was asked by the General Assembly to draft a statute for the court. The ILC's Draft Statute, finalized in 1994, was largely influenced by the ICTY Statute.[49] In that same year, an *ad hoc* Committee was set up by the

---

[43] Art. 5, ICTY Statute.

[44] Art. 3, ICTR Statute.

[45] Art. 1, ICTY Statute.

[46] Art. 1, ICTR Statute. It should be noted, however, that the fact that crimes were committed in Rwandan neighbouring States does not turn such crimes into crimes committed in an international armed conflict. This is because these crimes were committed by Rwandans against Rwandans.

[47] Letter dated 21 Aug. 1989 from the Permanent Representative of Trinidad and Tobago to the UN Secretary-General, UN GAOR, 47th Sess., Annex 44, Agenda Item 152, *UN Doc. A/ 44/ 195 (1989)*.

[48] UN GA Res. 44/ 39, UN GAOR, 44th Sess., Supp. No. 49, at 311, *UN Doc. A/ 44/ 49 (1989)*.

[49] Rep. of the ILC on the Work of Its 46th Sess, UN GAOR, 49th Sess., Supp. No. 10 (A/49/10). For an analysis of the ILC's Draft Statute for an International Criminal Court, see T. L. H. McCormack and G. J. Simpson, 'A New International Criminal Law Regime?' (1995) **42** *Netherlands Int'l L. Rev.* 177; S. R. Ratner and J. S. Abrams, *Accountability for Human Rights Atrocities in International Law: Beyond the Nuremberg Legacy* (Clarendon Press, 1997), 179–84.

General Assembly to review the issues raised in the Draft Statute. In the meantime, in 1991, the ILC adopted its Draft Code of Crimes Against the Peace and Security of Mankind, a project entrusted to it by the UN General Assembly since 1947.[50] The Draft Code was submitted to Governments for comment and was revised in 1996 in the light of the comments received. The 1994 Draft Statute and the 1996 Draft Code generally overlapped in terms of the content and scope of the offences within the jurisdiction of the future international criminal court.[51] The 1996 Draft Code provides, in essence, that offences against the peace and security of mankind are crimes under international law, for which the responsible individuals shall be punished, whether or not these crimes are punishable under national law. However, without prejudice to the jurisdiction of an international criminal court, each State Party to such a Code shall take necessary measures to establish its jurisdiction over the crimes of genocide, the crimes against humanity, the crimes against UN and associated personnel, and war crimes, leaving an international criminal court with the exclusive jurisdiction over the crime of aggression. As will be seen, the Draft Code has been overtaken by events.

The advent of the establishment of the ICTY and the ICTR in 1993 and 1994, respectively, fuelled the widespread belief that a permanent international criminal court was desirable and practical. Another committee set up by the General Assembly, called the Preparatory Committee for the Establishment of an International Criminal Court, met six times in 1996–98 to prepare a text of a convention to set up an international criminal court.

All these efforts culminated in the convening of the Rome Conference, attended by 160 States, from 15 June to 17 July 1998, which adopted the ICC Statute on the last day of the Conference.[52]

Details of the provisions of the ICC Statute will be analysed in the relevant parts of this book. The following is an overview of the ICC Statute so that readers can understand the discussion in the succeeding chapters of the book.[53]

The Statute comprises a Preamble and thirteen Parts covering 128 Articles. The Preamble affirms that the most serious crimes of concern to the international community as a whole must not go unpunished. It also emphasizes that the ICC shall be complementary to national criminal jurisdictions.

---

[50] The name 'Draft Code of Offences Against the Peace and Security of Mankind' was changed to 'Draft Code of Crimes Against the Peace and Security of Mankind' in 1988.

[51] For a detailed analysis of the 1994 Draft Statute, the 1991 and 1996 Draft Codes, see L. S. Sunga, *The Emerging System of International Criminal Law: Developments in Codification and Implementation* (Kluwer, 1997), *passim*.

[52] For a concise account of the negotiating process at the Rome Conference, see: P. Kirsch and John T. Holmes, 'The Rome Conference on an International Criminal Court: The Negotiating Process' (1999) **93** *AJIL* 2. Ambassador Kirsch of Canada was Chairman of the Committee of the Whole of the Conference; H-P. Kaul, 'Breakthrough in Rome: The Statute of the International Criminal Court' (1999) **59/60** *Law and State* 114.

[53] At this juncture, references to the specific Article numbers do not seem necessary; readers can always resort to the full text of the ICC Statute, which appears as an appendix to this book. For some preliminary impressions of the ICC Statute, see A. Cassese, 'The Statute of the International Criminal Court: Some Preliminary Reflections' (1999) **10** *Euro. J. Int'l L.* 144.

Part 1, entitled 'Establishment of the Court', provides that an independent ICC is hereby established, with the seat at The Hague. The ICC, which shall be brought into relationship with the UN, shall have the power to exercise its jurisdiction over the most serious crimes of international concern as referred to in the Statute, and shall be complementary to national criminal jurisdictions. The ICC shall have international legal personality as well as such legal capacity necessary as may be necessary for the exercise of its functions and the fulfilment of its purposes. It may exercise its functions and powers on the territory of any State Party and, by special agreement, on the territory of any other State.[54]

Part 2 is entitled 'Jurisdiction, Admissibility and Applicable Law'. It stipulates that the ICC shall have jurisdiction over four crimes; namely, genocide, crimes against humanity, war crimes, and the crime of aggression, once a provision is adopted to define the last-mentioned crime and set out the conditions under which the ICC shall exercise jurisdiction with respect to this crime consistent with the UN Charter. Elements of Crimes shall be adopted by a two-thirds majority of the members of the Assembly of States Parties to assist the ICC in the interpretation and application of Articles 6, 7, and 8 on the crime of genocide, crimes against humanity, and war crimes, respectively. The Elements of Crimes and amendments thereto must be consistent with the Statute. Article 10 provides that nothing in this Part is to be construed as limiting or prejudicing in any way existing or developing rules of international law for purposes other than the ICC Statute.

Pursuant to Article 11, the ICC has jurisdiction only with respect to 'crimes committed' after the entry into force of the Statute and only after the entry into force of the Statute for the State in question, unless that State has made a declaration acepting the exercise of jurisdiction by the ICC with respect to the crime in question. This must be read in conjunction with Article 24, under Part 3 (General Principles of Criminal Law) of the Statute, which stipulates that no person shall be criminally responsible under the Statute for 'conduct prior to' the entry into force of the Statute, and that in the event of a change in the law applicable to a given case prior to a final judgment, the law more favourable to the person being investigated, prosecuted, or convicted shall apply.[55]

Matters pertaining to the exercise of jurisdiction are elaborated in Articles 12–19. Where a situation[56] is referred to the Prosecutor by a State Party, the ICC may exercise

---

[54] See also F. Jarasch, 'Establishment, Organization and Financing of the International Criminal Court (Parts I, IV, XI–XIII)' (1998) 6 *Euro. J. Crime, Crim. L. & Crim. Justice* 9.

[55] For a legislative history of these articles, see Per Saland, 'International Criminal Law Principles', in R. S. Lee (ed.), *The International Criminal Court: The Making of the Rome Statute—Issues, Negotiations, Results* (Kluwer, 1999), 189 at 196–7.

[56] The term 'situation' was proposed by the US Delegation to allay concerns of several delegations with the regime provided in the ILC Draft Statute, which permitted a State Party to select individual cases of violations and lodge complaints with the Prosecutor in relation to these cases, thereby politicizing the process. The term 'situation' is less politicized—it is up to the Prosecutor to determine whether a situation referred by a State Party warrants a case against the individual(s) concerned (S. A. Fernandez de Gurmendi, 'The Role of the International Prosecutor', in Lee (ed.), *International Criminal Court*, 175 at 180; M. H. Arsanjani, 'The Rome Statute of the International Criminal Court' (1999) 93 *AJIL* 22 at 27).

jurisdiction if one or more of the following States are parties to the Statute or have accepted the ICC's jurisdiction: the State on whose *territory* the act or omission occurred, and the State of which the person being investigated or prosecuted is a *national*. In the case of a non-State Party, that State may, by declaration lodged with the Registrar, accept the exercise of the ICC's jurisdiction.[57] Any State Party to the ICC Statute or the UN Security Council acting under Chapter VII of the UN Charter may refer a situation to the Prosecutor. The Prosecutor may also initiate proceedings *proprio motu* on the basis of information on crimes within the ICC's jurisdiction, provided that the Pre-Trial Chamber determines that there is a reasonable basis to proceed. The Prosecutor shall notify all States Parties and those States which would normally exercise jurisdiction over the crimes in question. However, the Prosecutor will have to defer to the State's investigation unless the Pre-Trial Chamber decides to authorize the investigation by the Prosecutor. In any case, Article 16 provides that investigation or prosecution shall be deferred for a period of twelve months after the Security Council, in a resolution adopted under Chapter VII (Action with Respect to Threats to the Peace, Breaches of the Peace, and Acts of Aggression) of the UN Charter, has requested the ICC to that effect; that request may be renewed by the Council under the same conditions.

The ICC shall have jurisdiction only where a State is unable or unwilling genuinely to carry out the investigation or prosecution of the crimes within the ICC's jurisdiction, where such investigation or prosecution has been carried out but is a mere sham, where the person concerned has already been tried for the conduct, or where the case is not of sufficient gravity to justify further action by the ICC. In order to determine unwillingness in a particular case, the ICC shall consider whether: (a) the national proceedings or decision had the purpose of shielding the person concerned from criminal responsibility; (b) there has been an unjustifiable delay in the proceedings inconsistent with an intent to bring the person concerned to justice; or (c) the proceedings were not or are not conducted independently or impartially, but with intent not to bring the person concerned to justice. In order to determine inability in a particular case, the ICC shall consider whether, due to a total or substantial collapse or unavailability of its national judicial system, the State is unable to obtain the accused, or the necessary evidence and testimony, or otherwise unable to carry out its proceedings. The ICC shall be the final arbiter of whether a case is admissible.[58] Article 20 covers the principle of *ne bis in idem*. No person shall be tried before the ICC with respect to conduct which formed the basis of crimes for which the person has been convicted or acquitted by the ICC, or tried before another court for a crime within the ICC's jurisdiction for which that person has already been convicted or acquitted by the ICC. However, a person already tried by another court for conduct proscribed as

---

[57] For a legislative history of this provision, see: H-P. Kaul, 'Special Note: The Struggle for the International Criminal Court's Jurisdiction' (1998) 6 *Euro. J. Crime, Crim. L. & Crim. Justice* 364. See also E. Wilmshurst, 'Jurisdiction of the Court', in Lee (ed.), *International Criminal Court* 127.

[58] Arts. 17–19 of the Statute. See also J. T. Holmes, 'The Principle of Complementarity', in Lee (ed.), *International Criminal Court*, 41.

crimes within the ICC's jurisdiction shall be tried by the ICC if the proceedings in the other court were intended to shield the person from prosecution before the ICC or otherwise were a mere sham.

It should be noted that the ICC Statute makes no distinction between civilian and military jurisdictions in national criminal justice systems.

The applicable law of the ICC is to be applied in the following order: (a) the Statute and its Rules of Procedure and Evidence; (b) applicable treaties and the principles and rules of international law; and (c) general principles of law, provided that these principles are not inconsistent with the Statute, international law, or internationally recognized norms and standards. The ICC may apply principles and rules of law as interpreted in its previous decisions. In any case, the application and interpretation of the law must be consistent with internationally recognized human rights, and be without discrimination.

Part 3 of the Statute covers 'General Principles of Criminal Law'. Article 22 incorporates the basic principle of legality—*nullum crimen sine lege*: a person is not criminally liable unless his conduct constitutes a crime under the Statute. Moreover, the definition of a crime shall be strictly construed and shall not be extended by analogy; in case of ambiguity, the definition is to be interpreted in favour of the person being investigated, prosecuted, or convicted. Yet, as customary international law continues to develop while the Statute may be static, it is expressly provided that this Article shall not affect the characterization of any conduct as criminal under international law independently of the Statute. Article 23 of the Statute covers the principle of 'no punishment without a pre-existing law' (*nulla poena sine lege*).

Individual criminal responsibility is elaborated in Article 25. The ICC shall have jurisdiction over natural persons only. The proposal to include criminal responsibility of legal entities did not find consensus support at the Rome Conference because not all legal systems recognize such responsibility. The proposal was therefore withdrawn.[59] Under the Statute, a person shall be individually responsible and liable for punishment if he, with intent and knowledge, commits a crime; orders, solicits or induces the commission of such a crime; aids, abets or otherwise assists in the commission of the crime; or in any other way contributes to the commission or attempted commission of such a crime by a group of persons acting within a common purpose;[60] or attempts the commission of a crime. Incitement is a crime only in the case of genocide. This provision on individual criminal responsibility is without prejudice to the responsibility of States under international law.

Article 26 of the Statute stipulates that the ICC shall have no jurisdiction over any person under the age of eighteen at the time of the commission of a crime.[61]

[59] P. Saland, 'International Criminal Law Principles', 198–9.

[60] This mode is a paraphrase of the concept of conspiracy in the Common Law, but unknown in most Civil Law jurisdictions. The adopted formula is derived from that used in the 1998 UN Convention for the Suppression of Terrorist Bombings, adopted by UN General Assembly Resolution 52/164 of 15 Dec. 1997, UN GAOR, 52nd Sess., Supp. No. 49, at 389, *UN Doc. A/ 52/ 49 (1997)*. See ibid., 199–200; Arsanjani (1999) **93** *AJIL* 37.

[61] See further P. Saland, 'International Criminal Law Principles', 200–2.

By virtue of Article 27, official positions shall not bar the ICC's jurisdiction, nor shall they constitute a ground for reduction of sentence.

Responsibility of commanders and civilian superiors or conduct of their subordinates under their effective authority and control is covered under Article 28.

Article 29 states that the crimes within the ICC's jurisdiction shall not be subject to any statute of limitations. In the case of an offence against the administration of justice, the Rules of Procedure and Evidence adopted by the Preparatory Commission for the International Court (PCNICC) in June 2000 provides in Rule 164, entitled 'Periods of limitation' under Chapter 9 (Offences and misconduct against the Court) three periods of limitations. Firstly, the ICC shall apply the periods of limitation in the State Party requested by the ICC to exercise jurisdiction over the offence. Secondly, if the ICC exercises jurisdiction over the offence, it shall be subject to a period of limitation of five years from the date on which the offence was committed, provided that during this period no investigation or prosecution has been initiated. Finally, enforcement of sanctions imposed with respect to the offence shall be subject to a period of limitation of ten years from the date on which the sanction has become final.[62]

Article 30 stipulates that unless otherwise provided, a crime within the ICC's jurisdiction must be committed with the intent and knowledge of the perpetrator.

Grounds for excluding criminal responsibility are specified in Article 31. They cover mental disease or defect and a state of intoxication (unless voluntarily intoxicated), duress resulting from a threat of imminent death or of continuing or imminent serious bodily harm, and self defence or defence of another person (or property in the case of war crimes) essential for the survival of persons or for accomplishing a military mission. Article 32 provides that neither a mistake of fact nor a mistake of law is a defence unless it negates the mental element required by the crime in question. Pursuant to Article 33, a superior order is not a defence, unless the person did not know that the order was unlawful and the order itself was not manifestly unlawful. However, orders to commit genocide or crimes against humanity are deemed manifestly unlawful.

Part 4 of the Statute deals with compositions and administration of the ICC. The ICC shall be composed of: (a) the Presidency comprising the President and the First and Second Vice-Presidents of the ICC; (b) an Appeals Division, a Trial Division, and a Pre-Trial Division; (c) the Office of the Prosecutor; and (d) the Registry. There shall be eighteen judges of the ICC elected for a nine-year term by a two-thirds majority of States Parties present and voting. At the first election, six judges will be selected by lot to serve for a term of three years, another six for a term of six years, with the remaining serving for nine years. They shall not be eligible for re-election, except for the judges selected by lot to serve for a three-year term who shall be eligible for re-election to a full-term.

The Office of the Prosecutor shall act independently as a separate organ of the ICC. The Prosecutor is elected by an absolute majority of the Assembly of States Parties for

62 *Doc. PCNICC/2000/1/Add. 1*, 2 Nov. 2000.

a term of nine years. The Prosecutor is assisted by one or more Deputy Prosecutors elected in the same way but from a list of candidates provided by the Prosecutor. They shall not be eligible for re-election.

The ICC is serviced by the Registry, which also has a Victims and Witnesses Unit. The Registry is headed by the Registrar who is elected by an absolute majority of the judges, taking into account any recommendation by the Assembly of States Parties, to serve a five-year term, renewable only once.

The official languages of the ICC shall be the six official languages of the UN.

Article 51 deals with the Rules of Procedure and Evidence of the ICC, which shall enter into force upon adoption by a two-thirds majority of the members of the Assembly of States Parties. In case of conflict between the Statute and the Rules, the Statute shall prevail.

Part 5 (Investigation and Prosecution) details the steps to be taken by the Prosecutor in the initiation of an investigation, duties and powers of the Prosecutor relating to investigations, rights of persons during an investigation, the related powers and functions of the Pre-Trial Chamber, and arrest proceedings in the State having custody of the person sought by the Prosecutor. It should be noted that the Pre-Trial Chamber has the power to authorize the Prosecutor to take specific investigative steps within the territory of a State Party without having secured the cooperation of that State if it has determined that the State is clearly unable to execute a request for cooperation due to the unavailability of any authority or any component of its judicial system competent to execute the request for cooperation.

Part 6 (The Trial) makes clear that there shall be no trial *in absentia*. The rights of the accused are set out in Article 67, and the measures to protect the victims and witnesses and their participation in the proceedings before the ICC in Article 68. Article 72 deals with the protection of national security information. The State has the final say on whether the disclosure of information would prejudice its national security, but it must cooperate with the ICC to resolve this matter. The ICC may use *in camera* or *ex parte* proceedings, summaries, or redactions of disclosure of the information and other permissible protective measures. If the State still refuses to cooperate, the ICC may refer the matter to the Assembly of States Parties or, where the UN Security Council referred the matter to the ICC, to the Security Council, and the ICC may make such inference in the trial of the accused as to the existence or non-existence of a fact, as may be appropriate in the circumstances. Alternatively, the ICC may order disclosure or, to the extent it does not order disclosure, make such inference in the trial of the accused as to the existence or non-existence of a fact, as may be appropriate in the circumstances.

The ICC is empowered to award reparations to victims of the crimes within its jurisdiction, including restitution, compensation, and rehabilitation. It may make an order directly against a convicted person or order that the award be made through the Trust Fund set up by the Assembly of States Parties for the benefit of victims and their families.

Part 7 enumerates penalties to be imposed by the ICC. The ICC may impose one of the following penalties on a person convicted of a crime within its jurisdiction: imprisonment not exceeding thirty years, or life imprisonment, *plus* a fine and/or a forfeiture of proceeds, property, and assets derived directly or indirectly from a crime. The money or property may be transferred to the Trust Fund.

Article 80 of the Statute provides: 'Nothing in this part affects the application by States of penalties prescribed by their national law, nor the law of States which do not provide for penalties prescribed in this Part'. This provision was included in the Statute at the insistence of delegations whose national law imposes the death penalty. On 17 July 1998, at the conclusion of the Rome Conference, the President of the Conference, responding to a recommendation by the Conference's Working Group on Penalties, read out the following declaration regarding the non-inclusion of the death penalty in the Statute:

'The debate at this Conference on the issue of which penalties should be applied by the Court has shown that there is no international consensus on the inclusion of the death penalty. However, in accordance with the principles of complementarity between the Court and national jurisdictions, national justice systems have the primary responsibility for investigating, prosecuting, and punishing individuals, in accordance with their national laws, for crimes falling under the jurisdiction of the International Criminal Court. In this regard, the Court would clearly not be able to affect national policies in this field. It should be noted that not including the death penalty in the Statute would not in any way have a legal bearing on national legislations and practices with regard to the death penalty. Nor shall it be considered as influencing, in the development of customary international law or in any other way, the legality of penalties imposed by national systems for serious crimes.'

Part 8 on Appeal and Revision provides that appeal may be lodged by the Prosecutor or the convicted person against decision of acquittal, conviction, or against sentence, as the case may be. Other decisions that may be subject to appeal include decisions on jurisdiction and admissibility, those on granting or denying release of the person investigated or accused, those involving an issue that would significantly affect the fair and expeditious conduct of the proceedings or the outcome of the trial, as well as decisions of the Pre-Trial Chamber to act on its own initiatives to preserve evidence deemed by it to be essential for the defence at trial.

Part 9, International Cooperation and Judicial Assistance, stipulates the general obligation for States Parties to cooperate fully with the ICC in its investigation and prosecution of crimes within its jurisdiction. Non-States Parties may be invited to provide assistance. Where there are competing requests from both the ICC and another State to surrender an indicted person for the same crime, priority shall be given to the ICC's request if the ICC has already determined the case to be admissible.

Paragraph 2 of Article 98, under the heading 'Cooperation with respect to waiver of immunity and consent to surrender', will be crucial for the effective functioning of the ICC, especially with regard to the surrender of persons who are nationals of non-States Parties. It stipulates that the ICC may not proceed with a request for surrender if such request would make the requested State act inconsistently with its obligations under international agreements that require the prior consent of the original sending

State for the surrender of a person to the ICC. In this circumstance, the ICC must first obtain the cooperation of the original sending State for the giving of consent for the surrender. Under Article 98(1), the ICC may not proceed with a request for surrender or assistance which would require the requested State to act inconsistently with its obligations under international law relating to the State or diplomatic immunity of a person or property of a third State, unless the ICC can first secure the cooperation from that third State for the waiver of the immunity.

Article 87(7) provides that where a State Party fails to comply with a request to cooperate with the ICC, the ICC may make a finding to that effect and refer the matter to the Assembly of States Parties or, where the UN Security Council referred the matter to the ICC, to the Security Council. Article 93(4) permits a State Party to deny, in accordance with Article 72 (in Part 6), a request for assistance, in whole or in part, if the request concerns the production of any documents or disclosure of evidence relating to its national security. Once again, in the final analysis, it is the ICC that determines whether the refusal is a breach of the State's obligations under the Statute.

Part 10 is on Enforcement. A sentence of imprisonment shall be served in a State designated by the ICC from a list of States which have indicated their willingness to accept sentenced persons. If no State is so designated, the sentence shall be served in the host State. It is the ICC that supervises the enforcement of conditions of imprisonment, which are governed by the law of the State of enforcement and shall be consistent with widely accepted international treaty standards governing treatment of prisoners. The ICC alone has the right to decide any application for appeal and revision/reduction of the sentence of imprisonment. When the person has served two-thirds of the sentence, or twenty-five years in the case of life imprisonment, the ICC shall review the sentence to decide whether it should be reduced.

Article 112 is the sole provision in Part 11, Assembly of States Parties. The Assembly is hereby established, with one representative from each State Party. Other States which have signed the Statute may be observers in the Assembly. The Assembly's powers and functions include adopting recommendations of the PCNICC, overseeing the administration of the ICC, approving budget for the ICC, deciding on the number of judges of the ICC, considering questions of non-cooperation, and performing any other function consistent with the Statute or the Rules of Procedure and Evidence.

The Assembly is to meet at the seat of the ICC or at the Headquarters of the UN once a year and when circumstances so require. Decisions on matters of substance must be approved by a two-thirds majority of those present and voting provided that an absolute majority of States Parties constitutes the quorum for voting. Decisions on matters of procedure must be approved by a simple majority of States Parties present and voting.

Part 12 is on Financing. The ICC is to be financed from the following sources: (a) assessed contributions made by States Parties in accordance with an agreed scale of assessment, based on the UN scale; (b) funds provided by the UN, subject to the approval of the UN General Assembly, in particular in relation to the expenses incurred due to referrals by the UN Security Council; and (c) voluntary contributions.

Part 13 is entitled 'Final Clauses'. The ICC shall settle disputes concerning its judicial functions. Any other dispute is to be settled by negotiations or by the Assembly of States Parties. Amendments may be proposed and a Review Conference is to be held after the expiration of seven years from the entry into force of the Statute. At any time thereafter, at the request of a State Party, the UN Secretary-General shall, upon approval by a majority of States parties, convene a Review Conference.

Reservations are expressly prohibited by Article 120.

Article 124 is a transitional provision. A State, on becoming a party to the Statute, may declare that, for a period of seven years after its entry into force for that State, it does not accept the ICC jurisdiction over war crimes when a crime is alleged to have been committed by its nationals or on its territory. Such a declaration may be withdrawn at any time.

The ICC Statute was open to signature until 31 December 2000. It shall enter into force on the first day of the month after the sixtieth day following the date of the deposit of the sixtieth instrument of ratification.

A State party may, by written notification, withdraw from the Statute—with effect one year after the date of receipt of notification, unless a later date is specified.

The ICC Statute was adopted on 17 July 1998 by a non-recorded vote of 120 in favour, seven against, twenty-one abstentions. Although the vote was non-recorded at the US's suggestion, the following countries spoke to reveal their voting positions. The US, China, Israel, and India stated that they had voted against the Statute. Mexico, Singapore, Sri Lanka, Trinidad and Tobago, and Turkey explained why they had abstained.[63]

China could not accept the universal jurisdiction of the ICC without State consent. In its view, the power of the Prosecutor should be based on State consent. Moreover, the ICC Statute should be adopted by consensus.

India was concerned that the Statute gives to the UN Security Council a role in terms that violate international law—the Council has the power to refer a case to the ICC, the power to block the ICC's proceedings, and the power to bind non-States Parties to the ICC Statute—all these while some of the Security Council members may have no intention to become States Parties to the Statute. Secondly, India was also concerned that the Statute accepts the concept of universal or inherent jurisdiction, making no distinction between States Parties and non-States Parties. Finally, the ICC Statute has failed to incorporate India's proposal to proscribe as a war crime the use of 'weapons of mass destruction, i.e. nuclear, chemical, and biological weapons'.

Israel was against the inclusion in the list of the most heinous and grievous war crimes the transfer by the Occupying Power of parts of its own population into the territory it occupies.

Before the adoption of the Statute in the plenary of the Conference, the US delega-

---

[63] The following statements appeared in the Rome Conference's Press Release L/ROM/22 dated 17 July 1998.

tion proposed to exempt from the ICC's jurisdiction conduct arising from the official actions of a non-State party acknowledged as such by that non-State Party. This would require the non-State Party to acknowledge responsibility for an atrocity in order for its national(s) to be exempted, an unlikely event for States committing genocide or other serious violations of international humanitarian law. This proposal was rejected. The US therefore voted against the adoption of the Statute because some of its fundamental concerns had not been addressed. In particular, the US could not accept the concept of jurisdiction in the Statute and its application over non-States Parties. It was also concerned with the possible inclusion of the crime of aggression within the ICC's jurisdiction without the linkage to a prior determination by the UN Security Council.[64]

The other three States voting against the adoption of the ICC Statute were presumably Libya, Iraq, and either Algeria, Qatar, or Yemen.[65]

Mexico abstained because no reservation is permitted. It was also dissatisfied with the lack of a clearer definition of complementarity; the non-proscription of nuclear weapons; and a lack of requirement for the consent of the State having custody over a person sought by the ICC. It also had strong reservations on the important role given to the Security Council under the Statute.

Singapore was not happy with the negotiation process in the last hours of the Conference in which provisions were drafted by just a small group of delegations who produced a strange fix for the question of jurisdiction. Besides, proscription of use of chemical and biological weapons had been inexplicably dropped.

Sri Lanka abstained to vent its disappointment that the crime of terrorism is not included as a crime within the ICC's jurisdiction.

Trinidad and Tobago abstained to show its frustration at the non-inclusion of drug trafficking and the death penalty.

Turkey abstained because terrorism is not included as a crime against humanity, as proposed by it. Besides, Turkey opposed the lack of a satisfactory formulation allowing the opting in and the opting out of the ICC's jurisdiction. With regard to war crimes, Turkey found no adequate safeguard against the ICC intervening in the internal matters of States which take action to root out terrorism. Turkey was also against the *proprio motu* powers of the Prosecutor.

One hundred and twenty-seven States signed the Final Act of the Conference.[66] Five

---

[64] In his statement before the Senate Committee on Foreign Relations on 23 July 1998, the head of the US Delegation to the Rome Conference mentioned two additional objections to the ICC Statute. First, the US failed to obtain consensus on its proposal to allow States to 'opt out' of the ICC jurisdiction for up to ten years so that the opting-out States could assess the development regarding the ICC and decide whether it was operating effectively and impartially. The US was also dissatisfied with the ICC State's 'take it or leave it' approach. By prohibiting reservations, the Statute fails to accommodate domestic constitutional requirements and national judicial procedures that may not be strictly in line with the provisions in the Statute but which do not defeat the object or purpose of the Statute. Summarized in A. Frye (ed.), *Toward an International Criminal Court?* (Council on Foreign Relations, 1999), 75.

[65] J. I. Charney, 'Progress in International Criminal Law' (1999) 93 *AJIL* 452 at 452 and n. 17.

[66] *Doc. A/ CONF. 183/ 10* of 17 July 1998.

resolutions are annexed thereto. The sixth resolution, known as Resolution F, set up the Preparatory Commission for the International Criminal Court (PCNICC) composed of representatives of States which have signed the Final Act and other States invited to participate in its proceedings. The PCNICC has been meeting at the UN Headquarters in New York to prepare proposals for practical arrangements for the establishment and coming into operation of the ICC. It shall remain in existence until the conclusion of the first meeting of the Assembly of States Parties. The PCNICC finally adopted the Elements of Crimes and Rules of Procedure and Evidence on 30 June 2000.

As of 31 December 2000, one hundred and thirty-nine States, including the US and Israel, have signed the ICC Statute, and it has been ratified by twenty-seven States: Senegal, Trinidad and Tobago, San Marino, Italy, Fiji, Ghana, Norway, Belize, Tajikistan, Iceland, Venezuela, France, Belgium, Canada, Mali, Lesotho, New Zealand, Botswana and Luxemburg (on the same day), Sierra Leone, Gabon, Spain, South Africa, Marshall Islands, Germany, Austria, and Finland, in that order.

While the ICC Statute has not yet entered into force, it already possesses significant legal value as reflecting the legal views (*opinio juris*) of an overwhelming majority of States attending the Rome Conference and the Sixth Committee of the UN General Assembly.[67] As the ICTY states in *Furundzija*:

'Notwithstanding Article 10 of the Statute, the purpose of which is to ensure that existing or developing law is not "limited" or "prejudiced" by the Statute's provisions, resort may be had *cum grano salis* to these provisions to help elucidate customary international law. Depending on the matter at issue, the Rome Statute may be taken to restate, reflect or clarify customary rules or crystallize them, whereas in some areas it creates new law or modifies existing law. At any event, the Rome Statute by and large may be taken as constituting an authoritative expression of the legal views of a great number of States.'[68]

2.4 EXISTING SYSTEM OF CRIMINAL JUSTICE OUTSIDE THE FRAMEWORK OF INTERNATIONAL CRIMINAL TRIBUNALS

The existing system of prosecution of 'international criminals' outside of the ICTY Statute, the ICTR Statute, and the ICC Statute, can be summarized as follows.[69]

Jurisdiction over criminal matters is primarily territorial. Territorial jurisdiction

---

[67] *Prosecutor v. Dusko Tadic,* Case No. IT-94-1-A, ICTY App. Ch., 5 July 1999, para. 223; *Prosecutor v. Anto Furundzija,* Case No. IT-95-17/1-T, ICTY T. Ch. II, 10 Dec. 1998, para. 227.

[68] Ibid., para. 227.

[69] For an account of the existing system of international cooperation in criminal matters, especially from the US perspective, see N. E. Guffey-Landers, 'Establishing an International Criminal Court: Will It Do Justice?' (1996) **20** *Maryland J. Int'l L. & Trade* 199 at 203–19.

encompasses the power to enact law (legislative or prescriptive jurisdiction), the power to construe and apply the law (adjudicative jurisdiction), and the power to enforce the law (enforcement jurisdiction). States also assert extraterritorial jurisdiction over events outside their territory on the following bases: the conduct in question was perpetrated by a national of the State asserting the jurisdiction (the nationality or active personality principle); the perpetration is against nationals of the State asserting jurisdiction (the passive personality principle); and the conduct affects the security of the State asserting the jurisdiction (the protective principle). 'Universal jurisdiction' is asserted in certain circumstances to prosecute offences irrespective of where these offences were committed, the nationality of the offenders, or any connection with the State asserting this jurisdiction. Piracy is a crime long recognized as being subject to universal jurisdiction of any State interested in trying pirates. War crimes falling under the category of 'grave breaches' of the four Geneva Conventions relating to the protection of victims of armed conflict of 12 August 1949 are also subject to 'universal jurisdiction' of almost all States of the world who have ratified the Conventions.[70] In *Eichmann*, the District Court of Jerusalem upheld universal jurisdiction as a source of its jurisdiction to try the accused for crimes against humanity and war crimes committed against the Jewish people during the Nazi regime when the State of Israel did not exist. The Court stated that this 'universal source (pertaining to the whole of mankind) . . . vests the right to prosecute and punish crimes of this order in every State within the family of nations'.[71]

Extradition comes into play when a State asserting criminal jurisdiction over an offender requests another State having custody of the offender to 'extradite' him to stand trial in the requesting State. Some important conditions exist. Foremost among these conditions are that the offence in question must also be an offence in the requested State, although this could be under a different name (the rule of 'double criminality'); that the offence in question must not be a 'political' offence (the 'political offence exception'); and that the person extradited will be prosecuted only for the offence stipulated in the request for extradition (the rule of 'speciality').[72] The political offence exception has proved to be the most problematic. What is a 'political' offence is subject to determination of requested States, and there is no objective test that has attained universal acceptance.[73] After WWI, the Netherlands refused to extradite German Emperor Kaiser Wilhelm II to stand trial for his roles in the initiating and

---

[70] For cases and materials on the question of jurisdiction, see J. J. Paust, M. Cherif Bassiouni, S. A. Williams, M. Scharf, J. Gurulé, and B. Zagaris (eds.), *International Criminal Law: Cases and Materials* (Carolina Academic Press, 1996), 95–180.

[71] *Attorney-General of the Govt. of Israel v. Eichmann*, Dist. Ct. Jerusalem, 11 Dec. 1961 (1962) **56** *AJIL* 805, para. 30.

[72] Sir Robert Y. Jennings and Sir Arthur Watts (eds.), *Oppenheim's International Law*, 9th ed. (Longman, 1992), 948–71.

[73] See the detailed analysis by Reinhardt, J. in the US case of *Quinn v. Robinson*, 783 F. 2d 776 (9th Cir. 1986); C. van den Wijngaert, *The Political Offence Exception to Extradition: The Delicate Problem of Balancing the Rights of the Individual and the International Public Order* (Kluwer, 1980).

waging of WWI, contending that his crimes were 'political' in nature. In 1962, the UK decided not to accede to the Genocide Convention of 1948 because Article VII of the Convention stipulating that offences of genocide shall not be considered as political crimes for the purpose of extradition would compel the UK to derogate from its 'traditional right to grant political asylum'.[74] Some States are also prohibited by their legislation or constitution from extraditing their nationals.

The international community has endeavoured to circumvent difficulties inherent in the usual bases of criminal jurisdiction by resorting to multilateral or bilateral agreements. Methods typically used in these agreements include: (a) obligating the State having custody over an offender to either prosecute him or extraditing him to another State which has shown interest in his prosecution; (b) treating the offences covered by the agreements as 'non-political' ones; and (c) allowing States Parties to exercise jurisdiction over the offences covered under the agreements when such offences were committed in the territory of one of the States Parties.[75] Such agreements govern crimes of common concern such as hijacking of aircraft;[76] aircraft bombings;[77] attacks on internationally protected persons, including diplomats;[78] hostage taking;[79] torture;[80] drug trafficking;[81] and war crimes of 'grave breaches' under the four Geneva Conventions of 12 August 1949.[82]

'Mutual assistance in criminal matters' is supplementary to the other forms of international cooperation to bring a criminal to justice. It concerns providing assistance in the taking of evidence or statements of persons, effecting services of judicial documents, executing searches and seizures, examining objects and sites, providing information and evidentiary items, and so forth. It does not concern the arrest or detention of any person with a view to the extradition of that person, the transfer of persons in custody to serve sentences, the transfer of proceedings in criminal matters, or the enforcement in the requested State of criminal judgments imposed in the requesting State except to the extent permitted by the law of the requested State and any agreement between the States concerned. Generally, the assistance may be refused

[74] *per* Lord Privy Seal Edward Heath, 663 House of Commons Debate (5th Ser.) cols. 423–4 (18 July 1962), in Whiteman, *Digest of International Law*, 871–2.

[75] For a discussion of theoretical bases of the various heads of jurisdiction under these arguments, see Toshiyuki Tanaka, 'Implementation of International Criminal Law' (1995) **38** *Japanese Annual Int'l L.* 65.

[76] Convention for the Suppression of Unlawful Seizure of Aircraft (the Hague Convention) of 16 Dec. 1970, 860 *UNTS* 105.

[77] Convention for the Suppression of Unlawful Acts against the Safety of Civil Aviation (the Montreal Convention) of 23 Sept. 1971, 974 *UNTS* 177.

[78] Convention on the Prevention and Punishment of Crimes against Internationally Protected Persons, Including Diplomatic Agents of 14 Dec. 1973, 1035 *UNTS* 167.

[79] International Convention against the Taking of Hostages of 17 Dec. 1979 (*UN Doc. A/ 34/ 819*).

[80] International Convention against Torture and Other Cruel, Inhuman or Degrading Treatment or Punishment of 10 Dec. 1984, 1465 *UNTS* 85.

[81] UN Convention against Illicit Trafficking in Narcotic Drugs and Psychotropic Substances of 20 Dec. 1988 (1989) **28** *ILM* 493.

[82] See, e.g. Geneva Convention Relative to the Protection of Civilian Persons in Time of War, 75 *UNTS* 287, Art. 146.

if the offence in question is regarded by the requested State as having a political nature.[83]

Extradition and mutual assistance in criminal matters are to be distinguished from transfer of prisoners, or cooperation in the execution of penal sentences. In the last mentioned instance, States cooperate with each other to transfer offenders to serve the remainder of sentences of imprisonment, confinement, or other forms of deprivation of liberty in another State, often their national State, so as to facilitate their successful reintegration into society.

The existing system is by no means satisfactory for bringing to justice those committing crimes of international concern.[84] Adolf Eichmann had to be kidnapped in secret by the Israeli secret service to stand trial for his role in the 'Final Solution' of the Jews during WWII. Some key criminals have been abducted by the US from other States to stand trial in US courts despite the existence of an extradition treaty between the US and the States concerned.[85]

The existing system cannot work satisfactorily if the State having custody of the perpetrator of a crime does not prosecute or extradite him. In the case of crimes condoned or promoted by a State or the incumbent Government, like genocide or crimes against humanity, impunity is the common culture at the national level. A Government might also wish to contain scandals. Therefore, even where there is prosecution, it may amount to a travesty of justice. Such was the case of Lieutenant William Calley, who was tried by court martial for his role in the massacre in My Lai, Vietnam, during the Vietnam War, in which twenty-two infants, children, women, and old men were killed in cold blood. In 1971, he was convicted and sentenced to life imprisonment and hard labour. US President Richard M. Nixon ordered that he be confined to quarters pending appeal. Calley's sentence was reduced to twenty years by the Third Army Commander. In 1973, the Court of Military Review upheld Calley's conviction and sentenced him to twenty years' imprisonment. This decision was upheld by the Court of Military Appeals. In 1974, the US Secretary of Defence reduced Calley's sentence to ten years. A district court overturned Calley's conviction and he was released on bail pending appeal by the prosecution. In 1975, he was released on parole. In that same year, the US Court of Appeal for the Fifth Circuit

---

[83] See the Model Treaty on Mutual Assistance in Criminal Matters, adopted by the UN General Assembly on 3 Apr. 1991 (*UN Doc. A/ RES/ 45/ 117*).

[84] See E. Davidson, *The Nuremberg Fallacy* (University of Missouri Press, 1998).

[85] See, e.g. *US v. Alvarez-Machain*, US Sup. Ct. Judgment of 15 June 1992 (1992) **31** *ILM* 900, where the US Supreme Court held, in effect, that as the extradition treaty between the US and Mexico did not prohibit the forcible abduction of foreign nationals specifically, the treaty did not divest US federal courts of jurisdiction over the foreign nationals. Analysed in R. Rayfuse, 'International Abduction and the United States Supreme Court: The Law of the Jungle Reigns', in J. Dugard and C. van den Wyngaert (eds.), *International Criminal Law and Procedure* (Dartmouth, 1996), 882; L. S. Sunga, *The Emerging System of International Criminal Law: Developments in Codification and Implementation* (Kluwer, 1997), 262–71. See also *US v. Matta-Ballesteros*, 71 F. 3d 754 (9th Cir. 1995), where *Alvarez-Machain* was followed in relation to the forcible abduction of a national of Honduras from Honduras to appear before the US court despite the existence of the extradition treaty between the US and Honduras.

reversed the decision of the district court. Calley remained free on parole. In fact, he was released after serving only a total of six months of his sentence.[86]

In many instances, despite the genuine interest to secure prosecution of international criminals, the existing law or legal system in the State concerned may be too inadequate or antiquated to lead to successful prosecution.[87] For example, the French Cour de Cassation, Criminal Chamber, held that French courts cannot exercise universal jurisdiction accorded by the relevant provisions of the 1949 Geneva Conventions relating to the protection of victims of armed conflicts, which France has ratified, because France has not enacted law to implement the Conventions. In the case of the Convention on Torture and Other Cruel, Inhuman or Degrading Treatment or Punishment of 1984, there is an implementing legislation, but nothing could be done if the accused is not found in French territory.[88]

Some national systems permit amnesty as a means to promote national unity and reconciliation after long turbulent years of human rights abuse by those in power. South Africa has the Committee on Amnesty to grant amnesty for any act, omission, or offence to anyone who fully disclosed all relevant facts about human rights abuse associated with a political objective. The validity of such amnesty has been upheld by the Constitutional Court of South Africa.[89] Using amnesty as the route to national reconciliation is not generally accepted. Security Council Resolution 955 that set up the ICTR, for example, considers that prosecution of the persons responsible for atrocities would lead to the process of national reconciliation and the restoration and maintenance of peace in Rwanda. The ICTR itself considers that cessation of the atrocities in the Rwandan conflict does not necessarily imply that international peace and security had been restored, 'because peace and security cannot be said to be re-established adequately without justice being done'.[90]

---

[86] *US v. First Lieutenant William L. Calley, Jr.*, US Military Court of Military Appeals, 21 Dec. 1973, 22 US Ct. Mil. App. 534 (1973), 382 F. Supp. 65 (Military District, Georgia 1974), 519 F. 2d 184 (5th Cir. 1975), 425 US 911 (1976). Discussed in D. L. Anderson (ed.), *Facing My Lai: Moving Beyond the Massacre* (University Press of Kansas, 1998); H. McCoubrey, *International Humanitarian Law: The Regulation of Armed Conflicts* (Dartmouth, 1990), 218–9.

[87] See A. Marschik, 'The Politics of Prosecution: European National Approaches to War Crimes', in McCormack and Simpson (eds.), *Law of War Crimes*, 65; J. M. Wenig, 'Enforcing the Lessons of History: Israel Judges the Holocaust', ibid., 103; G. Triggs, 'Australia's War Crimes Trials: All Pity Choked', ibid., 123; and S. A. Williams, 'Laudable Principles Lacking Application: The Prosecution of War Criminals in Canada', ibid., 151.

[88] *In re Javor*, 26 Mar. 1996, and *In re Munyeshyaka*, 6 Jan. 1998, reported and analysed by B. Stern (1999) 93 *AJIL* 525.

[89] *Azanian Peoples Organization v. President of the Rep. of South Africa*, Case CCT 17/96, Const. Ct. of S. Africa, 25 July 1996, summarized in (1997) 91 *AJIL* 360. On non-prosecutorial options, see further Ratner and Abrams, *Accountability*, 193–215.

[90] *Prosecutor v. Kanyabashi*, Case No. ICTR-96-15-T, ICTR T. Ch., Decision on the Defence Motion on Jurisdiction, para. 26.

3

GENERAL PRINCIPLES OF INTERNATIONAL CRIMINAL LAW

3.1 PRINCIPLE OF LEGALITY

The principle of legality aims at preventing the prosecution and punishment of an individual for acts which he reasonably believed to be lawful at the time of their commission.[1] Inherent in this principle are the requirement of specificity and the prohibition of ambiguity in criminal law, its retroactive application, or its application by analogy.[2] The principle is enshrined in human rights instruments such as the International Covenant on Civil and Political Rights of 1966,[3] whose Article 15 stipulates:

'1. No one shall be held guilty of any criminal offence of any act or omission which did not constitute a criminal offence, under national or international law, at the time when it was committed. . . .
2. Nothing in this article shall prejudice the trial and punishment of any person for any act or omission which, at the time when it was committed, was criminal according to the general principles of law recognized by the community of nations.'

This provision is intended to avoid the situation faced by the Nuremberg Tribunal and the Tokyo Tribunal after WWII. However, the cardinal principles enunciated at Nuremberg and Tokyo, such as the principle of individual criminal responsibility on the international plane, cannot be refuted by an international tribunal. The ICTY has gone as far as considering as undisputed that acts such as murder, torture, rape, and inhuman treatment are criminal according to 'general principles of law' recognized by every legal system and those who commit these acts cannot escape prosecution before an international criminal tribunal by hiding behind the principle of legality.[4]

---

[1] *Prosecutor v. Zejnil Delalic, Zdravko Mucic, Hazim Delic, and Esad Landzo ('Celebici' case)*, Case No. IT-96–21-T, ICTY T. Ch. II *quater*, 16 Nov. 1998, para. 313.

[2] Ibid., paras. 402, 408–13.

[3] Adopted 16 Dec. 1966 (1967) **6** *ILM* 368.

[4] *Celebici*, para. 313.

3.2 APPLICABLE LAW AND RULES OF INTERPRETATION

There have been four occasions in which *ad hoc* international criminal tribunals were set up to prosecute international criminals. The first two were the Nuremberg and the Tokyo Tribunals established after WWII. The other two are the ICTY and the ICTR. Each international criminal tribunal interprets the law in accordance with the instrument creating the tribunal itself. So will the International Criminal Court to be established by the ICC Statute.

THE NUREMBERG AND TOKYO TRIBUNALS

The crimes enumerated in the Nuremberg Charter and the Tokyo Charter may seem somewhat at odds with international crimes as we understand them today. For example, genocide did not exist as a *sui generis* crime, and the distinction between war crimes and crimes against humanity lay in the fact that the former were committed in occupied territories, whereas the latter were committed in Germany and the territories annexed as part of the Third Reich.

While the Nuremberg Tribunal alleged that it was applying customary international law to interpret the Nuremberg Charter, rules of customary international law might have existed at that time in relation to war crimes, but certainly not crimes against humanity or crimes against peace. It transpired that judges also had to resort to their national criminal laws to interpret the law of the Tribunals. For example, the judges of these Tribunals dealt with the issue of duress, for which there was no guidance in international law, by resorting to their own national jurisdictions.[5] Tribunals applying Control Council Law No. 10 also took account of generally recognized principles of criminal law.[6] In the *Dachau Concentration Camp* case, for instance, the US Prosecution relied on principles of American criminal law on the subject of complicity.[7]

THE ICTY AND THE ICTR

With respect to the ICTY and the ICTR, their Statutes and Rules consist of a 'fusion and synthesis' of the Common Law tradition and the Civil Law tradition.[8]

Trial Chamber II of the ICTY held in *Kupreskic and Others* that the ICTY is an

---

[5] This was noted in the Joint Separate Opinion of Judge McDonald and Judge Vohrah in *Prosecutor v. Drazen Erdemovic*, Case No. IT-96–22-A, ICTY App. Ch., 7 Oct. 1997.

[6] Cf., e.g. *S. et al.* ('*Hechingen Deportation*'), Decision of a German court in the French occupied zone, cited by Trial Chamber II of the ICTY in *Prosecutor v. Anto Furundzija*, Case No. IT-95–17/1-T, ICTY T. Ch. II, 10 Dec. 1998, n. 248.

[7] *Trial of Martin Gottfried Weiss and 39 Others*, General Military Court of the US Zone, Germany, 15 Nov.-13 Dec. 1945, 16 UNWCC *Law Reports* 5, at 12–13. Also cited in *Furundzija*, n. 232.

[8] *Celebici*, para. 159.

international court which applies international law, although it may also draw upon national law to fill possible *lacunae* in the ICTY Statute or customary international law.[9]

The Appeals Chamber of the ICTY held in *Tadic* that although the ICTY Statute is legally a very different instrument from an international treaty, it is permissible to be guided by the principle applied by the International Court of Justice with regard to treaty interpretation; that is, a tribunal called upon to interpret and apply the provisions of a treaty must 'endeavour to give effect to these provisions in their natural and ordinary meaning in the context in which they occur.'[10] Where the wording of a provision is clear and unambiguous, it must be given a *literal* interpretation without any necessity to resort to supplementary means or secondary sources of interpretation such as the *travaux préparatoires* leading to the adoption of the treaty or any other international norm-creating agreement. For example, if there appears to be a manifest contradiction between the ICTY Statute adopted by the Security Council and secondary sources, such as the Report of the Secretary-General which was approved by the Security Council, the former must prevail.[11]

In case of doubt and wherever the contrary is not apparent from the text of a treaty provision, the provision must be interpreted in light of and in conformity with customary international law.[12] It must be presumed that the draftsmen of the treaty (including the Security Council in the case of the instruments establishing *ad hoc* international tribunals, such as the ICTY) intended to remain within the confines of general rules of international law, unless they departed explicitly or implicitly from such rules.[13] Thus, while it is open to the Security Council, subject to respect for peremptory norms of international law (*jus cogens*), to adopt definitions of crimes in the ICTY Statute that depart from customary international law, provisions of the ICTY Statute defining crimes within the ICTY's jurisdiction should, as a general principle, always be interpreted as reflecting customary international law, unless a contrary intention is expressed in the terms of the Statute or from other authoritative sources. In this latter situation, secondary sources should be taken into account to provide an authoritative interpretation of the instrument in question.[14]

---

[9] *Prosecutor v. Zoran Kupreskic and Others*, Case No. IT-95–16-T, ICTY T. Ch. II, 14 Jan. 2000, paras. 539–40.

[10] *Prosecutor v. Dusko Tadic*, Case No. IT-94-A, ICTY App. Ch. (hereinafter '*Tadic* Appeals Judgment'), 15 July 1999, para. 282, quoting the ICJ Advisory Opinion on *Competence of the General Assembly for the Admission of a State to the United Nations*, ICJ Rep. 1950, 8.

[11] *Tadic* Appeals Judgment, paras. 295–6, 303.

[12] For example, in *Erdemovic*, the Appeals Chamber of the ICTY, after finding the ICTY Statute silent on the applicability or non-applicability of duress as a complete defence, resorted to the examination of criminal law in Common Law and Civil Law States to ascertain whether either *opinio juris* or general principles of law existed on this issue. *Prosecutor v. Drazen Erdemovic*, Case No. IT-96–22-A, 7 Oct. 1997, Joint Separate Opinion of Judge McDonald and Judge Vohrah, Separate and Dissenting Opinion of Judge Li, and Separate and Dissenting Opinions of Judge Cassese and Judge Stephen. See also Olivia Swaak-Goldman (1998) **92** *AJIL* 282 at 283–7.

[13] *Tadic* Appeals Judgment, para. 287.

[14] Ibid., paras. 295–6, 303–4.

Therefore, although the ICTY Statute and the ICTR Statute differ from treaties in that they are concluded by an international organization and are made binding on States by virtue of the enforcement power of the UN Security Council under Chapter VII of the UN Charter, the rules of interpretation of these Statutes are essentially the same as rules of customary international law on treaty interpretation as codified Articles 31 and 32 of the Vienna Convention on the Law of Treaties of 1969.[15]

Article 31 of the 1969 Vienna Convention stipulates:

'1. A treaty shall be interpreted in good faith and in accordance with the ordinary meaning to be given to the terms of the treaty in their context and in the light of its object and purpose.

2. The context for the purpose of the interpretation of a treaty shall comprise, in addition to the text, including its preamble and annexes:

(a) any agreement relating to the treaty which was made between all the parties in connexion with the conclusion of the treaty;

(b) any instrument which was made by one or more parties in connexion with the conclusion of the treaty and accepted by the other parties as an instrument related to the treaty.

3. There shall be taken into account, together with the context:

(a) any subsequent agreement between the parties regarding the interpretation of the treaty or the application of its provisions;

(b) any subsequent practice in the application of the treaty which establishes the agreement of the parties regarding its interpretation;

(c) any relevant rules of international law applicable in the relations between the parties.

4. A special meaning shall be given to a term if it is established that the parties so intended.'

Article 32 of the 1969 Vienna Convention provides:

'Recourse may be had to supplementary means of interpretation, including the preparatory work of the treaty and the circumstances of its inclusion, in order to confirm the meaning resulting from the application of Article 31, or to determine the meaning when the interpretation according to Article 31:

(a) leaves the meaning ambiguous or obscure; or

(b) leads to a result which is manifestly absurd or unreasonable.'

Where there is no applicable treaty provision on a particular subject customary international law, general principles of international criminal law, or general principles of international law may be resorted to in that order.[16] Failing that, it is necessary to look for 'principles of criminal law common to the major legal systems of the world' that

---

[15] (1969) 8 *ILM* 679.   [16] *Furundzija*, paras. 177, 191.

may be derived, 'with all due caution', from national laws.[17] As Trial Chamber II of the ICTY puts it in *Furundzija*:

'Whenever international criminal rules do not define a notion of criminal law, reliance upon national legislation is justified, subject to the following conditions: (i) unless indicated by an international rule, reference should not be made to one national legal system only, say that of common-law or that of civil-law States. Rather, international courts must draw upon the general concepts and legal institutions common to all the major legal systems of the world. This presupposes a process of identification of the common denominators in these legal systems so as to pinpoint the basic notions they share; (ii) since "international trials exhibit a number of features that differentiate them from national criminal proceedings" (Paragraph 5, Separate and Dissenting Opinion of Judge Cassese, *Prosecutor v. Drazen Erdemovic*, Judgment, Case No. IT-96-22-A, 7 Oct. 1997), account must be taken of the specificity of international criminal proceedings when utilizing national law notions. In this way a mechanical importation or transposition from national law into international criminal proceedings is avoided, as well as the attendant distortions of the unique traits of such proceedings.'[18]

In *Furundzija* itself, the Trial Chamber found that despite the inevitable discrepancies, most legal systems in the Common Law and Civil Law States consider rape to be forcible sexual penetration of the human body by the penis or the forcible insertion of any other object into either the vagina or the anus. However, there is a lack of uniformity in the criminalization of forced oral penetration, with some States treating it as sexual assault while other States categorizing it as rape. The Trial Chamber then resorted to the general principles of international criminal law or, if such principles were of no avail, to the general principles of international law to find out how this act should be criminalized. After finding that the general principle of respect for human dignity forms the fundamental principle of international humanitarian law and human rights law as well as a principle permeating the whole body of international law, the Trial Chamber decided that the definition of rape should be broadened to encompass 'such an extremely serious sexual outrage as forced oral penetration'.[19]

In addition to the general rules of interpretation mentioned above, the principle of legality requires that criminal statutes be strictly interpreted and without giving retroactive effect to the provisions of the statutes.[20] In *Celebici*, the Trial Chamber of the ICTY resorted to 'a reasonable as well as purposive interpretation of the existing provisions of international customary law' to interpret the ICTY Statute and Rules of

[17] Ibid., para. 177. Cf. also *Celebici*, para. 414; *Kupreskic and Others*, para. 670.

[18] *Furundzija*, para. 178. Trial Chamber II *quater* of the ICTY held in *Celebici* that after resorting to the general principles of treaty interpretation, the rules of interpretation of national legal systems may be relied on, where applicable, under general principles of law unless such rules are inconsistent with the plain language of the Statute and Rules of Procedure and their object and purpose. *Celebici*, para. 1161. See also *Kupreskic and Others*, paras. 541–2, 678.

[19] *Furundzija*, paras. 179–86. Cf. also paras. 642–3 of the *Tadic* Judgment which defined civilians who are victims of crimes against humanity by resorting to decisions of French domestic courts.

[20] *Celebici*, paras. 408–12.

Procedure and Evidence.[21] After acknowledging the necessity to have regard to the different approaches of interpretation in the Common Law and the Civil Law traditions, the Trial Chamber concluded that since the essence of interpretation is to discover the true purpose and intent of the Statute and Rules in question, the task of the judge interpreting a provision under whichever system is necessarily the same.[22] The Trial Chamber resorted to the '*literal* rule' of interpretation, which is supplemented by the '*golden* rule' of interpretation, and the '*mischief* rule' of interpretation. Under the golden rule, the court will modify the grammatical sense of the word to avoid injustice, absurdity, anomaly, or contradiction, as clearly not to have been intended by the legislature. Under the mischief, or purposive, rule, the court is required to look into the legislative history for the 'mischief' that the statute intends to remedy.[23] Since the ICTY and the ICTR are *ad hoc* Tribunals, they must take into consideration the objects and purposes of the Statutes as well as the social and political considerations which gave rise to their creation.[24] According to the Trial Chamber:

'The rule of strict construction requires that the language of a particular provision shall be construed such that no cases shall be held to fall within it which do not fall both within the reasonable meaning of its terms and within the spirit and scope of the enactment . . . [I]f the legislature has not used words sufficiently comprehensive to include within its prohibition all the cases which should naturally fall within the mischief intended to be prevented, the interpreter is not competent to extend them. The interpreter of a provision can only determine whether the case is within the intention of a criminal statute by construction of the express language of the provision.

A strict construction requires that no case shall fall within a penal statute which does not comprise all the elements which, whether morally material or not, are in fact made to constitute the offence as defined by the statute. In other words, a strict construction requires that an offence is made out in accordance with the statute creating it only when all the essential ingredients, as prescribed by the statute, have been established.

It has always been the practice of courts not to fill omissions in legislation when this can be said to have been deliberate. It would seem, however, that where the omission was accidental, it is usual to supply the missing words to give the legislation the meaning intended. The paramount object in the construction of a criminal provision, or any other statute, is to ascertain the legislative intent. The rule of strict construction is not violated by giving the expression its full meaning or the alternative meaning which is more consonant with the legislative intent and best effectuates such intent.

The effect of strict construction of the provisions of a criminal statute is that where an equivocal word or ambiguous sentence leaves a reasonable doubt of its meaning which the canons of construction fail to solve, the benefit of the doubt should be given to the subject and against the legislature which has failed to explain itself. This is why ambiguous criminal statutes are to be construed *contra proferentem*.'[25]

---

[21] Ibid., para. 170.   [22] Ibid., para. 159, 170.   [23] Ibid., paras. 160–71.
[24] Ibid., para. 170.   [25] Ibid., paras. 410–3.

With respect to the principle of *res judicata*, it only applies *inter partes* in a case where a matter has already been judicially determined within that case itself.[26] In other words, in criminal cases, the *res judicata* doctrine is limited to the question of whether, when the previous trial of a particular individual is followed by another of the same individual, a specific matter has already been fully litigated.[27]

The issue of precedents (*stare decisis*) is analysed exhaustively by the ICTY Appeals Chamber in *Aleksovski*.[28] In general, in the administration of criminal law, where the liberty of the individual is at stake, the Court would not depart from a previous decision, except with circumspection, so that certainty, stability, and predictability in criminal law can be ensured.[29] A proper construction of the ICTY Statute itself leads to the same conclusion. The Appeals Chamber should follow its previous decisions, except where there are cogent reasons to depart from them in the interests of justice, and after the most careful consideration of previous decisions, both as to the law, including the authorities cited, and the facts. Examples for such departure include cases where the previous decision has been decided on a wrong legal principle or given *per incuriam* because the judge or judges were ill-informed about the applicable law.[30] According to the principle of *stare decisis*, what is followed in previous decisions is the legal principle (*ratio decidendi*) applicable in similar or substantially similar cases where the question raised by the facts in the subsequent case is the same as the question decided by the legal principle in the previous decision.[31] Where previous decisions are conflicting, the Appeals Chamber is to determine which decision it will follow, or whether to depart from both decisions for cogent reasons in the interests of justice.[32] In any case, the *ratio decidendi* of the Appeals Chamber binds Trial Chambers since the former is given the function of settling definitively the questions of law and fact arising from the decisions of the Trial Chamber in order to ensure a single, unified, coherent, and rational body of law.[33] However, decisions of Trial Chambers have no binding force on each other, although a Trial Chamber is free to follow the decision of another Trial Chamber if it finds that decision persuasive.[34]

So, the Trial Chamber of the ICTY in *Celebici* refused to follow the judgment of the Trial Chamber of the ICTY in *Tadic* that categorized the armed conflicts in the former Yugoslavia at the relevant time as an internal armed conflict.[35] Likewise, in *Kayishema and Ruzindana*, Trial Chamber II of the ICTR refused to follow the interpretation of Trial Chamber I of the ICTR in *Akayesu* on the elements of 'murder' as a crime

---

[26] *Kupreskic and Others*, para. 540.
[27] *Celebici*, para. 228.
[28] *Prosecutor v. Zlatko Aleksovski*, Case No. IT-95–14/1-A, ICTY App. Ch., 24 Mar. 2000, paras. 89–115.
[29] Ibid., para. 97.
[30] Ibid., paras. 107–9.
[31] Ibid., para. 110, and cf. para. 125.
[32] Ibid., para. 111.
[33] Ibid., para. 113.
[34] Ibid., para. 114.
[35] *Celebici*, paras. 233–4, declining to follow the *Tadic* Judgment.

against humanity.[36] Yet, decisions of the same Tribunal in previous cases are generally taken into consideration and cannot be dismissed without sound reasons.[37] The definition of rape adopted by the ICTR in *Akayesu* has been followed even by the ICTY in *Celebici* and relied upon as guidance by the ICTY in *Furundzija*.[38]

It is interesting to note that the Trial Chamber of the ICTY in *Celebici* warned of the dangers of relying on the reasoning and findings of a very different judicial body concerned with rather different circumstances from the case at issue; for example, the International Court of Justice's reasoning on the issue of State responsibility should not be transposed wholesale into the context of characterizing whether an armed conflict is an international or internal conflict for the purpose of a war crimes trial before an international criminal court.[39] To determine the authoritative value of case law, a case must be appraised within the context of the forum in which the case was heard as well as the law applied.[40] Thus, case law from the British military courts for the trials of war criminals whose jurisdiction was based on the rules and procedure of the domestic military courts were less helpful in establishing rules of international law than case law of tribunals set up to apply international law.[41]

In any case, international tribunals are not bound by past doctrines; they must apply customary international law as it stands at the time of the commission of offences. Thus, in *Tadic*, Trial Chamber II of the ICTY opined that it must interpret the notion of crimes against humanity as it stood at the relevant times when the offences were committed by the accused, and not at the time of WWII or soon thereafter when the notion was being developed.[42]

THE ICC STATUTE

The ICC Statute is a treaty binding on its States Parties. It is therefore directly subject to the rules of treaty interpretation as enshrined in the Vienna Convention on the Law of Treaties of 1969.

---

[36] *Prosecutor v. Clément Kayishema and Obed Ruzindana*, Case No. ICTR-95-1-T, ICTR T. Ch. II, 21 May 1999, paras. 137–40.

[37] See, e.g., *Furundzija*, paras. 198, 296, where Trial Chamber II of the ICTY follows previous decisions of the ICTY on the issue of complicity and imposition of sentence in case of multiple convictions.

[38] *Prosecutor v. Jean-Paul Akayesu*, Case No. ICTR-96-4-T, ICTR T. Ch. I, Judgment of 2 Sept. 1998, paras. 597–8, followed by *Celebici*, para. 479 and relied upon as a guidance by *Furundzija*, paras. 174–86. In *Prosecution v. Dusko Tadic* (ICTY T. Ch. II, Sentencing Judgment of 11 Nov. 1999), Judge Robinson, in his Separate Opinion, stated that the decision of the Appeals Chamber of the ICTY in *Erdemovic* as to the relative gravity of crimes against humanity and war crimes was binding on the Trial Chamber in *Tadic* and he was bound by it, otherwise he would have imposed the same sentence for war crimes as for crimes against humanity.

[39] *Celebici*, paras. 230–1. This warning was heeded by the Appeals Chamber of the ICTY in the *Tadic* Appeals Judgment, which chose not to transpose wholesale the ICJ's reasoning on State responsibility in *Military and Paramilitary Activities in and against Nicaragua (Nicaragua v. US)*, ICJ Rep. 1986, 14 into the context of characterization of armed conflicts in *Tadic*. See Chapter 6.

[40] *Furundzija*, para. 194.

[41] Ibid., para. 196.

[42] *Tadic* Judgment, para. 654.

Article 21 of the ICC Statute under the heading 'Applicable law' establishes the hierarchy of the rules of interpretation of the ICC Statute as follows:[43]

'(1) The Court shall apply:

    (a) In the first place, this Statute, Elements of Crimes and its Rules of Procedure and Evidence;

    (b) In the second place, where appropriate, applicable treaties and the principles and rules of international law, including the established principles of international law of armed conflict;

    (c) Failing that, general principles of law derived by the Court from national laws of legal systems of the world including, as appropriate, the national laws of States that would normally exercise jurisdiction over the crime, provided that those principles are not inconsistent with this Statute and with international law and internationally recognized norms and standards.

(2) The Court may apply principles and rules of law as interpreted in its previous decisions.

(3) The application and interpretation of law pursuant to this article must be consistent with internationally recognized human rights, and be without any adverse distinction founded on grounds such as gender, as defined in Article 7, paragraph 3,[44] age, race, colour, language, religion or belief, political or other opinion, national, ethnic or social origin, wealth, birth or other status.'

With respect to the first source of applicable law, it is obvious that the Statute is binding on the ICC. Article 9(1) of the ICC Statute provides that Elements of Crimes adopted by a two-thirds majority of the members of the Assembly of State Parties 'shall assist' the ICC in the interpretation and application of Articles 6, 7, and 8 of the ICC Statute dealing with genocide, crimes against humanity, and war crimes, respectively. Article 9 was a compromise between two positions. Some delegations, led by the US, wanted the Elements of Crimes to bind the ICC judges so as to ensure certainty and clarity of the law of the ICC Statute. Other delegations opposed restriction on the ICC judges in their interpretation of international criminal law. Article 9(1) therefore only provides that the Elements of Crimes 'shall assist' the ICC, and Article 9(3) requires that the Elements of Crimes 'be consistent with' the ICC Statute, and it is the ICC that determines such consistency in specific cases.[45] Thus, the Elements of Crimes and their amendments cannot override those elements already expressly stated in the ICC Statute itself, such as the definitions of the constituent elements of the crime of enslavement as provided in Article 7(2)(c).

---

[43] For a legislative history of this Article, see Per Saland, 'International Criminal Law Principles', in R. S. Lee (ed.), *The International Criminal Court: The Making of the Rome Statute—Issues, Negotiations, Results* (Kluwer, 1999), 189 at 213–6.

[44] Art. 7(3) stipulates: 'For the purpose of this Statute, it is understood that the term "gender" refers to the two sexes, male and female, within the context of society. The term "gender" does not indicate any meaning different from the above'. It is the sociological aspects of male and female, rather than biological distinctions between them, that matter. C. Steains, 'Gender Issues', in Lee, 357 at 371–5.

[45] See H. von Hebel and D. Robinson, 'Crimes within the Jurisdiction of the Court', in Lee, 79 at 87–8.

As for the Rules of Procedure and Evidence, Article 51(5) of the Statute makes it clear that the Statute shall prevail in the event of conflict between it and the Rules.

The second source is also obvious. The ICC, like the ICTY and the ICTR before it, must resort to applicable treaties and principles and rules of international law to interpret its Statute and Elements of Crimes so as to keep its 'applicable law' up to date and reflective of reality.

The third source allows the ICC to resort to drawing inspiration from case law in the criminal field decided by national courts of the various legal systems of the world. This is a supplementary means of construction to fill any lacuna in the first two sources.[46]

Article 21(2) allows, but not obliges, the ICC to follow its previous decisions. Part 8 of the ICC Statute sets out the provisions on appeal and revision. The approach of the ICTY and the ICTR relating to previous judgments of the respective Tribunals and their Appeals Chamber is rationally sound and, as such, likely to be followed by the ICC as well.

Article 21(3) intends to provide a general consistency test and prohibition on adverse distinction.[47] The term 'gender' was a sensitive issue at the Rome Conference. Certain delegations opposed its inclusion for fear that it might be interpreted as condoning homosexuality. Read in conjunction with Article 7(3) of the Statute, this provision means that since the social roles of male or female in a particular society may vary according to the context and time, a person should not suffer discrimination simply because he or she does not fit into the stereotype associated with the biological distinction between male and female.[48]

It should be noted also that Article 10 of the ICC Statute stipulates that nothing in Part 2, covering Articles 5 to 21, of the Statute 'shall be interpreted as limiting or prejudicing in any way existing or developing rules of international law for purposes other than this Statute'. This was intended to emphasize that the inclusion or non-inclusion in the ICC Statute of certain norms would not prejudice the positions of States on the customary law status of such norms, would not prejudice existing norms or future developments of international law, and would not authorize the ICC to apply existing or new norms omitted deliberately in the ICC Statute.[49]

The Preparatory Commission for the International Criminal Court (hereinafter 'the PCNICC') has been set up in accordance with Resolution F adopted by the Rome Conference to, *inter alia*, draft Elements of Crimes and Rules of Procedure and Evidence for approval by the Assembly of States Parties.[50] The PCNICC has adopted

---

[46] Cf. I. Caracciolo, 'Applicable Law', in F. Lattanzi and W. A. Schabas (eds.), *Essays on the Rome Statute of the International Criminal Court*, i (il Sirente, 1999), 211 at 227–8.

[47] P. Saland, 'Crimes within the Jurisdiction of the Court', 215.

[48] B. Bedont, 'Gender-Specific Provisions in the Statute of the International Criminal Court', Lattanzi and Schabas (eds.), *Essays on the Rome Statute*, 183 at 187–8.

[49] von Hebel and Robinson, 'Crimes within the Jurisdiction of the Court', in Lee, 88.

[50] *Doc. A/ CONF. 183/ 10* of 17 July 1998.

the Elements of Crimes for those crimes under Articles 6, 7, and 8 of the ICC Statute.[51]

The 'General Introduction', which is authoritative for the purposes of interpretation of the Elements of Crimes for each of the said crimes as adopted by the PCNICC, states as follows:

'1. Pursuant to Article 9, the following Elements of Crimes shall assist the Court in the interpretation and application of Article 6, 7, and 8, consistent with the Statute. The provisions of the Statute, including Article 21, and the general principles set out in Part 3 are applicable to the Elements of Crimes.

2. As stated in Article 30, unless otherwise provided, a person shall be criminally responsible and liable for punishment for a crime within the jurisdiction of the Court only if the material elements are committed with intent and knowledge. Where no reference is made in the Elements of Crimes to a mental element for any particular conduct, consequence, or circumstances listed, it is understood that the relevant mental element, i.e. intent, knowledge or both, set out in Article 30 applies. Exceptions to the Article 30 standard, based on the Statute, including applicable law under its relevant provisions, are indicated below.

3. Existence of intent and knowledge can be inferred from relevant facts and circumstances.

4. With respect to mental elements associated with elements involving value judgment, such as those using the terms 'inhumane' or 'severe', it is not necessary that the perpetrator personally completed a particular value judgment, unless otherwise indicated.

5. Grounds for excluding criminal responsibility or the absence thereof are generally not specified in the elements of crimes listed under each crime. [Footnote: this paragraph is without prejudice to the obligation of the Prosecutor under Article 54, paragraph 1, of the Statute.][52]

6. The requirement of 'unlawfulness' found in the Statute or in other parts of international law, in particular international humanitarian law, is generally not specified in the Elements of Crimes.

7. The Elements of Crimes are generally structured in accordance with the following principles:

   – As the Elements of Crimes focus on the conduct, consequences and circumstances associated with each crime, they are generally listed in that order;

   – When required, a particular mental element is listed after the affected conduct, consequence, or circumstance;

   – Contextual circumstances are listed last.

---

[51] Unless otherwise stated, the reference in this book to the Elements of Crimes adopted by the PCNICC are those adopted on 30 June 2000 and contained in *Doc. PCNICC/2000/1/ Add. 2*, 2 Nov. 2000. They are reproduced in Appendix 4.

[52] Art. 54(1) provides, *inter alia*, that the Prosecutor shall extend the investigation to cover all facts and evidence relevant to an assessment of whether there is criminal responsibility under the Statute, and, in doing so, investigate incriminating and exonerating circumstances equally.

8. As used in the Elements of Crimes, the term "perpetrator" is neutral as to guilt or innocence. The elements, including the appropriate mental elements, apply *mutatis mutandis*, to all those whose criminal responsibility may fall under Articles 25 and 28 of the Statute.

9. A particular conduct may constitute one or more crimes.

10. The use of short titles for the crimes has no legal effect.'

It should be noted that the Rome Conference decided to leave the issue of omission as a material element of a crime (*actus reus*) to the ICC's case law. Therefore, a conduct mentioned in an element of crime could encompass an act and an omission, as the case may be.[53] The word 'perpetrator' is used throughout the Elements of Crimes because the ICC Statute uses the word 'accused' from the provision of Article 61(9) onwards, that is, only after a charge against a person has been confirmed. The Elements of Crimes will have to be neutral in the sense that they may cover any stage of the proceedings involving a person involved in the conduct criminalized by the ICC Statute. The word 'perpetrator' has been chosen in preference to 'accused', 'person', 'actor', 'author', 'individual', or 'agent'.

With regard to the second paragraph of the General Introduction to the Elements of Crimes, Article 30 of the Statute, entitled 'Mental Element', stipulates:

'1. Unless otherwise provided, a personal shall be criminally responsible and liable for punishment for a crime within the jurisdiction of the Court only if the material elements are committed with intent and knowledge.

2. For the purposes of this Article, a person has intent where:

   (a) In relation to conduct, that person means to engage in the conduct;

   (b) In relation to a consequence, that person means to cause that consequence or is aware that it will occur in the ordinary course of events.

3. For the purposes of this Article, "knowledge" means awareness that a circumstance exists or a consequence will occur in the ordinary course of events. "Know" and "knowingly" shall be construed accordingly.'

In drafting the Elements of Crimes, the PCNICC had to be specific as to when the mental element of intent plus knowledge is not applicable, and when it is automatically applicable. It also had to make clear as to which material element(s) the mental element in question should be specifically related. For example, since a war crime must be committed in the context of an armed conflict, an element of a war crime is the perpetrator's *awareness*, not intent or intent plus knowledge, of *factual circumstances* that established the existence of an armed conflict.

---

[53] P. Saland, 'International Criminal Law Principles', 212–3.

3.3 DRAFT CODE OF CRIMES AGAINST THE PEACE AND SECURITY OF MANKIND

The ILC's Draft Statute for an International Criminal Court was revised substantially during a series of meetings of diplomatic delegations prior to the Rome Conference. In fact, the Rome Conference virtually replaced the Draft Statute with the ICC Statute that is much more extensive in terms of content. With respect to the ILC's parallel project of the Draft Code of Crimes Against the Peace and Security of Mankind, it has served the purpose of informing Governments of the content of the relevant rules of international law as it was and as it should be as of 1996.

The ICTY considers the Draft Code to be an authoritative international instrument which, depending on the specific question at issue, may either constitute evidence of customary law, or shed light on customary rules which are of uncertain content or are in the process of formation, or at least be indicative of the legal opinions of eminently qualified publicists in the ILC who represent the major legal systems of the world.[54] In *Furundzija*, Trial Chamber II of the ICTY relied substantially on the relevant provision of the Draft Code to arrive at its conclusion on the elements of the crime of aiding and abetting.[55] Similarly, in *Tadic*, the ILC Commentary on the threshold of crimes against humanity was adopted.[56] Nevertheless, since the Draft Code is not legally binding, international tribunals are free not to follow provisions of the Draft Code which they find to be contrary to the prevailing rules of international law. For instance, the ICTY Trial Chamber in *Celebici* did not adopt the position in the Draft Code to the effect that a lack of formal legal competence to take the necessary measures to prevent or repress the crime may preclude the criminal responsibility of the superior under the principle of command responsibility.[57]

3.4 APPRAISAL OF THE RELATIONSHIP BETWEEN GENERAL CONCEPTS OF PUBLIC INTERNATIONAL LAW AND CONCEPTS OF INTERNATIONAL HUMAN RIGHTS LAW AND THEIR EFFECTS ON INTERNATIONAL CRIMINAL LAW

Public international law sets the parameters of the exercise of jurisdiction over an offence. It also determines whether the proscription of certain conduct has attained the status of customary international law applicable to all. The crimes proscribed by

---

[54] *Furundzija*, para. 227.
[55] Ibid., paras. 228–32, 242–3.
[56] *Tadic* Judgment, paras. 648, 729.
[57] *Celebici*, para. 395.

the ICTY Statute, the ICTR Statute, and the ICC Statute are recognized under customary international law as crimes of serious concern to the international community
as a whole that deserve international criminal prosecution in an international criminal tribunal. To add other categories of crimes to the Statutes would encounter strong
opposition, insofar as those categories have not attained the said status, since such
inclusion would violate the principle of legality.[58]

Public international law also provides rules of interpretation of international
criminal statutes, especially where such statutes are international agreements.

Public international law works hand in hand with international human rights law.
The UN Charter and international human rights instruments are creatures of public
international law. The developments in public international law in tearing down the
sanctity of sovereignty of State and the shield of non-interference in domestic affairs
of another State set in motion legal actions to promote and protect human rights in
various fora, such as the European Court of Human Rights, and the Inter-American
Court of Human Rights. The jurisprudence of the ICTY and the ICTR is replete with
reference to the jurisprudence of international judicial bodies applying international
human rights law. Although the draftsmen of the ICC Statute were cautious not to
allow violations of international human rights law automatically to constitute crimes
within the ICC's jurisdiction as well, some conducts proscribed previously only in
international human rights law have found their way into the ICC Statute. Enforced
disappearance and apartheid are the two most obvious examples. Moreover, the ICC
draftsmen even went further. Whereas international human rights law requires an
official involvement in the case of torture, the ICC Statute omits this requirement
altogether. It is now settled that under the ICC Statute and the Elements of Crimes,
torture as a crime against humanity need not be committed for a specific purpose—
an element still required by international human rights law.

Therefore, public international law, international human rights law, and international criminal law are complementary to one another. Developments in one of
these fields affect developments in the other fields. The case of General Augusto
Pinochet of Chile should illustrate adequately the trilateral relationship and interaction among these branches of law.

In September 1973, General Augusto Pinochet staged a *coup d'état* to overthrow
President Allende's Socialist government in Chile. In Operation Condor, military
governments in Chile, Argentina, Bolivia, Paraguay, and Uruguay, and perhaps Brazil,
allegedly coordinated anti-leftist, anti-Communist, and anti-Marxist campaigns that
involved international terrorism, kidnapping across borders, exchange of prisoners,
torture, and murder. Spanish citizens, two Uruguayan Congressmen, students, and
political activists were among its victims. Chile was believed to be the centre of
Operation Condor.

---

[58] Report of the UN Secretary-General pursuant to para. 2 of Security Council Res. 808 (1993), introducing the ICTY Statute. Quoted by the International Court of Justice in its Advisory Opinion of 8 July 1996
on *Legality of the Threat or Use of Nuclear Weapons*, ICJ Rep. 1996, para. 81.

In 1988, Pinochet, convinced of his own popularity, held a referendum on whether he should continue in office for a further eight years. He lost, but forty-three per cent of the Chilean electorate voted in favour of his remaining in office. In 1990, Pinochet relinquished his power to a democratically-elected president in exchange for a secret amnesty. Pinochet had legal immunity as commander-in-chief of the army until he retired from that post on 11 March 1998. On 12 March 1998, he was sworn in as senator for life—a position giving him immunity which he arranged for himself in the 1980 constitution that provided for the restoration of limited democracy to Chile. Since March 1998, criminal proceedings have been initiated against Pinochet by alleged victims of his dictatorship. With regard to the other Chilean military officers, only a handful have been brought to justice. Chile has an amnesty law issued by a military decree in 1978 prohibiting prosecution of crimes committed by the military junta before the amnesty. The purpose of the amnesty was for the 'general tranquillity, peace, and order' of the nation. Unlike Uruguay, where an amnesty for military officers involved in gross human rights violations was submitted to and approved by referendum, the Chilean amnesty law has never been put to the vote.

In October 1998, Pinochet went to London as a guest of the British Ministry of Defence. He led a Chilean military delegation to buy military engineering equipment. While in London, he suffered a back injury and had to undergo medical treatment. On 16 October 1998, Pinochet, aged 82, was arrested in London on warrant issued by the Central Court of Criminal Proceedings in Madrid, Spain (led by Baltasar Garzon, a Spanish magistrate), alleging that he had murdered Spanish citizens in Chile. The arrest was undertaken after the Office of Legal Adviser of the UK Foreign and Commonwealth Office had advised the police that Pinochet's diplomatic passport did not give him diplomatic immunity.

On 22 October 1998, a second warrant was issued by the Spanish court accusing him of crimes of torture, hostage taking, and murder. On 3 November 1998, Spain requested Pinochet's extradition, accusing him of involvement in the deaths and disappearances of 3,178 people in Chile and abroad during his rule, as well as torture and kidnapping during that time, as a result of which seven Spanish citizens and their descendants died. It was alleged that Pinochet used these methods to consolidate his power, all in the name of 'fighting Marxism'. Spain alleged that these crimes were in breach of Spanish law relating to genocide, torture, and terrorism.

The *Pinochet* case is important because Pinochet is alleged to be one of the most notorious human rights violators, whose actions have injured the interests of numerous nations. For example, on 11 November 1998, Switzerland demanded Pinochet's extradition to face charges concerning the disappearance of a dual Swiss-Chilean national in 1979. On 12 November 1998, France, which had denied Pinochet a visa to visit Paris before his trip to London in October, requested that Pinochet be extradited from the UK to stand trial for the disappearance of several French nationals in Chile during Pinochet's rule. In the UK, Belgium, Italy, and Sweden, Chilean exiles have filed charges against Pinochet for crimes against humanity, including widespread murder, kidnapping, and torture. In Germany, Chilean exiles who have become

German nationals have brought charges of murder, torture, and kidnapping against Pinochet. The German Justice Minister said she would support an extradition request if there is evidence of injury suffered by German citizens.

Up to then, only low- or middle-level officials have been prosecuted in a foreign domestic court for human rights violations. National governments rarely punish former leaders who violated human rights. Rare exceptions include South Korea's punishment of two of its former presidents, and Argentina's imprisonment of former president General Jorge Rafael Videla, who led the first three military junta that ruled Argentina between 1976 and 1983, for his role in the repression in the 1970s. Former leaders who are punished are those who have lost all their power and have no place to live peacefully in exile. Most former heads of State, including Pinochet, are in a completely different situation.

The core question in the *Pinochet* case was the scope of the immunity enjoyed by a former head of State for acts committed when he was still head of State. Another related question was: If he was entitled to immunity only with respect to official acts performed in the exercise of his functions as head of State, what could constitute official acts in the exercise of his functions as head of State?

The Queen's Bench Division held that the acts of torture and hostage taking were done in the exercise of Pinochet's functions as head of State because, according to the Spanish warrant, they were committed under colour of the authority of the government of Chile. Pinochet was charged, not with personally torturing victims or causing their disappearance, but with using the power of the State of which he was the head to that end.[59]

In view of the importance of this case, a leapfrog appeal was made to the House of Lords. The House of Lords held, by a three to two majority (Lord Slynn and Lord Lloyd dissenting), that former sovereigns have narrower immunity than incumbent sovereigns; the immunity of former sovereigns does not apply to charges of torture or hostage taking. While Pinochet could not be charged with any act that was a 'legitimate function of government', he could be held accountable for actions proscribed by international law.[60] Lord Nicholls of Birkenhead said that the second warrant charged five offences but for the present purposes he need refer to only two of them— torture and hostage taking. The gist of His Lordship's reasoning is summarized in the following statement:

'[T]orture of his own subjects, or of aliens, would not be regarded by international law as a function of the head of State. All States disavow the use of torture as abhorrent, although from time to time some still resort to it. . . . Similarly, the taking of hostages, as much as torture, has been outlawed by the international community as an offence. International law recognizes, of course, that the functions of a head of State might include activities which are wrongful, even illegal, by the law of his own State or by the laws of other States. But

---

[59] (1999) **38** *ILM* 68.

[60] *R. v. Bow Street Metropolitan Stipendiary Magistrate and others, ex p. Pinochet Ugarte (Amnesty International and others intervening)* [1998] 4 ALL ER 897 (HL).

international law has made plain that certain types of conduct, including torture and hostage-taking, are not acceptable conduct on the part of anyone. That applies as much to heads of State, or even more so, as it does to everyone else; the contrary conclusion would make a mockery of international law. That was made clear long before 1973 and the events which took place in Chile then and thereafter.'[61]

Lord Steyn added that the development of international law since WWII justified the conclusion that by the time of the 1973 *coup d'état*, and certainly ever since, international law condemned genocide, torture, hostage-taking, and crimes against humanity as international crimes deserving of punishment. Given this state of international law, it was difficult to maintain that the commission of such high crimes might amount to acts performed in the exercise of the functions of a head of State.[62] Lord Hoffmann stated briefly that he concurred with Lord Nicholls of Birkenhead.

The dissenting Lord Slynn of Hadley stated that if the question were whether the allegations should be investigated by a criminal court in Chile or by an international tribunal, the answer, subject to the terms of any amnesty, would surely be yes to both. In his view, Pinochet was entitled to immunity when tried in the English court. Lord Lloyd of Berwick, also dissenting, opined that almost all revolutionary leaders were guilty of serious crimes, such as murder, and that it was impossible to give State immunity to some but not to others. In committing the crimes which are alleged against him, Senator Pinochet was acting in his sovereign capacity as head of State. English courts are not an international court, and by hearing Spain's case for Pinochet's extradition, an English court would in effect be pronouncing on the validity of the amnesty in Chile—against the will of the Government of Chile, and would assert jurisdiction over the internal affairs of that State at the very time when the Supreme Court in Chile was itself performing the same task.

All members of the House of Lords in the *Pinochet* case concurred that a current head of State is immune from criminal process under customary international law.

The *Pinochet* case decided by the House of Lords reflects the trend towards universal criminal jurisdiction over crimes under international law. Senator Pinochet is not a British national; his alleged crimes were committed outside England and Wales and they had no effects within England and Wales; and his victims are not British subjects. Nonetheless, the House of Lords held that his alleged crimes were extraditable offences because they were punishable under English law. The House, in effect, *enforced* universal jurisdiction *ratione materiae* and *ratione personae* over crimes under international law, such as torture, that have been proscribed by Acts of Parliament implementing international conventions on the matter. The House construed English statutes in the light of developments of international human rights law and international criminal law to draw the line against giving impunity to even a former head of State who committed international crimes while still in office.

---

[61] Ibid., at 939–40. His Lordship then referred to the Nuremberg Charter which specifically rejected the immunity of heads of State and diplomatic immunity, and to the fact that this rejection was endorsed by UN General Assembly Resolution 95(1) of 11 December 1946.

[62] Ibid., at 945–6.

Unfortunately, on a motion of the Counsel for Pinochet, another panel of the House of Lords held on 17 December 1998 that the House's judgment of 25 November 1998 had to be set aside and new hearings held before the House on the ground of conflict of interests and the appearance of bias. Lord Hoffmann and his wife had been actively affiliated with the activities of Amnesty International, one of the parties to the proceedings, and Lord Hoffmann had failed to disclose such a connection to the parties.

In its judgment of 24 March 1999,[63] the House curtailed a very large number of charges for which Senator Pinochet could be extradited to stand trial in Spain. It did so essentially on the grounds of lack of jurisdiction *ratione temporis* over the charges to be excluded, and apparently in due respect for the principle of legality (*nullum crimen sine lege*). All the crimes for which Pinochet's extradition was sought from Spain, except for torture, were not crimes under English law at the time the alleged offences were committed; hence, no double criminality, which is a fundamental prerequisite for extradition. By a majority of six to one, their Lordships ruled that Pinochet had no immunity for torture—an extraditable offence under the Criminal Justice Act of 1988 that implements the Convention against Torture and Other Cruel, Inhuman or Degrading Treatment or Punishment 1984[64] which the UK has ratified.[65] While there has been some disappointment with respect to the House's last judgment,[66] one cannot deny that universal jurisdiction over crimes against international law is a growing trend that cannot be reversed.[67] Pinochet was allowed to return to Chile in March 2000 after the UK Home Secretary had determined that he was unfit to stand trial. Back home in Chile, the Supreme Court of Chile decided in August 2000 to strip Pinochet of all immunity from judicial proceedings brought against him. This might not have been possible if the House of Lords' judgments against Pinochet, especially the first judgment, had not drawn widespread international reaction against the culture of impunity.

The Pinochet 'precedent' has propelled movement towards the end of impunity both at the national level and at the international level. In February 2000, following the 'precedent' of the proceedings against Pinochet in Britain, the Dakar Regional Court in Senegal indicted Hissene Habré, former Head of State of Chad, who had been living in exile in Senegal since 1990. He was charged with torture and murder of his own subjects during his rule from 1982 to 1990. It was the first time that a former African head of State has been charged with human rights violations by a court of another State. In that same month, Lieutenant Colonel Tharcisse Muvunyi, a former

---

[63] *R. v. Bow Street Metropolitan Stipendiary Magistrate and others ex p. Pinochet Ugarte (Amnesty International and others intervening) (No. 3)* [1999] 2 ALL ER 97, HL.

[64] (1984) 23 *ILM* 102.

[65] For the proper context in which the House of Lords' judgments are to be considered, see M. Byers, 'The Law and Politics of the Pinochet Case' (2000) 10 *Duke J. Comp. & Int'l L.* 415.

[66] See S. Villalpando, 'L'affaire Pinochet; beaucoup de bruit pour rien? L'apport au droit international de la décision de la chambre des Lords du 24 mars 1999' (2000) 104 *Revue Générale de Droit Int'l Public* 393. Cf. R. Wedgwood, 'International Criminal Law and Augusto Pinochet' (2000) 40 *Virginia J. Int'l L.* 829.

[67] See: Anne-Marie Slaughter, 'The Long Arm of the Law', *Foreign Policy* (Spring 1999), 34.

Rwandan army commander whose soldiers allegedly massacred over 100,000 people in 1994, was arrested at his London residence on an arrest warrant issued by the ICTR. He had been living in London with his family since twenty-two months earlier. He was accused of genocide and crimes against humanity. His arrest came right after General Augustin Ndindiliyimana, former Chief of Staff of the Rwandan Military Police, had been arrested in Belgium on an arrest warrant issued by the ICTR.

In February 1999, after the House of Lords had rendered its first judgment in the *Pinochet* case, a group of Belgian and French nationals of Cambodian origin accused three Khmer Rouge leaders; namely, Khieu Samphan, Noun Chea, and Ieng Sary, of murder, causing death by starvation, and torture committed against Cambodian nationals in the late 1970s. The Attorney-General of Belgium has agreed to pursue the matter by entrusting the investigation of these allegations to the Belgian judge who has been working on the extradition of General Pinochet to Belgium for his alleged crimes against humanity committed in Chile.[68]

A three-member Group of Experts for Cambodia was appointed by the UN Secretary-General to evaluate the existing evidence with a view to determining the nature of the crimes committed by the Khmer Rouge leaders in the years 1975–79, to assess the feasibility of their apprehension, and to explore legal options for bringing them to justice before an international or national jurisdiction. On 22 February 1999, the Group, led by Sir Ninian Stephen of Australia, submitted its report to the UN General Assembly and the UN Security Council. The report concluded that there was sufficient evidence of the commission of serious crimes under international law by the Khmer Rouge leaders, including crimes against humanity, genocide, war crimes, forced labour, torture, and crimes against internationally protected persons, as well as crimes under Cambodian law. The Group carefully considered the feasibility of a national tribunal to try the Khmer Rouge leaders, but concluded that the Cambodian judiciary in its present state was unlikely to meet minimal international standards of justice, even with external assistance. The UN Secretary-General concurred with the Group that the tribunal trying the Khmer Rouge leaders must be international in character, although this does not necessarily mean that it should be modelled after either of the existing *ad hoc* Tribunals or be linked to them institutionally, administratively, or financially.[69]

However, the Cambodian Government's initial reaction to the report was that peace and national reconciliation are a '*sine qua non* condition for rehabilitation, socio-economic development and alleviation of poverty of the Cambodian people', and that it would prefer to follow the experience of the South African Truth and Reconciliation Commission instead of putting the Khmer Rouge leaders on

---

[68] *The Cambodia Daily*, 19 Apr. 1999.

[69] Identical letters dated 15 Mar. 1999 from the Secretary-General to the President of the General Assembly and the President of the Security Council, *UN Doc. A/53/850; S/1999/231* of 16 Mar. 1999. For a detailed case study of the possible mechanisms and applicable law to prosecute the Khmer Rouge, see S. R. Ratner and J. S. Abrams, *Accountability for Human Rights Atrocities in International Law: Beyond the Nuremberg Legacy* (Clarendon Press, 1997), 229–87.

trial before a national or international tribunal.[70] Subsequently, it argued that the Cambodian courts, and not any international tribunal, are fully competent to conduct any such trial by virtue of Article VI of the Convention on the Prevention and Punishment of the Crime of Genocide of 1948[71] and Article 33 of the Cambodian Constitution, since the criminals are Cambodians, the victims were Cambodians, and the crimes were committed in Cambodia. Faced with international pressure, the Cambodian Government is, at the time of writing, working with the UN to find an acceptable formula to have foreign judges and foreign prosecutors participating in all stages of the proceedings.

In general, the municipal order all over the world is increasingly *enforcing* universal jurisdiction over international crimes.[72] Criminal jurisdiction based on territorial principle is no longer impervious to external challenge, as evidenced in the case of the proposed Khmer Rouge trial. These developments are conducive to the increasingly widespread acceptance of the ICC Statute by States.

The linkage between international criminal law, international human rights law, and public international law will be maintained in the ICC, as apparent from Article 36 of the ICC Statute on qualifications, nominations, and elections of ICC judges. Article 36(3)(b) stipulates that every candidate for election to the ICC shall:

'(i) Have established competence in criminal law and procedure, and the necessary relevant experience, whether as judge, prosecutor, advocate or in other similar capacity, in criminal proceedings; or

(ii) Have established competence in relevant areas of international law such as international humanitarian law and the law of human rights, and extensive experience in a professional legal capacity which is of relevance to the judicial work of the Court.'

Article 36(5) of the Statute provides that there shall be two lists of candidates. List 'A'

---

[70] Note from Prime Minister Hun Sen of Cambodia dated 3 Mar. 1999 to the UN Secretary-General. Similar arguments have been advanced by Chileans who are against the prosecution of Senator Pinochet outside Chile. See R. Lagos and H. Munoz, 'The Pinochet Dilemma', *Foreign Policy* (Spring 1999), 26.

[71] 78 *UNTS* 277. Art. VI states: 'Persons charged with genocide or any of the other acts enumerated in article III shall be tried by a competent tribunal of the State in the territory of which the act was committed, or by such international penal tribunal as may have jurisdiction with respect to those Contracting Parties which shall have accepted its jurisdiction'.

[72] E.g. Art. 7 of the Belgian Law of 16 June 1993 as amended by the Law of 10 Feb. 1999 establishes the universal jurisdiction of Belgian courts in relation to 'grave violations of international humanitarian law', irrespective of the presence or absence of the accused on Belgian territory, the territory in which the violations occurred, or the nationality of the accused or victims. Pursuant to this Law, on 11 April 2000 the Brussels Tribunal de première instance issued an international arrest warrant against the Democratic Republic of the Congo's then Minister for Foreign Affairs Yerodia Abdoulaye Ndombasi, seeking his detention and subsequent extradition to Belgium for alleged crimes constituting 'grave violations of international humanitarian law', including 'crimes against humanity', committed by him in the territory of the Democratic Republic of the Congo (DRC). On 17 Oct. 2000, the DRC filed a request before the International Court of Justice, asking the ICJ to order Belgium to discharge the international arrest warrant. At the time of writing, the case, entitled *Arrest Warrant of 11 April 2000 (Democratic Rep. of the Congo v. Belgium)*, is still pending.

contains the names of candidates with the qualifications specified in Article 36(3)(b)(i), whereas list 'B' contains the names of candidates with the qualifications specified in Article 36(3)(b)(ii). A candidate with sufficient qualifications for both lists may choose on which list to appear. At the first election to the ICC, at least nine judges are to be elected from list 'A' and at least five judges from list 'B'. Subsequent elections are to be so organized as to maintain the equivalent proportion on the ICC of judges qualified on the two lists.

PART II

PARTICULAR INTERNATIONAL CRIMES

4

GENOCIDE

Mass destruction of peoples took place several times in the twentieth century. Foremost in terms of notoriety were the destruction of Armenians by the Ottoman Empire in 1915–16 during WWI,[1] the Holocaust of the Jews by Nazi Germany, and the killing of millions of Cambodians by the Khmer Rouge regime in Cambodia in the mid-1970s.[2]

The term 'genocide' was coined by Raphael Lemkin using the combination of the Greek word *genos* (race or tribe) and the Latin *-cide* (killing).[3] There was no specific reference to the term 'genocide' in the Nuremberg Charter or the Judgment of the Nuremberg Tribunal, but it did appear in the indictment and was referred to by the Prosecution from time to time. What is now known as genocide was in fact prosecuted by the Nuremberg Tribunal under the heading of crimes against humanity. This was the only prosecution of perpetrators of this crime until the establishment of the ICTY and the ICTR in the 1990s. The court martial set up by the succession of post-WWI Ottoman governments to prosecute perpetrators of the Armenian genocide did not finish its work,[4] and, at the time of writing, the long-awaited trial of Khmer Rouge leaders is being discussed but has not yet materialized.

The proscription of the crime of genocide, as defined in the Convention on the Prevention and Punishment of the Crime of Genocide of 1948,[5] has become part of customary international law and a norm of *jus cogens*.[6] Article II of the Genocide Convention provides that genocide means:

---

[1] See: R. H. Kevorkian and P. B. Paboudjian, *Les Arméniens dans l'Empire ottoman à la veille du Génocide* (Arhis, 1992); R. H. Kevorkian (ed.), 'L'Extermination des déportés arméniens ottomans dans les camps de concentration de Syrie-Mésopotamie (1915–1916): la deuxième phase du génocide', *Revue d'histoire arménienne contemporaine*, ii (1996–1997–1998) (special number).

[2] See generally H. Fein (ed.), *Genocide Watch* (Yale University Press, 1992). According to the report of the Group of Experts for Cambodia dated 22 February 1999, genocide was one of the serious crimes under international law allegedly committed by the Khmer Rouge leaders. See above, 3.4.

[3] For a historical background, see R. Lemkin, 'Genocide as a Crime Under International Law' (1947) **41** *AJIL* 145; M. Lippman, 'The Drafting of the 1948 Convention on the Prevention and Punishment of the Crime of Genocide' (1985) **3** *Boston Univ. Int'l L. J.* 1; G. J. Andreopolous (ed.), *Genocide: Conceptual and Historical Dimensions* (University of Pennsylvania Press, 1994).

[4] See: V. N. Dadrian, 'A Textual Analysis of the Key Indictment of the Turkish Military Tribunal Investigating the Armenian Genocide' (1991) **44** *Armenian Review* 1.

[5] 78 *UNTS* 277.

[6] *Prosecutor v. Goran Jelisic*, Case No. IT-95–10, ITCY T. Ch. I, 14 Dec. 1999, para. 60.

'any of the following acts committed with intent to destroy, in whole or in part, a national, ethnical, racial or religious group, as such:

(a) Killing members of the group;

(b) Causing serious bodily or mental harm to members of the group;

(c) Deliberately inflicting on the group conditions of life calculated to bring about its physical destruction in whole or in part;

(d) Imposing measures intended to prevent births within the group;

(e) Forcibly transferring children of the group to another group.'

This provision is replicated in Article 4(2) of the ICTY Statute, Article 2(2) of the ICTR Statute, and Article 6 of the ICC Statute.

The nature of the crime of genocide is elaborated in the Advisory Opinion of the International Court of Justice (ICJ) in *Reservations to the Convention on the Prevention and Punishment of the Crime of Genocide*. According to the ICJ, genocide is:

'"a crime under international law" involving a denial of the right of existence of entire human groups, a denial which shocks the conscience of mankind and results in great losses to humanity, and which is contrary to moral law and to the spirit and aims of the United Nations . . . The first consequence arising from this conception is that the principles underlying the Convention are principles which are recognized by civilized nations as binding on States, even without any conventional obligation. A second consequence is the universal character both of the condemnation of genocide and of the cooperation required "in order to liberate mankind from such an odious scourge" (Preamble to the Convention).'[7]

Genocide, however, is not a crime under the national law of every State. There is no crime of genocide even in certain States that have ratified the Genocide Convention.[8]

Genocide is the gravest form of crime against humanity. While other crimes against humanity, as will be seen in the next chapter, require the civilian population to be targeted as part of a widespread or systematic attack, genocide requires the specific intent to destroy, in whole or in part, a national, ethical, racial, or religious group of persons. Where the Prosecution relies on the same elements and the same culpable conduct to prove both a crime against humanity and an act of genocide whose victims are the same, a crime against humanity may be subsumed in the crime of genocide and punished as such, provided that the requisite elements of the crime of genocide are proven.[9]

---

[7] ICJ Rep. 1951, 15 at 23. Also quoted in *Jelisic*, para. 60.

[8] In *re Thompson, ex p. Nulyarimma and Others* [1998] Aust. Capital Territory Sup. Ct. 136, it was held that Australia's Genocide Convention Act 1949 which ratified the Genocide Convention of 1948 did not incorporate the provisions of that Convention into Australian municipal law, and the crime of genocide was not recognized at common law, either. Upheld in *Nulyarimma v. Thompson* [1999] Federal Ct. Aust. 1192 (1 Sept. 1999), and see S. Peters, 'The Genocide Case: *Nulyarimma v. Thompson*' (1999) *Aust. Int'l L. J.* 233; M. Flynn, 'Genocide: It's a Crime Everywhere, But not in Australia' (2000) **59** *Univ. W. Aust. L. Rev.* 29.

[9] In *Prosecutor v. Clément Kayishema and Obed Ruzindana* (Case No. ICTR-95–1-T, ICTR T. Ch. II, 21 May 1999), the accused were charged with several counts of crimes against humanity for murder, extermination, and other inhumane acts. The Chamber found it improper to convict the accused for both genocide and crimes against humanity since, in the circumstances of the case, they amounted to the same offence.

An accused must be found guilty on the basis of his own individual criminal responsibility, without the necessity for the Prosecution having to establish that genocide has taken place throughout the country concerned. Nevertheless, the seriousness of the charge of genocide compels judges to examine scrupulously and meticulously all the inculpatory and exonerating evidence against the accused.[10]

The victim of the crime of genocide is the group itself and not the individual. A common criterion in the four types of groups protected by the Genocide Convention is that 'membership in such groups would seem to be normally not challengeable by its members, who belong to it automatically, by birth, in a continuous and often irremediable manner'.[11] The more 'mobile' groups which one joins through individual voluntary commitment, such as political, professional, or economic groups, are excluded from this category of crime.[12] Although the UN General Assembly adopted a resolution during its First Session to affirm that genocide was a crime under international law committed on 'religious, racial, political, or any other grounds',[13] the Genocide Convention omits the political group as a protected group. The exclusion of the political group has made it possible for the Genocide Convention to refer to the possibility that the perpetrator of genocide can also be tried by 'a competent international penal tribunal subject to the acceptance at a later date by the contracting party concerned of its jurisdiction'. Hitherto, a number of delegations had voted against any mention of such an international penal tribunal with jurisdiction over offences against political groups since it would allow interference in the domestic political affairs of States, thereby undermining their national security.[14]

Attempts by certain delegations at the Rome Conference to include 'social' and 'political' groups as protected groups under the rubric of the crime of genocide did not succeed because the Rome Conference intended to codify customary international law in the ICC Statute, and not to draft a new genocide convention.[15]

A national group is 'a collection of people who are perceived to share a legal bond based on common citizenship, coupled with reciprocity of rights and duties'.[16]

An ethnical group is one whose members share a common language and culture. An ethnical group may identify or distinguish itself as such, or may be identified as such by others, including perpetrators of genocide.[17]

A racial group is distinguished from other racial groups by hereditary physical

[10] *Prosecutor v. Jean-Paul Akayesu*, Case No. ICTR-96–4-T, ICTR T. Ch. I, 2 Sept. 1998, paras. 129–30.

[11] *Akayesu*, para. 511.

[12] Ibid., paras. 511, 521; *Kayishema and Ruzindana*, para. 118. Trial Chamber I of the ICTR in *Prosecutor v. Rutaganda*, Case No. ICTR-96–3, 6 Dec. 1999, para. 47, and Trial Chamber I of the ICTR in *Prosecutor v. Alfred Musema*, Case No. ICTR-96–13-T, 27 Jan. 2000, paras. 153–4, adhere to the elaboration of the crime of genocide in *Akayesu*.

[13] UN GA Res. 96 (1) of 11 Dec. 1946.

[14] UN Secretary-General, *Historical Survey of the Question of International Criminal Jurisdiction* (United Nations, 1949), 42.

[15] W. Schabas, 'Article 6 Genocide', in O. Triffterer (ed.), *Commentary on the Rome Statute of the International Criminal Court: Observers' Notes, Article by Article* (Nomos, 1999).

[16] *Akayesu*, para. 512.

[17] Ibid., para. 513; *Kayishema and Ruzindana*, para. 98.

traits frequently identified with geographical areas, irrespective of linguistic, cultural, national or religious factors.[18]

A religious group is a group whose members share the same religion, denomination or mode of worship, or common beliefs.[19]

Trial Chamber I of the ICTR held in *Akayesu* that 'it is particularly important to respect the intention of the drafters of the Genocide Convention, which according to the *travaux préparatoires*, was patently to ensure the protection of *any* stable and permanent group'.[20] This judicial pronouncement is likely to have limited impact, however. The drafters virtually excluded all 'stable' groups not enumerated specifically in the Genocide Convention itself. The most obvious stable group with permanent membership brought about automatically by birth that is excluded deliberately from the enumeration is the cultural group. Its inclusion was rejected by the Sixth (Legal) Committee of the UN General Assembly on the grounds that the Convention relates to physical destruction of a group, not to eliminating its cultural attributes, that the concept of cultural genocide was not susceptible to precise definition, that it might impede legitimate efforts by States to foster a national community and civilize 'primitive' peoples, and that the subject was better left to human rights law.[21] There is no judicial authority, treaty provision, or State practice to support the desire of indigenous peoples to make destruction of culture short of physical destruction of such protected groups an act of genocide.[22] Forcible transfer of children, an act characterized originally as cultural genocide, is now included in the enumerated acts of genocide because the ultimate result of such transfer is the actual physical destruction of a national, ethnic, racial, or religious group, as such.

A subjective criterion is used to determine whether a person falls within one of these enumerated groups. The perpetrator of genocide may adopt either a positive approach or a negative approach in this respect. Under the positive approach, the perpetrator distinguishes a group by reason of what he considers to be its national, ethnic, racial, or religious characteristic pertaining to that group. Pursuant to the negative approach, the perpetrator excludes individuals from the group of which the

---

[18] *Akayesu*, para. 514.

[19] Ibid., para. 515; *Kayishema and Ruzindana*, para. 98.

[20] *Akayesu*, para. 505. Emphasis added. Also ibid., para. 701; *Jelisic*, para. 69; *Rutaganda*, para. 56; *Musema*, para. 162. This seems to be in line with the opinion of the Commission of Experts appointed to investigate the atrocities in the former Yugoslavia that drafters of the Genocide Convention intended the definition of genocide to be flexible and progressive so as to meet evolving exigencies. J. Paust, M. Bassiouni, S. Williams, M. Scharf, J. Garulé, and B. Zugaris, *International Criminal Law: Cases and Materials* (Carolina Academic Press, 1996), 1083.

[21] S. R. Ratner and J. S. Abrams, *Accountability for Human Rights Atrocities in International Law: Beyond the Nuremberg Legacy* (Clarendon Press, 1997), 29, esp. the references that appear in n. 24.

[22] Cf. S. J. Anaya, *Indigenous Peoples in International Law* (Oxford University Press, 1996), esp. at 192, 209; C. C. Tennant and M. E. Turpel, 'A Case Study of Indigenous Peoples: Genocide, Ethnocide and Self-Determination' (1990) 59 *Nordic J. Int'l L.* 287; J. Burger and P. Hunt, 'Towards the International Protection of Indigenous Peoples' Rights' (1994) 4 *Neth. Quart. Hum. Rts.* 409. Raphael Lemkin remarked a long time ago that destruction of the culture of a group was 'as disastrous for civilization as was the physical destruction of nations' (quoted in M. Lippman (1985) 3 *Boston Univ. Int'l L. J.* 11).

perpetrator considers himself a member and which he considers to have its own national, ethnic, racial, or religious characteristic distinct from that of the group to which such individuals belong.[23] In *Rutaganda*, Trial Chamber I of the ICTR considers that membership of a group is essentially a subjective concept; the victim is perceived by the perpetrator of genocide as belonging to a group slated for destruction and in some circumstances the victim may perceive himself as belonging to the said group.[24] Thus, assessment has to be made on a case-by-case basis, taking into account the relevant evidence and the political and cultural context of the society concerned.[25] For example, while Hutu and Tutsi in Rwanda share the same language and culture and are not strictly distinct ethnic groups, in the context of the period of genocide in Rwanda in 1994, they themselves and the Rwandan authorities considered Hutu and Tutsi as belonging to two distinct ethnic groups as previously categorized by their colonizers.[26]

Membership of a group can also be determined objectively. In *Rutaganda*, Trial Chamber I of the ICTR finds a number of objective indicators of the Tutsi population as an ethnic group with a distinct identity. Every Rwandan citizen was required to carry an identity card showing his ethnic identity being either Hutu, Tutsi, or Twa. Moreover, the Rwandan Constitution and laws in force at the relevant time also identified Rwandans by reference to their ethnic group, and customary determination of membership of an ethnic group in Rwanda followed patrilineal lines.[27]

Genocide can be committed within a limited confine of a particular geographical area or region, provided that all the requisite elements of genocide are met.[28] In customary international law, as appeared from the Genocide Convention of 1948, genocide can be committed in the context of peace or of armed conflict.[29]

ACTUS REUS

Genocide need not involve the actual extermination of group—genocide is committed once any one of the acts enumerated above is committed with the requisite *mens rea*.[30] Genocide can be committed by acts or omissions.[31] In *Kambanda*, the accused was found guilty of genocide, *inter alia*, for his omission to fulfil his duty as Prime Minister of Rwanda to take action to stop on-going massacres which he had become

---

[23] *Jelisic*, paras. 70–2; *Kayishema and Ruzindana*, para. 98; *Akayesu*, para. 513.
[24] *Rutaganda*, para. 55.
[25] Ibid., para. 57. Followed in *Musema*, paras. 161, 163.
[26] *Akayesu*, paras. 122 (n. 56), 702–3.
[27] *Rutaganda*, paras. 400–1.
[28] *Jelisic*, para. 83.
[29] *Case Concerning Application of the Convention on the Prevention and Punishment of the Crime of Genocide (Bosnia-Herzegovina v. Yugoslavia)*, Preliminary Objections, ICJ Judgment of 11 July 1996, para. 31.
[30] *Akayesu*, para. 497; *Jelisic*, para. 62.
[31] *Prosecutor v. Jean Kambanda*, Case No. ICTR-97–23-S, ICTR T. Ch., 4 Sept. 1998, para. 40 (1)–(4).

aware of, or to protect children and the population from possible massacres, after he had been personally asked to do so and this omission resulted in massacres.[32] There is no need for the Prosecution to establish the precise number of victims of an act of genocide attributable to the accused.[33]

MENS REA

As the ICTY makes clear in *Jelisic,* 'it is in fact the *mens rea* which gives genocide its speciality and distinguishes it from an ordinary crime and other crimes against international humanitarian law. . . .'[34]

In order to convict an accused of genocide, it must be proven that the accused had the specific intent (*dolus specialis*), or a 'psychological nexus between the physical result and the mental state of the perpetrator',[35] to destroy, at least in part, a national, ethnic, racial, or religious group, as such,[36] or that the accused had at least the clear knowledge (*conscience claire*) that he was participating in genocide, that is, the destruction, at least in part, of a national, ethnic, racial, or religious group, as such.[37] Phrased differently, the requisite knowledge is that the accused knew or should have known that his act would destroy, in whole or in part, such protected group.[38] The special nature of this intent supposes the discriminatory nature of the act—a group is targeted discriminatorily as such, and, in this context, genocide is closely related to the crime against humanity of persecution.[39] It could be said that genocide in itself constitutes a crime against humanity of persecution.[40] What distinguishes persecution from genocide is that the perpetrator of persecution selects his victims by reason of their belonging to a specific community but he does not necessarily seek the destruction of that community as such.[41] Therefore, the discriminatory nature of the targeting is not the same thing as the specific intent to destroy a group or community as such. To find an accused guilty of genocide, his specific intent to destroy the group or community must be proved beyond all reasonable doubt. The fact that the accused discriminated against one group does not suffice because while discriminatory intent may be a predominant subjective element of guilt in the case of persecution, which is a crime against humanity, it is not a decisive subjective element to find an accused guilty of genocide. In *Jelisic,* the accused's intent to persecute the victimized group was

---

[32] Ibid., para. 39 (iii) (ix).

[33] *Jelisic,* para. 65.

[34] Ibid., para. 66.

[35] *Musema,* para. 166.

[36] *Akayesu,* para. 498; *Jelisic,* para. 66.

[37] *Prosecutor v. Goran Jelisic,* Case No. IT-95–10, ICTY T. Ch. I, Oral Judgment of 19 Oct. 1999 (hereinafter 'Jelisic Oral Judgment').

[38] *Akayesu,* para. 520.

[39] *Jelisic,* paras. 67–8.

[40] Ibid., para. 68, citing *Kayishema and Ruzindana,* para. 578 and *Attorney-General v. Eichmann,* District Court of Jerusalem (1968) 5 *ILR* 36 at 239, para. 201.

[41] *Jelisic,* para. 79.

proved, but he was found not guilty of genocide as he lacked the specific intent to destroy the group in question.[42]

The expression 'to destroy in whole or in part' means to destroy an important part from a quantitative or qualitative perspective; the accused must intend to destroy either a large proportion of the group or a representative fraction of the group, such as its political leaders, religious leaders, or its intellectuals.[43] The genocidal intent may be shown in two forms: the desire to exterminate a large number of members of a protected group, or the desire to destroy a more limited number of members of such group who are selected because of the potential impact of their destruction on the survival of the group as such.[44] In other words, each act or omission must be evaluated in the context of what would happen to the rest of the group in question.[45] For example, the destruction of all or almost all young, fertile women of child bearing age who account for only five to ten per cent of the entire population of the protected group is genocide.

The accused must choose the victim not because of his individual identity, but because of his membership of one of the groups mentioned above, since the accused must have an ulterior motive to destroy such group.[46] This does not mean that an ulterior motive is required in addition to the other elements of the crime of genocide already mentioned. What is meant here is that the accused must commit a proscribed act or omission against the victim because the victim is a member of the group the accused intends to destroy in whole or in part. This is also clear from the legislative history of the Genocide Convention of 1948. The Delegation of Venezuela tabled the proposal before the *ad hoc* Committee of UNESCO, which was drafting the Genocide Convention, to add the words 'as such' after the end of the enumerated list of protected groups. The Delegation explained that it would be 'useless and even dangerous' to enumerate motives for genocide since a restrictive enumeration would be manipulated by the guilty parties to help them avoid being charged with genocide. Therefore, the Delegation wished to ensure that it was sufficient to indicate that intent, not a motive, was a constituent factor of the crime.[47]

The *mens rea* must be formed prior to the commission of an act of genocide in the sense that the act should be done to further the genocidal intent.[48] In this context, it is not necessary that the accused intended to commit crimes over a vast geographical area or to eliminate an important or substantial part of the population. However, the

---

[42] Ibid., paras. 77, 93 ff.

[43] Ibid., paras. 81–2.

[44] Ibid., para. 82. While it is largely accepted that the intention to destroy must aim at a substantial part of the group, the ICTY considers that Trial Chamber II of the ICTR in *Kayishema and Ruzindana* (para. 97) goes further than this in holding that the term 'in part' requires the intention to destroy a 'considerable number' of individuals who are part of the group. It is hereby submitted that the opinion of the ICTY in *Jelisic* is the better of the two.

[45] *Jelisic,* para. 82.

[46] *Akayesu,* paras. 521–2; *Rutaganda,* para. 59; *Musema,* para. 165.

[47] UN GAOR, 3rd Sess, 1948, Summary Records of the Sixth Committee, iii, pt. I, 124–5.

[48] *Kayishema and Ruzindana,* para. 91.

crimes perpetrated by the accused must show that the perpetrator, whether he is placed in a high hierarchical position or is a mere ordinary person, had the clear knowledge or the intent to seek the total or at least partial destruction of such a given human group.[49]

The necessary element of intent may be inferred from a number of facts such as words or deeds or a pattern of purposeful action that deliberately, consistently, and systematically targets victims on account of their membership of a particular group while excluding the members of other groups. Circumstantial evidence that may be useful includes the general context of the commission of other criminal acts committed by the same offender or by others that were systematically directed against that same group, the physical targeting of a protected group or their property, the use of derogatory language towards members of the group, the weapons used and the extent of bodily injury, the methodical way of planning, the systematic way of killing, and the relative proportionate scale of the actual or attempted destruction of the group in a region or a country.[50] As a result, proving the *dolus specialis* required for genocide has become relatively easier than previously expected.

Such was the case in *Akayesu* where Trial Chamber I of the ICTR found that the accused in that case had the requisite *mens rea* to commit genocide through, *inter alia*, the systematic rape of Tutsi women in Rwanda in 1994. A Tutsi women married to a Hutu man was spared because her ethnic background was unknown. The systematic rape of Tutsi women was part of the propaganda campaign to mobilize the Hutu against the Tutsi, with the Tutsi women being presented as sexual objects to be subjected to sexual violence because they were Tutsi. This sexual violence was a step towards the destruction of the Tutsi group by destroying their spirit, will to live, or will to procreate.[51]

By contrast, the Prosecution did not succeed in proving the genocidal intent in *Jelisic*. The accused Jelisic, nicknamed 'Serb Adolf', was regarded as the chief executioner of detainees at the Luka camp, a makeshift detention facility in Brcko, northern Bosnia, following the takeover of that city by Bosnian Serb forces in 1992. Although he repeatedly killed Muslim detainees as well as a few Croats, he was found not guilty of genocide. This was also despite the fact that he had boasted, among other things, that he would sterilize Muslim women and deal with Muslim men in such a manner as to prevent multiplication or proliferation of Muslims.[52] According to Trial Chamber I of the ICTY, the Prosecution failed to prove the existence of a scheme to destroy the Muslim group in Brcko or outside Brcko of which acts of murder committed by the accused could form part.[53] While it is 'theoretically possible' to find an individual guilty of genocide on account of his own serial killings, it is very difficult in

---

[49] *Jelisic*, paras. 80–2.
[50] *Akayesu*, paras. 523–4, 728–30; *Kayishema and Ruzindana*, para. 93; *Jelisic*, paras. 73–7; *Rutaganda*, paras. 60–2; *Musema*, paras. 166–7.
[51] *Akayesu*, para. 732.
[52] *Jelisic*, para. 102.
[53] Ibid., paras. 94, 98, 108.

practice to prove the genocidal intention of an individual if the crimes committed are not widespread or backed up by an organization or a system.[54] In addition, Jelisic killed Muslims at the camp randomly, with his victims chosen arbitrarily without any logic or scheme.[55] For example, an eminent well-known figure in the local Muslim community was allegedly forced to play Russian roulette with the accused before the accused himself gave the person a travel pass to leave the camp. On the accused's own initiative and against all logic, the accused also issued travel passes to several Muslim detainees at the camp, some of them after being beaten by the accused.[56] Jelisic was considered a mentally disturbed person, a 'borderline' case, with anti-social and narcissistic behaviour, who was thrust into a position of authority at the camp and enjoyed the physical expression of his authority.[57] He was found not guilty of genocide in the absence of 'an affirmed resolve to destroy in whole or in part a group as such'.[58]

The facts in *Jelisic* are to be distinguished from those in *Ruggiu*. The accused in the latter case was a Belgian national employed at the *Radio Television Libre des Milles Collines* (RTLM) in Rwanda from January 1994 to July 1994. He used the RTLM to broadcast his messages inciting genocide against the Tutsis. Trial Chamber I of the ICTR, following *Akayesu*, held that the person who incites another to commit genocide must himself have a specific intent to commit genocide, namely, to destroy, in whole or in part, a national, ethnic, racial, or religious group, as such.[59] The accused in that case was found guilty of, *inter alia*, the crime of direct and public incitement to commit genocide.[60] The Trial Chamber noted, however, that on a few occasions the accused personally conveyed Tutsi children in his jeep, hidden under blankets, to a mission so that they would be cared for and protected, and that he was responsible for feeding a group of farmers and refugees including Tutsis.[61] The Trial Chamber considered that these acts constituted mitigating circumstances to reduce Ruggiu's sentence. No mention was ever made that they would negate Ruggiu's specific intent to destroy the Tutsis as such, and no reference was ever made to *Jelisic*. It is hereby submitted that Ruggiu is distinguishable from Jelisic for the following reasons. Ruggiu clearly intended to destroy the Tutsis and their sympathizers after he had been indoctrinated and enlisted by certain Hutu extremists.[62] Unlike the situation in *Jelisic*, the existence of a scheme to destroy the Tutsis was evident and Ruggiu served that scheme. The fact that he showed some compassion to a few Tutsis did not negate his resolve to eliminate the Tutsis, at least 'in part', especially those Tutsis holding political or military authority. Those Tutsis

[54] Ibid., paras. 100–1.

[55] Ibid., 106, 108.

[56] Ibid., 106.

[57] Ibid., paras. 102–5.

[58] Ibid., paras. 107.

[59] *Prosecutor v. Georges Ruggiu*, Case No. ICTR-97–32-I, ICTR T. Ch. I, 1 June 2000, para. 14.

[60] Ibid., para. 24.

[61] Ibid., paras. 73–4.

[62] Ibid., paras. 62–7.

benefiting from his generosity were not the political enemy he wanted destroyed. His motive might be political or idealistic, but motives are not an element of the crime of genocide. Although the reasons behind his incitement might be political or idealistic, the Tutsis are an ethnic group whose destruction in whole or in part constitutes genocide.

While the existence of a specific plan to destroy is not an element of genocide, the ICTR in *Kayishema and Ruzindana* concurs with the view expressed by the ICTY in *Jelisic* that, due to the magnitude of genocide, it is virtually impossible to carry out genocide without a plan or organization, with some or indirect involvement on the part of the State, although a individual need not have knowledge of all details of such plan or organization.[63] In other words, 'serial killings' cannot be always equated with genocide.

There can be no defence that the enumerated acts of genocide are committed for a eugenic reason or a welfare reason. The prohibition against each and every one of the enumerated acts is unequivocal and committing any one of them would be genocide. To allow such a defence would be tantamount to accepting the superiority of one group over another, something which can only be judged subjectively with the group who judges inevitably asserting its own superiority.

In Australia, there has been an on-going debate and controversy regarding measures taken to assimilate the Aborigines with the white race. The Aboriginals Ordinance 1918 (Northern Territory) provided the legal basis for the removal of Aboriginal children from families and communities in Australia's Northern Territory. In *Kruger and Others v. The Commonwealth of Australia; Bray and Others v. The Commonwealth of Australia*,[64] the plaintiffs who were members of 'the Stolen Generation of the Northern Territory', contended that the legislation was unconstitutional and invalid because it, among other things, constituted or authorized 'the crime against humanity of genocide'. The action failed. In essence, the High Court held that although the Ordinance might authorize the forcible transfer of the children from their racial group, the settled principle of statutory interpretation compelled the conclusion that it did not authorize persons to remove those children 'with intent to destroy in whole or in part' their racial group, as such. Some of the High Court judges in that case emphasized the presumption that a statute should be construed as being in conformity with international law,[65] while the other judges emphasized the benevolent intent of the legislature to further 'the interests' of the Aboriginals or half-caste.[66] It is hereby submitted that making a racial group disappear through its biological assimilation with another racial group is a crime of genocide under customary international law. One individual or group cannot arrogate to itself the right to conclude that it would

---

[63] *Kayishema and Ruzindana*, para. 94.

[64] (1997) 146 *ALR* 126. Also analysed in M. Storey, '*Kruger v. The Commonwealth*: Does Genocide Require Malice?' (1998) 21 *Univ. New South Wales L. J.* 224.

[65] *per* Toohey and Gaudron, JJ.

[66] *per* Dawson, Gummow, and McHugh, JJ.

be in the interests of a national, ethnic, racial, or religious group if that group somehow ceases to exist.

The foregoing legal analysis applies to all offences of genocide. The Elements of Crimes adopted by the PCNICC for each of the enumerated acts of genocide under Article 6 of the ICC Statute have the following common elements. The number of victim(s) may be one or more persons, provided that the victim(s) belonged to a particular national, ethnical, racial, or religious group, and that the perpetrator intended to destroy, in whole or in part, that national, ethnical, racial, or religious group, as such. The conduct must have taken place in the context of a manifest pattern of similar conduct directed against that group or was conduct that could itself effect such destruction. 'In the context of' would include the initial acts in an emerging pattern. The term 'manifest' is an objective qualification. Therefore, the prosecutor may charge a perpetrator where the act proscribed by Article 6 of the ICC Statute was directed against one person but the act took place within a manifest pattern of genocidal conduct. The phrase 'was conduct that could itself effect such destruction' has been inserted to cover the rare instance in which the perpetrator was not acting in the context of a manifest pattern of genocidal conduct but his conduct in itself was of such a magnitude that it constitutes genocide if accompanied by the requisite mental element, as where he used an atomic bomb to kill a protected group. It therefore envisages the situation where there is not any involvement, direct or indirect, on the part of the State. An insane perpetrator could steal an atomic bomb and use it to kill a protected group.

The Elements also make clear that, notwithstanding the normal requirement for a mental element provided for in Article 30 of the ICC Statute, and recognizing that knowledge of the circumstances will usually be addressed in proving genocidal intent, the appropriate requirement, if any, for a mental element regarding this circumstance will need to be decided by the ICC on a case-by-case basis.

The following are the elements of crimes peculiar to each of the enumerated acts of genocide.

4.1 KILLING

The French version of 'killing' in the case of genocide is '*meurte*', that is, unlawful and intentional killing. However, there is virtually no difference between the two versions in the context of genocide since both of them are linked to the intent to destroy in whole or in part, not a type of act that would normally happen by accident or as a result of mere negligence.[67] As the ICTR ruled in *Akayesu*, 'killing' is homicide

---

[67] *Kayeshima and Ruzindana*, paras. 101–4.

committed with the intent to cause death.[68] By its constituent physical elements, the very crime of genocide necessarily entails premeditation.[69]

The Elements of Crimes adopted by the PCNICC for the crime of genocide by killing under Article 6(a) of the ICC Statute makes clear that it is the act of killing, or causing death, that forms an essential element for this crime. Causing death as understood in the Elements connotes intentional omission that leads to death of the victim.

4.2 CAUSING SERIOUS BODILY OR MENTAL HARM

'Serious bodily harm' is to be determined on a case-by-case basis. It could be interpreted to mean 'harm that seriously injures the health, causes disfigurement, or causes any serious injury to the external, internal organs or senses'.[70] Thus, it can mean acts of torture, be they bodily or mental; inhumane or degrading treatment; rape; sexual violence; or persecution.[71] The harm need not be permanent or irremediable.[72] The international jurisprudence on this offence therefore negates the understanding of the US at the time of its ratification of the Genocide Convention which states, *inter alia*, that the term 'mental harm' in Article II(b) of the Genocide Convention means 'permanent impairment of mental faculties through drugs, torture, or similar techniques'.

Likewise, the phrase 'serious mental harm' is to be determined on a case-by-case basis.[73]

Forcing a victim to lie down in front of a vehicle and threatening to drive over her, forcing one victim to beat another victim, and tying two victims together thereby causing one of them to suffocate have been held to constitute acts causing serious bodily or mental harm.[74] Rape and sexual violence are considered one of the worst ways of inflicting harm on the victim as he or she suffers both bodily and mental harm.[75] As already mentioned, the systematic rape of Tutsi women in 1994 was a step to achieve the destruction of the Tutsi group by destroying their spirit, will to live, or will to procreate.[76]

The Elements of Crimes adopted by the PCNICC for the crime of genocide by

---

[68] *Akayesu*, para. 501; *Rutaganda*, para. 55; *Musema*, para. 155. However, Trial Chamber I of the ICTR in *Rutaganda* and in *Musema* arrived at this conclusion on the ground of presumption of innocence and the general principles of criminal law that the version more favourable to the accused should be adopted.

[69] *Akayesu*, para. 501.

[70] *Kayishema and Ruzindana*, para. 109, and see also para. 108.

[71] *Akayesu*, para. 504; *Rutaganda*, para. 50; *Musema*, para. 156.

[72] Ibid.

[73] *Kayishema and Ruzindana*, paras. 110–3.

[74] Ibid., paras. 722–3.

[75] Ibid., para. 731.

[76] *Akayesu*, para. 732.

causing serious bodily or mental harm under Article 6(b) of the ICC Statute follow faithfully existing international jurisprudence. The pertinent part of the Elements stipulates that the perpetrator must have caused serious bodily or mental harm to one or more persons, and that this conduct may include, but is not necessarily restricted to, acts of torture, rape, sexual violence, or inhuman or degrading treatment.

4.3 DELIBERATELY INFLICTING CONDITIONS OF LIFE CALCULATED TO BRING ABOUT PHYSICAL DESTRUCTION

This act connotes methods of destruction not leading immediately to the death of members of the targeted group, but which seek ultimately their physical destruction. Examples of such conditions of life include starving the targeted group; depriving the targeted group of proper housing (including systematic expulsion from homes), clothing, hygiene, and medical care for an extended period; subjecting the targeted group to a subsistence diet; compelling the targeted group to do excessive work or undergo excessive physical exertion.[77]

The Elements of Crimes adopted by the PCNICC for the offence under Article 6(c) of the ICC Statute stipulate that the perpetrator must have inflicted certain conditions of life upon one or more persons. The conditions of life must have been calculated to bring about the physical destruction of that group, in whole or in part. The term 'conditions of life' may include, but is not necessarily restricted to, deliberate deprivation of resources indispensable for survival, such as food or medical services, or systematic expulsion from homes.

It should be noted that the US submitted a proposal to the PCNICC to require that the intended results must occur before the accused can be guilty of this offence. This proposal was not accepted by other delegations because the provision of the ICC Statute is unequivocal. To constitute this offence, it is enough to inflict conditions of life 'calculated to bring about physical destruction'; that is, mere 'calculation' suffices without any need for the results to materialize.[78] This conclusion is consistent with the decision of the Israeli court in *Eichmann*, where the accused was found guilty of this offence for having sent his Jewish victims to hard labour camps with intent to kill them irrespective of the fact that some of them eventually survived.[79]

Despite the fact that the intended result is not an element for this offence, it is still

---

[77] *Kayishema and Ruzindana*, paras. 115–6, *Akayesu*, paras. 505–6; *Rutaganda*, para. 51; *Musema*, para. 157.

[78] See, e.g. Proposal submitted by Colombia—Comments on the proposal submitted by the United States of America on Article 6: the crime of genocide (PCNICC/ 1999/ DP. 4), *Doc. PCNICC/ 1999/ WGEC/ DP. 2* of 18 Feb. 1999.

[79] *Attorney-General of the Govt. of Israel v. Eichmann*, Supreme Ct. of Israel sitting as Court of Criminal Appeals, 29 May 1962 (1968) **36** *ILR* 5 at 235–6.

difficult to prove the commission of this crime, as shown by a decision of the International Court of Justice.

In *Legality of Use of Force*, the Federal Republic of Yugoslavia (FRY) initiated proceedings against each of the ten Members of the North Atlantic Treaty Organization (NATO) that undertook a bombing campaign against it during the so-called 'humanitarian intervention' in the Kosovo crisis in 1999. The FRY asked the ICJ to order provisional measures enjoining the States involved to 'cease immediately [their on-going] acts of use of force' and to 'refrain from any act of threat or use of force' against the FRY while the FRY was instituting proceedings against these States before the ICJ. The FRY contended that the dispute concerned, among other things, acts of each NATO Member which had violated its international obligations under the Genocide Convention 'not to deliberately inflict conditions of life calculated to cause the physical destruction of a national group'. In the FRY's view, the sustained and intensive bombing of the entire territory of the FRY, including the most heavily populated areas, constituted 'a serious violation of Article II of the Genocide Convention'. More specifically, the FRY alleged that it was the Yugoslav nation as a whole and 'as such' that was being targeted, and that the use of certain weapons whose long-term hazards to health and the environment are already known, and the destruction of the largest part of the country's power supply system, with catastrophic consequences of which the NATO Members must have been aware, implied 'the intent to destroy, in whole or in part', the Yugoslav national group as such.

Yugoslavia referred, as a basis for the ICJ's jurisdiction, to Article IX of the Genocide Convention, to which all of these ten NATO States and the FRY were party. The Article provides:

'Disputes between the Contracting Parties relating to the interpretation or fulfilment of the present Convention, including those relating to the responsibility of a State for genocide . . . shall be submitted to the International Court of Justice at the request of any of the parties to the dispute.'

The ICJ held that it manifestly lacked jurisdiction *vis-à-vis* the US and Spain because of the unequivocal reservations made by the two States with respect to the acceptance of the ICJ's jurisdiction under Article IX of the Genocide Convention as well as under the relevant provision of the ICJ Statute. The ICJ ordered that the cases against these two States be removed from its List. With respect to the other eight NATO Members, they did not make any reservation to Article IX of the Genocide Convention. Nonetheless, they argued that in order for Article IX of the Genocide Convention to be applicable, the claims submitted by the FRY had to relate, even indirectly or tenuously, to the concept of genocide, but that it was impossible to discern any genocidal intention, or even any appearance of such intention. The NATO action was said not to be directed against the FRY population, but against the FRY's 'military machine and military-industrial complex'. The ICJ accepted this argument and found that it lacked *prima facie* jurisdiction, which is a precondition for the order of provisional measures. In its view, the essential characteristic of genocide under the Genocide Convention is the intended destruction of a national, ethnical, racial, or religious group, as such. The threat or use of force against a State cannot in itself constitute an act of genocide within the meaning of Article II of the Genocide Convention. Furthermore, it did not appear at that time that the bombings which formed the subject of the FRY's application entailed the element of intent, towards a national group as such, as required by Article II of the Genocide Convention. Consequently, the ICJ was not in a position to find, at that stage of the proceedings, that the acts imputed by the FRY to the eight NATO Members were capable of coming within the provisions of the Genocide Convention. Therefore, no provisional measures were ordered.[80]

4.4 IMPOSING MEASURES INTENDED TO PREVENT BIRTHS

Imposing measures to prevent birth within the group includes sexual mutilation, the practice of sterilization, forced birth control, forced separation of the sexes, prohibition of marriages, and forced pregnancy in a patriarchal society for the mother to give birth to a child who will consequently not belong to its mother's group. Such measures may be physical or mental (such as rape that traumatizes the victim), provided that, through threats or trauma, they cause the victim not to procreate.[81]

The pertinent elements of the Elements of Crimes laid down by the PCNICC for the crime of genocide by imposing measures intended to prevent births under Article 6(d) of the ICC Statute merely require that the perpetrator must have imposed certain measures upon one or more persons with intent to prevent births within that group.

The US again proposed that the intended result of the conduct must occur before its perpetrator could be held guilty of this offence. The proposal was rejected. Article 6(d) of the ICC Statute refers to 'measures intended' to prevent births within the group, not 'measures having the effect' of preventing births within the group.

4.5 FORCIBLY TRANSFERRING CHILDREN

In *Akayesu*, Trial Chamber I of the ICTR held that the objective of criminalizing forcibly transferring children of the protected group to another group as an act of genocide is, as in the case of measures intended to prevent births, 'not only to sanction

---

[80] *Legality of Use of Force (Yugoslavia v. Belgium)*, Request for the Indication of Provisional Measures, ICJ Order of 2 June 1999, para. 40. Also *Legality of Use of Force (Yugoslavia v. Canada)*, *(Yugoslavia v. France)*, *(Yugoslavia v. Germany)*, *(Yugoslavia v. Italy)*, *(Yugoslavia v. Netherlands)*, *(Yugoslavia v. Portugal)*, and *(Yugoslavia v. UK)*, Request for the Indication of Provisional Measures, ICJ Orders of 2 June 1999.

[81] *Akayesu*, paras. 507–8, *Kayishema and Ruzindana*, para. 117; *Rutaganda*, para. 52; *Musema*, para. 158.

a direct act of forcible physical transfer, but also to sanction acts of threats or trauma which would lead to the forcible transfer'.[82] It could be argued that forced removal of children of the group to another group causes serious mental harm to these children as well as to their parents and close relatives, and that the perpetrator of such forced removal could also be punished under the rubric of the genocidal crime of 'causing serious bodily or mental harm to members of the group' as well.

Trial Chamber II of the ICTR in *Kayishema and Ruzindana* also concurs with *Akayesu* on this point.[83]

The US proposal at the PCNICC to define a 'child' as a 'person under the age of fifteen' was opposed by other delegations on the ground that the Convention on the Rights of the Child of 1989, which is ratified by virtually every State, defines a child as every human being below the age of 18.[84] Likewise, the US proposal to qualify that the transfer must be made from the child's lawful residence was rejected. It would confuse the crime of genocide by forcibly transferring children under Article 6(d) of the ICC Statute with the crime against humanity of deportation or forcible transfer of population under Article 7(1)(d) of the Statute. It is only in relation to the latter Article that the Statute, in Article 7(2)(d), mentions that the forced displacement of persons must be 'from the area in which they are lawfully present'. Neither customary international law nor applicable conventional law requires an element of lawful presence of the child in the case of this offence of genocide. The protection accorded to the child is not contingent on the child's presence in his lawful residence, but extends to his actual place of residence, wherever he may be and irrespective of whether it is lawful or not.[85]

The pertinent part of the Elements of Crimes laid down by the PCNICC for the crime of genocide by imposing measures intended to prevent births under Article 6(d) of the ICC Statute is quite straightforward. The perpetrator must have forcibly transferred one or more persons under the age of eighteen years from one protected group to another group, and the perpetrator must have known, or should have known, that the person or persons were under the age of eighteen years. What is meant by 'forcibly' is not restricted to physical force, but may include threat of force or coercion, such as that caused by fear of violence, duress, detention, psychological oppression or abuse of power, against such person or persons or another person, or by taking advantage of a coercive environment.[86] This meaning is adopted in order to

---

[82] *Akayesu*, para. 509. Followed in *Rutaganda*, para. 53; *Musema*, para. 159.

[83] *Kayishema and Ruzindana*, para. 118.

[84] (1989) **28** *ILM* 1448.

[85] See, e.g. Proposal submitted by Colombia—Comments on the proposal submitted by the United States of America on Article 6: the crime of genocide (PCNICC/ 1999/ DP. 4), *Doc. PCNICC/ 1999/ WGEC/ DP. 2* of 18 Feb. 1999, and Proposal by Algeria, Bahrain, Comoros, Djibouti, Egypt, Iraq, Jordan, Kuwait, Lebanon, Libyan Arab Jamahiriya, Mauritania, Morocco, Oman, Palestine, Qatar, Saudi Arabia, the Sudan, the Syrian Arab Republic, Tunisia, United Arab Emirates, and Yemen—Comments on the proposal submitted by the United States of America concerning terminology and the crime of genocide (PCNICC/ 1999/ DP. 4), *Doc. PCNICC/ 1999/ WGEC/ DP. 4* of 22 Feb. 1999.

[86] Report of the Preparatory Commission for the International Criminal Court, *Doc. PCNICC/2000/1/ Add. 2*, 2 Nov. 2000.

harmonize the meaning of 'forcibly' as used in this provision with the one already adopted by the PCNICC's Working Group on Elements of Crimes for the crime against humanity of deportation or forcible transfer of population under Article 7(1)(d) of the ICC Statute,[87] and to reflect the international jurisprudence of the ICTR and the ICTY, which defines the meaning of the term in the context of sexual crimes to encompass all situations where the victim could not be justifiably considered to have consented to the conduct of the accused. It derives from the pronouncement of the ICTR in *Akayesu* which explains what amounts to 'coercion' and 'coercive circumstances',[88] and from that of the ICTY in *Furundzija* which elaborates that threats of force may be against the victim or a third person, and that such threats may be expressed or implied and 'must place the victim in reasonable fear that he, she, or a third person will be subjected to violence, detention, duress, or psychological oppression'.[89]

4.6 CONCLUSIONS

The ICTY and the ICTR have contributed significantly towards the clarification of the concept of genocide and the improvement of the prosecution's chance of success in the following ways.

First of all, they have clarified what each of the protected groups means. The test to identify the membership of a protected group eases the burden of proof for the prosecution while, at the same time, taking into account the political and cultural context of the society in question.

Secondly, in terms of the elements of the crime of genocide, it has now been made clear that genocide can be committed by an act or an omission. Furthermore, the qualitative and quantitative tests ease the burden of proof of the prosecution with respect to the requirement that the act or omission must be committed with intent to destroy a protected group as such 'in whole or in part'. The prosecution could discharge such a burden by evaluating the potential or actual impact of such act or omission in the context of what would happen or has happened to the group concerned.

Thirdly, the fact that specific intent to destroy could be inferred from a number of facts facilitates immensely the task of the prosecution. The task of the prosecution that was long considered insurmountable now becomes surmountable.

Fourthly, the ICTR and the ICTY have shown gender as well as cultural sensitivity and realism in categorizing sexual crimes that could be tantamount to genocide. Indeed, rape or other forms of sexual violence could be used to cause serious bodily or

---

[87] *Doc. PCNICC/ 2000/ WGEC/ L. 1/ Add. 1*, 29 June 2000.
[88] *Akayesu*, para. 688.
[89] *Prosecutor v. Anto Furundzija*, Case No. IT-95–17/1-T, ICTY T. Ch. II, 10 Dec. 1998, para. 174.

mental harm to members of the group, or to prevent births within the group, or to create conditions of life calculated to bring about physical destruction, especially in view of the social and/or religious taboo against victims of rape and other sexual violence in some societies.

On the whole, these developments have assisted the PCNICC in drafting the Elements of Crimes for genocide and they provide much optimism for success in prosecuting the crime of genocide under international criminal law.

5

CRIMES AGAINST HUMANITY

A crime against humanity is a crime against 'humaneness' that offends certain general principles of law and which becomes the concern of the international community. It has repercussions beyond international frontiers or exceeds in magnitude or savagery any limits tolerated by modern civilization.[1] Crimes against humanity differ from genocide in that no *dolus specialis* to destroy members of a particular group is required in case of crimes against humanity.[2]

The expressions 'humanity', 'laws of humanity', and 'dictates of humanity' were used in, for example, the Preamble to the 1907 Hague Convention IV Respecting the Laws and Customs of War on Land.[3] Paragraph 2 of the Preamble states that the contracting Parties desire to serve even in the case of war 'the interests of humanity and the ever-progressive needs of civilization'. Paragraph 8 of the Preamble (the so-called 'Martens Clause') provides that they declare, among other things, that 'the inhabitants and belligerents remain under the protection and governance of the principles of the law of nations, derived from the usages established among civilized peoples, from the laws of humanity, and from the dictates of the public conscience'. As pointed out by Egon Schwelb, the Preamble treats the 'interests of humanity' as the purpose which the laws and customs of war serve, and the 'laws of humanity' as one of the sources of the law of nations; there is no intention to indicate a set of norms different from war crimes.[4]

The terminology 'crimes against humanity' was used in a non-technical sense as far back as 1915, in the Declaration of 28 May 1915 of the Governments of France, Great Britain, and Russia denouncing the massacres of the Armenian population by Turkey as 'crimes against humanity and civilization for which all the members of the Turkish Government will be held responsible together with its agents implicated in the massacres'.[5] The terminology was also used in subsequent statements concerning WWI. The Commission of Fifteen Members was established by the Preliminary Peace Conference in January 1919 to inquire into the responsibilities relating to WWI. Chapter

---

[1] E. Schwelb, 'Crimes Against Humanity' (1946) **23** *BYBIL* 178 at 195–7.

[2] *Prosecutor v. Jean-Paul Akayesu*, Case No. ICTR-96–4-T, ICTR T. Ch. I, 2 Sept. 1998, paras. 565–8; *Attorney-General of Israel v. Eichmann*, District Ct. of Jerusalem (11 Dec. 1961) **36** *ILR* 5 at 41.

[3] *UK Treaties Series* 9 (1910), Cd. 5030; 8 *UNTS* 279.

[4] Schwelb, 180. For the use of 'dictates of humanity', see ibid., 183, n. 1.

[5] The Armenian Memorandum presented by the Greek delegation to the Commission of Fifteen on 14 Mar. 1919. Quoted in ibid., at 181.

II of the Commission's report, dated 29 March 1919, stated, *inter alia*, that 'all persons belonging to enemy countries . . . who have been guilty of offences against the laws and customs of war or the laws of humanity, are liable to criminal prosecution'. Annex I of the report listed, in addition to the charge of war crimes as they were generally understood at that time, the charges of murder and massacre, systematic terrorism, killing of hostages, torture of civilians, rape, abduction of female civilians for the purpose of enforced prostitution, deportation of civilians, and pillage, committed by Turkish and German authorities against Turkish subjects, as well as a charge of pillage by Austrian troops against the population of an Austrian town. The addition of the laws of humanity failed on an objection by the American members of the Commission essentially on the grounds that a judicial tribunal could only enforce existing law, not the vague notions of laws and principles of humanity that fall within the realm of moral law.[6]

Crimes against humanity were prosecuted at the Nuremberg and Tokyo trials after WWII. Article 6(c) of the Nuremberg Charter[7] enumerated the following as crimes against humanity:

'. . . murder, extermination, enslavement, deportation and other inhumane acts committed against any civilian populations, before or during the war; or persecutions on political, racial, or religious grounds in execution of or in connection with any crime within the jurisdiction of the Tribunal, whether or not in violation of the domestic law of the country where perpetrated.'

The semi-colon before 'or persecutions . . . ' in the English and French texts was replaced subsequently by a comma by the Protocol signed at Berlin on 6 October 1945.[8] The change was made to harmonize these texts with the Russian text, all of which were equally authentic. As a result, the provisos 'in execution of or in connection with any crime within the jurisdiction of the Tribunal' and ', whether or not in violation of the domestic law of the country where perpetrated' applied to the whole text of Article 6(c).[9]

Although this was the first technical use of the terminology 'crimes against humanity', and the statesmen involved fully appreciated that crimes against humanity under the Nuremberg Charter were in a different category from war crimes,[10] they were not treated by the Nuremberg Tribunal as a new concept. The Nuremberg Tribunal did not question the legality of the inclusion of crimes against humanity in the Nuremberg Charter, merely noting that 'from the beginning of the War in 1939 War Crimes were committed on a vast scale, which were also Crimes against Humanity'.[11] The

  [6] Ibid., 180–3.
  [7] *UK Treaty Series* 27 (1946), Cd. 6903.
  [8] US Dept. of State Publication 2461, Executive Agreement Series 472 (US Govt. Printing Office, 1946), 45 ff.
  [9] Schwelb, 188, 192–5, 204–5.
  [10] Ibid., 186–7.
  [11] *Trial of the Major War Criminals*, Proceedings of the International Military Tribunal, Nuremberg, pt. 22 (H.M. Stationery Office, 1950) (hereinafter '*Nuremberg Proceedings*'), 468; (1947) **41** *AJIL* 249.

Nuremberg Tribunal simply ruled that the Nuremberg Charter was decisive and binding on it, and that it was 'the expression of international law existing at the time of its creation; and to that extent [was] itself a contribution to international law'.[12] This was despite the fact that the Nuremberg Charter extended the jurisdiction of the Nuremberg Tribunal beyond war crimes in the traditional sense to encompass other serious crimes falling outside the purview of traditional war crimes, such as crimes where the victim was stateless, had the same nationality as the perpetrator, or had the nationality of a State allied with that of the perpetrator.[13] Indeed, crimes against humanity under the Nuremberg Charter corresponded roughly to violations of the 'laws of humanity' mentioned in the report of the 1919 Commission of Fifteen Members.[14] The Nuremberg Tribunal, in practice, treated crimes against humanity and war crimes as overlapping and interchangeable, with the major discernible difference being that crimes against humanity were those committed in Germany or in Austria and Czechoslovakia annexed as part of Germany, whereas war crimes were committed in territories occupied by Germany.[15] As one commentator puts it, crimes against humanity under the Nuremberg Charter aimed to ensure that inhumane acts in violation of general principles of the laws of all civilized nations committed in connection with war should be punished; therefore, a crime against humanity was treated as an 'accompanying' or 'accessory' crime to either crimes against peace or war crimes.[16]

Crimes against humanity under the Nuremberg Charter fell into two main categories: (i) murder, extermination, enslavement, deportation, and other inhumane acts committed against any civilian populations, before or during the war; and (ii) persecutions on political, racial, or religious grounds. As mentioned, the commission of a crime against humanity under either of these categories had to be in execution of or in connection with any crime within the jurisdiction of the Nuremberg Tribunal.

Control Council Law No. 10, dated 20 December 1945, enumerated the following as crimes against humanity:

'Atrocities and Offences, including but not limited to murder, extermination, enslavement, deportation, imprisonment, torture, rape, or other inhumane acts committed against any civilian population or persecution on political, racial or religious grounds, whether or not in violation of the domestic laws of the country where perpetrated.[17]

Control Council Law No. 10 added imprisonment, torture, and rape to the list of crimes against humanity under the Nuremberg Charter. Although the list of crimes against humanity under the Nuremberg Charter was exhaustive and that under

---

[12] *Nuremberg Proceedings*, 443; (1947) **41** *AJIL* 216.

[13] *Prosecutor v. Dusko Tadic*, Case No. IT-94–1-T, ICTY T. Ch. II, 7 May 1997 (hereinafter '*Tadic* Judgment'), para. 619.

[14] Schwelb, 181.

[15] R. S. Clark, 'Nuremberg and Tokyo in Contemporary Perspective', in T. H. L. MacCormack and G. J. Simpson (eds.), *The Law of War Crimes: National and International Approaches* (Kluwer, 1997), 171 at 179.

[16] Schwelb, 206.

[17] **36** *ILR* 31.

Control Council Law No. 10 was illustrative, there was no practical difference between the two as the words 'other inhumane acts' in Article 6(c) of the Nuremberg Charter were sufficiently broad to cover other crimes of similar nature. Most changes in the wording adopted by Law No. 10 resulted in practically no difference between crimes against humanity under that Law and those under the Nuremberg Charter. However, the omission in Law No. 10 of the words 'in execution of or in connection with any crime within the jurisdiction of the Tribunal' had the effect of doing away with the requirement that a crime against humanity had to be committed in execution of, or in connection with, a crime against peace or a war crime.[18]

Article 5(c) of the Tokyo Charter[19] conferred jurisdiction on the Tokyo Tribunal to prosecute and punish crimes against humanity. The provision of the Nuremberg Charter on crimes against humanity, as amended by the Berlin Protocol, was followed in the Tokyo Charter, except that religious grounds of persecution were omitted, probably because persecutions on religious grounds had not been committed on a large scale in connection with the Japanese war effort. It has been noted that crimes against humanity prosecuted before the Tokyo Tribunal were in fact war crimes, being always committed against persons other than Japanese nationals and outside Japan.[20] This observation is correct, especially in light of the modification of the Tokyo Charter just before the commencement of the Tokyo proceedings by deleting from the definition of crimes against humanity the requirement that the crimes had to be directed against the civilian population. This modification was intended to make it possible to punish the wholesale killing of military personnel in an unlawful war. As a result, Counts 37 and 38 were the only counts dealing with the crimes not falling under the category of either crimes against peace or war crimes. Count 37 charged certain accused with 'conspiring to murder members of the armed forces and civilians of the United States, the Philippines, the British Commonwealth, the Netherlands, and Thailand by initiating unlawful hostilities against those countries in breach of the Hague Convention No. III of 18th October 1907'. Similarly, Count 38 charged these same accused with 'conspiring to murder the soldiers and civilians by initiating hostilities in violation of the [agreements]'.[21]

The prosecution of crimes against humanity was upheld subsequently by the UN General Assembly on 11 December 1946[22] and by the International Law Commission.[23] The concept of crimes against humanity continued to be refined in domestic courts of Israel and France, among others.[24] Now, it is a settled rule of customary

---

[18] Schwelb, 217–9.

[19] 4 *Bevans* 20.

[20] Schwelb, 215–6.

[21] B. V. A. Röling and C. F. Rüter (eds.), *The Tokyo Judgment: The International Military Tribunal for the Far East (IMTFE) 29 April 1946–12 November 1948*, i (APA—University Press Amsterdam BV, 1977), xii, 21.

[22] Resolution on the Affirmation of the Principles of International Law Recognized by the Charter of the Nuremberg Tribunal. UN GA Res. 95 (1) of 11 Dec. 1946.

[23] Principle VI. c of the Principles of International Law Recognized in the Judgement of the Tribunal ('Nuremberg Principles') (1950) ii *Yearbook of the ILC* 374–8.

[24] See *Akayesu*, paras. 567–77.

international law that crimes against humanity are international crimes and the perpetrators of these crimes incur individual criminal responsibility. Moreover, crimes against humanity under customary international law need not be linked to international armed conflict, as required in the Nuremberg and Tokyo Charters, or any conflict at all.[25]

Article 5 of the ICTY Statute, under the heading 'Crimes against humanity', stipulates that the ICTY shall have the power to prosecute persons responsible for the following crimes 'when committed in armed conflict, whether international or internal in character, and directed against any civilian population: (a) murder; (b) extermination; (c) enslavement; (d) deportation; (e) imprisonment; (f) torture; (g) rape; (h) persecutions on political, racial and religious grounds; (i) other inhumane acts'.

While Article 3 of the ICTR Statute enumerates the same crimes against humanity as those in Article 5 of the ICTY Statute, it does away with the requirement in the ICTY Statute that such crimes be committed in armed conflict. However, Article 3 of the ICTR Statute confines the jurisdiction of the ICTR to the prosecution of persons responsible for these enumerated crimes 'when committed as part of a widespread or system attack against any civilian population on national, political, ethnic, racial or religious grounds'. Thus, the ICTR Statute contains a requirement of discriminatory intent in each of the enumerated crimes against humanity additional to the other requirements in the Nuremberg Charter, the Tokyo Charter, and the ICTY Statute.[26] Yet, the ICTR Statute is specifically tailor-made to punish the atrocities occurring in Rwanda in 1994, where Tutsis were singled out for attacks because of their ethnic origin. Tutsis and those Hutus who were believed to be political supporters of the Tutsi-dominated government were also singled out for attacks because of their political leaning.[27] Discrimination on the basis of a person's political ideology has been held to satisfy the requirement of 'political' grounds.[28] Inhumane acts committed against persons not falling within any one of the discriminatory categories could constitute crimes against humanity if the perpetrator intends to commit such acts to further his attacks on the group discriminated against on one of the discriminatory grounds.[29]

Article 7 of the ICC Statute, under the heading 'Crimes against humanity', stipulates in paragraph 1 that these crimes mean any of the acts enumerated therein 'when committed as part of a widespread or systematic attack directed against any civilian population, with knowledge of the attack'. The enumerated acts are murder; extermination; enslavement; deportation or forcible transfer of population;

---

[25] *Prosecutor v. Dusko Tadic*, Case No. IT-94-1, ICTY App. Ch., Decision on the Defence Motion for Interlocutory Appeal on Jurisdiction of 2 Oct. 1995 ('*Tadic* Jurisdiction Decision'), para. 141.

[26] The ICTR itself recognizes this fact. See *Prosecutor v. Kayishema and Obed Ruzindana*, Case No. ICTR-95-1-T, ICTR T. Ch. II, 21 May 1999, para. 130.

[27] Ibid.

[28] *Akayesu*, para. 583.

[29] Ibid., para. 584.

imprisonment or other severe deprivation of physical liberty in violation of fundamental rules of international law; torture; rape, sexual slavery, enforced prostitution,
forced pregnancy, enforced sterilization, or any other form of sexual violence of
comparable gravity; persecution against any identifiable group or collectivity on political, racial, national, ethnic, cultural, religious, gender, or other grounds that are
universally recognized as impermissible under international law, in connection with
any act referred to in Article 7, paragraph 1, or any other crime within the ICC's
jurisdiction; enforced disappearance of persons; the crime of apartheid; other
inhumane acts of a similar character intentionally causing great suffering, or serious
injury to the body or mental or physical health.[30]

The definition of crimes against humanity under the ICC Statute is not an innovation; it reflects developments of international humanitarian law since Nuremberg.[31]
The ICC Statute also adds 'forcible transfer of population' as an alternative offence to
'deportation'. Besides, it expands the offence of imprisonment to include 'other severe
deprivation of physical liberty in violation of fundamental rules of international law'.
In the case of sexual offences, the ICC Statute adds to the offence of rape those of
'sexual slavery, enforced prostitution, forced pregnancy, enforced sterilization, or any
other form of sexual violence of comparable gravity'. With regard to the crime of
persecution, the ICC Statute elaborates that it must be 'against any identifiable group
or collectivity' on discriminatory grounds, with gender, national, ethnic, cultural, 'or
other grounds that are universally recognized as impermissible under international
law' added to the discriminatory grounds enumerated in the ICTY and the ICTR
Statutes. The ICC Statute lists enforced disappearance of persons and the crime of
apartheid as new grounds. As for 'other inhumane acts', the ICC Statute elucidates
that they must be 'of a similar character intentionally causing great suffering, or
serious injury to body or to mental, or physical health'.

In general, the essential elements shared among crimes against humanity are as
follows: the act is inhumane in nature and character, causing great suffering, or
serious injury to body or to mental or physical health; the act is committed as part of a
widespread or systematic attack; and the act is committed against members of the
civilian population.[32]

ACTUS REUS

The *actus reus* of a crime against humanity thus comprises commission of an attack
that is inhumane in nature and character, causing great suffering, or serious injury
to body or to mental or physical health. The inhumane act must be committed

---

[30] For a legislative history, see H. von Hebel and D. Robinson, 'Crimes within the Jurisdiction of the
Court', in R. S. Lee (ed.), *The International Criminal Court: The Making of the Rome Statute—Issues, Negotiations, Results* (Kluwer, 1999), 79 at 90–103.

[31] See D. Robinson, 'Defining "Crimes against Humanity" at the Rome Conference' (1999) 93 *AJIL* 43 at
43–4.

[32] Cf. *Akayesu*, para. 578.

as part of a widespread or systematic attack against members of a civilian population.[33]

In the case of the ICTR Statute, the act must be committed on one or more discriminatory grounds; namely, national, political, ethnic, racial, or religious grounds. In the case of the ICTY Statute, the ICTY has jurisdiction *ratione materiae* over crimes against humanity that are committed in armed conflict only.

MENS REA

In addition to the specific elements contained in each individual crime against humanity, in order to transform a crime into a crime against humanity, the perpetrator must *knowingly* commit the crime in the sense that he must understand the overall or broader context in which his act occurs. He must have actual or constructive knowledge that his act or acts is or are part of a widespread or systematic attack on a civilian population and pursuant to a policy or plan.[34] It must be proved that the accused knew that his crimes were related to the attack on a civilian population in the sense of forming part of a context of mass crimes or fitting into such a pattern.[35] Article 7(1) of the ICC Statute affirms that a crime against humanity must be committed by the perpetrator 'with knowledge of the attack [directed against a civilian population who are the victim of that crime]'. Without this knowledge, the perpetrator would have the *mens rea* for an ordinary crime, not a crime against humanity.

Knowledge is examined on an objective level and factually can be implied from circumstances, and it is not necessary that the accused must know exactly what will happen to the victims.[36] It is also not necessary to prove that the accused knows of the criminal policy or plan; it suffices that the accused deliberately takes a risk that the crime might be committed, even with the hope that the risk would not lead to any damage or harm.[37] Therefore, a person who voluntarily assumes political or military functions and exercises his functions by collaborating periodically with the author of the plan, policy, or organization and by participating in its realization thereby implicitly accepts the context in which his functions, collaboration, and participation would in all probability take place.[38] The requisite knowledge can be inferred from a

---

[33] Ibid.; *Prosecutor v. George Rutaganda*, Case No. ICTR-96-3, ICTR T. Ch. I, 6 Dec. 1999, para. 65; *Prosecutor v. Alfred Musema*, Case No. ICTR-96-13-T, ICTR T. Ch. I, 27 Jan. 2000, para. 201.

[34] *Kayishema and Ruzindana*, paras. 133–4; *Tadic* Judgment, paras. 626, 638, 656–7; *Prosecutor v. Dusko Tadic*, Case No. IT-94-1-A, ICTY App. Ch., 15 July 1999 (hereinafter '*Tadic* Appeals Judgment'), para. 271; *Rutaganda*, para. 69; *Prosecutor v. Zoran Kupreskic and Others*, Case No. IT-95-16-T, ICTY T. Ch. II, 14 Jan. 2000, paras. 556–7; *Musema*, para. 206; *Prosecutor v. Georges Ruggiu*, Case No. ICTR-97-32-I, ICTR T. Ch. I, 1 June 2000, para. 20.

[35] Ibid.; *Prosecutor v. Tihomir Blaskic*, Case No. IT-95-14-T, T. Ch. I of the ICTY, 3 March 2000, paras. 244–50.

[36] *Tadic* Judgment, paras. 657, 659.

[37] *Blaskic*, paras. 251–4.

[38] Ibid., paras. 255–7.

number of concrete facts; for example, the historical or political circumstances in which the acts occur, the functions of the accused at the time of the crimes in question, his responsibilities in the political or military hierarchy, the direct or indirect relationship between the military hierarchy and the political hierarchy, the widespreadness and seriousness of the acts committed, and the nature of the crimes committed as well as their notoriety.[39] Thus, the accused in *Blaskic* was found to be part of a design whose purpose was the persecution of the Muslim population because of his political will to get involved with the Croat defence council known as the HVO which had military and civilian structures. The HVO took decisions on the organization of life in the town, and, as such, the accused, who was a general, was deemed to be perfectly aware that the scope of his activities was not and could not be a strictly military one, and to be aware of the policy of discrimination against Muslims to systematically exclude them from the organs of political life.[40]

It is not necessary to prove the accused's motive.[41] A motive is generally irrelevant in criminal law, except at the sentencing stage when it might be relevant to mitigation or aggravation of the sentence. That an accused committed a crime with 'purely personal motives or reasons' does not exonerate him from being guilty of a crime against humanity if his act fits into the pattern of crimes against humanity as described above.[42] Thus, when, during the widespread persecution of the Jews by the Nazi regime in Germany, a neighbour or a relative denounced another person to the Gestapo so that that other person would be arrested and punished, the act of denunciation could be punished as a crime against humanity despite the fact that it was in pursuance of personal motives such as getting rid of a wife who would not agree to a divorce, getting rid of a contemptuous father-in-law, or taking revenge on a landlord.[43]

Except in the case of the ICTR Statute,[44] a discriminatory intent is required only with regard to the various types of persecution.[45]

Compared to the ICTY and the ICTR Statutes, the ICC Statute adds to the defin-

---

[39] Ibid., para. 259.

[40] Summary of the Judgment in *Blaskic* as read by the President of Trial Chamber I of the ICTY.

[41] *Tadic* Appeals Judgment, paras. 248, 250, 255, 269, 270–2. The Appeals Chamber (ibid., paras. 266–7) cited the decision of the majority of the Supreme Court of Canada in *R. v. Finta* (1994) 1 SCR 701, at 819 in support of its decision on this point. Followed in *Kupreskic and Others*, para. 558.

[42] *Tadic* Appeals Judgment, paras. 255, 268–70.

[43] Ibid., paras. 257–63, citing decisions of the Supreme Court for the British Zone (Criminal Chamber) in the case of *Mrs K. and P.* (Decision of 9 Nov. 1948), *H.* (Decision of 20 Apr. 1949), and *Sch.* (Decision of 26 Oct. 1948), respectively. In *Tadic* Appeals Judgment, Presiding Judge Shahabudeen and Judge Nieto-Navia disagreed with the majority of the Appeals Chamber on this point. They reasoned that where an act was motivated by purely personal reasons which were completely unrelated to the attack on civilian population, no crime against humanity was committed, even if the accused was aware of the attack. *Tadic* Appeals Judgement, Separate Opinion of Judge Shahabudeen, paras. 37–38; Declaration of Judge Nieto-Navia, para. 12.

[44] See *Rutaganda*, paras. 71–4; *Musema*, paras. 208–11.

[45] *Tadic* Appeals Judgment, paras. 283–4, 288–92, 297–302, 305; *Kupreskic and Others*, paras. 558, 570; *Blaskic*, para. 244.

ition of crimes against humanity the requirement that the act must be committed 'with knowledge of the attack'. It is doubtful whether anything novel is added to the existing international jurisprudence on this point. The phrase was added at the Rome Conference to ensure that the accused be aware of the context of a widespread or systematic attack directed against any civilian population in which his conduct occurs, so that unrelated events, such as a 'crime wave' with no connection between these crimes, would not be crimes against humanity.[46]

NEXUS WITH AN ARMED CONFLICT

Article 5 of the ICTY Statute requires that crimes against humanity subject to the jurisdiction of the ICTY must be 'committed in armed conflict'. The type and nature of such conflict, be it international or internal, is immaterial, and it is not necessary for the perpetrator of the crime to have the intention to participate directly in the armed conflict, provided that the act be linked geographically and temporally with the armed conflict.[47] It is also not necessary that such a crime forms part of an official policy or practice approved or tolerated by one of the belligerents or that it serves a policy linked to the conduct of war or that it is in the interest of a party to the conflict.[48] However, the armed conflict requirement is a jurisdictional element that defines the *ratione materiae* of the ICTY, and not a legal ingredient of the subjective element of crimes against humanity in general.[49] Thus, there is no need to prove a nexus between the specific acts allegedly committed by the accused and the armed conflict.[50] Crimes against humanity in customary international law may also be committed in peacetime as well as in armed conflict.[51]

The inclusion in the ICTY Statute of the requirement that crimes against humanity be committed in armed conflict may blur the distinction between war crimes and crimes against humanity. However, such distinction does still exist even in this case. The draftsmen of the ICTY Statute intended that those war crimes which, besides targeting civilians as victims, possess special features peculiar to crimes against humanity, such as the fact of being part of a widespread or systematic practice, must be categorized as crimes against humanity and punished as such.[52]

---

[46] von Hebel and Robinson, 'Crimes within the Jurisdiction of the Court', 94–5, 98 (n. 55).

[47] *Kupreskic and Others*, paras. 545–6; *Blaskic*, para. 71.

[48] *Tadic* Judgment, para. 573; *Prosecutor v. Delalic, Mucic, Delic, Landzo* ('*Celebici*' case), Case No. IT-96–21-T, ICTY T. Ch. II *quater*, 16 Nov. 1998, para. 195; *Blaskic*, para. 70.

[49] *Tadic* Appeals Judgment, para. 249.

[50] Ibid., para. 272; *Blaskic*, paras. 66–8.

[51] *Tadic* Appeals Judgment, para. 251; *Kupreskic and Others*, paras. 573–7.

[52] *Tadic* Appeals Judgment, para. 286. Also *Prosecutor v. Mile Mrksic et al.*, Case No. IT-95–13-R61, ICTY T. Ch., 3 Apr. 1996, Decision on the Review of Indictment Pursuant to Rule 61 of the Rules of Procedure and Evidence ('*Vukovar Hospital Rule 61 Decision*'), para. 30.

ATTACK

Article 7(2)(a) of the ICC Statute defines 'attack directed against any civilian population' as 'a course of conduct involving the multiple commission of acts [enumerated as crimes against humanity] against any civilian population, pursuant to or in furtherance of a State or organizational policy to commit such attack'. The term 'multiple commission of acts' is chosen instead of 'commission of multiple acts' because the latter might be interpreted as requiring more than one type of inhumane act.[53]

Thus, the attack is the event in which the enumerated crimes must form part, and there may be a combination of the enumerated crimes (for instance murder, rape, and deportation) within a single attack.[54] The attack involved is an unlawful act that may be violent or non-violent in nature, like apartheid or exerting pressure on the population to act in a particular manner.[55]

The attack may be an act or omission.[56] In *Kambanda*, the accused was also found guilty of crimes against humanity for having omitted to fulfil his duty as Prime Minister of Rwanda to protect the children and population of Rwanda from the massacres which eventually took place, especially after he had been personally asked to do so.[57]

NEXUS BETWEEN SPECIFIC CRIMES AND ATTACK

A crime against humanity must be committed as part of a widespread or systematic attack against any civilian population. The provision 'as part of' means being related to the attack. As the ICTY Appeals Chamber states in *Tadic*:

'The Trial Chamber correctly recognized that crimes which are unrelated to widespread or systematic attacks on a civilian population should not be prosecuted as crimes against humanity. Crimes against humanity are crimes of a special nature to which a greater degree of moral turpitude attaches than to an ordinary crime. Thus to convict an accused of crimes against humanity, it must be proved that the crimes were *related to the attack on a civilian population* . . . and that the accused knew that his crimes were *so related*.'[58]

COMMITTED AGAINST ANY CIVILIAN POPULATION

The notions 'attack on any civilian population' and 'the armed conflict' are separate notions. Although the attack on any civilian population may be part of an armed

---

[53] von Hebel and Robinson, 'Crimes within the Jurisdiction of the Court', 95 (n. 47).

[54] *Kayishema and Ruzindana*, para. 122; *Rutaganda*, para. 68. However, the ICTR in *Kayishema and Ruzindana* opines that the attack must not be carried out for purely personal motives (ibid., paras. 122–3). The Appeals Chamber in *Tadic* has now ruled that the existence or absence of personal motives is irrelevant as an element of a crime against humanity.

[55] *Akayesu*, para. 581; *Rutaganda*, para. 70; *Musema*, para. 205.

[56] *Prosecutor v. Jean Kambanda*, Case No. ICTR 97–23-S, ICTY T. Ch., 4 Sept. 1998, para. 40 (5) (6).

[57] Ibid., para. 39 (ix).

[58] *Tadic* Appeals Judgment, para. 271.

conflict, there is no need to prove a nexus between the accused's acts and the armed conflict; what is to be proved is a nexus between the accused's acts and the attack on any civilian population.[59] It has been observed, however, that under customary international law the victims of crimes against humanity need not necessarily be civilians but may include military personnel.[60]

'Civilian' must be given a broad definition to cover not only the general population, but also members of the armed forces and resistance forces who are *hors de combat* by sickness, wounds, detention, or any other cause.[61] It is the situation faced by the victim at the time of the commission of the crime that must be taken into account to determine whether they have the 'civilian' status.[62] For instance, where the head of family is compelled to use arms to defend his family, he does not lose his civilian status; neither do the police or local defence force who act in this manner although they are formed in an attempt to prevent the cataclysm of armed conflicts.[63] The word 'any' before 'civilian population' makes it clear that crimes against humanity can be committed against stateless persons or civilians of the same nationality of the perpetrator as well as against foreign citizens.[64]

Where there is no armed conflict or where there is relative peace, the definition of civilian includes all persons except those who have the duty to maintain public order and the legitimate means to exercise force.[65]

The 'population' element does not mean that the entire population of a given State or territory must be targeted; it is intended to indicate the collective nature of crimes against humanity that excludes single or isolated acts punishable as war crimes or crimes against municipal law not rising to the level of crimes against humanity.[66] The targeted population must be predominantly civilian in nature although the presence of certain non-civilians in their midst does not change the character of that population.[67] In other words, the individual victim is victimized because of his membership of a civilian population targeted by the accused.

---

[59] Ibid., para. 251.

[60] *Kupreskic and Others*, para. 568.

[61] *Tadic* Judgment, paras. 626, 641–3; *Akayesu*, paras. 574–6, 582; *Tadic* Appeals Judgment, paras. 636–43; *Rutaganda*, para. 70; *Prosecutor v. Goran Jelisic*, Case No. IT-95–10, ICTY T. Ch. I, 14 Dec. 1999, para. 54; *Musema*, para. 207; *Blaskic*, paras. 208–10, 214. Trial Chamber II of the ICTY observes in *Kupreskic and Others* that there is no reason for protecting only civilians but not combatants under the rules against crimes against humanity, particularly rules proscribing persecution (*Kupreskic and Others*, paras. 547–9).

[62] *Blaskic*, para. 214.

[63] Ibid., para. 213, quoting the Final Report of the Committee of Experts established pursuant to Res. 780 of the UN Security Council (1992), S/1994/674, para. 78.

[64] *Tadic* Judgment, para. 635. See also Schwelb (1946) 23 *BYBIL* 188–9, 203.

[65] *Kayishema and Ruzindana*, para. 127.

[66] *Tadic* Judgment, para. 644.

[67] *Kayishema and Ruzindana*, para. 128, citing *Tadic* Judgment, at para. 638; *Rutaganda*, para. 70; *Kupreskic and Others*, para. 549; *Musema*, para. 207; *Blaskic*, paras. 211, 214.

ON A WIDESPREAD OR SYSTEMATIC BASIS

Crimes against humanity must be related to widespread or systematic attacks, and not just a random act of violence, against a civilian population.[68] This requirement is expressly stipulated in Article 3 of the ICTR Statute and Article 7 of the ICC Statute. Although it is not expressly mentioned in Article 5 of the ICTY Statute, the ICTY has consistently considered the requirement that the attack be directed against any civilian population to imply the widespread or systematic nature of such attack.[69]

The act can be part of either a widespread or systematic attack and need not be a part of both.[70] In practice, however, it is difficult to separate the widespread and the systematic nature of the attack since the widespread attack aimed at a large number of victims is generally carried out with some kind of planning or organization.[71] The existence of a political agenda or ideology to destroy, persecute or weaken a particular community coupled with institutions to implement that policy, the involvement of political or military authorities at high level, the extent of financial, military or other means, as well as the extent of the repetitious, uniform, and continuous perpetration against the same civilian population are among the factors that may evince the widespread or systematic character of an attack.[72]

Under established international jurisprudence, a widespread attack is an attack directed against a multiplicity of *victims*, whereas a systematic attack is an attack carried out pursuant to a preconceived policy or plan.[73] As explained by the ICTR, 'widespread' means 'massive, frequent, large scale action, carried out collectively with considerable seriousness and directed against a multiplicity of victims'; while 'systematic' means 'thoroughly organized and following a regular pattern on the basis of a common policy involving substantial public or private resources' although this policy may not be adopted formally as the policy of a State.[74]

Article 7 of the ICC Statute does not define what 'a widespread or systematic attack' means. It merely stipulates that such attack must be 'directed against any civilian population'. Article 7(2)(a) of the ICC Statute defines 'attack directed against any civilian population' to mean 'a course of conduct involving the multiple commission of acts' enumerated in Article 7(1) directed against any civilian population, 'pursuant to or in furtherance of a State or organizational policy to commit such attack'. Unfortunately, this provision is a rather awkward piece of draftsmanship. The phrase 'pursuant to or in furtherance of a State or organizational policy to commit such attack' inadvertently blurs the distinction between 'a widespread attack' and 'a

---

[68] *Tadic* Appeals Judgment, para. 271.

[69] *Blaskic,* paras. 202–3.

[70] *Tadic* Judgment, paras. 646–7; T. Ch. I of the ICTR in *Akayesu* (para. 579) ruled that the French version using the word '*et*' ('and') between 'widespread' and 'systematic' is in error. Followed in *Rutaganda,* para. 66; *Musema,* paras. 202–3.

[71] *Blaskic,* para. 207.

[72] *Jelisic,* para. 53; *Blaskic,* para. 203.

[73] *Kayishema and Ruzindana,* para. 123. Cf. also *Tadic* Judgment, para. 648; *Blaskic,* para. 206.

[74] *Akayesu,* para. 580; *Rutaganda,* para. 67; *Musema,* para. 204.

systematic attack' which exists under established international jurisprudence. Article 7 of the ICC Statute requires that both a widespread attack and a systematic attack be carried out pursuant to or in furtherance of a State or organizational policy to commit such attack. To reconcile the provision under Article 7 of the ICC Statute with established international jurisprudence, it is hereby submitted that the difference between the two types of attack is one of degree of organization of the attack. A widespread attack is proved when it is directed against a multiplicity of victims as part of a course of conduct involving multiple commission of acts in pursuant to or in furtherance of a State or organizational policy to commit such attack, as in the case of the policy of persecution of Jews under Nazi Germany. A systematic attack shares the same elements as a widespread attack just mentioned, with the exception that a systematic attack is orchestrated, coordinated, or organized by a group of people so that the attack is carried out in a systematic manner. In other words, systematicity is a higher threshold test than widespreadness because the latter involves unorganized, uncoordinated, and unorchestrated multiple commission of acts that somehow serve a policy to commit a crime against humanity.

In any event, one single act against a single victim or a limited number of victims could qualify as a crime against humanity as long as there is a link with the widespread or systematic attack against a civilian population,[75] or where its effect is widespread in scope.[76] For instance, the act of denouncing a Jewish neighbour to the Nazi authorities committed against the background of widespread persecution against the Jews has been held to be a crime against humanity.[77]

THE POLICY ELEMENT

Although the Nuremberg Charter did not include the requirement of existence of a State or organizational policy, the Nuremberg Tribunal stressed that the inhumane acts qualified as crimes against humanity were committed as part of the policy of terror and were in many cases organized and systematic.[78] As the ICTR explains in *Kayishema and Ruzindana*, the requirement of committing a crime against humanity pursuant to a policy is intended to exclude the situation where an individual commits an inhumane act on his own initiative pursuant to his own criminal plan without any encouragement or direction from either a Government or a group or an organization. It is the existence of such a policy that endows the criminal

---

[75] *Vukovar Hospital Rule 61 Decision*, para. 30. Cited with approval in *Tadic* Judgment, para. 649.

[76] *Blaskic*, para. 206. See also *Vukovar Hospital Rule 61 Decision*, para. 30.

[77] See *Kupreskic and Others*, para. 550 and the authorities cited therein.

[78] *Tadic* Judgment, para. 648. See also the *Justice* case decided under Control Council Law No. 10, where the Tribunal held that crimes against humanity must be strictly construed to exclude isolated cases of atrocity or persecution whether committed by private individuals or by governmental authority; there must be proof of 'conscious participation in systematic government organized or approved procedures amounting to atrocities and offences of the kind specified in the act and committed against populations or amounting to persecution on political, racial, or religious grounds'. TWC, iii (1951), 982.

act with a great dimension which warrants its punishment as a crime against humanity.[79]

Such a policy need not be conceived at the highest level of the State organ, formalized, or expressly, clearly, or precisely announced but can be inferred from the manner in which the acts take place—the widespread or systematic manner of the act may evince a policy to commit these acts.[80] This is despite the fact that the connection between the act and the policy concerned may be denied by the relevant authorities or apparatus of that policy.[81] Facts that may be inferred to show such a policy include the general historical circumstances and the entire political context in which the criminal acts take place; the creation and implementation in the territory in question of autonomous political institutions of whatever level of power; the general tenor of a political programme as evidenced in writings by its authors and their speeches; media propaganda; creation and implementation of autonomous military institutions; mobilization of armed forces; repeated and coordinated military offensives in the relevant time and case; connections between the military hierarchy and the political institution and its programme; modifications of the ethnic composition of the population; discriminatory measures, be they administrative or otherwise (such as banking restrictions and a requirement of a travel pass); and the scope of the executions carried out, in particular, deaths and other forms of physical violence, thefts, arbitrary detentions, deportations and expulsions, or destruction of non-military property, especially religious edifices.[82]

That a crime against humanity may be committed in pursuance of a policy of either a State or a non-State actor is not disputed. The law regarding crimes against humanity has developed to the extent that crimes against humanity can be committed on behalf of entities with *de facto* control over a particular territory although those entities have no international recognition or formal status of a *de jure* State; it can be also committed by a terrorist group or organization.[83] Private individuals with the aforesaid *de facto* power or organized in criminal gangs or groups might also be in the position to commit crimes against humanity.[84] Indeed, Article 7(2)(a) of the ICC Statute states, *inter alia,* that the attack is a course of conduct 'pursuant to or in furtherance of a State or organizational policy'.

The policy in question may be localized in a particular geographical region alone. For example, the policy of ethnic cleansing over the region of Vlasenica alone, or the policy to commit inhumane acts against the civilian population of the territory of Opstina Prijedor in order to achieve the creation of a Greater Serbia, have each been

---

[79] *Kayishema and Ruzindana,* paras. 124–6, quoting the ILC's commentary to the 1996 Draft Code of Crimes Against the Peace and Security of Mankind on this point. See also *Akayesu,* paras. 572–4, 576, quoting *dicta* of French domestic courts on this point.

[80] *Tadic* Judgment, para. 653; *Blaskic,* paras. 204–5.

[81] *Kupreskic and Others,* paras. 551–5, and the cases cited therein.

[82] *Blaskic,* para. 204.

[83] *Kupreskic and Others,* paras. 654–5.

[84] Ibid., para. 655; *Blaskic,* para. 205, citing Art. 18 of the ILC's 1996 Draft Code of Crimes Against the Peace and Security of Mankind.

held to fulfil the policy requirement for the ICTY to exercise its jurisdiction over the crimes against humanity brought before it.[85]

In the case of the ICC Statute, Article 7(2)(a) stipulates that the attack directed against any civilian population must be 'pursuant to or in furtherance of a State or organizational policy to commit such attack'. The terminology 'such attack' is preferred to 'such acts' so as to allay the concern of the Women's Caucus of the coalition of the non-governmental organizations that the latter terminology might be interpreted as requiring proof of a specific policy to commit rape in the case of a crime against humanity based on rape.[86]

The drafting of the Elements of Crimes for the crimes against humanity under Article 7 of the ICC Statute was much more difficult than the drafting of the Elements of Crimes for either genocide or war crimes. Unlike war crimes which have been well-established in customary international law, crimes against humanity are of more recent origin. While the crime of genocide has the extremely high threshold of the specific intent (*dolus specialis*) to destroy a protected group as such, there is a relatively unclear dividing line between crimes against humanity under international criminal law, on the one hand, and violations of human rights that are subject to litigation in domestic courts or regional human rights judicial bodies, on the other.

In order to exclude acts occurring in a household context or according to some religious or cultural practices from being characterized as crimes against humanity within the ICC's jurisdiction, several Arab States proposed that the act or acts described in the Elements of Crimes as constituting crimes against humanity 'do not affect family matters recognized by different national laws of the States Parties [to the ICC Statute]'.[87] In a separate but related proposal, Egypt attempted to raise the threshold of this genus of crimes by requiring that the widespread attack against victims of crimes against humanity be 'massive, frequent, or large scale, carried out collectively with considerable seriousness and directed against a multiplicity of victims', whereas the systematic attack against victims of crimes against humanity be 'thoroughly organized and followed a regular pattern on the basis of a common policy that was evident'.[88] These States subsequently withdrew their proposals after there was general consensus in favour of the requirement that the policy to commit an attack directed against a civilian population must be 'actively promoted or encouraged' by the State or organization in question. Nonetheless, the delegations that seemed to endorse this compromise later changed their position on the ground that such compromise would run counter to customary international law as pronounced by the

[85] *Prosecutor v. Dragan Nikolic*, Case No. IT-94-2-R61, ICTY Decision on Review of Indictment pursuant to Rule 61 of the Rules of Procedure and Evidence, 20 Oct. 1995, para. 27, and *Tadic* Appeals Judgment, para. 660, respectively.

[86] von Hebel and Robinson, 'Crimes within the Jurisdiction of the Court', 96 (n. 47).

[87] Proposal submitted by Bahrain, Iraq, Kuwait, Lebanon, Libyan Arab Jamahiriya, Oman, Qatar, Saudi Arabia, the Sudan, Syrian Arab Republic, and the United Arab Emirates concerning the elements of crimes against humanity, *Doc. PCNICC/ 1999/ WGEC/ DP. 39*, 3 Dec. 1999.

[88] Proposal submitted by Egypt on common elements to be included in all crimes against humanity, *Doc. PCNICC/ 1999/ WGEC/ DP. 42*, 7 Dec. 1999.

ICTY and the ICTR in their judgments rendered after the Third Session of the PCNICC in November and December 1999.[89] Besides, it would be inconsistent with Article 7(2)(i) of the ICC Statute itself, which provides that the crime against humanity of enforced disappearance can be committed 'by, or with, the authorization, support or acquiescence of, a State or a political organization'. Thus, during the Fifth Session of the PCNICC in June 2000, there was a heated and protracted confrontation between the proponents and opponents of the requirement that a policy needs to be 'actively promoted or encouraged'.

A concept closely related to and often discussed in the same package as the 'policy' question was that of the universal nature of the recognition that a particular conduct deserved to be criminalized as a crime against humanity. During the Rome Conference, a number of Arab States proposed that the reference in the ICC Statute to 'fundamental rules of international law' in the case of the crime against humanity of imprisonment or other severe deprivation of physical liberty, as well as to 'fundamental rights' in the definition of the crime against humanity of persecution, be qualified by the requirement that such rights must have attained 'universal recognition'. The proposed requirement of 'universal recognition', they believed, would be a safeguard against any attempted imposition of human rights standards that are alien to a particular State or region in disregard of the 'civilization' or 'way of life' practised there. The majority of delegations at the Conference opposed this proposal.

Barely a few days before the end of the Rome Conference, the leadership of the Conference decided to omit any reference to 'universal recognition' in all the relevant provisions of the draft ICC Statute without seeking the prior concurrence of the delegations favouring its inclusion. The draft ICC Statute as amended was then put before the Conference for adoption.[90] However, the proponents of 'universal recognition' did not consider their cause a lost one; they tried to resurrect it at the PCNICC. Their oft-reiterated position was that there was a need to understand each others' legal systems and civilization. The principle of legality (*nullum crimen sine lege*) was often cited in support. The Delegation of Iran, for example, pointed out the possibility that ordinary people in a remote village might find that their long-established norms of behaviour were now criminalized as crimes against humanity within the ICC's jurisdiction although the norms were lawful under their domestic law. According to Iran and Egypt, such criminalization would be squarely against the principle of legality. Iran also argued that 'fundamental rights' are enshrined in the Universal Declaration of Human Rights, the United Nations Charter, and various human rights

[89] The Delegation of Switzerland mentioned *Kupreskic and Others* decided by the ICTY after the 3rd Session of the PCINCC. (Statement of the Delegation of Switzerland at the meeting of the Working Group on Elements of Crimes, 13 June 2000.) In that case, it was held that the State's tolerance, encouragement, or otherwise endorsement of the criminal conduct in question is sufficient to prove the policy element. (*Kupreskic and Others*, paras. 551–5.)

[90] Information shared with this author by several delegates who attended the Rome Conference. During the meeting of the Working Group on Elements of Crimes on 14 June 2000, the Delegation of Canada made a statement that the concept of 'universal recognition' was debated at the Rome Conference but was rejected and replaced by that of 'fundamental rules of international law'.

documents that are too numerous and that have diversity of States Parties. Therefore, in its view, only violation of those 'fundamental rights' that are 'universally recognized' as having the status of *jus cogens*, with *erga omnes* effects, should be punished by the ICC Statute, which is an international instrument of 'universal' application and free of domination by one system of law and rights.[91]

The compromise package that was finally accepted was presented by the Sub-Coordinator on 29 June 2000, at 4 p.m. That was the penultimate day of the Fifth Session of the PCNICC, which was mandated to finalize the Elements of Crimes and Rules of Procedure and Evidence by the end of June 2000. Most notably, the term 'generally applicable international law' had been chosen by the Sub-Coordinator as the compromise solution for the diverging preferences for 'applicable international law', 'general international law', and 'customary international law'.[92] After listening to the views expressed on the floor, the Sub-Coordinator refused to make any change to the text, saying that the text represented the best compromise that could be attainable. It was submitted to the Plenary of the PCNICC on the following day, and was adopted as such.

The package appears as paragraph 1 and as the footnote to paragraph 3 of the Introduction to the Elements of Crimes for the crimes against humanity under Article 7 of the ICC Statute. Paragraph 2 of the Introduction is not controversial and was adopted by the Working Group on Elements of Crimes early in the Fifth Session of the PCNICC. The Introduction now reads:

'1. Since Article 7 pertains to international criminal law, its provisions, consistent with Article 22, must be strictly construed, taking into account that crimes against humanity as defined in Article 7 are among the most serious crimes of concern to the international community as a whole, warrant and entail individual criminal responsibility, and require conduct which is impermissible under generally applicable international law, as recognized by the principal legal systems of the world.

2. The last two elements for each crime against humanity describe the context in which the conduct must take place.[93] These elements clarify the requisite participation in and knowledge of a widespread or systematic attack against a civilian population. However, the last element should not be interpreted as requiring proof that the

---

[91] Statement of the Delegation of Iran at the meeting of the Working Group on Elements of Crimes, 15 June 2000. Iran repeated this argument several times throughout the 5th Session of the PCNICC.

[92] This author, after consulting with a few delegations, told the meeting early in the afternoon of 29 June 2000 that the Delegation of Thailand had some reservations regarding the use of 'applicable' or 'general' before 'international law'. It would be difficult to prove which rule or rules of international law were 'applicable' to a particular case, and that the term 'general international law' might be understood to mean international law of general application (*lex generalis*) as opposed to rules of international law of specific application (*lex specialis*), and this would be unhelpful because the rule of international criminal law applicable to a particular prosecution before the ICC could be of the latter type.

[93] These elements read:

'– The conduct was committed as part of a widespread or systematic attack directed against a civilian population.

– The perpetrator knew that the conduct was part of or intended the conduct to be part of a widespread or systematic attack against a civilian population.'

perpetrator had knowledge of all characteristics of the attack or the precise details of the plan or policy of that State or organization. In the case of an emerging widespread or systematic attack against a civilian population, the intent clause of the last element indicates that this mental element is satisfied if the perpetrator intended to further such an attack.

3. "Attack directed against a civilian population" in these context elements is understood to mean a course of conduct involving the multiple commission of acts referred to in Article 7, paragraph 1, of the Statute against any civilian population, pursuant to or in furtherance of a State or organizational policy to commit such attack. The acts need not constitute a military attack. It is understood that "policy to commit such attack" requires that the State or organization actively promote or encourage such an attack against a civilian population. [Footnote: A policy which has a civilian population as the object of the attack would be implemented by State or organizational action. Such a policy may, in exceptional circumstances, be implemented by a deliberate failure to take action, which is consciously aimed at encouraging such attack. The existence of such a policy cannot be inferred solely from the absence of governmental or organizational action.]'[94]

On the whole, the policy element as adopted by the PCNICC does not depart significantly from the established international jurisprudence.

The enumerated offences of crimes against humanity are analysed in the following sections.

5.1 MURDER

Murder is a crime against humanity pursuant to Article 6(c) of the Nuremberg Charter, Article II(1)(c) of Control Council Law No. 10, Article 5(c) of the Tokyo Charter, Article 5(a) of the ICTY Statute, Article 3(a) of the ICTR Statute, and Article 7(1)(a) of the ICC Statute.

The French version of 'murder' under Article 7(1)(a) of the ICC Statute uses the word '*meurte*'. However, Article 3(a) of the French version of the ICTR Statute and Article 5(a) of the ICTY Statute use the term '*assassinat*' for the English term of 'murder' as a crime against humanity. In *Akayesu*, Trial Chamber I of the ICTR held that under customary international law it is the act of murder (or '*meurte*' in French), not '*assassinat*'—unlawful killing with premeditation, which constitutes a crime against humanity, and that there were sufficient reasons to assume that the French version of the ICTR Statute suffers from an error in translation.[95] Hence, murder is defined as 'the unlawful, intentional killing of a human being' with the following requisite elements:

[94] Report of the Preparatory Commission for the International Criminal Court, *Doc. PCNICC/ 2000/ 1/ Add.* 2, 2 Nov. 2000, at 9.
[95] *Akayesu*, para. 588.

'1. the victim is dead;

2. the death resulted from an unlawful act or omission of the perpetrator or a subordinate;

3. at the time of the killing the perpetrator or a subordinate had the intention to kill or inflict grievous bodily harm on the deceased having known that such bodily harm is likely to cause the victim's death, and is reckless whether death ensues or not.'[96]

However, Trial Chamber II of the ICTR in *Kayishema and Ruzindana* disagrees with this reasoning in *Akayesu*, arguing that since the text was drafted in English and French, both being original and authentic, there was no translation between English and French, and that therefore the word '*assassinat*' was chosen deliberately. Unlike murder (or '*meurte*') where mere intention or recklessness suffices and premeditation may not be always necessary, '*assassinat*' under the civil law system requires a higher standard of *mens rea* in the form of premeditation. Yet, even if the draftsmen of the ICTR Statute intended that only the standard of *mens rea* for '*assassinat*' would be sufficient, they would still need to use the term 'murder' in English for lack of choice of technical legal terms.[97] In case of doubt, Trial Chamber II of the ICTR in *Kayishema and Ruzindana* gives the benefit of the doubt to the accused and sets a higher standard of *mens rea* in favour of the accused by requiring the prosecution to establish intentional and premeditated killing by the accused. In this context, the result is premeditated when the actor formed his intent to kill after a cool moment of reflection, whereas the result is intended when it is the actor's purpose, or the actor is aware, that it will happen in the ordinary course of events.[98] To commit murder as a crime against humanity, the actor, engaging in conduct which is unlawful, must cause the death of another, by a premeditated act or omission, with intent to kill or cause grievous bodily harm to that person.[99]

Trial Chamber II of the ICTY held in *Kupreskic and Others* that the constituent elements of murder 'comprise the death of the victim as a result of an unlawful act or omission of the accused, where the conduct of the accused was a substantial cause of the death of the victim'; that is, 'the accused is guilty of murder if he or she, engaging in conduct which is unlawful, intended to kill another person or to cause this person grievous bodily harm, and has caused the death of that person'.[100] However, Trial Chamber II of the ICTY in that case prefers to adopt the standard of *mens rea* as formulated in *Kayishema and Ruzindana*.[101]

---

[96] Ibid., para. 589.

[97] *Kayishema and Ruzindana*, paras. 137–8 and accompanying footnotes.

[98] Ibid., para. 139.

[99] Ibid., para. 140. The ICTR cites as an example of this category of murder extrajudicial killings carried out with the order of a Government or with its complicity or acquiescence. Cf. also Art. 33(4) of the Vienna Convention on the Law of Treaties of 1969, which provides in its pertinent part that when a comparison of the authentic texts discloses a difference of meaning, the meaning which best reconciles the texts, having regard to the object and purpose of the treaty, shall prevail. As noted in Chapter 2, the rules of interpretation of the ICTY Statute and those of treaties are not dissimilar.

[100] *Kupreskic and Others*, para. 560.

[101] Ibid., para. 561.

The word '*assassinat*' in the French version in the case of murder as a crime against humanity, as appeared in the ICTR Statute, is a remnant of Article 6(c) of the Nuremberg Charter. That provision of the Nuremberg Charter uses the term '*l'assassinat*' in the French version for 'murder' in the English version. On the other hand, Article 7(1)(a) of the ICC Statute uses the terminology '*meurte*' in the French version and 'murder' in the English version. Murder as a crime against humanity under the ICC Statute is thus the unlawful killing of a human being as part of a widespread or systematic attack against a civilian population of which the victim is a member. The requisite elements of this crime are that the victim is dead as a result of an unlawful act or omission of the accused or his subordinate who, at the time of the killing, intended to kill or cause grievous bodily harm to the deceased with the knowledge that such bodily harm was likely to cause the victim's death, and was reckless whether death ensued or not.[102] This is in line with international customary law, as appeared from the judgment of Trial Chamber I of the ICTY in *Jelisic* and in *Blaskic*, and Trial Chamber I of the ICTR in *Rutaganda* and in *Musema*. In these cases, the ICTY and the ICTR adopt the reasoning of Trial Chamber I of the ICTR in *Akayesu* on the grounds that the word '*meurte*' reflects international customary law, and that elements of murder as a crime against humanity are the same as murder as a war crime.[103] Trial Chamber I of the ICTY in *Blaskic* held that the constitutive elements of murder are comprised of the death of the victim as a result of an act or omission of the accused or his subordinate, where the accused or his subordinate had the intention to kill the victim or to cause grievous bodily harm to him which harm could reasonably be foreseen to be likely to cause his death.[104]

There was not much debate on this crime against humanity at the PCNICC. The Elements of Crimes finally adopted by the PCNICC for this crime seem to follow *Blaskic*. They merely require that the perpetrator must have killed or caused death to one or more persons. Causing death includes situations where death ensues from intentional omission.

5.2 EXTERMINATION

Extermination is proscribed as a crime against humanity under Article 6(c) of the Nuremberg Statute, Article II(1)(c) of Control Council Law No. 10, Article 5(c) of the Tokyo Charter, Article 5(b) of the ICTY Statute, Article 3(b) of the ICTR Statute, and Article 7(1)(b) of the ICC Statute.

Article 7(2)(b) of the ICC Statute gives an illustrative statement of 'extermination' as including 'the intentional infliction of conditions of life, *inter alia*, the deprivation

---

[102] Cf. *Akayesu*, paras. 589–90; *Rutaganda*, paras. 78–9.
[103] *Jelisic*, para. 51; *Blaskic*, para. 216; *Rutaganda*, para. 77; *Musema*, paras. 214–5.
[104] *Blaskic*, para. 217, citing *Akayesu*, para. 589.

of access to food and medicine, calculated to bring about the destruction of part of a population'.

The most elucidating definition of the requisite elements of extermination is given by Trial Chamber II of the ICTR in *Kayishema and Ruzindana*, as follows:

'The actor participates in the mass killing of others or in the creation of conditions of life that lead to the mass killing of others, through his act(s) or omission(s); having intended the killing, or being reckless, or grossly negligent as to whether the killing would result and; being aware that his act(s) or omission(s) forms part of a mass killing event; where, his act(s) or omission(s) forms part of a widespread or systematic attack against any civilian population. . . .[105]

. . .

An actor may be guilty of extermination if he kills, or creates the conditions of life that kills, a single person providing the actor is aware that his act(s) or omission(s) forms part of a mass killing event. For a single killing to form part of extermination, the killing must actually form part of a mass killing event. An "event" exists when the (mass) killings have close proximity in time and place.'[106]

The actor need not have a specific individual in mind.[107]

The ICTR Trial Chamber then cites a hypothetical example in which ten Hutu officers fire into a crowd of 200 Tutsis, killing them all. Officer X is a poor shot and kills just one person, while Officer Y kills sixteen. Because both officers participated in the mass killing and were both aware that their actions formed part of the mass killing event, they will be both guilty of extermination.[108] In other words, a perpetrator could be held guilty of extermination even if he kills only one person, provided all the requisite elements for extermination are proved.

According to the ICTR, the term 'mass' may mean 'large scale' and is to be determined on a case-by-case basis using a common sense approach.[109] In *Akayesu*, for example, the accused was found guilty of extermination for ordering the killing of sixteen people.[110]

The creation of conditions of life that lead to extermination is the institution of circumstances (such as imprisoning a large number of people and withholding the necessities of life; and introducing deadly virus into a population and preventing

---

[105] *Kayishema and Ruzindana*, para 144. Cf. *Rutaganda*, paras. 81–2.

[106] *Kayishema and Ruzindana*, para. 147. Cf. *Akayesu*, para. 592, where Trial Chamber I of the ICTR defines the essential elements of extermination as the following: the accused or his subordinates participated in the killing of certain named or described persons; the act or omission was unlawful and intentional; the unlawful act or omission must be part of a widespread or systematic attack; the attack must be against the civilian population; and the attack must be on discriminatory grounds, namely: national, political, ethnic, racial, or religious grounds.

[107] *Kayishema and Ruzindana*, paras. 145–6.

[108] Ibid., para. 147, n. 49. This author must caution that in the given example the ICTR must have assumed that for some reason the killing could not qualify as genocide because certain elements of genocide are absent.

[109] Ibid., paras. 145–6.

[110] *Akayesu*, paras. 735–43.

medical care) which ultimately causes the mass death of others. Extermination also includes the planning of the implementation of extermination or the creation of conditions of life leading to extermination, provided that a nexus between the planning and the actual extermination can be proved.[111]

On the whole, the difference between murder and extermination is the scale, with extermination being mass destruction or murder on a massive scale.[112] Moreover, steps that are too remote from an individual act of murder to constitute complicity in that act may be punishable as complicity in the crime of extermination.[113]

The Elements of Crimes for this offence under the ICC Statute as adopted by the PCNICC closely follow international jurisprudence on this matter. The perpetrator must have killed one or more persons, including inflicting conditions of life calculated to bring about the destruction of part of a population. The conduct could be committed by different methods of killing, either directly or indirectly, provided that it constituted, or took place as part of, a mass killing of members of a civilian population. The infliction of such conditions could include the deprivation of access to food and medicine. 'As part of' would include the initial conduct in a mass killing.

5.3 ENSLAVEMENT

Enslavement is proscribed as a crime against humanity pursuant to Article 6(c) of the Nuremberg Charter, Article II(1)(c) of Council Control Law No. 10, Article 5(c) of the Tokyo Charter, Article 5(c) of the ICTY Statute, Article 3(c) of the ICTR Statute, and Article 7(1)(c) of the ICC Statute.

Article 7(2)(c) of the ICC Statute defines 'enslavement' as 'the exercise of any or all the powers attaching to the right of ownership over a person and includes the exercise of such power in the course of trafficking in persons, in particular women and children'. This definition is similar to that given under the Slavery Conventions.[114]

In the *Foca* case, the ICTY Prosecutor's Indictment accuses Stankovic of enslavement for his alleged detention of his victims in a house against their will. Although they had food and were neither guarded nor locked in they could not escape because the territory was surrounded by their adversaries, both soldiers and civilians. They were forced to do manual work for the Serb soldiers during the day, and if any one of them refused to obey orders she would be beaten.[115] In a related case, the ICTY

---

[111] Ibid., para. 146.

[112] *Akayesu*, para. 591; *Kayishema and Ruzindana*, para. 142; *Rutaganda*, para. 80.

[113] Schwelb (1946) 23 *YBIL* 192.

[114] Art. 1 of the Convention to Suppress the Slave Trade and Slavery of 25 Sept. 1926 (6 *League of Nations Treaties Series* 253) and the Supplementary Convention on the Abolition of Slavery, the Slave Trade, and Institutions and Practices Similar to Slavery of 1956 (266 *UNTS* 3) stipulate: 'Slavery is the status or condition of a person over whom any or all of the powers attaching to the right of ownership are exercised'.

[115] *Gagovic and Others*, Case No. IT–96–23 (Indictment of 26 June 1996), paras. 10.6–10.8.

convicted the accused of enslavement for their detention of women for one to three months during which the women were forced to perform household chores before some of them were sold to other Serb soldiers.[116]

This offence was subject to extensive discussion in the PCNICC as to whether it should encompass 'forced labour'. Various delegations opposed its extension to cover forced labour on the ground that the issue of forced labour is within the competence of the International Labour Organization (ILO) and forced labour is not an international crime under either customary international law or conventional law.[117] Besides, it is arguable that the ICC Statute has confined the ICC's jurisdiction to serious violations of international criminal law, not international human rights law.

The PCNICC has decided that there is no need to prove pecuniary benefits before a person could be found guilty of the crime against humanity of enslavement since the central element of enslavement is the exploitation of one or more persons through the exercise of the right of ownership. Although forced labour was not included in the Nuremberg Charter, it was prosecuted by a US Military Tribunal under Control Council Law No. 10 in *Pohl and Others*, which shows that forced labour as a form of enslavement is not new. The Tribunal considered the word 'liberty' the most precious word in any language and likened forced labour to enslavement in the following statement:

'Slavery may exist even without torture. Slaves may be well fed and well clothed and comfortably housed, but they are still slaves if without lawful process they are deprived of their freedom by forceful restraint. We might eliminate all proof of ill-treatment, overlook the starvation and beatings and other barbarous acts, but the admitted fact of slavery— compulsory uncompensated labour—would still remain. There is no such thing as benevolent slavery. Involuntary servitude, even if tempered by humane treatment, is still slavery.'[118]

Therefore, forced labour and trafficking in persons, in particular women and children, are modern forms of slavery as a crime against humanity of enslavement, as well as a crime against humanity of sexual slavery and the corresponding war crime of enslavement under the ICC Statute.

The proposal at the PCNICC to include the term 'servile status' to define the state of enslavement was also subject to heated debates at the PCNICC due to its rather vague meaning. It certainly should not be construed to encompass acceptable practices like compulsory military service. In the end, it was agreed that the term

---

[116] *Prosecutor v. Kunarac, Kovac and Vukovic*, ICTY T. Ch. II, 22 Feb. 2001.

[117] Art. 2(1) of the Convention (No. 29) concerning Forced or Compulsory Labour of 28 June 1930 defines 'forced or compulsory labour' for the purposes of that Convention as 'all work or service which is exacted from any person under the menace of any penalty and for which the said person has not offered himself voluntarily'. However, Art. 2(2) of the Convention lists the exceptions which include any work or service exacted by virtue of compulsory military service laws for work of a purely military character, or as a consequence of a conviction in a court of law, and so forth. (*UN Doc. ST/HR/ Rev. 5* (vol. I/ Part 1), 216). Cf. the Convention (No. 105) concerning the Abolition of Forced Labour of 25 June 1957 (*UN Doc. ST/ HR/ Rev. 5* (Vol. I/ Part 1), 229).

[118] *Trial of Oswald Pohl and Others*, US Military Tribunal, Nuremberg, Germany, 3 Nov. 1947, TWC, v, (1950), 958, quoted in M. M. Whiteman, *Digest of International Law* (US Dept. of State, 1968), 905–6.

would be qualified by reference to the definition under the Supplementary Convention on the Abolition of Slavery, the Slave Trade, and Institutions and Practices Similar to Slavery of 1956.[119] Article 7(b) of the Convention defines 'a person of servile
status' as 'a person in the condition or status resulting from any of the institutions or
practices mentioned in article 1 of this Convention'. Article 1 of the Convention
enumerates the following 'situations and practices similar to slavery':

'(a) Debt bondage, that is to say, the status or condition arising from a pledge by a debtor
of his personal services or of those of a person under his control as security for a debt,
if the value of those services as reasonably assessed is not applied towards the liquid-
ation of the debt or the length and nature of those services are not respectively
limited and defined;

(b) Serfdom, that is to say, the condition or status of a tenant who is by law, custom or
agreement bound to live and labour on land belonging to another person and to
render some determinate service to such other person, whether for reward or not, and
is not free to change his status;

(c) Any institution or practice whereby:

(i)   A woman, without the right to refuse, is promised or given in marriage on
payment of a consideration in money or in kind to her parents, guardian, family
or any other person or group; or

(ii) The husband of a woman, his family, or his clan, has the right to transfer her to
another person for value received or otherwise; or

(iii) A woman on the death of her husband is liable to be inherited by another
person;

(d) Any institution or practice whereby a child or young person under the age of 18 years,
is delivered by either or both of his natural parents or by his guardian to another
person, whether for reward or not, with a view to the exploitation of the child or
young person or of his labour.'

It should be noted that confinement is not necessary. This is clear from the definition
of 'debt bondage'. The *Foca* situation mentioned above also involves no 'confinement'
in the literal sense of being locked up. A sale or exchange or trade in persons is also
not necessary.

5.4 DEPORTATION OR FORCIBLE TRANSFER OF POPULATION

Deportation is proscribed as a crime against humanity under Article 6(c) of the
Nuremberg Charter, Article II(1)(c) of Control Council Law No. 10, Article 5(c) of the
Tokyo Charter, Article 5(d) of the ICTY Statute, and Article 3(d) of the ICTR Statute.

---

[119] Done at Geneva on 7 Sept. 1956, in force 30 Apr. 1957. 266 *UNTS* 3.

Article 7(1)(d) of the ICC Statute proscribes 'deportation or forcible transfer of population', which Article 7(2)(d) defines as 'forced displacement of the persons concerned by expulsion or other coercive acts from the area in which they are lawfully present, without grounds permitted under international law'.[120]

Deportation is generally understood as the forcible removal of persons to the territory of another State, whereas forcible transfer refers to the forcible transfer of persons to another location within the same State.[121] They involve an act of expulsion or other types of coercive acts.

The proviso 'without grounds permitted by international law' qualifies the conduct or perpetration, whereas 'lawfully present' qualifies the condition in which the deportee or transferee finds himself in a territory. Although the lawfulness or otherwise of the presence is determined by national law, that national law must also be measured against the yardstick of international law. In other words, lawful presence cannot be terminated by national law in violation of applicable rules of international law. The PCNICC has concluded that for the perpetrator to be criminally liable for this offence, he must have been aware of the factual circumstances establishing the lawfulness of such presence.

It is clear that the proviso does not proscribe deportation of forcible transfer of illegal immigrants, or resettlement or evacuation for the sake of safety or welfare of a population.

Blaskic provides an example of illegal forcible transfer of population. Two hundred and forty-seven Muslim civilians from a town were forced by a paramilitary group to march to another town and sit down facing a building as human shields for approximately three hours before being led to live in seven houses where there was only space for them to stand up, and then led off in trucks and evacuated by force out of the village.[122]

The charge of 'unlawful deportation *and* forcible transfer' is included in the Indictments of the ICTY Prosecutor against Slobodan Milosevic, Milan Milutinovic, Dragoljub Ojdanic, Vlajko Stojiljkovic, and Nikola Sainovic. The alleged acts involve forcibly expelling and deporting, in 1999, thousands of Kosovo Albanians from their homes in the Kosovo Province of the Federal Republic of Yugoslavia in 1999, and, between 1991 and 1995, non-Serbs in Croatia and Bosnia and Herzegovina from areas under Serbian control. Apart from the outright acts of forced transfer and deportation of non-Serbian population, the following more indirect methods were alleged to have been used by the accused in well-planned and coordinated efforts: heavy shelling and armed attacks on villages, widespread killings, and destruction of non-Serbian residential areas as well as cultural and religious sites.[123]

---

[120] Quoted by Trial Chamber I of the ICTY in *Blaskic*, para. 234.

[121] See, e.g. the Proposal submitted by Canada and Germany on Art. 7 of the ICC Statute, *Doc. PCNICC/ 1999/ WGEC/ DP. 36* of 23 Nov. 1999.

[122] *Blaskic*, paras. 549–50.

[123] Case No. IT-99–37, Indictment of 24 May 1999.

It should be noted that the Elements of Crimes adopted by the PCNICC are consistent in defining the meaning of the term 'forcibly'. It is not restricted to physical force, but may include 'threat of force or coercion, such as that caused by fear of violence, duress, detention, psychological oppression or abuse of power against such person or persons or another person, or by taking advantage of a coercive environment'.[124]

5.5 IMPRISONMENT OR OTHER SEVERE DEPRIVATION OF PHYSICAL LIBERTY

Imprisonment is proscribed as a crime against humanity under Article II(1)(c) of Control Council Law No. 10, Article 5(e) of the ICTY Statute, and Article 3(e) of the ICTR Statute. Article 7(1)(e) of the ICC Statute proscribes imprisonment or other severe deprivation of physical liberty in violation of fundamental rules of international law. The latter was added to avoid an unduly restrictive interpretation of the term 'imprisonment'.[125] The ICC Statute makes clear that in order to be a crime against humanity an imprisonment or other forms of severe deprivation of physical liberty must be in violation of fundamental rules of international law.

One question raised during the drafting of the Elements of Crimes for this offence was how to ensure that the word 'severe' does not require subjective evaluation or judgment, on the part of the perpetrator. The accepted formula, proposed by the Delegation of Belgium, would require the perpetrator to be aware of the factual circumstances that established the gravity of the conduct. The formula, according to Professor Roger S. Clark of the Delegation of Samoa, would get rid of the 'mistake of law' problem in the sense that the perpetrator could not allege that he did not know that his conduct was against the law; all that needs to be proved is his awareness of the factual circumstances.[126]

5.6 TORTURE

Torture is proscribed as a crime against humanity pursuant to Article II(1)(c) of Control Council Law No. 10, Article 5(f) of the ICTY Statute, Article 3(f) of the ICTR Statute, and Article 7(1)(f) of the ICC Statute.

Under customary international law, torture is the intentional infliction of severe

---

[124] See 4.5 above.

[125] von Hebel and Robinson, 'Crimes within the Jurisdiction of the Court', 99.

[126] Statement of the Delegation of Belgium and that of the Delegation of Samoa, Informal Consultations on Elements of Crimes, 5th Sess. of the PCNICC, 16 June 2000.

physical or mental pain or suffering upon the victim by an official or someone acting at the instigation of, or with the consent or acquiescence of, an official or person acting in an official capacity, for one of the following purposes—to obtain information or confession from the victim or a third person; to punish the victim or a third person; to intimidate or coerce the victim or the third person, or for any reason based on discrimination of any kind.[127] The enumerated purposes do not constitute an exhaustive list, and there is no requirement that the conduct must be solely for a prohibited purpose.[128] It suffices that the prohibited purpose is part of the motivation behind the conduct although it need not be the predominating or sole purpose.[129] With regard to the person or persons involved, it is required that at least one of the persons involved in the torture process be a public official or at any rate act in a non-private capacity, for instance as a *de facto* organ of a State or any other authority-wielding entity.[130] Examples of torture include severe beatings, death threats, rapes, burning of hands, attempted suffocation, sexual violence, and forcing someone to watch sexual violence and other kinds of torture.[131]

Article 7(2)(e) of the ICC Statute defines 'torture' as 'the intentional infliction of severe pain or suffering, whether physical or mental, upon a person in the custody or under the control of the accused; except that torture shall not include pain or suffering arising only from, inherent in or incidental to, lawful sanctions'. The Rome Conference considered that crimes against humanity could be instigated or directed by State or non-State actors; therefore the requirement of official involvement is not included in the definition of torture under Article 7(2)(e) of the ICC Statute.[132] The 'purpose' element is not included, either. The exclusion of 'lawful sanctions' was to alleviate the concerns of Muslim States that some Islamic forms of punishment would be considered as 'torture' within the meaning of the Statute.[133]

Since the provision makes no mention of official involvement in the torture, the PCNICC's Elements of Crime for the crime against humanity of torture do away with this requirement altogether. Although some delegation to the PCNICC preferred to include a purpose element, the PCNICC decided against it on the ground that specifying the requisite purposes may be restrictive to the development of the law in this matter.

As will be seen in the next chapter, the Elements of Crimes adopted by the PCNICC for war crimes of torture still retain the 'purpose' element that distinguishes torture from other war crimes involving the infliction of harm. The crime against humanity of torture does not have this 'purpose' element anywhere, be it in the ICC Statute or in the Elements of Crimes. Therefore, what distinguishes the crime against humanity

---

[127] *Akayesu*, paras. 593–4, and cf. paras. 682–4; *Celebici*, para. 494.
[128] *Celebici*, para. 470.
[129] Ibid.
[130] *Prosecutor v. Anto Furundzija*, Case No. IT-95–17/1-T, ICTY T. Ch. II, 10 Dec. 1998, para. 162.
[131] *Akayesu*, paras. 392–4; *Celebici*, paras. 913–4, 936–43, 955–65; *Furundzija*, paras. 163, 264, 267.
[132] von Hebel and Robinson, 'Crimes within the Jurisdiction of the Court', 99.
[133] M. H. Arsanjani, 'The Rome Statute of the International Criminal Court' (1999) **93** *AJIL* 22 at 31.

of torture from other crimes against humanity which involve the infliction of harm to the body, mental state of mind, or health is the severity of the harm inflicted in the case of torture. In the case of torture, it is the 'severe' physical or mental pain or suffering. As will be seen, in the case of 'other inhumane acts', it is 'great suffering, or serious injury to body or to mental or physical health'.

5.7 SEXUAL CRIMES

The debate at the PCNICC centred around the choice of terminology to qualify 'consent'. Some delegations preferred the wording 'voluntary' or 'freely given' instead of 'genuine'. In the end, it was felt that 'genuine consent' already connotes that the consent is 'voluntary' and 'freely given'.

RAPE

Rape is proscribed as a crime against humanity under Article II(1)(c) of Control Council Law No. 10, Article 5(g) of the ICTY Statute, Article 3(g) of the ICTR Statute, and Article 7(1)(g) of the ICC Statute.

Rape has been held by the ICTR in *Akayesu* to be 'a form of aggression' whose central elements 'cannot be captured in a mechanical description of objects and body parts'. The 'conceptual framework' is used to define rape by recognizing that the essential elements of rape are not the particular details of the body parts and the objects involved, but 'rather the aggression that is expressed in a sexual manner under conditions of coercion'. Rape is thus defined as 'a physical invasion of a sexual nature, committed on a person under circumstances which are coercive'; it may or may not involve sexual intercourse.[134] Coercive circumstances need not be evidenced by a show of physical force; threats, intimidation, extortion, and 'other forms of duress which prey on fear or desperation' may be coercion.[135] Besides, coercion may be inherent in certain situations, such as armed conflict, in which the victim finds herself or him-self.[136] While rape and sexual violence are committed on a person under coercive circumstances, rape is distinguishable from other forms of sexual violence in that the former is 'a physical invasion of sexual nature' short of 'a physical invasion' of the body of another person.[137] Thrusting a piece of wood into the sexual organ of a woman as she lies dying is rape.[138] Forced penetration of the mouth which is a humiliating and degrading attack on human dignity can be considered rape.[139]

---

[134] *Akayesu*, paras. 597–8; *Musema*, para. 226.
[135] *Akayesu*, para. 688.
[136] Ibid.
[137] *Musema*, para. 227.
[138] *Akayesu*, para. 686.
[139] *Furundzija*, paras. 181–6; *Musema*, para. 228.

Therefore, forcing two men to perform fellatio on one another could constitute rape 'if pleaded in the appropriate manner'.[140]

The ICTR in *Akayesu* and *Musema* as well as the ICTY in *Celibici* adopted such conceptual definition of rape, believing that it is flexible enough to meet evolving norms of criminal justice in sexual crimes.[141] However, the ICTY in *Furundzija* preferred a more traditional approach of 'a mechanical description of objects and body parts' to define rape. In that case, rape is defined as:

'(i) the sexual penetration, however slight:

(a) of the vagina or anus of the victim by the penis of the perpetrator or any other object used by the perpetrator; or

(b) of the mouth of the victim by the penis of the perpetrator;

(ii) by coercion or force or threat of force against the victim or a third person.'[142]

Under existing international jurisprudence, rape can be torture when inflicted by or at the instigation of or with the consent or acquiescence of a public official or other person acting in an official capacity.[143]

The Elements of Crimes adopted by the PCNICC for this crime follows more closely the mechanical description of objects and body parts used in *Furundzija*, with elaboration to permit the possibility that the victim can be male or female. The conceptual definition was found to be too vague to be satisfactory for criminal prosecution before the ICC.

SEXUAL SLAVERY

Sexual slavery is a crime against humanity under Article 7(1)(g) of the ICC Statute. There is no similar provision in any other international criminal statute.

The alleged acts indicted by the ICTY Prosecutor in the *Foca* case as enslavement and rape might also qualify as sexual slavery if prosecuted under the ICC Statute. The victims in that case were allegedly confined in a house which was being run similar to a brothel where they were treated as personal property of the perpetrator and were subjected to repeated rapes and sexual assaults.

It has also been pointed out that some Rwandan women acquiesced to forced temporary marriage and performing sexual services to their so-called 'husband' in order to save their children from the on-going genocide. Some of the women were locked up or confined, while others stayed at their home to protect themselves or their family members from danger threatened by their 'husband' should they attempt to escape.[144]

The PCNICC modelled the Elements of Crimes for the crime against humanity of

---

[140] *Celebici*, para. 1066.

[141] *Musema*, paras. 228–9.

[142] *Furundzija*, para. 185.

[143] *Akayesu*, para. 597.

[144] Women's Caucus for Gender Justice, 'Recommendation and Commentary for the Elements Annex, Part I', submitted to the PCNICC, 29 Nov.–17 Dec. 1999, at 9.

sexual slavery on that of enslavement. Forced labour could also be sexual slavery. For example, in a situation of women taken as sexual slaves they are forced to provide 'sexual services' and these services fall within the definition of forced labour under the International Labour Organization (ILO) Forced Labour Convention of 1930 (No. 29). The Convention defines 'forced labour' as 'all work or service which is extracted from any person under the menace of any penalty and for which the said person has not offered himself [or herself] voluntarily'. Besides, sexual acts often form part of the process of forced labour.[145] The Elements of Crimes adopted by the PCNICC for this crime also take cognizance of the complex nature of the crime which, like the crime of enforced disappearance, could be committed by more than one person.

ENFORCED PROSTITUTION

Enforced prostitution is proscribed as a crime against humanity pursuant to Article 7(1)(g) of the ICC Statute. What distinguishes this offence from sexual slavery is the pecuniary or other advantage the perpetrator or another person obtained or expected to obtain in exchange for or in connection with the victim's acts of a sexual nature. In this light, the so-called 'Comfort Women' detained by Japanese troops during WWII to provide sexual gratification to Japanese soldiers are not enforced prostitutes, but are more likely to be sexual slaves.

FORCED PREGNANCY

Forced pregnancy is a crime against humanity under Article 7(1)(g) of the ICC Statute. Article 7(2)(f) of the ICC Statute defines 'forced pregnancy' as 'the unlawful confinement, of a woman forcibly made pregnant, with the intent of affecting the ethnic composition of any population or carrying out other grave violations of international law'. However, this definition is not in any way to be interpreted as 'affecting national laws relating to pregnancy'. This rider is added to allay the concerns of several delegations at the Rome Conference. It makes clear that proscription of forced pregnancy as a crime against humanity does not give rise to a universal right to abortion and does not in any way restrict the competence of States to regulate birth control and abortion pursuant to their own constitutional, philosophical, or religious principles.[146] Situations covered by this crime include those where women are forcibly impregnated and confined so as to force them to bear children of a conquering ethnic group with a view to affecting the ethnic composition of a population, or so as to serve as a medical experiment.[147]

---

[145] These two examples were cited in an unofficial memorandum issued on 20 June 2000 by the coalition of the non-governmental organizations that were observers at the 5th Sess. of the PCNICC.

[146] Robinson (1999) 93 *AJIL* 53, n. 63. According to Arsanjani, who was Secretary of the Committee of the Whole of the Rome Conference, the term 'forced pregnancy' is preferred to 'enforced pregnancy' in the hope that the former could not be used in support of legalizing abortion (Arsanjani (1999) 93 *AJIL* 31).

[147] Robinson (1999) 93 *AJIL* 53, n. 63.

The Elements of Crimes adopted by the PCNICC for this crime against humanity of forced pregnancy simply follow the letter of Article 7(2)(f) of the ICC Statute.

ENFORCED STERILIZATION

Enforced sterilization is a crime against humanity under Article 7(1)(g) of the ICC Statute. The PCNICC has considered it unnecessary to include the term 'forcibly' to qualify the conduct of the perpetrator of this crime because the phrase 'not carried out with . . . genuine consent' of the victim or victims is sufficient for the purpose.

China is concerned about this offence because China has adopted a one-child policy to control its population growth. China proposed that birth-control measures that are not to be considered as measures of enforced sterilization criminalized under the ICC Statute are those having 'a non-permanent effect', and not just 'a short-term effect' as appeared in the existing draft Elements of Crimes. This proposal received support from Israel, Greece, and Mexico. At the other end of the spectrum were delegations like Canada and Germany who considered any reference to birth-control measures as unsatisfactory. In their opinion, read literally, it would nullify the entire crime; since all sterilization involves 'birth-control measures'.[148] In the end, a compromise was achieved to use the term 'a non-permanent effect in practice' so as to allow the ICC flexibility to determine whether the birth-control measure in question has a practical effect of depriving the victim permanently of biological productive capacity. This compromise is also incorporated in the Elements of Crimes for the war crime of enforced sterilization under Article 8(2)(b)(xxii) and (e)(vi) of the ICC Statute.

The Elements of Crimes adopted by the PCNICC for this crime against humanity require that the perpetrator must have deprived one or more persons of biological reproductive capacity, and that the conduct must have been neither justified by the medical or hospital treatment of the person or persons concerned nor carried out with their genuine consent. However, 'genuine consent' does not include consent obtained through deception; it must be an informed consent.[149]

SEXUAL VIOLENCE

As explained by the ICTY in *Furundzija*, international criminal law prohibits 'all serious abuses of a sexual nature inflicted upon the physical and moral integrity of a person by means of coercion, threat of force, or intimidation in a way that is degrading and humiliating for the victim's dignity'.[150] The ICTR in *Akayesu* defines sexual violence as 'any act of a sexual nature which is committed on a person under

---

[148] Proposal submitted by Canada and Germany on Art. 7, *Doc. PCNICC/ 1999/ WGEC/ DP. 36* of 23 Nov. 1999, at 7, n. 11.

[149] This was proposed by the Delegation of Ecuador at the 5th Sess. of the PCNICC to make it clear that the consent in question is also an 'informed' one.

[150] *Furundzija*, para. 186.

circumstances which are coercive and is not limited to physical invasion of the human body [but] may include acts which do not involve penetration or even physical contact'.[151] It was held in that case that the act of undressing a female victim and forcing her to do gymnastics naked in the public courtyard in front of the crowd constituted sexual violence.[152]

Sexual violence of comparable gravity to rape, sexual slavery, enforced prostitution, forced pregnancy, or enforced sterilization is a crime against humanity pursuant to Article 7(1)(g) of the ICC Statute.

The Elements of Crimes finally adopted by the PCNICC for the crime against humanity of sexual violence clarify further that the perpetrator must have committed 'an act of a sexual nature against one or more persons or caused such person or persons to engage in one or more acts of a sexual nature by force, or by threat of force or coercion, such as that caused by fear of violence, duress, detention, psychological oppression or abuse of power, against such person or persons or another person, or by taking advantage of a coercive environment or such person's or persons' incapacity to give genuine consent'. In addition, the perpetrator must have been aware of the factual circumstances that established the gravity of the conduct in question.

5.8 PERSECUTION

Persecution is a crime against humanity under Article 6(c) of the Nuremberg Charter, Article II(1)(c) of Control Council Law No. 10, Article 5(c) of the Tokyo Charter, Article 5(h) of the ICTY Statute, Article 3(h) of the ICTR Statute, and Article 7(1)(h) of the ICC Statute.

Persecution is the violation of the right to equality in some serious fashion that infringes on the enjoyment of a basic or fundamental right.[153] Only extreme forms of discrimination amounting to deliberate persecution are to be punished as a crime against humanity. Thus, persecution as a crime against humanity is defined in Article 7(2)(g) of the ICC Statute as 'the intentional and severe deprivation of fundamental rights contrary to international law by reason of the identity of the group or collectivity'. This statutory definition is similar to the one given by Trial Chamber II of the ICTY in *Kupreskic and Others*, which defines the crime against humanity of persecution as 'the gross or blatant denial, on discriminatory grounds, of a fundamental right, laid down in international customary or treaty law, reaching the same level of gravity as the other [crimes against humanity]'.[154]

In essence, the constituent elements of the crime of persecution are an act or

---

[151] *Akayesu*, para. 598.
[152] Ibid., para. 688.
[153] *Tadic* Judgment, para. 697; *Blaskic*, para. 220, and the authorities cited in paras. 221–6.
[154] *Kupreskic and Others*, para. 621.

omission that persecutes another person on a discriminatory ground, committed with intent to cause an infringement of an individual's enjoyment of a basic fundamental right, and that act or omission does result in such infringement.[155] The discrimination involved concerns the specific intent to attack a human person insofar as he belongs to a community or a group.[156] In charging the perpetrator of persecution as a crime against humanity, the Prosecution, therefore, must prove the existence of the following elements: (a) those elements required for all crimes against humanity; (b) a gross or blatant denial of a fundamental right reaching the same level of gravity as the other crimes against humanity; and (c) discriminatory grounds.[157]

In terms of the *actus reus*, Trial Chamber I of the ICTY held in *Blaskic* that the crime of persecution covers not only attacks on physical or mental integrity or the liberty of the individual, but also acts aimed at property provided that the victims are selected specifically because of their belonging to a certain community.[158]

The crime of persecution encompasses acts of varying severity, from killing to a limitation on the type of professions open to the targeted group, as well as acts of a physical, economic, or judicial nature in violation of the right of an individual to equal enjoyment of basic rights.[159] In *Tadic*, for example, the accused was convicted by the ICTY of persecution for his role in, *inter alia*, the attack on a village and its surrounding areas, the seizure, collection, segregation, and forced transfer of civilians to camps, beatings, and killings that infringed the enjoyment of fundamental rights by non-Serbs on the basis of religious and political discrimination.[160] However, persecution does not always require a physical element. Streicher was convicted of persecution on political and racial grounds by the Nuremberg Tribunal for his incitement through virulent speech and publication preaching hatred of the Jews at the time when Jews in Eastern Europe were being killed under the most horrible conditions.[161] In the *Justice* case, the accused who were former judges, prosecutors, or officials in the Reich Ministry of Justice were convicted for their role in furthering the persecution of Jews and Poles on political, racial, or religious grounds through their application of laws to these victims in a discriminatory and arbitrary manner.[162]

As clarified by Trial Chamber II of the ICTY in *Kupreskic and Others*, acts of persecution 'must be evaluated not in isolation but in context, by looking at their cumulative effect'. This is because although individual acts may not be inhumane, their overall consequences may offend humanity in such a way that they may be termed 'inhumane'.[163] While persecution is used frequently to connote a series of acts,

---

[155] Cf. ibid., para. 572; *Tadic* Judgment, para. 715.
[156] *Blaskic*, para. 235.
[157] *Kupreskic and Others*, para. 627.
[158] *Blaskic*, para. 233, and see the authorities cited in paras. 228–32.
[159] *Tadic* Judgment, paras. 704, 708–10; *Kupreskic and Others*, paras. 610–4 and the cases cited therein.
[160] *Tadic* Judgment, para. 717.
[161] *Nuremberg Proceedings*, 501–2; (1947) **41** *AJIL* 293–6. Also cited in *Tadic* Judgment, para. 708; *Ruggiu*, para. 19.
[162] TWC, i, 51–2. Cited in *Tadic* Judgment, para. 709.
[163] *Kupreskic and Others*, para. 622.

there is a possibility that a single act may constitute persecution, provided that there is clear evidence of the discriminatory intent, as, for instance, a single murder of a Muslim person in the former Yugoslavia as part of a widespread and systematic persecutory attack against a civilian population and committed with discriminatory intent.[164]

Acts constituting persecution may overlap with one another, as, for example, in the case of murder and extermination, torture and rape, enslavement and imprisonment, and each of these crimes may in itself constitute persecution.[165] In *Blaskic*, Trial Chamber I of the ICTY found the accused guilty of the crime against humanity of persecution that comprised attacks upon cities, towns and villages; murder and causing serious bodily injury; destruction and plunder of property and, in particular, of institutions dedicated to religion or education; inhumane treatment of civilians, in particular, their being taken hostage and used as human shields; and the forcible transfer of civilians. This charge of persecution arose out of the same set of acts charged as violations of the laws or customs of war, for which the accused was also found guilty. However, with regard to the charge of persecution, the prosecution had to prove that the acts were committed against the victims on discriminatory grounds.[166]

However, there is a limit to the acts which can constitute persecution within the meaning of crimes against humanity. For instance, in the *Flick* case, offences against industrial property were held not to constitute crimes against humanity because the compulsory taking of the property could not be said to affect the life and liberty of oppressed peoples,[167] while it might be said that economic measures of a personal type can constitute persecutory acts, especially if committed by terror or linked with other acts of violence, or as part of a comprehensive process, such as the comprehensive destruction of homes and property that are the livelihood of a certain population.[168] The test is whether the property or economic rights in question can be considered so fundamental that their denial amounts to persecution.[169]

While the *actus reus* of persecution may be identical to other crimes against humanity, persecution is distinguishable from the other crimes against humanity in that it is committed on discriminatory grounds.[170] Nonetheless, it is not necessary to prove that the accused has taken part in the formulation of a discriminatory policy or practice of a government authority.[171]

In customary international law, there are no definitive grounds for persecution.[172] The three discriminatory grounds against the group or collectivity included in the

---

[164] Ibid., para. 624.
[165] Ibid., paras. 571, 594–605 and the authorities cited therein.
[166] *Blaskic*, paras. 234–5, 260.
[167] *Kupreskic and Others*, para. 631.
[168] Ibid.; *Tadic* Judgment, para. 707, citing *Flick* case.
[169] *Kupreskic and Others*, paras. 630–1.
[170] Ibid., para. 607.
[171] Ibid., para. 625.
[172] *Tadic* Judgment, para. 711.

Nuremberg Charter and Control Council Law No. 10 were race, religion, and politics. On the other hand, the Tokyo Charter omitted religion as a discriminatory ground due to its irrelevance in the Japanese war effort. Article 5(h) of the ICTY Statute and Article 3(h) of the ICTR Statute proscribe crimes against humanity of 'persecutions on political, racial and religious grounds', thus following the Nuremberg Charter and Control Council Law No. 10. The Appeals Chamber of the ICTY in *Tadic* recognizes that since the aim of the draftsmen of the ICTY Statute was to make all crimes against humanity punishable, the discriminatory grounds enumerated in Article 5(h) of the ICTY Statute cannot be exhaustive. Otherwise, such an interpretation of Article 5(h) would create significant *lacuna* by failing to protect victim groups not covered by the discriminatory grounds enumerated in Article 5(h) of the ICTY Statute, such as physical or mental disability, age or infirmity, or sexual preference. The Appeals Chamber cites the example of the extermination of 'class enemies' in the Soviet Union during the 1930's and the deportation of the urban educated of Cambodia by the Khmer Rouge between 1975–79 as other instances that would not fall within the purview of crimes against humanity on the basis of the grounds enumerated in the ICTY Statute.[173] It is submitted that, for the same reason, the discriminatory grounds enumerated in Article 3(h) of the ICTR Statute, which are identical to Article 5(h) of the ICTY Statute, cannot be exhaustive, either. Moreover, since each of the crimes against humanity under the ICTR Statute must be committed with discriminatory intent on 'national, political, ethnic, racial or religious grounds', it is inconceivable that the list of discriminatory grounds in the case of persecution—in which discriminatory intent plays the most prominent role of all types of crimes against humanity—would be the most restrictive of all.

The discriminatory grounds against the group or collectivity are stipulated in Article 7(1)(h) of the ICC Statute to encompass political, racial, national, ethnic, cultural, religious, gender, or other grounds that are universally recognized as impermissible under international law. The last proviso is added to ensure that while the enumerated grounds are not exhaustive, they are not open-ended.[174] The national, ethnic, or gender grounds are added to the list of grounds for persecution in previous international criminal statutes so as to reflect modern developments. Gender is to be understood as referring to the two sexes, male and female, within the context of society.[175]

Whatever grounds are enumerated are alternatives; any one of such grounds suffices to constitute persecution.[176] With regard to the group of victims, it is the

---

[173] *Kayishema and Ruzindana*, para. 285.

[174] Robinson (1999) 93 *AJIL* 54. In Robinson's opinion, although any other prohibited grounds of discrimination which become universally recognized as impermissible under international law can be incorporated automatically without amending the ICC Statute, universal recognition is a high threshold and, consequently, the ICC Statute may have to be amended to reflect future developments (ibid.)

[175] Art. 7(3), ICC Statute.

[176] *Tadic* Judgment, paras. 712–3. In this connection, the conjunctive 'and' between the various listed bases under Art. 5(h) of the ICTY Statute is treated as an attempt by the drafters 'to define, in a cumulative sense, the [ITCY's] adjudicative powers under Article 5'; and that the ICTY Statute should be read in accordance with custom whereby any one of the listed grounds suffices as a basis for persecution. Ibid., para. 713.

one to which the perpetrator of persecution does not consider himself to belong.[177]

The requisite *mens rea* for this crime is the discriminatory intent with the aim of removing the victims from the society in which they live alongside the perpetrators, or eventually even from humanity itself, on the ground that people who share ethnic, racial, religious, or other bonds different from those of a dominant group are to be treated as inferior to the dominant group, resulting in the fundamental human rights of the victim group being grossly and systematically trampled upon.[178] Thus, the *mens rea* requirement is higher than other crimes against humanity since persecution as a crime against humanity belongs to the same genus of offence as genocide, although the *mens rea* of genocide is 'an extreme and most inhuman form of persecution'.[179] While the *mens rea* of genocide is the intent to destroy the protected group in whole or in part, the *mens rea* of persecution is the intent to discriminate forcibly against a group or members thereof by grossly and systematically violating their fundamental human rights.[180] However, 'when persecution escalates to the extreme form of wilful and deliberate acts designed to destroy a group or part of a group, it can be held that such persecution amounts to genocide'.[181] In *Kupreskic and Others*, the ICTY Trial Chamber imposed the heaviest sentence on persecution, higher than the crime against humanity of murder and other inhumane acts. In that case, the Prosecution lumped together all acts of ethnic cleansing against the victims under Count 1 (Persecution), charging the accused with persecuting Bosnian Muslim inhabitants of Ahmici-Santici and its environs on political, racial, or religious grounds by planning, organizing, and implementing an attack which was designed to remove or 'cleanse' all Bosnian Muslims from the village and surrounding areas. This persecution, described by the Trial Chamber as a widespread pattern of 'persecutory violence', resulted in some 116 inhabitants of the village being killed, about twenty-four wounded, and 169 houses and two mosques destroyed.[182] In contrast, the charges of murder, inhumane acts, and cruel treatment specified the names of the individual victims instead of using the more general term of 'the Bosnian Muslim inhabitants of Ahmici-Santici and its environs' as in the charge of persecution.

In *Ruggiu*, the accused pleaded guilty to the charge of direct and public incitement to genocide as well as to that of crime against humanity of persecution, and his plea was upheld by Trial Chamber I of the ICTR as being based on sufficient facts. The facts behind these two charges were essentially the same. In the case of persecution, the accused's acts involved direct and public radio broadcasts aimed at singling out and attacking the Tutsi ethnic group and Belgians on discriminatory grounds, by depriving them of the fundamental rights to life, liberty, and basic humanity enjoyed

---

[177] *Blaskic*, para. 236, citing *Tadic* Judgment, para. 714.
[178] *Kupreskic and Others*, paras. 633–4, 751.
[179] Ibid., para. 636.
[180] Ibid., para. 751.
[181] Ibid., para. 636.
[182] Ibid., paras. 749–54, 761–3.

by members of a wider society. The goal was the death and removal of those persons from the society in which they lived alongside the accused, or eventually even from humanity itself.[183] It seems that in persecution, as opposed to genocide, the Belgians were not targeted for destruction, in whole or in part, as a national, racial, ethnical, or religious group, as such. On the contrary, they, together with the Tutsis targeted with them, were a 'political' group which the accused despised and wanted 'removed',[184] and a political group is not a protected group in relation to genocide.

The crime of persecution under the ICC Statute must be committed '*in connection with any act [enumerated as crimes against humanity in Article 7(1) of the ICC Statute] or any crime within the jurisdiction of the [ICC].*'[185] This 'connection' requirement appeared only in the Nuremberg Charter and the Tokyo Charter. The other international criminal statutes, including the ICTY and the ICTR Statutes, set no such jurisdictional threshold requirement. As the ICTY puts it in *Tadic*, if there is an infringement of an individual's fundamental right through discrimination on one of the stipulated grounds, then it not necessary to have a separate act of an inhumane nature to constitute persecution.[186] Likewise, the ICTY states in *Kupreskic and Others* that persecution under customary international law need not be committed in connection with other international crimes; hence, the provision of Article 7(1)(h) of the ICC Statute 'is not consonant with customary international law'.[187] The reason why this 'connection' requirement is added as a jurisdictional threshold of crimes against humanity under Article 7 of the ICC Statute is because several delegations at the Rome Conference considered the notion of persecution to be vague and potentially elastic.[188] One commentator argues that since persecution is a crime in itself, and not an auxiliary offence to be used as an additional charge or aggravating factor, it will suffice to prove a connection between persecution and any instance of murder, torture, rape, or any other inhumane act enumerated in Article 7 of the ICC Statute which need not constitute a crime against humanity in its own right. In other words, it is not necessary to prove that the 'connected' inhumane acts were committed on a widespread or systematic basis or pursuant to a policy.[189]

At the Fifth Session of the PCNICC, some delegations wanted to make sure that persons who are not members of an identifiable group or collectivity but who sympathize with the group or collectivity and are somehow 'associated with' or 'identified with' such group or collectivity should also be protected from persecution. Examples of such persons include members of non-governmental organizations or humanitarian assistance personnel. Other delegations, however, feared that this terminology would expand the scope of protection under Article 7(1)(h) of the ICC Statute. As a

---

[183] *Ruggiu*, para. 22.
[184] Ibid., verdict on Count 2 of the Indictment.
[185] Art. 7(1)(h), ICC Statute.
[186] *Tadic* Judgment, para. 697.
[187] *Kupreskic and Others*, para. 580.
[188] Robinson (1999) **93** *AJIL* 54–5.
[189] Ibid., at 55. See also von Hebel and Robinson, 'Crimes within the Jurisdiction of the Court', 101–2.

compromise, the UK Delegation proposed that the phrase 'by reason of the identity of the group' used in the Statute be copied in the relevant element of the Elements of Crimes for this crime, and this proposed compromise was accepted.

The Elements of Crimes adopted by the PCNICC for this offence provide in their pertinent part:

'1. The perpetrator severely deprived, contrary to international law,[190] one or more persons of fundamental rights.
2. The perpetrator targeted such person or persons by reason of the identity of a group or collectivity or targeted the group or collectivity as such.
3. Such targeting was based on political, racial, national, ethnic, cultural, religious, gender as defined in Article 7, paragraph 3, of the Statute, or other grounds that are universally recognized as impermissible under international law.
4. The conduct was committed in connection with any act referred to in Article 7, paragraph 1, of the Statute or any crime within the jurisdiction of the Court. . . .'

5.9 ENFORCED DISAPPEARANCE OF PERSONS

Enforced disappearance of persons is a crime against humanity under Article 7(1)(i) of the ICC Statute. Although neither the ICTY Statute or the ICTR Statute explicitly proscribes enforced disappearance of persons as a crime against humanity, it might be prosecuted under the offence 'other inhumane acts' pursuant to Article 5(i) of the ICTY Statute and Article 3(i) of the ICTR Statute. The Rome Conference merely decided to highlight explicitly enforced disappearance and apartheid instead of leaving them included implicitly under the crimes against humanity of other inhumane acts.[191]

Article 7(2)(i) of the ICC Statute defines 'enforced disappearance of persons' as 'the arrest, detention or abduction of persons by, or with the authorization, support or acquiescence of, a State or a political organization, followed by a refusal to acknowledge that deprivation of freedom or to give information on the fate or whereabouts of those persons, with the intention of removing them from the protection of the law for a prolonged period of time'.

The people who commit this crime may be numerous, and the time span may be

---

[190] The phrase 'contrary to international law' has been added at the insistence of the Delegation of Turkey at the 5th Sess. of the PCNICC in June 2000. According to that Delegation, some measures to protect the safety or welfare of a group or collective are permissible under international law; hence, they are not persecution. Other delegations found nothing wrong with including this phrase in the element.

The footnote accompanying this phrase reads: 'This requirement is without prejudice to paragraph 6 of the General Introduction to the Elements of Crimes'. Paragraph 6 of the General Introduction to the Elements of Crimes, in turn, states that the requirement of 'unlawfulness' mentioned in the Statute or in other parts of international law, in particular international humanitarian law, is generally not specified in the Elements of Crimes.

[191] von Hebel and Robinson, 'Crimes within the Jurisdiction of the Court', 102.

long or indefinite. Let us consider the following hypothetical example. Police Officer X arrests A for theft which A has actually committed. A is detained with the authorization of the State. Subsequently, some State officials, after finding out that A is a left-wing activist, want A to disappear for ever and without trace and they instruct Police Inspector Y to order Police Officer Z to make A 'disappear' (for example, by making him jump into the sea from a helicopter 400 feet above the sea with a heavy cement block tied to his back). A's relatives cannot find A in prison and the people involved in his disappearance refuse to tell them about A's fate or whereabouts. Police Officer X, for his part, honestly has no idea about A's fate so he cannot tell A's relatives what he does not know.

The crime of enforced disappearance has been called an 'octopus crime' as well as a 'permanent crime'.[192] Several persons could be prosecuted at different stages of the disappearance although some of them may or may not be aware of acts committed by others in the chain of events. This crime also begs the issue of jurisdiction *ratione temporis* of the ICC under Article 11 of the ICC Statute. Under that Article, the ICC shall have jurisdiction over the crimes committed after the entry into force of the Statute *vis-à-vis* the State concerned. Criminal responsibility must be duly allocated. In our hypothetical example, Police Officer X should not be held criminally liable for A's disappearance.

With regard to the jurisdiction *ratione temporis* of the ICC over this crime, the draft submitted to the PCNICC by the Sub-Coordinator on this crime provided: 'Consistent with the Statute it is understood that this crime falls under the jurisdiction of the Court only if the arrest, detention or abduction occurs after the entry into force of the Statute'. This proposal was rejected by the Informal Consultation on the Elements of Crime on the ground that it would amount to interpretation of the ICC's jurisdiction *ratione temporis* under Article 11 of the ICC Statute, which the PCNICC was not mandated to do.

The Elements of Crimes adopted finally by the PCNICC for this offence read:

'**Crime against humanity of enforced disappearance of persons** [1st Footnote: Given the complex nature of this crime, it is recognized that its commission will normally involve more than one perpetrator as a part of a common criminal purpose.] [2nd Footnote: This crime falls under the jurisdiction of the Court only if the attack referred to in elements 7 and 8 occurs after the entry into force of the Statute.]

1. The perpetrator:

   (a) Arrested, detained[193] [194]or abducted one or more persons; or

---

[192] At the PCNICC, it was the Delegation of the UK that first used the term 'octopus crime', while the delegations from a number of Latin American States considered it a 'permanent crime'.

[193] **Footnote:** 'The word "detained" would include a perpetrator who maintained an existing detention.'

[194] **Footnote:** 'It is understood that under certain circumstances an arrest or detention may have been lawful.'

(b) Refused to acknowledge the arrest, detention or abduction, or to give information on the fate or whereabouts of such person or persons.

2. (a) Such arrest, detention or abduction was followed or accompanied by a refusal to acknowledge that deprivation of freedom or to give information on the fate or whereabouts of such person or persons; or

(b) Such refusal was preceded or accompanied by that deprivation of freedom.

3. The perpetrator was aware that:[195]

(a) Such arrest, detention or abduction would be followed in the ordinary course of events by a refusal to acknowledge that deprivation of freedom or to give information on the fate or whereabouts of such person or persons;[196] or

(b) Such refusal was preceded or accompanied by that deprivation of freedom.

4. Such arrest, detention or abduction was carried out by, or with the authorization, support, or acquiescence of, a State or a political organization.

5. Such refusal to acknowledge that deprivation of freedom or to give information on the fate or whereabouts of such person or persons was carried out by, or with the authorization or support of, such State or political organization.

6. The perpetrator intended to remove such person or persons from the protection of the law for a prolonged period of time.

7. The conduct was committed as part of a widespread or systematic attack directed against a civilian population.

8. The perpetrator knew that the conduct was part of or intended the conduct to be part of a widespread or systematic attack directed against a civilian population.'

In *Velasquez Rodriquez*, the Inter-American Court of Human Rights held that when the existence of a policy or practice of disappearances has been shown, the disappearance of a particular individual may be proved 'through circumstantial or indirect evidence or by logical inference'; otherwise, it would be impossible to prove that an individual has disappeared because 'this type of repression is characterized by an attempt to suppress any information about the kidnapping or the whereabouts and fate of the victim'.[197] This is especially so where investigation by an international body will have to depend on the cooperation of the State implementing a policy of enforced disappearance and in whose territory the investigation will be carried out.[198] It is submitted that this logical inference is also applicable to the prosecution of the crime of enforced disappearance before the ICC. However, for an accused to be found guilty

---

[195] **Footnote:** 'This element, inserted because of the complexity of this crime, is without prejudice to the General Introduction to the Elements of Crimes.'

[196] **Footnote:** 'It is understood that in the case of a perpetrator who maintained an existing detention, this element would be satisfied if the perpetrator was aware that such a refusal had already taken place.'

[197] Inter-American Ct. of Human Rights, 1988, Ser. C, No. 4, (1988) 9 *Human Rights L. J.* 212, paras. 124, 131.

[198] Ibid., paras. 135–6.

for this offence under the ICC Statute, the requisite elements for this offence will have to be satisfied beyond all reasonable doubt.[199]

5.10 APARTHEID

Article I of the International Convention on the Suppression and Punishment of the Crime of Apartheid of 30 November 1973[200] declares that apartheid is a crime against humanity, and that inhumane acts resulting from apartheid are crimes against international law. Article III of the Apartheid Convention attaches individual criminal responsibility on the international plane for the crime of apartheid.

Apartheid is a crime against humanity under Article 7(1)(j) of the ICC Statute. Article 7(2)(h) of the ICC Statute defines 'the crime of apartheid' as 'inhumane acts of a character similar to [other crimes against humanity], committed in the context of an institutionalized regime of systematic oppression and domination by one racial group over any other racial group or groups and committed with the intention of maintaining that regime'.[201]

There was little discussion on the Elements of Crimes for this offence. The Elements of Crimes adopted by the PCNICC for the crime against humanity of apartheid adds little to the definition given in Article 7(2)(h) of the ICC Statute. They merely clarify that an inhumane act amounting to apartheid could be committed against one or more persons; that the term 'character' as used in Article 7(2)(h) of the Statute refers to the nature and gravity of the act; and that the perpetrator must have been aware of the factual circumstances that established the character of the act.

Since the definition of apartheid under Article 7(2)(h) of the ICC Statute closely follows the definition of the crime of apartheid under Article II of the Apartheid Convention, the Convention's enumerated list of proscribed acts of apartheid may serve as illustrations for the ICC to consider when dealing with this crime.

Article II of the Apartheid Convention stipulates that the crime of apartheid means any of the following inhumane acts committed for the purpose of establishing and maintaining domination by one racial group of persons over any other racial group of persons and systematically oppressing them:

---

[199] The Inter-American Court of Human Rights in *Velasquez Rodriguez* was dealing with allegations of violations by Honduras of the American Convention on Human Rights (Pact of San José) of 1969 ((1970) **9** *ILM* 673). The Court upheld 'the principle that the silence of the accused or elusive or ambiguous answers on its part may be interpreted as an acknowledgment of the truth of the allegations, so long as the contrary is not indicated by the record or is not compelled as a matter of law', but '[t]his result would not hold under criminal law, which does not apply in the instant case . . . ' ((1988) **9** *Human Rights L. J.* para. 138).

[200] 1015 *UNTS* 243.

[201] It should be noted that the ICC Statute departs from the proposal in Art. 18(f) of the ILC's 1996 Draft Code of Crimes Against the Peace and Security of Mankind which encompasses not only racial groups but also ethnic groups as well as religious groups.

'(a) Denial to a member or members of a racial group or groups of the right to life and liberty of person:

   (i)   By murder of members of a racial group or groups;

   (ii) By the infliction upon the members of a racial group or groups of serious bodily or mental harm, by the infringement of their freedom or dignity, or by subjecting them to torture or to cruel, inhuman, or degrading treatment or punishment;

   (iii) By arbitrary arrest and illegal imprisonment of the members of a racial group or groups;

(b) Deliberate imposition on a racial group or groups of living conditions calculated to cause its or their physical destruction in whole or in part;

(c) Any legislative measures and other measures calculated to prevent a racial group or groups from participation in the political, social, economic, and cultural life of the country and the deliberate creation of conditions preventing the full development of such a group or groups, in particular by denying to members of a racial group or groups basic human rights and freedom, including the right to work, the right to form recognized trade unions, the right to education, the right to leave and return to their country, the right to a nationality, the right to freedom of movement and residence, the right to freedom of opinion and expression, and the right to freedom of peaceful assembly and association;

(d) Any measures, including legislative measures, designed to divide the population along racial lines by the creation of separate reserves and ghettos for the members of a racial group or groups, the prohibition of mixed marriages among members of various racial groups, the expropriation of landed property belonging to a racial group or groups or to members thereof;

(e) Exploitation of the labour of the members of a racial group or groups, in particular by submitting them to forced labour;

(f) Persecution of organizations and persons, by depriving them of fundamental rights and freedoms, because they oppose apartheid.'

5.11 OTHER INHUMANE ACTS

This category of 'other inhuman acts', first included in Article 6(c) of the Nuremberg Charter, has been maintained since then to ensure that there be no *lacuna* in the law with regard to categories of crimes against humanity that need to evolve to catch up with the imagination and creativity of criminals against humanity. It is included in Article II(1) of Control Council Law No. 10, Article 5(c) of the Tokyo Charter, Article 5(i) of the ICTY Statute, Article 3(i) of the ICTR Statute, and Article 7(1)(k) of the ICC Statute.

Article 7(1)(k) of the ICC Statute specifies that such other inhumane acts must be 'of a similar character [to the other crimes against humanity already enumerated in

Article 7 of the ICC Statute] intentionally causing great suffering, or serious injury to body or to mental or physical health'. This is intended to rein in the imprecise and open-ended nature of this provision. However, it was noted by Trial Chamber II of the ICTY in *Kupreskic and Others* that this provision fails to provide any indication of the legal standards to identify the prohibited inhumane acts.[202] The Trial Chamber in that case resorts to international standards on human rights such as those set out in the Universal Declaration of Human Rights of 1948 and the 1966 International Convention on Civil and Political Rights[203] and the 1996 International Convention on Economic, Social, and Cultural Rights[204] in order to identify 'a set of basic rights appertaining to human beings, the infringement of which may amount, depending on the accompanying circumstances, to a crime against humanity'; that is, they must be carried out in a systematic manner and on a large scale, as serious as the other classes of crimes proscribed as crimes against humanity.[205] In this context, one may use the *ejusdem generis* rule to compare and assess the gravity of the proscribed act.[206]

Trial Chamber II of the ICTR held in *Kayishema and Ruzindana* that these 'other inhumane acts' are acts or omissions that deliberately cause serious mental or physical suffering or injury or constitute a serious attack on human dignity of comparable seriousness or gravity to the other crimes against humanity already enumerated in the relevant provisions of the international instruments concerned.[207] Acts that rise to the level of inhumane acts are to be determined on a case-by-case basis, and there must be a nexus between an inhumane act and the serious suffering or injury to the mental or physical health of the victim.[208] Mutilation, beatings, and other types of violence, including sexual violence, causing severe bodily harm also qualify.[209] Forced undressing of a woman in public, forcing a naked woman to march in public or to perform exercises naked in public have been held to be 'other inhumane acts' falling within the purview of crimes against humanity.[210] It has been held that the legal meaning of 'inhumane treatment' is the same as that of 'cruel treatment'.[211]

One may question whether 'other inhumane acts' that are crimes against humanity extend to acts against property. The preferred view is that such inhumane acts are not confined to acts against life and limb. Pillage, plunder, arbitrary destruction or expropriation of public and private property may cause 'great suffering, or serious injury to the . . . mental . . . health' of the victim.[212]

---

[202] *Kupreskic and Others*, para. 565.

[203] (1967) 6 *ILM* 368.

[204] Ibid., 360.

[205] *Kupreskic and Others*, para. 566.

[206] Ibid.

[207] *Kayishema and Ruzindana*, para. 151. See also *Akayesu*, para. 585; *Musema*, paras. 230–3.

[208] *Kayishema and Ruzindana*, *Akayesu*, *Musema*.

[209] *Tadic* Judgment, paras. 729–30, 753–4; *Akayesu*, para. 688.

[210] *Akayesu*, para. 697.

[211] *Jelisic*, para. 52, following *Celebici*, para. 552.

[212] Cf. H. Lauterpacht, 'The Law of Nations and the Punishment of War Crimes' (1944) 21 *BYBIL* 58 at 79.

Thus, the *actus reus* and *mens rea* of this offence is that the actor commits an act of similar gravity and seriousness to the other crimes against humanity enumerated in the relevant instrument, with intent to cause that other inhumane act, and with knowledge that the act is committed within the overall context of a widespread or systematic attack directed against a civilian population.[213] The constitutive elements of serious attacks on the physical or mental integrity as a form of other inhumane acts comprise the act of the accused or his subordinate that causes serious suffering to the mental or physical health of the victim (with the seriousness being determined on a case-by-case basis), with intent to cause serious attack on the mental or physical health of the victim as a result of the volition or recklessness of the accused or his subordinate.[214]

To find the accused guilty of such inhumane act against a third party, it must be proved that the accused intended to cause serious mental suffering on that third party, or knew that his act was likely to cause serious mental suffering but was reckless as to whether such suffering would result with regard to the third party. Where the accused did not know that the third party was witnessing his acts committed against others, particularly against family or friends, then the accused lacks the necessary intent to inflict serious mental suffering on the third party and, consequently, cannot be held responsible for the mental suffering of the third party.[215] Thus, live broadcasting through a loudspeaker of the cries of prison camp inmates who were being subject to physical violence committed by prison camp guards constitute serious psychological violence, an act of inhumane treatment, against other camp detainees although these detainees themselves were not subject to the physical violence.[216]

As a crime against humanity, an inhumane act must be one inflicted on a living individual. However, it should be noted that certain acts against dead bodies (for example, cannibalism, mutilation of and the failure to bury dead bodies in breach of specific provisions of the laws and usages of war relating to the mistreatment of the war dead) have been punished as war crimes.[217]

The Elements of Crimes adopted by the PCNICC for this crime against humanity of other inhumane acts do not depart from established jurisprudence. The Elements require that the nature and gravity of an act amounting to an inhumane act be at the level of great suffering, or serious injury to body or to mental or physical health, and that the perpetrator must have been aware of the factual circumstances that established the nature and gravity of the act.

---

[213] *Kayishema and Ruzindana*, para. 154.

[214] *Blaskic*, para. 243.

[215] *Kayishema and Ruzindana*, para. 153.

[216] Cf. *Prosecutor v. Aleksovski*, ICTY T. Ch. I, 3 Nov. 1999, para. 190. Trial Chamber I of the ICTY in *Aleksovski* considered inhumane treatment in the context of humiliating and degrading treatment proscribed by the laws and customs of war (ibid., paras. 48–54, 228).

[217] *Tadic* Judgment, para. 748.

6

WAR CRIMES

War crimes are crimes committed in violation of international humanitarian law applicable during armed conflicts.[1] According to this law, in the conduct of hostilities the opposing forces are to be governed by three principles: necessity, humanity, and chivalry. Necessity ensures that only conduct essential to achieving victory is permitted; hence, the proportionality between the contribution an attack on a target will make to the ultimate victory and the damage or injury inflicted upon the target. In other words, necessity is invoked only to achieve a military objective on the battlefield, but not political or other objectives.[2] Humanity, or humanitarianism, governs the degree of permitted violence, thereby outlawing unnecessary or excessive action. Chivalry demands the exercise of fairness and mutual respect between the opposing forces; hence, the outlawing of dishonourable means and methods of combat like perfidy, wrongful use of protected emblems while engaging in attack, and denying quarter.[3]

The International Committee of the Red Cross (ICRC) has summarized the basic rules of international humanitarian law in armed conflicts as follows:

'1. Persons *hors de combat* and those who do not take a direct part in hostilities are entitled to respect for their lives and their moral, and physical integrity. They shall in all circumstances be protected and treated humanely without any adverse distinction.

2. It is forbidden to kill or injure an enemy who surrenders or who is *hors de combat.*

3. The wounded and sick shall be collected and cared for by the party to the conflict which has them in its power. Protection also covers medical personnel, establishments, transports, and equipment. The emblem of the red cross or the red crescent is the sign of such protection and must be respected.

4. Captured combatants and civilians under the authority of an adverse party are entitled to respect for their lives, dignity, personal rights, and convictions. They shall be protected against all acts of violence and reprisals. They shall have the right to correspond with their families and to receive relief.

---

[1] For a legal history and sources of war crimes, see L. C. Green, *The Contemporary Law of Armed Conflict* (Manchester University Press, 1993), chaps. 2, 18–19.

[2] B. M. Carnahan, 'Lincoln, Lieber and the Laws of War: The Origins and Limits of the Principle of Military Necessity' (1998) **92** *AJIL* 213, esp. at 215, 219.

[3] Green, *Contemporary Law of Armed Conflict*, 122, 327–37; C. Greenwood, 'Historical Development and Legal Basis', in D. Fleck (ed.), *The Handbook of Humanitarian Law in Armed Conflicts* (Oxford University Press, 1995), 1 at 30–3.

5. Everyone shall be entitled to benefit from fundamental judicial guarantees. No one shall be held responsible for an act he has not committed. No one shall be subjected to physical or mental torture, corporal punishment, or cruel or degrading treatment.

6. Parties to a conflict and members of their armed forces do not have an unlimited choice of methods of warfare of a nature to cause unnecessary losses or excessive suffering.

7. Parties to a conflict shall at all times distinguish between the civilian population and combatants in order to spare civilian population and property. Neither the civilian population as such nor civilian persons shall be the object of attack. Attacks shall be directed solely against military objectives.'[4]

These basic rules summarize the relevant provisions of international conventions relating to international humanitarian law. Such conventions include: the 1907 Hague Regulations Respecting the Laws and Customs of War on Land dated 18 October 1907 annexed to the 1907 Hague Convention IV Respecting the Laws and Customs of War on Land;[5] the Geneva Convention for the Amelioration of the Conditions of the Wounded and Sick in Armed Forces in the Field of 12 August 1949 (GC I);[6] the Geneva Convention for the Amelioration of the Condition of Wounded, Sick and Shipwrecked Members of the Armed Forces at Sea of 12 August 1949 (GC II);[7] the Geneva Convention Relative to the Treatment of Prisoners of War of 12 August 1949 (GC III);[8] and the Geneva Convention Relative to the Protection of Civilian Persons in Time of War of 12 August 1949 (GC IV).[9] The Geneva Conventions of 12 August 1949 are supplemented by the Protocol Additional to the Geneva Conventions of 12 August 1949, and Relating to the Protection of Victims of International Armed Conflicts of 12 December 1977 (AP I),[10] and the Protocol Additional to the Geneva Conventions of 12 August 1949, and Relating to the Protection of Victims of Non-International Armed Conflicts of 12 December 1977 (AP II).[11] AP I treats 'guerrilla warfare' in the exercise of self-determination against alien domination as an international armed conflict entitled to the protection accorded by AP I. AP I also widens the scope of protection accorded to victims of international armed conflicts under the four Geneva Conventions. Article 3, common to the four Geneva Conventions, provides a minimum protection for victims of armed conflict not of an international character. This is supplemented by AP II.

The meaning of the basic rules, including the terms used, will be analysed later on in this chapter.

---

[4] *Basic Rules of the Geneva Conventions and Their Additional Protocols* (ICRC, 1987) (hereinafter '*ICRC, Basic Rules*'), 7. See further: *Legality of the Threat or Use of Nuclear Weapons*, ICJ Advisory Opinion of 8 July 1996, ICJ Rep. 1996, para. 78; Green, *Contemporary Law of Armed Conflict*, chaps. 10–12, 14, 21.

[5] *UK Treaties Series* 9 (1910), Cd. 5030.

[6] 75 *UNTS* 31.

[7] 75 *UNTS* 85.

[8] 75 *UNTS* 135.

[9] 75 *UNTS* 287.

[10] 1125 *UNTS* 3.

[11] 1125 *UNTS* 609.

International humanitarian law applies from the initiation of an armed conflict and extends beyond the cessation of hostilities until a general conclusion of peace in the case of an international conflict, or a peaceful settlement in the case of an internal conflict. During that time, international humanitarian law applies in the whole territory of the warring States or, in the case of an internal conflict, the whole territory under the control of a party, irrespective of whether or not actual combat takes place there.[12]

The Appeals Chamber of the ICTY in the *Tadic* Jurisdiction Decision laid down the test to determine the existence of an armed conflict as follows:

'[A]n armed conflict exists whenever there is a resort to armed force between States or protracted armed violence between governmental authorities and organized armed groups or between such groups within a State.'[13]

The latter situation is to be distinguished from mere civil unrest or terrorist activities.

It should be noted that the customary international law of armed conflict does not require that there be declarations of hostilities before the law becomes applicable.[14]

Not every crime committed during an armed conflict is a war crime. A war crime must be sufficiently linked to an armed conflict itself although it suffices that the crime is closely related to the hostilities taking place in other parts of the territories controlled by the parties to the conflict.[15] It need not be part of a policy or of practice officially sanctioned or tolerated by one of the parties to the conflict, or committed in furtherance of a policy associated with the conduct of war or in the actual interest of a party to the conflict.[16]

War crimes under the Nuremberg and Tokyo Charters were those committed during international armed conflicts.

War crimes covered by the ICTY Statute are of two categories. Article 2 of the ICTY Statute proscribes grave breaches of the relevant provisions of the four Geneva Conventions of 1949 relating to the protection of victims of international armed conflicts, that is, grave crimes committed in an international armed conflict. Article 3 of the ICTY Statute proscribes 'violations of laws or customs of war', with an enumeration of a non-exhaustive list of such violations. Article 3 has been held to cover any such serious violation other than grave breaches irrespective of whether the violation

---

[12] *Prosecutor v. Dusko Tadic*, Case No. IT-94–1-AR72, App. Ch. of the ICTY, Decision of 2 Oct. 1995 on the Defence Motion for Interlocutory Appeal on Jurisdiction ('*Tadic* Jurisdiction Decision'), para. 70; *Prosecutor v. Tihomir Blaskic*, Case No. IT-95–14-T, ICTY T. Ch. I, 3 Mar. 2000, paras. 63–4.

[13] *Tadic* Jurisdiction Decision, ibid., quoted with approval *in Prosecutor v. Anto Furundzija*, Case No. IT-95–17/1-T, ICTY T. Ch. II, 10 Dec. 1998, para. 59; *Prosecutor v. Zejnil Delalic, Zdravko Mucic, Hazim Delic, Esad Landzo* ('*Celebici*' case), Case No. IT-96–21-T, ICTY T. Ch. II *quater*, 16 Nov. 1998, para. 183; *Prosecutor v. Jean-Paul Akayesu*, Case No. ICTR-96–4-T, ICTR T. Ch. I, 2 Sept. 1998, para. 619; *Prosecutor v. Goran Jelisic*, Case No. IT-95–10, ICTY T. Ch. I, 14 Dec. 1999, para. 29.

[14] Cf. Green, *Contemporary Law of Armed Conflict*, 69–70.

[15] *Tadic* Jurisdiction Decision, para. 70; *Celebici*, paras. 193–4.

[16] *Celebici*, para. 195.

occurs within the context of an international or non-international armed conflict.[17] Article 3 is also considered to constitute an 'umbrella rule' in the sense that serious violations of any international rule of humanitarian law may be regarded as crimes falling within its ambit if the requisite conditions are satisfied.[18] These conditions are set out by the Appeals Chamber of the ICTY in *Tadic* Jurisdiction Decision as follows:

'(i)   the violation must constitute an infringement of a rule of international humanitarian law;

(ii)   the rule must be customary in nature or, if it belongs to treaty law, the required conditions must be met;

(iii)   the violation must be "serious", that is to say, it must constitute a breach of a rule protecting important values, and the breach must involve grave consequences for the victim;

(iv)   the violation of the rule must entail, under customary or conventional law, the individual criminal responsibility of the person breaching the rule.'[19]

Therefore, Article 3 of the ICTY Statute covers such crimes as torture and outrages upon personal dignity including rape despite the fact that these crimes are not listed specifically in Article 3 itself.[20]

War crimes covered by the ICTR are those committed in an internal conflict. Article 4 of the ICTR Statute is under the heading 'Violations of Article 3 common to the Geneva Conventions and of Additional Protocol II [of the Geneva Conventions of 12 August 1949, and Relating to the Protection of Victims of Non-International Armed Conflicts of 8 June 1977]'.

War crimes under the ICC Statute are divided into four main categories.[21] War crimes in international armed conflicts are covered by Article 8(2)(a), which proscribes grave breaches of the Geneva Conventions of 12 August 1949, and by Article 8(2)(b), which proscribes 'other serious violations of the laws and customs applicable in international armed conflict, within the established framework of international law'. War crimes in non-international armed conflicts are covered by Article 8(2)(c), which proscribes serious violations of Article 3 common to the four Geneva Conventions of 12 August 1949, and by Article 8(2)(e), which proscribes 'other serious

---

[17] *Tadic* Jurisdiction Decision, paras. 86–94; *Celebici*, para. 297. Indeed, Art. 3 of the ICTY Statute is not limited to offences under the 'Hague law' that regulates the conduct of hostilities, especially the 1907 Hague Convention (IV) Respecting the Laws and Customs of War on Land ('Hague Convention IV'), but includes some violations of the Geneva Conventions of 1949. *Celebici*, para. 278.

[18] *Furundzija*, para. 133; *Jelisic*, para. 33; *Prosecutor v. Zlatko Aleksovski*, Case No. IT-95-14/1-A, ICTY App. Ch., 24 Mar. 2000 (hereinafter '*Aleksovski* (App. Ch.)'), para. 21.

[19] *Tadic* Jurisdiction Decision, para. 94. Also quoted in *Celebici*, para. 279; *Furundzija*, para. 258; *Aleksovski* (App. Ch.), para. 20.

[20] *Furundzija*, para. 158 and cf. paras. 137–42, 173.

[21] For a legislative history, see H. von Hebel and D. Robinson, 'Crimes within the Jurisdiction of the Court', in R. S. Lee (ed.), *The International Criminal Court: The Making of the Rome Statute—Issues, Negotiations, Results* (Kluwer, 1999), 79 at 103–22.

violations of the laws and customs applicable in armed conflicts not of an international character, within the established framework of international law'.

The ICC Statute enumerates war crimes in an exhaustive manner. Article 8(1) of the ICC Statute provides that the ICC shall have jurisdiction in respect of war crimes 'in particular when committed as a part of a plan or policy or as part of a large-scale commission of such crimes'. This is a jurisdictional threshold rather than an additional requirement for the elements of war crimes. The jurisdictional threshold is aimed at preventing the ICC from being overburdened with minor or isolated cases. It derived from the US proposal to provide a safeguard against the exercise of jurisdiction by the ICC over isolated cases of war crimes committed by US soldiers serving abroad.[22] However, the proviso 'in particular' does not rule out the ICC's exercising jurisdiction over war crimes 'not committed as a part of a plan or policy or as part of a large-scale commission of such crimes'. This is clear when one considers the fact that the US proposal to stipulate that the ICC shall have jurisdiction over war crimes 'only when committed as part of a plan or policy or as part of a large-scale commission of such crimes' was not accepted.[23]

The Introduction to the Elements of Crimes adopted by the Preparatory Commission for the International Criminal Court (PCNICC) for war crimes under Article 8 of the ICC Statute states explicitly that the elements 'shall be interpreted within the established framework of the international law of armed conflict including, as appropriate, the international law of armed conflict applicable to armed conflict at sea'.[24] This proviso takes into account the fact that customary international law of armed conflict, or international humanitarian law, has continued to evolve.[25]

CLASS OF PERPETRATORS

All types of persons could be held criminally liable for war crimes. Not only soldiers, but also men in the street, members of government, party officials and administrators, industrialists and businessmen, judges and prosecutors, doctors and nurses, executioners, and concentration camp inmates were found guilty of war crimes in

---

[22] Ibid., 107–108. Mr. von Hebel was Coordinator on the definition of war crimes at the Rome Conference.

[23] Ibid., 108, 124. See also M. H. Arsanjani, 'The Rome Statute of the International Criminal Court' (1999) 93 *AJIL* 22 at 33. Ms. Arsanjani served as the Secretary of the Committee of the Whole of the Rome Conference.

[24] Report of the Preparatory Commission for the International Criminal Court, *Doc. PCNICC/2000/1/ Add. 2*, 2 Nov. 2000. Such law has been codified in, e.g., *San Remo Manual on International Law Applicable to Armed Conflicts at Sea*, prepared by international lawyers and naval experts convened by the International Institute of Humanitarian Law, adopted in June 1994. See also D. P. O'Connell, *The International Law of the Sea*, ed. I. A. Shearer, ii (Clarendon Press, 1984), chaps. 29–30; W. H. von Heinegg, 'The Law of Armed Conflicts at Sea', in Fleck (ed.), *Handbook of Humanitarian Law*, 405.

[25] See T. Meron, *War Crimes Law Comes of Age: Essays* (Clarendon Press, 1998), chap. xiv ('The Continuing Role of Custom in the Formation of International Humanitarian Law').

post-WWII trials.[26] However, this is clarified by Trial Chamber II of the ICTR in *Kayishema and Ruzindana* as follows:

'. . . [I]ndividuals of all ranks belonging to the armed forces under the military command of either of the belligerent Parties fall within the class of perpetrators. If individuals do not belong to the armed forces, they could bear the criminal responsibility only when there is a link between them and the armed forces. It cannot be disregarded that the governmental armed forces are under the permanent supervision of public officials representing the government who had to support the war efforts and fulfil a certain mandate. On this issue, in the *Akayesu* Judgment, Trial Chamber I was correct to include in the class of perpetrators, "individuals who were legitimately mandated and expected as public officials or agents or persons otherwise holding public authority or *de facto* representing the Government to support or fulfil the war efforts".'[27]

Each crime is to be considered on a case-by-case basis, taking into account the material evidence and facts.[28] Thus, civilians may be held responsible for war crimes as well, as in the case of Hirota, the former foreign minister of Japan, who was convicted by the Tokyo Tribunal for war crimes committed during the 'Rape of Nanking', and that of the three civilians found guilty of the war crime of killing of unarmed prisoners of war in the *Essen Lynching* case.[29] In *Akayesu*, the accused wore a military jacket, carried a rifle, and assisted the military on their arrival in his commune where he was mayor by undertaking a number of tasks, including reconnaissance and mapping of the commune, and the setting up of radio communications. He also allowed the military to use his office premises. Yet, Trial Chamber I of the ICTR ruled that the accused could not incur individual criminal responsibility for war crimes because the Prosecution had failed to prove beyond reasonable doubt that the accused was a member of the armed forces, or that he was legitimately mandated and expected, as a public official or agent or person otherwise holding public authority or representing the government, to support or fulfil the war efforts.[30]

---

[26] See the authorities cited in in *Doc. PCNICC/1999/WGEC/INF. 1* of 19 Feb. 1999 (which was submitted on behalf of the ICRC), at 7–9.

[27] *Prosecutor v. Kayishema and Ruzindana*, Case No. ICTR-95–1, ICTR T. Ch. II, 21 May 1999, para. 175, quoting *Prosecutor v. Alfred Musema*, Case No. ICTR-96–13-T, para. 631. Followed in *Prosecutor v. George Rutaganda*, Case No. ICTR-96–3, ICTR T. Ch. I, 6 Dec. 1999, para. 96.

[28] *Kayishema and Ruzindana*, para. 176.

[29] *In re Heyer and Others* (*Essen Lynching* case), British Military Court, Essen, Germany, 22 Dec. 1945, *Ann. Dig.* 13 (1946), 287. Also cited in *Kayishema and Ruzindana*, paras. 633–4. See also *In re Tesch and Others* (*Zyklon B* case), British Military Court, Hamburg, 8 Mar. 1946, *Ann. Dig.* 13 (1951), 250; and *Prosecutor v. Alfred Musema*, Case No. ITCR-96–13-T, ICTR T. Ch. I, 27 Jan. 2000, paras. 264–75 and the cases cited therein.

[30] *Akayesu*, paras. 640–4.

CHARACTERIZATION OF A CONFLICT AS EITHER INTERNATIONAL OR INTERNAL

An armed conflict is international if it takes place between two or more States. An internal armed conflict breaking out on the territory of one State may become international or, depending upon the circumstances, be international in character alongside an internal armed conflict, if another State intervenes in that conflict through its troops,[31] or if some of the participants in the internal armed conflict act on behalf of that other State.[32]

If certain legal conditions are met, armed forces fighting in a *prima facie* internal armed conflict may be regarded as acting on behalf of a foreign Power, thereby rendering the conflict international because one State is deemed to be using force against another State.[33] The Appeals Chamber of the ICTY held in *Tadic* that the test is one of *control* by a foreign Power over paramilitary units and other irregulars in the conduct of hostilities in the territory of another State 'and, by the same token, *a relationship of dependence and allegiance*' of these irregulars *vis-à-vis* that foreign Power.[34] The Appeals Chamber reasoned that the test involves establishing the criteria for the legal imputability to a State of acts performed by individuals, and that reliance must be had upon the criteria established by general rules on State responsibility.[35] In the case of private individuals not having the status of State officials of a foreign State, the International Court of Justice ruled in *Military and Paramilitary Activities in and against Nicaragua* (*Nicaragua v. US*) that for State responsibility to be incurred, the private individuals must not only be paid or financed by that foreign State, and their action be coordinated or supervised by that State, but also that that State should issue specific instructions concerning the commission of the unlawful acts in question.[36] Nevertheless, the Appeals Chamber of the ICTY rejects the argument that the threshold for the test of control should be so high in each and every circumstance as set by *Nicaragua*. According to the ICTY Appeals Chamber:

'the requirement of international law for the attribution to States of acts performed by private individuals is that the State exercises control over the individuals. The *degree of control* may, however, vary according to the factual circumstances of each case . . .'[37]

---

[31] *Celebici*, paras. 208–34; *Blaskic*, paras. 83–94.

[32] *Prosecutor v. Dusko Tadic*, Case No. IT-94-A, ICTY App. Ch., 15 July 1999 (hereinafter '*Tadic* Appeals Judgment'), para. 84.

[33] Ibid., paras. 88–162. The issue was put more clearly by Presiding Judge Shahabudeen in his Separate Opinion, paras. 17–18, 26, 32.

[34] Ibid., para. 94. The test would ensure that the irregulars in fact 'belong' to a foreign Power and, as such, the foreign Power is a party to the armed conflict in question (ibid). That is to say, the question turns on the issue whether the irregulars could be considered as *de jure* or *de facto* organs of a foreign Power (ibid., para. 87).

[35] Ibid., paras. 98, 104–5.

[36] ICJ Rep. 1986, p. 14 at p. 62 *et seq.*, as interpreted by the ICTY Appeals Chamber in *Tadic* Appeals Judgment, para. 114.

[37] *Tadic* Appeals Judgment, para. 117. Emphasis in original.

There are three tests to determine whether an individual is acting as a *de facto* State organ.

First of all, in the context of armed conflicts, individuals having the formal status of organs of a State or individuals who make up organized and hierarchically structured groups, such as a military unit or armed bands of irregulars or rebels, are under the control of the State sponsoring them whether or not that State has issued specific instructions to those individuals.[38] After reviewing judicial decisions and State practice on this point, the ICTY Appeals Chamber states as follows:

'In order to attribute the acts of a military or paramilitary group to a State, it must be proved that the State wields *overall control* over the group, not only by equipping and financing the group, but also by coordinating or helping in the general planning of its military activity . . . However, it is not necessary that, in addition, the State should also issue, either to the head or to members of the group, instructions for the commission of specific acts . . .'[39]

Coordinating or helping in the general planning does not necessarily involve the controlling authorities planning all the operations of the units dependent on them, choosing their targets, or giving specific instructions concerning the conduct of military operations. The requisite control may be deemed to exist when a State or a Party to an armed conflict has 'a role in organizing, coordinating or planning the military actions of the military group, in addition to financing, training and equipping or providing operational support to that group' regardless of any specific instruction to the group.[40] The ICTY Appeals Chamber in *Aleksovski* clarifies that the 'overall control' test 'calls for an assessment of all the elements of control taken as a whole, and a determination to be made on that basis as to whether there was the required degree of control'.[41]

Another test is to be applied where individuals or groups are not organized into military structures. In this case, an overall or general level of control is not sufficient. There must be specific instructions or directives aimed at the commission of specific acts issued by a State to the individual or group in question, or it must be established that the act has been publicly endorsed or approved *ex post facto* by the State concerned.[42]

Finally, when private individuals act within the framework of, or in connection with, armed forces, or in collusion with State authorities, their acts may be assimilated

---

[38] Ibid., paras. 120–3.

[39] Ibid., para. 131. Emphasis added.

[40] Ibid., para. 137. Since the Appeals Chamber of the ICTY considered that the Bosnian Serb armed forces constituted a 'military organization', it applied the test of overall control to determine whether these armed forces acted as *de facto* organs of the Federal Republic of Yugoslavia (FRY). It found that the test was satisfied by the FRY's financial, logistical, and other assistance and support given to the Bosnian Serb armed forces, and, more importantly, the FRY's participation in the general direction, coordination and supervision of the activities and operations of the forces as well as an *ex post facto* confirmation of this overall control over the forces as evidenced in the process of negotiation and conclusion of the Dayton-Paris Accord of 1995 to end ethnic conflicts in the former Yugoslavia. It was therefore held in *Tadic* that the armed conflict in these circumstances was an international armed conflict. (Ibid., paras. 145–62.)

[41] *Aleksovski* (App. Ch.), para. 145.

[42] *Tadic* Appeals Judgment, paras, 131, 137.

to that of organs of the State in question on account of their actual behaviour within the structure of that State and regardless of any specific instructions by that State.[43] Thus, concentration camp inmates of Polish nationality and an Austrian Jew appointed by the German armed forces to oversee the Jewish concentration camps in Belsen and Auschwitz, Poland, during WWII 'could be regarded as having approximated to membership of the armed forces of Germany'.[44] Similarly, a Dutch national who was not formally a member of any German authority was found to have behaved in fact as a member of German special forces (SD or *Einsatzkommandos*) and was held to be criminally liable for war crimes and crimes against humanity for having killed a number of civilians in Poland during WWII on behalf of the German special forces.[45]

In all circumstances, it is recognized that while it may be relatively easy to establish the threshold of control where the controlling State in question is adjacent to the State in whose territory an armed conflict is taking place, more extensive and compelling evidence is required when the controlling State is not adjacent to such territorial State or where the general situation of turmoil, civil strife, and weakened authority exists in the territorial State.[46]

The tests formulated by the Appeals Chamber in *Tadic* were followed by Trial Chamber I of the ICTY in *Blaskic*.[47]

INTERNAL ARMED CONFLICTS OR ARMED CONFLICTS NOT OF AN INTERNATIONAL CHARACTER

In the light of the foregoing characterization of international armed conflicts, an internal armed conflict may be defined as an armed conflict that takes place in the territory of a State and which does not qualify as an international armed conflict as mentioned above. In other words, it is protracted armed conflict between government authorities and organized armed groups or between such groups within a State.[48] However, situations of internal disturbances and tensions, unorganized and short-lived insurrections, banditry, or terrorist activities are not subject to international humanitarian law.[49]

---

[43] Ibid., paras. 141, 144.

[44] *Trial of Joseph Kramer and 44 Others*, British Military Court, Luneberg, 17 Sept.–17 Nov. 1945, UNWCC *Law Reports*, ii, 1, at 152. Cited in *Tadic* Appeals Judgment, para. 142.

[45] *Public Prosecutor v. Menten*, Dutch Court of Cassation Judgment of 29 May 1978. (1987) 75 *ILR* 331 *et seq.* Cited in *Tadic* Appeals Judgment, para. 143.

[46] *Tadic*, Appeals Judgment, paras. 138–40. In this light, the Appeals Chamber reconciled its reasoning in *Tadic* with that of the ICJ in *Nicaragua* by stating that in order to establish the responsibility of the US for acts of irregular forces operating in and against Nicaragua, the circumstances of the case warrant that the ICJ demand proof of a higher threshold of control (the so-called 'effective control') that requires relatively more extensive and compelling evidence, including specific instructions issued by the US, over those irregular forces (ibid., para. 138). Followed in *Celebici*, App. Ch., 20 Feb. 2001, para. 47.

[47] *Blaskic*, paras. 95–123.

[48] *Tadic* Jurisdiction Decision, para. 70, also cited with approval in *Akayesu*, para. 619, and followed in Art. 8(2)(f) of the ICC Statute.

[49] *Prosecutor v. Dusko Tadic*, Case No. IT-94-1-T, ICTY T. Ch. II, 7 May 1997 (hereinafter '*Tadic* Judgment'), para. 562.

With respect to the ICC, this is made clear by Article 8(2)(d) and (f) of its Statute. Article 8(3) of the Statute adds that nothing in Article 8(2)(c) and (e) on war crimes in internal conflicts 'shall affect the responsibility of a Government to maintain or re-establish law and order in the State or to defend the unity and territorial integrity of the State, by all legitimate means'.

It should be noted that the PCNICC has made clear that with respect to the Elements of Crimes in the case of each of the war crimes under the ICC Statute:

'• There is no requirement for a legal evaluation by the accused as to the existence of an armed conflict or its character as international or non-international;

• In that context there is no requirement for awareness by the accused of the facts that established the character of the conflict as international or non-international;

• There is only a requirement for the awareness of the factual circumstances that established the existence of an armed conflict that is implicit in the terms "took place in the context of and was associated with" [as appeared in one of the elements of each war crime].'[50]

The list of war crimes in Article 8 of the ICC Statute is the most exhaustive of all such lists in international criminal statutes. This chapter will, therefore, proceed according to the order of the war crimes enumerated in Article 8 of the ICC Statute.

6.1 WAR CRIMES IN INTERNATIONAL ARMED CONFLICT

GRAVE BREACHES OF THE 1949 GENEVA CONVENTIONS OF 12 AUGUST 1949[51]

'Grave breaches' are serious war crimes that are subject to the universal jurisdiction of all States. Moreover, if a State does not prosecute the offender it shall extradite him to any party to the respective Geneva Conventions that will prosecute and punish that person.[52]

The international nature of the armed conflict is a prerequisite for the applicability of grave breaches of the Geneva Conventions of 1949.[53] The PCNICC has made clear

---

[50] *Doc. PCNICC/2000/1/ Add. 2*, 2 Nov. 2000.

[51] The author wishes to acknowledge his appreciation to the ICRC for the valuable analysis of the sources of law for each offence listed under Art. 8(2)(a) of the ICC Statute. See *Doc. PCNICC/1999/WGEC/INF. 1* of 19 Feb. 1999, submitted by the ICRC to the PCNICC.

[52] Arts. 49–50, GC I; Arts. 50–51, GC II; Arts. 129–130, GC III; and Arts. 146–7, GC IV.

[53] *Tadic* Jurisdiction Decision, paras. 79–84; *Celebici*, paras. 201–2. However, Trial Chamber II *quater* of the ICTY in *Celebici* alluded to the possibility of the customary law having developed the provisions of the four Geneva Conventions since 1949 by extending their customary scope to cover internal armed conflicts as well (*Celebici*, para. 202).

that, at least in the case of the ICC, the term 'international armed conflict' includes military occupation.[54]

Grave breaches must be committed against persons or property protected by any of the four Geneva Conventions of 1949, in particular civilians in the hands of a party to a conflict of which they are not nationals.[55] Since the four Geneva Conventions of 1949 are a part of customary international law,[56] so is the grave breach regime under these Geneva Conventions.

AP I extends the definition of grave breaches.[57] The reason why Article 8(2)(a) of the ICC Statute is confined to grave breaches of the 1949 Geneva Conventions only is because AP I has not enjoyed the same universal acceptance as the four Geneva Conventions.

Protected persons or property

The chapeau of Article 8(2)(a) of the ICC Statute provides that grave breaches of the Geneva Conventions of 1949 are the acts enumerated in that provision 'against persons or property protected under the provisions of the relevant Geneva Conventions'. This chapeau intends to take into account the differing lists of grave breaches in the respective Geneva Conventions and the differing categories of protected persons or property and the corresponding different systems of protection.[58]

In essence, protected persons are those who, for some reason, are not taking a direct or active part in the hostilities, for example, because they are wounded, sick, *hors de combat*, or are civilians.[59] As Trial Chamber II *quater* of the ICTY held in *Celebici* and Trial Chamber I of the ICTY held in *Blaskic*, there is no gap between the various Geneva Conventions of 1949—an individual is entitled to protection as a prisoner of war under GC III, protection against grave breaches afforded to soldiers under GC I or GC II, or protection under GC IV; there is no intermediate status.[60] This protection arises *ipso facto* and *ipso jure*. Thus, it is not even necessary for the adversary in whose hands a protected person finds himself to recognize that the person is entitled to the protection. In the trial of *Hideki Tojo*, the Tokyo Tribunal convicted the accused of having conspired to order, authorize, or permit the Japanese Army to commit war crimes against Chinese prisoners of war by disregarding their status and rights under the pretext that Japan did not recognize Japan's military action against China as a war.[61]

---

54 *Doc. PCNICC/2000/L. 1/Rev. 1/Add. 2*, at 16, n. 40.

55 *Tadic* Judgment, paras. 558–60.

56 *Tadic* Jurisdiction Decision, paras. 79–85.

57 See, e.g. Arts. 11, 44, 45, 73, 85(2) and (3). See also Green, *Contemporary Law of Armed Conflict*, 287–9.

58 von Hebel and Robinson, 'Crimes within Jurisdiction of the Court', 108.

59 Cf. also *Prosecutor v. Dragan Nikolic*, Case No. IT-94-2-R61, ICTY T. Ch. I, 20 Oct. 1995, para. 30; *Vukovar Rule 61 Decision*, Case No. IT-95-13-R61, ICTY T. Ch. I, 3 Apr. 1996, para. 25.

60 *Celebici*, para. 271; *Blaskic*, para.147. Protected persons are defined in, e.g. Arts. 13, 24, 25, and 26 of GC I; Arts. 13, 36, and 37 of GC II, Art. 4 of GC III; and Arts. 4, 13, 20 of GC IV.

61 B. V. A. Röling and C. F. Rüter (eds.), *The Tokyo Judgment*, i (APA—University Press Amsterdam BV, 1977), 461 at 463.

In general, civilians enjoy the protection against effects of hostilities unless, and as long as, they take a direct or active part in the hostilities.[62] Thus, civilians are all persons who are not combatants.[63] When civilians are compelled to use arms for the sole purpose of protecting their own lives, they are not thereby deprived of protection under international humanitarian law.[64]

To be entitled to the protection from grave breaches, protected persons must, at the relevant time, be 'in the hands of a party to the conflict or Occupying Power of which they are not nationals'.[65] The expression 'in the hands of' is to be understood not only in the physical sense of being held prisoner, but also in the sense of being present in territory under the control of an opposing party to the conflict.[66] Territory is under the control of an opposing party even if there exists a defended place or zone still in possession of the national forces within an occupied area, provided that such place or zone is surrounded and effectively cut off from the rest of the occupied area.[67] The precise date when the victims of the acts of the accused fall into the hands of the opposing armed forces is of critical relevance to the evaluation of their status as protected persons under international humanitarian law.[68]

The requirement that the persons to be protected must not be nationals of the adversary or Occupying Power in whose hands they find themselves is not to be applied strictly. Protection of individuals under international humanitarian law applies very broadly and the nationality test must be applied flexibly. As explained by the Appeals Chamber of the ICTY in *Tadic*, even as early as in 1949 when the four Geneva Conventions of 1949 were adopted the legal bond of nationality was not considered crucial in every case. In the case of civilians, GC IV, when interpreted in light of its object and purpose, is directed to the protection of civilians to the maximum extent possible. Its primary purpose is to safeguard those civilians who do not enjoy the diplomatic protection, and are not subject to the allegiance and control, of the State in whose hands they may find themselves. Thus, it protects not only civilians in enemy territory, occupied territory, or the combat zone who do not have the nationality of the belligerent in whose hands they find themselves, but also stateless persons and those civilians who are refugees and thus no longer owe allegiance to or had diplomatic protection by the Party to the conflict in whose hands they find

---

[62] This is clarified by Art. 51(3), AP I.

[63] *Celebici*, para. 272, and cf. Art. 50 of AP I. Since mercenaries are not considered by customary international law to be combatants, they would presumably be civilians, but since they take a direct or active part in the hostilities, the scope of their protection is relatively more limited than that of civilians taking no active part in the hostilities. They would, for example, be entitled to the right to a fair trial and the fundamental guarantees under Art. 75 of AP I, which extends to all 'persons who are in the power of a Party to the conflict and who do not benefit from more favourable treatment under the [Geneva Conventions] or under [AP I]' (Green, *Contemporary Law of Armed Conflict*, 112).

[64] *Prosecutor v. Zoran Kupreskic and Others*, Case No. IT-95–16-T, ICTY T. Ch. II, 14 Jan. 2000, para. 335.

[65] See, e.g. Art. 4(1) of GC IV.

[66] *Celebici*, para. 246; *Tadic* Judgment, para. 579. See also *Prosecutor v. Ivica Rajic*, Case No. IT-95–12-R61, ICTY T. Ch. II, 13 Sept. 1996, para. 37.

[67] *Tadic* Judgment, para. 580.

[68] Ibid., para. 579.

themselves and of which they are nationals. An example of this last mentioned situation is the case of German Jews who had fled to France before 1940 and thereafter found themselves in the hands of German forces occupying France. Nationals of a neutral State or a co-belligerent State are treated automatically as 'protected persons' when they lose or do not enjoy the normal diplomatic protection of the State of which they are nationals. In the complexity of present-day international armed conflicts that are inter-ethnic armed conflicts, like the one in the former Yugoslavia, ethnicity rather than nationality may become determinative of national allegiance.[69] Hence, the allegiance to a party to the conflict and control by that party over persons in a given territory may be the crucial test. It is the substance of relations between the persons and the State in whose hands they find themselves that matters the most, not formal bonds or purely legal relations in a domestic law applicable to these persons.[70] The Appeals Chamber of the ICTY held that even if, in the circumstances in *Tadic*, the Bosnian Serb perpetrators and their victims were to be regarded as nationals of Bosnia and Herzegovina (or of Yugoslavia before the enactment of a citizenship law in Bosnia and Herzegovina on 6 October 1992), the victims were 'protected persons' because they did not owe allegiance to and did not receive the diplomatic protection of the Federal Republic of Yugoslavia on whose behalf the Bosnian Serb armed forces had been fighting.[71] Similarly, in *Celebici*, Bosnian Serbs in the hands of Bosnian authorities were also treated as 'protected persons'.[72] The Elements of Crimes adopted by the PCNICC for the ICC, therefore, only requires that, with regard to nationality, the accused needs only to know that the victim belonged to an adverse party to the conflict.[73]

'Protected property' is not defined in any provision of the four Geneva Conventions of 1949 or Additional Protocol I, which merely provide a description of what cannot be attacked, destroyed, or appropriated. These include medical units and establishments, medical transports, and hospital ships, among others.[74] In customary international law, as enshrined in Article 53 of GC IV, any destruction by the Occupying Power of real or personal property is prohibited except in case of military necessity. Therefore, 'protected property' is that found in territories occupied by foreign forces, including those acting as a *de facto* organ or agent of a foreign State to the extent that it transforms the armed conflict concerned into an international one.[75]

---

[69] Cf. *Celebici*, paras. 263–5; *Blaskic*, paras. 126–33.

[70] *Tadic* Appeals Judgment, paras. 164–6, 168.

[71] Ibid., paras. 167–9. Cf. also the case of Muslims of Bosnia in *Blaskic*, paras. 145–6.

[72] *Celebici*, paras. 245–66, 274–5. Affirmed by the ICTY App. Ch. Judgment, paras. 54–99.

[73] Doc. *PCNICC/2000/ 1 /Add. 2*, n. 33. The four Geneva Conventions of 1949 introduce the term 'adverse party' in preference to 'enemy', as previously used, so as to extend the principles of international humanitarian law to every conflict, not just situations amounting to war in the traditional sense. (Green, *Contemporary Law of Armed Conflict*, 84.)

[74] See, e.g. Arts. 19, and 33–35 of GC I; Arts. 22, 24, 25, and 27 of GC II; Arts. 19, 21, 22, 33, 53, and 57 of GC IV.

[75] *Blaskic*, paras. 149–50, citing the *Rajic* Rule 61 Decision of 13 Sept. 1996, para. 42.

Property used for military purposes becomes a military object for so long as it is so used and, therefore, loses its status as protected property during that time.[76]

Constituent elements of the crimes

Trial Chamber I of the ICTY held in *Blaskic* that the *mens rea* of each of the grave breaches encompass such intention as recklessness that can be assimilated to serious criminal negligence.[77] Recklessness means the taking of an excessive risk.[78]

In the case of the ICC, however, the PCNICC's Elements of Crimes apply to the offences of grave breaches the general *mens rea* stipulated in Article 30 of the ICC Statute, namely, intent or knowledge, or both. The Elements of Crimes emphasize the perpetrator's knowledge of the factual circumstances that established the protected status of the individual victim or property under one or more of the Geneva Conventions of 1949 as well as factual circumstances that established the existence of an armed conflict, and the fact that the victim belonged to an adverse party to the conflict. The perpetrator's criminal conduct in question must also have taken place in the context of and been associated with an international armed conflict.

It is hereby submitted that the ICC should also take into consideration the jurisprudence of the ICTY regarding the *actus reus* and *mens rea* for grave breaches, so that international criminal law can develop in a coherent and harmonized manner as far as possible.

Article 8(2)(a)(i) of the ICC Statute—Wilful killing

According to existing international jurisprudence, the *actus reus* of this offence is the taking of lives of protected persons by whatever means.[79] It can be committed either by an act or an omission, provided that the conduct of the accused is a substantial cause of the death of the victim.[80] One study of post-WWII trials by the ICRC leads to the conclusion that the notion of 'wilful killing' must be limited to those acts or omissions contrary to existing treaty and customary law of armed conflict. Instances cited include the killing of a captured member of the opposing armed forces or a civilian inhabitant of occupied territory without a fair trial, reduction of rations for prisoners of war resulting in their starvation, and ill-treatment of prisoners of war in violation of the laws and usages of war causing their death.[81]

The *mens rea* required to establish the crimes of wilful killing (or *'l'homicide intentionnel'* in French) and murder as recognized by the Geneva Conventions is present where there is demonstrated an intention on the part of the accused to kill, or inflict serious injury, in reckless disregard of human life.[82] For example, if someone severely

---

[76] Cf. the general protection accorded to 'civilian objects' provided in Art. 52 of AP I.
[77] *Blaskic*, para. 152.
[78] *Celebici*, para. 437–9.
[79] Cf. *Celebici*, para. 431.
[80] Ibid., para. 424.
[81] *Doc. PCNICC/1999/WGEC/INF. 1*, at 12.
[82] *Celebici*, paras. 437–9; *Blaskic*, para. 153. Also *Celebici*, App. Ch. Judgment, para. 422.

beats his elderly victim over an extended period of time and leaves him without medical treatment in disregard of the risk that he might die from his injuries, and he actually dies therefrom, then the perpetrator is guilty of wilful killing.[83]

The *mens rea* may be inferred from the circumstances to determine whether the accused foresees death as a consequence of his acts or omissions, or the taking of an excessive risk that shows recklessness.[84] The accused could also be convicted of this offence if the Prosecution can prove his wilful neglect that amounts to recklessness in the sense of gross criminal or wicked negligence, or gross and criminal disregard of the accused's duties.[85]

With regard to the ICC Statute, the Elements of Crimes adopted by the PCNICC for this war crime simply stipulate that the perpetrator must have killed, or caused death to, one or more persons.

Article 8(2)(a)(ii) of the ICC Statute—Torture or inhuman treatment, including biological experiments

Torture: Torture may be prosecuted as a grave breach, a serious violation of humanitarian law, a crime against humanity, or genocide. In general, the crime of torture under customary international law comprises 'acts or omissions, by or at the instigation of, or with the consent or acquiescence of an official, which are committed for a particular prohibited purpose and cause a severe level of mental or physical pain or suffering'.[86]

Torture is the most specific of those offences of mistreatment constituting 'grave breaches'.[87] In the context of torture as a war crime, the following elements are required:

'(i) torture consists of the infliction, by act or omission, of severe pain or suffering, whether physical or mental; in addition

(ii) this act or omission must be intentional;

(iii) it must aim at obtaining information or a confession, or at punishing, intimidating, humiliating or coercing the victim or a third person, or at discriminating, on any ground, against the victim or a third person;

(iv) it must be linked to an armed conflict;

---

[83] These were the circumstances involving the wilful killing of the victim named Simo Jovanovic in *Celebici* (ibid., paras. 842, 845, and Annex B—The Indictment, para. 18).

[84] Ibid., para. 437.

[85] *Doc. PCNICC/1999/WGEC/INF. 1*, at 14.

[86] *Celebici*, para. 442. See also paras. 443, 452–74. The ICTY Trial Chamber reaches this definition after comparing the three existing definitions of torture under the 1984 Convention Against Torture and Other Cruel, Inhuman or Degrading Treatment or Punishment (UN Doc. A/RES/39/46 of 10 Dec. 1984), the Declaration on the Protection of all Persons from Being Subjected to Torture and Other Cruel, Inhuman or Degrading Treatment or Punishment (UN Doc. GA Res. 3452 (XXX) of 9 Dec. 1975), and the 1985 Inter-American Convention to Prevent and Punish Torture (1986) **25** *ILM* 519. These elements are upheld as correct by the ICTY Appeals Chambers in *Prosecutor v. Anto Furundzija*, Case No. IT-95–17/1-A, 21 July 2000 [hereinafter '*Furundzija* (App. Ch.)'], para. 111.

[87] *Celebici*, para. 442.

(v)at least one of the persons involved in the torture process must be a public official or must at any rate act in a non-private capacity, e.g. as a *de facto* organ of a State or any other authority-wielding entity.'[88]

International jurisprudence has not specifically set the threshold level of suffering or pain required for this crime—all depends on the circumstances of each case.[89]

Official involvement covers situations where officials take a passive attitude or turn a blind eye to torture, 'most obviously by failing to prevent or punish torture under national penal or military law, when it occurs'.[90]

The jurisprudence of the ICTY does not mention one important part of the definition of torture under the relevant conventions, that is, the pain or suffering arising only from, inherent in, or incidental to lawful sanctions are excluded from the scope of this crime. It seems that what is permissible is to be judged according to international law—what is lawful under domestic law may not be lawful from the perspective of international law, especially international criminal law.

It has now been held that rape can be torture if the act meets the criteria involved.[91] This should lay to rest the debate as to whether rape could be among the grave breaches subject to universal jurisdiction.[92]

The Appeals Chamber of the ICTY in *Furundzija* upheld the conclusion of the Trial Chamber in that case that an act short of rape could also be torture. In that case, amidst the laughter and stares of on-looking soldiers, the accused rubbed a knife against a nude woman's thighs and stomach, threatening to insert the knife into her vagina if she did not tell the truth in answer to the interrogation by the accused. These acts altogether were held to be intimidating and humiliating to the extent that they had devastating impact on the physical and mental state of the victim.[93]

With regard to the requisite *mens rea*, the accused must inflict torture on the victim for a prohibited purpose, and there is no exhaustive list of these purposes.[94] However, that prohibited purpose must not be a purely private one, since the prohibition of torture is not concerned with private conduct, which is normally sanctioned under national law.[95] Yet, it would be very exceptional to find the infliction of severe pain or suffering by a public official during armed conflict not an act of torture on the ground that he acts for purely private reasons.[96]

In the case of the ICC, the PCNICC has done away with the requirement of official involvement in all offences of torture and the purpose of torture as a crime of

[88] *Furundzija*, para. 162.
[89] Doc. PCNICC/1999/WGEC/INF. 1, at 16–20.
[90] *Celebici*, para. 474.
[91] *Celebici*, paras. 475–93, 496; *Furundzija*, paras. 163, 171; *Akayesu*, paras. 597–8.
[92] See, e.g., T. Meron, 'Rape as a Crime under International Humanitarian Law' (1993) 87 *AJIL* 424 at 425–7.
[93] *Furundzija* (App. Ch.), para. 112.
[94] *Celebici*, para. 470.
[95] Ibid., para. 471.
[96] Ibid.

genocide or a crime against humanity, but it still retains the purpose element for torture as a war crime. This is because torture in war crimes is committed in a different context from that committed in genocide or a crime against humanity: torture in war crimes is committed with a specific purpose to further the war effort.

Thus, the pertinent part of the Elements of Crimes for the war crime of torture as a grave breach stipulates that the perpetrator must have inflicted severe physical or mental pain or suffering upon one or more persons for such purposes as: obtaining information or a confession, punishment, intimidation or coercion, or for any reason based on discrimination of any kind.

Inhuman treatment: Inhuman treatment is an intentional act or omission which, if judged objectively, is deliberate and not accidental, and which (a) causes serious mental or physical suffering or injury, or (b) constitutes a serious attack on physical or mental integrity or health, or (c) is contrary to the fundamental principle of human treatment, in particular an attack on human dignity.[97]

Inhuman treatment includes subjecting others to 'inhumane conditions'.[98] What is inhuman must be considered in the light of the circumstances of each case.[99]

Examples of inhuman treatment include forcing brothers to perform fellatio on one another and forcing a father and son to beat one another repeatedly over a period of at least ten minutes.[100] However, the mere fact that inmates of a prison camp have to be content with overcrowding, and a lack of appropriate medical care or nourishment, may not be sufficient in themselves to amount to inhuman treatment if this situation mirrors the general conditions prevailing in a territory ravaged by armed conflict, independently of the wish of the accused, and the accused has no intent to treat an inmate or inmates inhumanely by his act or omission.[101] It would be different if the inmates were subjected to physical or mental violence or the atmosphere of terror in the camp, or were forced to serve as human shields or to dig trenches in the frontline thereby being exposed to the danger of death, or were deliberately detained for a long period in conditions of hardship.[102] It is relevant to consider whether the poor conditions of detention are a result of the deliberate intention, negligence, failure to act, or intentional discrimination of the person responsible for the detention. The *mens rea* of the offence is the intent to humiliate or ridicule the victim;

---

[97] Ibid., paras. 442, 543, 558; *Blaskic*, para. 155. Affirmed in *Celebici*, App. Ch., para. 426.

[98] *Celebici*, para. 558.

[99] Ibid., para. 544; *Blaskic*, para. 155.

[100] *Celebici*, paras. 1066, 1070.

[101] Cf. *Prosecutor v. Zlatko Aleksovski*, ICTY T. Ch. I, 25 June 1999 (hereinafter '*Aleksovski* Judgment'), paras. 158, 164, 173, 182, 212–5, 219, 221. Although the ICTY in that case rules in para. 46 (albeit wrongly in the light of *Tadic* Appeals Judgment) that the armed conflict in that case was an internal conflict, it rules in paras. 49–51 and 228 that the laws and customs of war in the context of Common Article 3 of the Geneva Conventions proscribe 'inhuman treatment in a general manner'. Therefore, its legal opinion on this point is relevant to the consideration of 'inhuman treatment' in cases of international armed conflicts as well.

[102] *Blaskic*, paras. 700, 709, 713.

however, the Prosecution need not prove a discriminatory intent, which is not a necessary element of the offence.[103]

In general, torture is the most aggravated form of inhuman treatment.[104] All cruel treatment falling short of torture because they fail to meet the purpose and severity required in case of torture is inhuman treatment.[105] For example, in *Celebici*, one of the defendants was found guilty of inhuman and cruel treatment through his use of an electrical shock device on his victims.[106] Of the offences within the framework of mistreatment, inhuman treatment extends the furthest to other acts that violate the fundamental principle of humane treatment, particularly human dignity.[107] In *Tadic*, the accused was charged alternatively with torture or inhuman treatment but the Appeals Chamber of the ICTY for some unexplained reason failed to specify in respect of which of the two offences it found him guilty. At the sentencing stage, the Trial Chamber applied the principle of *in dubio pro reo*—any ambiguity must accrue to the defendant's advantage, and sentenced the accused for the lesser offence of inhuman treatment.[108]

The victim of the war crime of 'inhumane act' need not be a living human being since certain acts against a dead body offend philosophical and religious notions of respect for the human being upon death. Thus, in *Trial of Max Schmid*, the accused was convicted of having wilfully, deliberately, and wrongfully participated in the maltreatment of a dead prisoner of war by mutilating his corpse and denying him an honourable burial.[109]

With regard to the ICC Statute, the PCNICC has defined the distinctive element of the Elements of Crimes for this war crime simply as the infliction by the perpetrator of severe physical or mental pain or suffering upon one or more persons.

Biological experiments: Biological experiments are a form of inhuman treatment that is a grave breach. The formulation 'torture or inhuman treatment, including biological experiments' is copied from the one appearing in Article 50 of GC I, Article 51 of GC II, Article 140 of GC III, and Article 147 of GC IV. Unfortunately, the term 'biological experiments' is not defined in any provision of the four Geneva Conventions of 1949 or their Additional Protocols. The relevant provisions of the Conventions just proscribe any form of 'scientific experiment', even where carried out with the consent of the victim, if such experiment is not justified by the medical, dental, or hospital treatment of the victim and not carried out in his interest. The procedure to be followed in any scientific experiment must be dictated by the state of

---

[103] *Aleksovski* (App. Ch.), paras. 18–28. The ICTY Appeals Chamber in that case held that the prohibition of outrages upon personal dignity is a category of the broader proscription of inhuman treatment under Art. 2(b) of the ICTY Statute as a grave breach of the Geneva Conventions of 1949 (ibid., para. 26).

[104] *Greek Case*, European Commission of Human Rights, (1969) 12 *Y.B. Eur. Conv. Hum. Rights* 186.

[105] See the cases and international instruments cited in *Furundzija*, n. 179–80, 196. Cf. also *Jelisic*, para. 52.

[106] *Celebici*, para. 1264.

[107] Ibid., para. 544.

[108] *Prosecutor v. Dusko Tadic*, ICTY T. Ch. II, Sentencing Judgment of 11 Nov. 1999, paras. 30–1.

[109] *Trial of Max Schmid*, UNWCC *Law Reports*, xiii, 151–2. Cited in *Tadic* Judgment, para. 748.

health of the person concerned and consistent with generally accepted medical stand-ards applicable under similar medical circumstances to persons who are nationals of the authority conducting the procedure and who are in no way deprived of liberty.[110]

The Elements of Crimes adopted by the PCNICC to guide the ICC in this instance add very little. The perpetrator must have subjected one or more persons to a particu-lar biological experiment which seriously endangered the physical or mental health or integrity of such person or persons. The intent of the experiment must have been non-therapeutic and neither justified by medical reasons nor carried out in such person's or persons' interest.

Article 8(2)(a)(iii) of the ICC Statute—Wilfully causing great suffering, or serious injury to body or health

This offence is distinguishable from torture primarily on the basis that the alleged act or omissions need not be committed for a prohibited purpose such as is required for an offence of torture.[111] Trial Chamber II *quater* of he ICTY held in *Celebici* that the constituent elements of this offence are:

'an act or omission that is intentional, being an act which, judged objectively, is deliberate and not accidental, which causes serious mental or physical suffering or injury. It covers those acts that do not meet the purposive requirements for the offence of torture, although clearly all acts constituting torture could also fall within the ambit of this offence.'[112]

The words 'great suffering' are not qualified by the words 'to body or health' as in the case of 'serious injury'; hence, 'great suffering' includes mental as well as physical suffering.[113] According to the Oxford English Dictionary, 'great' means 'much above average in size, amount, or intensity', whereas 'serious' means 'not slight or negligible'.[114]

In *Celebici* itself, three of the accused were found guilty of this offence as well as the offence of cruel treatment for having subjected the inmates of the Celebici prison-camp to an atmosphere of terror created by the killing and abuse of detainees and to inhumane living conditions by being deprived of adequate food, water, medical care, as well as sleeping and toilet facilities, thereby causing the detainees to suffer severe psychological and physical trauma.[115]

The use of 'or' between 'great suffering' and 'serious injury' as well as between 'body' and 'health' makes it clear that it suffices for the Prosecution to prove that an act or omission meets the *actus reus* and *mens rea* concerning 'great suffering' or 'serious injury' to either the 'body' or 'health'.[116] This offence also includes rape.[117]

---

[110] See, e.g. Art. 13 of GC III, Art. 32 of GC IV, and Art. 11 of AP I.

[111] *Celebici*, para. 442.

[112] Ibid., para. 511; *Blaskic*, para. 156. Also *Celebici*, App. Ch. Judgment, para. 424.

[113] *Celebici*, para. 509.

[114] Ibid., para. 510.

[115] *Celebici*, para. 1119.

[116] Ibid., para. 506; *Blaskic*, para. 156.

[117] This was the position of the ICRC at the Rome Conference. Mentioned in *Furundzija*, n. 192.

In the case of the ICC, the Elements of Crimes adopted by the PCNICC follow established international jurisprudence for this offence.

Article 8(2)(a)(iv) of the ICC Statute—Extensive destruction and appropriation of property, not justified by military necessity and carried out unlawfully and wantonly

The ICTY held in *Celebici* that the prohibition against unjustified appropriation of public and private property is general in scope, and extends both to acts of looting committed by individual soldiers for their private gain, and to the organized seizure of property undertaken within the framework of a systematic economic exploitation of occupied territory.[118] Violation of this prohibition is a breach of a rule protecting important values.[119]

Unjustifiable extensive destruction of property. One essential distinction between the war crime of extensive destruction of property not justified by military necessity and carried out unlawfully and wantonly as a grave breach, on the one hand, and war crimes involving intentional attacks against non-military objects which are 'other serious violations of the laws and customs applicable in international armed conflict'[120] which are not grave breaches, on the other, is the extensive nature of the war crimes in the former category. An isolated act would not suffice to constitute a grave breach.[121]

In post-WWII trials, setting fire to, pulling down, mutilating, or damaging property were held to be destruction of property.[122]

Unjustifiable appropriation of property. Unjustifiable appropriation of property includes pillage and plunder. The concept of pillage in the traditional sense implies an element of violence not necessarily present in the offence of plunder which embraces all forms of unlawful appropriation of property in armed conflict for which individual criminal responsibility attaches in international law, including those acts traditionally described as 'pillage'.[123]

The term 'plunder' is used interchangeably with the words 'spoliation' and 'exploitation'. They all mean appropriation in which the owner is deprived of his property involuntarily and against his will by threats, intimidation, pressure, or by using the position or power of the military occupant under circumstances indicating that the owner is induced to part with his property against his will.[124] Spoliation is the widespread and systematic acts of dispossession and acquisition of property in viola-

---

[118] *Celebici*, para. 590.

[119] Ibid., para. 1154.

[120] As in, e.g. Art. 8(2)(b)(ii) and (iii) of the ICC Statute.

[121] Pictet (ed.), *Commentary IV Geneva Convention* (ICRC, 1958), Art. 147, at 601.

[122] *Doc. PCNICC/1999/WGEC/INF. 1*, at 38–9.

[123] *Celebici*, para. 591.

[124] *In re Krauch and Others* ('*I. G. Farben*' case), US Military Tribunal at Nuremberg, 29 July 1948, TWC, viii (1952), at 1133; also in (1953) 15 *Ann. Dig.* 668 at 672–7.

tion of the owner's rights.[125] Any form of deprivation of property, including theft or requisition, is appropriation.[126] With regard to plunder, Trial Chamber I of the ICTY found the accused in *Jelisic* guilty of plunder of public or private property in violation of the laws or customs of war, as proscribed by Article 3(e) of the ICTY Statute, for his acts of robbing money, watches, jewellery, and other valuable objects belonging to the detainees in a makeshift detention facility in the former Yugoslavia in 1992, accompanied by threats to kill those who refused to give him all their possessions.[127] In the opinion of the Trial Chamber, plunder is a fraudulent or arbitrary appropriation of public or private property belonging to the enemy or adverse party, committed in the context of an armed conflict and is connected thereto. It may be committed by isolated acts of soldiers for their own private gain or to satisfy their personal greed, or by organized appropriation within the framework of systematic economic exploitation of an occupied territory.[128]

In order to be a war crime, which is a 'serious' violation of international humanitarian law, although the unjustifiable appropriation is *per se* a breach of a rule protecting important values, it must also have grave consequences for the victim. Thus, where it is not proven that any property taken from the victim is of 'sufficient monetary value for its unlawful appropriation to involve grave consequences for the victim', then it is not a serious violation of international humanitarian law.[129] In *Blaskic*, the accused was held to be responsible for, *inter alia*, pillage that comprised the theft of money belonging to private persons, seizure of 2,000 DM, and jewellery belonging to one victim as well as seizure of money in the wallet of another victim, and the taking of the amount of 400 DM from a corpse.[130] Therefore, the issue of 'seriousness' is to be determined on a case-by-case basis. Likewise, to be a grave breach, the destruction or appropriation must be extensive and carried out unlawfully and wantonly and without justifiable military necessity.[131]

This offence requires proof of the unlawfulness of the act in question and of the fact that it exceeds military necessity. The lawfulness or unlawfulness in question must refer to that of international law, especially the relevant provisions of the four Geneva Conventions and the Hague Regulations (1907), as well as any newly established rules of customary international law. For instance, Article 53 of GC IV generally prohibits the Occupying Power from destroying real or personal property belonging individually

---

[125] Ibid.

[126] Cf. *Doc. PCNICC/1999/WGEC/INF. 1*, at 43–4.

[127] *Jelisic*, para. 49.

[128] *Jelisic*, para. 48, following *Celebici*, para. 590. It is hereby submitted that the term 'fraudulent' or 'arbitrary' appropriation may be understood as 'unlawful' appropriation, as used in *Celebici*.

[129] *Celebici*, para. 1154. The Trial Chamber of the ICTY in *Celebici* was considering the charge of plunder in the context of the *ratione materiae* of the ICTY under the ICTY Statute. Art. 1 of the ICTY Statute stipulates that the ICTY shall have the power to prosecute persons responsible for 'serious violations of international humanitarian law' committed in the territory of the former Yugoslavia since 1991 in accordance with the provisions of that Statute.

[130] *Blaskic*, para. 424.

[131] Ibid., para. 157.

or collectively to private persons, the State, other public authorities, or social or cooperative organizations, except where military operations render it absolutely necessary. Article 33 of GC IV makes it unlawful to undertake reprisals against private persons and their property. Article 56 of the Hague Regulations (1907) prohibits all seizure of, destruction or wilful damage done to institutions dedicated to religion, charity, and education, the arts and sciences, even when they are State property.[132]

The requisite *mens rea* for this offence is 'wantonly'. It has been noted by the ICRC that the *mens rea* required in post-WWII trials for this kind of offence is that the offence must be committed 'wilfully and knowingly' or 'intentionally'.[133]

The Elements of Crimes adopted by the PCNICC to guide the ICC regarding this war crime state the obvious. The perpetrator must have extensively and wantonly destroyed or appropriated certain property. Such destruction or appropriation must not have been justified by military necessity.

Article 8(2)(a)(v) of the ICC Statute—Compelling a prisoner of war or other protected person to serve in the forces of a hostile Power

The US Military Tribunal operating under Control Council Law No. 10 held in the *Ministries* case that while it is not illegal to recruit prisoners of war who volunteer to fight against their own country, 'pressure or coercion to compel such persons to enter into the armed services obviously violates international law'.[134] Therefore, the term 'compelling' means using pressure or coercion to force someone to do something.

As for the *mens rea*, the US Military Tribunal held the accused in the *Milch* case guilty of 'unlawfully, wilfully, and knowingly' guilty of participating in 'plans and enterprises involving the use of prisoners of war in war operations and work having a direct relation with war operations'.[135]

The Elements of Crimes adopted by the PCNICC to guide the ICC in the case of this war crime provide simply that the perpetrator must have coerced one or more persons, by act or threat, to take part in military operations against that person's own country or forces or otherwise serve in the forces of a hostile power.

Article 8(2)(a)(vi) of the ICC Statute—Wilfully depriving a prisoner of war or other protected person of the rights of fair and regular trial

This provision is derived directly from Article 130 of GC III and Article 147 of GC IV. The rights of fair and regular trial enshrined in these instruments include: the right of the accused to be judged by an independent and impartial court (Article 84(2) of GC III), the right to be promptly informed of the offences with which the accused is charged (Article 104 of GC III, and Article 71(2) of GC IV), the right against collective penalty (Article 87 of GC III, and Article 33 of GC IV), the right to the protection

---

[132] See further *Doc. PCNICC/1999/WGEC/INF. 1*, at 35–41.
[133] Ibid., at 43–4.
[134] *In re Weizsaecker and* Others, US Military Tribunal at Nuremberg, 14 Apr. 1949 (1955) **16** *Ann. Digest* 344 at 357.
[135] TWC, vii, at 27 *et seq.*

under the principles of legality (Article 99 (1) of GC III, and Article 67 of GC IV), the right not to be punished more than once for the same act (*ne bis in idem*)(Article 86 of GC III, and Article 117(3) of GC IV), the right to be informed of his rights of appeal (Article 106 of GC III, and Article 73 of GC IV), and the right not to be sentenced or executed without previous judgment pronounced by a regularly constituted court that affords all the judicial guarantees recognized as indispensable by civilized peoples (Common Article 3 of the four Geneva Conventions).[136]

Of course, other internationally recognized rights to ensure fair and regular trials which are not included in GC III or GC IV are to be observed also.

The ICRC considers that the case law of post-WWII trials show that the offence must be committed 'wilfully and knowingly'.[137]

In the case of the ICC, the distinctive element as adopted by the PCNICC for this war crime is that the perpetrator must have deprived one or more persons of a fair and regular trial by denying judicial guarantees as defined, in particular, in the third and the fourth Geneva Conventions of 1949.

Article 8(2)(a)(vii) of the ICC Statute—Unlawful deportation or transfer or unlawful confinement

This offence is derived directly from Article 147 of GC IV. Since GC IV was concluded in 1949 after the post-WWII trials, it must be presumed that GC IV incorporates the law pronounced by these trials[138] that the international community considered to be reflective of customary law.

Unlawful deportation or transfer. Article 45 of GC IV proscribes as unlawful the transfer of protected persons to a State not party to GC IV unless it is their country of residence to which they are to be repatriated after the cessation of hostilities. Protected persons may be transferred to a State Party to GC IV only after the detaining State has satisfied itself of the willingness and ability of such transferee State to apply GC IV and shall take effective measures to rectify the situation or shall request the return of the protected persons if the transferee State fails to carry out its obligations under GC IV in any important respect. It is prohibited to transfer a protected person to any State where he may have reason to fear persecution for his political opinions or religious beliefs. However, it is permissible to extradite protected persons accused of offences against ordinary criminal law pursuant to extradition treaties concluded before the outbreak of hostilities.

In addition, Article 49 of GC IV proscribes as unlawful individual or mass 'transfers, as well as deportations' of protected persons from occupied territory to the territory of the Occupying Power or to that of any other State, occupied or not, regardless of their motive. However, the Occupying Power may undertake total or partial evacuation of a given area to another area within the occupied territory if

---

[136] See further *Doc. PCNICC/1999/WGEC/INF. 1*, at 46–9.
[137] Ibid., at 49–50. See also Green, *Contemporary Law of Armed Conflict*, 297–8.
[138] Cf. the cases cited in *Doc. PCNICC/ 1999/ WGEC/ INF. 1*, at 52.

necessitated by the security of the population or imperative military reasons. Displacement of protected persons outside the occupied territory is prohibited unless it is impossible to avoid this for material reasons. In any event, persons so evacuated must not be detained in an area particularly exposed to the dangers of war unless necessitated by the security of the population or imperative military reasons. They must be transferred back to their homes as soon as hostilities in the area in question have ceased. Above all, it is unlawful for the Occupying Power to deport or transfer parts of its own population into the territory it occupies.

The ICRC notes that in several post-WWII trials, the accused were found guilty of these types of offences on the basis that they committed the offences 'wilfully and knowingly in violation of international conventions'.[139]

As for the ICC, the distinctive element adopted by the PCNICC for the war crime of unlawful deportation and transfer as a grave breach provides simply that the perpetrator must have deported or transferred one or more persons to another State or to another location.

Unlawful confinement. Under international humanitarian law, during armed conflict the individual freedom of civilians in the territory of a party to an armed conflict remains unimpaired, irrespective of whether they are nationals or aligned with an enemy party, subject to certain exceptions.[140] Article 27(4) of GC IV permits 'such measures of control and security as may be necessary as the result of war'. The general exception laid down in Article 5 of GC IV is that those definitely suspected of or engaged in activities hostile to the security of the State, spies, or saboteurs, may be lawfully confined because of their activities that are prejudicial or hostile to the security of that State. The adversary may intern people or place them in an assigned residence if it has 'serious and legitimate reasons' to think that they may seriously prejudice its security by means such as sabotage or espionage. Such activities must involve material, direct harm to the adversary, and not just mere support to the forces of the party with which the civilian is sided.[141] While the decision of whether a civilian is a security threat is largely left to the decision of the State, the State cannot take security measures to confine civilians on a collective basis. Thus, in *Celebici* while a number of civilians detained in the Celebici prison-camp were in possession of weapons at the time of their capture which could have been used or were in fact used against the forces of the detaining authority, the confinement in the prison-camp of other civilians could not be justified by any means since they could not 'reasonably have been considered to pose any sufficiently serious danger to the detaining forces as to warrant their detention'.[142]

Security measures taken to confine a civilian must be taken on the justification of absolute necessity, with no less severe alternative means available. As stipulated in Article 42 of GC IV:

---

[139] Ibid.   [140] *Celebici*, paras. 565–83.   [141] Ibid., para. 575.   [142] Ibid., paras. 1131–2.

'The internment or placing in assigned residence of protected persons may be ordered only if the security of the Detaining Power makes it absolutely necessary.

If any person, acting through the representatives of the Protecting Power, voluntarily demands internment, and if his situation renders this step necessary, he shall be interned by the Power in whose hands he may be.'

If a civilian is confined in violation of Article 42 of GC IV, such confinement is unlawful. An initially lawful confinement becomes unlawful if it violates Article 43 of GC IV, which provides:

'Any protected person who has been interned or placed in assigned residence shall be entitled to have such action reconsidered as soon as possible by an appropriate court or administrative board designated by the Detaining Power for that purpose. If the internment or placing in assigned residence is maintained, the court or administrative board shall periodically, and at least twice yearly, give consideration to his or her case, with a view to the favourable amendment of the initial decision, if circumstances permit.'

This was the case concerning the detainees of the Celebici prison-camp. Even if it might be argued that the initial confinement of a number of the detainees was lawful, their continued confinement became unlawful because they were not granted the procedural rights required by Article 43 of GC IV in the sense that no judicial body existed to review their detention.[143] The ICTY emphasizes that respect of the procedural rights of the protected persons is a fundamental principle of GC IV as a whole.[144]

GC I, GC II, and GC III also prohibit unlawful confinement of protected persons within the scope of these respective instruments. They encompass both the conditions as well as modalities of confinement and necessary judicial guarantees. The following are some important examples of the relevant provisions of these instruments.

Article 28 of GC I permits retention of medical personnel, chaplains attached to the armed forces, and staff of National Red Cross Societies and that of other Voluntary Aid Societies only insofar as the state of health, the spiritual needs, and the number of prisoners of war require. Article 30 of GC I requires that personnel whose retention is not indispensable pursuant to Article 28 shall be returned to the Party to the conflict to whom they belong, as soon as a road is open for their return and military requirements allow. Article 32 of GC I proscribes detention of medical personnel of a recognized Society of a neutral State who have fallen into the hands of the adverse party.

GC II provides in Article 36 that the religious, medical, and hospital personnel of hospital ships and their crews may not be captured during the time they are in the service of the hospital ship, whether or not there are wounded and sick on board. Article 37 of GC II requires that these persons who fall into the hands of the adverse party be sent back after they have finished their duties in taking care of the wounded and sick under their responsibility as soon as the Commander-in-Chief of that adverse party considers it practicable.

---

[143] Ibid., paras. 1135, 1141.   [144] Ibid., para. 582. Affirmed on appeal.

GC III contains rather extensive conditions and modalities concerning confinement of prisoners of war. In general, prisoners of war may not be confined in close confinement except where necessary to safeguard their health and only during the continuation of the circumstances which make such confinement necessary. It is unlawful to confine them in premises not located on land and affording every guarantee of hygiene, healthiness, and safety. They may not be confined in penitentiaries except where justified by their own interest. It is unlawful to confine any prisoner of war to more than thirty days for any single punishment even if the prisoner of war is answerable for several acts at the same time, whether or not such acts are related. A prisoner of war shall not be confined while awaiting trial or disciplinary hearing unless a member of the armed forces of the Detaining Power would be so confined if he were accused of a similar offence, or if it is essential to do so in the interests of camp order and discipline or national security, respectively. It is unlawful to confine seriously wounded and seriously sick prisoners of war who are fit to travel back to their own State. It is also unlawful to confine prisoners of war after the cessation of hostilities.[145]

The distinctive element adopted by the PCNICC to guide the ICC regarding the war crime of unlawful confinement as a grave breach simply stipulates that the perpetrator must confine or continue to confine one or more persons to a certain location.

Article 8(2)(a)(viii) of the ICC Statute—Taking of hostages

'Hostages' are innocent non-combatants in the occupied territory who are unlawfully deprived of their liberty, often arbitrarily and sometimes under threat of death;[146] they are seized and held in custody as an anticipatory precaution against the enemy or in order to secure a promise from the enemy, such as using them as a screen against the enemy for the advancing or retreating force or killing them in order to terrorize and repress a resistance movement.[147] Their detention could be lawful in certain circumstances, notably when it is necessary to protect civilians or when it is so required by reason of security.[148] To find the accused guilty under this offence, the Prosecution has to establish that at the relevant time of the detention, the condemned act was committed with a view to obtaining a concession or an advantage.[149]

---

[145] See GC III, Arts. 21–23, 25, 87, 90–91, 95, 97, 103, 109, and 118.

[146] *Blaskic*, paras. 158, 187.

[147] Cf. Lord Wright, 'The Killing of Hostages as a War Crime' (1948) **25** *BYBIL* 296 at 298, 301; Green, *Contemporary Law of Armed Conflict*, 272–3. Under Art. 1(1) of the International Convention Against the Taking of Hostages of 1979 (1979) **18** *ILM* 1456, the offence of taking of hostages means seizing, detaining, threatening to kill, injure, or continue to detain another person (the 'hostage') in order to compel a third party, namely, a State, an international intergovernmental organization, a natural or juridical person, or a group of persons, to do or abstain from doing any act as an explicit or implicit condition for the release of the hostage. Art. 12 of the Convention, however, excludes expressly the application of this Convention to hostage taking covered by the Geneva Conventions of 1949 and their additional Protocols.

[148] *Blaskic*, para. 158.

[149] Ibid.

Article 6(b) of the Nuremberg Charter stipulates that 'ill-treatment . . . of civilian population of or in occupied territory . . . killing of hostages . . .' shall be a war crime. The Nuremberg Tribunal held that this provision is declaratory of the existing laws and customs of war as appeared in Article 46 of the Hague Regulations (1907), which provided: 'Family honour and rights, the lives of persons and private property, as well as religious convictions and practices must be respected'.[150] The US Military Tribunal at Nuremberg stated in the *Hostages* case that it was:

'concerned with the subject of reprisals and the detention of members of the civilian population for the purpose of using them as the victims of subsequent reprisal measures. The most common purpose of holding them is for the general purpose of securing the good behaviour and obedience of the civilian population in occupied territory. The taking of reprisals against the civilian population by killing members thereof in retaliation for the hostile acts against the armed forces or military operations of the occupant seems to have been originated in Germany in modern times. It has been invoked by Germany in the Franco-Prussian War, World War I and in World War II. No other nation has resorted to the killing of the civilian population to secure peace and order in so far as our investigation has revealed . . .'[151]

One may question whether the mere act of taking of hostages without also killing them is a war crime. The US Military Tribunal at Nuremberg in the *High Command* case stated, after referring to the *Hostages* case:

'It was therein held that under certain very restrictive conditions and subject to certain rather extensive safeguards, *hostages may be taken*, and after a judicial finding of strict compliance with all pre-conditions and as a last desperate remedy hostages may even be sentenced to death. It was held further that similar drastic safeguards, restrictions, and judicial pre-conditions apply to the so-called 'reprisal prisoners'. If so inhumane a measure as the killing of innocent persons for offences of others, even when drastically safeguarded and limited, is ever permissible under any theory of international law, killing without full compliance with all requirements would be murder. If the killing is not permissible under any circumstances, then a killing with full compliance with all the mentioned prerequisites still would be murder.'[152]

The accused in the *High Command* case were convicted on the count of killing of hostages because they had killed the hostages without fulfilling certain very restrictive conditions or certain rather extensive safeguards. It has been pointed out that the *Hostages* case did not establish any exculpatory pre-conditions that would make killing of hostages not unlawful, and that in fact no such exculpatory ground had ever been put forward, still less sanctioned, in any previous cases.[153] Therefore, it is

---

[150] Lord Wright (1948) 25 *BYBIL* 298–9.

[151] *Trial of Wilhelm List and others*, UNWCC *Law Reports*, viii, at 63. Also in (1953) 15 *Ann. Dig.* 632 at 644.

[152] *Trial of Wilhem von Leeb and others*, UNWCC *Law Reports*, xii. Also in (1953) 15 *Ann. Dig.* 376 at 393. Emphasis added.

[153] Lord Wright (1948) 25 *BYBIL* 308–9.

doubtful whether the Tribunal in the *High Command* case stated the law correctly on this point. The applicable customary norm is stipulated in Article 50 of the Hague Convention IV that:

'No collective penalty, pecuniary or otherwise, shall be inflicted upon the population on account of the acts of individuals for which it cannot be regarded as collectively responsible'.

When read in conjunction with Article 46 of the Hague Regulations (1907), which was held by the Nuremberg Tribunal as being the legal foundation for the proscription of killing of hostages, it is clear that 'rights' of innocent non-combatant civilians 'must be respected' and the mere act of taking of hostages without more would amount to the deprivation of the right to freedom and liberty of the persons taken hostage on account of a 'collective penalty' inflicted on them because of the acts of other individuals. As one jurist points out, the Occupying Power not only has no right to kill hostages, but the practice of taking hostages itself is illegitimate and constitutes a violation of the law of nations because it is contrary to customary international law and to the rules under the Hague Regulations (1907) as well as the general principles of law recognized by civilized nations.[154] It should be noted that in connection with the charge of hostage taking Trial Chamber I of the ICTY in *Blaskic* merely examined whether the victims were detained or otherwise deprived of liberty by the accused for some of the purposes discussed above without considering whether the victims were in fact killed.[155] The accused in that case was found guilty of the taking of hostages for the purpose of exchange of prisoners and forcing the enemy to cease military operations against his force.[156]

Members of the armed forces of the adversary who are captured are prisoners of war whose protection can be found in GC III. It was probably for this reason that Article 2(h) of the ICTY Statute uses the terminology 'taking civilians as hostages' as a war crime of grave breaches. This terminology is in line with the definition given in the *Hostages* case that hostages are 'those persons of the civilian population' taken into custody for the purpose of guaranteeing with their lives the future good conduct of the population of the community from which they are taken.[157] The terminology used in the ICTY Statute is not followed by the ICC Statute, however. Such terminology is not helpful and may be misleading; civilians who benefit from the protection of international humanitarian law include soldiers and members of resistance movements who are *hors de combat* for whatever reason.

Thus, the pertinent part of the Elements of Crimes adopted by the PCNICC to guide the ICC with respect to this war crime stipulates:

'1. The perpetrator seized, detained, or otherwise held hostage one or more persons.

---

[154] Alexander-Czeslaw Melen, *Revue de Droit international, de sciences diplomatiques et politiques* (1946), 17. Translation by this present author from the passage quoted in ibid., 306.

[155] *Blaskic*, para. 187.

[156] Ibid., para. 701.

[157] Quoted in *Doc. PCNICC/1999/WGEC/INF. 1*, at 61.

2. The perpetrator threatened to kill, injure, or continue to detain such person or persons.

3. The perpetrator intended to compel a State, an international organization, a natural or legal person or a group of persons to act or refrain from acting as an explicit or implicit condition for the safety or the release of such person or persons.'

It should be noted that the persons who are 'hostages' are not necessarily persons used as 'human shields' against military operations. The use of persons as human shields comes under the offence of inhuman or cruel treatment,[158] or the one proscribed by Article 8(2)(b)(xxiii) of the ICC Statute.

OTHER SERIOUS VIOLATIONS OF THE LAWS AND CUSTOMS APPLICABLE IN INTERNATIONAL ARMED CONFLICT[159]

Article 3 of the ICTY Statute confers jurisdiction on the ICTY to prosecute persons violating the laws or customs of war. This Article has been held to be a general provision covering, subject to certain conditions, all violations of international humanitarian law not qualified as grave breaches, acts of genocide, or crimes against humanity.[160] The Appeals Chamber of the ICTY held in the *Tadic* Jurisdiction Decision that the following conditions must be satisfied to fulfil the requirement of Article 3 of the ICTY Statute: the violation must constitute an infringement of a rule of international humanitarian law; the rule must be customary in nature or, if it belongs to treaty law, the required conditions must be satisfied; the violation must be 'serious'; and the violation of the rule must give rise, under customary or conventional law, to the individual criminal responsibility of the person violating the rule.[161]

'Serious' means breach of a rule protecting important values, and the breach must involve grave consequences for the victim.[162] The ICC Statute omits war crimes that are not serious enough to warrant prosecution before the ICC. For example, the war crime of grave breach of 'unjustifiable delay in the repatriation of prisoners of war or civilians' under Article 85(4)(b) of AP I which is not proscribed by Article 8(2)(a) of the Statute is also not proscribed by Article 8(2)(b) of the Statute. Otherwise, all serious war crimes under AP I and the Hague Regulations are proscribed as war crimes under Article 8(2)(b) of the ICC Statute.

---

[158] See *Blaskic*, paras. 739–43.

[159] The author is indebted to the ICRC's text on Art. 8, para. 2 (b) of the ICC Statute submitted to the PCNICC on 14 July 1999 (*Doc. PCNICC/1999/WGEC/INF. 2* of 14 July 1999, at 9–62), the ICRC's text on Art. 8, para. 2(b)(i)–(vii), (ix), (xi), and (xii), and para. 2(e)(v)–(viii), (xi)–(xii) of the ICC Statute submitted to the PCNICC on 30 July 1999 as contained in *Doc. PCNICC/1999/WGEC/INF. 2/Add. 1* of 30 July 1999, and the ICRC's Working Paper on Art. 8, para. 2(b)(xvii)–(xx), (xxiii)–(xxv) of the ICC Statute submitted to the PCNICC on 3 Aug. 1999. See also Green, *Contemporary Law of Armed Conflict*, 290–2.

[160] *Tadic* Judgment, para. 559.

[161] *Tadic* Jurisdiction Decision, para. 94.

[162] Ibid. Quoted with approval in *Celebici*, paras. 279–80.

The common elements in the Elements of Crimes adopted by the PCNICC for the war crimes under Article 8(2)(b) of the ICC Statute are as follows:

'– The [perpetrator's] conduct took place in the context of and was associated with an international armed conflict.

– The perpetrator was aware of factual circumstances that established the existence of an armed conflict.'

Article 8(2)(b)(i) of the ICC Statute—Intentionally directing attacks against the civilian population as such or against individual civilians not taking direct part in hostilities

This offence is derived from Article 51(2) of AP I, which stipulates: 'The civilian population as such, as well as individual civilians, shall not be the object of attack . . .' Article 51(3) of AP I provides that civilians shall enjoy the protection 'unless and for such time as they take a direct part in hostilities'. Article 49(1) of AP I defines 'attacks' as 'acts of violence against the adversary, whether in offence or in defence'.

The civilian population comprises all persons who are civilians, and a civilian is any person who does not belong or no longer belongs to the various types of combatants.[163] The civilian population as such does not participate in the armed conflict, and the presence within the civilian population of individuals who do not come within the definition of civilian does not deprive the population of its civilian character.[164] When an individual civilian takes a direct part in hostilities, he ceases to be a 'civilian'.

According to the ICTY Trial Chamber in *Blaskic*, the *actus reus* of this offence is an attack or targeting of a civilian population or civilians, without justifiable military necessity, that causes deaths or serious corporal damage to the civilian population or individual civilians.[165] This judicial pronouncement is consistent with the requirement in the chapeau of Article 85(3) of AP I which requires that such attack is a grave breach under AP I when it causes death or serious injury to body or health.

The parties to the conflict must endeavour to distinguish between military targets and civilian targets. Therefore, the *mens rea* of this offence is the intention to carry out the attack in the knowledge (also in the sense of not being able to ignore) that civilians would be targeted without military necessity.[166]

The rationale and illustration of this offence are neatly summarized in the following pronouncement of the US Military Tribunal in the *Einsatzgruppen* case:

'A city is bombed for tactical purposes: communications are to be destroyed, railroads wrecked, ammunition plants demolished, factories razed, all for the purpose of impeding the military. In these operations, it inevitably happens that non-military persons are killed. This is an incident, a grave incident to be sure, but an unavoidable corollary of hostile battle

---

[163] Art. 50 of AP I, Art. 4(A)(1), (2), (3), and (6) of GC III, and Art. 43 of AP II. Also *Kayishema and Ruzindana*, para. 179; *Blaskic*, para. 180.

[164] Art. 50, AP I of 1977.

[165] *Blaskic*, para. 180.

[166] Ibid.

action. The civilians are not individualized. The bomb falls, it is aimed at the railroad yards, houses along the tracks are hit and many of their occupants killed. But that is entirely different, both in fact and in law, from an armed force marching up to these same railroad tracks, entering those houses abutting thereon, dragging out the men, women and children and shooting them.'[167]

Thus, the proscribed act of intentionally directing attacks against the civilian population as such or against individual civilians not taking direct part in hostilities certainly includes reprisals against the civilian population as such or against non-combatants, as explicitly stipulated in Article 51(6) of AP I, and implicitly provided in common Article 1 of the four Geneva Conventions and Article 4(2)(b) of AP II.[168] Carrying out indiscriminate attacks which are not directed against specific military objectives, or which employ a method of combat that is indiscriminate in its effects,[169] qualifies as a crime under this heading.[170]

According to the Elements of Crimes adopted by the PCNICC to guide the ICC in relation to this offence, the perpetrator must have directed an attack, with the intended object of the attack being a civilian population as such or individual civilians not taking direct part in hostilities.

Article 8(2)(b)(ii) of the ICC Statute—Intentionally directing attacks against civilian objects, that is, objects which are not military objectives

In the case of the ICC, the *actus reus* and *mens rea* for this offence are identical to the ones required for Article 8(2)(b)(i) of the ICC Statute, with 'civilian objects' replacing 'the civilian population as such or against individual civilians not taking direct part in hostilities' as the target of the attacks.

The attack must have caused damage to civilian objects. Civilian objects are all objects which cannot be legitimately considered as military objectives. The perpetra-tor of the attack must have carried out the attack in the knowledge (also in the sense of not being able to ignore) that civilian objects would be targeted without military necessity.[171]

'Military objectives' that may be objects of the attack are those objects which, by their nature, location, purpose, or use, make an effective contribution to military action, and whose total or partial destruction, capture, or neutralization, in the prevail-ing circumstances at the relevant time, offer a definite military advantage.[172] In case of doubt whether an object normally dedicated to civilian purposes is being used to make an effective contribution to military action, it shall be presumed not to be so used.[173]

---

[167] *Ohlendorf and Others* (1953) **15** *Ann. Dig.* 656 at 660–1.

[168] Common Art. 1 of GC I–GC IV obligates the High Contracting Parties to respect and to ensure respect for the respective GC's in all circumstances, whereas the fundamental guarantee under Art. 4(2)(b) of AP II proscribes 'collective punishment'.

[169] See Art. 51(4) and (5) and Art. 35(2) of AP I.

[170] The ICRC considers that it is such a crime. See *Doc. C/1999/WGEC/INF. 2/Add. 1*, at 13–17.

[171] *Blaskic*, para. 180.

[172] See Art. 52(2) of AP I.

[173] Art. 52(3) of AP I.

It should be noted that the ICTY Statute includes in Article 3(b) in the category of violations of the laws or customs of war 'wanton destruction of cities, towns or villages, or devastation not justified by military necessities'. It was held in *Blaskic* that the devastation must be committed intentionally or must be a foreseeable consequence of the act of the accused.[174]

Article 8(2)(b)(iii) of the ICC Statute—Intentionally directing attacks against personnel, installations, material, units or vehicles in a humanitarian assistance or peacekeeping mission in accordance with the UN Charter, as long as they are entitled to the protection given to civilians or civilian objects under the international law of armed conflict

This war crime is a new international crime. It was added at the Rome Conference in response to the overwhelming demand for the inclusion of 'crimes against UN personnel' as a separate category of international crime within the ICC's jurisdiction. [175]

The *actus reus* and the *mens rea* for this crime are identical to those of the two preceding war crimes, with the exception that the targets of the present crime are personnel, installations, material, units, or vehicles in (a) a humanitarian assistance mission, or (b) a peace-keeping mission in accordance with the UN Charter, 'as long as they are entitled to the protection given to civilian objects under the international law of armed conflict'. This prerequisite may seem superfluous; if these persons or objects are taking no direct part in the hostilities, they are entitled automatically under the international law of armed conflict to protection against attack. Nevertheless, the inclusion of this war crime in the ICC Statute has symbolic significance as a signal that the international community of nations attaches great importance to these missions and any attack on them would be a serious crimes of concern to the international community as a whole.[176]

The relevant Elements of Crimes adopted by the PCNICC stipulate that the perpetrator must have directed an attack, with the intended object of the attack being personnel, installations, material, units, or vehicles involved in a humanitarian assistance or peacekeeping mission in accordance with the Charter of the United Nations. Such personnel, installations, material, units, or vehicles must have been entitled to that protection given to civilians or civilian objects under the international law of armed conflict, and the perpetrator must have been aware of the factual circumstances that established such protection.

The meaning of an 'attack' in this context may be further clarified by reference to the 1994 Convention on the Safety of United Nations and Associated Personnel, Article 7(1) of which proscribes attacks against UN and associated personnel, their

---

[174] *Blaskic*, para. 183.

[175] See further, the 1994 Convention on the Safety of United Nations and Associated Personnel (1995) **34** *ILM* 482, which obligates its States Parties to criminalize under its national law, *inter alia*, a murder, kidnapping, or other attack, or threat thereof, as well as an attempt to commit such act, against any UN or associated personnel.

[176] von Hebel and Robinson, 'Crimes within the Jurisdiction of the Court', 110.

equipment and premises. Article 9 of the Convention obligates States Parties to criminalize under their respective national laws the intentional commission of:

'(a) A murder, kidnapping, or other attack upon the person or liberty of any United
Nations or associated personnel;

(b) A violent attack upon the official premises, the private accommodation, or the means
of transportation of any United Nations or associated personnel likely to endanger
his or her person or liberty.'

The words 'or other attack' make it clear that murder or kidnapping are also
'attacks' upon the UN or associated personnel.[177]

The protection against the attack is accorded as long as any of the personnel are not
engaged as combatants against organized armed forces because in such situation the
law of armed conflict would apply instead.[178] According to one authority on the
subject, using force in self-defence *per se* does not transform peace-keepers into combatants and thereby deprive them of protection under international humanitarian
law.[179] However, the UN itself officially recognizes as 'combatants' UN forces engaged
in situations of armed conflict, including those engaged in enforcement actions or
those using force in self-defence during peace-keeping operations.[180]

Since the peace-keeping missions covered by this Article must be the ones undertaken in accordance with the UN Charter, unilateral military actions not engaged or
deployed by the United Nations fall outside the scope of protection under this Article.

With respect to the humanitarian assistance mission, it must be different from the
ones 'using the distinctive emblems of the Geneva Conventions in conformity with
international law' because international attacks against them is a separate crime under
Article 8(2)(b)(xxiv) of the ICC Statute. It is hereby submitted that the humanitarian
mission covered by Article 8(2)(b)(iii) of the ICC Statute can be any mission undertaken by any individual, group of individuals, or organization in the pursuit of
humanitarian relief purposes and undertaken impartially without any adverse
distinction to the recipients of such relief.[181]

If a humanitarian assistance mission or a UN peace-keeping mission takes a direct
part in hostilities, then it loses the protection afforded by this Article as long as it takes
such a direct part. This is because protection afforded to civilians ceases when, and for

---

[177] This is further confirmed by Art. 9(c) of the Convention which proscribes a 'threat to commit any such
attack . . .'

[178] Cf. Art. 2(2) of the 1994 Convention on the Safety of United Nations and Associated Personnel, which
stipulates: 'This Convention shall not apply to a United Nations operation authorized by the Security Council
as an enforcement action under Chapter VII of the Charter of the United Nations in which any of the
personnel are engaged as combatants against organized armed forces and to which the law of international
armed conflict applies'. See also Green, *Contemporary Law of Armed Conflict*, 319–23 (on UN enforcement
operations), and cf. 323–6 (on UN peace-keeping operations).

[179] Cf. Green, *Contemporary Law of Armed Conflict*, 324–5.

[180] UN Secretary-General's Bulletin, Observance by United Nations forces of international humanitarian
law, *Doc. ST/ SGB/ 1999/ 13*, 6 Aug. 1999, Sec. 1.1.

[181] Cf. Arts. 70 and 71 of AP I on 'relief actions' and 'personnel participating in relief actions', respectively.

such time as, they take a direct part in hostilities.[182] Likewise, civilian objects become military objectives when they by their nature, location, purpose, or use make an effective contribution to military action and whose total or partial destruction, capture, or neutralization, in the prevailing circumstances at the relevant time, offers a definite military advantage.[183]

Article 8(2)(b)(iv) of the ICC Statute—Intentionally launching an attack in the knowledge that such attack will cause incidental loss of life or injury to civilians or damage to civilian objects or widespread, long-term and severe damage to the natural environment which would be clearly excessive in relation to the concrete and direct overall military advantage anticipated

This provision is derived from combining the provisions of Articles 35(3), 51(5)(b), 55(1), 57(2)(a)(iii), and 85(3) of AP I. The Rome Conference added the words 'clearly' and 'overall', at the suggestion of the US, to the said provisions of AP I, to permit a wider margin of appreciation to the soldiers in the field and exclude their errors of judgment from being war crimes under the ICC Statute.[184] The ICRC considers the word 'overall' redundant: it is apparently intended to indicate that a particular target can have a significant military advantage which can be felt over a lengthy period of time and affect military action beyond the vicinity of the target itself, and this is already included in the relevant provisions of AP I.[185] However, it is hereby submitted, the word is still helpful since not all States Parties to the ICC Statute will necessarily be States Parties to AP I also.

Article 56 of AP I prohibits any attack on dams, dykes, and nuclear electrical generating stations if it would result in the release of dangerous forces and consequent severe losses among the civilian population.

The *actus reus* of this offence is the launching of an attack to cause incidental loss of life or injury to civilians or damage to civilian objects or widespread, long-term, and severe damage to the natural environment in violation of the principles of necessity and proportionality.[186] Thus, an attack might be legitimate if, for instance, dangerous forces are far away from populated areas and would not affect the civilian population.[187] Similarly, it is not illegal to destroy an enemy tanker or nuclear-powered vessel simply because its destruction would result in damage to the environment or create widespread, long-term, and serious effects on the civilian population.[188] The expres-

---

[182] See, e.g. Art. 51(3) of AP I.

[183] Art. 52 of AP I.

[184] von Hebel and Robinson, 'Crimes within the Jurisdiction of the Court', 111.

[185] *UN Doc. A/CONF. 183/INF/10* of 13 Jul. 1998.

[186] Cf. ICJ Advisory Opinion, *Legality of the Threat or Use of Nuclear Weapons*, 8 Jul. 1996, at para. 30, where the ICJ states: '. . . States must take environmental considerations into account when assessing what is necessary and proportionate in the pursuit of legitimate military objectives. Respect for the environment is one of the elements that go to assessing whether an action is in conformity with the principles of necessity and proportionality'.

[187] Green, *Contemporary Law of Armed Conflict*, 149–50.

[188] Ibid., 290.

sion 'widespread, long-term, and severe damage' connotes 'the extent of intensity of the damage, its persistence in time, and the size of the geographical area affected by the damage', with the word 'long-term' signifying 'the long-lasting nature of the effects and not the possibility that the damage would occur a long time afterwards'.[189] The ICRC considers that the *travaux préparatoires* of AP I and other grounds support the construction of the word 'long-term' to mean decades rather than months, although it is not easy to know beforehand precisely the scope and duration of some environmentally damaging acts.[190]

The *mens rea* for this offence is the intent to launch the attack in the knowledge, in the sense of knowing with certainty, that it will be disproportionate to the military advantage anticipated in the circumstances.[191] The test of the *mens rea* would require both the objective and the subjective elements. It can be objectively determined whether a reasonable man would find the incidental injury or damage clearly excessive when compared to the military advantage expected to be gained from the attack. If the military value of an object to be attacked is determined by the broader strategic purpose of a particular military operation comprising various individual actions, the foreseeable military advantage of that particular military operation must be weighed against the foreseeable casualties of that operation in its totality.[192] Nonetheless, one must defer to 'the honest judgment of responsible commanders, based on the information reasonably available to them at the relevant time, and taking fully into account the urgent and difficult circumstances under which such judgments must usually be made'.[193]

This alleged war crime was a subject matter of investigation by the committee set up by the ICTY Prosecutor in May 1999 to assess the allegations that senior political and military personnel from the North Atlantic Treaty Organization (NATO) Member States committed serious violations of international humanitarian law during NATO's bombing campaign against the Federal Republic of Yugoslavia from 24 March 1999 to 9 June 1999, during the so-called NATO's 'humanitarian intervention' in Kosovo. The committee's Final Report of June 2000 exonerated NATO personnel from all blame by deferring to the honest judgment of the soldiers in the field and the military strategists at the relevant time. For example, it accepted NATO's explanation that the Serbian TV and Radio Station in Belgrade served a dual object, and that its destruction would give NATO a military advantage proportionate to the action taken. The Final Report went on to concede that although the civilian casualties were 'unfortunately high' they did not appear to be clearly disproportionate.[194]

---

[189] ILC's Report on the Work of Its 43rd Sess (1991), UN GAOR, 46th Sess., Supp. No. 10 (A/46/10), at 276. Quoted in *Doc. PCNICC/1999/WGEC/INF. 2/Add. 1*, at 33.

[190] ICRC's Report to the UN General Assembly, *UN Doc. A/48/269*, at 9. Quoted in *Doc. PCNICC/1999/ WGEC/INF. 2/Add. 1*, at 34.

[191] Cf. *Doc. PCNICC/1999/WGEC/INF. 2/Add. 1*, at 34.

[192] Ibid., at 30–2.

[193] Canadian Law of Armed Conflict Manual (2nd Draft, 1986), quoted in ibid., at 29–30.

[194] Final Report to the ICTY Prosecutor by the Committee Established to Review the NATO Bombing Campaign Against the Federal Republic of Yugoslavia (available from *http://www.un.org/icty/pressreal/ nato061300.htm*), paras. 71–79, esp. at paras. 77–78.

The Elements of Crimes adopted by the PCNICC for this war crime would also support the conclusion reached by the said Final Report. The PCNICC has taken pains to clarify that:

'... The expression "concrete and direct overall military advantage" refers to a military advantage that is *foreseeable by the perpetrator at the relevant time. Such advantage may or may not be temporally or geographically related to the object of the attack.* The fact that this crime admits the possibility of lawful incidental injury and collateral damage does not in any way justify any violation of the law applicable in armed conflict. It does not address justifications for war or other rules related to *jus ad bellum.* It reflects the proportionality requirement inherent in determining the legality of any military activity undertaken in the context of an armed conflict.'[195]

In terms of the perpetrator's *mens rea*, the Elements depart from the general rule that it is not necessary for the perpetrator to have personally completed a particular value judgment. To be guilty of this war crime, the perpetrator must have known, in the sense of making the value judgment, that the attack launched by him would cause incidental death or injury to civilians or damage to civilian objects or widespread, long-term, and severe damage to the natural environment and that such death, injury, or damage would be of such an extent as to be clearly excessive in relation to the concrete and direct overall military advantage anticipated. However, an evaluation of that value judgment must be based on the requisite information available to the perpetrator at the time.[196]

It should be noted that there is no result requirement as part of the *actus reus* of this war crime. What is required is the act of launching the attack of the nature and with the perpetrator's state of mind as described above.

Article 8(2)(b)(v) of the ICC Statute—Attacking or bombarding, by whatever means, towns, villages, dwellings or buildings which are undefended and which are not military objectives

This offence is derived directly from Article 25 of the Hague Regulations (1907), with the exception of the words 'and which are not military objectives' being added thereto.

The rule of Article 25 of the Hague Regulations (1907) is reiterated in Article 59(1) of AP I which proscribes attacking or bombarding non-defended localities. In essence, a non-defended locality is the inhabited place open for occupation, where all combatants as well as mobile weapons and mobile military equipment have been evacuated, no hostile use is made of fixed military installations or establishments, no acts of hostility are committed by the authorities or by the population, and no activities in support of military operations are undertaken.[197]

---

[195] *Doc. PCNICC/2000/1/Add. 2*, 2 Nov. 2000, n. 36. Emphasis added.
[196] Ibid., n. 37.
[197] *Doc. PCNICC/1999/WGEC/INF. 2/Add. 1*, at 37–8; Green, *Contemporary Law of Armed Conflict*, 97–8.

Undefended localities must not be military objectives as well. 'Military objectives' are those objects which, by their nature, location, purpose, or use, make an effective contribution to military action, and whose total or partial destruction, capture, or neutralization, in the prevailing circumstances at the relevant time, offers a definite military advantage.[198] In case of doubt whether an object normally dedicated to civilian purposes is being used to make an effective contribution to military action, it shall be presumed not to be so used.[199]

It is in this sense that the Elements of Crimes adopted by the PCNICC to guide the ICC in relation to this war crime must be understood. The pertinent part of the Elements of Crimes reiterates the provision of Article 8(2)(b)(v) of the ICC Statute and clarifies the term 'undefended' to mean being 'open for unresisted occupation'. It is also made clear that the presence in the locality of the attacked town(s), village(s), dwelling(s), or building(s) of persons specially protected under the Geneva Conventions of 1949 or of police forces retained for the sole purpose of maintaining law and order does not by itself render the locality a military objective.

Article 8(2)(b)(vi) of the ICC Statute—Killing or wounding a combatant who, having laid down his arms or having no longer means of defence, has surrendered at discretion

This offence is derived directly from Article 23(c) of the Hague Regulations (1907). This is similar to Article 41(1) of AP I which provides that a person *hors de combat* shall not be made the object of attack. A person is *hors de combat* if (a) he is in the power of an adverse party; (b) he has clearly expressed an intention to surrender; or (c) he has been rendered unconscious or is otherwise incapacitated by wounds or sickness, and is consequently incapable of defending himself. In any of these cases, the person must abstain from any hostile act and does not attempt to escape.[200] Similarly, Article 42(1) of AP I prohibits making parachutists in distress the objects of attack during their descent.

Article 41(1) of AP I prefers not to use the terminology 'killing or wounding' as in Article 23(c) of the Hague Regulations (1907). The terminology 'to be made the object of attack' is used to make clear that what is forbidden is the deliberate attack against persons *hors de combat*, and not the act of killing or wounding them as the incidental consequence of attacks not directed at them *per se*.[201] The fact that the Rome Conference deliberately adheres to the formulation in the Hague Regulations (1907) might give rise to the presumption that Article 8(2)(b)(vi) of the ICC Statute in effect lowers the requisite threshold under Article 41(1) of AP I. However, post-WWII cases decided with reference to Article 23(c) of the Hague Regulations (1907) reveal the consistent pattern that the accused were convicted for having deliberately

---

[198] See Art. 52(2) of AP I.
[199] Art. 52(3) of AP I. See further: Green, *Contemporary Law of Armed Conflict*, 147–9.
[200] Art. 41(2) of AP I.
[201] *Doc. PCNICC/1999/WGEC/INF. 2/Add. 1*, at 45.

killed or wounded combatants who had surrendered after laying down their arms or having no means of defence.[202]

The words 'at discretion' have been defined as meaning 'unconditionally'.[203]

The ICRC has noted the overlap between this offence and the offence of wilful killing as a grave breach under Article 8(2)(a)(i), as well as the offence of declaring that no quarter will be given under Article 8(2)(b)(xii) of the ICC Statute.[204]

The Elements of Crimes adopted by the PCNICC with regard to Article 8(2)(vi) of the ICC Statute simply require that the perpetrator must have killed or injured one or more persons who were *hors de combat*, being aware of the factual circumstances that established this *hors de combat* status.

Article 8(2)(b)(vii) of the ICC Statute—Making improper use of a flag of truce, of the flag or of the military insignia and uniform of the enemy or of the UN, as well as of the distinctive emblems of the Geneva Conventions, resulting in death or serious personal injury

This formulation is taken from Article 23(f) of the Hague Regulations (1907), with the word 'emblems' replacing the word 'badges' under the Hague Regulations (1907) and the UN being added as another entity whose flag and uniform must not be used improperly. Article 8(2)(b)(vii) of the ICC Statute criminalizes the improper use only where it results in death or serious personal injury.

The terminology 'improper use' covers a wide range of prohibited conduct, and what is improper use naturally depends on the prevailing circumstances at the relevant time. It certainly includes 'perfidy', which is defined by Article 37 of AP I as '[a]cts inviting confidence of an adversary to lead him to believe that he is entitled to, or is obliged to accord, protection under the rules of international law applicable in armed conflict, with intent to betray that confidence'. The feigning of an intent to negotiate under a flag of truce or of a surrender, and the feigning of protected status by the use of signs, emblems, or uniforms of the UN are two of the examples of perfidy specifically mentioned in Article 37 of AP I. Other widely recognized examples of such improper use include: firing from a building or tent displaying the emblem of the Red Cross, and misusing the emblem of the Red Cross to give a ship the appearance of a hospital ship for the purpose of camouflage.[205] What is still disputed is whether such flag, military insignia, uniforms, or emblems may be properly used at other times than during combat *on land*, such as when used for the purpose of approach or withdrawal.[206]

---

[202] See, e.g. the *P. Back* case (UNWCC, *Law Reports of Trials of War Criminals*, iii, at 60); and the *Peleus* case (British Military Court, Hamburg, ibid., i, at 2). Cited in *Doc. PCNICC/1999/WGEC/INF. 2/Add. 1*, at 42.

[203] British Manual of Military Law (1958), at 43. Cited in *Doc. PCNICC/1999/WGEC/INF. 2/Add. 1*, at 46.

[204] *Doc. PCNICC/1999/WGEC/INF. 2/Add. 1*, at 40.

[205] Ibid., at 56, quoting the US Dept. of the Army Field Manual, FM 27–10, *The Law of Land Warfare* (1958), at 23 and *German Military Manual, Joint Services Regulation (ZDv) 15/2* (1992), no. 1019.

[206] The British Military Manual states that there is no unanimity on this point, whereas the US Military Manual adopts the view that it is not improper to use such flags etc. except during combat (the Law of War on Land being Part III of the Manual of Military Law 91958), at 103, and US Dept. of the Army Field Manual, FM 27–10, *The Law of Land Warfare* (1958), at 23, quoted in ibid., at 52.

The ambiguity probably derives from the fact that under customary international law ruses of war to deceive the enemy are allowed in naval warfare, provided that warships display their true colours prior to an actual armed engagement.[207] However, warships and auxiliary vessels are prohibited at all times from actively simulating the status of vessels protected by the UN flag, hospital ships, small coastal rescue craft, or medical transports, vessels on humanitarian missions, or vessels entitled to be identified by the emblem of the Red Cross or Red Crescent.[208] Besides, aircraft are never entitled to false markings because an aircraft is generally unable to change its markings once it is airborne.[209]

The Elements of Crimes adopted by the PCNICC in relation to Article 8(2)(b)(vii) of the ICC Statute do not improve upon or provide the answer to the ambiguity just pointed out.

In the case of the war crime of improper use of a flag of truce, the perpetrator must have used a flag of truce in order to feign an intention to negotiate when there was no such intention on the part of the perpetrator. In doing so, the perpetrator must have known or should have known of the illegality of such use, which did result in death or serious personal injury, and the perpetrator must have known that the conduct could result in death or serious personal injury.

To be guilty of the war crime of improper use of a flag, insignia, or uniform of the hostile party under the ICC Statute, the perpetrator must have made such use in a manner prohibited under international law of armed conflict while engaged in an attack. In doing so, the perpetrator must have known or should have known of the illegality of such use, which did result in death or serious personal injury, and the perpetrator must have known that the conduct could result in death or serious personal injury.

To be guilty of the war crime of improper use of the distinctive emblems of the Geneva Conventions, the perpetrator must have made such use for combatant purposes in a manner prohibited under the international law of armed conflict. 'Combatant purposes' in these circumstances means purposes directly related to hostilities and not including medical, religious, or similar activities. In doing so, the perpetrator must have known or should have known of the illegality of such use, which did result in death or serious personal injury, and the perpetrator must have known that the conduct could result in death or serious personal injury. The Elements of Crimes in the case of the war crime of improper use of a flag, insignia, or uniform of the UN make it more difficult for the prosecution to prove the accused's *mens rea* than in the other offences under Article 8(2)(b)(vii) of the ICC Statute. The 'should have known'

[207] *San Remo Manual on International Law Applicable to Armed Conflicts at Sea* (Cambridge University Press, 1995) hereinafter '*San Remo Manual*', No. 110, at 184; *US Commander's Handbook on the Law of Naval Operations* (NWP 1–14M) (1995) (hereinafter '*US Commander's Handbook*'), at 12–1 (12.5.1); *German Military Manual, Joint Services Regulation (ZDv) 15/2* (1992), no. 1018. Quoted in *Doc. PCNICC/1999/WGEC/INF. 2/Add. 1*, at 52–3.

[208] *San Remo Manual*, No. 110, at 184 ff.

[209] *San Remo Manual*, No. 109, at 184; *US Commander's Handbook*, at 12–1 (12.3.2) and (12.5.2).

test required in the other offences found in Article 8(2)(b)(vii) is not applicable here because of the variable and regulatory nature of the relevant prohibitions. What is required to find the perpetrator guilty is as follows. The perpetrator must have used a flag, insignia, or uniform of the United Nations in a manner prohibited under the international law of armed conflict in the knowledge of the illegality of such use, which did result in death or serious personal injury. Like the other offences under Article 8(2)(b)(vii) of the ICC Statute, in doing so the perpetrator must have known that the conduct could result in death or serious personal injury.

Article 8(2)(b)(viii) of the ICC Statute—The transfer, directly or indirectly, by the Occupying Power of parts of its own civilian population into the territory it occupies, or the deportation or transfer of all or parts of the population of the occupied territory within or outside this territory

Article 49 of GC IV proscribes individual or mass deportations or transfers of all or parts of protected persons from occupied territory to the territory of the Occupying Power or to that of any other country, occupied or not, regardless of their motive.[210] Article 85(4)(a) of AP I proscribes as a grave breach the transfers by the Occupying Power of parts of its own civilian population into the territory it occupies, or the deportation or transfer in violation of Article 49 of GC IV.

Article 8(2)(b)(viii) of the ICC Statute is derived largely from Article 85(4)(a) of AP I, with two exceptions. Firstly, the Rome Conference adds the words 'directly or indirectly' to the provision under Article 85(4)(a) of AP I. This addition resulted from the efforts of the Arab Group of States to make clear that an Occupying Power is to be responsible for this crime if it deliberately organizes the transfer of its own population into occupied territory, but also where it takes no effective steps to prevent its own population from organizing such a transfer.[211] Secondly, the Rome Conference found it unnecessary to refer to Article 49 of GC IV after incorporating its wording into Article 8(2)(b)(viii) of the ICC Statute.

The Elements of Crimes adopted by the PCNICC for this war crime merely reiterate the provision of Article 8(2)(b)(viii) of the ICC Statute, adding that the term 'transfer' needs to be interpreted in accordance with the relevant provisions of international humanitarian law.

In relation to international humanitarian law, Article 49 of GC IV has already been dealt with when analysing Article 8(2)(a)(vii) of the ICC Statute. It expressly proscribes forcible transfers or deportations of protected persons from occupied territories to the territory of the Occupying Power or to that of any other State, occupied or not. Forcible transfer or deportation within an occupied territory, or outside that territory when it is impossible to avoid this for material reasons, may be carried out temporarily if necessitated by the security of the population or imperative military

---

[210] See also Meron, *War Crimes Law Comes of Age: Essays* (Oxford University Press, 1998), chap. VI ('Deportation of Civilians as a War Crime under Customary Law').

[211] von Hebel and Robinson, 'Crimes within the Jurisdiction of the Court', 113.

reasons. On the other hand, Article 8(2)(b)(viii) of the ICC Statute is the inverse of Article 49 of GC IV and Article 8(2)(a)(vii) of the ICC Statute. What this Article criminalizes is the transfer, directly or indirectly, by the Occupying Power of parts of its own civilian population *into* the territory it occupies, *or* the deportation or transfer of all or parts of the population of the occupied territory *within or outside* the occupied territory. It should be understood, however, if the latter situation is justified by the security of the population or imperative military reasons, then that is permissible, as provided in Article 49 of GC IV. What is proscribed is the transfer or deportation of the population of the occupied territory within or outside that territory without the said justification, for instance, in order to make room for the population of the Occupying Power who are to be transferred into the occupied territory and settle there.[212]

The word 'indirectly' indicates that the population of the Occupying Power need not be physically forced or otherwise compelled to be transferred to the occupied territory, but may be induced or facilitated to be transferred there. It could also mean that the population of the Occupying Power might be transferred via a third State to the occupied territory. However, there might be an exception, as in the case of children. Article 78 of AP I provides that a party to the conflict may arrange for the temporary evacuation of children who are its nationals to a foreign country where compelling reasons of the health or medical treatment of the children so require. There is nothing to indicate that such foreign country must not be an occupied territory.

The ICRC notes that the terminology 'by the Occupying Power' necessitates government involvement and the conduct of a private person for private ends, not imputable to the government of the Occupying Power, would not incur criminal responsibility under this provision.[213] Besides, the term 'parts of the population' means that more than one person is deported or transferred.[214]

Article 8(2)(b)(ix) of the ICC Statute—Intentionally directing attacks against buildings dedicated to religion, education, art, science or charitable purposes, historic monuments, hospitals and places where the sick and wounded are collected, provided they are not military objectives

This provision is derived largely from Articles 27 and 56 of the Hague Regulations (1907) and provisions of the Geneva Conventions and AP I on the protection of hospitals and places where the sick and wounded are collected, such as Articles 19–23 of GC I, Articles 22, 23, 34, and 35 of GC II, Articles 18–19 of GC IV, and Articles 12 and 53 of AP I. The protection accorded to the historic monuments, works of art or places of worship under customary law exists alongside that accorded by conventional

---

[212] This provision compels Israel to vote against the ICC Statute. Israel does not accept GC IV and considers the inclusion into the list of the most heinous and grievous war crimes the action of transferring population into occupied territory unacceptable.

[213] *Doc. PCNICC/1999/WGEC/INF. 2*, at 13.

[214] Ibid., at 14.

law, especially the Hague Convention for the Protection of Cultural Property in the Event of Armed Conflict of 14 May 1954[215] and the Second Protocol to the Hague Convention of 1954 adopted on 26 March 1999.[216] The Rome Conference added 'buildings dedicated to . . . education' to the list of protected objects under these existing international instruments.

Article 3(d) of the ICTY Statute proscribes as a war crime in violation of the laws or customs of war 'seizure of, destruction or wilful damage done to institutions dedicated to religion, charity and education, the arts and sciences, historic monuments and works of art and science'. It was held in *Blaskic* that the damage or destruction must have been committed intentionally to the edifices which can be clearly identified as being dedicated to the aforesaid purposes and which were not being used at the time of the attack for military objectives. Furthermore, the edifices must not be situated within the immediate vicinity of military targets.[217]

There is no reason to consider that the Elements of Crimes adopted by the PCINCC for Article 8(2)(b)(ix) of the ICC Statute are in any way different from those under existing jurisprudence. According to the Elements, the perpetrator must have directed an attack against one or more buildings specified in that Article, with intent that such buildings be the object of the attack. Like the war crime of attacking undefended places under Article 8(2)(b)(v) of the ICC Statute, it is made clear that the presence in the locality of such buildings of persons specially protected under the Geneva Conventions of 1949 or of police forces retained for the sole purpose of maintaining law and order does not by itself render the locality a military objective.

Article 8(2)(b)(x) of the ICC Statute—Subjecting persons who are in the power of an adverse party to physical mutilation or to medical or scientific experiments of any kind which are neither justified by the medical, dental or hospital treatment of the person concerned nor carried out in his or her interest, and which cause death to or seriously endanger the health of such person or persons

This provision is derived directly from Article 11(1), (2), and (4) of AP I.

Mutilation: Mutilation is proscribed by numerous provisions of the Geneva Conventions and Additional Protocols, such as Articles 13 of GC III, 32 of GC IV, Articles 11(2)(a), 75(2)(a)(iv) of AP I, and Article 4(2)(a) of AP II. Scientific or medical experiments are also proscribed alongside mutilation by most of these provisions.

---

[215] 249 *UNTS* 215.

[216] *UNESCO Doc. HC/ 1999/ 7* of 26 Mar. 1999. See further, *Doc. PCNICC/1999/WGEC/INF. 2/Add. 1*, at 59–62. The Hague Convention only protects 'movable or immovable property of great cultural importance to the cultural heritage of every people'. Thus, it does not protect every object regarded as of cultural heritage by the State of location. The First Protocol to the Hague Convention only protects places of worship 'which constitute the cultural or spiritual heritage of peoples' (Green, *Contemporary Law of Armed Conflict*, 145–6). The Second Protocol aims at improving the application and effectiveness of the Hague Convention. See: J-M. Henckaerts, 'New rules for the protection of cultural property in armed conflict' (1999) **81** *Int'l Rev. Red Cross* 593; J. Hladik, 'The 1954 Hague Convention for the Protection of Cultural Property in the Event of Armed Conflict and the notion of military necessity', ibid., 621.

[217] *Blaskic*, para. 185.

'Physical' is sometimes inserted in front of 'mutilation'. The dictionary meaning of mutilation is the severe damage, injury or disfigurement by breaking, maiming, tearing, or cutting off a body part.[218] The ICTR in *Musema* defines mutilation as 'causing severe physical injury or damage to victims'.[219] Physical mutilation and mutilation are therefore synonymous.

The Elements of the crime of mutilation under this provision as adopted by the PCNICC emphasizes particular forms of mutilation—that of permanently disfiguring the person who was in the power of an adverse party, or permanently disabling or removing his organ or appendage. The mutilation must have caused death or seriously endangered the physical or mental health of the victim without any justification in terms of the medical, dental, or hospital treatment of the victim or in terms of his interest.

Consent is not a defence to this crime. It is a crime under this provision to undertake any medical procedure which is not indicated by the state of health of the person concerned and which is not consistent with generally accepted medical standards which would be applied under similar medical circumstances to persons who are nationals of the party conducting the procedure and who are in no way deprived of liberty. The notion 'in the power of' seems to be identical in its meaning to 'in the hands of' already discussed.

Medical or scientific experiments. The Elements of the crime of medical or scientific experiments as adopted by the PCNICC reiterates the pertinent part of the provisions of Article 8(2)(b)(x) of the ICC Statute. Like the war crime of mutilation, consent is not a defence to this crime. This present provision, in effect, prohibits any medical procedure which is not indicated by the state of health of the person concerned and which is not consistent with generally accepted medical standards which would be applied under similar medical circumstances to persons who are nationals of the party conducting the procedure and who are in no way deprived of liberty.

Further guidance in relation to the elements of the war crime of medical or scientific experiments may be sought from the judgment of the US Military Tribunal at Nuremberg in the *Medical* case. The Tribunal laid down ten basic principles to satisfy moral, ethical, and legal concepts, violation of which would entail criminal culpability and punishment. These principles, which deserve to be quoted in full, are as follows:

'1. The voluntary consent of the human subject is absolutely essential. This means that the person involved should have legal capacity to give consent; should be so situated as to be able to exercise free power of choice, without the intervention of any element of force, fraud, deceit, duress, over-reaching, or other ulterior form of constraint or coercion; and should have sufficient knowledge and comprehension of the elements of the subject-matter involved as to enable him to make an understanding and

---

[218] See, e.g., *Chambers's Twentieth Century Dictionary* (Villafield Press, 1952), 707; *Oxford Advanced Learner's Dictionary* (Oxford University Press, 1992), 819; *Cambridge International Dictionary of English* (Cambridge University Press, 1995), 933.

[219] *Musema*, para. 285.

enlightened decision. This latter element requires that before the acceptance of an affirmative decision by the experimental subject there should be made known to him the nature, duration, and purpose of the experiment; the method and means by which it is to be conducted; all inconveniences and hazards reasonably to be expected; and the effects upon his health or person which may possibly come from his participation in the experiment.

The duty and responsibility for ascertaining the quality of the consent rests upon each individual who initiates, directs, or engages in the experiment. It is a personal duty and responsibility which may not be delegated to another with impunity.

2. The experiment should be such as to yield fruitful results for the good of society, unprocurable by other methods or means of study, and not random and unnecessary in nature.

3. The experiment should be so designed and based on the results of animal experimentation and a knowledge of the natural history of the disease or other problem under study that the anticipated results will justify the performance of the experiment.

4. The experiment should be so conducted as to avoid all unnecessary physical and mental suffering and injury.

5. No experiment should be conducted where there is *a priori* reason to believe that death or disabling injury will occur; except, perhaps, in those experiments where the experimental physicians also serve as subjects.

6. The degree of risks to be taken should never exceed that determined by the humanitarian importance of the problem to be solved by the experiment.

7. Proper preparations should be made and adequate facilities provided to protect the experimental subject against even remote possibilities of injury, disability, or death.

8. The experiment should be conducted only by scientifically qualified persons. The highest degree of skill and care should be required through all stages of the experiment of those who conduct or engage in the experiment.

9. During the course of the experiment the human subject should be at liberty to bring the experiment to an end if he has reached the physical or mental state where continuation of the experiment seems to him to be impossible.

10. During the course of the experiment the scientist in charge must be prepared to terminate the experiment at any stage, if he has probable cause to believe, in the exercise of good faith, superior skill, and careful judgment required of him that a continuation of the experiment is likely to result in injury, disability, or death to the experimental subject.'[220]

Article 8(2)(b)(xi) of the ICC Statute—Killing or wounding treacherously individuals belonging to the hostile nation or enemy

This provision has its genesis in Article 23(b) of the Hague Regulations (1907), which, in turn, derives from the prohibition of perfidy under customary international law.

---

[220] *Trial of Rudolf Brandt et al.*, US Military Tribunal at Nuremberg, 19 and 20 Aug. 1947, TWC, ii, 171–300, excerpted in G. K. McDonald and O. Swaak-Goldman (eds.), *Substantive and Procedural Aspects of International Criminal Law*, ii (Kluwer, 2000), 1697 at 1704–5.

The keyword here is 'treacherously', which has never been defined in any international instrument.

According to the ICRC, perfidious acts defined by Article 37 of AP I are constituted by two elements. Firstly, 'the act in question must objectively be of a nature to cause or at least induce the confidence of an adversary'. Such confidence arises out of 'a precisely specified legal protection which either the adversary himself is entitled to or is a protection which [the accused] is legally obliged to accord to the adversary' as prescribed by rules of international law applicable in armed conflict. Article 37(1) of AP I lists examples of treacherous acts as including: the feigning of an intent to negotiate under a flag of truce or of a surrender; the feigning of an incapacitation by wounds or sickness; the feigning of civilian, non-combatant status; and the feigning of protected status by the use of signs, emblems, or uniforms of the United Nations or other States not party to the conflict. Secondly, the act inviting confidence must be carried out intentionally to mislead the adversary into relying upon the protection he expects. Thus, the *mens rea* of this offence is the 'intent to betray' confidence in order to kill or wound individuals belonging to the hostile nation or enemy.[221]

Nonetheless, Article 37(2) of AP I permits ruses of war. It defines ruses of war as 'acts which are intended to mislead an adversary or to induce him to act recklessly but which infringes no rule of international law applicable in armed conflict and which are not perfidious because they do not invite confidence of an adversary with respect to protection under the law'. Examples of ruses of war include the use of camouflage, decoys, mock operations, and misinformation.[222]

The PCNICC has adopted the Elements of Crimes for this war crime to require that the perpetrator must have invited the confidence or belief of one or more persons belonging to an adverse party that they were entitled to, or were obliged to accord, protection under rules of international law applicable in armed conflict, with intent to betray that confidence or belief. Thereafter, the perpetrator must have killed or injured such person or persons harbouring such confidence or belief.

Article 8(2)(b)(xii) of the ICC Statute—Declaring that no quarter will be given

This provision is derived from Article 23(d) of the Hague Regulations (1907). Article 40 of AP I prohibits ordering that there shall be no survivor to threaten an adversary therewith or to conduct hostilities on this basis. This offence is closely similar to that proscribed by Article 8(2)(b)(vi) of the ICC Statute, with the difference being that ordering or threatening to spare no one amounts to a war crime in itself.

This is made clear in the Elements of this crime as adopted by the PCNICC. The perpetrator must have declared or ordered that there shall be no survivors in order to threaten an adversary or to conduct hostilities on the basis that there shall be no survivor. At the relevant time, the perpetrator must have been in a position of effective

---

[221] *Doc. PCNICC/1999/WGEC/INF. 2/Add. 1* at 70.
[222] See further: Green, *Contemporary Law of Armed Conflict*, 138–9, 169–70, 178–9.

command or control over the subordinate forces to which the declaration or order was directed.

In the *K.-H. Moehle* case, a British Military Court found as a war crime the mere passing of an order that subordinate German U-boat commanders were to destroy ships and kill their crew, provided that such order could be interpreted by a reasonable subordinate only as an order not to allow an adversary party to survive.[223]

A question has been raised whether the making of surrender impossible by choosing particular methods or means of warfare amounts to a denial of quarter.[224] The answer should be in the affirmative if it could be proved that the accused intended to conduct hostilities on the basis that there be no survivors.

Article 8(2)(b)(xiii) of the ICC Statute—Destroying or seizing the enemy's property unless such destruction or seizure be imperatively demanded by the necessities of war

This provision is derived directly from Article 23(g) of the Hague Regulations (1907) and overlaps to some extent with Article 8(2)(a)(iv) of the ICC Statute—extensive destruction and appropriation of property, not justified by military necessity and carried out unlawfully and wantonly. The differences between Article 8(2)(a)(iv) and Article 8(2)(b)(xiii) of the ICC Statute are as follows. Firstly, the former concerns destruction and appropriation that are extensive in scope. Secondly, the latter uses the term 'seizure/seizing' instead of 'appropriation'. Finally, while the former criminalizes acts not justified by military necessity and carried out unlawfully and wantonly, the latter criminalizes acts not imperatively demanded by the necessities of war.

The Elements of this crime as adopted by the PCNICC provide that the perpetrator must have destroyed or seized, without any justification of military necessity, certain property belonging to a hostile party. At the time of its destruction or seizure, such property must have been protected from that destruction or seizure under the international law of armed conflict, and the perpetrator must have been aware of the factual circumstances that established the status of the protected property.

Acts amounting to destruction are the same as the ones already discussed when analysing Article 8(2)(a)(iv) of the ICC Statute. It also includes plunder of property, which is a violation of the laws and customs of war as stipulated in Article 47 of the Hague Regulations (1907), and also proscribed by Article 3(e) of the ICTY Statute.[225]

There is no definition under international instruments or judicial decisions on the law of armed conflict for 'seizure' of property.[226] It is hereby submitted that seizure encompasses any kind of depriving a person of the property legally belonging to him; it may be temporary or permanent in nature. This is apparent from the *A. Krupp* trial, in which the US Military Tribunal rejected the Defence's contention that the laws and

---

[223] British Military Court, Hamburg (UNWCC *Law Reports*, ix, at 75–80). Cited in *Doc. PCNICC/1999/ WGEC/INF. 2/Add. 1*, at 43.

[224] The ICRC raises this question in *Doc. PCINCC/1999/WGEC/INF. 2/Add. 1*, at 73.

[225] *Celebici*, para. 584.

[226] *Doc. PCNICC/1999/WGEC/INF. 2*, at 29.

customs of war do not prohibit the seizure and exploitation of property in belliger-ently occupied territory so long as there is 'no definite transfer of title'. The Tribunal stated that if, for example, a factory is being taken over and its rightful owner is prevented from using it and deprived from lawfully exercising his prerogative as owner, it cannot be said that his property is respected under the Hague Regulations (1907).[227]

The protected property can be private or public property, as is made clear, for instance, by Article 53 of GC IV.[228]

Article 8(2)(b)(xiv) of the ICC Statute—Declaring abolished, suspended or inadmissible in a court of law the rights and actions of the nationals of the hostile party

The provision is derived directly from Article 23(h) of the Hague Regulations (1907). The rule in the Hague Regulations (1907) was added at the suggestion of two German delegates in order to prohibit belligerents from depriving enemy subjects by legisla-tion or depriving them of the means of enforcing their legal rights by recourse to courts of law.[229]

The Elements of this crime as adopted by the PCNICC require that the perpetrator must have effected the abolition, suspension, or termination of admissibility in a court of law of certain rights or actions, directed and intended to be directed at the nationals of a hostile party.

Article 8(2)(b)(xv) of the ICC Statute—Compelling the nationals of the hostile party to take part in the operations of war directed against their own country, even if they were in the belligerent's service before the commencement of the war

This provision is derived directly from the second sentence of Article 23 of the Hague Regulations (1907). It also overlaps with the offence under Article 8(2)(a)(v) of the ICC Statute—compelling a prisoner of war or other protected person to serve in the forces of the hostile Power.

The Elements of this crime as adopted by the PCNICC stipulate that the perpetra-tor must have coerced a national or nationals of a hostile party by act or threat to take part in military operations against that person's own country or forces.

Article 8(2)(b)(xvi) of the ICC Statute—Pillaging a town or place, even when taken by assault

This provision is derived directly from Article 28 of the Hague Regulations (1907). The ICTY held in *Celebici* that the concept of pillage in the traditional sense implies an element of violence; whereas the offence of plunder embraces all forms of unlawful appropriation of property in armed conflict for which individual

---

[227] UNWCC *Law Reports*, x, at 137. Quoted in ibid., at 33.
[228] See further, *Doc. PCNICC/1999/WGEC/INF. 2*, at 30–3.
[229] Ibid., at 34.

criminal responsibility attaches in international law, be it committed with or without violence. Therefore, plunder includes those acts traditionally described as 'pillage'.[230]

The element of violence is included, for example, in the offence of pillage under Article 221 of the French Code of Military Service, which proscribes 'pillage committed in gangs by military personnel with arms or open force'. Likewise, Article 440 of the French Penal Code proscribes the looting of personal belongings and other property of the civilian evicted from their homes prior to their destruction.[231]

It is surprising that the elements of this offence as adopted by the PCNICC contain no element of violence. The delegations to the PCNICC wished to distinguish clearly the war crime of pillage and that of destroying and seizing the enemy's property. While military necessity could justify the latter, it could not justify the former. As the ICRC noted during the Fourth Session of the PCNICC in March 2000, pillage was an old offence related to 'war booty' and the taking of civilian property for one's own private use.

The Elements of Crime adopted by the PCNICC in the case of this offence stipulate that the perpetrator must have appropriated certain property, with intent to deprive the owner of the property and to appropriate it for private or personal use without the owner's consent. However, appropriations justified by military necessity, and not or private or personal use, cannot constitute the crime of pillaging.

As they stand, the Elements of this crime are almost identical to those of the offence under Article 8(2)(a)(iv) of the ICC Statute. There are two essential differences: the Elements of crime under Article 8(2)(a)(iv) require an extensive and wanton nature of the appropriation, while those under Article 8(2)(b)(xvi) require that the appropriation be for private or personal use.

Therefore, the ICC might refer to the existing rule of international law, as stated by the ICTY in *Celebici*, to hold that the appropriation under this offence requires an element of violence, although it need not be perpetrated on an extensive scale and wantonly, as in the case of the offence under Article 8(2)(a)(iv) of the ICC Statute.

Article 8(2)(b)(xvii) of the ICC Statute—Employing poison or poisoned weapons

This provision is derived directly from Article 23(a) of the Hague Regulations (1907). The prohibition can be traced to at least since the late Middle Ages, and is probably the most ancient prohibition of a means of combat in international law.[232] However,

---

[230] *Celebici*, para. 591. Followed in *Blaskic*, para. 184.
[231] *PCNICC/1999/WGEC/INF. 2*, at 45, citing the *F. Holstein and Others* case (Permanent Military Tribunal at Dijon, France, UNWCC *Law Reports*, viii (1949), 22 at 31), and the *H. Szabadcs* case (Permanent Military Tribunal at Clermont-Ferrand, France, UNWCC *Law Reports*, ix (1949), 59 at 60 ff).
[232] ICRC Working Paper (3 Aug. 1999), 9.

the International Court of Justice has not interpreted this prohibition as extending to cover nuclear weapons.[233]

According to the Elements of Crimes adopted by the PCNICC for this offence, the perpetrator must have employed a substance or a weapon that releases a substance as a result of its employment, and the substance must have been such that it causes death or serious damage to health in the ordinary course of events, through its toxic properties. Thus, the ordinary meaning of the word 'poison' is adopted by the PCNICC. The term is defined, for example, in the *Cambridge International Dictionary of English* as 'a substance that causes illness or death if taken into a living thing, esp. a person's or animal's body'.[234] A more complex definition of the term 'poison' can be found, for instance, in the US Military Manual, which defines poisons as 'biological or chemical substances causing death or disability with permanent effects when, in even small quantities, they are ingested, enter the lungs or bloodstream, or touch the skin'.[235] Adopting such a complex definition of poison would unnecessarily require the Prosecution to prove the permanent nature of the damage caused, the biological or chemical quality of the substance, and so forth. Therefore, the PCNICC is wise to adopt the simplest formulation. It also logically excludes from the scope of this war crime 'unintentional and insignificant poisonous secondary effects of otherwise permissible munitions'.[236]

The prohibition is absolute in the sense that poisoning is not made lawful by giving a notice informing the enemy of the use of the poison, as, for example, that the water has been poisoned.[237]

Article 8(2)(b)(xviii) of the ICC Statute—Employing asphyxiating, poisonous or other gases, and all analogous liquids, materials or devices

The prohibition is derived directly from the 1925 Geneva Protocol for the Prohibition of the Use of Asphyxiating, Poisonous or Other Gases, and of Bacteriological Methods of Warfare.[238] While the preamble of the 1925 Geneva Protocol extends the prohibition to the use of bacteriological agents, Article 8(2)(b)(xviii) of the ICC Statute does

---

[233] ICJ Advisory Opinion of 8 July 1996 on *Legality of the Threat or Use of Nuclear Weapons*, ICJ Rep. 1996, paras. 55 ff. Cf. R. A. Falk, 'Nuclear Weapons, International Law and the World Court: A Historic Encounter' (1997) **91** *AJIL* 64. It should be noted that at the 3rd Sess. of the PCNICC (29 Nov.–17 Dec. 1999), Mexico proposed in the Working Group on the Elements of Crimes that the word 'poison' be used instead of 'substance' because 'poison' is the word used by Art. 8(2)(b)(xvii) of the ICC Statute. However, the majority of States preferred the word 'substance' and its accompanying elucidation because it would clarify the meaning of the word 'poison' used in that provision.

[234] *Cambridge International Dictionary of English* (1995), 1090.

[235] Dept. of the Airforce, AF Pamphlet 110–31, *International Law—The Conduct of Armed Conflict and Air Operations* (1976), 5–6.

[236] The term appears in *German Military Manual, Joint Services Regulation (ZDv) 15/2* (1992), No. 434, as quoted in ICRC's Working Paper (3 Aug. 1999), 10–11.

[237] *British Military Manual, The Law of War on Land being Part III of the Manual of Military Law* (1958), 42; *Canadian Law of Armed Conflict Manual*, 2nd Draft (1986), 5–18. Cited in ICRC's Working Paper (3 Aug. 1999), 10.

[238] 94 *League of Nations Treaty Series* 65.

not cover such use. In the ICRC's opinion, the use of bacteriological agents would probably be tantamount to an attack on civilians within the meaning of Article 8(2)(b)(i) of the Statute due to the impossibility of biological agents being able to distinguish between civilians and combatants.[239]

Use of nuclear weapons is outside the scope of the prohibition under the 1925 Geneva Protocol. As the ICJ opined in 1996, the term 'analogous materials or devices' under the 1925 Geneva Protocol has been understood in State practice in its ordinary sense as covering 'weapons whose prime, or even exclusive effect is to poison or asphyxiate', and therefore does not refer to nuclear weapons.[240] As for chemical weapons, the Chemical Weapons Convention of 1993 aims at regulating development, production, stockpiling, and use of chemical weapons.[241] Once the prohibition of chemical weapons and/or nuclear weapons has attained the status of customary law, its use could be a war crime under Article 8(2)(b)(xx) of the ICC Statute.[242]

The Elements of Crimes adopted by the PCNICC for this offence provide in broad term that the perpetrator must have employed a gas or other analogous substance or device which causes death or serious damage to health in the ordinary course of events, through its asphyxiating or toxic properties. However, this shall not be interpreted as limiting or prejudicing in any way existing or developing rules of international law with respect to development, production, stockpiling, and use of chemical weapons.

Article 8(2)(b)(xix) of the ICC Statute—Employing bullets which expand or flatten easily in the human body, such as bullets with a hard envelope which does not entirely cover the core or is pierced with incisions

This prohibition is derived directly from the Declaration IV(3) concerning Expanding Bullets, The Hague, 29 July 1899. The words 'such as' before 'bullets with a hard envelope . . . ' make it clear that such bullets constitute just one example of the proscribed bullets. The preamble of The Hague Declaration stated that the undersigned were inspired by the sentiments expressed in the Declaration of St. Petersburg of 29 November (11 December) 1868. The sentiments were to the effect that the only legitimate object to accomplish during war is to weaken the military forces of the enemy by disabling the greatest possible number of men without uselessly aggravating the sufferings of disabled men, or rendering their death inevitable. Thus, the use of any bullets which uselessly aggravate the sufferings of disabled men, or render their

---

[239] ICRC Working Paper (3 Aug. 1999), 12.

[240] *Legality of the Threat or Use of Nuclear Weapons*, ICJ Rep. 1996, para. 55 ff.

[241] Convention on the Prohibition of the Development, Production, Stockpiling and Use of Chemical Weapons and on Their Destruction of 13 Jan. 1993 (1993) 32 *ILM* 800.

[242] The PCNICC sessions to draft the weapon-related crimes under Art. 8(2)(xvii), (xviii), and (xix) of the ICC Statute were largely dominated by the US, the UK, the Netherlands, Sweden, Belgium, and France—all of whom lead the world in weapon technology. Most of the developing States played no significant role in this area apart from remarking that the Elements of Crimes for these war crimes must not depart from the pertinent rules of international law or international law of armed conflicts.

death inevitable because they expand or flatten easily in the human body violates the international law of armed conflict.[243]

During discussion at the PCNICC, it was generally felt that a soldier to whom his commander issued bullets without the soldier's awareness of the prohibited status of the bullets under international law should not be held criminally liable therefor. The Elements of Crimes adopted by the PCNICC for this offence thus require that the perpetrator employing bullets whose use violates the international law of armed conflict because they expand or flatten easily in the human body must have been aware (and not 'should have known') that the nature of the bullets was such that their employment would uselessly aggravate suffering or the wounding effect.

It has been pointed out, however, that a tribunal would have to consider whether the ordinary soldier to whom such weapons were issued could reasonably be expected to disobey, particularly if he had no other weapon to defend himself against the adverse party. In this kind of situation, it could be argued that only those responsible for issuing the weapons would be liable.[244]

Article 8(2)(b)(xx) of the ICC Statute—Employing weapons, projectiles and material and methods of warfare which are of a nature to cause superfluous injury or unnecessary suffering or which are inherently indiscriminate in violation of the international law of armed conflict, provided that such weapons, projectiles and materials and methods of warfare are the subject of a comprehensive prohibition and are included in an annex to the ICC Statute, by an amendment in accordance with the relevant provisions set forth in Articles 121 and 123

Employing weapons, projectiles, and material and methods of warfare of a nature to cause superfluous injury or unnecessary suffering is prohibited by Article 35(2) of AP I, which traces its origin to Article 23(e) of the Hague Regulations (1907).

Under the customary international law of armed conflict, as enshrined in Article 48 of AP I, the parties to the conflict must always distinguish between the civilian population and combatants and between civilian objects and military objectives and must direct their operations only against military objectives. Article 51(4) therefore proscribes indiscriminate attacks. Such attacks are those not directed at a specific military objective, or employing a method or means of combat which cannot be directed against a specific military objective or limited in its effects, thereby being of a nature to strike military objectives and civilians or civilian objects without distinction. Article 51(5) of AP I gives the following illustrations of indiscriminate attacks:

'(a) an attack by bombardment by any methods or means which treats as a single military objective a number of clearly separated and distinct military objectives located in a city, town, village, or other area containing a similar concentration of civilians or civilian objects; and

(b) an attack which may be expected to cause incidental loss of civilian life, injury to

---

[243] ICRC Working Paper (3 Aug. 1999), 15–16.
[244] Green, *Contemporary Law of Armed Conflict*, 129.

civilians, damage to civilian objects, or a combination thereof, which would be excessive in relation to the concrete and direct military advantage anticipated.'

That these rules are rules of customary law is beyond doubt.[245] The problem, nevertheless, is that at present the international community of nations has not been able to universally endorse a comprehensive ban on the use of the most obvious candidates for this prohibition—nuclear weapons, chemical and biological weapons, and anti-personnel landmines, among others.[246] When the international community has reached the stage where such comprehensive ban is practicable, then the ICC Statute will be amended with an annex listing such weapons, projectiles, and materials and methods of warfare the use of which will be a war crime under Article 8(2)(b)(xx) of the ICC Statute.[247]

The PCNICC has deferred drafting elements of this crime. The Elements of Crimes for this war crime will have to be drafted by the States Parties to the ICC Statute once such weapons, projectiles, or material or methods of warfare have been included in an annex to the ICC Statute.

A controversy has been caused by France's Interpretative Declaration at the time of its ratification of the ICC Statute on 9 June 2000. Paragraph 2 of the Interpretative Declaration states:

'The provisions of Article 8 of the Statute, and in particular paragraph(2)(b) thereof, relate solely to conventional weapons and can neither regulate nor prohibit the possible use of nuclear weapons nor impair the other rules of international law applicable to other weapons necessary to the exercise of France of its inherent right of self-defence, unless nuclear weapons or the other weapons referred to herein become subject in the future to a comprehensive ban and are specified in an annex to the Statute by means of an amendment adopted in accordance with the provisions of Articles 121 and 123.'

It could be argued that the 'possible use' (*l'emploi eventuel*) of these weapons must be subject to the rules of proportionality and other relevant rules of international humanitarian law laid down by the ICJ in its Advisory Opinion in *Legality of the Threat or Use of Nuclear Weapons*. Otherwise, France's Interpretative Declaration would amount to a reservation to the ICC Statute, something prohibited by Article 120 of the Statute. This contention can be supported by the decision of the ICTY Trial

---

[245] *Legality of the Threat or Use of Nuclear Weapons*, ICJ Advisory Opinion of 8 July 1996, ICJ Rep. 1996, paras. 78 ff.

[246] See ibid., paras. 35, 95. See also ICRC Working Paper (3 Aug. 1999), 17–30. For a legislative history behind this Article, see R. S. Clark, 'The Rome Statute of the International Criminal Court and Weapons of a Nature to Cause Superfluous Injury or Unnecessary Suffering, or Which Are Inherently Indiscriminate', in J. Carey and R. John Pritchard (eds.), *International Humanitarian Law: Origins, Challenges and Prospects* (Edwin Mellon Press, forthcoming 2000).

[247] In the meantime, the ICRC has initiated the SirUS (Superfluous Injury or Unnecessary Suffering) Project to bring objectivity to the legal notion of 'superfluous injury or unnecessary suffering' in order to facilitate the review of the legality of weapons. Proposals on this matter were submitted, e.g. to the 27th International Conference of the Red Cross and Red Crescent in late 1999. For a legislative history of Art. 8(2)(xx) of the ICC Statute, see von Hebel and Robinson, 'Crimes within the Jurisdiction of the Court', 113–6.

Chamber in the *Martic* Rule 61 Hearing, where the Chamber stated that although there was no formal prohibition of the use of cluster bombs as such, the use of the Orkan rocket with a cluster bomb warhead in that case constituted evidence of the accused's intent to deliberately attack the civilian population. The warhead was inaccurate and landed in an area with no military objectives in its vicinity, killing at least five civilians and injuring several others.[248]

Article 8(2)(b)(xxi) of the ICC Statute—Committing outrages upon personal dignity, in particular humiliating and degrading treatment

This provision is derived directly from Article 75(2)(b) of AP I. The term 'in particular' before 'humiliating and degrading treatment' makes it clear that such treatment is just one example of the outrages, albeit the one that the provision wishes to criminalize.

Since the victim of a war crime of 'inhumane act' need not be a living human being, certain acts against dead bodies that offend philosophical and religious notions of respect for the human being upon death may amount to outrages on personal dignity.[249]

This offence is identical to the one proscribed by common Article 3(1)(c) of the four Geneva Conventions, and criminalized in Article 8(2)(c) of the ICC Statute. The ICTY and the ICTR have dealt with this offence in detail in the context of an internal conflict. Therefore, a legal analysis of the Elements of this crime will be undertaken later on in this chapter, with the understanding in the case of Article 8(2)(b)(xxi) of the ICC Statute that the proscribed conduct took place in the context of and was associated with an international conflict.

The Elements of this crime as adopted by the PCNICC rightly stipulate that the perpetrator must have humiliated, degraded, or otherwise violated the dignity of one or more persons, including dead persons. The victim need not personally be aware of the existence of the humiliation or degradation, or other violation. Relevant aspects of the cultural background of the victim are to be taken into account as well. What is required to find the perpetrator criminal liable is that the severity of the humiliation, degradation, or other violation must be of such degree as to be generally recognized as an outrage upon personal dignity.

Article 8(2)(b)(xxii) of the ICC Statute—Committing rape, sexual slavery, enforced prostitution, forced pregnancy, as defined in Article 7(2)(f) of the ICC Statute, enforced sterilization, or any other form of sexual violence also constituting a grave breach of the Geneva Conventions

Rape. Rape can be a torture, which is a grave breach of the Geneva Conventions and proscribed by Article 8(2)(a)(ii) of the ICC Statute, if the act meets the criteria

---

[248] *Prosecutor v. Milan Martic*, Case No. IT-95–11-R61, ICTY T. Ch., 8 Mar. 1996, paras. 18, 23–31. Cited in the Final Report to the Prosecutor by the Committee Established to Review the NATO Bombing Campaign Against the Federal Rep. of Yugoslavia, para. 27.

[249] Cf. *Trial of Max Schmid*, UNWCC *Law Reports*, xiii, 151–2. Cited in *Tadic* Judgment, para. 748.

involved.[250] It can also be a violation of the laws or customs of war, an act of genocide, or a crime against humanity, if the requisite elements are met.[251]

The definition of rape has already been dealt with in the chapter on crimes against humanity. The definition of rape as a war crime and as a crime against humanity differ only in terms of the context in which rape is perpetrated. This difference is, accordingly, reflected in the Elements of Crimes adopted by the PCNICC for the war crime of rape under Article 8(2)(b)(xxii) of the Statute.

Sexual slavery. The most obvious example of sexual slavery during war is the case of 'comfort stations' maintained by the Japanese armed forces during WWII. More recent instances include the 'rape camps' maintained by some of the parties to the conflicts in the former Yugoslavia. The UN Special Rapporteur of the Working Group on Contemporary Forms of Slavery defines sexual slavery as 'the status or condition of a person over whom any or all of the powers attaching to the right of ownership are exercised, including sexual access through rape or other forms of sexual violence'.[252] It could be committed by States actors or private individuals, and no government involvement or State action needs to be proved. Nor does it require that a person subjected to sexual slavery be bought, sold, or traded as a chattel.[253] The Elements of Crimes adopted by the PCNICC stipulate in the case of sexual slavery that the perpetrator must have exercised any or all of the powers attaching to the right of ownership over one or more persons, such as by purchasing, selling, lending, or bartering such a person or persons, or by imposing on them a similar deprivation of liberty, and caused such person or persons to engage in one or more acts of a sexual nature. Given the complex nature of this crime, it is recognized that its commission could involve more than one perpetrator as a part of a common criminal purpose. Like the crime against humanity of sexual slavery under Article 7(1)(g) of the ICC Statute, it is understood that the deprivation of liberty in question may, in some circumstances, include exacting forced labour or otherwise reducing a person to servile status as defined in the Supplementary Convention on the Abolition of Slavery, the Slave Trade, and Institutions and Practices Similar to Slavery of 1956, and that the perpetrator's aforesaid conduct may include trafficking in persons, in particular women and children.

Enforced prostitution. In *W. Awochi*, before the Netherlands Temporary Court-Martial in Batavia after WWII, the accused, a Japanese, was charged with the offence of 'abduction of girls and women for the purpose of enforced prostitution' and was found guilty. He ran a club restaurant where his victims were confined against their will under the threat that the Japanese Military Police would harm them unless they

---

[250] *Celebici*, paras. 475–93.

[251] *Furundzija*, paras. 164–72.

[252] Final Report of the Special Rapporteur of the Working Group on Contemporary Forms of Slavery, on systematic rape, sexual slavery, and slavery-like practices during armed conflict, *UN Doc. E/CN. 4/ Sub. 2/ 1998/ 13* of 22 June 1998, para. 27.

[253] Ibid.

gave themselves to the Japanese visitors, under which threats they were forced to prostitute themselves.[254]

Enforced prostitution is a form of sexual slavery, with the element of pecuniary or other gains by the accused or another person being added to the elements of sexual slavery in general. The term 'forced prostitution' and 'enforced prostitution' have been treated as synonymous.[255]

The Elements of Crimes adopted by the PCNICC therefore provide in the case of enforced prostitution that the perpetrator must have caused one or more persons to engage in one or more acts of a sexual nature by force, or by threat of force or coercion, such as that caused by fear of violence, duress, detention, psychological oppression or abuse of power, against such person or persons or another person, or by taking advantage of a coercive environment or such person's or persons' incapacity to give genuine consent. In doing so, the perpetrator or another person must have obtained or expected to obtain pecuniary or other advantage in exchange for or in connection with the acts of a sexual nature.

Forced pregnancy. The Elements of Crimes in the case of the war crime of forced pregnancy as adopted by the PCNICC require that the perpetrator must have confined one or more women forcibly made pregnant, with the intent of affecting the ethnic composition of any population or carrying out other grave violations of international law.

Enforced sterilization. In certain post-WWII trials, the accused were charged with acts of enforced sterilization in the context of medical experiments.[256]

The Elements of Crimes for the war crime of enforced sterilization as adopted by the PCNICC duplicate those for the crime against humanity of enforced sterilization, except for the context in which the crime is committed.

Sexual violence. To be a war crime under Article 8(2)(b)(xxii) of the ICC Statute, 'any other form of sexual violence' apart from the ones already enumerated in this same provision must also constitute a grave breach of the Geneva Conventions. What this means is that the sexual violence must be of such gravity so as to be comparable to the other enumerated sexual crimes in that provision. It also affirms that sexual violence can constitute a grave breach and may be charged as such under the relevant provisions of Article 8(2)(a) or (b) of the ICC Statute.[257] The war crime of 'any other form of sexual violence' under Article 8(2)(b)(xxii) of the ICC Statute is qualified by the proviso 'also constituting a grave breach of the Geneva Conventions'.

---

[254] UNWCC *Law Reports*, xiii, 123. Cited in *Doc. PCNICC/1999/WGEC/INF. 2*, at 54.

[255] See, e.g. Final Report of the Special Rapporteur of the Working Group on Contemporary Forms of Slavery, *UN Doc. E/CN. 4/ Sub. 2/ 1998/ 13* of 22 June 1998, para. 31.

[256] The *Hoess* case, Supreme National Tribunal, Poland, UNWCC *Law Reports*, vii, 15; *K. Brandt and Others* (the '*Doctors' Trial*'), ibid., i, 11 ff. Cited in *Doc. PCNICC/1999/WGEC/INF. 2*, at 55.

[257] von Hebel and Robinson, 'Crimes within the Jurisdiction of the Court', 117, n. 111.

Serious sexual assault falling short of actual penetration, all serious abuses of a sexual nature inflicted on the physical and moral integrity of a person by means of coercion, threat of force, or intimidation in any way that is degrading and humiliating for the victim's dignity are proscribed, although their distinction from rape is primarily relevant for the purposes of sentencing.[258] All these acts also constitute outrages on personal dignity and sexual integrity of the victim.[259]

Hence, the PCNICC's adopted Elements of Crimes for this offence of sexual violence provide that the perpetrator must have committed an act of a sexual nature against one or more persons or caused such person or persons to engage in an act of a sexual nature by force, or by threat of force or coercion, or by taking advantage of a coercive environment or such person's or persons' incapacity to give genuine consent. The perpetrator's conduct must have been of a gravity comparable to that of a grave breach of the Geneva Conventions, and the perpetrator must have been aware of the factual circumstances that established the gravity of the conduct.

Article 8(2)(b)(xxiii) of the ICC Statute—Utilizing the presence of a civilian or other protected person to render certain points, areas, or military forces immune from military operations

This prohibition is derived from numerous provisions, in particular, Article 23 of GC III, Article 28 of GC IV, and Article 51(7) of AP I.

Use of 'human shields' to deter military operations have been widespread, for example, during the Gulf War and the Kosovo military operations in 1999. The Prosecution in *Blaskic* charged the accused of inhuman and cruel treatment for the use of Muslim civilians as human shields and thereby causing them considerable mental suffering.[260] It is submitted that the accused could have been charged with the war crime of utilizing the presence of a civilian or other protected person to render certain points, areas, or military forces immune from military operations as well. Moreover, unlike the case of inhuman or cruel treatment, it is not necessary to prove the victim's physical or mental suffering; all that is needed is that the accused intentionally uses the victim as a human shield. In *Karadzic and Mladic*, the accused were charged with 'taking United Nations Peacekeepers hostage and using them as "human shields"' by tying the Peacekeepers to potential targets of NATO air-strikes, thus being grave breaches of the Geneva Conventions and violations of the laws and customs of war.[261]

Thus, the PCNICC is right to have adopted the elements of this crime to require that the perpetrator must have moved or otherwise taken advantage of the location of one or more civilians or other persons protected under the international law of armed

---

[258] *Furundzija*, para. 186.
[259] Cf. ibid., para. 272.
[260] *Blaskic*, paras. 709–16.
[261] *Prosecutor v. Karadzic and Mladic*, Case No. IT-95-5-R61 and Case No. IT-95-18-R61, ICTY Rule 61 Decisions, **108** *ILR* at 91, 96. Also quoted in ICRC Working Paper (3 Aug. 1999), 31–2.

conflict, with the intent to shield a military objective from attack or shield, favour, or impede military operations.

Article 8(2)(b)(xxiv) of the ICC Statute—Intentionally directing attacks against buildings, material, medical units and transport, and personnel using the distinctive emblems of the Geneva Conventions in conformity with international law

This prohibition is derived from numerous prohibitions of attack as stipulated in the Geneva Conventions and AP I, including Articles 24–27, 36, 39, 40–44 of GC I, Articles 42–44 of GC II, Articles 18–22 of GC IV, Articles 12–13, 15, 18, 23, and 24 of AP I.

The Elements of Crimes as adopted by the PCNICC for this war crime stipulate that the perpetrator must have intentionally attacked one or more persons, buildings, medical units, or transports or other objects using, in conformity with international law, a distinctive emblem or other method of identification indicating protection under the Geneva Conventions.

The wording 'other method of identification indicating the protection under the Geneva Conventions' is added because, in practice, when armed conflict is taking place it may be necessary to use some other method of identification besides the distinctive emblems of the Geneva Conventions to indicate the protected status under these Conventions. The emphasis is thus on the protection from attacks against those entitled to such protection under the Geneva Conventions, rather than on the use of the distinctive emblems. This would also accommodate the evolution of practice in this area where new methods of identification are replacing traditional emblems of the Geneva Conventions.

Article 8(2)(b)(xxv) of the ICC Statute—Intentionally using starvation of civilians as a method of warfare by depriving them of objects indispensable to their survival, including wilfully impeding relief supplies as provided for under the Geneva Conventions

This prohibition is derived from Article 54, under the heading 'Protection of objects indispensable to the survival of the civilian population', of AP I.

Article 54(1) of AP I stipulates that starvation as a method of warfare is prohibited. There is no definition given for 'starvation' since its ordinary meaning is well understood. Using starvation of civilians as a method of warfare means causing civilians to starve in order to attain military objectives.

Starvation by means of depriving civilians of objects indispensable to their survival is elaborated in Article 54(2) of AP I as follows:

'It is prohibited to attack, destroy, remove, or render useless objects indispensable to the survival of the civilian population, such as foodstuffs, agricultural areas for the production of foodstuffs, crops, livestock, drinking water installations and supplies and irrigation works, for the specific purpose of denying them for their sustenance value to the civilian population or to the adverse Party . . . in order to starve out civilians . . .'

Since impeding humanitarian assistance has become widespread during armed conflicts, Article 8(2)(b)(xxv) of the ICC Statute makes 'wilfully impeding relief supplies as provided for under the Geneva Conventions' a war crime of starvation of civilians. The provisions under the Geneva Conventions protecting relief supplies destined for civilians are Articles 23, 55, 59–62, 108–9, and 142 of GC IV, and Articles 70–71 of AP I. In essence, such relief supplies must be humanitarian and impartial in character and provided without any adverse distinction.

There are exceptions to the rule in Article 54 of AP I, though. Article 54(3) of AP I stipulates that the prohibition under paragraph 2 of that Article does not apply to such of the objects used by an adverse Party 'as sustenance solely for the members of its armed forces', or 'if not as sustenance, then in direct support of military action'. However, even if the objects indispensable to the survival of civilians were used in direct support of military action, the adverse Party shall not take actions against these objects which may be expected to leave them with such inadequate food or water as to cause their starvation or cause their movement. Paragraph 5 of Article 54 of AP I provides an even more sweeping exception to the prohibition under paragraph 2 of that Article 54 as follows:

'In recognition of the vital requirements of any Party to the conflict in the defence of its national territory against invasion, derogation from the prohibition contained in paragraph 2 may be made by a Party to the conflict within such territory under its own control where required by imperative military necessity.'

The Elements of Crimes adopted by the PCNICC for the war crime of starvation as a method of warfare do not incorporate such a sweeping exception under Article 54(5) of AP I. The Elements only provide that the perpetrator must have deprived civilians of objects indispensable to their survival, with the intent to starve civilians as a method of warfare.

Article 8(2)(b)(xxvi) of the ICC Statute—Conscripting or enlisting children under the age of fifteen years into the national armed forces or using them to participate actively in hostilities

Children have been used in armed conflicts in non-combatant roles from time immemorial. However, use of children as combatants in armed conflicts in the past few decades has been a growing worldwide phenomenon that arouses the concern of the international community of nations. Children are vulnerable to intimidation, manipulation, and indoctrination.[262]

Article 77(2) of AP I obligates its High Contracting Parties who are parties to the conflict to take 'all feasible measures in order that children who have not attained the age of fifteen years do not take a direct part in hostilities, and in particular, they shall refrain from recruiting them into their armed forces'. In recruiting children who are fifteen years of age or older, 'but who have not attained the age of eighteen years, the

---

[262] See I. Cohn and G. Goodwin-Gill, *Child Soldiers: the role of children in armed conflict* (Clarendon Press, 1994).

Parties to the conflict shall endeavour to give priority to those who are oldest'. This provision is adopted in Article 38(2) and (3) of the United Nations Convention on the Rights of the Child (CROC) of 1989,[263] which has been ratified by 191 States; that is, all members of the international community of nations, except the US and Somalia. Thus, the prohibition of conscripting or enlisting children under the age of fifteen years into the national armed forces or using them to participate actively in hostilities can be considered a norm of customary international law, albeit a norm that lacks sanction.

Article 8(2)(b)(xxvi) of the ICC Statute intends to remedy this absence of enforcement of the customary norm. However, the Rome Conference considered that there was no sufficient support under customary international law for raising the relevant age from fifteen to eighteen.[264] 'Conscripting or enlisting' relates to the administrative act of placing the name of a child soldier on the list, and the terminology 'national armed forces' means the official armed forces of a State.[265]

The ICTR in *Akayesu* held that 'direct part in hostility' and 'active part in hostilities' are so similar that they may be treated as synonymous.[266] The issue is further clarified by the ICTR in *Rutaganda* that taking a 'direct' part in the hostilities means 'acts of war which by their very nature or purpose are likely to cause actual harm to the personnel and equipment of the enemy armed forces'.[267] These judicial pronouncements seem to be consistent with the objectives of the draftsmen of the ICC Statute in this matter. The words 'using' and 'participate' which appear in Article 8(2)(xxvi) are intended to cover direct or active participation in combat and military activities connected with combat like scouting, spying, sabotage, and the use of children as decoys, couriers or at military checkpoints or at the frontline.[268]

There are divergent approaches in national legal systems regarding the accused's knowledge of the age of the child. In Common Law jurisdictions, like the US as well as England and Wales, the accused's misunderstanding of the age of the child is not a defence although that misunderstanding may be reasonably well-founded. On the other hand, the laws of France, Switzerland, and Germany, among others, accept such a defence.[269] As will be seen shortly, the Elements of Crimes adopted by the PCNICC follow the latter approach in this case.

The Optional Protocol to CROC on the involvement of children in armed conflict has raised the age of prohibited recruitment of children from fifteen years to eighteen years. The rationale for the Optional Protocol is to afford greater protection to children by setting a higher minimum age for their recruitment.[270]

---

[263] *UN Doc. ST/ HR/ Rev. 5* (Vol. I/Part 1), at 174.
[264] von Hebel and Robinson, 'Crimes within the Jurisdiction of the Court', 117–8.
[265] Ibid., 118.
[266] *Akayesu*, para. 629.
[267] *Rutaganda*, para. 98.
[268] von Hebel and Robinson, 'Crimes within the Jurisdiction of the Court', 118.
[269] See the authorities cited in *Doc. PCNICC/1999/WGEC/INF. 2* at 61–2.
[270] As of Sept. 2000, there were 59 signatories to the Optional Protocol and two ratifiers.

Should the minimum age of eighteen become a new norm of customary international law, then there would be a divergence between the criminal sanction under the ICC Statute and the new customary international norm. In this situation, Article 10 of the ICC Statute provides that nothing in Part 2, that includes Article 8, of the ICC Statute 'shall be interpreted as limiting or prejudicing in any way existing or developing rules of international law for purposes other than this Statute'. Thus, the minimum age limit of fifteen years would continue to apply to States Parties to the ICC Statute as a matter of conventional law unless and until this provision under the ICC Statute is amended in accordance with the ICC Statute itself.

In any case, Article 26 of the ICC Statute provides that the ICC shall have no jurisdiction over children under eighteen at the time of the alleged commission of a crime. This recognizes tacitly the fact that children under eighteen are victims of international crimes and should not be punished as a result.

The Elements of Crimes adopted by the PCNICC stipulate in the case of this war crime that the perpetrator must have conscripted or enlisted one or more persons under the age of fifteen years into the national armed forces or used one or more persons to participate actively in hostilities. The perpetrator must have known or should have known that such person or persons were under the age of fifteen years.

6.2 WAR CRIMES IN NON-INTERNATIONAL ARMED CONFLICT

The four Geneva Conventions of 1949 generally apply to international armed conflicts only. So does AP I of 1977 which supplements the four Geneva Conventions.

When the Diplomatic Conference for the Establishment of International Conventions for the Protection of Victims of War was convened in Geneva in 1949, it was the common understanding among delegates that they would be concluding Conventions applicable to international armed conflicts. The effort by the ICRC to try to make these Conventions applicable to internal armed conflicts as well was rejected as an attempt to interfere in the internal affairs of States and to protect all forms of insurrections, rebellion, anarchy, and the disintegration of States. As a compromise, and out of the desire to protect victims of internal armed conflicts, the Conference approved Common Article 3 as it now appears in the four Geneva Conventions.[271] The International Court of Justice in *Nicaragua* opines that Common Article 3 serves as a minimum rule to be imperatively applied to all types of armed conflict and corresponds to the elementary considerations of humanity.[272] It has attained the status of a rule of customary international law.[273]

---

[271] For a historical background of Common Art. 3, see *Kayishema and Ruzindana*, paras. 159–65.

[272] ICJ Rep. 1986, 14 at 114. Cited by Trial Chamber I of the ICTY in *Aleksovski* Judgment, para. 50. See also *Celebici*, para. 314; *Tadic* Appeals Judgment, para. 137; *Furundzija*, para. 132; *Blaskic*, para. 161.

[273] ICJ Rep. 1986, 114; *Akayesu*, para. 608; *Celebici*, para. 301; *Blaskic*, paras. 164–8.

Paragraph 1 of Article 3 common to the four Geneva Conventions of 1949 proscribes the following acts:

'(a) violence to life and person, in particular murder of all kinds, mutilation, cruel treatment and torture;

(b) taking of hostages;

(c) outrages upon personal dignity, in particular humiliating and degrading treatment;

(d) the passing of sentences and the carrying out of executions without previous judgment pronounced by a regularly constituted court, affording all the judicial guarantees which are recognized as indispensable by civilized peoples.'

Common Article 3 applies to an armed conflict of an internal or mixed character, as distinct from mere acts of banditry, internal disturbances and tensions, unorganized and short-lived insurrections, or terrorist activities, which are not subject to international humanitarian law.[274] It is the intensity of the conflict and the organization of the parties to the conflict that distinguish an internal armed conflict from internal strife not qualified as an internal armed conflict.[275]

Common Article 3 has been supplemented by AP II.[276] While Common Article 3 applies in the case of 'armed conflict not of an international character', Article 1 of AP II stipulates that this Protocol shall apply to all armed conflicts not covered by AP I and 'which take place in the territory of a High Contracting Party between its armed forces and dissident armed forces or other organized armed groups which, under responsible command, exercise such control over a part of its territory as to enable them to carry out sustained and concerted military operations and to implement this Protocol'. This distinction emanates from the differing intensity of the conflict, with a higher threshold in the case of AP II.[277] The criteria establishing the threshold are to be applied objectively, irrespective of the subjective evaluations of the parties involved in the conflict.[278] In the case of AP II, the parties to the conflict are normally either the government confronting dissident armed forces, or the government fighting insurgent organized armed groups.[279] The term 'armed forces' is to be understood in the broadest sense to cover all armed forces as described within national legislation.[280] Similarly, in the case of AP II, situations of internal disturbances and tensions, such as riots, isolated and sporadic acts of violence, and other acts of a similar nature do not qualify as internal armed conflicts; there must be protracted armed conflict between governmental authorities and organized armed groups or between such groups.[281] However, the dissident forces need not have a hierarchical system of military organization similar to that of regular armed forces; it must be an organization capable of planning

---

[274] *Tadic* Judgment, para. 562; *Rutaganda*, para. 90; *Musema*, para. 248.

[275] *Akayesu*, para. 120.

[276] For a historical background of AP II, see *Aleksovski* Judgment, paras. 166–8.

[277] *Akayesu*, paras. 602, 618; *Musema*, para. 250.

[278] *Akayesu*, para. 624.

[279] Ibid., paras. 825–6.

[280] *Musema*, para. 256.

[281] See Art. 1(2) of AP II; Art. 8(2)(f) of the ICC Statute; *Akayesu*, paras. 619–21, 625.

and carrying out sustained and concerted military operations carried out continu-
ously and according to a plan while at the same time imposing discipline on its
members.[282] Moreover, it must be able to dominate a sufficient part of the territory
and in a position to implement AP II.[283] The goal of AP II is to improve the protection
afforded to victims in non-international armed conflicts and to develop objective
criteria independent of the subjective judgments of the parties to an armed conflict
without thereby modifying the existing conditions of applicability of Common Article 3. If an armed conflict meets the criteria under AP II, it also automatically meets
the threshold requirements of Common Article 3.[284]

Paragraph 2 of Article 4 of AP II under the heading 'Fundamental guarantees'
proscribes the following acts:

'(a) violence to the life, health and physical or mental well-being of persons, in particular
    murder as well as cruel treatment such as torture, mutilation or any form of corporal
    punishment;

(b) collective punishments;

(c) taking of hostages;

(d) acts of terrorism;

(e) outrages upon personal dignity, in particular humiliating and degrading treatment,
    rape, enforced prostitution and any form of indecent assault;

(f) slavery and the slave trade in all their forms;

(g) pillage;

(h) threats to commit any of the foregoing acts.'

The fundamental guarantees under Article 4 of AP II thus overlap to a considerable
extent with the minimum guarantees provided in Common Article 3 of the Geneva
Conventions. Article 4 of the ICTR Statute under the heading 'Violations of Article 3
common to the Geneva Conventions and of Additional Protocol II' proscribes the acts
enumerated in Article 4 of AP II, with the sole exception that 'slavery and slave trade
in all their forms' is replaced by 'the passing of sentences and carrying out of executions without previous judgment . . . ' proscribed in paragraph (d) of Common
Article 3. Moreover, Article 4 of the ICTR Statute states that the violations listed
therein are not exhaustive. However, since AP II as a whole does not reflect customary
international law, it has legal binding force as custom insofar as it overlaps with
Common Article 3, which is already part of customary international law.[285] This is the
case of the fundamental guarantees contained in Article 4(2) of AP II which reaffirm
and supplement Common Article 3.[286] Since Rwanda ratified AP II on 19 November
1984 and had enacted implementing legislation before the relevant date when

---

[282] *Musema*, para. 257.

[283] Ibid., para. 258.

[284] *Rutaganda*, para. 92; *Musema*, para. 252.

[285] *Akayesu*, paras. 608–9.

[286] Ibid., paras. 610; *Musema*, paras. 240–1.

offences under the ICTR Statute were committed, AP II also applies to Rwanda as a matter of conventional law.[287] Likewise, Croatia, as well as Bosnia-Herzegovina has ratified both AP I and AP II since 1992.[288]

SERIOUS VIOLATIONS

The phrase 'serious violations' of Common Article 3 and AP II has been held to be synonymous with 'breaches of a rule protecting important values [which] must involve grave consequences for the victim'.[289] While it may be possible that a violation of some of the prohibitions of Common Article 3 may be so minor as to not involve grave consequences for the victim, all depending on facts of a particular case,[290] it has been held that the list of prohibited acts provided in Common Article 3 as well as AP II 'undeniably should be recognized as serious violations entailing individual criminal responsibility'.[291]

The ICTR in *Kayishema and Ruzindana* held that for an act to violate Common Article 3 and AP II, the following elements must be established: the existence of a non-international armed conflict at the relevant time, a nexus between the accused and the armed forces, the commission of a crime *ratione loci* and *ratione personae*, and a nexus between the crime and the non-international armed conflict.[292]

RATIONE PERSONAE

With respect to the class of victims, they must be civilians or the civilian population as such. Common Article 3 of the Geneva Conventions protects 'persons taking no active part in the hostilities', whereas AP II stipulates in Article 4 that it intends to protect 'all persons who do not take a direct part or who have ceased to take part in hostilities'. These phrases have been treated as synonymous.[293] It should be noted, however, that whereas the concept of 'protected person' under the four Geneva Conventions is defined positively, the class of persons protected under Common Article 3 is defined negatively. In the latter case, a Trial Chamber is to ask whether, at the time of the alleged offence, the alleged victim was directly taking part in the hostilities in the context of which the alleged offence is said to have been committed; the victim will enjoy the protection of Common Article 3 if the answer to that question is in the negative.[294] Taking a 'direct' part in the hostilities means 'acts of war which by their very nature or purpose are likely to cause actual harm to the personnel and

---

[287] *Akayesu*, para. 617; *Rutaganda*, para. 90.
[288] *Blaskic*, para. 172.
[289] *Akayesu*, para. 616.
[290] *Tadic* Judgment, para. 612.
[291] *Aleksovski*, para. 184. See also *Akayesu*, paras. 616–7; *Rutaganda*, para. 104; *Musema*, paras. 286–8.
[292] *Kayishema and Ruzindana*, para. 169. Cf. also *Tadic* Judgment, para. 614.
[293] *Akayesu*, para. 629.
[294] *Tadic* Judgment, para. 615; *Rutaganda*, para. 98; *Blaskic*, para. 177.

equipment of the enemy armed forces'.[295] Whether someone qualifies as a person not taking part in the hostilities is a question of fact to be determined on a case-by-case basis.[296] Thus, where civilians bear their arms as a desperate and futile attempt at survival against thousands of armed assailants, these civilians are not considered to be taking a direct part in the hostilities.[297]

The determination of the 'civilian' or 'civilian population' status in an internal armed conflict is the same as in the case of international armed conflicts discussed above.[298]

Common Article 3(1) of the Geneva Conventions of 1949 provides that persons taking no active part in the hostilities shall in all circumstances be treated humanely, 'without any adverse distinction founded upon race, colour, religion or faith, sex, birth or wealth, or any other similar criteria'. The ICTY Appeals Chamber held in *Aleksovski* that the reference to 'without any adverse distinction' was intended to remove any possible basis for an argument that inhuman treatment of a particular class of persons may be justified.[299] Furthermore, there is no basis in Common Article 3 to the Geneva Conventions of 1949, or in provisions of AP I and AP II, for a requirement that customary international law imposes a requirement of proof of a discriminatory intent or motive.[300]

RATIONE LOCI

The rules contained in Common Article 3 apply not only to the narrow geographical context of the actual theatre of combat operations. Until a peaceful settlement to an internal armed conflict is reached, international humanitarian law continues to apply in the whole territory under the control of a Party to the armed conflict, whether or not actual armed combat occurs there, and the crimes committed in these circumstances are to be treated as crimes committed in the context of an armed conflict.[301]

AP II applies 'to all persons affected by an armed conflict as defined in Article 1'. It has been held in the case of the ICTR Statute that where an armed conflict meets the threshold requirements of Common Article 3 and AP II, the protection under these international instruments applies over the whole territory because it is impossible to apply rules of Common Article 3 in one part of the country and other rules under Common Article 3 plus AP II in other parts of the country.[302]

---

[295] *Rutaganda*, para. 98.

[296] *Tadic* Judgment, para. 616; *Akayesu*, para. 629; *Musema*, paras. 276–81.

[297] *Rutaganda*, para. 456.

[298] Trial Chamber II of the ICTR in *Kayishema and Ruzindana* treats civilians and the civilian population as such in an internal armed conflict by also referring to international instruments governing international armed conflicts (*Kayishema and Ruzindana*, paras. 179–81).

[299] *Aleksovski* (App. Ch.), para. 22, citing Pictet (ed.), *Commentary to the Geneva Conventions of 12 Aug. 1949, Geneva Convention IV Relative to the Protection of Civilian Persons in Time of War* (ICRC, 1958), at 40.

[300] *Aleksovski*, paras. 18–28, esp. at para. 23.

[301] *Tadic* Jurisdiction Decision, paras. 69–70. Followed in *Kayishema and Ruzindana*, paras. 182–3; *Akayesu*, paras. 635–6; *Rutaganda*, para. 104; *Musema*, paras. 283–4.

[302] *Akayesu*, paras. 635–6. Cf. also *Rutaganda*, para. 101.

NEXUS BETWEEN THE ARMED CONFLICT AND THE CRIME

Not all the crimes committed during an internal conflict are war crimes. There must be a direct, obvious link between the crime and the armed conflict in the sense of being closely related to or committed in conjunction with, or in the context of and is associated with, the armed conflict.[303] Whether such nexus exists is a matter of fact to be adjudged on a case-by-case basis.[304] For example, the fact that genocide has been proved does not establish automatically that there is an armed conflict in conjunction with which a war crime is committed.[305]

In the *Tadic* Jurisdiction Decision, the ICTY summarizes the international humanitarian law applicable to non-international armed conflicts in the following statement:

'The emergence of . . . general rules on internal armed conflicts does not imply that internal strife is regulated by general international law in all aspects. Two particular limitations may be noted: (i) only a number of rules and principles governing international armed conflicts have gradually been extended to apply to internal conflicts; and (ii) this extension has not taken place in the form of a full and mechanical transplant of those rules to internal conflicts; rather the general essence of those rules, and not the detailed regulation they may contain, has become applicable to internal conflicts.'[306]

Not all war crimes in international armed conflicts under the non-grave breach regime of Article 8(2)(b) of the ICC Statute are transposed into the comparable provisions under Article 8(2)(c) or (e) of the Statute. For example, the proscription of starvation under Article 8(2)(b)(xxv) of the Statute, which is also included explicitly in Article 14 of AP II, proved too controversial at the Rome Conference for it to be included in the Statute's regime of war crimes in internal conflicts.[307] There is also no provision comparable to Article 8(2)(b)(xvii)—(xx) on the proscription of the use of certain types of weapon.

To allay the concerns of a number of States, including China and Russia, that the inclusion of internal armed conflicts might open the door to interference in domestic affairs,[308] Article 8(3) of the ICC Statute provides explicitly:

'Nothing in paragraphs 2(c) and (e) shall affect the responsibility of a Government to maintain or re-establish law and order in the State or to defend the unity and territorial integrity of the State by all legitimate means.'

As if this provision is not enough, the eighth preambular paragraph of the Statute

---

[303] *Kayishema and Ruzindana*, paras. 186–8; *Rutaganda*, para. 102, and the cases cited therein; *Musema*, paras. 260–2. Cf. Trial Chamber I of the ICTR's statement in *Akayesu* (para. 636) that the crimes must not be committed by the perpetrator for purely personal motives.

[304] *Kayishema and Ruzindana*, para. 188; *Rutaganda*, para. 103.

[305] *Rutaganda*, paras. 461–2.

[306] *Tadic* Jurisdiction Decision, para. 67. See also Green, *Contemporary Law of Armed Conflict*, chap. 19; Meron, *War Crimes Law Comes of Age: Essays*, chap. xiii ('International Criminalization of Internal Atrocities').

[307] von Hebel and Robinson, 'Crimes within the Jurisdiction of the Court', 125, n. 122.

[308] Ibid., 121–2.

emphasizes that 'nothing in this Statute shall be taken as authorizing any State Party to intervene in an armed conflict in the internal affairs of any State'.

The Elements of Crimes adopted by the PCNICC for war crimes under Article 8(2)(c) and (e) of the ICC Statute have the following common elements. The perpetrator's conduct took place in the context of and was associated with an armed conflict not of an international character. The perpetrator was aware of factual circumstances that established the existence of an armed conflict.

SERIOUS VIOLATIONS OF ARTICLE 3 COMMON TO THE FOUR GENEVA CONVENTIONS OF 12 AUGUST 1949

Article 8(2)(c) of the ICC Statute proscribes violations of Common Article 3 of the Geneva Conventions, without any reference to AP II. Article 8(2)(d) of the ICC Statute sets the threshold by stipulating that:

'Paragraph 2(c) applies to armed conflicts not of an international character and thus does not apply to situations of internal disturbances and tensions, such as riots, isolated and sporadic acts of violence or other acts of a similar nature.'

The Elements of Crimes adopted by the PCNICC provide that the victim or victims of the perpetrator's proscribed conduct were either *hors de combat*, or were civilians, medical personnel, or religious personnel, including those non-confessional non-combatant military personnel carrying out a similar function, who were taking no active part in the hostilities. The perpetrator must have been aware of the factual circumstances that established this status of the victim or victims.

Violence to life and person, in particular murder of all kinds, mutilation, cruel treatment, and torture

The mental element required for this offence is the intention to cause violence to life or person of the victim as a result of the perpetrator's volition or recklessness.[309] The words 'in particular' signify that the list is not exhaustive.

Murder. While the prohibition of grave breaches in an international armed conflict, as it appears also in Article 8(2)(a)(i) of the ICC Statute, covers the crime of 'wilful killing', or '*l'homicide intentionnel*' in French, the word 'murder', or '*meurte*' in French, is used instead with regard to Common Article 3. However, it has been held that there can be no reason to attach meaning to the difference of terminology; it is equally prohibited to kill protected persons during an international armed conflict and persons taking no active part in hostilities in an internal armed conflict.[310] The nature and purpose of the prohibition in the Geneva Conventions are to proscribe the

---

[309] *Blaskic*, para. 182.
[310] *Celebici*, paras. 422–3; *Blaskic*, para. 181.

deliberate taking of the lives of defenceless and vulnerable persons who fall under the protection of the Conventions.[311]

The *actus reus* of murder is the taking of the lives of persons taking no active part in hostilities in an internal armed conflict. The requisite *mens rea* is the intention to kill, or inflict serious injury, in reckless disregard of human life. Recklessness means the taking of an excessive risk.[312] The specific elements of murder in this case are identical to murder as a crime against humanity, except for the context in which it takes place.[313]

The Elements of Crimes adopted by the PCNICC thus provide in this case that the perpetrator must have killed one or more persons who were either *hors de combat*, or were civilians, medical personnel, or religious personnel taking no active part in the hostilities, including those non-confessional non-combatant military personnel carrying out a similar function. The perpetrator must have been aware of the factual circumstances that established this status of such person or persons.

Mutilation. As already pointed out, the act of 'physical mutilation' proscribed under Article 8(2)(b)(x) of the ICC Statute and that of 'mutilation' proscribed under Article 8(2)(c)(i) of the same Statute are synonymous, except for the nature of the armed conflict at hand and the class of victims.

Torture. The characteristics of the offence of torture under Common Article 3 and under the grave breaches provisions in the case of international armed conflicts do not differ, except for the nature of the armed conflict involved and the class of victims.[314]

Cruel Treatment. There is no definition of cruel treatment in international instruments since it is impossible to find any satisfactory solution to this general concept. Whether a particular treatment is cruel must be determined in light of the circumstances of each specific case. However, guidance in terms of the form of cruel treatment may be sought from Article 4 of AP II which proscribes 'violence to the life, health and physical or mental well-being of persons, in particular murder as well as *cruel treatment such as torture, mutilation or any form of corporal punishment*'.[315]

In the case of the ICTY Statute, cruel treatment is brought either in the alternative charge of torture or, in case of international armed conflicts, alternative to charges of grave breaches by wilfully causing great suffering or serious injury or inhuman treatment.[316] Therefore, three of the accused in *Celebici* could be found guilty of cruel treatment or the offence of wilfully causing great suffering or serious injury or

---

[311] *Celebici*, para. 431; *Jelisic*, para. 34.
[312] *Celebici*, paras. 431, 437–9. Cf. also *Jelisic*, para. 35.
[313] *Musema*, para. 285. Also *Celebici*, App. Ch. Judgment, para. 423.
[314] *Celebici*, paras. 442–3, 452–74. See also *Musema*, para. 285.
[315] *Tadic* Judgment, paras. 724–6. Emphasis added.
[316] *Celebici*, para. 545. Cf. also *Jelisic*, para. 52.

inhuman treatment for having subjected the Celebici prison-camp to an atmosphere of terror created by the killing and abuse of detainees and to inhumane living conditions by being deprived of adequate food, water, medical care, as well as sleeping and toilet facilities, thereby causing the detainees to suffer severe psychological and physical trauma. The sentences imposed for each of these two offences were the same; namely, five years' imprisonment for each offence in the case of one convict, and seven years' imprisonment for each offence for the other two convicts. Likewise, forcing brothers to perform fellatio on one another and forcing father and son to beat one another repeatedly over a period of ten minutes could be held to constitute acts of either inhuman treatment or cruel treatment if the relevant elements exist.[317]

The prohibition against cruel treatment under the Common Article 3 is 'a means to an end, the end being that of ensuring that persons taking no part in the hostilities shall in all circumstances be treated humanely'; there is no narrow or special meaning given to the term, but it includes torture, mutilation or any form of corporal punishment.[318] It extends to all acts or omissions which, judged objectively, are deliberate and not accidental, which cause serious mental or physical suffering or injury or constitute a serious attack on human dignity, including treatment that does not meet the purposive requirement for the offence of torture.[319] It was held in *Blaskic* that the use of civilian detainees to serve as human shields and to dig trenches in the war front constitutes cruel treatment.[320]

The distinctive element adopted by the PCNICC for this war crime of cruel treatment under Article 8(2)(c)(i) of the ICC Statute simply requires that the perpetrator must have inflicted severe physical or mental pain or suffering upon one or more persons.

Committing outrages upon personal dignity, in particular humiliating and degrading treatment

Committing outrages upon personal dignity is a form of inhuman treatment which constitutes particularly abominable acts causing more serious suffering than most other proscribed acts of its genre.[321]

It is an act motivated by the contempt on the dignity of another person. Such an act must be gravely humiliating or degrading for the victim although it need not be an attack directed against the physical or mental well-being of the victim. It suffices that the act inflicts genuine and lasting suffering upon the victim as a result of the

---

[317] *Celebici*, paras. 1066, 1070. The act of severe beating and kicking of victims was held to be cruel treatment in *Tadic* Judgment, para. 752. Now see *Celebici*, App. Ch. Judgment, paras. 424, 426.

[318] *Tadic* Judgment, paras. 723, 725.

[319] *Celebici*, paras. 443, 552. Followed in *Blaskic*, para. 186. Cf. also *Jelisic*, paras. 41–5.

[320] *Blaskic*, para. 186.

[321] *Aleksovski* Judgment, para. 54. However, the Appeals Chamber in that case states *obiter* that the Trial Chamber's reasoning in relation to this mental element is not always entirely clear, and that the *mens rea* 'intent to humiliate or ridicule' the victim may impose a requirement that the Prosecution is not obliged to prove. (*Aleksovski* (App. Ch.), para. 27.)

humiliation or ridicule. Although the degree of suffering varies from one person to another, depending on temperament of each person, the *actus reus* of the culpable act must satisfy an objective test; namely, the perpetrator must commit a humiliating or degrading act upon the victim to the extent that a reasonable man would feel outraged thereby. With regard to the requisite *mens rea*, the perpetrator must wilfully or intentionally act or omit to act with intent to humiliate or ridicule the victim, being aware of the foreseeable and logical consequences that his act or omission will humiliate or degrade the victim.[322] The degree of gravity of an act and its consequences may depend on the character of the act itself, as well as its repetition which could transform an act that is not outrageous into an outrageous act when repeated several times. The form of violence inflicted on the victim, its duration and seriousness, and the intensity of the physical or moral suffering may also be used to determine whether a set of facts in question would amount to the crime.[323]

Inhuman treatment constituting outrages upon personal dignity includes insults, threats, thefts, physical violence, as well as physical and psychological ordeals of having to serve as human shields and to excavate trenches in dangerous areas.[324] As the ICTY Appeals Chamber rules in *Aleksovski*, these acts are 'serious' because their victims are not merely inconvenienced or made uncomfortable—they have to endure, under prevailing circumstances, 'physical and psychological abuse and outrages that any human being would have experienced as such'.[325]

It should be noted that Article 4(e) of the ICTR Statute proscribes 'outrages upon personal dignity, in particular humiliating and degrading treatment, rape, enforced prostitution and any form of indecent assault'. Trial Chamber I of the ICTR held in *Akayesu* that sexual violence, which includes rape, falls within the scope of 'outrages upon personal dignity' set forth in Article 4(e) of the ICTR Statute.[326] Sexual violence is defined by the Trial Chamber as 'any act of a sexual nature which is committed on a person under circumstances which are coercive'. It is not confined to physical invasion of the human body but may include acts not involving penetration or physical contact. For instance, forcing a woman to undress and do gymnastics naked in public in front of a crowd is sexual violence. Coercive circumstances may be evidenced by a show of physical force or by threats, intimidation, extortion, and other forms of duress that prey on the fear or desperation of the victim.[327] Trial Chamber I of the ICTR in *Musema* defines 'humiliating and degrading treatment' as the act of 'subjecting victims to treatment designed to subvert their self-regard'; it may be considered a lesser form of torture but without the motives required for torture or committed

---

[322] *Aleksovski* Judgment, para. 56. Therefore, culpable negligence is not sufficient.

[323] Ibid., para. 57.

[324] Ibid., paras. 87–9. Although the relevant domestic law requires citizens to perform certain work in dangerous conditions, such law would not be applicable to those civilians who benefit from the protection of international humanitarian law. Ibid., para. 127.

[325] *Aleksovski* (App. Ch.), para. 37.

[326] *Akayesu*, para. 688.

[327] Ibid.

under State authority.[328] 'Indecent assault', which is another form of outrage upon personal dignity, is defined as 'infliction of pain or injury by an act which was of a sexual nature ... by means of coercion, force, threat or intimidation and was non-consensual'.[329]

Like war crimes in international armed conflict, the victim of a war crime of 'inhumane act' need not be a living human being; hence, certain acts against dead bodies that offend philosophical and religious notions of respect for the human being upon death may amount to inhumane treatment or outrages on personal dignity.[330]

The Elements of Crimes adopted by the PCNICC in the case of this crime under Article 8(2)(c)(i) of the ICC Statute read as follows:

'1. The perpetrator humiliated, degraded, or otherwise violated the dignity of one or more persons. (For this crime, "persons" can include dead persons. It is understood that the victim need not personally be aware of the existence of the humiliation or degradation, or other violation. This element takes into account relevant aspects of the cultural background of the victim.)

2. The severity of the humiliation, degradation, or other violation was of such degree as to be generally recognized as an outrage upon personal dignity.'

Taking of hostages

Taking of hostages in non-international armed conflict is prohibited by both Common Article 3 of the four Geneva Conventions of 1949 and Article 4(2)(c) of AP II. Taking of hostages is now generally considered contrary to the customary law of human rights and is criminalized by most legal systems.[331]

The constituent Elements of this offence under Common Article 3 of the 1949 Geneva Conventions are similar to those required for the offence of taking of hostages as a war crime of grave breach committed in an international armed conflict.[332]

The passing of sentences and the carrying out of executions without previous judgment pronounced by a regularly constituted court, affording all judicial guarantees which are generally recognized as indispensable

With regard to this offence, the Rome Conference changed the phrase 'recognized as indispensable by civilized people' as originally appeared in Common Article 3 of the Geneva Conventions to become 'generally recognized as indispensable' as currently appeared in Article 8(2)(c)(iv) of the ICC Statute.

The Elements of Crimes adopted by the PCNICC stipulate in the case of this war crime that the perpetrator must have passed sentence or executed one or more persons without any previous judgment pronounced by a court, or if there was a previous

---

[328] *Musema*, para. 285.
[329] Ibid.
[330] Cf. *Trial of Max Schmid*, UNWCC *Law Reports*, xiii, 151–2. Cited in *Tadic* Judgment, para. 748.
[331] See, e.g. the 1979 Hostages Convention. Also Green, *Contemporary Law of Armed Conflict*, 309.
[332] *Blaskic*, para. 158.

judgment the court that rendered judgment did not afford the essential guarantees of independence and impartiality,[333] or did not afford all other judicial guarantees generally recognized as indispensable under international law. The perpetrator must have been aware of the absence of a previous judgment or of the denial of relevant guarantees and the fact that they are essential or indispensable to a fair trial. In this connection, the ICC should consider whether, in light of all relevant circumstances, the cumulative effect of factors with respect to guarantees deprived the person or person of a fair trial.

The ICC will certainly have to consider all judicial guarantees recognized by different legal systems, including the European Court of Human Rights, the Inter-American system of human rights, and those judicial guarantees incorporated into widely accepted international instruments such as the International Covenant on Civil and Political Rights.[334]

OTHER SERIOUS VIOLATIONS OF THE LAWS AND CUSTOMS APPLICABLE IN ARMED CONFLICTS NOT OF AN INTERNATIONAL CHARACTER[335]

Article 8(2)(e) of the ICC Statute does not incorporate explicitly the fundamental guarantees under Article 4 of AP II, which has not been ratified by a number of prospective ratifiers of the ICC Statute anyway. Article 8(2)(e) of the ICC Statute intends to add to the regime of protection under Common Article 3 of the four Geneva Conventions of 1949 'other serious violations of the laws and customs applicable in armed conflicts not of an international character, within the established framework of international law'. The norms covered by this provision are derived from a variety of sources, such as the Hague Regulations (1907), the four Geneva Conventions of 1949, and AP II where the provisions of AP II have been considered part of customary international law.

The threshold requirement is stipulated in Article 8(2)(f) as follows:

'Paragraph 2(e) applies to armed conflicts not of an international character and thus does not apply to situations of internal disturbances and tensions, such as riots, isolated and sporadic acts of violence or other acts of a similar nature. It applies to armed conflicts that take place in the territory of a State when there is protracted armed conflict between governmental authorities and organized armed groups or between such groups.'

This provision is identical to the threshold provision for Article 8(2)(c) of the

---

[333] Art. 6(2) of AP II replaces the term 'regularly constituted court' as stipulated in Common Article 3(1)(d) of the Geneva Conventions with 'a court offering the essential guarantees of independence and impartiality'. This covers the situation where the victim is tried by a court set up by an insurgent party. See *Doc. PCNICC/1999/WGEC/INF. 2*, at 92.

[334] These judicial guarantees are quite exhaustively analysed by the ICRC in ibid., 89–113.

[335] The author is indebted to the ICRC's text on Art. 8(2)(e) of the ICC Statute submitted to the PCNICC on 24 Nov. 1999 as contained in *Doc. PCNICC/1999/WGEC/INF/2/ Add.3*.

Statute as provided in Article 8(2)(d) of that Statute, with one exception. The second sentence of Article 8(2)(e) is a novel provision to cover a 'protracted armed conflict' and a situation where organized armed groups fight each other without any involvement of governmental authorities. The threshold for the applicability of Article 8(2)(e) is therefore much lower than that of Article 8(2)(c).[336] It is also much lower than the threshold for the applicability of AP II. Like Article 8(2)(c) of the ICC Statute, Article 8(3) provides that nothing in Article 8(2)(e) shall affect the responsibility of a government to maintain or re-establish law and order in the State or to defend the unity and territorial integrity of that State, by all legitimate means.

Article 8(2)(e)(i) of the ICC Statute corresponds to Article 13(2) of AP II, Article 8(2)(e)(ii) of the ICC Statute corresponds to Article 11 of AP II, Article 8(2)(e)(iii) of the ICC Statute reflects Article 16 of AP II, and Article 8(2)(e)(viii) of the ICC Statute reflects Article 17 of AP II. The provisions of Article 8(2)(e)(v), (ix), (x), (xi), and (xii) reflect the attempt to incorporate norms of the customary international humanitarian law applicable to international armed conflicts (the Hague Regulations (1907)) to be applicable to cases of conflicts not of an international character. Article 8(2)(e)(iii) intends to satisfy the overwhelming demand of the international community that intentional attacks against international humanitarian assistance or peacekeeping missions be made an international crime. Article 8(2)(e)(vii) proscribes the use of child soldiers, in response to the international outrage against this phenomenon. Article 8(2)(e)(vi), which proscribes the commission of rape, sexual slavery, enforced prostitution, forced pregnancy, and enforced sterilization, may be said to incorporate the international customary humanitarian law in international armed conflicts to be applicable in non-international armed conflicts as well. The phrase 'and any other form of sexual violence also constituting a serious violation of article 3 common to the four Geneva Conventions' at the end of that provision seems to mean any other form of sexual violence that is an outrage upon personal dignity, in particular humiliating and degrading treatment, as proscribed by Common Article 3 and incorporated into Article 8(2)(c)(ii) of the ICC Statute.

In general, the Elements of Crimes adopted by the PCNICC for the war crimes in Article 8(2)(e) of the ICC Statute are identical to the ones adopted for the corresponding war crimes under Article 8(2)(b) of the Statute except for the nature of the conflict at hand.

Intentionally directing attacks against the civilian population as such or against individual civilians not taking direct part in hostilities

This provision is derived from the first sentence of Article 13(2) of AP II, which provides: 'The civilian population as such, as well as individual civilians, shall not be the object of attack'. This prohibition, which includes, prohibition of reprisals

---

[336] See von Hebel and Robinson, 'Crimes within the Jurisdiction of the Court', 120–1.

against civilians, has been held by the ICTY to be part of customary international law.[337]

The elements of this crime are identical to those of the war crime of attacking civilians in Article 8(2)(b)(i) of the ICC Statute with the sole exception of the nature of the armed conflict involved.

Intentionally directing attacks against buildings, material, medical units and transport, and personnel using the distinctive emblems of the Geneva Conventions in conformity with international law

The offence is derived from numerous prohibitions of attacks stipulated in AP II, including Articles 9 and 11 of AP II.[338]

This war crime is identical to the one in Article 8(2)(b)(xxiv) of the ICC Statute except for the nature of the armed conflict.

Intentionally directing attacks against personnel, installations, material, units or vehicles in a humanitarian assistance or peacekeeping mission in accordance with the UN Charter, as long as they are entitled to the protection given to civilian objects under the international law of armed conflict

This war crime corresponds to that in Article 8(2)(b)(iii) of the ICC Statute. Although Article 2(2) of the 1994 Convention on the Safety of United Nations and Associated Personnel provides guidance as to the duration of the protection against such attacks during an international armed conflict only, there is no substantive difference between the elements of this type of war crimes as committed in international armed conflicts or in internal conflicts. This is because, in the case of internal armed conflicts, Article 13(3) of AP II sets essentially the same standard regarding the protection as in international armed conflicts. It provides that 'civilians' shall enjoy the protection unless and for such time as they take a direct part in hostilities. In the case of civilian objects, they logically lose protection for such time as they are used to make an effective contribution to military action or a party to a conflict.[339] This same rationale applies to humanitarian assistance missions.[340]

Thus, the Elements of Crimes for this offence under Article 8(2)(b)(iii) and those for the war crime under Article 8(2)(e)(iii) are identical, except that in the latter case

---

[337] See *Tadic* Jurisdiction Decision, para. 127; *Prosecutor v. Milan Martic*, ICTY App. Ch. Decision on Review of Indictment pursuant to Rule 61 of the Rules of Procedure and Evidence, Case No. IT-95–11-R61, paras. 11, 15, 17.

[338] See further, *Doc. PCNICC/ 1999/ WGEC/ INF/ 2/ Add. 3*, at 11–14.

[339] This deduction is arrived at by the ICRC by considering analogous provisions in Art. 52(2) of AP I which is followed and made applicable to both internal and international conflicts in Art. 2(6) of the Protocol on Prohibitions or Restrictions on the Use of Mines, Booby-Traps and Other Devices as amended on 3 May 1996 (Protocol II to the 1980 Convention as amended), and in Art. 1(6) of the Second Protocol to the Hague Convention of 1954 for the Protection of Cultural Property in the Event of Armed Conflict of 26 Mar. 1999 (*Doc. PCNICC/ 1999/ WGEC/ INF/ 2/ Add. 3*, at 16–17). See also Art. 11(2) of AP II in the case of medical units and transports.

[340] ICRC, *Doc. PCNICC/ 1999/ WGEC/ INF/2/ Add. 3*, at 18–19.

the perpetrator's proscribed conduct took place in the context of and was associated with an armed conflict not of an international character.

Intentionally directing attacks against buildings dedicated to religion, education, art, science or charitable purposes, historic monuments, hospitals and places where the sick and wounded are collected, provided they are not military objectives

This war crime corresponds to the war crime in Article 8(2)(b)(ix) of the ICC Statute. The provision is derived from Articles 27 and 56 of the Hague Regulations (1907). While the Hague Regulations (1907) do not directly apply to internal conflicts, their relevant provisions have been incorporated into the 1954 Hague Convention for the Protection of Cultural Property in the Event of Armed Conflict, which is applicable to internal conflicts, and AP II.[341]

The pertinent element of the Elements of Crimes adopted by the PCNICC for this war crime substitutes 'an armed conflict not of an international character' for 'an international armed conflict' in the corresponding element of the Elements of Crimes for the war crime in Article 8(2)(b)(ix) of the Statute, however.

Pillaging a town or a place, even when taken by assault

This war crime corresponds to the one in Article 8(2)(b)(xvi) of the ICC Statute. Instead of 'an international armed conflict' in the Elements of Crimes adopted by the PCNICC for the war crime in Article 8(2)(b)(xvi), 'an armed conflict not of an international character' is used in the Elements of Crimes for this present war crime.

Committing rape, sexual slavery, enforced prostitution, forced pregnancy, as defined in Article 7(2)(f) of the ICC Statute, enforced sterilization, or any other form of sexual violence also constituting a serious violation of Article 3 common to the four Geneva Conventions

The Elements of Crimes adopted by the PCNICC for the war crimes listed in this Article are identical to the ones adopted for the war crimes listed in Article 8(2)(b)(xxii) of the ICC Statute, with the exception of the phrase 'an international armed conflict' being replaced by 'an armed conflict not of an international character'.

Besides, the Elements of Crimes for the war crime of sexual violence under Article 8(2)(e)(vi) substitutes 'a serious violation of article 3 common to the four Geneva Conventions' for 'a grave breach of the Geneva Conventions' in the Elements for the war crime of sexual violence under Article 8(2)(b)(xxii) of the ICC Statute. The phrase 'also constituting a serious violation of article 3 common to the four Geneva Conventions' in Article 8(2)(e)(vi) has a dual purpose. It aims at ensuring that any other type of sexual acts that deserves to be criminalized as a war crime under that provision must be of gravity comparable to the other sexual crimes enumerated

---

[341] Ibid. at 19–23. See also, e.g., Arts. 11 and 16 of AP II.

therein. In addition, it allows this offence to be charged as a serious violation of the Common Article 3.

Conscripting or enlisting children under the age of fifteen years into the national armed forces or using them to participate actively in hostilities

Article 4(3)(c) of AP II stipulates that 'children who have not attained the age of fifteen years shall neither be recruited in the armed forces or groups nor allowed to take part in hostilities'.

Although this provision is not followed verbatim in CROC, which prefers to adopt the formulation of Article 77(2) of AP I, there is no reason to assume that there are differences between the prohibition of recruitment or use of children under fifteen years old in case international armed conflict and that in internal armed conflict. The essential elements as well as the rationale for the prohibition are identical in both cases.

Thus, the Elements of Crimes adopted by the PCNICC for this war crime are identical to the ones adopted for the war crime in Article 8(2)(b)(xxvi) of the ICC Statute, with two exceptions. First of all, the words 'an armed force or group' replace the words 'national armed forces' for the purpose of the war crime under Article 8(2)(e)(vii), so as to cover the conscription or enlistment of children into rebel forces or the use by rebel forces of children to actively participate in hostilities. Secondly, the phrase 'an armed conflict not of an international character' replaces 'an international armed conflict' in the Elements of Crimes for the war crime under Article 8(2)(b)(xxvi).

Ordering the displacement of the civilian population for reasons related to the conflict, unless the security of the civilians involved or imperative military reasons so demand

This war crime is derived directly from the first sentence of Article 17(1) of AP II. It is the only war crime under Article 8(2)(e) of the ICC Statute that has no comparable provision in Article 8(2)(b) of the Statute.

The PCNICC has adopted the Elements of Crimes for this war crime as follows:

'1. The perpetrator ordered a displacement of a civilian population.

2. Such order was not justified by the security of the civilians involved or by military necessity.

3. The perpetrator was in a position to effect such displacement by giving such order.'

Instances of unlawful displacement include displacement for the purpose of 'ethnic cleansing' within a State.[342]

Killing or wounding treacherously a combatant adversary

The offence is derived from Article 23(b) of the Hague Regulations (1907), which

---

[342] *Prosecutor v. Karadzic and Mladic,* Cases No. IT-95–5-R61 and No. IT-95–18-R61, paras. 66 ff. Cited in *Doc. PCNICC/ 1999/ WGEC/ INF. 2* at 128.

do not directly apply to internal conflicts. In the *Tadic* Jurisdiction Decision, the ICTY held that the prohibition of perfidy in international armed conflicts also applies to internal conflict, relying on a case before the Nigerian Supreme Court to the effect that rebels must not feign civilian status while engaging in military operations.[343]

This war crime is almost identical to the war crime of killing or wounding treacherously individuals belonging to the hostile nation or enemy under Article 8(2)(b)(xi) of the ICC Statute. The Elements of Crimes adopted by the PCNICC for the war crimes in these two Articles are identical, with two exceptions. First of all, the war crime under Article 8(2)(e)(ix) is committed in an internal armed conflict, not an international armed conflict as in the case of the war crime under Article 8(2)(b)(xi). Secondly, the Elements of Crimes for the war crime in Article 8(2)(e)(ix) use the term 'combatant adversaries' to describe the victims, whereas the Elements for the war crime under Article 8(2)(b)(xi) describe the victims as persons belonging to 'an adverse party'.

Although the legal instruments applicable to armed conflicts not of an international character, including AP II, do not contain the concept of 'combatant', Articles 4(1) and 13(3) of AP II make it clear that persons not taking an active or direct part in the hostilities are entitled to fundamental guarantees of humane treatment and protection against the dangers arising from military operations. Thus, a combatant adversary in non-international armed conflicts is a person taking an active or direct part in the hostilities against the accused.[344] The term 'combatant adversary' that is used instead of 'individuals belonging to the hostile nation or army' as used in Article 8(2)(b)(xi) of the Statute has the consequence of excluding from the ambit of the war crime in an internal conflict the treacherous killing or wounding of a civilian adversary. Instead such killing or wounding of a civilian adversary in an internal armed conflict is only a war crime of violence to life and person under Article 8(2)(c)(i) of the ICC Statute, although the treacherous nature of the conduct may be an aggravating factor in sentencing.[345]

Declaring that no quarter will be given

The fundamental guarantees under Article 4 of AP II provide, *inter alia*, that '[i]t is prohibited to order that there shall be no survivors'.[346]

In pith and substance, this war crime is identical to the one in Article 8(2)(b)(xii) of the ICC Statute, with one exception. The phrase 'an international armed conflict' is replaced by 'an armed conflict not of an international character' in the case of the war crime in Article 8(2)(e)(x).

---

[343] *Tadic* Jurisdiction Decision, para. 125, citing *Pius Nwaoga v. The State* (1979) 52 *ILR* 496 ff. Also cited in *Doc. PCNICC/ 1999/ WGEC/ INF/ 2/ Add. 3*, at 24 and n. 25.

[344] Cf. ICRC, *Doc. PCNICC/ 1999/ WGEC/ INF/2/ Add. 3*, at 25.

[345] Ibid.

[346] See further *Doc. PCNICC/ 1999/ WGEC/ INF/ 2/ Add. 3*, at 26–7.

Subjecting persons who are in the power of another party to the conflict to physical mutilation or to medical or scientific experiments of any kind which are neither justified by the medical, dental or hospital treatment of the person concerned nor carried out in his or her interest, and which cause death to or seriously endanger the health of such person or persons

The war crimes listed in this Article correspond to the ones in Article 8(2)(b)(x) of the ICC Statute. The two differences in the Elements of Crimes are, firstly, that in the case of the war crimes listed in Article 8(2)(e)(xi) the criminalized conduct took place in the context of and was associated with 'an armed conflict not of an international character', and, secondly, Article 8(2)(e)(xi) uses the phrase 'in the power of another party to the conflict' instead of 'in the power of an adverse party' as in Article 8(2)(b)(x).

Destroying or seizing the property of an adversary unless such destruction or seizure be imperatively demanded by the necessities of the conflict

This war crime corresponds to the one in Article 8(2)(b)(xiii) of the ICC Statute. However, the term 'an international armed conflict' in the Elements of Crimes adopted by the PCNICC for the war crime in Article 8(2)(b)(xiii) is replaced by 'an armed conflict not of an international character' in the case of the war crime under Article 8(2)(e)(xii). In addition, the term 'property of an adversary' replaces 'property of a hostile party' in Article 8(2)(b)(xiii).

7

AGGRESSION AND OTHER INTERNATIONAL CRIMES

7.1 AGGRESSION

Pursuant to Article 5(1)(d) of the ICC Statute, the ICC has jurisdiction in accordance with the Statute with respect to the crime of aggression. However, Article 5(2) of the Statute provides that the ICC shall exercise jurisdiction over this crime once a provision is adopted in accordance with Articles 121 and 123 defining the crime and setting out the conditions under which the ICC shall exercise jurisdiction with respect to this crime. In any case, such a provision 'shall be consistent with the relevant provisions of the Charter of the United Nations'.[1]

Article 121 of the ICC Statute governs the amendment procedure. After the expiry of seven years from the entry into force of the ICC Statute, any State Party may propose amendments to the Statute which must be adopted by consensus or a two-thirds majority of States Parties. An amendment shall enter into force for all States Parties one year after the instruments of ratification or acceptance have been deposited with the UN Secretary-General by seven-eighths of the States Parties, but any State Party which has not accepted the amendment may withdraw from the Statute with immediate effect by giving notice no later than one year after the entry into force of such amendment. However, any amendment to Articles 5 to 8 is the sole exception to this general rule; it shall enter into force only for those States Parties which have accepted the amendment one year after the deposit of their instruments of ratification or acceptance. The ICC shall not exercise its jurisdiction regarding a crime covered by the amendment to these Articles when committed by nationals or on the territory of a State Party which has not accepted the amendment.

Article 123 of the ICC Statute concerns amendments by a Review Conference which shall be convened seven years after the entry into force of the ICC Statute or at any time thereafter. Rules governing the binding effect of amendments adopted by the Review Conference are identical to those stipulated in Article 121.

Of all the crimes listed in Article 5 of the ICC Statute, the crime of aggression is

---

[1] For a concise legislative history, see H. von Hebel and D. Robinson, 'Crimes within the Jurisdiction of the Court', in R. S. Lee (ed.), *The International Criminal Court: The Making of the Rome Statute—Issues, Negotiations, Results* (Kluwer, 1999), 79 at 80–5.

exceptional in many ways. It has no definition, no enumerated list of acts falling within that definition, and no indication of constituent elements of the crime. Above all, determination of aggression by a State is a *sine qua non* condition for the attribution of individual criminal responsibility for the crime of aggression.[2]

The inclusion of the crime of aggression in the ICC's jurisdiction is borne out by the desire to ensure that this crime be punished, as it was punished under the rubric of 'crimes against peace' under the Nuremberg Charter and the Tokyo Charter at the end of WWII. Indeed, it was in the context of the crimes against peace that the Nuremberg Tribunal made the now classic pronouncement that 'crimes against international law are committed by men, not by abstract entities, and only by punishing individuals who commit such crimes can the provisions of international law be enforced'.[3] According to the Nuremberg Tribunal, war is essentially an evil thing because its consequences affect the whole world. Therefore, to initiate a war of aggression is 'not only an international crime; it is the supreme international crime differing only from other war crimes in that it contains within itself the accumulated evil of the whole'.[4]

The crimes against peace enumerated in Article 6(a) of the Nuremberg Charter were: 'planning, preparation, initiation or waging of a war of aggression, or a war in violation of international treaties, agreements or assurances, or participation in a common plan or conspiracy for the accomplishment of any of the foregoing'. One study finds that the US wanted to include a definition of 'aggression' in the Nuremberg Charter so that the Defence would not be able to argue that 'crimes against peace' lacked precise elements and were thus not enforceable. The Soviet Union and France were opposed to the inclusion of such definition. For the Soviet Union, the Allies were meeting to enumerate the acts for which the Nazi leaders were to be held criminally responsible. For France, it doubted whether starting a war itself, as distinguished from committing crimes in the conduct of war (that is, war crimes), had incurred individual criminal responsibility.[5] Nevertheless, this lack of definition in no way deterred the Nuremberg Tribunal, and subsequently the Tokyo Tribunal, from punishing the accused charged with this offence. The Tokyo Charter merely inserted the words 'declared or undeclared' before 'wars of aggression' to pre-empt any argument that Japan was not technically at war with any State since it had not formally declared war against anyone. Judge B. V. A. Röling of the Netherlands, who dissented from the majority opinion of the Tokyo Tribunal, notes the Japanese doubt as to the fairness of the trial because the Tokyo Charter presumed that Japan had carried out an

---

[2] Report of the International Law Commission, UN GAOR, 51st Sess., Supp. No. 10, *UN Doc. A/ 51/ 10 (1996)*, 84–5.

[3] *Trial of the Major War Criminals*, Proceedings of the International Military Tribunal, Nuremberg, pt. 22 (H.M. Stationery Office, 1950) (hereinafter '*Nuremberg Proceedings*'), 447; (1947) **41** *AJIL* 172 at 221.

[4] *Nuremberg Proceedings*, 421; (1947) **41** *AJIL* 186.

[5] L. S. Sunga, *The Emerging System of International Criminal Law: Development in Codification and Implementation* (Kluwer, 1997), 41–3.

aggressive war, which the Tokyo Tribunal had, as yet, to establish.[6] For instance, owing to the assumption of the existence of a conspiracy to wage war in the Pacific, border incidents like the ones on Lake Khazan in 1938 and the Khalkin-Gol River in 1939 were treated as wars waged by Japan against the Soviet Union.[7] The vanquished were deemed to have committed aggression and those involved were to be punished.

The ICC Statute, on the other hand, is a product of multilateral negotiations among 160 sovereign States, many of whom have been engaged in some kind of armed conflict against other States. Above all, some of the Permanent Members of the UN Security Council have taken military actions without prior approval of the UN Security Council, and, arguably, for purposes not authorized by the UN Charter. The line dividing aggression and international 'humanitarian intervention' by external armed forces is not clearly delineated.[8] Neither are the parameters of self-defence. The international legal order governing international peace and security under the UN Charter is, therefore, somewhat flawed, and, when the international community has to define the crime of aggression to be prosecuted by the ICC, there is no consensus on how to do it.

Press releases of the statements made at the Rome Conference show at least eight positions of States concerning the crime of aggression as a crime under the ICC's jurisdiction.[9]

First of all, some delegations were in favour of the inclusion of the crime of aggression within the ICC's jurisdiction. Benjamin B. Ferencz, a former prosecutor at the Nuremberg Trials, noted the fact that the UN Charter does not provide for criminal prosecution of those who have committed aggression, and this gap would have to be filled by an independent court. In his opinion, excluding aggression from international judicial scrutiny would grant immunity to those responsible for the 'supreme international crime' and would encourage war rather than peace. The following States shared his view: Afghanistan, Azerbaijan, Bahrain, Bulgaria, Cape Verde, Cyprus, Denmark, Gabon, Georgia, Ghana, Greece, Guinea, Indonesia, Iran (as the

---

[6] B. V. A. Röling, 'Introduction', in B. V. A. Röling and C. F. Rüter (eds.), *The Tokyo Judgment; The International Military Tribunal for the Far East (I.M.T.F.E.), 29 April 1946–12 November 1948*, i, (APA—University Press Amsterdam BV, 1977) hereinafter '*Tokyo Judgment*', xiii.

[7] Ibid., xii.

[8] Cf. V. P. Nanda, 'The Validity of United States Intervention in Panama under International Law', (1990) **84** *AJIL* 494 at 498–500; T. J. Farer, 'Panama: Beyond the Charter Paradigm', ibid., 503 at 508–15; A. D'Amato, 'The Invasion of Panama Was a Lawful Response to Tyranny', ibid., 516 at 519–24; C. Greenwood, 'Is there a right of humanitarian intervention?', *The World Today* (Feb. 1993), 34; L. F. Damrosch (ed.), *Enforcing Restraint: Collective Intervention in Internal Conflicts* (West View Press, 1995), *passim*; T. M. Franck, *Fairness in International Law and Institutions* (Clarendon Press, 1995), 272–4; S. D. Murphy, *Humanitarian Intervention: The United Nations in an Evolving World Order* (University of Pennsylvania Press, 1996), *passim*; R. Mullerson, 'Book Reviews and Notes: *Humanitarian Intervention: The United Nations in an Evolving World Order. By Sean D. Murphy*', (1998) **92** *AJIL* 583; A. Orford, 'Locating the International: Military and Monetary Interventions after the Cold War' (1997) **38** *Harvard Int'l L. J.* 443; A. Cassese, '*Ex iniuria ius oritur.* Are We Moving towards International Legitimation of Forcible Humanitarian Countermeasures in the World Community?' (1999) **10** *Euro. J. Int'l L.* 23.

[9] The Press Releases are accessible from the website *http://www.un.org/icc/pressrel/lrom*. The Press Releases are from No. L./ROM/6. R1 of 15 June 1998 onwards.

Spokesman of the Non-Aligned Movement), Ireland, Italy, Macedonia, the Philippines, Slovakia, Tanzania, Uganda, Vietnam, and Zambia.

A second, slightly different position, would include the crime of aggression in the ICC's jurisdiction only if there was a clearly defined definition of the actual crime. Those expressing their position to this effect were Angola, Brunei, Croatia, Estonia, Kazahkstan, Latvia, Malta, Mexico, Mozambique, Namibia, the Netherlands, Portugal, and Sierra Leone.

Pursuant to a third position, the crime of aggression to be included in the ICC's jurisdiction had to follow the definition adopted by the UN General Assembly in its Resolution 3314 (XXIX) on the Definition of Aggression of 14 December 1974. Those adopting this position were Egypt, Oman, Syria, and the League of Arab States. However, the League would make a distinction between an act of aggression and the 'legitimate struggle of peoples for self-determination'.

A fourth instance was taken by Armenia, who wished to see the crime of aggression included within the ICC's jurisdiction, with an expanded definition of the crime to cover the blockade of ports, coasts, territory, and air routes of a State by the armed force of another State.

A fifth position was that of Cuba, who wanted the crime of aggression and the 'threat or use of force' included within the ICC's jurisdiction.

A sixth position, that of Libya, would include 'aggression to the environment' within the ICC's jurisdiction.

Some delegations would include the crime of aggression within the ICC's jurisdiction only if the UN Security Council first determines that a State has committed an act of aggression. The States endorsing this position were the Czech Republic, France, Germany, Hungary, Lithuania, Poland, Russia, Turkey, the UK, and the US. The Netherlands simply assumed that there was a generally acceptable solution on the role of the Security Council on this issue.

The last position opposed the inclusion of the crime of aggression in the ICC's jurisdiction. According to Morocco, the ICC should steer clear of political issues such as the question of aggression.

Many States, including Azerbaijan, Guinea, and Latvia, declared that they had been victims of aggression. On the other hand, it was remarkable to see that several States that have launched large-scale armed invasions against another sovereign State spoke in favour of the inclusion of the crime of aggression within the ICC's Statute. This inevitably causes suspicion in the minds of neutral observers as to the ulterior motives of these States.

Benjamin B. Ferencz summarizes what happened at the Rome Conference as follows:

'When the final plenipotentiary negotiating sessions began in Rome in the summer of 1998, most States, including the European Union and about 30 nations united in the Non-Aligned Movement, insisted that without the inclusion of aggression as a crime they would be unable to support the new court. Many Arab States wanted the [UN General Assembly Resolution of 14 December 1974 on the Definition of Aggression] consensus definition, with possibly some improvements in their favour, included in the ICC Statute. Germany's delegate, Dr

Hans-Peter Kaul, pressed various compromise solutions. India and Pakistan, busy testing new nuclear weapons, were not inclined to subject themselves to possible charges of aggression. China stressed the protection of its national sovereignty. The US, mindful of military and political considerations, remained aloof on the question of including aggression and insisted on preserving the Security Council's veto rights as guaranteed by the UN Charter. A host of real or politically motivated concerns about including aggression that had been voiced during earlier meetings remained unaltered. There simply was not enough time in Rome to reach agreement on these sensitive questions. In the end, the agile and adroit Chairman Philippe Kirsch of Canada found the only compromise possible: the resolution of the differences was postponed to a later day.'[10]

DEFINITION OF AGGRESSION

The Nuremberg Tribunal did not define 'aggression' but it distinguished between 'aggressive actions' and 'aggressive wars'. The annexation of Austria and the imposition of German administration on parts of Czechoslovakia, both in March 1938, were considered aggressive actions or steps in a plan to wage aggressive war against other States, and the individuals responsible were held guilty of a conspiracy to commit a crime against peace. The Nuremberg Tribunal held that aggressive wars had been waged, starting from September 1939, against Poland, Denmark, Norway, the Netherlands, Belgium, Luxembourg, Yugoslavia, Greece, the USSR, and the US. In the latter case, the individuals responsible were held guilty of waging aggressive war. The Tribunal left open the question whether the armed conflicts with Britain and France were aggressive wars. In the case of aggressive actions, the governments of Austria and Czechoslovakia had agreed to submit to Hitler's demands *before* the entrance of German troops. As for aggressive wars, the governments concerned had resisted Hitler's demands, in most cases *after* the entrance of German troops.[11]

Control Council Law No. 10 permitted each occupying authority in Germany to carry out its own trials of persons in custody. The definition of the crimes against peace under Control Council Law No. 10 was expanded from that of Article 6 of the Nuremberg Charter to include 'initiation of invasions' which were not resisted, as in the cases of the German annexation of Austria and Czechoslovakia. Thus, in the *Ministries* case the US Military Tribunal held the German annexation of Austria and Germany's action in Czechoslovakia to be an 'aggressive invasion' and a crime against peace *per se*.[12]

The Tokyo Charter closely followed the formulation of the offence of crimes against peace in the Nuremberg Charter, with no definition of aggression given. The Tokyo Charter merely replaced 'a war of aggression' and 'international treaties' in Article 6(a) of the Nuremberg Charter with 'a declared or undeclared war of aggression' and 'international law, treaties', respectively.

[10] B. B. Ferencz, 'Can Aggression be Deterred by Law?' (1999) 11 *Pace Int'l L. Rev.* 304 at 310–1.
[11] *Nuremberg Proceedings*, 421 ff; (1947) 41 *AJIL* 186 ff.
[12] *In re von Weizsaecker and Others*, US Military Tribunal at Nuremberg, 14 Apr. 1949 (1955) 16 *Ann. Dig.* 344 at 347.

The world order after WWII is governed by the UN Charter. The UN's first and foremost purpose, as provided in Article 1(1) of the UN Charter, is:

'To maintain international peace and security, and to that end: to take effective collective measures for the prevention and removal of threats to the peace, and for *the suppression of acts of aggression or other breaches of the peace*, and to bring about by peaceful means, and in conformity with the principles of justice and international law, adjustment or settlement of international disputes or situations which might lead to a breach of the peace.'[13]

To this end, Article 2(4) of the Charter stipulates:

'All Members shall refrain in their international relations from the threat or use of force against the territorial integrity or political independence of any States or in any other manner inconsistent with the Purposes of the United Nations.'

The only permissible exception is provided in Article 51 of the Charter, which allows individual or collective self-defence against an 'armed attack' ('*aggression armée*' in the French version) undertaken before the UN Security Council takes the measures necessary to maintain international peace and security.[14]

The UN is entrusted by Article 2(6) of its Charter to ensure that even States not members of the UN also act in accordance with the UN Principles as necessary to maintain international peace and security.

The term 'aggression' is deliberately left undefined in the UN Charter because it was feared that the progress of the technique of modern warfare would render futile the definition of all cases of aggression and, as such, the list of cases of aggression would be incomplete, thereby allowing the aggressor to exploit the loophole and distort the definition to its advantage. In addition, it was felt that even in the cases listed as aggression automatic action by the Security Council might lead to a premature application of the Council's enforcement measures under Chapter VII of the UN Charter.[15] Thus, Article 39 of the UN Charter leaves it to the Security Council to determine the existence of 'any threat to the peace, breach of the peace, or act of aggression' and take appropriate actions accordingly.

Leaving this matter in the hands of the Security Council has proved counterproductive at times. For example, when Korea was being invaded in 1950, the Soviet Union was boycotting Security Council meetings in protest against the Republic of China occupying the 'Chinese' seat at the Council. Therefore, the Security Council, in the Soviet absence, was able to 'recommend' that States provide assistance to South Korea to repel the armed attack and to restore international peace and security, including providing military forces and other assistance available to a unified

---

[13] Emphasis added.

[14] For arguments that Art. 2(4) of the UN Charter and the international order under the UN Charter in general do not work effectively, see A. C. Arend and R. J. Beck, *International Law and the Use of Force: Beyond the UN Charter Paradigm* (Routledge, 1993), 29 ff., esp. 177–202.

[15] Security Council Enforcement Arrangements, *UN SC Doc. 881, III/3/46, 12 UN C.I.O. Doc. 505 (1945)*. Quoted in A. C. Carpenter, 'The International Criminal Court and the Crime of Aggression' (1995) **64** *Nordic J. Int'l L.* 223 at 239, n. 35.

command under the US.[16] On 1 August 1950, the Soviet Union resumed its seat at the Council and the Council could not continue to deal with the Korean conflict any longer. After troops from the People's Republic of China had entered the conflict in October 1950 and subsequently advanced to the south, a draft Security Council resolution to condemn the Chinese use of force was vetoed by the Soviet Union on 30 November 1950, leaving the international community with no choice but to resort to the UN General Assembly to sustain the on-going international efforts to end the conflict. It was the General Assembly, not the Security Council, that passed a resolution stating that the People's Republic of China's direct aid and assistance to those who were 'already committing aggression in Korea' as well as China's 'engaging in hostilities against United Nations forces' meant that China 'itself engaged in aggression in Korea'.[17] An armistice in Korea was achieved in July 1953, as a result of the truce negotiations between a Chinese-North Korean delegation and the unified command under the US. The constitutionality of the UN Security Council resolutions has been subject to question. The Soviet Union always insisted that these Council resolutions as well as the subsequent General Assembly resolution were unconstitutional. On the other hand, it could be argued that the Council resolutions were not strictly enforcement measures under Chapter VII of the UN Charter as they only served to 'recommend', not 'bind', States to take a particular course of action. In any case, it was only through sheer luck, brought about by the Soviet temporary absence from the Council, that the Council could proceed the way it did and the Soviet veto of further roles by the Council was ineffective in practice after the unified military command had been put in place.

The abstract nature of the essential concepts of international peace and security as set out in the UN Charter, such as 'territorial integrity or political independence', has left some legal scholars in doubt as to whether 'indirect aggressions' like intervention in civil strife or civil wars are prohibited by the UN Charter.[18] It is also questionable when a State can legitimately exercise the right of self-defence and whether a State can pre-empt an 'armed attack' against it through the exercise of the so-called 'anticipatory self-defence'.[19] The failure to control or prevent the use of force in international

---

[16] UN SC Res. 82 of 25 June 1950; UN SC. Res. 83 of 27 June 1950; UN SC. Res. 84 of 7 July 1950.

[17] UN GA Res. 498 (V) of 1 Feb. 1951, UN GAOR, 5th Sess., Suppl. 20A, at 1.

[18] L. Henkin, *How Nations Behave: Law and Foreign Policy* (Columbia University Press, 1968), at 133, 141, 143–5, 149–50, 249; E. Luard, *Conflict and Peace in the Modern International System* (State University of New York Press, 1968), at 72, 74–5, 77, 320. Cf. also S. M. Schwebel, 'The Brezhnev Doctrine Repealed and Peaceful Co-existence Enacted' (1972) **66** *AJIL* 816; E. Korovin, 'Jungle Law Versus the Law of Nations' (1957) 1 *New Times* 16; Yi Shin, 'What Does Bourgeois International Law Explain About the Question of Intervention' (1960) 4 *Research on Int'l Problems* 47; J. N. Moore (ed.), *Law and Civil War in the Modern World* (Johns Hopkins University Press, 1974); R. T. Bohan, 'The Dominican Case: Unilateral Intervention' (1966) **60** *AJIL* 809; C. H. M. Waldock, 'The Regulation of the Use of Force by Individual States in International Law' (1952–II) **81** *Hague Recueil* 467.

[19] As in the case of the Israeli aerial attack against Iraqi nuclear reactors on 7 June 1981. See *Hearings before the Committee on Foreign Relations, United States Senate*, 97th Congress, 1st Sess., on the Israeli Air Strike and Related Issues, held on 18, 19, and 25 June 1981 (US Govt. Printing Office, 1981), at 219 ff. See also Franck, *Fairness in International Law*, 266–72, 292–8.

law is often attributed to the lack of a firm and clear definition on the limit of 'permissible' use of force under the UN regime.

The UN General Assembly, by Resolution 2330 (XXII) of 18 December 1967, set up a Special Committee on the Question of Defining Aggression. This culminated in the General Assembly's adoption by consensus of Resolution 3314 of 14 December 1974 on the Definition of Aggression.[20]

The objective of the Definition, as elaborated in its Preamble, is to deter potential aggressors by providing authoritatively the parameters of how far a State can act without encroaching upon the international norm against the use of force or unfriendly relations with other States.

However, in order to achieve the consensus in its adoption by the General Assembly, it was necessary to include several ambiguous phrases that States might construe manipulatively to their own advantage.

Article 1 of the Definition provides:

'Aggression is the use of armed force by a State against the sovereignty, territorial integrity, or political independence of another State, or in any other manner inconsistent with the Charter of the United Nations, as set out in this Definition. . . .'

Article 2 of the Definition adds that:

'The first use of armed forces by a State in contravention of the Charter shall constitute *prima facie* evidence of an act of aggression although the Security Council may, in conformity with the Charter, conclude that a determination that an act of aggression has been committed would not be justified in the light of other relevant circumstances, including the fact that the acts concerned or their consequences are not of sufficient gravity.'

Article 2 of the Definition, therefore, empowers the Security Council to decide whether the first use of armed forces is an act of aggression. It also introduces a distinction between low-intensity conflicts and the other types of conflicts, with the former not qualifying as 'aggression'.

Article 3 of the Definition illustratively lists, in a non-exhaustive manner, the incidents which qualify as acts of aggression. It includes invasion, attack, military occupation (however temporary), or annexation by the armed forces of one State by another; bombardment of one State by another; blockade of ports; attack on land, sea, or air; allowing the territory to be used by another State to attack a third State; and sending, or being substantially involved in sending, armed bands, groups, irregulars, or mercenaries to carry out armed attack against another State of such gravity as to amount to the acts listed in the preceding paragraphs of this Article.

Article 4 of the Definition gives the Security Council the discretion to decide whether other acts may constitute aggression under the provisions of the UN Charter.

---

[20] UN GAOR, Supp. No. 19, *UN Doc. A/9615 (1974)*. See also B. B. Ferencz, 'Defining Aggression: What It Stands for and Where It Is Going' (1972) **66** *AJIL* 491. For an excellent analysis of legal debates prior to the adoption of the Definition in 1974, see S. M. Schwebel, 'Aggression, Intervention and Self-Defence in Modern International Law' (1972–II) **136** *Hague Recueil* 413.

Article 5 of the Definition stipulates that no consideration of whatever nature, be it political, economic, military, or otherwise, may justify an act of aggression. It is, thus, questionable whether the use of forces on 'humanitarian' grounds (the so-called 'humanitarian intervention') can be justified. Paragraph 2 of this Article distinguishes between 'a war of aggression' which is a crime against international peace and 'aggression' which gives rise to international responsibility. The Definition does not clarify where to the draw the line separating the two notions and what the consequences would be for each of them. It has been argued that the definition of aggression under the Declaration was intended as a definition of the crime of aggression, especially in view of the fact that the General Assembly's original mandate to define aggression was based on the Nuremberg Principles.[21] Nonetheless, the Definition merely stipulates in Article 5(2) that a war of aggression is 'a crime against international peace' which 'gives rise to international responsibility'. The nature of such responsibility is not elaborated to clarify whether it includes both State responsibility and individual criminal responsibility.

Article 6 of the Definition seems to return any progress in defining aggression back to square one. It provides that nothing in this Definition is to be interpreted as in any way enlarging or diminishing the scope of the UN Charter, including its provisions concerning cases in which the use of force is lawful. Furthermore, Article 7 of the Definition excludes from the scope of the Definition acts of peoples exercising their right to self-determination, freedom, and independence.

Article 8 of the Definition states that the preceding provisions of the Declaration are interrelated in terms of interpretation and application, and that each provision should be construed in the context of the other provisions.

Only when there is consensus among the Permanent Members of the UN Security Council can a finding of aggression be made, as in the case of the Security Council's finding of South Africa's 'aggression' against Angola in the late 1970s, drawing on the 1974 Definition.[22] Even after the Cold War, such determinations by the Security Council are rare owing to the continued existence of conflict of interests among the

---

[21] Ferencz (1999) 11 *Pace Int'l L. Rev.* 304 at 315. *Contra*: S. Laurenti, 'The Crime of Aggression', Discussion Paper submitted by the Lelio Basso International Foundation to the PCNICC (26 Jul.–13 Aug. 1999), at 1–2, where the author opines that the Definition 'does not deal with aggression as an individual crime'; and also J. Hogan-Doran and B. T. van Ginkel, 'Aggression as a Crime under International Law and the Prosecution of Individuals by the Proposed International Criminal Court' (1996) 43 *Netherlands Int'l L. Rev.* 321 at 335, where the authors point out that the Definition does not include an element of criminal intent for an individual to be guilty of committing an act of aggression.

[22] T. W. Bennett, 'A Linguistic Perspective of the Definition of Aggression' (1988) 31 *German Y. B. In'tl L.* 48 at 48. Bennett notes that that was the only occasion up to 1988 in which the Security Council used the term 'aggression' in its resolution.

Security Council Resolution 418 of 4 Nov. 1977 cites in its preamble 'the military build-up by South Africa and its persistent acts of aggression against the neighbouring States' as a basis for invoking Chapter VII of the UN Charter to impose a mandatory arms embargo against South Africa. It has been pointed out, nevertheless, that South Africa's attacks against neighbouring States might, in fact, be an exercise of the right of self-defence in response to attacks by South African guerrillas from bases in those States. M. E. Tzartzouras, 'The Law of Humanitarian Intervention after Somalia' (1993) 46 *Revue Héllénique de Droit Int'l* 197 at 212, n. 91.

Permanent Five. It was remarkable that in the case of the Gulf War of 1990–1, the Security Council never branded any State an 'aggressor'.[23]

Since UN General Assembly resolutions have no legally binding force, the General Assembly has set up, as a parallel measure, the Special Committee on Enhancing the Effectiveness of the Principle of Non-Use of Force in International Relations to draft a World Treaty on the Non-Use of Force in International Relations.[24] The Special Committee has not been successful in drafting the Treaty because the interplay between international law and international politics makes this impossible.[25] The lack of success is caused, among other things, by the problem of prohibiting the use of nuclear weapons and the adoption of practical measures to limit and reduce armaments.[26] Besides, it has been rightly observed that such a Treaty would create a parallel regime in an instrument having neither the solemnity nor the universality of the UN Charter, thereby creating instability and confusion about the norms applicable to non-use of force.[27]

The elusiveness of the international rule governing aggression is also demonstrated by the Judgment of the International Court of Justice (ICJ) in *Military and Paramilitary Activities in and against Nicaragua (Nicaragua v. US)* in 1986.

In 1981, the US took action against Nicaragua on the grounds of the latter's alleged involvement in logistical support, including provision of arms, for guerrillas in El Salvador, and cross-border military attacks on Honduras and Costa Rica. The US supported the *contras*—armed opposition to the Government in Nicaragua along the borders with Honduras and Costa Rica.

In late 1983 or early 1984, the US President authorized a US government agency to lay mines in Nicaraguan ports. The US claimed the right of collective self-defence under Article 51 of the UN Charter, and the Inter-American Treaty of Reciprocal Assistance, arguing that it was providing, upon request, proportionate and appropriate assistance to third States not before the ICJ (namely, El Salvador, Honduras, and Costa Rica) in their self-defence against aggression by Nicaragua.

In its Judgment, the ICJ distinguishes between 'an armed attack' and 'a mere frontier incident' according the scale and effects involved. It rules that the prohibition of the sending of armed bands, groups, irregulars or mercenaries to carry out acts of armed force against another State under Article 3(g) of the Declaration on the Definition of Aggression is a rule of customary international law. The ICJ holds, however, that, in customary international law, assistance to rebels in the form of the provisions of weapons or logistical or other support may be regarded as a threat or use of force, or intervention in internal or external affairs of other States, but it is not an 'armed attack' that gives rise to the right of self-defence. Moreover, it is the

---

[23] Cf. Franck, *Fairness in International Law*, 222–3, also 231–6, 287–8.

[24] Resolution 31/9 of 8 Nov. 1976, UN GAOR, 34th Sess., Supp. No. 41, *UN Doc. A/34/41* and *Corr. 1.*

[25] See Report of the Special Committee on Enhancing the Effectiveness of the Principle of Non-Use of Force in International Relations, UN GAOR, 38th Sess., Supp. No. 41 (*UN Doc. A/38/41*).

[26] Ibid., paras. 18–20.

[27] Ibid., para. 33.

victim of an armed attack that must form and declare the view that it has been so attacked. In that particular case, El Salvador made an official declaration to that effect and did ask for the US to exercise its right of collective self-defence, but this is held to be invalid because it occurred much later than the start of the US activities which this request sought to justify. Thus, by using force against Nicaragua and by laying the mines, the US violated the principle prohibiting recourse to the threat or use of force. Moreover, the US's training, arming, equipping, financing, and supplying the *contra* forces or otherwise encouraging, supporting and aiding military and paramilitary activities in and against Nicaragua was in breach of the US obligation under customary international law not to intervene in the affairs of another State.

In his Dissenting Opinion, the British Judge Sir Robert Jennings opines that the majority opinions were 'neither realistic nor just' in the real world. For him, provision of arms coupled with other kinds of involvement may amount to an armed attack that gives rise to the right of self-defence.

The Dissenting Opinion of US Judge Stephen M. Schwebel further reveals the fallacy of the Definition of Aggression. He believes that:

'The Definition has its conditions, its flaws, its ambiguities and uncertainties. It is open-ended. Any definition of aggression must be, because aggression can only be ultimately defined and found in the particular case in the light of particular facts. . . .'[28]

Judge Schwebel reads Article 3(g) of the Declaration on the Definition of Aggression conjunctively with Article 2 of that Declaration and holds that Nicaragua was the '*prima facie* aggressor' in this case because the first international use of armed force was by Nicaragua. In his view, the majority opinions of the ICJ would deprive States of the power to intervene effectively to preserve the political independence of another State being overthrown by force from a stronger State.[29]

Where do we go from here?

The proposals submitted to the PCNICC reveal two major trends in the definition of the crime of aggression.[30] These trends have existed since the time of the Preparatory Commission on the Establishment of an International Criminal Court in 1996–98.

The first trend is to define it by providing a generic definition, or a definition based on the object or result of occupying or annexing the territory of the attacked State or

[28] ICJ Rep. 1986, p. 14, Dis. Op. of Judge Schwebel, para. 168.

[29] See also S. M. Schwebel, 'The Roles of the Security Council and the International Court of Justice in the Application of International Humanitarian Law' (1995) **27** *Int'l L. & Politics* 731. The developments of this case before the ICJ were summarized in Shabtai Rosenne, *The World Court: What It Is and How It Works*, 5th ed. (Martinus Nijhoff, 1995), chap. 5. Rosenne reports that discovery in May 1993 of a weapons cache and documents in the capital of Nicaragua proved that Nicaragua had provided material assistance to the Salvadorean guerrillas all along—a crucial fact alleged by the US but denied by Nicaragua before the ICJ. The ICJ, in Rosenne's opinion, had been misled by Nicaragua in its appreciation of facts (ibid., 152–3).

[30] Consolidated text of proposals on the crime of aggression, Discussion paper proposed by the Coordinator of the Working Group on the Crime of Aggression, *Doc. PCNICC/1999/WGCA/RT. 1* of 9 Dec. 1999, at 1–5.

part thereof, or a general definition plus the detailed list of acts enumerated in General Assembly Resolution 3314 (XXIX) of 14 December 1974.

The other trend is to cover both the definition of the crime, which is based on Article 6(a) of the Nuremberg Charter, and the relationship between the ICC and the UN Security Council. It would stipulate simply: 'For the purposes of the present Statute and subject to a prior determination by the United Nations Security Council of an act of aggression by the State concerned, the crime of aggression means any of the following acts: planning, preparing, initiating, or carrying out a war of aggression'.

An important, related question is how to set an appropriate threshold in the definition of aggression so as to avert frivolous or vexatious prosecutions. Not every use of force in violation of international law should incur individual criminal responsibility for the crime of aggression. Otherwise, minor incidents like border skirmishes or a single bomb straying onto the territory of another State would burden the ICC's workload and exhaust its resources.

It is doubtful whether an iron-clad definition of aggression that satisfies the principle of legality required in international criminal law could ever be agreed upon.

CONDITIONS FOR THE ICC'S EXERCISE OF JURISDICTION

The ICJ has highlighted one important point in the rules of international law regulating use of force in the present international legal system that lacks a supranational enforcement authority or legislative body. It was observed in *Military and Paramilitary Activities in and against Nicaragua* that when States violated customary law on the use of force they did not assert the right to do so; they tried to characterize their use of force as justifiable under the exceptions permitted by the law.[31] There must be a neutral body to determine whether such an assertion is legally correct, and if it is not, what action is to be taken.

Article 39 of the UN Charter entrusts this role to the UN Security Council. The problem is that the UN Security Council has not been able to respond with consistency and objectivity to incidents of international armed conflicts. According to one study, of the 112 inter-State uses of force during the years 1945–91, most of them were not punished or even officially determined by the international community to be unlawful; only 'rhetorical criticism' and disapproval were expressed.[32]

Even after the Cold War, the five Permanent Members of the Council often have diverging views on how to solve the problem of internal conflicts caused by ethnic and religious differences that replace international conflicts based on political ideological differences during the Cold War. This was manifest in the episode of NATO's 'humanitarian intervention' in the Kosovo crisis in 1999. China and Russia would not

---

[31] ICJ Rep. 1986, 14 at 98.

[32] A. M. Weisburd, *Use of Force: The Practice of States Since World War II* (Pennsylvania State University Press, 1996), *passim*, esp. at 11, 226, 312–3.

have permitted the UN Security Council to authorize the intervention, leaving the other three Permanent Members to pursue this option without the Council's prior authorization.

The proposals submitted at the PCNICC and views expressed by delegations reveal three main approaches each of which enjoys considerable support.[33]

The first approach would reconcile the prerogatives of the UN Security Council with the ICC's independence. Article 5(2) of the ICC Statute provides that the definition of this crime and the conditions under which the ICC shall exercise jurisdiction with respect thereto shall be consistent with the relevant provisions of the UN Charter, and Article 39 of the Charter gives the Security Council the responsibility for establishing the existence of an act of aggression. Therefore, the Security Council, acting in accordance with its power to refer a situation to the ICC Prosecutor under Article 13(b) of the ICC Statute, must first make a decision establishing that an act of aggression has been committed by a State before proceedings against a national of that State can take place in the ICC with regard to the crime of aggression. Thus, when the ICC receives a complaint relating to this crime, it shall first request the Security Council to determine whether or not an act of aggression has been committed by the State whose national is concerned, and the Security Council shall make a decision on this request within a specific time-frame. If the Security Council fails to make such a decision within that time-frame, there are three possible options. According to the first option, the ICC may proceed. Under the second option, the ICC must request the UN General Assembly to make a recommendation within a specific time-frame, and if the General Assembly fails to do so, the ICC may proceed. The third option would authorize the ICC to request the UN General Assembly either to make a recommendation or to seek an advisory opinion of the ICJ within a specific time-frame. In the absence of such recommendation or request, the ICC may proceed only if the State Party referring a situation to the ICC pursuant to Article 14 of the ICC Statute has been held by ICJ, acting in conformity with its competence over contentious cases under Article 36 of its Statute, to be a victim of an act of aggression in violation of the UN Charter. [34]

The second approach is similar to the first one. The ICC shall exercise its jurisdiction over the crime of aggression subject to a determination by the UN Security Council in accordance with Article 39 of the UN Charter that an act of aggression has been committed by the State in question. After receiving a complaint related to this crime, the ICC shall first seek to discover whether the Security Council has made a determination with respect to the alleged aggression by that State and, if not, the ICC will request, subject to the provisions of the ICC Statute, the Security Council to make such a determination. If the Security Council does not take such determination or, within twelve months of the request from the ICC, has not adopted a resolution under

---

[33] Consolidated text of proposals on the crime of aggression, *Doc. PCNICC/1999/WGCA/RT. 1* of 9 Dec. 1999, at 3–6.

[34] Proposal of Bosnia-Herzegovina, Portugal, Australia, New Zealand, and Romania, submitted to the 7th Sess. of the PCNICC in Feb./Mar. 2001.

Chapter VII of the UN Charter to request the ICC to defer investigation or prosecution as provided by Article 16 of the ICC Statute, the ICC shall proceed with the case in question.[35]

The third approach follows closely the proposal in Article 23(2) of the International Law Commission's Draft Statute for an International Criminal Court, which provides that a complaint of or directly related to an act of aggression may not be brought before the ICC unless the Security Council has first determined that a State has committed the act of aggression.[36] This approach therefore defers to the primary responsibility of the Security Council in the maintenance of international peace and security under the UN Charter. By the same token, it also immunizes nationals of each Permanent Member of the Security Council from prosecution before the ICC for this crime because it is just not conceivable that any Permanent Member of the Council will ever fail to cast a veto against determination by the Security Council that its has committed an act of aggression.[37] However, this approach would accommodate the view that the classical international law on the use of force is currently undergoing change, and that it is the Security Council that can determine realistically which use of force is or is not an act of aggression. One example which could probably be cited in support of this contention is Nigeria's military action in Liberia through the Economic Community of West African States which was welcomed by the Security Council after the armed intervention had taken place.[38] Another example could be the use of force by NATO against the Federal Republic of Yugoslavia in 1999 to end the Kosovo crisis. Although the military action was undertaken without prior approval of the Security Council, the Council has not condemned the action. Instead, it adopted Resolution 1244 (1999) of 10 June 1999 to authorize UN Member States and international organizations to set up a security presence in Kosovo under UN auspices after NATO had secured its military victory. Resolution 1244 (1999) might be interpreted as either an *ex post facto* authorization of NATO's use of force against Yugoslavia, or as a damage control measure in response to NATO's *de facto* authority over Kosovo.

Any option chosen finally must be consistent with the provisions of the UN Charter, as required by Article 5(2) of the ICC Statute itself. Article 103 of the UN Charter stipulates that if there is a conflict between the obligations of the UN

---

[35] The first two approaches are variations of the proposal submitted by Cameroon at the Rome Conference. See *Doc. A/CONF. 183/C. 1/L. 39* of 2 July 1998, at 3, reproduced in Compilation of Proposals on the Crime of Aggression submitted at the Preparatory Committee on the Establishment of an International Criminal Court (1996–1998), the UN Diplomatic Conference of Plenipotentiaries on the Establishment of an International Criminal Court (1998), and the Preparatory Commission for the International Criminal Court (*Doc. PCNICC/1999/INF/2* of 6 Aug. 1999, at 15).

[36] Report of the ILC to the General Assembly on the Work of its 46th Session, UN GAOR, Supp. No. 10 (A/49/10) (1994), at 43–161.

[37] See further A. Pyrich, 'United Nations: Authorizations of Use of Force—Security Council Resolution 665' (1991) 32 *Harvard Int'l L. J.* 265 at 269; C. T-H. Lin, 'The International Criminal Court: Taiwan's Last Hope?' (1997) 6 *Pacific Rim L. & Policy Assoc.* 755 at 765.

[38] R. Wedgwood, 'The International Criminal Court: An American View' (1999) 10 *Euro. J. Int'l L.* 93 at 106–7.

Members under the UN Charter and their obligations under any other international agreement, their obligations under the UN Charter shall prevail.[39] If this issue of consistency is not settled by the consensus of the international community of States, including the Permanent Members of the Council, there is a high possibility that a defendant charged with the crime of aggression might argue successfully before the ICC that the ICC is usurping the Security Council's Charter authority and is acting outside its own judicial competence (*ultra vires*).

ELEMENTS OF THE CRIME OF AGGRESSION

Only when the definition of the crime of aggression and the conditions of the ICC's exercise of jurisdiction have been settled can one discuss the material and mental elements for this crime. The following is a conjecture about the elements of this crime, based on international jurisprudence on this matter to date.

Actus reus

Crimes against peace under the Nuremberg Charter and the Tokyo Charter were committed by the 'planning, preparing, initiating, or waging' what will be prosecuted by the ICC as the crime of aggression, or 'participating in a common plan or conspiracy to accomplish the same'. This kind of description of punishable acts is unhelpful for our purpose. It in fact merely describes the various modes of commission of the crime. The ICC Statute has its own regime of the modes of commission of the crimes within the ICC's jurisdiction as stipulated in Articles 25 and 28, which will be discussed in the next chapter of this book. Conspiracy is not among those modes specified therein, and all the modes must now be interpreted in the light of the more recent jurisprudence.

At the PCNICC, there is widespread support for the principle that the planning, preparation, or ordering of aggression should be criminalized only when an act of aggression actually takes place.[40] Certain delegations even doubt whether it is possible to 'attempt' to commit aggression, since the substantial step required by Article 25(3) of the ICC Statute for an attempt would be an armed attack which is an act of aggression in itself.

What is clear is that omission can amount to an *actus reus* of this crime. The US Military Tribunal in the *High Command* case held that, in certain circumstances, omission or inaction could incur criminal liability of the accused just like 'active participation'. This happens in the following situation:

'If . . . , after the policy to initiate and wage aggressive wars was formulated, a defendant came into possession of knowledge that the invasions and wars to be waged were aggressive

---

[39] See, *Questions of Interpretation and Application of the 1971 Montreal Convention arising from the Aerial Incident at Lockerbie (Libyan Arab Jamahiriya/ United Kingdom)*, Provisional Measures, Order of 14 Apr. 1992, ICJ Rep. 1992, 3 at 14–15. See also Franck, *Fairness in International Law*, 242–4.

[40] Consolidated text of proposals on the crime of aggression, Discussion paper proposed by the Coordinator of the Working Group on the Crime of Aggression, *PCNICC/1999/WGCA/RT. 1* of 9 Dec. 1999, at 4.

and unlawful, then he will be criminally responsible if he, being on the policy level, could have influenced such policy and failed to do so.'[41]

Mens rea

The requisite mental elements for the crime of aggression are intent plus knowledge. In the *High Command* case, the US Military Tribunal stated that those guilty of this offence must have:

'actual knowledge that an aggressive war is being intended and that if launched it will be an aggressive war. It requires in addition that the possessor of such knowledge, after he acquires it shall be in a position to shape or influence the policy that brings about its initiation or its continuance after its initiation, either by furthering, or by hindering or preventing it. If he then does the former, he becomes criminally responsible; if he does the latter to the extent of his ability, then his action shows the lack of criminal intent with respect to such policy. . . .'[42]

The Tokyo Tribunal found the publicist Hashimoto guilty of waging a war of aggression for having been 'fully apprised that the war against China was a war of aggression' and being one of those who had conspired to bring about that war, he did everything within his power to secure its success.[43] In the case of Foreign Minister Hirota, it was held that all the plans to wage aggressive wars and activities related thereto were 'fully known to and supported' by him; hence, his liability for having participated in the common plan or conspiracy to wage aggressive wars.[44] In the case of Itagaki, he was convicted for, *inter alia*, having taken an active and important part in waging aggressive wars against China, the United States, the British Common-wealth, the Netherlands, and the USSR 'which he knew were wars of aggression'.[45] Such knowledge includes recognition that a conduct will lead to war, as in this case Itagaki was held to have been a strong supporter of Japan's 'New Order' in East Asia and the South Seas, recognizing that the attempt to set up that 'New Order' must lead to war with the USSR, France, and Britain who would defend their possessions in these areas.[46]

INDIVIDUAL CRIMINAL RESPONSIBILITY

The individuals subject to prosecution under this charge fall into a special category. Not just any individual can be criminally responsible for an offence of aggression.

Article 6 of the Nuremberg Charter provides in its pertinent part: Leaders, organizers, instigators, and accomplices participating in the formulation or execution of a common plan or conspiracy to commit any of the foregoing crimes are responsible for all acts performed by any persons in execution of such plan.

---

[41] *Wilhelm von Leeb and Others*, US Military Tribunal at Nuremberg, 28 Oct. 1948 (1953) **15** *Ann. Dig.* 376 at 381, also quoted in G. Brand, 'The War Crimes Trials and the Law of War' (1949) **26** *BYBIL* 414 at 421.

[42] Ibid.

[43] *Tokyo Judgment*, at 445.

[44] Ibid., at 447.

[45] Ibid., at 449.

[46] Ibid.

The Tokyo Charter restricts the identity of the individuals to be prosecuted for the crime against peace to '[a]ll of those who at any time were parties to the criminal conspiracy or who at any time with guilty knowledge played a part in its execution. . . .' Twenty-eight defendants were selected by the Executive Committee of the Prosecution. The criteria for selection were: (1) they could be charged with crimes against peace, and this criteria resulted in Japanese industrialists being excluded; (2) they were representatives of the defendants which had played a vital role in Japan's policy of aggression; (3) they were the principal leaders who ought to bear primary responsibility for the acts committed, and this criteria excluded the Emperor of Japan who was a mere ceremonial head of State; and (4) there was sufficient evidence to convict them.

Article II(2)(f) of Control Council Law No. 10 provided that for an individual to be deemed to have committed a crime of aggression he must have 'held a high political, civil, or military (including General Staff) position in Germany or in one of its Allies, co-belligerents or satellites or held high position in financial, industrial, or economic life of any such country'.

The rationale was explained in the *High Command* case. Somewhere between the dictator and supreme commander of the armed forces of a nation and the common soldier is the boundary between criminal and excusable participation in the waging of an aggressive war by an individual engaged in it. The Tribunal reasoned as follows:

'If and as long as a member of the armed forces does not participate in the preparation, planning, initiating, or waging of aggressive war on a policy level, his war activities do not fall under the definition of crimes against peace. *It is not a person's rank or status, but his power to shape or influence the policy of his State, which is the relevant issue for determining his criminality under the charge of crimes against peace.*

International law condemns those who, due to their *actual power* to shape and influence the policy of their nation, prepare for, or lead their country into or in an aggressive war. But we do not find that, at the present stage of development, international law declares as criminals those below that level who, in the execution of this war policy, act as the instruments of the policy makers. Anybody who is on the policy level and participates in the war policy is liable to punishment. But those under them cannot be punished for the crimes of others. The misdeed of the policy makers is all the greater in as much as they use the great mass of the soldiers and officers to carry out an international crime; however, the individual soldier or officer below the policy level is but the policy makers' instrument, finding himself, as he does, under the rigid discipline which is necessary for and peculiar to military organization.

We do not hesitate to state that it would have been eminently desirable had the commanders of the German armed forces refused to implement the policy of the Third Reich by means of aggressive war. It would have been creditable to them not to contribute to the cataclysmic catastrophe. This would have been the honourable and righteous thing to do; it would have been in the interest of their State. Had they done so they would have served their fatherland and humanity also. But however much their failure is morally reprimandable, we are of the opinion and hold that international common law, at the time they so acted, had not developed to the point of making the participation of military officers below the policy making or policy influencing level into a criminal offence in and of itself.'[47]

Whether an individual can be classified as being on a policy level is a question of fact to be proved on a case-by-case basis.[48]

This was also the approach utilized by the Tokyo Tribunal. For example, in the case of Muto, the Tribunal found that he was a soldier and before his holding the important post of Chief of the Military Affairs Bureau of the Ministry of War held no appointment which involved the making of high policy, or, alone or with others, tried to affect the making of high policy. He was held to have joined the conspiracy once he became Chief of the Military Affairs Bureau.[49] The same reasoning was applied to the case of Sato, Muto's successor as Chief of the Military Affairs Bureau in 1942. It was not until 1941, when Sato became Chief of the Military Affairs Section of that Bureau that he was able to influence policy making, and the Tribunal found no evidence that before then he had indulged in plotting to influence policy making.[50] On the other hand, Hashimoto, an Army officer, who never held high government offices, was convicted for his publications and support or establishment of the societies devoted to warlike purposes.[51]

There is no general presumption of responsibility inherent in a high office, however. Hideki Tojo, Prime Minister of Japan from October 1941 to July 1944, and Umezu, who was Chief of the Army General Staff from July 1944 until Japan's surrender, were convicted of the conspiracy in as well as the initiation and waging of aggressive wars because they had been actively involved in the pursuit and carrying out of invasions of other countries for years.[52] On the other hand, Shigemitsu, Japan's Minister to China, and Ambassador to the USSR, Great Britain, and China, was found to have never exceeded the functions proper to these offices; indeed he repeatedly advised his Foreign Office to oppose the policies of the conspirators of war of aggression. He was held not to be guilty of the conspiracy. In contrast, two of his colleagues at the Japanese Foreign Office, Oshima and Shiratori, were convicted of the conspiracy because they went beyond the call of their duties to conspire to wage aggressive wars, even in defiance of their Foreign Minister. Shigemitsu became Foreign Minister in April 1943, by which time Japan had been deeply involved in execution of the conspiracy of waging the war in the Pacific and the military was in complete control of Japan. The Tokyo Tribunal convicted Shigemitsu of waging the war in the Pacific on the grounds that he now played a principal part in waging that war until he resigned on 13 April 1945.[53]

One lesson to be drawn from this case is that if a person 'on a policy level' wishes to

---

[47] (1953) 15 *Ann. Dig.* 376 at 381–2. Emphasis added.
[48] See, e.g., *Alfred Krupp von Bohlen and Others*, TWC, xv, at 145–6.
[49] *Tokyo Judgment*, at 455.
[50] Ibid., at 456–7.
[51] Ibid., at 444–5.
[52] Ibid., at 461–4.
[53] Ibid., at 458.

be exonerated from crimes against peace or aggression, he must withdraw once he becomes 'fully aware' of the conspiracy to wage an aggressive war, or of the war being waged, which he disapproves of. This was made clear in the case of Togo, who was Foreign Minister of Japan from October 1941 until September 1942 when he resigned, and again in 1945. Togo pleaded that he joined the Cabinet in 1941 on the assurance that every effort would be made to bring negotiations with the US to a successful conclusion. Nevertheless, when the negotiations collapsed and war became unavoidable, Togo did not resign but continued in office and supported the war. Although he argued that to do anything else would have been cowardly, he did resign in September 1942 over a dispute in the Cabinet on the treatment of occupied territories. Therefore, the Tribunal found unconvincing his reason not to resign right after finding that war had become inevitable.[54]

Another remarkable feature of the Tokyo Judgment was the fact that the Judgment traced a course of conduct of the defendants from early in their respective careers up to their prosecution before the Tribunal. This should not be construed as indicating that junior officers were also held liable for crimes against peace. Since the prosecution had already selected 'major war criminals' for indictments, the Tribunal merely looked at the course of conduct of each defendant to establish the pattern of his behaviour in relation to Japan's policy to wage aggressive wars, and determine whether a charge of conspiracy, initiation of a war of aggression, and/or waging of an aggressive war, as in the case may be, could be proven beyond any reasonable doubt. According to Judge Röling of the Tokyo Tribunal, the parts played by the accused in the events leading to and during WWII had to be investigated, 'and again every foot of the way was fought' because both the facts and the meaning of each incident 'were the subject of controversy and the topic towards which a wealth of evidence was directed'.[55]

The jurisprudence of the post-WWII tribunals is now encapsulated in Article 16 of the ILC's Draft Code of Crimes Against the Peace and Security of Mankind of 1996. It reads:

'Crime of aggression
An individual who, as leader or organizer, actively participates in or orders the planning, preparation, initiation or waging of aggression committed by a State, shall be responsible for a crime of aggression.'[56]

In its Commentary to this draft Article, the ILC emphasized that the perpetrators of an act of aggression are those individuals who have 'the necessary authority or power to be in a position of potentially to play a decisive role in committing aggression'. They include the members of a Government, persons occupying the high-level posts in the military, the diplomatic corps, political parties, and industry.[57]

---

[54] *Tokyo Judgment*, at 461. The Tribunal states: 'We are disposed to judge his action and sincerity in the one case by the same considerations as in the other'.

[55] Ibid., at 23.

[56] *UN Doc. A/ CN. 4/ L. 532* of 8 July 1996.

[57] (1996) ii *Yearbook of the ILC*, Part Two, 42.

In the PCNICC, there is widespread support for the principle under which the crime of aggression is committed by political or military leaders of a State.[58] This is likely to be the position finally endorsed by the PCNICC or the Assembly of States Parties of the ICC Statute.

CONCLUSIONS

Besides the issues of defining aggression, conditions of the ICC's exercise of jurisdiction over this crime, and the elements of the crime, there remain some other related issues awaiting to be decided. For example, the *ne bis in idem* provision in Article 20 of the ICC Statute only refers to the crimes proscribed in Articles 6, 7, and 8 of the Statute. Therefore, when the crime of aggression is included by an amendment to the Statute, it needs to be determined whether the principle of *ne bis in idem* also applies to the crime of aggression as well.

Is there any realistic hope to include the crime of aggression as a crime under the ICC's jurisdiction?

Ferencz envisages four scenarios faced by the international community. First of all, beginning at the most negative end of the spectrum, there is no agreement on an acceptable definition of aggression or the role of the UN Security Council; hence, the ICC will have no jurisdiction over the crime of aggression. Secondly, in the absence of the ICC's jurisdiction, the aggressor may still be prosecuted by the victor who defeats the aggressor, or by a new national government. Thirdly, an *ad hoc* tribunal may be established by the Security Council to try the aggressor. Finally, the ICC is able to exercise its jurisdiction over the crime of aggression pursuant to the ICC Statute.[59]

The last scenario would be possible despite a lack of precise definition of the crime. This is so if one bears in mind that criminal prosecution, conviction, and punishment are a fact of life in municipal criminal law even in States whose national criminal code does not yet include a 'full general part', or which do not even have a criminal code.[60] In any case, the conditions for the ICC's exercise of jurisdiction over the crime of aggression must be settled once and for all.

---

[58] Consolidated text of proposals on the crime of aggression, Discussion paper proposed by the Coordinator of the Working Group on the Crime of Aggression, *PCNICC/1999/WGCA/RT. 1* of 9 Dec. 1999, at 4. The Delegations of the UK, Italy, and Thailand spoke in support of this opinion at the Working Group on the Crime of Aggression, 5th Sess. of the PCNICC in June 2000.

[59] Ferencz (1999) 11 *Pace Int'l L. Rev.* 304 at 313–4.

[60] Cf. K. J. Keith, 'The Proposed International Criminal Court: Over What Crimes Should It Have Jurisdiction?' (1998) 6 *Proc. Aust.-NZ Soc. Int'l L. Annual Conf.* 69 at 72–3.

7.2 OTHER INTERNATIONAL CRIMES

Apart from the eventuality of the ICC exercising jurisdiction over the crime of aggression, other international crimes in addition to those listed in Article 5 of the ICC Statute may also come under the ICC's jurisdiction through the amendments made under Article 121 or Article 123 of the Statute.

The prime candidates are international trafficking of narcotic drugs and psychotropic substances, and international terrorism. They were the so-called 'treaty-based crimes' included in the early versions of the ILC's Draft Statute for an International Criminal Court. The US opposed legislating new crimes that were not already established, and urged other States to avoid defining crimes that were not yet clearly criminalized under international law. It would be unwilling to share confidential information on international drug traffickers or terrorists with the ICC for fear that its sources of intelligence would be put in danger. The majority of States at the Rome Conference agreed that the Conference should codify pre-existing rules of customary international law, and only genocide, war crimes, and crimes against humanity had attained this customary status. Terrorism and international drug trafficking are merely 'treaty-based' in the sense that they are punishable only in the territory of States Parties to the treaties on the respective subjects and these States may not necessarily be States Parties to the ICC Statute.

As a compromise, Resolution E adopted by the Rome Conference as part of the Final Act of the Conference recommended that the Review Conference consider including these two crimes within the ICC's jurisdiction.[61]

INTERNATIONAL DRUG TRAFFICKING[62]

The successful drive towards the establishment of the ICC emanated from the initiative of Trinidad and Tobago in the UN General Assembly in 1989. That State proposed the establishment of an ICC to prosecute transnational drug traffickers. During the Rome Conference, Trinidad and Tobago, Barbados, Dominica, and Jamaica formally proposed to include such a crime within the ICC's jurisdiction.[63] Those speaking in support of the inclusion of this crime within the ICC's jurisdiction included Algeria, Argentina, the Holy See, Kyrgyz Republic, Libya, Macedonia, Madagascar, Nigeria, Tajikistan, Thailand, Turkey, and Member States of the Caribbean Community (Caricom).

In contrast, Kazakhstan opposed the inclusion of this crime on the ground that its inclusion would negate the principle of complementarity. The majority of delegations

---

[61] *Doc. A/ CONF. 183/ 10* of 17 July 1998.

[62] For the existing legal regime of international cooperation see J. J. Paust, M. C. Bassiouni, S. A. Williams, M. Scharf, J. Gurulé, and B. Zagaris (eds.), *International Criminal Law: Cases and Materials* (Kluwer, 1996), 1245–86.

[63] *Doc. A/ CONF. 183/ C. 1/ L. 48* of 3 July 1998.

felt that its inclusion would flood the ICC's docket and the ICC would not have sufficient resources to deal with the lengthy and complicated process of investigations which should be more efficiently left to the respective national authorities and their bilateral or multilateral cooperative arrangements.[64]

INTERNATIONAL TERRORISM

International terrorism is one of the most heinous crimes that strike at the heart of peoples in virtually every corner of the globe. Its indiscriminate nature claims the lives and limbs of innocent victims and its suppression is far from satisfactory in its present state of enforcement of municipal law to combat terrorism through judicial assistance and cooperation among States.

At the Rome Conference, those speaking in favour of its inclusion as a crime within the ICC's jurisdiction were Algeria, Armenia, Congo, India, Israel, Kyrgyz Republic, Libya, Macedonia, Russia, Sri Lanka, Tajikistan, and Turkey. According to Algeria, international terrorism is a threat against the foundation of a State and a denial of democratic values. For Israel, there needs to be a correct balance between recognizing terrorism as an international crime and focusing on the most practical and effective means of cooperation in bringing international terrorists to justice. It is interesting to note that Algeria, India, Sri Lanka, and Turkey wished to have international terrorism included as a crime against humanity.[65] The eventual non-inclusion of this crime within the ICC's jurisdiction compelled Sri Lanka and Turkey to abstain from voting to adopt the ICC Statute.

An essential reason behind the resistance to the inclusion of terrorism within the ICC's jurisdiction is the fear of politicization of the ICC. The League of Arab States opposed the inclusion of international terrorism in the ICC Statute on the ground that the international community has not been able to define 'terrorism' in such a way as to be generally acceptable. On 16 November 1937, the League of Nations adopted the Convention for the Prevention and Punishment of Terrorism,[66] Article 1(2) of which defines terrorism as 'criminal acts directed against a State and intended to or calculated to create a state of terror in the minds of particular persons, or a group of persons or the general public'. It has never entered into force. For so long, certain types of act that terrorize the general public were part of the struggle by the oppressed against their oppressors. One Resolution of the UN General Assembly states explicitly that 'the struggles of peoples under colonial and alien domination and racist regimes for the implementation of their right of self-determination and independence is

---

[64] Trinidad and Tobago was one of the 21 States that abstained from voting to adopt the ICC Statute; it did so on the ground that drug trafficking and death penalty have not been included in the Statute. Nevertheless, on 6 April 1999, it became the second State to ratify the Statute.

[65] *Doc. A/ CONF. 183/ C. 1/ L. 27/ Corr. 1* of 29 June 1998. This proposal did not succeed, either.

[66] League of Nations Publication C.94.M.47.V.

legitimate and in full accordance with the principles of international law'.[67] Article 7 of the UN General Assembly Resolution on the Definition of Aggression also states that nothing in the Definition should prejudice the right of self-determination or struggle of peoples under colonial and racist regimes or other forms of alien domination. As such, while there is general agreement that it is unlawful for States to aid attacks on neighbouring States, there is little consensus on whether Palestinian Liberation Organization-sponsored attacks on Israel during the height of the Middle East conflicts were unlawful in international law.[68] The matter has become even more confused when, during the Cold War, insurgent forces aimed at undermining the regime of one State was regarded by the opponent of that regime as legitimate movements for self-determination. What States have been able to do quite successfully is concluding international agreements to prosecute and punish certain types of acts of such gravity that they cannot be tolerated, for example, hijacking of airplanes or ships, hostage taking, and attacks on internationally protected persons including diplomats.

One study published in 1993 finds three crucial aspects inherent in acts of terrorism that distinguish such acts from non-terrorist acts. They are: violence, actual or threatened; a 'political' objective, however conceived; and an intended audience, typically though not exclusively a wide one. Its proposed definition of an act of terrorism is 'the threat or use of violence with the intent of causing fear in a target group, in order to achieve political objectives'.[69] Recognition of the existence of a 'political' aspect in acts of terrorism can impede efforts to prosecute perpetrators of this kind of conduct; political offences are a classic exception to extradition.

After the Cold War and after the era of colonialism, insurgence against the central Government receives less support from the international community. Therefore, terrorism is now being looked at in a new light. General Assembly resolutions have been passed to state that there is no justification for terrorist acts. General Assembly Resolution 53 on 'Measures to Eliminate Terrorism' adopted on 11 December 1995, for instance, adopts implicitly and improves on the definition of terrorism under the now defunct 1937 Convention. It 'reiterates' that 'criminal acts intended or calculated to provoke a state of terror in the general public, a group of persons or particular persons for political purposes are in any circumstances unjustifiable, whatever the considerations of a political, philosophical, ideological, racial, ethnic, religious or any other nature that may be invoked to justify them'.[70] The latest multilateral effort to define 'terrorism' in an international agreement appears in Article 5 of the UN Convention for the Suppression of Terrorist Bombings of 1998. It provides:

---

[67] UN GA Res. 3103 on the Basic Principles of the Legal Status of the Combatants Struggling against Colonial and Alien Domination and Racist Regimes, *UN Doc. A/ 9120 (1973)*.

[68] per Robert H. Bork, J., and Harry T. Edwards, J. in *Tel-Oren v. Libyan Arab Rep.* (1984) 726 F. 2d 774, US Ct. App., District of Columbia Circuit, 3 Feb. 1984.

[69] Arend and Beck, *International Law and the Use of Force*, 141. The authors derive this definition from opinions of eminent international lawyers mostly in the West and Israel, and the US Department of State. It is doubtful whether this definition will be universally accepted. Cf. Sunga, *Emerging System of International Criminal Law*, 191–202; Paust et al., *International Criminal Law*, 1175–1228.

[70] *UN Doc. A/RES/ 5/ 53.*

'Each State Party shall adopt such measures as may be necessary, including, where appropriate, domestic legislation to ensure that *criminal acts* within the scope of this Convention, in particular where they are *intended or calculated to provoke a state of terror in the general public or in a group of persons or particular persons*, are under no circumstances justifiable by considerations of a political, philosophical, ideological, racial, ethnic, religious or other similar nature and are punished by penalties consistent with their grave nature.'[71]

It remains to be seen how successful this Convention will be. If it is successful, there may be no need to include terrorism as a crime within the ICC's jurisdiction. If it is not, opposition to its inclusion in the ICC Statute will probably be even stronger than that encountered at the Rome Conference.

OTHER CRIMES

Madagascar proposed orally the inclusion of trafficking in small arms, and the deposit of nuclear waste in other States as crimes within the ICC's jurisdiction. Madagascar and the Comoros wished the ICC Statute to include the crime of mercenaryism in the ICC's jurisdiction.[72] Nigeria proposed orally that money laundering be included as well.

None of these proposed inclusions received serious consideration at the Rome Conference. They were not even included in Resolution E of the Final Act of the Conference as crimes whose possible inclusion would be reconsidered by the Review Conference.

---

[71] Adopted by UN GA Res. 52/164 of 15 Dec. 1997, UN GAOR, 52nd Sess., Supp. No. 49, *UN Doc. A/ 52/ 49 (1997)*. Emphasis added.

[72] *Doc. A/ CONF. 183/ C. 1/ L. 46 and Corr. 1* of 3 and 7 July 1998. For a legal analysis on this issue, see Sunga, *Emerging System of International Criminal Law*, 183–91.

PART III

MODES OF PARTICIPATION AND GROUNDS FOR EXCLUDING CRIMINAL RESPONSIBILITY

8

MODES OF PARTICIPATION IN INTERNATIONAL CRIMES

The underlying basic assumption of individual criminal responsibility is founded upon the principle of personal culpability; that is, no one may be held criminally responsible for acts or transactions in which he has not personally engaged or in some other way participated (*nulla poena sine culpa*).[1] Under customary international law and general principles of criminal law, individuals may be held criminally liable for their participation in the commission of offences in any of the several capacities or modes of participation.[2] Article 7(1) of the ICTY Statute and Article 6(1) of the ICTR Statute under the heading 'individual criminal responsibility' stipulate:

'A person who planned, instigated, ordered, committed or otherwise aided and abetted in the planning, preparation or execution of a crime referred to in . . . the present Statute, shall be individually responsible for the crime.'

The ICTY has held that where the Prosecution relies on Article 7(1) of the ICTY Statute without specification and leaves the Trial Chamber with the discretion to allocate criminal responsibility, the Trial Chamber is empowered and obliged, if satisfied beyond any reasonable doubt that the accused has committed the crimes as charged in the indictment, to convict the accused under the appropriate head of criminal responsibility.[3]

Article 25 of the ICC Statute, under the heading 'Individual criminal responsibility' is even more elaborate with regard to modes of participation in international crime. It provides in paragraphs 1 and 2 that the ICC shall have jurisdiction over natural persons, and that a person shall be individually responsible for a crime within the ICC's jurisdiction. The French proposal at the Rome Conference to include 'legal' or 'juridical' persons within the ICC's jurisdiction was not accepted. While 'legal' or 'juridical' persons could be in a better position than 'natural' persons to provide restitution and compensation to victims of crimes, it would be impractical to

---

[1] *Prosecutor v. Dusko Tadic*, Case No. IT-94–1-A, ICTY App. Ch., 5 July 1999 (hereinafter '*Tadic* Appeals Judgment'), para. 264.

[2] *Prosecutor v. Clément Kayishema and Obed Ruzindana*, Case No. ICTR-95–1 -T, ICTR T. Ch. II, 21 May 1999, paras. 195–7; *Prosecutor v. Zejnil Delalic, Zdravko Mucic, Hazim Delic and Esad Landzo* ('*Celebici*' case), Case No. IT-96–21-T, ICTY T. Ch. II *quater*, 16 Nov. 1998, para. 321.

[3] *Prosecutor v. Anto Furundzija*, Case No. IT-95–1 7/1-T, ICTY T. Ch. II, 10 Dec. 1998, para. 189.

empower the ICC to punish 'legal' or 'juridical' persons on whose behalf natural persons commit crimes. There are no generally recognized common standards for corporate liability, and the fact that the concept of corporate liability is not recognized in some principal legal systems would make this form of liability violate the principle of legality as well as make the principle of complementarity unworkable.[4]

Article 25(3) of the ICC Statute stipulates that a person shall be criminally responsible and liable for punishment for a crime within the ICC's jurisdiction if that person:

'(a) Commits such a crime, whether as an individual, jointly with another or through another person, regardless of whether that other person is criminally responsible;

(b) Orders, solicits or induces the commission of such a crime which in fact occurs or is attempted;

(c) For the purpose of facilitating the commission of such a crime, aids, abets or otherwise assists in its commission or its attempted commission, including providing the means for its commission;

(d) In any other way contributes to the commission or attempted commission of such a crime by a group of persons acting with a common purpose. Such contribution shall be intentional and shall either:

   (i)   be made with the aim of furthering the criminal activity or criminal purpose of the group, where such activity or purpose involves the commission of a crime within the jurisdiction of the [ICC]; or

   (ii) be made in the knowledge of the intention of the group to commit the crime;

(e) In respect of the crime of genocide, directly and publicly incites others to commit genocide;

(f) Attempts to commit such a crime by taking action that commences its execution by means of a substantial step, but the crime does not occur because of circumstances independent of the person's intentions. However, a person who abandons the effort to commit the crime or otherwise prevents the completion of the crime shall not be liable for punishment under this Statute for the attempt to commit that crime if that person completely and voluntarily gave up the criminal purpose.'

The modes of participation in a crime specified in Article 25(3)(a) and (b) are direct commission of the crime by the perpetrator, often called the 'principal'. Common Law systems call the person who pursues the conduct in Article 25(3)(c) and (d) an 'accessory' or 'secondary participant' in 'complicity'. Complicity is when two or more persons join together to play some part in the commission of a crime. The modes stipulated in Article 25(3)(e) and (f) are known in the Common Law as 'inchoate offences'. 'Inchoate' means 'just begun', 'undeveloped'. Inchoate offences under the Common Law are incitement, conspiracy, and attempt; they are punishable

---

[4] Cf. K. Ambos, 'Article 25 Individual criminal responsibility', in O. Triffterer (ed.), *Commentary on the Rome Statute of the International Criminal Court: Observers' Notes, Article by Article* (Nomos, 1999).

even though the substantive crime which a person conspires, incites, or attempts is not committed and no harm results.[5]

The ICC Statute differs from the ICTY Statute and the ICTR Statute with regard to modes of participation in international crimes in the following ways.

First of all, in the case of the ICTY Statute and the ICTR Statute, a perpetrator incurs individual criminal responsibility in an offence other than genocide only if the offence is completed.[6] On the other hand, the ICC Statute proscribes an attempt to commit any crime within the ICC's jurisdiction, and not just a crime of genocide.

Secondly, while the ICTR Statute and the ICTY Statute use the term 'instigation' as a mode of commission of any crime, the ICC Statute uses the terms 'solicitation' and 'inducement'. There seems to be no substantive difference between these terms, however. According to Black's Law Dictionary, 'to instigate' means 'to stimulate or goad into an action', and 'instigation' also means 'solicitation'.[7] Instigation involves prompting another to commit an offence and it leads to the actual commission of an offence desired by the instigator.[8]

Thirdly, Article 4(3) of the ICTY Statute and Article 2(3) the ICTR Statute copy verbatim Article III of the Genocide Convention of 1948 which provides that the following acts are punishable: (a) genocide; (b) conspiracy to commit genocide; (c) direct and public incitement to commit genocide; (d) attempt to commit genocide; and (e) complicity in genocide. On the other hand, Article 25 of the ICC Statute does not include conspiracy. At the Rome Conference, there were two opposing positions on the inclusion of conspiracy. The Common Law States treat conspiracy as an inchoate offence punishable when two or more persons conspire to commit an offence irrespective of whether that offence is actually committed. On the other hand, the Civil Law States consider conspiracy as a form of complicity, punishable only when the crime in question is committed or attempted. In the end, no consensus was reached to incorporate it directly in Article 25 of the ICC Statute, and it is only covered indirectly in Article 25(3)(d).[9]

Finally, 'planning' as specified in Article 7(1) of the ICTY Statute and Article 6(1) of the ICTR Statute is not specifically mentioned in Article 25 of the ICC Statute. Planning is similar to the notion of complicity in Civil Law or conspiracy in Common Law, the difference being that, unlike complicity or plotting, planning can be an act committed by one person who contemplates designing the commission of a crime at both the preparatory and execution phases.[10] In effect, therefore, this mode of commission of a crime is also covered by complicity in Article 25(3)(d) of the ICC Statute.

---

[5] A. Ashworth, *Principles of Criminal Law*, 3rd ed. (Oxford University Press, 1999), 425–6, 460.

[6] *Prosecutor v. Jean-Paul Akayesu*, Case No. ICTR-96–4-T, ICTR T. Ch. I, 2 Sept. 1998, paras. 473–5.

[7] *Black's Law Dictionary*, 6th ed. (West Publishing, 1990), 799.

[8] *Akayesu*, paras. 481–2; *Prosecutor v. George Rutaganda*, Case No. ICTR-96–3-T, ICTR T. Ch. I, 6 Dec. 1999, para 38; *Prosecutor v. Alfred Musema*, Case No. ICTR-96–13-T, ICTR T. Ch. I, 27 Jan. 2000, para. 120.

[9] W. Schabas, 'Article 6 Genocide', in Triffterer (ed.), *Commentary on the Rome Statute*.

[10] *Akayesu*, para. 480; *Rutaganda*, para. 37; *Musema*, para. 119; *Prosecutor v. Tihomir Blaskic*, Case No. IT-95–14-T, ICTY T. Ch. I, 3 Mar. 2000, para. 279.

The case of direct physical perpetration of a crime by the principal as appeared in Article 25(3)(a) of the ICC Statute has been discussed in Part II of this book. Ordering, soliciting, or inducing the commission of a crime as provided in Article 25(3)(b) of the Statute is no different from direct physical perpetration of the crime. As Lord Steyn puts it in *Pinochet*, 'there is no distinction between the man who strikes, and a man who orders another to strike'.[11] However, ordering implies a superior-subordinate relationship between the person giving the order and the person implementing it.[12] The order may be explicit or implicit, in writing or in any other form.[13] Thus, in *Blaskic*, the accused wrote orders for his subordinates to undertake 'cleansing' of the ground, using the following words: '[K]eep in mind that the lives of the Croats in the Lasva region depend on your mission. This region could become our grave if you do not demonstrate resolve'. It is not necessary that the order is given directly by the superior to the person who commits the material element of the crime, and, since it is the criminal intention of the person who gives the order which incurs the criminal liability of that person, it matters little whether the order appears to the subordinate to be manifestly unlawful or not.[14]

This chapter is going to deal with the modes of participation other than direct physical perpetration of the crime by the principal offender. For the sake of an orderly presentation, such modes will be divided into complicity and inchoate offences along the line adopted by the Common Law systems. The chapter will also deal with the responsibility of military commanders or civilian superiors who order the commission of a crime by their subordinates.

8.1 COMPLICITY

When the accused gets involved in complicity in a crime, he would be an accomplice, that is, 'someone who associates himself in [a principal] offence committed by another'.[15] The law of complicity is re-stated in the *Ministries* case that 'he who participates [in a crime] or plays a consenting part therein' is guilty of a crime.[16]

According to one school of thought, the physical act constituting complicity 'borrows' the criminality of the act committed by the principal perpetrator of the criminal enterprise; hence, the act of complicity is a crime only when the crime has been consummated by the principal perpetrator. According to this school of thought, a

---

[11] *R. v. Bow Street Metropolitan Stipendiary Magistrate, ex p. Pinochet Ugarte* [1998] 4 ALL ER 897, HL at 946.

[12] *Akayesu*, para. 483.

[13] *Blaskic*, para. 281.

[14] Ibid., para. 282.

[15] *Akayesu*, paras. 527–9; *Rutaganda*, para. 39; *Musema*, para. 121.

[16] *US v. Ernst von Weizsaecker et al.*, TWC, xiv, 611, 470–1. Cited in *Tadic* Appeals Judgment, para. 264. The ICTY Appeals Chamber itself re-states the law as follows: 'Whoever contributes to the commission of crimes by the group of persons or some members of the group, in execution of a common purpose, may be held to be criminally liable, subject to certain conditions . . .' (ibid., para. 190).

person cannot be both the principal perpetrator of a particular act and the accomplice thereto.[17]

Whatever the merit of the aforesaid school of thought, two separate categories of criminal participation have been held to have crystallized in international law—(i) co-perpetrators participating in a joint criminal enterprise or design, and (ii) aiders and abettors.[18]

COMMON CRIMINAL DESIGN OR CO-PERPETRATION

Most of the time, international crimes do not result from the criminal acts of single individuals but from collective criminal enterprises, pursuant to a common criminal design. The logic behind holding each of these individuals criminally liable as principals, and not aiders and abettors, is summed up cogently by the Appeals Chamber of the ICTY in *Tadic* as follows:

' . . . Although only some members of the group may physically perpetrate the criminal act the participation and contribution of the other members of the group is often vital in facilitating the commission of the offence in question. It follows that the moral gravity of such participation is often no less—or indeed no different—from that of those actually carrying out the acts in question.[19]

Under these circumstances, to hold criminally liable as a perpetrator only the person who materially performs the criminal act would disregard the role as co-perpetrators of all those who in some way made it possible for the perpetrator physically to carry out that criminal act. At the same time, depending upon the circumstances, to hold the latter liable only as aiders and abettors might understate the degree of their criminal responsibility'.[20]

Two central issues are involved here. Firstly, whether specific acts of one person can incur the criminal culpability of another where both participate in the execution of a common criminal plan, and what degree of *mens rea* is required in such a case.[21]

---

[17] *Akayesu*, paras. 527–32. Followed in *Musema*, paras. 170–3.

[18] *Furundzija*, para. 216. It should be noted that Trial Chamber II of the ICTR in *Akayesu* resorted to the Rwanda Penal Code in categorizing acts of complicity which include incitement, aiding and abetting, and instigation (*Akayesu*, para. 537). In *Prosecutor v. Kupreskic and Others* (Case No. IT-95-16-T), Trial Chamber II of the ICTY held that the mode of participation under Art. 7(1) of the ICTY Statute is either direct commission (sole perpetration), or co-perpetration, or as aiding and abetting (*Kupreskic and Others*, para. 772).

[19] *Tadic* Appeals Judgment, para. 191.

[20] Ibid., para. 192.

[21] This is how the issues are framed by the ICTY Appeals Chamber in *Tadic* Appeals Judgment, para. 185. Since the ICTY Statute does not specify the *actus reus* and *mens rea* of this category of collective criminality, the Appeals Chamber turns to customary international law, chiefly case law and a few instances of internal legislation, for guidance (ibid., paras. 194, 221–2, 224–6). The Appeals Chamber concedes that the major legal systems of the world do not take the same approach to the notion of common purpose, and that domestic law to a large extent runs parallel to, and precedes, international regulation in the area in question. However, the Appeals Chamber finds that the consistency and cogency of case law and treaties, as well as their consonance with the general principle on criminal responsibility set forth in the ICTY Statute and general international criminal law and in national legislation, are sufficient to warrant the conclusion that case law reflects customary rules of international criminal law (ibid., paras. 225–6).

Actus reus

The objective elements (*actus reus*) of this mode of participation in commission of an international crime are as follows:[22]

A plurality of persons. They need not be organized in a military, political or administrative structure. This is evidenced, for example, in cases of mob violence, where multiple offenders act out a common purpose in situations of disorder.[23]

The existence of a common plan, design, or purpose which amounts to or involves the commission of a crime. There is no necessity for this plan, design, or purpose to have been previously arranged or formulated. The common plan or purpose may materialize extemporaneously and be inferred from the fact that a plurality of persons acts in unison to put into effect a joint criminal enterprise.

Participation of the accused in the common design involving the commission of a crime. This participation need not involve commission of a specific crime (e.g. murder, extermination, torture, rape), but may take the form of assistance in, or contribution to, the execution of the common plan or purpose, as will be shown below.

This notion of common purpose is not linked to that of causation; hence, it is not necessary that the participation of an accused be a *sine qua non*, or that the offence would not have been committed but for his participation.[24]

Mens rea

The subjective elements (*mens rea*) of this mode of participation in the commission of an international crime differ according to the category of common design.[25]

In the first category, cases of co-perpetration, what is required is the *intent* to commit a certain crime (this being the shared intent on the part of all co-perpetrators). In other words, all participants in the common design possess the same criminal intent to commit a crime although each co-perpetrator may carry out a different role within this common design, and one or more of them actually commit the crime, with intent. Therefore, the prerequisite *actus reus* and *mens rea* to hold criminally liable a person who did not or cannot be proven to have effected the commission of a certain crime are as follows: (i) that person voluntarily participates in one aspect of the common design (for example, by inflicting non-fatal violence on the victim in the case of murder, or by furnishing material assistance to or facilitating the activities of his co-perpetrators); and (ii) that person, although not personally

---

[22] Ibid., para. 227.

[23] As in *re Heyer and Others* ('*Essen Lynching*' case), British Military Court, Essen, Germany, 22 Dec. 1945 (1951) 13 *Ann. Dig.* 287, cited in *Tadic* Appeals Judgment, paras. 205–9.

[24] *Tadic* Appeals Judgment, para. 199, citing, with approval, the submission of the Judge Advocate in *Trial of Feurstein and others* ('*Ponzano*' case), Proceedings of a War Crimes Trial held at Hamburg, Germany, Judgment of 24 Aug. 1948, pp. 7–8.

[25] *Tadic* Appeals Judgment, paras. 220, 228.

effecting the crime himself, must intend the result of the action taken by his perpetrators.[26]

The point is put elegantly in the *Einsatzgruppen* case decided by a United States Military Tribunal sitting at Nuremberg with regard to members of *Einsatz* units whose express mission, well known to all the members, was to carry out a large-scale programme of murder:

'. . . Any member who assisted in enabling these units to function, knowing what was afoot, is guilty of the crimes committed by the unit. The cook in the galley of a pirate ship does not escape the yardarm merely because he himself does not brandish a cutlass. The man who stands at the door of a bank and scans the environs may appear to be the most peaceable of citizens, but if his purpose is to warn his robber confederates inside the bank of the approach of the police, his guilt is clear enough . . . Far from being a defence or even a circumstance in mitigation, the fact that [certain of the commanders] did not personally shoot a great many people, but rather devoted themselves to directing the over-all operations of the *Einsatzgruppen*, only serves to establish their deeper responsibility for the crimes of the men under their command.'[27]

It also seems necessary to prove knowledge on the part of the accused as to the intended purpose of the criminal enterprise, even if such knowledge may be deducible only by implication in the sense that everybody, particularly persons in the accused's position, should know about the situation that bears upon the commission of the crime in question. Otherwise, the accused could not have been able to participate consciously in a common criminal enterprise and intend a particular outcome of that enterprise.[28]

The second category of cases concerns instances where the offences charged are alleged to have been committed by members of military or administrative units acting pursuant to a concerted plan, such as running concentration camps. The requisite *actus reus* is the active participation in the enforcement of that concerted plan, and this could be inferred from the position of authority and the specific functions held by each accused. In terms of *mens rea, personal knowledge* of the nature of the system of ill-treatment is required (whether proved by express testimony or a matter of reasonable inference from the accused's position of authority), as well as the *intent* to further this common concerted system or design of ill-treatment. The requisite intent could also be inferred from the position of authority held by each accused which, in and of itself, is indicative of the level of awareness of the common design and an intent to participate in it.[29]

The third category of cases concerns a common design to pursue a course of

---

[26] Ibid., paras. 196–9, 220, 228.

[27] *United States of America v. Otto Ohlendorf et al.*, TWC, iv, 3 at 373.

[28] Although the ICTY Appeals Chamber in *Tadic* Appeals Judgment does not include the requirement of knowledge as part of the first category of cases, when discussing the first category of cases, the Appeals Chamber cites extensively, and without any disapproval, a number of post-WWII cases that stressed the necessity of knowledge on the part of the accused as to the intended purpose of the criminal enterprise. See *Tadic* Appeals Judgment, paras. 199–200 and accompanying footnotes 243–5.

[29] Ibid., paras. 202–3, 220, 228.

conduct where one of the perpetrators commits an act which, while outside the common design, was nevertheless a natural and foreseeable consequence of the implementation of that common purpose. What is to be proved is the *intent* to participate in and further—individually and jointly—the criminal activity or the criminal purpose of a group and to contribute to the joint criminal enterprise or in any event to the commission of a crime by that group. In addition, a person shall be responsible for a crime other than the one agreed upon in the common plan only if, under the circumstances of the case, (i) it was *foreseeable* that such a crime might be committed by one or other members of the group; and (ii) the accused *willingly took that risk*.[30] In order for responsibility for the crime to be imputable to the others, everyone in the group must have been able to *predict* the result of the risk, and this requires more than negligence.[31] As the Appeals Chamber of the ICTY states in *Tadic*:

'What is required is a state of mind in which a person, although he did not intend to bring about a certain result, was aware that the actions of the group were most likely to lead to that result but nevertheless willingly took that risk. In other words, the so-called *dolus eventualis* is required (also called "advertent recklessness" in some national legal systems).'[32]

In *Tadic* itself, the armed group to which the Appellant Tadic belonged killed five men in the village of Jaskici and the Appellant was convicted of the killing of the five men although it was not proven that the Appellant himself actually pulled the trigger. He was guilty because he had the intention to further the common criminal purpose (a 'recognizable plan' or policy of ethnic cleansing), and actively took part in that purpose to rid the Prijedor region, where the village of Jaskici is situated, of the non-Serb population by committing inhumane acts against them. The common criminal purpose was not to kill all non-Serb men, but killings frequently occurred in the effort to effect that purpose and the Appellant was aware of them. Therefore, the fact that non-Serbs might be killed in the implementation of this common criminal purpose was, in the circumstances in that case, foreseeable, and the Appellant was aware that the actions of the group to which he belonged were likely to lead to such killings, but he nevertheless willingly took that risk.[33]

The Appeals Chamber of the ICTY in *Tadic* has noted that 'a substantially similar notion' is stipulated in Article 25(3)(d) of the ICC Statute.[34] However, the Appeals

---

[30] Ibid., para. 228.

[31] Ibid., para. 220.

[32] Ibid.

[33] Ibid., paras. 183, 230–7. Cf. also *Kupreskic and Others*, paras. 782–3.

[34] *Tadic* Appeals Judgment, para. 222. The other international agreement cited by the ICTY Appeals Chamber in that case is the UN Convention for the Suppression of Terrorist Bombing, adopted by consensus by the UN General Assembly through Resolution 52/164 of 15 Dec. 1997 and opened for signature on 9 Jan. 1998. Article 2(3)(c) of the Convention stipulates that offences under the Convention may be committed by any person who in any other way other than participating as an accomplice, or organizing or directing others to commit an offence, contributes to the commission of one or more of the offences by a group of persons 'acting with a common purpose, such contribution shall be intentional and either be made with the aim of furthering the general criminal activity or purpose of the group or be made in the knowledge of the intention of the group to commit the offence or offences concerned' (ibid., para. 221).

Chamber adds that should it be argued that the *actus reus* and *mens rea* of the crime stipulated in Article 25(3) of the ICC Statute differ to some extent from those stipulated by the Appeals Chamber in that case, the consequences of this difference may only be appreciable in the long run, once the ICC is established.[35] Nonetheless, it should be noted that the ICTR in *Kayishema and Ruzindana* has interpreted the *actus reus* and *mens rea* in this situation as similar to those set out in Article 25(3)(d) of the ICC Statute. The ICTR has ruled that the Prosecutor must satisfy a two-stage test that requires the demonstration of participation and knowledge or intent, that is awareness by the actor of his participation in a crime.[36] In other words, the Prosecutor must prove that:

'through [each of his modes] of participation, whether be by act(s) or omission(s), the accused contributed substantially to the commission of a crime and that, depending on the mode of participation in question, he was at least aware that his conduct would so contribute to the crime.'[37]

What constitutes the *actus reus* and the requisite degree of contribution varies with each mode of participation and are questions of fact for a Trial Chamber to consider. The accused need not be present at the scene of the crime, and his contribution need not always be a tangible one.[38] For example, an approving spectator who is held in such respect by the other perpetrators that his presence encourages them in their conduct may be guilty of complicity if the spectator knows the effect that his presence would have.[39]

AIDING AND ABETTING

Aiding means giving assistance to someone, whereas abetting involves facilitating the commission of an act by being sympathetic thereto, including providing mere exhortation or encouragement.[40]

Actus reus

The *actus reus* of aiding and abetting requires practical assistance, encouragement, or moral support, which has substantial effect on the perpetration of the crime.[41] The

---

[35] According to the Appeals Chamber, this is because Art. 10 of the ICC Statute [which appears in Part 2 of the ICC Statute and which provides that nothing in Part 2 of the Statute shall be interpreted as limiting or prejudicing in any way existing or developing rules of international law for purposes other than the ICC Statute] is inapplicable to Art. 25(3) appearing in Part 3 of the ICC Statute. Ibid., n. 282.

[36] *Kayishema and Ruzindana*, para. 198.

[37] Ibid., para. 207.

[38] Ibid., paras. 199–201.

[39] *Furundzija*, para. 207. Cited with approval in *Kayishema and Ruzindana*, paras. 200–1.

[40] *Akayesu*, para. 484; *Furundzija*, para. 231.

[41] *Furundzija*, paras. 235–6, 249 and also paras. 199–209, 217–26. Cf. also *Prosecutor v. Jean Kambanda*, Case No. ICTR-97-23-S, ICTR T. Ch., 4 Sept. 1998, paras. 39(v), (viii), (xi), 40(4); *Tadic* Appeals Judgment, para. 229; *Prosecutor v. Zlatko Aleksovski*, Case No. IT-95-14/1-A, ICTY App. Ch., 24 Mar. 2000 (hereinafter '*Aleksovski* (App. Ch.)'), para. 162.

accused's conduct may in itself be perfectly lawful; it becomes criminal only when combined with the unlawful conduct of the principal.[42] Either aiding or abetting alone suffices to incur criminal liability of the perpetrator.[43]

Assistance rendered to the commission of a crime need not be tangible in the sense of providing material means or physical help, but may consist of omission that has a decisive effect on the perpetration of a crime provided that such omission is accompanied by the requisite *mens rea*.[44] Such omission is often in the form of mere presence to give moral support or encouragement (the so-called 'silent approval'), as long as the requisite intent is present.[45] Presence alone is not sufficient if it is an ignorant or unwilling presence, unless the presence can be shown or inferred, by circumstantial or other evidence, to be knowing and to have a direct and substantial effect, such as encouragement, on the commission of the illegal act. To have such effect, the presence is usually combined with authority in the sense that the supporter must be of a certain status for his presence to be interpreted as giving moral support or approval to the commission of the crime by the principal offender. Therefore, while the presence of a spectator in civilian dress was held to be insufficient to find the spectator guilty of aiding and abetting a crime,[46] intermittent presence on the crime scene by a long-time militant member of the Nazi Party was held to be aiding and abetting the commission of the crime by the principal offenders.[47] Likewise, in *Aleksovski*, the warden of a prison camp who was present during the interrogation of camp detainees was held to have aided and abetted, or even incited, the commission of the crime by his subordinates against the detainees because his presence could be interpreted as giving tacit approval to his subordinates to commit the crime.[48] Maybe the only exception is in case of aiding and abetting genocide. Trial Chamber I of the ICTR held in *Akayesu* that in order to find a person guilty of aiding and abetting in the planning, preparation, or execution of genocide it must be proven that the person did have the specific intent to commit genocide, 'namely that he or she acted with the intent to destroy in whole or in part, a national, ethnical, racial or religious group, as such'.[49] It would be difficult to infer such specific intent from mere presence.

While presence may be important in many circumstances, it is an act of participa-

---

[42] *Furundzija*, para. 243.

[43] *Akayesu*, para. 484.

[44] *Blaskic*, para. 284.

[45] Ibid.; *Kambanda*, paras. 39(v), (viii), (xi), 40(4); *Celebici*, para. 327; *Furundzija*, paras. 199–209. Cf. also *Kupreskic and Others*, para. 845.

[46] The *Pig-cart Parade* case, Judgment of the German Supreme Court in the British Occupied Zone of Germany, cited in *Furundzija*, paras. 208–9.

[47] The *Synagogue* case, Judgment of the German Supreme Court in the British Occupied Zone of Germany, cited in *Furundzija*, paras. 205–9.

[48] *Prosecutor v. Zlatko Aleksovski*, ICTY T. Ch. I, 25 June 1999 (hereinafter 'Aleksovski Judgment'), paras. 87–89, 229. In that case, the accused sometimes ordered that violence be used against the detainees, but at other times kept his silence when violence was actually used by his subordinates. See also *Akayesu*, paras. 451–2, 693–4, 706–7.

[49] *Akayesu*, para. 485. Conversely, the accused need not have such specific intent to destroy in case of complicity in genocide. Ibid., and para. 545.

tion with knowledge that gives rise to the criminal responsibility of the principal.[50] Actual physical presence when the crime is committed is not necessary, provided that the accused is found to have knowingly participated in the commission of an offence and his participation substantially effected the commission of that offence through supporting the actual commission before, during, or after the incident. He will also be responsible for all that naturally results from the commission of the act in question.[51]

Whether the accused's participation substantially effects the commission of the crime is a question of fact to be determined on a case-by-case basis.[52] However, an aider and abettor is not exonerated by the mere fact that his assistance could easily have been obtained from another.[53]

The act contributing to the commission of a crime can be spread geographically and temporally, that is, before, during, or after its commission. It suffices that the act of participation substantially facilitates or contributes to the commission of a crime, and that the accused participates in it voluntarily with knowledge of the unlawful nature of the act in question.[54]

The requirement that the assistance facilitates the commission of the crime means that such assistance need not even constitute a *conditio sine qua non* for the acts of the principal offender.[55] For example, when the crimes are already taking place, the accused, who is in a position to stop them, allows them to go on and facilitates their commission through his words of encouragement, thereby sending a clear signal of official tolerance for these crimes.[56] The accused's aiding and abetting is not a *conditio sine qua non* for the perpetrators' commission of the crimes in the first place; it merely sustains and facilitates the commission of the crimes. Hence, in *Furundzija*, Trial Chamber II of the ICTY dismisses the use of the term 'direct' in qualifying the nexus between the assistance and the principal act because it might give a misleading connotation that the assistance needs to be tangible one, or to have a causal effect on the crime.[57] The term 'direct' is not used in Article 25(3)(c) of the ICC Statute, either.

---

[50] *Prosecutor v. Dusko Tadic*, Case No. IT-94-1-T, ICTY T. Ch. II, 7 May 1997 (hereinafter '*Tadic* Judgment'), paras. 689–90, *Celebici*, paras. 327–9.

[51] *Tadic* Judgment, paras. 691–2; *Musema*, paras. 125–6. As noted by Trial Chamber II of the ICTY in *Furundzija* (n. 227), the English law relating to accessories after the fact, as appeared in Section 4(1) of the Criminal Law Act 1967, is a separate offence of 'assisting an offender' rather than a form of aiding and abetting.

[52] Cf. *Furundzija*, paras. 217–25.

[53] *S. et al.* ('*Hechingen Deportation*' case), Decision of a German court in the French Occupied Zone of Germany, cited in *Furundzija*, para. 224.

[54] *Aleksovski* Judgment, paras. 61–5, 87–9, 129, 138; *Rutaganda*, para. 43. Cf. also *Kupreskic and Others*, paras. 803–4: *Blaskic*, para. 285.

[55] *Furundzija*, paras. 209, 233; *Blaskic*, para. 285.

[56] *Furundzija*, para. 209, referring to the actual events in *Akayesu* and inferring from the pronouncement in para. 692 of the ICTR's judgment in that case to this effect.

[57] *Furundzija*, para. 232. Cf. *Tadic* Judgment, where Trial Chamber II of the ICTY held that the elements inherent in the forms of participation in a crime are that the perpetrator 'knowingly participated in the commission of an offence', and that 'his participation directly and substantially affected the commission of that offence through supporting the actual commission before, during, or after the incident' (*Tadic* Judgment, para. 692, quoted with approval in *Akayesu*, para. 477).

In the *Case against R. Mulka et al.* ('*Auschwitz Concentration Camp*' case), it was held that the defendants were guilty of being aiders and abettors if it could be proved that they performed their assigned duty in the concentration camp without the specific intent to actually identify themselves with the aims of the Nazi regime to exterminate the Jews in the camp. If it could be proved that they actually identified themselves with the said aims, then they would be guilty as principal offenders because they wanted the offence as their own. However, in order to be guilty of aiding and abetting, a person must act to further the commission of the main offence by the principal offenders in a concrete manner. Thus, the physician in charge of taking care of the guard personnel of the Auschwitz concentration camp who confined himself to doing just that, as well as the physician who treated prisoners in the camp and saved their lives, and those subordinates who unsuccessfully put little obstacles in the way of the destruction programme with regard to the Auschwitz concentration camp would not be guilty of aiding and abetting.[58]

Mens rea

The requisite *mens rea* of aiding and abetting in customary international law is the knowledge (in the sense of being aware) that the accused's act assists the commission of the offence by the principal;[59] he need not share the *mens rea* of the principal in the sense of positive intention to commit the crime.[60] Besides, if he knows that one of a number of crimes will probably be committed, and one of those crimes is in fact committed, he has intended to facilitate the commission of the crime, and is guilty as an aider and abettor. In other words, he need not know the precise crime that was intended and which was actually committed.[61] The existence of this *mens rea* need not be explicit, but may be inferred from all relevant circumstances.[62] Such inference of aiding and abetting is made in *Aleksovski*, where the accused was aware that the prisoners of the prison camp under his command were being mistreated repeatedly by the Croatian Defence Council (HVO) soldiers over a period of time, yet he continued to send the prisoners outside the prison camp to work under those soldiers without taking measures open to him to stop them from going out to work in such conditions.[63]

Article 30 of the ICC Statute stipulates that, 'unless otherwise provided, a person shall be criminally responsible and liable for punishment for a crime within the [ICC's] jurisdiction only if the material elements are committed with intent and knowledge'. In light of what has been stated above, the intent in this case must be the intent of the aider and abettor to facilitate the commission of the crime. As Trial Chamber I of the ICTY puts it in *Tadic*, the test of *mens rea* that emerged from

---

58 Cited in *Tadic* Appeals Judgment, n. 254.
59 Ibid., para. 229; *Celebici*, para. 328; *Furundzija*, paras. 247, 249; *Aleksovski* (App. Ch.), para. 164.
60 *Furundzija*, paras. 247, 249; *Akayesu*, paras. 538–9.
61 *Furundzija*, para. 246. Quoted with approval in *Blaskic*, para. 287.
62 *Celebici*, para. 328.
63 *Aleksovski* (App. Ch.), paras. 169, 172.

post-WWII trials is 'awareness of the act of participation coupled with a conscious decision to participate'.[64] The aider and abettor need not share the intent of the principal to commit the crime. This is followed by Trial Chamber I of the ICTY in *Blaskic*. After finding it appropriate to distinguish between 'knowledge' and 'intent' with reference to Article 30 of the ICC Statute, the Trial Chamber concludes what must be proved is (a) the accused's knowledge that his act or omission would contribute to the commission of the crime, and (b) the intent of the accused to provide assistance thereto, or at least his knowledge that his assistance would have a possible or foreseeable consequence of supporting the commission of that crime.[65]

In complex situations like torture which typically involve a great number of people, each performing his individual function, allocation of criminal liability (which also matters for stigmatization of the offenders and for sentencing purposes) is as follows. To be guilty as a principal, the accused must 'participate in an integral part of the crime and partake of the purpose behind the [crime]'. In the case of the crime of torture under customary international law, such purpose is the intent to obtain information or a confession, to punish or intimidate, humiliate, coerce or discriminate against the victim or a third person.[66] To be guilty as an aider and abettor, the accused must 'assist in some way which has a substantial effect on the perpetration of the crime and with knowledge that torture is taking place'.[67]

Distinction between the two categories of complicity

The Appeals Chamber of the ICTY held in *Tadic* that aiding and abetting is distinguishable from acting pursuant to a common purpose or design to commit a crime as follows.

'(i)   The aider and abettor is always an accessory to a crime perpetrated by another person, the principal.

(ii)   In the case of aiding and abetting no proof is required of the existence of a common concerted plan, let alone of the pre-existence of such a plan. No plan or agreement is required: indeed, the principal may not even know about the accomplice's contribution.

(iii)   The aider and the abettor carries out acts specifically directed to assist, encourage or lend moral support to the perpetration of a certain specific crime (murder, extermination, rape, torture, wanton destruction of civilian property, etc.), and this support has a substantial effect upon the perpetration of the crime. By contrast, in the case of acting in pursuance of a common purpose or design, it is sufficient for the participant to perform acts that in some way are directed to the furthering of the common plan or purpose.

(iv)   In the case of aiding and abetting, the requisite mental element is knowledge that the

---

[64]   *Tadic* Judgment, para. 674, quoted in *Furundzija*, paras. 241, 247.
[65]   *Blaskic*, para. 286.
[66]   *Furundzija*, paras. 257, 529–31.
[67]   Ibid. See also paras. 250–6, 273–4, 281–2.

acts performed by the aider and abettor assist the commission of a specific crime by the principal.'

By contrast, in the case of common purpose or design more is required (i.e. either intent to perpetrate the crime or intent to pursue the common criminal design plus foresight that those crimes outside the criminal common purpose were likely to be committed), as stated above.[68]

COMPLICITY IN GENOCIDE

Genocide and complicity in genocide are two distinct, mutually exclusive crimes.[69] Complicity in genocide necessarily implies the existence of a principal offence; that is, the completed, consummated offence, although the perpetrator of the principal offence himself has not been tried.[70] However, an individual cannot be guilty of both an act of genocide and an act of complicity in genocide for the same act since the two offences are mutually exclusive.[71]

The *mens rea*, or special intent, required for complicity in genocide is knowledge of the genocidal plan, coupled with the *actus reus* of participation in the execution of such plan. Thus, the accused is liable as an accomplice to genocide if he 'knowingly and wilfully' aided or abetted or instigated one or more persons in the commission of genocide, while being aware of the genocidal plan even though the accused himself did not have the specific intent to destroy, in whole or in part, a national, ethical, racial or religious group, as such.[72] In other words, the accused who, without himself sharing the goal of partial or total destruction of a protected group as such, knew that his act or omission contributed to or would have contributed to such destruction could be responsible for complicity in genocide, but not genocide itself.[73] However, if the accused was unaware of the principal's genocidal intent, the accused could not be

---

[68] *Tadic* Appeals Judgment, para. 229. Cf. also *Kayishema and Ruzindana*, paras. 204–5. In *Furundzija* (paras. 210–5, 249), Trial Chamber II of the ICTY also tried to distinguish, albeit less elaborately than the ICTY Appeals Chamber in *Tadic* Appeals Judgment, aiding and abetting from the case of co-perpetration by a group of persons pursuing a common criminal design. It is somewhat surprising that the Trial Chamber in *Furundzija* at one point treats both modes of participation as the same. See *Furundzija*, para. 231, which contradicts para. 216.

[69] *Akayesu*, para. 700.

[70] Ibid., paras. 527; *Musema*, paras. 172–4.

[71] *Musema*, para. 175.

[72] *Akayesu*, paras. 545, 725–6. In paragraph 536 of its judgment in *Akayesu*, Trial Chamber I of the ICTR stated: 'Complicity by aiding and abetting implies a positive action which excludes, in principle, complicity by failure to act or omission'. However, in paragraphs 546–8 of the same judgment, the Trial Chamber distinguished between 'complicity in genocide' and 'aiding and abetting' of genocide, stating that 'in theory, complicity requires a positive act, i.e. an act of commission, whereas aiding and abetting may consist in failing to act or refraining from action'. This is confusing. In any case, it is hereby submitted that what the Trial Chamber meant by 'complicity' is complicity through common criminal design or co-perpetration. As for aiding and abetting, it was held that in order to find a person guilty of aiding and abetting in the planning, preparation, or execution of genocide, it must be proven that the person did have the specific intent to commit genocide. Ibid., para. 485. Cf. also ibid., para. 705.

[73] *Jelisic*, para. 86, citing *Akayesu*, paras. 544–7. Also *Musema*, paras. 180–3.

prosecuted for complicity in genocide although he might be prosecuted for, for example, complicity in murder.[74]

8.2 INCHOATE OFFENCES

INCITEMENT IN GENOCIDE

Incitement is the mode of participation in international crime that is punishable in the case of genocide only.

Incitement can be defined as encouraging or persuading another to commit an offence, or committing an act intended to directly provoke another to commit a crime through speeches, shouting or threats, or any other means of audiovisual communication. There is also authority which would consider threats or other forms of pressure as incitement.[75] It is necessary to prove the causal connection between the incitement and the material commission of the crime.[76]

Incitement must be both direct and public. The public nature of incitement is to be considered in the light of the place where the incitement took place and whether or not it was selective or limited. The incitement must not be made in private, but must be made in a public place or to members of the general public at large.[77] Incitement can be made at public meetings or through radio broadcasts encouraging others to commit genocide, or by congratulating people who committed genocide so that they and/or others would emulate the genocide already committed.[78]

The 'direct' element of incitement means that the incitement is made in a direct form and specifically provokes another to commit a crime. Vague or indirect suggestions may not qualify as incitement.[79] However, the incitement may be implicit; it need not specifically ask others to commit genocide, provided that it leaves no doubt what it means. For example, the incendiary phrase 'you refuse to give your blood to your country and the dogs drink it for nothing' was interpreted in the context in which it was uttered to mean that something had to be done out of patriotism to eliminate from Rwanda the Tutsi minority group and their sympathizers.[80] In any case, the incitement must aim at causing a specific offence to be committed.[81] The direct element must be considered on a case-by-case basis and in the light of its cultural and linguistic content and the circumstances in which it took place,

---

[74] *Musema*, para. 182.
[75] Cf. *Akayesu*, paras. 482, 555.
[76] *Blaskic*, para. 280.
[77] *Akayesu*, para. 556.
[78] *Kambanda*, paras. 39(vii), (viii), (x), 40(3).
[79] *Akayesu*, para. 557.
[80] *Kambanda*, para. 39(x).
[81] *Akayesu*, para. 557.

particularly whether the persons for whom the incitement was intended understood immediately the implication of the inciting message.[82]

The *actus reus* of incitement in genocide may be summarized as 'directly provoking the perpetrator(s) to commit genocide, whether through speeches, shouting or threats uttered in public places or at public gatherings, or through the sale or display of written material or printed matter in public places or at public gatherings, or through the public display of placards or posters, or through any other means of audiovisual communication'.[83]

The *mens rea* of incitement in genocide may be defined as the intent to directly prompt or provoke another to commit genocide. The person who is inciting to commit genocide must have himself the specific intent to commit genocide.[84] Addressing a public gathering to call on the audience to unite in order to get rid of an ethnic group, with full awareness of the impact of that address, has been held to constitute direct and public incitement to commit genocide.[85]

Since genocide is such a serious international crime, direct and public incitement to commit genocide must be punished as such even where the incitement failed to produce the result desired by the person who incited. Incitement in genocide belongs to the genre of inchoate offences which are punishable irrespective of the result thereof which may or may not have been achieved.[86]

CONSPIRACY

Article 6 of the Nuremberg Charter provided: 'Leaders, organizers, instigators and accomplices participating in the formulation or execution of a common plan or conspiracy to commit any of the foregoing crimes are responsible for all acts performed by any persons in execution of such plan'. This was copied verbatim in Article 5 of the Tokyo Charter. However, the Nuremberg and Tokyo Tribunals limited their consideration of liability in respect of the common plan or conspiracy to the charge of waging aggressive war, but not the charges of war crimes and crimes against humanity.

The Nuremberg Charter went further by providing in Articles 9 and 10 that the Nuremberg Tribunal may declare that a group or organization was a criminal organization whose members might be tried before national, military, or occupation courts for their membership therein. In any such cases, the criminal nature of the group or organization was considered proved and not open to question. When applying these

---

[82] See *Prosecutor v. Georges Ruggiu*, Case No. ICTR-97-32-I, ICTR T. Ch. I, 1 June 2000, paras. 14, 17, 44.

[83] *Akayesu*, para. 558.

[84] Ibid., para. 560.

[85] Ibid., paras. 709–10.

[86] Ibid., paras. 561–2. Trial Chamber I of the ICTR in *Akayesu* noted that the drafters of the Genocide Convention considered providing explicitly to this effect, but a majority decided against it. The Trial Chamber concluded that it could not thereby be inferred that the drafters did not intend to punish unsuccessful acts of incitement; rather, when considered 'in light of the overall *travaux*', they simply 'decided not to specifically mention that such a form of incitement could be punished' (ibid., para. 561).

provisions, the Tribunal emphasized that this procedure was novel and was to be properly safeguarded so as not to produce great injustice. A criminal organization was considered analogous to criminal conspiracy—the members joined the group or organization voluntarily in full knowledge of its criminal purpose and activities. The rationale for such procedure was to save time and efforts in proving the criminal acts and intent in the later trial of members of a large organization who were accused of participating in its criminal purposes. The Tribunal held the Leadership Corps of the Nazi Party, the Gestapo and the SD, and the SS, to be criminal organizations. It acquitted the Reich Cabinet, and the General Staff and High Command of being criminal organizations because of their relatively small size and because many of their members were being prosecuted individually before the Tribunal. This procedure has been subject to criticisms on the ground that it upheld the notion of 'collective guilt' or 'guilt by association' not recognized by the general principles of criminal law.[87] The seven Nuremberg Principles formulated by the International Law Commission in 1950 merely refers, in Principle VII, to 'complicity in a crime', whereas 'criminal organization' or even 'conspiracy' is not mentioned anywhere in the Principles.

The term 'conspiracy' is used explicitly in Article 4(3)(b) of the ICTY Statute and Article 2(3)(b) of the ICTR Statute, which confer jurisdiction on the ICTY and the ICTR, respectively to punish 'conspiracy to commit genocide'. The rationale for including this offence, as gleaned from the *travaux préparatoires* of the Genocide Convention, is to ensure that even mere agreement to commit genocide should be punishable even if no preparatory act has taken place.[88] Conspiracy to commit genocide is defined as an agreement between two or more persons to commit genocide.[89] The *mens rea* required is the concerted intent to commit genocide, that is, the *dolus specialis* of genocide itself.[90] In *Kambanda*, the accused, who was Prime Minister of Rwanda, was found to have conspired with others to commit genocide. This conspiracy took the form of participation in meetings to discuss actions to commit genocide.[91]

Conspiracy is an inchoate offence punishable by virtue of the process of conspiracy itself and not as a consequence of the result of that conspiracy.[92] Hence, an accused cannot be convicted of both genocide and conspiracy to commit genocide on the basis of the same set of acts.[93]

In sum, conspiracy is distinguishable from complicity in the following ways. No distinction is made in the case of conspiracy between direct perpetrators and indirect

---

[87] For an excellent analysis of the judgment of the Nuremberg Tribunal on this matter as well as the criticisms it has been subject to, see R. K. Woetzel, *The Nuremberg Trials in International Law* (Stevens & Sons, 1962), 190–217.

[88] *Musema*, para. 185.

[89] Ibid., para. 191.

[90] Ibid., para. 192.

[91] *Kambanda*, paras. 39 (iii)–(iv), 40(2).

[92] *Musema*, para. 193.

[93] Ibid., para. 198.

perpetrators, perpetrators and co-perpetrators, or perpetrators and accomplices: all the participants are associated in the framework of a common plan and have joinly decided to commit the crime.[94]

As mentioned previously, the concept of conspiracy is covered indirectly in Article 25(3)(d) of the ICC Statute. The ICC will likely construe this provision in the case of genocide by seeking guidance from the well-established jurisprudence of the ICTR on this point.

ATTEMPT

The concept of attempt was not included in the Nuremberg Charter or the Tokyo Charter. The ILC *Special Rapporteur* on the Draft Code of Crimes Against the Peace and Security of Mankind noted in 1990 that the theory of attempt could be of limited application in such crimes. For example, it would be difficult to see what form an attempt to commit an act of aggression could take and how to differentiate between commencement of execution of an act of aggression and the act itself; the idea of an attempt at a threat of aggression was 'even more bewildering'. However, the concept is entirely conceivable for most crimes against humanity and genocide which consist of a series of specific criminal acts.[95]

The ICTY Statute and the ICTR Statute specifically criminalize attempts in cases of genocide only. The Statutes have to reflect customary international law on individual criminal responsibility, and there was no such responsibility for attempts under the Nuremberg Charter or the Tokyo Charter. However, Article III of the Genocide Convention of 1948 includes attempt to commit genocide as a punishable act and since the Convention codifies customary international law on genocide, the ICTY Statute and the ICTR Statute find no difficulty in replicating the Convention.

Article 25(3)(f) of the ICC Statute goes further by including attempts as a mode of participation in any crime within the ICC's jurisdiction. It follows the general principle recognized by national jurisdictions. There must be a substantial step to commit a crime, but the crime does not occur because of circumstances beyond the control of the person. Nonetheless, if the person abandons his intention and effort to commit the crime voluntarily or otherwise prevents the completion of the crime, he is not liable for the attempt.

---

[94] Report of the ILC Special *Rapporteur* on the Draft Code of Crimes Against the Peace and Security of Mankind, *Yearbook of the ILC*, ii (1990), pt. II, at 16.

[95] Ibid., at 16–17.

8.3 COMMAND RESPONSIBILITY

The principle of command responsibility or superior responsibility is well-established in international law,[96] as recognized by, for example, Article 87 of AP I, Article 7(3) of the ICTY Statute, Article 6(3) of the ICTR Statute, and Article 28 of the ICC Statute. Under this principle, a superior is criminally responsible for the acts committed by his subordinates if he knew or had reason to know that the subordinate was about to commit such acts or had done so and the superior failed to take the necessary and reasonable measures to prevent such acts or to punish the perpetrators thereof. This command responsibility emanates from failure to act in breach of a clear, affirmative duty or moral obligation imposed by the law of war or by international law upon those in authority to act.[97]

An accused may be found guilty of command responsibility additionally or in the alternative to the other modes of responsibility already discussed in this chapter, depending on the facts of each case.[98] When the superior acts positively by ordering, instigating, or planning criminal acts carried out by his subordinates, he incurs 'direct' responsibility, like all other individuals who bear individual criminal responsibility pursuant to Article 7(1) of the ICTY Statute, Article 6(1) of the ICTR Statute, and Article 25(3) of the ICC Statute. However, if he fails to take measures to prevent or repress his subordinates' criminal acts, his culpable omissions thereby incur 'indirect' command responsibility or command responsibility *strictu sensu*, as proscribed by Article 7(3) of the ICTY Statute, Article 6(3) of the ICTR Statute, and Article 28 of the ICC Statute.[99] Where a superior fails to prevent or repress his subordinates' criminal acts, he could be held liable for aiding and abetting or inciting the crimes if all the necessary elements for aiding and abetting or incitement, as the case may be, are present.[100]

This principle is also applicable to civilian, non-military commanders, who wield the requisite authority. International instruments and case law do not restrict its application to military commanders only but extend it to cover political leaders and other civilian superiors in positions of authority.[101] A former civilian prime minister, politicians, and industrialists have been found guilty under this principle for crimes committed by their subordinates.[102] Therefore, the crucial question is not the civilian

---

[96] *Celebici*, paras. 333–43. Although the term 'commander' normally connotes a military commander and the term 'superior' connotes a civilian superior, both terms are treated interchangeably here for ease of reference.

[97] *Celebici*, paras. 334, 338–9, citing, *inter alia*, *In Re Yamashita*, 327 US 1 (1946), *United States v. Karl Brandt and Others* ('Doctors' Trial'), TWC, ii, 186 at 212; *United States v. Wilhelm von Leeb et al.* ('High Command' case), TWC, xi, 462 at 512.

[98] *Kayishema and Ruzindana*, para. 210; *Celebici*, para. 333.

[99] Cf. *Celebici*, paras. 333–4.

[100] *Blaskic*, paras. 337–9.

[101] *Celebici*, paras. 356–63; *Musema*, paras. 136, 146–8.

[102] *Kayishema and Ruzindana*, paras. 213–5. Cf. *Kambanda*, para. 39 (ii), (xii).

or military status of the superior, but the degree of authority the superior exercises over his subordinates.[103] In *Kayishema and Ruzindana*, the ICTR found Kayishema, a local politician, in his capacity as prefect of Kibuye, Rwanda, responsible for the acts of the *gendarmes*, the *bourgmestres* (mayors), police and prison guards who were his subordinates. In *Aleksovski*, the accused who was a civilian who had been appointed by the minister of justice to be warden of a prison camp was held criminally responsible for crimes committed by prison guards inside the camp, but not those committed by soldiers not under his command that took place outside the camp compound.[104] In *Musema*, the accused, who was director of an important tea factory, was held to have a superior relationship over employees of the factory. He exercised *de jure* authority over them while they were on the factory premises and while they were engaged in their professional duties as employees of the factory even if those duties were performed outside factory premises. He was also found to have exercised legal and financial control over these employees, particularly through his power to appoint and remove the employees from their positions at the tea factory. Thus, the accused was in a position to take reasonable measures to attempt to prevent or to punish these employees concerning their crimes, and his omission to do so gave rise to his superior responsibility.

Three cumulative elements must be proved to find command responsibility. Firstly, there must be a superior-subordinate relationship. Secondly, the superior knew or had reason to know that the subordinate was about to commit a crime or had committed a crime. Finally, the superior failed to take necessary and reasonable measures to prevent the crime or to punish the perpetrator thereof.[105] With regard to the affirmative duty or moral obligation to act, it seems to be imposed by the law of war or by international law on the commander or superior by virtue of his position and/or authority.[106]

Since the superior-subordinate relationship lies at the heart of the principle of command responsibility, this principle is 'ultimately predicated upon the power of the superior to control the acts of his subordinates'.[107] However, the Trial Chamber may look beyond the *de jure* powers wielded by the accused and consider the *de facto* power or influence he actually exercises.[108] This is a question of facts to be decided on a case-by-case basis.[109] Therefore, while the US Military Tribunals held in the *Hostage* and *High Command* cases that military chiefs of staff could not be held criminally

---

[103] *Kayishema and Ruzindana*, para. 216; *Aleksovski* Judgment, paras. 75–8, 103; and see also *Akayesu*, para. 491.

[104] *Aleksovski* Judgment, paras. 118–9, 133–7.

[105] Ibid., paras. 69–72; *Celebici*, para. 346; *Blaskic*, para. 294.

[106] Cf. *Celebici*, paras. 333–4, 338–9, 373, 377 and the cases cited therein.

[107] *Celebici*, para. 377; *Musema*, para. 135.

[108] *Kayishema and Ruzindana*, paras. 217–20: *Celebici*, paras. 370–1; *Musema*, paras. 141–2; *Blaskic*, paras. 300–1. For example, in the case of the *bourgmestre* (mayor) in Rwanda, his *de facto* authority in the maintenance of public order within his commune is significantly greater than that which is conferred on him *de jure* (*Akayesu*, para. 77).

[109] *Akayesu*, para. 483; *Musema*, para. 135.

responsible on the basis of command responsibility because they did not have command authority in the chain of command,[110] the Tokyo Tribunal held Lieutenant General Akira Muto, Chief of Staff to General Yamashita in the Philippines, who had no formal powers of command, responsible on the basis of command responsibility due to his *de facto* position to exert control over the conduct of war by Japanese troops in the Far East.[111]

The superior-subordinate relationship includes not only 'direct subordination' by persons formally under the authority in the chain of command, but also 'indirect subordination' by persons not formally under the authority in the chain of command such as the civilian population in the territory controlled by a military commander who maintains peace and order.[112] Such relationship often exists in the form of psychological pressure.[113] In a chaotic situation prevailing in the locality where a crime was committed, any consideration as to the *de jure* powers exercised by the accused must be subject to an elucidation of the *de facto* power, or absence thereof, that he wielded over the perpetrators of the crime.[114] Article 28 of the ICC Statute uses the test of 'effective' command or control to incur command responsibility. The ICTY in *Celebici* and the ICTR in *Kayishema and Ruzindina* use this test of effective control in their consideration of the command responsibility of the accused in these cases, although the relevant provision of the ICTY Statute and the ICTR Statute is, respectively, silent as to the test to be used.[115] Effective control must be understood in the sense of 'having the material ability to prevent and punish' the commission of a crime.[116] Such material ability includes hierarchical and supervisory authority.[117] It includes, for example, the ability to make reports to the competent authorities so that appropriate measures could be taken.[118] Thus, this principle of command responsibility extends to civilian superiors only to the extent that they exercise a degree of effective control over their subordinates in the manner similar to that of military

[110] *Hostages* case, TWC, xi, 1230 at 1286, 1288 (also in (1953) **15** *Ann. Dig.* 632 at 649–53); *High Command* case, TWC, xi, 462 at 513–4 (also in (1953) **15** *Ann. Dig.* 376 at 385–92).

[111] Tokyo Trial Official Transcript, reprinted in R. John Pritchard and Sonia Bagbanua Zaide (eds.), *The Tokyo War Crimes Trial* (Garland Publishing, 1981), 49, 820–1. Also cited in *Celebici*, paras. 368–9, 375. Cf. *Akayesu*, para. 691. Now see *Celebici*, App. Ch. Judgment, paras. 188–98, 268, 302–4.

[112] *Celebici*, paras. 371–2; *Musema*, para. 143.

[113] *Musema*, para. 140.

[114] *Kayishema and Ruzindana*, paras. 477–8. See also *Celebici*, para. 354.

[115] *Celebici*, para. 378; *Kayishema and Ruzindana*, paras. 217–23. Art. 6(3) of the ICTR Statute, which is identical to Art. 7(3) of the ICTY Statute, stipulates:

'The fact that any of the acts referred to in the present Statute was committed by a subordinate does not relieve his superior of criminal responsibility if he knew or had reason to know that the subordinate was about to commit such acts or had done so and the superior failed to take the necessary and reasonable measures to prevent such acts or to punish the perpetrators thereof.'

[116] *Celebici*, para. 378. Quoted with approval by the ICTR in *Kayishema and Ruzindana*, para. 230.

[117] Cf. *Kayishema and Ruzindana*, para. 481, where the ICTR observes that in Rwanda the Prefect's position as regards the *bourgmestre* (mayor) is 'evidently one of hierarchical authority and supervisory jurisdiction. [These], coupled with the Prefect's overarching duty to maintain public order and security, reflect the ultimate hierarchical authority enjoyed by the Prefect over the *bourgmestre*'.

[118] *Blaskic*, para. 302.

commanders.[119] If this test of effective control is met, a superior may be held criminally liable even for his failure to prevent the execution of an illegal order issued by his superiors which has been passed down to his subordinates independent of him.[120] It also implies that several superiors or commanders could be held responsible for the same crime committed by a subordinate.[121]

Actus reus

When a *de jure* or *de facto* superior orders a person under his control to commit a crime, he is directly guilty without the necessity of establishing whether he tried to prevent or punish the commission of the crime. If he did not order it, to find his command responsibility, it must be established that he knew or had reason to know and failed to prevent or punish the commission of the crime.[122] The ability to prevent and punish a crime in question is a question of fact.[123] In any case, the superior does not have the option to either prevent the commission of a crime by his subordinate or let the crime be committed first and subsequently punish his subordinate for its commission. In order to exonerate himself from superior responsibility, the superior must undertake both to prevent and to punish the commission of a crime by his subordinate.[124]

Necessary and reasonable measures are measures that are within the superior's material capability. This is a question of fact to be considered on a case-by-case basis in the light of the circumstances of each case.[125]

A causal nexus may exist between the superior's failure to fulfil his duty to prevent the commission of an offence by his subordinates and the commission of the offence by the subordinate which would not have taken place but for such failure. On the other hand, while it is both possible and likely to find a causal connection between the failure of a superior or a commander to punish past crimes committed by subordinates and the commission of any such future crimes, no such causal link can possibly exist between an offence committed by a subordinate and the subsequent failure of a superior to punish the perpetrator of that same offence. Therefore, there is no requirement of causality as a separate element of the doctrine of superior responsibility.[126]

Mens rea

The principle of command responsibility is not based on a standard of strict liability.[127] The *mens rea* requirement for command responsibility is serious negligence that

---

[119] *Celebici*, para. 378.

[120] *High Command* case, TWC, xi, 462 at 512 (also in (1953) 15 *Ann. Dig.* 376 at 389–92). Cited in *Celebici*, para. 373.

[121] *Aleksovski* Judgment, para. 106; *Blaskic*, para. 303.

[122] *Kayishema and Ruzindana*, para. 223.

[123] Ibid., para. 231.

[124] *Blaskic*, para. 336.

[125] *Aleksovski* Judgment, paras. 81, 117, 136; *Celebici*, paras. 394–5.

[126] *Celebici*, paras. 398–400.

[127] Ibid., para. 383.

is tantamount to acquiescence or even malicious intent.[128] For example, Hirota, foreign minister of Japan during WWII, was convicted by the Tokyo Tribunal of atrocities, including mass rape, committed in the 'Rape of Nanking' because he had 'recklessly disregarded his legal duty by virtue of his office to take adequate steps to secure the observance and prevent breaches of the law and customs of war'.[129]

Such *mens rea* exists where '(1) the superior had actual knowledge, established through direct or circumstantial evidence that his subordinates were committing or about to commit crimes, or (2) where he had in his possession information of a nature, which at least, would put him on notice of the risk of such offences by indicating the need for additional investigation in order to ascertain whether such crimes were committed or were about to be committed by his subordinates'.[130] While such knowledge cannot be presumed but must be established, it may be inferred from various facts; for example, the number, type, and effect of the unlawful acts in question; the period when they are committed; the number and type of soldiers participating in committing them; the logistic means used; the geographical location of the acts; the general character of the acts; the speed of the operations; the *modus operandi* of similar unlawful acts; the officers and personnel implicated; and the whereabouts of the commander or superior at the time of commission of the acts.[131] Indeed, an individual's position of superior or commander constitutes in and of itself a serious indication that he has knowledge of the crimes committed by his subordinates.[132] In *Blaskic*, a solid chain of command set up by the accused that operated satisfactorily under him and the organized nature of the attacks against towns and villages were sufficient to incur command responsibility on the accused.

The superior must know, or had reason to know, of his subordinates' criminal activities. The former requirement is clear, while the latter is rather ambiguous. Under customary international law, a superior can be held criminally liable only if some specific information was in fact available to him which would put him on notice of offences committed by his subordinates.[133] As the Trial Chamber of the ICTY puts it in *Celebici*:

'This information need not be such that it by itself was sufficient to compel the conclusion of the existence of such crimes. It is sufficient that the superior was put on further inquiry by the information, or, in other words, that it indicated the need for additional investigation in order to ascertain whether offences were being committed or about to be committed by his subordinates . . .'[134]

If such information is available, the superior cannot plead ignorance in his defence; he

---

[128] *Akayesu*, para. 489; *Musema* para. 131.

[129] *Akayesu*, para. 490; *Celebici*, paras. 357, 376; *Musema*, para. 133.

[130] *Celebici*, para. 383. Affirmed on appeal. *Celebici*, App. Ch. Judgment, paras. 222–41.

[131] *Blaskic*, paras. 307–8.

[132] Ibid., para. 308, citing *Aleksovski* Judgment, para. 80.

[133] *Celebici*, para. 393.

[134] Ibid., and see also the authorities cited in paras. 387–92.

must inform himself of what his subordinates are doing or about to do.[135] A superior is responsible for the crimes of his subordinates if he has not put in place a means within his disposal to keep him informed of the violation of the law by his subordinates if, in the circumstances, he would have known of such violation and his ignorance constitutes an omission or serious personal negligence to the extent that it incurs his criminal liability.[136] In other words, if a superior has exercised due diligence in discharging his duty while being ignorant that the crimes are about to be committed or have been committed by his subordinates, this ignorance cannot incur his superior responsibility; however, bearing in mind his personal position in the hierarchy of authority and the circumstances at the time, ignorance resulting from negligence in the discharge of his duty would incur his criminal responsibility because he 'should have known' or 'had reason to know' about the crimes.[137]

The ICC Statute makes one distinction between military commanders and other superiors. In the case of military commanders, Article 28(1)(a) of the Statute imposes a more active duty on the superior to inform himself of the activities of his subordinates when he 'knew or, owing to the circumstances at the time, should have known that the forces [under his command] were committing or about to commit such crimes'. On the other hand, Article 28(2)(a) of the Statute requires that non-military superiors must have either known, 'or consciously disregarded information which clearly indicated, that the subordinates were committing or about to commit such crimes'. The French version is even clearer when it states that the non-military superiors must have 'deliberately neglected to take into account' the information which clearly indicated ('*delibérément negligé de tenir compte d'informations qui l'indiquaient clairement*') that the subordinates were committing or about to commit such crimes. The ICTR in *Kayishema and Ruzindana* endorses this test of *mens rea* as it appeared in Article 28 of the ICC Statute.[138]

In the absence of direct evidence of the requisite knowledge, it cannot be presumed but must be established by way of circumstantial evidence.[139] Actual or constructive knowledge may be inferred from the circumstances of each case, especially in terms of time and place. The more remote in time or place of commission of a crime by a subordinate, the more difficult it will be to impute the knowledge thereof to the superior in the absence of other indicators. On the other hand, the commission of a crime in the immediate vicinity of the place where the superior usually works would

---

[135] Ibid., para. 388, quoted in *Blaskic*, para. 309.

[136] *Blaskic*, paras. 322, 330, and see also the authorities cited in paras. 314–21.

[137] Ibid., para. 332, and see the authorities cited in paras. 323–31.

[138] *Kayishema and Ruzindana*, paras. 225–8. The ICTY Trial Chamber in *Celebici* merely notes the distinction made in Art. 28(1)(a) of the ICC Statute (*Celebici*, para. 393). One commentator criticizes this provision of the ICC Statute on the ground that a weaker civilian command responsibility standard will not deter civilian superiors to the same extent as military commanders (G. R. Vetter, 'Command Responsibility of Non-Military Superiors in the International Criminal Court (ICC)' (2000) 25 *Yale J. Int'l L.* 89 at 94. See also the comparisons of case law on the *mens rea* for command responsibility and elements of such responsibility in Table 1 at 123 and Table 2 at 142, respectively).

[139] *Celebici*, para. 386.

seriously indicate the existence of the knowledge on the part of the superior about the commission of the crime, especially when the crime is committed repeatedly.[140]

In *Celebici*, Zdravko Mucic (or 'Pavo'), one of the defendants in that case, was in a *de facto* position of superior authority as the commander of the prison-camp called Celebici. He had overall authority over the officers, guards and detainees, and the persons to whom the officers and guards were subordinate. The inhumane conditions of the prison-camp were held to have been perpetrated by Mucic who selected the guards and chose his deputy to exert harsh discipline. He was found guilty of war crimes on the basis of command responsibility as a result of his 'deliberate neglect of his duty to supervise his subordinates, thereby enabling them to mistreat the detainees' in the prison-camp. He made no effort to prevent or punish his subordinates who mistreated or even killed the prisoners, or even to investigate specific incidents of mistreatment or killing. He was aware that detainees were being mistreated or killed, but he apparently tolerated these incidents throughout the entire period he was commander of the prison-camp. Mucic was held to have been 'imputed with knowledge' of the crimes committed by his subordinates.[141]

---

[140] *Kayishema and Ruzindana*, paras. 80, 114; *Celebici*, para. 386.

[141] *Celebici*, paras. 1242–3, 1250. His staying away from the prison-camp at night in order to 'save himself from the excesses of the guards and the soldiers' was considered an aggravating factor in sentencing him.

9

GROUNDS FOR EXCLUDING CRIMINAL RESPONSIBILITY

The term 'grounds for excluding criminal responsibility' is interchangeable with the term 'defences': they both prevent the punishability and/or prosecution of a crime.[1]

The Nuremberg Charter did not recognize any defence to the crimes under the Charter, and when the accused were acquitted it was because of insufficient evidence. Superior orders were permitted in mitigation of the punishment, if the Tribunal determined that justice so required.

Neither the ICTY Statute nor the ICTR Statute provide grounds for excluding criminal responsibility of the individual. Article 7 of the former and Article 6 of the latter exclude explicitly the official position of any accused person as a defence or mitigating factor, but allows superior orders as a factor in mitigation if the ICTY or the ICTR, as the case may be, determines that justice so requires. However, the possibility of raising defences exists in their respective Rules of Procedure and Evidence. Rule 67(A)(ii) of the ICTY Rules and the ICTR Rules provides that the Defence shall notify the Prosecutor of its intent to offer (a) the defence of alibi, and/or (b) 'any special defence, including that of diminished or lack of mental responsibility'.[2] Therefore, in practice, Counsel for the accused before these Tribunals raise all defences recognized in national jurisdictions.

The ICC Statute is more detailed in terms of defences to prosecution. Article 26 excludes persons under eighteen from the ICC's jurisdiction, while Article 27 rejects official capacity as irrelevant to prosecution before the ICC. The non-applicability of statute of limitations is affirmed in Article 29. Article 31 lists the following as grounds for excluding criminal responsibility under the Statute: (a) a mental disease or defect; (b) intoxication; (c) self-defence; (d) duress; and (e) other grounds deriving from applicable law as set forth in Article 21. Article 32 allows mistake of fact or mistake of law as a ground for excluding criminal responsibility if it negates the mental element required by a crime or, in the case of mistake of law, as required by Article 33 on superior orders and prescription of law. Article 33, in turn, provides that superior

---

[1] A. Eser, '"Defences" in War Crimes Trials', in Y. Dinstein and M. Tabory (eds.), *War Crimes in International Law* (Martinus Nijhoff, 1996), 251.

[2] Rule 67(B) stipulates that the failure of the Defence to provide notice under this Rule shall not limit the right of the accused to testify to the said defences.

orders do not relieve a person of criminal responsibility unless certain conditions are met, including the fact that the order was not manifestly unlawful.

The following sections will analyse each of the grounds listed in the ICC Statute in the order provided in that Statute itself.

9.1 AGE

The minimum age of criminal responsibility under the criminal law of each State is a matter of public policy of that State. There is no uniform rule. The minimum age in England and Wales is ten years old, while that in other States varies from fourteen, sixteen, or eighteen.

The ICC Statute adopts the minimum age of eighteen. By virtue of Article 26 of the ICC Statute, the ICC shall not have jurisdiction over any person who was under the age of eighteen at the time of the alleged commission of a crime. The rationale is to treat children as victims, not perpetrators of international crimes. Therefore, although the Statute proscribes as war crimes conscripting or enlisting children under fifteen or using them to participate actively in hostilities, the jurisdiction of the ICC is confined in all cases to adults over eighteen at the time of the alleged commission of a crime.

9.2 OFFICIAL CAPACITY

The defence of official capacity has been rejected at least since the Nuremberg Trials. Concurring with the argument of Sir Hartley Shawcross, Chief Prosecutor of the UK, that State actions were the actions of men who 'should not be able to seek immunity behind the intangible personality of the State',[3] the Nuremberg Tribunal held:

'The principle of International Law, which under certain circumstances, protects the representatives of a State, cannot be applied to acts which are condemned as criminal by International Law. The authors of these acts cannot shelter themselves behind their official position in order to be freed from punishment in appropriate proceedings. . . .'[4]

The defence of diplomatic immunity was raised before the Tokyo Tribunal by Hiroshi Oshima, Japan's first Military Attaché and subsequently Ambassador to Germany, in relation to his activities in Germany during his diplomatic posting there. The Tribunal rejected this defence in the following words:

'Diplomatic privilege does not import immunity from legal liability, but only exemption

---

[3] *Trials of German Major War Criminals: Proceedings of the International Military Tribunal, Nuremberg*, pt. 2 (H.M. Stationery Office, 1946), 56.

[4] Ibid., pt. 22 (hereinafter 'Nuremberg Proceedings'), 447; (1947) **41** *AJIL* 221.

from trial by the Courts of the State to which the Ambassador is accredited. In any event this immunity has no relation to crimes against international law charged before a tribunal having jurisdiction.'[5]

Article 7(2) of the ICTY Statute and Article 6(2) of the ICTR Statute provide that the official position of a person, whether as Head of State or Government or as a responsible government official shall not relieve that person of criminal responsibility nor mitigate punishment.

Article 27 of the ICC Statute, under the heading 'Irrelevance of official capacity', is even more detailed. It stipulates:

'1. This Statute shall apply equally to all persons without any distinction based on official capacity. In particular, official capacity as a Head of State or Government or a government official shall in no case exempt a person from criminal responsibility under this Statute, nor shall it, in and of itself, constitute a ground for reduction of sentence.

2. Immunities or special procedural rules which may attach to the official capacity of a person, whether under national or international law, shall not bar the Court from exercising its jurisdiction over such a person.'

Nonetheless, by virtue of Article 98(1) of the Statute, the ICC may not proceed with a request for surrender or assistance which would require the requested State to act inconsistently with its obligations under international law in relation to State or diplomatic immunity of a person or property of a third State unless the ICC first obtained a waiver of immunity from that third State. It is doubtful whether this provision will shield international criminals who happen to be Heads of State or accredited diplomats. The Nuremberg Tribunal and its Tokyo counterpart have made this clear in the above judicial pronouncements. The rejection of such immunity in the ILC's Principles of the Nuremberg Judgment has been endorsed by the UN General Assembly. Hence, States have no obligation under international law to grant State or diplomatic immunity to international criminals. The two judgments of the British House of Lords in *Pinochet* denying immunity to a 'former' Head of State for crimes of international concern, but not to an incumbent Head of State, does not reflect the position of international law. It was only an English court constructing the relevant provisions of the English law in question.[6]

---

[5] B. V. A. Röling and C. F. Rüter (eds.), *The Tokyo Judgment: The International Military Tribunal for the Far East (I.M.T.F.E.), 29 April 1946–12 November 1948*, i (APV—University Press Amsterdam BV, 1977), 456.

[6] *R. v. Bow Street Metropolitan Stipendiary Magistrate and others, ex p. Pinochet Ugarte (Amnesty International and others intervening)*, [1998] ALL ER 897; [1999] 2 ALL ER 97. The House of Lords was interpreting s. 20(1) of the State Immunity Act 1978, which provides that the Diplomatic Privilege Act of 1964 shall apply *mutatis mutandis* to a sovereign or other head of State as it applies to a head of a diplomatic mission. Under s. 39 of the Act of 1964, the ambassador shall enjoy diplomatic privileges and immunities from the moment he takes up his accredited post. Such privileges and immunity shall normally cease when he leaves his accredited post or on expiry of a reasonable period to do so, but the immunity shall continue to subsist with respect to acts performed by him 'in the exercise of his functions as a member of the mission'. Other salient aspects of these judgments are discussed in Chapter 3 of this book.

9.3 STATUTE OF LIMITATIONS

The Convention on the Non-Applicability of Statutory Limitations to War Crimes and Crimes Against Humanity[7] excludes the applicability of statute of limitations in case of war crimes and crimes against humanity.

Article 29 of the ICC Statute, in recognition of the gravity of international crimes that should not go unpunished, stipulates that the crimes within the ICC's jurisdiction shall not be subject to any statute of limitations.

9.4 DIMINISHED RESPONSIBILITY AND INSANITY

Article 31(1)(a) of the ICC Statute excludes criminal responsibility of the person who 'suffers from a mental disease or defect that destroys his or her capacity to appreciate the unlawfulness or nature of his or her conduct, or capacity to control his or her conduct to conform to the requirements of law'.

Insanity is based on the premise that, at the time of commission of the criminal act the accused is unaware of what he is doing or is incapable of forming a rational judgment as to whether such an act is right or wrong.[8]

Diminished responsibility is based on the premise that, while the accused recognizes the wrongful nature of his actions, he is unable to control his actions because of his abnormality of mind.[9] The abnormality of mind means a state of mind so different from that of ordinary human beings that it substantially impairs his ability to control his actions. The ability to exercise self-control in relation to one's physical acts is a question of fact and is to be distinguished from the ability to form a rational judgment which indicates the accused's level of intelligence.[10] Thus, in *Celebici*, Trial Chamber II *quater* of the ICTY rejected the plea of diminished responsibility raised by the defendant Esad Landzo because, despite his personality disorder, Landzo was 'quite capable of controlling his actions'.[11] However, the accused's abnormality of mind may arise from a condition of arrested or retarded development of mind or any inherent causes or induced by disease or injury.[12] To be relevant, diminished responsibility must occur at the time the person raising this plea was committing the crime in question.[13]

---

[7] 75 *UNTS* 73.

[8] *Prosecutor v. Zejnil Delalic et al.* ('*Celebici*' case), Case No. IT-96–21-T, ICTY T. Ch. II *quater*, 16 Nov. 1998, para. 1156.

[9] Ibid.

[10] Ibid., paras. 1167–9.

[11] Ibid., para. 1186.

[12] See s. 2(1) of the English Homicide Act of 1957. 5 & 6 *Eliz.* 2. c.11.

[13] *Celebici*, para. 1181.

The plea of diminished responsibility does not usually exonerate the accused completely from his crimes. In some Common Law jurisdictions, including England and Wales, a person found to have diminished responsibility may not be tried for murder, but must make a plea of manslaughter. For the ICTY, it is not a full defence, but may be a matter to be considered in mitigation of sentence.[14]

Since there is a presumption of sanity of the person alleged to have committed a criminal act, the person who pleads diminished responsibility must discharge the burden of proof to rebut the presumption of sanity.[15] English law and the Rules of Procedure and Evidence of the ICTY and the ICTR merely require that diminished responsibility be established on the balance of probabilities.[16]

9.5 INTOXICATION

Article 31(1)(b) of the ICC Statute accepts intoxication as a ground for excluding criminal responsibility insofar as the intoxication 'destroys a person's capacity to appreciate the unlawfulness or nature of his or her conduct, or capacity to control his or her conduct to conform to the requirements of law'. However, there is no defence where a person has become intoxicated voluntarily under such circumstances that the person knew, or disregarded the risk, that, as a result of intoxication, he or she was likely to engage in conduct constituting a crime within the ICC's jurisdiction.

9.6 SELF DEFENCE

Self defence is recognized by Article 31(1)(c) of the ICC Statute as a ground for excluding criminal responsibility. To be a defence, the accused must act 'reasonably to defend himself or herself or another person or, in the case of war crimes, property which is essential for the survival of the person or another person or property which is essential for accomplishing a military mission, against an imminent and unlawful use of force in a manner proportionate to the degree of danger to the person or the other person or property protected'. However, the fact that the accused was involved in a defensive operation conducted by forces shall not in itself constitute a self defence that excludes his criminal responsibility.[17]

---

[14] Ibid., paras. 1162–71; *Celebici*, App. Ch. Judgment, 20 Feb. 2001, paras. 590, 839–41.

[15] *Celebici*, paras. 1157–8.

[16] Ibid., paras. 1160, 1172.

[17] For a legislative history of this provision, see Per Saland, 'International Criminal Law Principles', in R. S. Lee (ed.), *The International Criminal Court: The Making of the Rome Statute—Issues, Negotiations, Results* (Kluwer, 1999), 189 at 207–8.

9.7 DURESS

The ICTY Statute and the ICTR Statute are silent as to the availability of duress, or coercion, as a defence. However, the ICTY has ruled that duress is not a complete defence although it may be taken into account by way of mitigation.[18] In *Erdemovic*, the accused, a member of the Bosnian Serb army, was proved to be capable of taking positive action to resist orders to kill on other occasions after weighing up his options and risks. However, he had no choice when ordered to summarily execute unarmed Bosnian Muslim men at a collective farm on 16 July 1995: he had to kill or be killed.[19] Duress was therefore taken into account in mitigating his sentence.[20]

Article 31(1)(d) of the ICC Statute permits duress as a ground to exclude criminal responsibility for a crime within the ICC's jurisdiction where the duress results from 'a threat of imminent death or of continuing or imminent serious bodily harm against that person, or another person, and the person acts necessarily and reasonably to avoid this threat, provided that the person does not intend to cause a greater harm than the one sought to be avoided.' Such a threat may either be made by other persons, or constituted by other circumstances beyond that person's control.

The jurisprudence of the ICTY can be reconciled to some extent with Article 31(1)(d) of the ICC Statute. The majority of the Appeals Chamber of the ICTY held in *Erdemovic* that 'duress does not afford a complete defence to a soldier charged with a crime against humanity and/or a war crime involving the killing of innocent human beings.'[21] Judge Cassese and Judge Stephen dissented on the grounds that duress can be a defence, provided that the following conditions are fulfilled: (1) the act charged was committed under an immediate threat of severe and irreparable harm to the life or limb; (2) there was no adequate means to avert such threat; (3) the crime committed was not disproportionate to the evil threatened; and (4) the situation leading to duress must not have been voluntarily brought about by the person under duress. In the case of killing, the condition of proportionality is usually not satisfied, although it might be in exceptional circumstances, such as when the killing of another person would take place in any event, and it is not disproportionate to save one's life when the other will be taken anyway. The dissenting Judges opined that when duress fails to provide a defence because the aforesaid conditions are not fulfilled, it may still be considered in mitigation of the sentence.[22] In light of the factual circumstances of

[18] *Celebici*, para. 1229. Cf. *Prosecutor v. Erdemovic*, Case No. IT-96–22-A, ICTY App. Ch., 7 Oct. 1997 (hereinafter '*Erdemovic* (App. Ch.)'), para. 19.

[19] *Prosecutor v. Erdemovic*, Case No. IT-96–22-S, ICTY T. Ch., Sentencing Judgment of 5 Mar. 1998 (hereinafter '*Erdemovic* (T. Ch.)'), para. 17. The Trial Chamber alluded to duress rather obliquely, stating that 'the accused's reluctance to participate and his reaction to having to perform this gruesome task have already been discussed elsewhere in this Judgment'.

[20] *Erdemovic* (App. Ch.), para. 19.

[21] Ibid.

[22] Ibid., Separate Opinions of Judge McDonald and Judge Vohrah, Separate and Dissenting Opinion of Judge Li, and Separate and Dissenting Opinions of Judge Cassese and Judge Stephen. Summarized in Olivia Swaak-Goldman (1998) **92** *AJIL* 282 at 283–7.

Erdemovic, the accused in that case, who killed about seventy to one hundred persons, would never be able to resort to duress as a complete defence, irrespective of whether it is the opinion of the majority or that of those who dissented that correctly states the law on this point. By the same token, all the judges would consider duress in mitigation of his sentence. As a matter of *law*, however, Article 31(1)(d) of the ICC Statute is more in line with the opinion of those who dissented than that of the majority in *Erdemovic*.[23] The requirement that no 'greater harm' is intended can be safely treated as synonymous with the condition of proportionality, and, it is submitted, is a question of facts to be decided on a case-by-case basis.

9.8 MISTAKE OF FACT

Article 32(1) of the ICC Statute recognizes a mistake of fact as a ground for excluding criminal responsibility 'only if it negates the mental element required by the crime'. This is in accord with the maxim *actus non facit reum nisi mens sit rea*—the act does not constitute guilt unless the mind is guilty.

The mistake of fact must be honestly, and reasonably, made on the basis of the conditions prevailing at the time of commission of the unlawful act. In *W. List and Others* (the '*Hostages*' case), one of the accused was charged with the wanton destruction of cities, towns, and villages, and the commission of other acts of devastation not warranted by military necessity, in the occupied territories in his retreat from Finland to western Norway. The accused misunderstood that the Russian army was right behind him, so he ordered complete devastation so that there would be nothing useful for the Russian army that was hot on his trail. After finding 'physical evidence' that the Russian army was expected to attack the accused on his retreat, the US Military Tribunal held that it was obliged to judge the situation as it appeared to the defendant at the time. If the facts were such as would justify the action by the exercise of honest judgment, after giving due consideration to all factors and existing possibilities, 'even though the conclusion reached may have been faulty, it cannot be said to be criminal' although when viewed in retrospect, the facts that gave rise to the accused's response did not actually exist.[24]

A more recent and notorious example of a mistake of fact was NATO's bombing of the Embassy of the People's Republic of China in Belgrade at the height of the Kosovo crisis in 1999. The aircrew involved in the attack were given the wrong target. A committee was set up by the ICTY Prosecutor to assess allegations and evidence of crimes within the ICTY's jurisdiction committed by the individuals involved in the

---

[23] According to one commentator, under the majority view of the ICTY Appeals Chamber in that case, 'Jews in Nazi concentration camps compelled to assist in operating the crematoria would have been denied the defence of duress. Would this be just?' (T. Meron, 'Crimes and Accountability in Shakespeare' (1998) **92** *AJIL* 1 at 18).

[24] US Military Tribunal at Nuremberg, 19 Feb. 1948 (1953) **15** *Ann. Dig.* 632 at 648–9.

NATO bombing campaign against the Federal Republic of Yugoslavia. It recommended that no action be taken against the aircrew since they had been given the wrong target, or against senior leaders in NATO since they had been provided with wrong information by officials of another agency.[25]

9.9 MISTAKE OF LAW

Under general principles of criminal law, ignorance of the law is no excuse (*ignorantia iuris neminem excusat* or *ignorantia iuris nocet*)—the perpetrator who did not know that his conduct was criminalized can be held criminally liable nevertheless. Therefore, by virtue of Article 32(2) of the ICC Statute, a mistake of law as to whether a particular type of conduct is a crime within the ICC's jurisdiction shall not be a ground for excluding criminal responsibility. However, it permits a mistake of law as a defence if the mistake negates the mental element required by such a crime, or is defensible in the context of superior orders.

It is hard to imagine how a mistake of law can negate the mental element required by such a crime. One example is a mistake regarding the legal ownership of property as a defence to a charge of pillage.[26] In such a situation, the perpetrator mistakenly believes that he is the lawful owner of the property in question. However, the perpetrator does not hold a mistaken view that pillaging property belonging to another person is not a crime within the ICC's jurisdiction.

Since every person is presumed to know the law, the party raising the defence has a heavier burden of proof than the one raising the defence of mistake of fact.

The participants involved in the drafting of the Elements of Crimes under the ICC Statute generally felt that Article 32 provides sufficient guidance on the issues of mistake of fact and mistake of law, and on the distinction between 'ignorance of law' and mistake of law negating a mental element. Hence, the Elements of Crimes do not provide any further elaboration on these issues.[27]

Article 32(2) of the ICC Statute provides two situations in which a mistake of law excludes criminal responsibility: when it negates the mental element required by a crime, or when it fulfils the condition under Article 33 on superior orders and prescription of law, to which we now turn.

---

[25] *Final report to the Prosecutor by the Committee Established to Review the NATO Bombing Campaign Against the Federal Republic of Yugoslavia*, June 2000, paras. 80–5. Available at *http://www.un.org/icty/ pressreal/nato061300.htm*.

[26] This example was given by the Delegation of Samoa during the 3rd Sess. of the UN Preparatory Commission on the Establishment of an International Criminal Court in Feb. 1997. (C. K. Hall, 'The Third and Fourth Sessions of the UN Preparatory Commission on the Establishment of an International Criminal Court' (1998) **92** *AJIL* 124 at 130.)

[27] Outcome of an inter-sessional meeting held in Siracusa, Italy, 31 Jan.–6 Feb. 2000, *Doc. PCNICC/ 2000/ WGEC/ INF/ 1* of 10 Mar. 2000, para. 6.

9.10 SUPERIOR ORDERS[28]

It was established as early as in 1900 that if a soldier 'honestly believes' he is doing his duty in obeying orders and the orders are 'not so manifestly illegal' that he ought to have known they were unlawful, the soldier could invoke superior orders in his defence.[29] This rule was further refined in *The Llandovery Castle* before the German Supreme Court at Leipzig. The accused in this latter case were charged with the sinking of a hospital ship and firing on lifeboats with survivors on board. It was held that the fact that the firing on the lifeboats was an offence against the law of nations must have been well-known to the accused, therefore the accused should not have obeyed the orders to fire.[30]

Article 8 of the Nuremberg Charter rejected expressly superior orders as a defence, but permitted the Nuremberg Tribunal to consider the orders in mitigation of the punishment, if the Tribunal determined that justice so required.

Article 6 of the Tokyo Charter and Article II(4)(b) of Control Council Law No. 10 had provisions on superior orders similar to the one in the Nuremberg Charter. The rationale for the test adopted by the Nuremberg Tribunal became clearer with the pronouncement of the US Military Tribunal in the *High Command* case decided under Control Council Law No. 10. This Tribunal alluded to the position and authority of Hitler as Commander in Chief of the Armed Forces and the Supreme Civil and Military Authority of the Third Reich. Hitler's personal decrees had the force of law. If a plea of superior order exonerated the superiors and the subordinates, all criminal liability would have rested with Hitler alone.[31]

Article 7(4) of the ICTY Statute and Article 6(4) of the ICTR Statute provide that acting pursuant to a superior or Government order is not a complete defence but may be considered in mitigation of punishment if justice so requires. Therefore, the Statutes closely follow the Nuremberg Charter in this matter.

Article 33 of the ICC Statute goes further by defining the situations where superior orders may be a defence. Paragraph 1 of the Article provides that commission of a crime within the ICC's jurisdiction pursuant to an order of a Government or of a superior, whether military or civilian, may be a defence only where the accused was under a legal obligation to obey the orders, and the accused did not know that the

---

[28] See Eser, '"Defences" in War Crimes Trials', 251–61; Y. Dinstein, *The Defence of Obedience to Superior Orders in International Law* (Sijthoff, 1965); J. L. Bakker, 'The Defence of Obedience to Superior Orders: the *Mens Rea* Requirement' (1989) **17** *Amer. J. Crim. L.* 55; L. C. Green, 'The Defence of Superior Orders in the Modern Law of Armed Conflict' (1993) **31** *Alberta L. Rev.* 320; S. Yeo, 'Mistakenly Obeying Unlawful Superior Orders' (1993) **5** *Bond L. Rev.* 1; J. W. Grayson, 'The Defence of Superior Orders in the International Criminal Court' (1995) **64** *Nordic J. Int'l L.* 243.

[29] *R. v. Smith* (1900) 17 Supreme Ct. (Cape of Good Hope) 561, *per* Solomon J.

[30] *The Llandovery Castle*, Germany, Reichsgericht, 16 July 1921 (1933) **2** *Ann. Dig.* 436–8. Followed in *In re Eck and Others* (*The Peleus*), British Military Court, Hamburg, 20 Oct. 1945 (1951) **13** *Ann. Dig.* 248–50.

[31] *In re Von Leeb and Others*, US Military Tribunal at Nuremberg, Germany, 28 Oct. 1948 (1953) **15** *Ann. Dig.* 376 at 395–9.

order was unlawful and the order was not manifestly unlawful. This replicates the reasoning of the US Military Tribunal in the *Einsatzgruppen* Trial that:

' ... The obedience of a soldier is not the obedience of an automaton. A soldier is a reasoning agent. He does not respond, and is not expected to respond, like a piece of machinery. ... And what the superior officer may not militarily demand of his subordinate, the subordinate is not required to do. Even if the order refers to a military subject it must be one which the superior is authorized under the circumstances to give. The subordinate is bound only to obey the lawful orders of his superior and if he accepts a criminal order and executes it with a malice of his own, he may not plead Superior Orders in mitigation of his offence. If the nature of the ordered act is manifestly beyond the scope of the superior's authority, the subordinate may not plead ignorance of the criminality of the order. . . .'[32]

The second situation envisaged in Article 32(2), under the heading 'Mistake of Law', of the Statute, which relates to superior orders, is illustrated in the *Ponzano* case decided by a War Crimes Trial held at Hamburg, Germany in 1948. The accused were charged with the killing of four British prisoners of war in violation of the rules of warfare. It was held that to find the accused guilty as charged, it was necessary to prove that when they did take part in the commission of a criminal offence, they knew the intended purpose of it. Thus, if any accused were to have been given an order to execute the prisoners of war, believing, albeit erroneously, that it was a perfectly legal execution pursuant to the death sentence passed by a properly instituted court, then that accused would not be guilty because 'he would not have any guilty knowledge'.[33] In other words, the order was not manifestly illegal, and the person who carried out the order made a mistake of law as to its legality and he, therefore, would not be guilty of a criminal charge resulting therefrom.

The term 'manifestly unlawful' has been construed by numerous national courts. In *R. v. Finta*, the Supreme Court of Canada ruled that an order is manifestly unlawful if it 'offends the conscience of every reasonable, right-thinking person, it must be an order which is obviously and flagrantly wrong, patently and obviously wrong'.[34] The US Court of Military Appeals in *US v. Calley* upheld the test that the order in question must be one which 'a man of ordinary sense and understanding would, under the circumstances, know to be unlawful, or if the order in question is actually known to be unlawful'.[35] One commentator contends the 'ought to know' principle traced back to pre-1945 decisions is still valid—it is a defence if the subordinate had no good reason for thinking that the order in question was unlawful or was assured by his superior, credibly, that it was in fact lawful.[36]

---

[32] *In re Ohlendorf & Others*, US Military Tribunal, Nuremberg, 10 Apr. 1948 (1953) 15 *Ann. Dig.* 566 at 665–6.

[33] *Trial of Feurstein and others*, Proceedings of a War Crimes Trial held at Hamburg, Germany (4–24 Aug. 1948), Judgment of 24 Aug. 1948, p. 8. Quoted in *Prosecutor v. Dusko Tadic*, Case No. IT-94-1-A, ICTY App. Cg., 15 July 1999 ('*Tadic* Appeals Judgment'), n. 242.

[34] [1994] 1 Sup. Ct. Rep. 701.

[35] *US v. Willaim Calley, Jr.*, 22 US Ct. Mil. App. 534 (1973), at 541–2.

[36] H. McCoubrey, *International Humanitarian Law: The Regulation of Armed Conflicts* (Dartmouth, 1990), 219–21.

Article 33(2) of the ICC Statute provides explicitly that orders to commit genocide or crimes against humanity are manifestly unlawful.[37] Since only people on a national policy level can commit a crime of aggression, superior orders would not be applicable in practice to the crime of aggression. They would, therefore, be available only in war crimes.

Given the relatively narrow applicability and scope of superior orders as a ground to exclude criminal responsibility, it might be advisable for the Defence to resort to duress in the alternative, circumstances permitting. After all, the 'moral choice' test applied by the Nuremberg Tribunal when it was dealing with the issue of superior orders would be more in line with the defence of duress.[38] The Nuremberg Tribunal laid down the following test 'in conformity with the law of nations':

'. . . The true test, which is found in varying degrees in the criminal law of most nations, is not the existence of the order, but whether moral choice was in fact possible. . . . [I]ndividuals have international duties which transcend the national obligations of obedience imposed by the individual State. . . . Superior orders, even to a soldier, cannot be considered in mitigation where crimes have been committed consciously, ruthlessly and without military excuse or justification. . . . Participation in such crimes as these has never been required of any soldier. . . .'[39]

This close relationship between superior orders and duress in the case of military personnel or subordinates under the authority of persons in effective control is borne out by the following statement of the US Military Tribunal in the *Einsatzgruppen* Trial:

'If one claims *duress* in the execution of an illegal order it must be shown that the harm caused by *obeying the illegal order* is not disproportionately greater than the harm which would result from not obeying the illegal order. It would not be an excuse, for example, if a subordinate under orders killed a person known to be innocent, because by not obeying it he himself would risk a few days of confinement. . . .'[40]

In other words, the element of moral choice is relevant when, although a superior order is manifestly illegal and the subordinate was aware of its illegality, he might have no choice but to obey, in which case he could only plead duress, not superior orders, in his defence.

Where there is no superior-subordinate relationship, only duress would be relevant.[41]

---

[37] For a legislative history of this Article, see Saland, 'International Criminal Law Principles', 210–2.

[38] Cf. ibid., 220–1.

[39] *Nuremberg Proceedings*, 447. Followed in relation to 'duress' in the *Einsatzgruppen* Trial (1953) 15 *Ann. Dig.* 665–8.

[40] *In re Ohlendorf and Others*, TWC, iv, 470. Quoted in McCoubrey, *International Humanitarian Law*, 220. Emphasis added.

[41] As in the *Zyklon B* case, where owners and scientists of the company supplying the gas to the SS for use in the death concentration camps were sentenced to death by the British Military Court in Hamburg despite the defence that they were under pressure, or duress, to obey the SS. Cited in McCoubrey, *International Humanitarian Law*, 220–1.

9.11 OTHERS

The grounds for excluding criminal responsibility enumerated in the ICC Statute are not exhaustive. Article 31(3) of the ICC Statute provides that at trial, the ICC may consider a ground for excluding criminal responsibility other than those already enumerated in the ICC Statute where such a ground is derived from applicable law.[42] The procedures relating to the consideration of such a ground are to be provided for in the Rules of Procedure and Evidence. The PCNICC has not adopted a Rule on this point, leaving the matter to the ICC.

Article 31(3) of the Statute was a compromise to allay the concerns of those delegations at the Rome Conference, led by the US, who wanted military necessity, reprisals, and probably self defence under Article 51 of the UN Charter to be included as grounds to exclude criminal responsibility. Since the grounds included in Article 31(1) are grounds under criminal law, there is no place for defences under public international law. Thus, paragraph 3 of Article 31 refers to 'applicable law as set forth in Article 21', namely, general principles of law.[43] Article 31(2) stipulates that the ICC will determine the applicability of the grounds for excluding criminal responsibility to the case before it. So, it is still not certain how the ICC will proceed in relation to Article 31(3).

The following are defences or grounds for excluding criminal responsibility that have been raised in practice.

BREACHES OF THE PRINCIPLE OF LEGALITY

The argument that prosecution in an international criminal tribunal is a breach of the principles of legality may be rebutted by the reasoning of the ICTY in *Celebici*. In the ICTY's view, it is not certain to what extent this principle has been admitted as part of international legal practice, separate and apart from the existence of the national legal systems since the methods of criminalization of conduct in national and international criminal justice systems differ in their application and standards. While the criminalization process in a national criminal justice system depends upon legislation which prescribes the time when conduct is prohibited and the content of such prohibition, the international criminal justice system achieves this objective through treaties or conventions, or after a customary practice of the unilateral enforcement of a prohibition by States. The latter aims at maintaining a balance between the preservation of justice and fairness towards the accused and taking into consideration the preservation of world order, with due regard to, *inter alia*, the nature of international law; the absence of international legislative policies and standards; the *ad hoc* nature of technical drafting of norms; and the basic assumption that international criminal law

---

[42] For the meaning of 'applicable law' in the case of the ICC, see Chapter 3.

[43] Saland, 'International Criminal Law Principles', 209–10.

norms will be embodied in the national criminal law of the various States.[44] The
pertinent question is to determine which of the acts proscribed by general or particular international law are international crimes *ipso jure*, and which ones are not such
crimes.[45] In the case of the ICTY Statute, the principle of *nullum crimen sine lege* is
respected by the explanation given in the Report of the UN Secretary-General on the
establishment of the ICTY that the ICTY is to apply rules of international humanitarian law which are beyond any doubt part of existing customary law. Such law is
specified as being the Geneva Conventions of 12 August 1949 for the Protection of
War Victims, the Hague Convention (IV) Respecting the Laws and Customs of War
on Land and the Regulations annexed thereto of 18 October 1907, the Convention on
the Prevention and Punishment of the Crime of Genocide of 9 December 1948, and
the Nuremberg Charter of 8 August 1945.[46] In other words, the ICTY exercises jurisdiction in respect of offences already recognized as such in existing international
humanitarian law.[47]

The same explanation is proffered by the ICTR in the case of the ICTR Statute.[48]
Unlike the ICTY Statute, the ICTR Statute also proscribes violations of AP II. While
AP II as a whole has not been universally recognized as part of customary international law, the ICTR notes that many provisions of this Protocol, especially those
enumerated in Article 4 of the ICTR Statute, can now be regarded as declaratory of
existing rules or as having crystallized in emerging rules of customary law. In any
event, the Protocol was ratified by Rwanda on 19 November 1984 and was therefore in
force in the territory of Rwanda at the relevant time. Moreover, all the offences
enumerated under Article 4 of the ICTR Statute constituted crimes under Rwandan
law in 1994.[49]

The ICTY Appeals Chamber in *Aleksovski* rejects this defence outright. It rules that
the principle of *nullem crimen sine lege*:

'does not prevent a court, either at the national or international level, from determining an
issue through a process of interpretation and clarification as to the element of a particular
crime; nor does it prevent a court from relying on previous decisions which reflect an
interpretation as to the meaning to be ascribed to particular ingredients of a crime.'[50]

The defence of breach of the principles of legality is unlikely to be of use in the case of
the ICC Statute. Article 22 of the ICC Statute stipulates that a person shall not be
criminally responsible under the ICC Statute unless the conduct in question constitutes, at the time it takes place, a crime within the ICC's jurisdiction, and that the

---

[44] *Celebici*, paras. 402–5. The ICTY Trial Chamber in this case was considering the principles of legality in
the context of interpretation of criminal statutes, especially the ICTY Statute.

[45] Ibid., para. 406.

[46] Ibid., paras. 415–6.

[47] Ibid., para. 417.

[48] *Prosecutor v. Jean-Paul Akayesu*, Case No. ICTR-96–4-T, ICTR T. Ch. I, 2 Sept. 1998, para. 605.

[49] Ibid., paras. 608–10, 617.

[50] *Prosecutor v. Zlatko Aleksovski*, Case No. IT-95–14/1A, ICTY App. Ch., 24 Mar. 2000, para. 127, and cf.
also para. 126.

definition of a crime shall be strictly construed and is not to be extended by analogy. Article 11 of the ICC Statute provides that the ICC shall have jurisdiction only with respect to crimes committed after the entry into force of the ICC Statute. If a State becomes a Party thereafter the ICC may exercise its jurisdiction only with respect to crimes committed after the entry into force of the ICC Statute for that State, or, in the case of a non-Party, after the date that non-Party lodges its declaration accepting the ICC's jurisdiction with respect to the crime(s) in question. Furthermore, Article 24 of the ICC Statute ensures non-retroactivity *ratione personae* by providing that a person shall not be criminally responsible under the Statute for his conduct prior to the Statute's entry into force, and that in the case of a change in the law applicable to a given case prior to a final judgment of the ICC, the law more favourable to the person being investigated, prosecuted, or convicted shall apply.

The second prong of the principles of legality, that is, *nulla peona sine lege*, is satisfied by the requirement under Article 23 of the ICC Statute that a person convicted by the ICC may be punished only in accordance with the ICC Statute. In the light of Articles 11 and 22 of the ICC Statute, such a person will know in advance of the entry into force of the ICC Statute in the relevant case what punishments are encapsulated in the ICC Statute. However, the same might not be said of *ad hoc* international tribunals like the ICTY and the ICTR whose Statutes bind UN Member States irrespective of their prior consent to be bound. In *Celebici*, one of the accused submitted that any sentence greater than that authorized in the former Yugoslavia, where the offence was committed, at the time of the commission of the offence, would violate the principles of legality.[51] The Trial Chamber of the ICTY in that case rejected this defence on the ground that all that is required by these principles is 'the existence of a punishment with respect to the offence', and the fact that there exists a new punishment of the offence which is greater than the former punishment does not offend the principles.[52] Since these principles are 'founded upon the existence of an applicable law', the fact that the new maximum punishment under an international instrument exceeds the erstwhile maximum under the national legislation of the State in question (for example, the former Yugoslavia in the case of the ICTY) does not bring the new law within the principles.[53]

In any event, when an international tribunal deals with the principle of legality, it tends to construe it restrictively. For example, in *Furundzija*, Trial Chamber II of the ICTY opined that it is not contrary to the general principle of *nullum crimen sine lege* to charge an accused with forcible oral sex as rape when in some national jurisdictions, including his own, he could only be charged with sexual assault with regard to the same act. In the Trial Chamber's view, it was not criminalizing acts which were not criminal when they were committed by the accused, but was simply attaching a greater stigma and a heavier sentence on the criminal act of the accused.[54] This line of

---

[51] *Celebici*, para. 1197.

[52] Ibid., para. 1212.

[53] Ibid., para. 1210.

[54] *Prosecutor v. Anto Furundzija*, Case No. IT-95–17/1-T, ICTY T. Ch. II, 10 Dec. 1998, paras. 184, 186.

reasoning is not at variance with the guarantee under the principle of legality as encapsulated in the ICC Statute. For example, Article 22(3) of the Statute stipulates that the principle of *nullum crimen sine lege*, including the prohibition of extension of the definition of a crime by analogy, as provided in that Article, 'shall not affect the characterization of any conduct as criminal under international law independently of this Statute'.

TU QUOQUE

The defence of *tu quoque*, or 'you also', was raised by the Defence before the Nuremberg Tribunal. The Defence submitted documentary evidence to support its allegations that the Allies had committed breaches of the Hague Regulations (1907) and crimes against humanity.[55] Counsel for one of the defendants reasoned:

'It is well known that at the beginning of this war International Law was respected by both sides and that the war was conducted humanely. It was only in the second phase of the war that a terrible bitterness among the fighting powers developed and on both sides things occurred which International Law cannot sanction. In my opinion, it is exceedingly important in judging a crime, whatever crime that may be, to consider the motive. If one does not know the motive of the action, one cannot judge the action itself. And the bitterness which was caused, purely psychologically, by the manner in which the war was conducted on one side and on the other, was the motive for actions which normally cannot be justified.'[56]

The Nuremberg Tribunal did not directly allude to this defence of *tu quoque*. It seemed to take this defence into account only in relation to the unrestricted submarine warfare under the command of Admiral Donitz. The Nuremberg Tribunal took note of the 8 May 1940 order of the British Admiralty to sink all vessels at sight in the Skagerrak as well as the view of Admiral Nimitz of the US Navy that unrestricted submarine warfare was carried out on the Pacific Ocean by the US from the first day the US entered WWII. The Nuremberg Tribunal then proceeded not to assess the sentence of Donitz on the ground of his breaches of the international law of submarine warfare.[57]

It was the US Military Tribunal sitting at Nuremberg under Control Council Law No. 10 that rejected *tu quoque* as a defence. It was held in the *Ministries* Trial that assuming, *arguendo*, that the allegations about the Allied Powers' violations of international law were true, '[i]t has never been suggested that a law duly passed [i.e. the Nuremberg Charter and Control Council Law No. 10 in that case] becomes ineffective when it transpires that one of the legislators whose vote enacted it was himself

---

[55] See the objection by the Prosecution (Sir David Maxwell Fife) to admissibility of evidence on the issue of '*tu quoque*', *Trial of German Major War Criminals: Proceedings of the International Military Tribunal, Nuremberg,* Part 7 (H.M. Stationery Office, 1946), at 257.

[56] Statement of Prof. Exner, Counsel for the defendant Jodl. Ibid., at 260.

[57] *Nuremberg Proceedings,* 509 (1947) 41 *AJIL* 302–6.

guilty of the same practice or that he himself intended, in the future, to violate the law'.[58]

This defence has also been rejected by the ICTY. It was held in *Kupreskic and Others* that the obligations under international humanitarian law are applicable *erga omnes*, absolute, and non-derogable.[59] Therefore, the fact that an adversary engages in unlawful behaviour cannot justify similar and reciprocal conduct because obligations under international humanitarian law are not based on reciprocity, but on the protection of individuals as human beings.[60] This was despite the fact that in that case the Trial Chamber found persuasive the Defence assertion that the conflict was caused by the Muslims who subsequently became victims of the accused's crimes.[61] Reprisals against civilian populations are absolutely prohibited, and when civilians abuse their rights by taking part in the hostilities and thereby making themselves subject to legitimate reprisals by the adversary forces the rules of proportionality proscribe widespread and indiscriminate attacks against civilians who take no part in the hostilities.[62] This reasoning was followed in *Blaskic*. When reading the summary of the judgment in that case, the President of Trial Chamber I of the ICTY admits the possibility that crimes were committed by Muslim forces against Croatian civilians, but he condemns the argument which would have crimes committed by the Croats against Muslim civilians excused by crimes committed by the Muslim forces—all perpetrators of these crimes must be prosecuted.

NECESSITY

At the Rome Conference, there was an attempt to combine duress and necessity due to the similarity of the two.[63] The difference between them is slight. The defence of duress relates to the situation where a person is subject to an immediate threat to his life or physical well-being or that of another if he fails to commit a crime, whereas the defence of necessity arises where a person finds himself in circumstances beyond his control and has to choose between not committing a crime and his own interest.[64] In other words, necessity arises out of natural causes which places a person in a condition of danger, where duress is the pressure brought to bear on a person by another person.[65] Necessity is sometimes called 'duress of circumstances', whereas duress caused by threats from another person is sometimes called 'duress *per minas*'.[66]

---

[58] *In re Weizsaecker and Others*, US Military Tribunal, Nuremberg, 14 Apr. 1949 (1955) 16 *Ann. Dig.* 344 at 348.

[59] *Prosecutor v. Zoran Kupreskic and Others*, Case No. IT-95-16-T, ICTR T. Ch. II, 14 Jan. 2000, paras. 23, 511, 519.

[60] Ibid., paras. 125, 511, 515–21, 765.

[61] Ibid., para. 162.

[62] Ibid., paras. 513, 522–4, 527–35.

[63] Saland, 'International Criminal Law Principles', 208.

[64] S. R. Ratner and J. S. Abrams, *Accountability for Human Rights Atrocities in International Law: Beyond the Nuremberg Legacy* (Clarendon Press, 1997), 123–4.

[65] *R. v. Imre Finta* [1994] 1 Sup. Ct. Rep. 265 (Sup. Ct. Canada), *per* Cory, J.

[66] A. Ashworth, *Principles of Criminal Law*, 3rd ed. (Oxford University Press, 1999), 227.

It was held by the US Military Tribunal in the *Flick* Trial that while some of the defendants in that case had not succeeded in bringing themselves under the concept of 'coercion' or 'duress', they did succeed in raising the defence of necessity. Four defendants, businessmen during the Third Reich's reign of terror, were obliged to use slave labour to support Nazi industrialization efforts. The Tribunal found such necessity substantiated by the 'clear and present danger' caused by the Third Reich's hordes of enforcement officials and secret police always ready to go into instant action and to 'mete out savage and immediate punishment against anyone doing anything that could be construed as obstructing or hindering the carrying out of Government regulations or decrees'. Necessity is considered a defence when the conduct in question was perpetrated to avoid an evil both serious and irreparable without any other adequate means of escape, and the remedy was not proportionate to the evil.[67]

Examples of the defence of necessity would include the burning down of premises during the 1898 Spanish-American War to prevent a yellow fever epidemic from spreading to US forces stationed in Cuba, the epidemic being a direct and immediate threat to the US forces.[68] Another example is the holding of some prisoners of war on ships during the 1982 Falklands War in contravention of GC III, but which met no complaints as it was the only practical and humanitarian measure in light of the circumstances.[69]

The defence of necessity was raised on appeal in *Aleksovski*. However, the Appellant's ground of appeal of necessity was entirely misplaced. He was arguing, in effect, that he had the choice between mistreatment of the victims or freeing them to face danger outside the prison camp under his command. The Appeals Chamber considered that the Appellant was not convicted for having detained anyone, but was convicted of the mistreatment of the victims who were detainees in his prison camp. The Appellant, faced with the actual choice of mistreatment of the detainees or not, was convicted of choosing the former.[70] Therefore, the Appeals Chamber considered it unnecessary to decide whether necessity constitutes a defence under international law, or whether it is the same as the defence of duress.[71]

Military necessity does not constitute a defence. This is because rules governing the conduct of hostilities already take into account the needs of military necessity; hence, generally, if an activity in question fulfils the test of military necessity, it is

---

[67] *Trial of Friedrich Flick and Five Others*, US Military Tribunal, Nuremberg, 22 Dec. 1947, UNWCC *Law Reports*, ix, 1–30. Excerpted in G. K. McDonald and O. Swaak-Goldman (eds.), *Substantive and Procedural Aspects of International Criminal Law*, ii, pt. 2: Documents and Cases (Kluwer, 2000), 1913 at 1928–30.

[68] This was the subject of the decision of the Anglo-American Arbitral Tribunal in the *Hardman Claim* in 1913. It was held that the act constituted 'military necessity'. (McCoubrey, *International Humanitarian Law*, 201.) It is hereby submitted, however, that the defence accepted in that case would better be characterized as 'necessity'. It was not 'military necessity' as the act did not target military objectives in order to secure military victory over the enemy.

[69] Ibid., 202.

[70] *Aleksovski* (App. Ch.), paras. 52–4.

[71] Ibid., para. 55.

not a war crime, unless there exists a contrary rule governing the situation in question.[72] If an activity fails the test of military necessity, whenever such a test is applicable, the perpetrator of the activity cannot invoke military necessity in his defence.[73]

Arguably, the accused cannot plead personal necessity relating to his own life or comfort that allegedly compels him to commit a war crime either although this may be a mitigation in his sentence.[74]

SELF-DEFENCE UNDER ARTICLE 51 OF THE UN CHARTER

Self-defence under international law is 'never available either to individuals or nations who are aggressors'.[75] If use of force by one State against another State is not an act of aggression because it qualifies as self-defence, then there is no State responsibility for the act. Since State responsibility for aggression is a *sine qua non* for individual criminal responsibility, the lack of State responsibility exonerates the individual involved in such use of force.[76]

DISCRIMINATORY JUSTICE

Trial Chamber I of the ICTY states succinctly in *Jelisic* that it has as a mission the contribution to the restoration of peace in the former Yugoslavia. To achieve this goal, it needs to identify, punish and pursue the political and military leaders responsible for the atrocities committed there since 1991. However, if the crimes committed during the armed conflicts could be attributable especially to these persons, such persons could not have achieved their objective without the enthusiastic cooperation or the direct or indirect contribution from individuals like Goran Jelisic. Therefore, Jelisic could not be heard to say that it would be unjust to punish small fry like him instead of punishing the big fish.[77]

This defence was raised in a broader context in *Kanyabashi*, where the Defence Counsel contended that there were numerous other areas of conflicts and incidents, e.g. the Congo, Liberia, and Somalia, in which the UN Security Council took no action to create an international tribunal, and that in light of the lack of such action in those cases individual criminal responsibility should not be taken in the case of Rwanda. Trial Chamber II of the ICTR rejected this argument outright. In its view:

---

[72] In the *High Command* Trial, the US Military Tribunal accepted a plea of military necessity as a defence to the war crime of spoliation because devastation of property would be a crime only when not justified by military necessity. UNWCC *Law Reports*, xii, 93–4.

[73] *Hostages* Trial, ibid., viii, 66–7.

[74] L. C. Green, *The Contemporary Law of Armed Conflict* (Manchester University Press, 1993), 293.

[75] *Ministries* Trial (1955) **16** *Ann. Dig.* 349.

[76] Para. 7 of the ILC Commentary to Article 14 (Defences) of its Draft Code of Crimes Against the Peace and Security of Mankind, *UN Doc. A/ 51/ 10 (1996)*, 26 July 1996.

[77] *Prosecutor v. Goran Jelisic*, Case No. IT-95–10-T, ICTY T. Ch. I, 14 Dec. 1999, para. 133.

'The fact that the Security Council, for previously prevailing geo-strategic and international political reasons, was unable in the past to take adequate measures to bring to justice the perpetrators of crimes against international humanitarian law is not an acceptable argument against introducing measures to punish serious violations of international humanitarian law when this becomes an option under international law. . . .'[78]

---

[78] *Prosecutor v. Kanyabashi*, Case No. ICTR-96–15-T, ICTR T. Ch. II, Decision on the Defence Motion on Jurisdiction, 18 June 1997, para. 36. See also *Celebici*, App. Ch. Judgment, 20 Feb. 2001, paras. 611, 617.

PART IV

PROCEDURAL AND OTHER ASPECTS

10

INITIATION OF PROCEEDINGS AND INTERNATIONAL COOPERATION

10.1 INITIATION OF PROCEEDINGS

Pursuant to the ICTY Statute and the ICTR Statute, the Prosecutor shall initiate investigations *ex officio* or on the basis of information obtained from any source, particularly from Governments, UN organs, intergovernmental, and non-governmental organizations. The Prosecutor shall assess the information received or obtained and decide whether there is sufficient basis to proceed.[1] The Prosecutor's indictment is then reviewed by a judge of the Trial Chamber to whom the indictment has been transmitted. If satisfied that a *prima facie* case has been established by the Prosecutor, the judge shall confirm the indictment; if not, the judge shall dismiss the indictment. Upon confirmation of an indictment, the judge may, at the request of the Prosecutor, issue such orders and warrants for the arrest, detention, surrender or transfer of persons, and any other orders as may be required for the conduct of the trial.[2]

The decision as to whom to indict is that of the Prosecutor alone. Once such an indictment has been confirmed, it is incumbent on the Trial Chambers to perform their judicial function when the accused persons are brought before them.[3] In *Celebici*, one of the defendants alleged that he was just one of thousands of individuals who might be prosecuted for similar offences, and that this placed him in the unfair position of being made into a kind of representative of all such persons who were not being subject to proceedings before the ICTY.[4] This was rejected by the Trial Chamber of the ICTY on the grounds that the decision to indict is solely the Prosecutor's, and that 'it is preposterous to suggest that unless all potential indictees who are similarly

[1] Art. 18, ICTY Statute; Art. 17, ICTR Statute.
[2] Art. 19, ICTY Statute; Art. 18, ICTR Statute.
[3] *Prosecutor v. Zejnil Delalic, Zdravko Mucic, Hazim Delic, and Esad Landzo* ('*Celebici*' case), Case No. IT-96–21-T, ICTY T. Ch. II *quater*, 16 Nov. 1998, para. 180.
[4] Ibid., para. 175.

situated are brought to justice, there should be no justice done in relation to a person who has been indicted and brought to trial'.[5]

It is the duty of the Prosecutor to devise the prosecution strategy and to decide whether any proceedings serve the interest of his mandate as Prosecutor. This is recognized by Rule 51(A) of the Rules of Procedure and Evidence of the ICTY and the ICTR, which allows the Prosecutor to apply for leave to withdraw an indictment at any stage of the proceedings. In *Ntuyahaga*, the accused was indicted for the murder of the Prime Minister of Rwanda and ten Belgian soldiers serving the UN Assistance Mission for Rwanda (UNAMIR), which murders were allegedly committed as part of a widespread or systematic attack against a civilian population on a national or political ground. The Prosecutor applied subsequently for leave to withdraw the indictment after the indictment had been confirmed and the initial appearance of the accused had taken place. The Prosecutor argued, *inter alia*, that the judicial proceedings instituted by the Prosecutor should be 'within the framework of a global policy aimed at shedding light on the events that occurred in Rwanda in 1994 and highlighting the complete landscape of the criminal acts perpetrated at the time', and that this objective would not be attained through the prosecution of a single count indictment that related only to the murders of the aforesaid eleven persons. Since the indictment 'narrowed the scope of prosecution', leaving the Prosecutor no opportunity to execute her strategy of prosecuting the accused for 'the totality of his criminal involvement', the Prosecutor wished to withdraw the indictment so that the accused could be prosecuted in Belgium instead. While the ICTR considers all accused persons are equal before the law and no distinction or ranking may be made among them on the basis of the number of counts with which they are charged, the ICTR granted leave to the Prosecutor to withdraw the indictment.[6]

The ICTY also follows the same approach. In *Furundzija*, Trial Chamber II of the ICTY allowed the Prosecutor to withdraw an indictment because the latter considered it would be 'in the interests of a fair and expeditious trial and the judicial economy of the Trial Chamber' to do so.[7]

With respect to parties to proceedings before the ICTY and the ICTR, it has been held that the Registrar is not a party to the proceedings and therefore has no *locus standi* to submit advisory briefs.[8] However, *amicus curiae* briefs from scholars and representatives of non-governmental organizations are permitted, and the parties to the proceedings are invited to make written submissions regarding the briefs, if they so wish.[9]

In the case of the ICC, the 'trigger mechanism' is more complex.

Pursuant to Article 13 of the ICC Statute, there are three modes of triggering the ICC's jurisdiction: (a) referral of a situation to the Prosecutor by a State Party;

---

[5] Ibid., para. 180, and see also para. 179.

[6] *Prosecutor v. Bernard Ntuyahaga*, Case No. ICTR-98–40-T, ICTR T. Ch. I, Decision on the Prosecutor's Motion to Withdraw the Indictment, 18 Mar. 1999, paras. 1–2.

[7] *Prosecutor v. Anto Furundzija*, Case No. IT-95–17/1-T, ICTY T. Ch. II, 10 Dec. 1998, paras. 7–8.

[8] *Ntuyahaga*, para. 1.

[9] *Furundzija*, para. 35.

(b) referral of a situation to the Prosecutor by the UN Security Council acting under Chapter VII of the UN Charter; and (c) initiation of an investigation by the Prosecutor on his own initiative (*proprio motu*). In the third mentioned case, the Prosecutor's request for authorization of an investigation, together with any supporting material collected, shall be reviewed by the Pre-Trial Chamber of the ICC.[10] There are a number of opportunities for the accused, the Prosecutor, and States to request the Pre-Trial Chamber to review decisions of the Prosecutor and to appeal decisions of the Pre-Trial Chamber before the start of a trial.

It should be remembered that, by virtue of Article 16 of the Statute, the Security Council may adopt a resolution under Chapter VII of the UN Charter to request the ICC to defer investigation or prosecution for a period of twelve months. The request may be renewed by the Security Council under the same conditions.

The trigger mechanism is subject to the principle of complementarity enunciated in paragraph 10 of the preamble to the ICC Statute, and Article 1 of the Statute. The ICTY and the ICTR do not have to respect this principle; their jurisdiction is concurrent with that of national courts but their primacy over national courts is provided explicitly in Article 9 of the ICTY Statute and Article 8 of the ICTR Statute.

Article 17 of the ICC Statute relates to admissibility. The ICC shall determine that a case is inadmissible where it is being, or has been, investigated or prosecuted by a State which has jurisdiction over it, unless that investigation or prosecution shows the inability, or an unwillingness, to genuinely carry out the investigation or prosecution. A case is also inadmissible where it is not of sufficient gravity to justify further action by the ICC.

10.2 INTERNATIONAL COOPERATION

The ICTY and the ICTR are subsidiary organs of the UN Security Council, and all States are obligated to render cooperation. The same cannot be said in relation to the ICC, set up by a mutilateral treaty which binds only States Parties thereto. Non-cooperation is subject to sanction by the Assembly of States Parties, or by the Security Council where the Council has referred the situation in question to the Prosecutor. The cooperation sought includes surrender of persons to the ICC and giving judicial assistance. Cooperation in the enforcement of the ICC's judgments, as provided in Part 10 of the Statute, should also be mentioned in this context.

The following are some practical issues encountered or likely to be encountered by an international criminal tribunal.

PROTECTION OF NATIONAL SECURITY INFORMATION

States are reluctant to share national security information with an international tribunal. The confidential information that may jeopardize national security interests is

---

[10] Arts. 15, 61(5) of the ICC Statute.

covered by several provisions of the ICC Statute. For instance, Article 54(3)(f) of the ICC Statute provides that the Prosecutor may 'take necessary measures, or request that necessary measures be taken, to ensure the confidentiality of the information' obtained by the Prosecutor. Article 57(3)(c) of the Statute obligates the Pre-Trial Chamber to provide the necessary protection of national security information. Article 93(4) and Article 99(5) allow States Parties to deny the ICC's request for assistance to the extent that the request concerns the production of any documents or disclosure of evidence which relates to its national security. Article 72 of the Statute is the core provision in this matter. It allows the State concerned the right to intervene in the proceedings in order to resolve the issue. Steps involved may include agreement on conditions under which confidential information may be provided to the ICC, such as through summaries or redactions, limitations on disclosure, use of *in camera* or *ex parte* proceedings, or other protective measures permissible under the ICC Statute and the Rules of Procedure and Evidence. If the State is still not satisfied with the steps taken or to be taken, and if the ICC determines that the evidence is relevant and necessary to establish the guilt or innocence of the accused, the ICC may request further consultations or it may determine that the State is not acting in accordance with its obligations under the Statute and refer the matter to the Assembly of States Parties, or to the Security Council where the Security Council refers the situation to the ICC for prosecution. The ICC may also make such inference in the trial of the accused, as to the existence or non-existence of a fact, as may be appropriate in the circumstances.

The Rules of Procedure and Evidence adopted by the PCNICC deal with this matter in just one provision. Rule 81, entitled 'Restrictions on Disclosure', stipulates in paragraph 4:

'The Chamber dealing with the matter shall, on its own motion or at the request of the Prosecutor, the accused or any State, take the necessary steps to ensure the confidentiality of information in accordance with Articles 54, 72 and 93 [of the ICC Statute] . . . .'

Neither the ICTY Statute nor the ICTR Statute has a comparable elaborate set of provisions relating to confidential security information to that which appears in the ICC Statute. Article 28 of the ICTR Statute and Article 29 of the ICTY Statute simply impose a duty on States to cooperate and provide judicial assistance to the ICTR and the ICTY, respectively. Nonetheless, some practical methods and procedure to accommodate the legitimate and *bona fide* security concerns of States have been considered by the ICTY Appeals Chamber in *Blaskic*.[11] The Appeals Chamber also held that a Trial Chamber could make a determination as to whether the State raising national security concerns is acting in good faith, particularly by scrutinizing that State's record of assistance and cooperation with the ICTY as well as its general attitude towards the ICTY.

---

[11] *Prosecutor v. Tihomir Blaskic*, Case No. IT-95–14-AR108 *bis*, Judgment of 29 Oct. 1997 on the Request of the Republic of Croatia for Review of the Decision of Trial Chamber II of 18 July 1997, paras. 67–8.

These guidelines were applied in the case of General Philippe Morillon, a former UNPROFOR officer, whose immunity had been lifted by the UN Secretary-General. When subpoenaed by the ICTY to testify, Morillon, a French national, raised objections based on the French law of 'national defence secrecy' and the duty of 'discretion of public servants'. He alleged that his testimony might endanger his own safety and that of the French civilian and military personnel assigned to the territory of the Former Yugoslavia as well as the 'essential security interests of France'. The Trial Chamber ordered him to testify and set the conditions to ensure the confidentiality as follows:

'ORDERS that the scope of the questions asked by the Prosecutor and the Defence be limited to the scope of the Witness' initial statement with the Trial Chamber reserving for itself the right to settle any dispute in that respect;

AUTHORIZES the Witness to state to the Judges that the requested information is, wholly or in part, confidential;

AUTHORIZES the representatives of the United Nations Secretary-General and the French government to be present in the courtroom while the Witness testifies with a maximum of two persons per delegation and to address the Trial Chamber, if necessary outside the presence of the Witness and/or parties, and to present any reasoned request which they believe necessary for the protection of the higher interests they have been assigned to protect. . . .'[12]

The ICC Statute's regime of protection of national security information appears balanced. It is partly derived from the *Blaskic* Subpoena Decision of the ICTY Appeals Chamber with regard to the possibility of holding hearings *in camera* and *ex parte*. If the ICTY has striven to protect the confidentiality of national security information even though there is no statutory provision obligating it to do so, it is to be expected that the ICC, with the elaborate regime of protection under the Statute, would, *a fortiori*, be even more vigilant in this matter.

SURRENDER OF A PERSON

The obligation to surrender a person to an international tribunal is quite problematic for States whose law only permits 'extradition' of a person to stand trial in another State, but not to an international tribunal. The law or even the constitution of some States prohibits extradition of their own nationals to another State. The relevant law or constitution will have to be amended for the States in question to fulfil their international obligations.

Transferring a requested person to stand trial before an international criminal

---

[12] *Prosecutor v. Tihomir Blaskic*, Case No. IT-95–14, ICTY T. Ch. I, Decision on Protective Measures for General Philippe Morillon, witness of the Trial Chamber, Order of 12 May 1999. Reproduced in John R. W. D. Jones, *The Practice of the International Criminal Tribunals for the Former Yugoslavia and Rwanda*, 2nd ed. (Transnational Publishers, 2000), 287.

tribunal may involve a complex process. The person may be found in State A which is obligated to surrender him to, say, the ICC. However, the person is previously extradited from State B on the condition that the extradition of that person to another State or entity would require the prior consent of State B, the original sending State; or that the person be returned to State B after the investigation or prosecution or execution of a sentence in State A. In another scenario, the person sought by the ICC may be a soldier from State B who is being stationed in State A. At present, the US, the world's number one military power, has status-of-forces (SOFA) agreements with the host States in whose territory US troops are stationed. These agreements protect US forces from local arrest for actions in the course of their duties. By virtue of Article 98(2) of the ICC Statute, the ICC may not proceed with a request for surrender which would make the requested State act inconsistently with its obligations under international agreements which require the consent of the original sending State for the surrender of a person of that original sending State to the ICC, unless the ICC can first obtain the cooperation of the original sending State for the giving of consent for the surrender. Insofar as the US is not party to the ICC Statute, SOFA agreements would allow the US Government an opportunity to withhold the consent for surrender of US military personnel to the ICC by the other party to the respective SOFA agreements.[13] Yet, the US is still concerned that its nationals might be surrendered to the ICC outside SOFA agreements or other international agreements, in disregard of the requirement for the US's prior consent. Therefore, during the Fifth Session of the PCNICC in June 2000, the US Delegation put forward a proposal concerning the Rules of Procedure and Evidence relating to Article 98(2) of the ICC Statute. The Rule, then numbered Rule 9.19(2), as proposed by the US, would read: 'The Court shall proceed with a request for surrender or an acceptance of a person into the custody of the Court only in a manner consistent with international agreements applicable to the surrender of the person'.[14] The US delegation explained that its proposal was based on:

'a procedural reality about the virtual surrender of a person to the Court in those circumstances where the consent of the sending State remains applicable. Where a person who is the subject of the Court's surrender request actually surrenders himself to the Court independently of the requested State or *is delivered to the Court by means other than by action of the requested State*, the Court's response must still be consistent with the international agreement applicable to the surrender of the person. The intent of Article 98(2) would be circumvented if efforts were undertaken, by whomever, to negate the relevance of the Court's request for surrender to the requested State with an operation that resulted in the person's arrival in The Hague by other means, either voluntarily *or forcibly*. Rule 9.19(2) establishes the procedure for these circumstances to ensure the consistent implementation of Article 98(2).'[15]

---

[13] R. Wedgwood, 'The United States and the International Criminal Court: Achieving a Wider Consensus Through the "Ithaca Package"' (1999) 32 *Cornell Int'l L. J.* 535 at 541.

[14] *Doc. PCNICC/2000/WGRPE(9)/DP. 4*, 13 June 2000.

[15] US Statement on Proposed Rule 9.19(2), 19 June 2000. Emphasis added.

This proposal met strong opposition from the majority of delegations, including the Member States of the European Communities many of whom are NATO Members, Canada (also a NATO Member), Norway, Switzerland, South Africa, Angola, Australia, New Zealand, Chile, Cuba, Liechtenstein, Trinidad and Tobago, Namibia, and Japan. Indeed, only Israel, and Turkey, and probably the Russian Federation, seemed to indicate that they had no objection to the US proposal. The US proposal would obligate the ICC, States, or international organizations, to enter into agreements to provide for surrender of a person to the ICC. Such a proposal would prevent the ICC from having custody of the persons accused of crimes within the ICC's jurisdiction unless the State of nationality of these persons consents to their surrender to the ICC. This would render meaningless the rationale behind Article 12 of the ICC Statute that permits the ICC to exercise its jurisdiction if the territorial State *or* the State of nationality of the accused is party to the ICC Statute or has accepted its jurisdiction. In the end, a compromise was reached in the form of what is now Sub-Rule 2 of Rule 195 (Provision of Information) under Section V: 'Cooperation under article 98'. It reads:

'The Court may not proceed with a request for the surrender of a person without the consent of a sending State if, under Article 98, paragraph 2, such a request would be inconsistent with obligations under an international agreement pursuant to which the consent of a sending State is required prior to the surrender of that State to the Court.'[16]

This was just a redraft of the US proposal and it did not satisfy all the delegations. An understanding, now incorporated in the final report of the PCNICC, has been adopted to clarify this provision as follows:

'It is generally understood that [Rule 195(2)] should not be interpreted as requiring or in any way calling for the negotiation or provisions in any particular international agreement by the Court or by any other international organization or State.'[17]

The understanding would eliminate any need for the ICC, a State, or an international organization to enter into a new international agreement in order to specifically permit the surrender of the accused to the ICC. However, this understanding still would not take care of the concern that the Rule as it stands would pre-empt the surrender of an accused to the ICC in the scenario envisaged by the US in its explanatory statement of 19 June 2000. Therefore, during the last meeting of the Plenary of the Fifth Session of the PCNICC on 30 June, Cote d'Ivoire proposed that a vote be taken on the Rule. After consultations held in the corridor, Cote d'Ivoire withdrew its request for the vote on the ground that Article 51(5) of the ICC Statute already provides unequivocally that in the event of conflict between the Statute and the Rules

---

[16] Report of the Working Group on Rules of Procedure and Evidence, *Doc. PCNICC/2000/WGRPE/L. 14/ Add. 2*, 29 June 2000, and Report of the PCNICC, *Doc. PCNICC/2000/1/ Add. 1*, 2 Nov. 2000. The phrase 'acceptance of a person into the custody of the Court' which appeared in the US proposal has been deleted because it does not appear in Art. 98 of the ICC Statute and is vague in its meaning.

[17] *Doc. PCNICC/2000/WGRPE(9)/RT. 3*, 29 June 2000.

of Procedure and Evidence, the Statute shall prevail. Some other delegations, including Cuba, Nigeria, and Portugal who spoke on behalf the European Communities, also made statements along the line of Cote d'Ivoire's and requested that their statements appear in an official record of the PCNICC.[18] Ambassador Philippe Kirsch, Chairman of the PCNICC, concluded that: 'The ICC Statute cannot be changed, and its integrity must be preserved.' Thus, it is safe to conclude that the US has failed to achieve its goal in this respect.

The ICTY Statute and the ICTR Statute compel States to render cooperation to the ICTY and the ICTR, respectively. The obligations prevail over any legal impediments to the surrender or transfer of the accused to the Tribunals which may exist under the national law or extradition treaties of the State concerned.

---

[18] Doc. PCNICC/2000/INF/4.

11

RIGHTS OF PARTIES

The credibility of every international criminal tribunal depends on the way in which it fairly balances the rights of parties involved in a case before it.

Parties before an international criminal tribunal include the Prosecution, the accused, and victims and witnesses.

As stated in Rule 2 of the ICTY Rules of Procedure and Evidence and the ICTR Rules, an accused is a person against whom one or more counts in an indictment have been confirmed pursuant to the relevant provision of the Rule, whereas a suspect is a person about whom the Prosecution possesses reliable information which tends to show that he may have committed a crime over which the ICTY has jurisdiction. So, an accused is a 'suspect' from the time of his arrest until the indictment against him is confirmed and his status is changed to become an 'accused'.[1]

Since the Prosecution has the authority to start the entire legal process, from investigation and submission of an indictment for confirmation, it has the duty to exercise due diligence to ensure that, within the scope of its authority, the case proceeds to trial in such a way that respects the rights of the suspect and the accused.[2]

The ICC Statute does not distinguish between a suspect and an accused. The Statute uses the term 'person' until the charge against a person is confirmed by the Pre-Trial Chamber under Article 61, from which point the person becomes an 'accused'.[3]

11.1 RIGHTS OF SUSPECTS

A suspect is entitled to a guarantee of his fundamental rights, including the right to be informed promptly of the reasons for his arrest and the charges against him, and the right to be brought to trial without undue delay.

The right to be promptly informed of the charges serves to counterbalance the interest of the prosecuting authority in seeking continued detention of the suspect as well as to enable the suspect to deny the offence and secure his release prior to the initiation of trial proceedings. There is no requirement that the suspect be informed

---

[1] *Jean-Bosco Barayagwiza v. Prosecutor*, Case No. ICTR-97–19-I, ICTR App. Ch., 3 Nov. 1999, para. 41.
[2] Ibid., paras. 91–9.
[3] The word 'accused' is used from Art. 61(9) onwards.

in any particular way; he need not be notified in writing, and the information may be given to the suspect in stages, as long as it is provided promptly. Whether this requirement is met is to be determined on a case-by-case basis.[4]

Also, a suspect is entitled to recourse to an independent judicial officer for review of his detention—the so-called right to be heard on a *writ of habeas corpus*. Even if an indictment against the suspect is confirmed subsequently and he makes his initial appearance, this fact does not excuse the failure to resolve the *writ* in a timely manner.[5]

According to a well-established principle of international human rights law, pre-trial detention is lawful as long as it does not exceed a reasonable period of time.[6] In the case of the ICTY and the ICTR, whose Statutes bind UN Member States, and which have primacy of jurisdiction over national courts, when a State detains a suspect at the behest of the Prosecutor of the ICTY or the ICTR, the suspect is deemed to be in constructive custody of the ICTY or the ICTR, as the case may be.[7]

A criminal justice system is founded upon the presumption of innocence until guilt if proven; hence, unnecessary delay or unjustifiable detention of a suspect undermines the heart of this system.[8]

While the ICTY Statute and the ICTR Statute do not contain provisions on the rights of suspects, the Rules of Procedure and Evidence of these Tribunals safeguard such rights. For example, Rule 42 lay down rights of suspects during investigation, while Rule 40*bis*(D) limits the provisional detention of a suspect.

With regard to the ICC Statute, a person arrested on a request of the ICC Prosecutor shall be brought promptly before the competent judicial authority in the custodial State which shall determine, according to the law of that State, among other things, that the person's rights have been respected.[9] That person also has the right to apply to the competent authority in the custodial State for interim release pending his surrender to the ICC.[10] Article 85(1) of the ICC Statute specifically provides that a victim of unlawful arrest or detention 'shall have an enforceable right to compensation'.

11.2 RIGHTS OF ACCUSED

NE BIS IN IDEM

The Civil Law principle of *ne bis in idem* and the corresponding Common Law principle of double jeopardy entitle the accused not to be tried twice for the same

---

[4] *Barayagwiza*, paras. 80–5.
[5] Ibid., paras. 87–90.
[6] Ibid., paras. 63–7.
[7] Ibid., paras. 52–61.
[8] Ibid., paras. 104–5.
[9] Art. 59(2)(c), ICC Statute.
[10] Art. 59(3), ICC Statute.

crime or offence. Double jeopardy is a double exposure to sentencing which is applicable to all the different stages of the criminal justice process in the *same* legal system:
prosecution, conviction, and punishment.[11] Unlike double jeopardy, *ne bis in idem*
averts the possibility of repeated prosecutions for the same conduct be it in the same
system or in *different* legal systems.[12]

Article 10 of the ICTY Statute and Article 9 of the ICTR Statute incorporate the
principle of *ne bis in idem* to protect a person tried by the ICTY from subsequent
prosecution by a national court. A person already tried by a national court may not be
tried by the ICTY or the ICTR, as the case may be, unless the original charge was
categorized as an ordinary crime, or the national court proceedings were not
impartial or independent, were designed to shield the accused from international
criminal responsibility, or the case was not prosecuted diligently. In considering the
penalty to be imposed on a person convicted of a crime under either Statute, the
Tribunal concerned shall take into account the extent to which any penalty imposed
by a national court on the same person for the same act has already been served. In
Tadic, the accused raised an objection to the ICTY's jurisdiction contending that he
was being prosecuted in Germany at the time of his transfer to the ICTY. His objection was rejected on the ground that he had not yet been tried in Germany and once
he was tried by the ICTY no State could try him for the same alleged conduct.[13]

Article 10(2)(a) of the ICTY Statute and Article 9(2)(a) of the ICTR Statute permit
prosecution before the respective Tribunals where the act for which a person was tried
by a national court was characterized as an ordinary crime. This permission should be
not interpreted too literally. In *Bagasora*, Trial Chamber I of the ICTR considered that
it was not possible for the Prosecutor to prosecute a person for genocide or crimes
against humanity after that person had already been tried for the same conduct in
question under Belgian jurisdiction. This was despite the fact that the said person had
been tried for murder and serious violations of the Geneva Conventions of 12 August
1949, AP I and AP II, and not genocide or crimes against humanity as Belgian law did
not contain any provision concerning these latter two crimes.[14] It would seem that 'an
ordinary crime' would be interpreted as a crime considered by national jurisdictions
as 'trivial offences' deserving light punishment contrary to international expectation
or standards. In other words, when a national authority prosecutes a crime of serious
concern to the international community as a whole as a 'trivial crime', the intention
to shield the perpetrator of that crime from justice is to be inferred and the ICTY or
the ICTR, as the case may be, can step in.

---

[11] See the authorities cited in *Prosecutor v. Zlatko Aleksovski*, Case No. IT-95–14/1-A, ICTY App. Ch., 24
Mar. 2000 (hereinafter '*Aleksovski* (App. Ch.)'), n. 363.

[12] M. C. Bassiouni, 'Human Rights in the Context of Criminal Justice: Identifying International Procedural Protections and Equivalent Protections in National Constitutions' (1993) 3 *Duke J. Comp. & Int'l L.*
235 at 288. Cf. *Prosecutor v. Dusko Tadic*, Case No. IT-94–1, ICTY T. Ch. II, Decision on Defence Motion on
the Principle of *Non-bis-in-idem*, 14 Nov. 1995, para. 9.

[13] *Tadic*, Decision on Defence Motion on the Principle of *Non-bis-in-idem*, para. 13.

[14] *Prosecutor v. Theoneste Bagosora*, Case No. ICTR-96–7-D, ICTY T. Ch. I, Decision on the Application by
the Prosecutor for a Formal Request for Deferral, 17 May 1996, para. 13.

A question has been raised as to whether the Prosecution's appeals against acquittals of the accused by a lower court would violate the principle of *ne bis in idem*. In *Tadic*, the Appeals Chamber of the ICTY allowed the Prosecutor's appeal against acquittals by the Trial Chamber of the ICTY and reversed the Trial Chamber's verdict.[15] Therefore, it can be safely assumed that the principle of *ne bis in idem* is not compromised in this kind of situation. As Judge Rafael Nieto-Navia explains in his Declaration appended to the judgment, there is no general principle of law that would prohibit Prosecution appeals against acquittals. While the Civil Law system generally allows appeals against decisions at first instance, the Common Law bars appeals against acquittals, except, as in the case of the law of the UK, in certain clearly circumscribed instances such as bribery, threats, or other interference with a witness or juror that tainted an acquittal. However, the rationale underpinning the Common Law's special weight given to acquittals is the desire to prevent the Government from abusing its power to prosecute accused persons by re-prosecuting them until they are finally convicted. This rationale is absent in the context of prosecutions before international tribunals where the Prosecution prosecutes on behalf of the international community and, like the Defence in that case, must rely on the cooperation of external entities without support by a governmental apparatus with abundant resources. In other words, unlike the situation in domestic courts where the Government has greater resources at its disposal than an accused person does, the Prosecution and the accused before an international tribunal enjoy equality of arms in fact and in law.[16]

Double jeopardy may also be a factor in reducing or mitigating a sentence. In *Aleksovski*, the ICTY Appeals Chamber, in imposing a revised sentence, took into account the element of double jeopardy in that the Appellant had had to appear for sentence twice for the same conduct, thereby suffering anxiety and distress, and also that he had been detained a second time after his release for nine months. The ICTY Appeals Chamber stated that without these factors the accused's sentence would have been considerably longer.[17]

Article 20 of the ICC Statute recognizes the principle of *ne bis in idem*. It provides that no person shall be tried before the ICC with respect to conduct which formed the basis of crimes for which that person has been convicted or acquitted by the ICC. Moreover, no person shall be tried before another court for a crime within the ICC's jurisdiction for which that person has already been convicted or acquitted by the ICC. However, in two circumstances, the ICC may try a person who has been tried by another court for conduct also proscribed as a war crime, an act of genocide, or a crime against humanity under the ICC Statute. The ICC may try such a person if the

---

[15] *Prosecutor v. Dusko Tadic*, Case No. IT-94–1-A, ICTY App. Ch., 15 July 1999 (hereinafter '*Tadic* Appeals Judgment'), para. 327(4), (5).

[16] Declaration of Judge Nieto-Navia, ibid., paras. 1–10. However, Judge Nieto-Navia thinks that the Appeals Chamber should analyse at the sentencing stage 'whether a successful Prosecution appeal should put the person in a worse position than that at the end of trial ('*reformatio in pejus*')'. Ibid., para. 11.

[17] *Aleksovski* (App. Ch.), para. 190.

proceedings in the other court were intended to shield the person from criminal responsibility for crimes within the ICC's jurisdiction, or otherwise were not conducted independently or impartially in accordance with the norms of due process recognized by international law and were conducted in a manner which, in the circumstances, was inconsistent with an intent to bring the person concerned to justice. This provision replicates Article 10(2)(b) of the ICTY Statute and Article 9(2)(b) of the ICTR Statute.

Article 20 of the ICC Statute appears in Part 2 on jurisdiction, admissibility, and applicable law, not Part 3 on general principles of criminal law in which grounds for excluding criminal responsibility are found. This is because *ne bis in idem* is closely related to the Articles on admissibility. It is a procedural bar to the ICC's jurisdiction rather than a ground for excluding criminal responsibility.

RIGHTS TO A FAIR TRIAL

Rights to a fair trial are guaranteed by all the international criminal statutes. The rights under the ICTY and ICTR Statutes and Rules are based on Article 14 of the International Covenant on Civil and Political Rights and are similar to the ones incorporated in Article 6 of the European Convention on Human Rights.[18]

The rights under the ICC Statute include the presumption of innocence as provided in Article 66, and the detailed provision on the rights of the accused as appeared in Article 67.

The following represents some important issues encountered by international criminal tribunals.

No trial in absentia. Article 21(4)(d) of the ICTY Statute and Article 20(4)(d) of the ICTR Statute stipulate that the accused is entitled to the right to be tried in his presence. Article 63 of the ICC Statute provides that the accused shall be present during the trial, except where the accused continues to disrupt the trial, in which case the accused will be removed. However, the removed accused can still observe the trial and instruct counsel from outside the court room through the use of communications technology, if required.

The meaning of this right is not be to interpreted too literally. In *Barayagwiza*, the accused refused to attend his trial on the ground that the ICTR was incapable of giving him a fair trial. He also instructed his Counsel, assigned for him by the ICTR, not to attend the trial but otherwise to continue to represent him. The ICTR Trial Chamber in that case held that, in the circumstances where the accused has been duly informed of his on-going trial, neither the ICTR Statute nor human rights law prevents the case against him from proceeding in his absence. As for the Defence Counsel, the Rules of the ICTR and its Code of Professional Conduct for Defence

---

[18] *Prosecutor v. Kanyabashi*, Case No. ICTR-96–15-T, ICTR T. Ch., Decision on the Defence Motion on Jurisdiction, 18 June 1997, 44.

Counsel obligate Counsel to mount an active defence in the best interests of the accused as well as represent the interests of the Tribunal to ensure that the accused receive a fair trial.[19]

Equality of Arms Between the Prosecution and the Defence. The principle of equality of arms falls within the fair trial guarantee.[20] It obligates a judicial body to ensure that neither party is put in a disadvantaged position when presenting its case.[21] Thus, in *Furundzija*, Trial Chamber II of the ICTY, cognizant of its duty to search for the truth and applying the 'interests of justice' test, decided to re-open the proceedings to allow the Defence to remedy the prejudice it suffered as a result of the late disclosure of Prosecution evidence that prejudiced the strategy of the whole Defence case.[22] The Trial Chamber expressed its grave concern over the Prosecution's failure to comply with its obligations under the relevant provisions of the ICTY Rules of Procedure and Evidence in this respect, and declared that it was appalled by this 'conduct close to negligence'.[23]

Unlike domestic courts which have the capacity to control matters that could materially affect the fairness of a trial, an international court must rely on the cooperation of States without the power to compel them to cooperate through enforcement measures. Since evidence is frequently in the custody of a State and that State can impede efforts by Counsel to obtain that evidence, the principle of equality of arms before international courts must be given a more liberal interpretation than that normally upheld with respect to proceedings before domestic courts. Before an international court, this principle means the equality of the parties, with the court providing every practicable facility within its power when faced with a request by either of the parties for assistance in presenting its case, such as issuing such orders, summonses, subpoenas, warrants, and transfer orders as may be necessary for the purposes of an investigation or for the preparation or conduct of the trial. Wherever the measures taken within the power of the court have proved to be to no avail, it may, upon the request of a party or *proprio motu*, order that proceedings be adjourned or

---

[19] *Jean-Bosco Barayagwiza v. Prosecutor*, Case No. ICTR-97–19, ICTR T. Ch. I, Decision on the Defence Counsel's Motion for Withdrawal from the Proceedings, 3 Oct. 2000.

[20] See, e.g. Art. 21 of the ICTY Statute and Art. 20 of the ICTR Statute, which provide, *inter alia*, that the accused shall be entitled to a fair and public hearing, as well as other minimum guarantees, including the right to a legal counsel; the right to have adequate time and facilities to prepare his defence; and the right to examine, or have examined, the witnesses against him and to obtain the attendance and examination of witnesses on his behalf under the same conditions as witnesses against him. See also *Tadic* Appeals Judgment, para. 44.

[21] *Tadic* Appeals Judgment, para. 48.

[22] *Prosecutor v. Anto Furundzija*, Case No. IT-95–17/1-T, ICTY T. Ch. II, 10 Dec. 1998, paras. 90–3, 107. The late-disclosed material was relevant to the issue of credibility of the testimony of the key witness and victim of the accused's alleged crimes.

[23] Ibid., paras. 10–11, 15, 22.

stayed.[24] Provided that the international court is not negligent in responding to a request for assistance, the principle of equality of arms is not violated.[25] Thus, the Appeals Chamber in *Tadic* dismissed the Defence's allegation that there was no equality of arms between the Defence and the Prosecution because the lack of cooperation and the obstruction by certain entities in a State prevented it from properly presenting its case at trial while the Prosecution was able to secure witnesses living in other States that cooperated fully. The Appeals Chamber ruled that what the Defence should have done was to bring the difficulties to the attention of the Trial Chamber forthwith so that the latter could determine whether any assistance could be provided within its power to alleviate the situation, failing which a stay of proceedings may be granted.[26] In *Tadic*, both parties faced limited access to evidence in the territory of the former Yugoslavia due to the unwillingness of the authorities of the Republic of Srpska to cooperate with the ICTY. The Trial Chamber in that case took a number of steps to assist the parties and alleviate the inherent difficulties of the situation. They included setting up a video-conference link from a secure location in the territory of the former Yugoslavia to allow numerous Defence witnesses otherwise unable or unwilling to give evidence to be able to do so; concealing from the public identities of witnesses who demanded anonymity; and granting safe conduct against arrest or other legal process to some Defence witnesses coming to the seat of the ICTY to testify.[27]

Likewise, the principle of equality of arms does not mean that the Defence is entitled to the same means and resources as the Prosecution. What is meant is that both parties have at their disposal adequate means to present their respective cases. Should there be difficulties that might prevent a trial from being fair, the dissatisfied party must bring them to the attention of the court to seek redress without undue delay.[28]

Specificity of the Indictment. The right of the accused to a fair trial includes the requirement that there be sufficient certainty to enable an adequate defence to be advanced.[29] Nonetheless, in some cases it may not be possible to be precise as to exact events, especially during the period of widespread chaos. Therefore, it is not necessary for the Prosecution to prove an exact date of an offence where the date or time is not also a material element of the offence.[30] The date may be a material element if an act is

---

[24] *Tadic* Appeals Judgment, paras. 51–52. Examples of the measures within the power of the ICTY include partial or full protection of witnesses; taking evidence by video-link or by way of deposition; summoning witnesses and ordering their attendance; issuing binding orders to States for the taking and production of evidence; and issuing binding orders to States to assist a party or to summon a witness and order his attendance under the Rules of Procedure and Evidence of the ICTY. Ibid., para. 52.

[25] Ibid., para. 53.

[26] Ibid., para. 55, and cf. para. 29.

[27] *Prosecutor v. Dusko Tadic*, Case No. IT-94–1-T, ICTY T. Ch. II, 7 May 1997 (hereinafter '*Tadic* Judgment'), paras. 530–1.

[28] See *Prosecutor v. Clément Kayishema and Obed Ruzindana*, ICTR T. Ch. II, 21 May 1999, paras. 55–64.

[29] Ibid., paras. 81, 83.

[30] Ibid., para. 85; *Tadic* Judgment, para. 534. Cf. also *Prosecutor v. Rutaganda*, Case No. ICTR-96–3, ICTR T. Ch. I, 6 Dec. 1999, para. 201.

criminal only if done, or only if the consequences of the act manifest themselves, within a certain period of time, or if the date is an essential element of the offence, or if a statute of limitations or its equivalent is applicable.[31] Even where the date of the offence is an essential element, it is not necessary to consider with what precision the timing of the offence must be specified; what is needed is for the indictment to specify the location and matter of offence to allow a comprehensive defence to be raised. However, where timing is of material significance to the charges, then the wording of the indictment concerned must be specific.[32]

The precision in the indictment therefore varies from case to case and depends on the nature of the alleged crimes in question.[33]

Disclosure of Defence Witness Statements. A trial chamber may order, depending on the circumstances of the case in question, the disclosure of Defence witness statements after examination-in-chief of the witness. Such disclosure does not amount to having the Defence assisting the Prosecution in trying the accused. Rather, the power to order the disclosure is inherent in the jurisdiction of any criminal court, be it national or international, and irrespective of the absence of an explicit or implicit provision in its statute or rules of procedure, to ascertain the credibility of the testimony of Defence witnesses. In its quest for truth and fair trial, if a Defence witness has made a prior statement, a Trial Chamber must be able to evaluate the testimony in the light of this statement.[34]

No Prosecution Case. An accused is to be acquitted if the Prosecution cannot prove that the accused is guilty beyond any reasonable doubt of the crime he is charged with. However, if after the Prosecution's presentation of its case-in-chief the court considers that there is lack of sufficient evidence to substantiate the charge against the accused, then there is no case for the Defence to answer, and the accused must be released. Thus, in *Jelisic*, after the Prosecution had come to the end of its presentation of evidence against the accused and Trial Chamber I of the ICTY had considered that the evidence was not sufficient to substantiate the charge of genocide against the accused, the Trial Chamber ruled that the accused could not be found guilty of genocide. This was despite the fact that the Defence still had not commenced its case. In order to ensure a good administration of justice in this instance, the Trial Chamber

---

[31] *Tadic* Judgment, para. 534.

[32] *Kayishema and Ruzindana*, paras. 85–6.

[33] Ibid. For instance, in *Tadic*, the indictment which was amended twice by the Prosecutor before trial made no reference to the accused's alleged murder of two Muslim policemen in the custody of a group of Serb paramilitary forces. Yet, the Trial Chamber found the accused guilty of this murder on the ground that the list of acts alleged in the general prosecution charge was preceded by the word 'including'. *Tadic* Judgment, para. 393. See also *Prosecutor v. Dusko Tadic*, Sentencing Judgment of 14 July 1997, paras. 44, 75.

[34] *Tadic* Judgment, paras. 322–6. Cf. also *Prosecutor v. Tihomir Blaskic*, Case No. IT-95–14-AR108 *bis*, ICTY App. Ch., Decision of 29 Oct. 1997 on the Request of the Republic of Croatia for Review of the Decision of Trial Chamber II of 18 July 1997, para. 25.

proceeded to pronounce its official ruling orally without having to wait until its decision could be put into writing.[35]

Guilty Plea. By virtue of Rule 62(B) of the ICTY as well as the ICTR Rules of Procedure and Evidence, the Trial Chamber is to be satisfied that the guilty plea entered by the accused was made voluntarily in cognizance of the consequence of the plea, was not equivocal, and that there is a sufficient factual basis for the crime and the accused's participation in it. That a plea must be voluntary has been interpreted to mean that the plea is made by an accused who is mentally fit to comprehend the consequences of pleading guilty without any threats, inducements, or promises.[36] An unequivocal plea is one which is not accompanied by words amounting to a defence contradicting an admission of criminal responsibility.[37] Besides, a plea must be informed in the sense that the accused must understand the nature of the charge against him and the consequences of pleading guilty to them.[38] This Rule responds to the decision of the ICTY Appeals Chamber in *Erdemovic*. It was held that Erdemovic's plea of guilty to crimes against humanity was not informed since he had not fully understood the distinction between war crimes and crimes against humanity, with the result that he pleaded guilty to the more serious crimes that normally entailed a heavier penalty. The case was remitted to a new Trial Chamber so that he could replead.[39] In *Jelisic*, Trial Chamber I of the ICTY accepted the accused's guilty plea after being satisfied that the accused understood the nature of the charges against him and the consequences of the guilty plea which was made after long discussions between the Prosecution and the Defence, and that the testimonies produced by the Prosecution left no doubt as to the actual commission of the accused of the crimes he admitted.[40] The ICTR has followed these same steps to verify the validity of a guilty plea.[41]

A plea bargain agreement was presented to any international tribunal for the first time in *Erdemovic*. It is to be treated as simply an agreement between the parties, concluded on their own initiative without the contribution or encouragement of the Trial Chamber and has no binding effect on the Trial Chamber.[42] In *Erdemovic* itself,

[35] *Prosecutor v. Goran Jelisic*, Case No. IT-95–10, ICTY T. Ch. I of the ICTY, Oral Judgment of 19 Oct. 1999 (*http://www.un.org/icty/brcko/judgement/judgement191099.htm*). See also written judgment of 14 Dec. 1999, paras. 14–17.

[36] *Prosecutor v. Drazen Erdemovic*, Case No. IT-96–22-A, ICTY App. Ch., 7 Oct. 1997, Joint Sep. Op. of Judge McDonald and Judge Vohrah, para. 10; *Jean Kambanda v. Prosecutor*, Case No. ICTR 97–23-A, ICTR App. Ch., 19 Oct. 2000 (hereinafter '*Kambanda* Appeals Judgment'), paras. 61–4.

[37] Joint Sep. Opinion of Judge McDonald and Vohrah in *Erdemovic*, para. 31; *Kambanda* Appeals Judgment, para. 84.

[38] Joint Sep. Opinion of Judges McDonald and Vohrah in *Erdemovic*, paras. 14–19; *Kambanda* Appeals Judgment, para. 75.

[39] *Erdemovic*, para. 20 of the Judgment and para. 5 of the Disposition.

[40] *Prosecutor v. Goran Jelisic*, ICTY T. Ch. I, Judgment of 14 Dec. 1999, paras. 26–8.; *Prosecutor v. Georges Ruggiu*, Case No. ICTR-97–32-I, ICTR T. Ch. I, 1 June 2000, paras. 10–24.

[41] *Prosecutor v. Jean Kambanda*, Case No. ICTR 97–23S, ICTR T. Ch. I, 4 Sept. 1998, paras. 6–7; *Kambanda* Appeals Judgment, paras. 49–95.

[42] *Prosecutor v. Drazen Erdemovic*, Case No. IT-96–22-S, ICTY T. Ch., Sentencing Judgment of 5 Mar. 1998, para. 19.

the Trial Chamber of the ICTY imposed the sentence of five years' imprisonment instead of the seven years agreed upon by the parties.[43]

Implications of Withdrawal of an Indictment. Withdrawal of an indictment amounts to a termination of proceedings and the accused must be released immediately and unconditionally if he is not held for any other cause. The court has no jurisdiction to order the release of a person who is no longer under indictment into the custody of any State, including the host State.[44]

Abuse of Process. An international tribunal may exercise its discretion to apply the 'abuse of process' doctrine to decline jurisdiction over an accused if to proceed with his trial would amount to an act of injustice. Under this doctrine, proceedings that have been lawfully initiated may be terminated after an indictment has been issued if improper or illegal procedures are used in pursuing an otherwise lawful process. It is irrelevant which entity or entities within the tribunal were responsible for such injustice resulting from serious and egregious violations of the accused's rights that would prove detrimental to the tribunal's integrity.[45] The tribunal may exercise its supervisory powers over judicial proceedings to rely on the abuse of process doctrine, in the interests of justice, in two distinct situations: '(1) where delay has made a fair trial for the accused impossible; and (2) where in the circumstances of a particular case, proceeding with the trial of the accused would contravene the [tribunal's] sense of justice, due to pre-trial impropriety or misconduct'.[46]

In *Barayagwiza*, the Appeals Chamber of the ICTR, while noting that the crimes for which the accused was charged were very serious, exercised its discretion to apply the abuse of process doctrine to remedy the cumulative breaches of the accused's rights by dismissing all the charges against the accused and directing the immediate release of the accused with prejudice to the Prosecutor, meaning that the Prosecutor is deprived of any right to proceed further against the accused. The Appeals Chamber found that the accused was detained at the behest of the Prosecutor for eleven months before he was informed of the general nature of the charges against him, and was denied the right to be heard on the *writ of habeas corpus*—all owing to the Prosecutor's failure to prosecute the case with due diligence.[47] Subsequently, however, the Appeals Chamber reviewed its decision on the Prosecutor's request for review or reconsideration of that decision on the basis of new facts not known at the time of the original proceedings without the lack of due diligence of the Prosecutor. While affirm-

---

[43] Ibid., paras. 18, 23. The Trial Chamber imposed this sentence after the accused had repleaded that he was guilty of violation of the laws or customs of war, instead of crimes against humanity as appeared in the plea bargain agreement. Before that, another Trial Chamber of the ICTY had sentenced Erdemovic to ten years' imprisonment, which sentence was overturned by the Appeals Chamber.

[44] *Prosecutor v. Bernard Ntuyahaga*, Case No. ICTR-98-40-T, ICTR T. Ch. I, Decision on the Prosecution's Motion to Withdraw the Indictment, 18 Mar. 1999, para. 3. This is different from the provisional release of an accused or a suspect while proceedings or investigations are still pending.

[45] *Barayagwiza*, paras. 72–7.

[46] Ibid., para. 77.

[47] Ibid., paras. 102–12.

ing that the accused's rights were violated, and that all violations demanded a remedy, the Appeals Chamber found the violations suffered by the accused and the omissions of the Prosecutor were not the same as those which emerged from the acts on which the earlier Decision was founded. It, therefore, altered the remedy ordered in that Decision, which consisted in the dismissal of the indictment and the release of the accused. The Appeals Chamber then decided that for the violation of his rights the accused was entitled to a remedy, to be fixed at the time of judgment at first instance, as follows. If he was found not guilty, he was to receive financial compensation; but if he was found guilty, his sentence was to be reduced to take account of the violation of his rights.[48] This decision was followed in *Semanza*,[49] whose facts were essentially similar to those in *Barayagwiza*.

Under Article 85(3) of the ICC Statute, in exceptional circumstances, where the ICC finds conclusive facts showing a grave and manifest miscarriage of justice, it may exercise its discretion to award compensation to a person who has been released from detention following a final decision of acquittal or a termination of the proceedings for that person. By virtue of Article 85(2) of the ICC Statute, where the conviction of a person has been reversed on the ground that a new or newly discovered fact reveals conclusively a miscarriage of justice, that person shall be compensated according to law, unless it is proved that the non-disclosure of the unknown fact in time is wholly or partly attributable to that person.

Impartiality of Judges. Persons running for election as judges of international criminal tribunals are more likely than persons serving as judges in national courts or regional courts to be advocates of human rights and have been involved in activities related to human rights. What is required of a judge of the ICTY and the ICTR is that he or she 'shall be persons of high moral character, impartiality and integrity'.[50] The same requirement appears in paragraph 3 of Article 36 of the ICC Statute regarding qualifications of judges of the ICC.

This matter was tested in *Furundzija*. The fourth ground of the Appellant's appeal in that case was that of recusal, namely, whether or not Judge Mumba, the Presiding Judge in the Appellant's trials, was impartial or gave the appearance of bias to the extent that it violated the Appellant's right to a fair trial. Prior to her election to the ICTY, Judge Mumba was a representative of the Government of Zambia on the UN Commission on the Status of Women (UNCSW), an organization whose primary function is to act for social change which promotes and protects human rights of women. This fact should have been known to the Appellant at the time of trial and the Appeals Chamber could have found that the Appellant had waived his right to raise the matter at the appellate stage. However, the Appeals Chamber held that such waiver

---

[48] *Jean-Bosco Barayagwiza v. Prosecutor*, Case No. ICTR-97–19-AR72, Decision on the Prosecutor's Request or Review or Reconsideration, ICTR App. Ch., 31 Mar. 2000. Unless otherwise stated, the reference in this chapter to the case is to the Decision of the Appeals Chamber on 3 Nov. 1999.

[49] *Laurent Semanza v. Prosecutor*, Case No. ICTR-97–20, ICTR App. Ch., 30 May 2000.

[50] Art. 13(1) of the ICTY Statute, and Art. 12(1) of the ICTR Statute.

would still not relieve an individual judge of his duty to withdraw from a particular case if he believes that his impartiality is in question.[51] The Appeals Chamber sets the following principles on the impartiality requirement for a judge:

'A. A judge is not impartial if it is shown that actual bias exists.

B. There is an unacceptable appearance of bias if:

(i) a Judge is a party to the case, or has a financial or proprietary interest in the outcome of a case, or if the Judge's decision will lead to the promotion of a cause in which he or she is involved, together with one of the parties. Under these circumstances, a Judge's disqualification from the case is automatic; or

(ii) the circumstances would lead a reasonable observer, properly informed, to reasonably apprehend bias.[52]

It was held that neither of these principles was applicable to this case. Firstly, unlike Lord Hoffmann in the *Pinochet* case in the House of Lords, Judge Mumba's membership was not contemporaneous with the period of her tenure as a Judge in the instant case, and the link between Judge Mumba and the UNCSW was tenuous, and did not compare with the close link between Lord Hoffmann and Amnesty International in the *Pinochet* case.[53] Secondly, there is a presumption of impartiality that attaches to a Judge, and Judge Mumba merely represented her Government in the UNCSW and was, as such, subject to instructions and control of her Government. There was no evidence to suggest that Judge Mumba identified personally with the views of her Government. In any case, even if Judge Mumba expressly shared the goal of the UNCSW, her inclination to promote and protect the human rights of women was of a general nature and was therefore distinguishable from an inclination to implement those goals and objectives as a Judge in a particular case. The Appeals Chamber observed that these goals merely reflected the objectives of the UN and were contemplated by the Security Council resolutions, condemning the systematic rape and detention of women in the Former Yugoslavia, that led to the setting up of the ICTY.[54]

The ICTY Appeals Chamber in *Furundzija* rightly recognizes that judges do have personal convictions. Paragraph 1 of Article 13 of the ICTY Statute requires that in the overall composition of the Chambers due account shall be taken of the experiences of judges in criminal law, international law, including international humanitarian law and human rights law. Therefore, the possession of experience in any one of these areas by a judge cannot, in the absence of the clearest evidence to the contrary, constitute evidence of bias or partiality.[55] This rationale would be equally applicable to ICC judges as well, since the qualifications of the ICC judges in Article

---

[51] *Prosecutor v. Anto Furundzija*, Case No. IT-95–17/1-A, ICTY App. Ch., 21 July 2000 (hereinafter '*Furundzija* (App. Ch.)'), paras. 164–75.

[52] Ibid., para. 189.

[53] This matter has already been discussed in Chapter 3 of this book.

[54] *Furundzija* (App. Ch.), paras. 192–201.

[55] Ibid., paras. 203–5. See also *Celebici*, App. Ch. Judgment, 20 Feb. 2001, paras. 694–709, esp. at para. 704.

36(3) of the Statute are closely similar to those provided in Article 13(1) of the ICTY Statute.

11.3 RIGHTS OF VICTIMS

DEFINITION OF VICTIMS

The definition of victims was subject to lengthy debate at the PCNICC. As adopted finally, 'victims' for the purpose of the ICC Statute and the ICC's Rules of Procedure and Evidence means 'natural persons who have suffered harm as a result of the commission of any crime within the jurisdiction of the [ICC]'. The term may include 'legal entities that have sustained direct harm to any of their property, which is dedicated to religion, education, art or science or charitable purposes, and to their historic monuments, hospitals and other places and objects for humanitarian purposes'.[56] Victims or their legal representatives may participate in the proceedings to present their views and concerns.[57]

Suggestions to mention specifically 'family members' within the definition were not accepted since it was generally felt that 'family members' would need a long and complex definition of its own. Besides, the 'harm' suffered by victims may already include harm to their family members due to a possible causal connection between the harm suffered by the victims' family and the harm suffered by the victims themselves. Reference to legal entities reflects the reality that perpetration of certain crimes, for example the war crimes under Article 8(2)(b)(ix) and Article 8(2)(e)(ii) and (iv), are directed against legal entities, which therefore deserve to be characterized as victims.

PROTECTION OF VICTIMS AND WITNESSES

The rights of the accused have to be balanced with those of victims and witnesses. For example, Article 20(1) of the ICTY Statute and Article 19(1) of the ICTR Statute provide that the Trial Chamber shall ensure that a trial is fair and expeditious, 'with full respect for the rights of the accused and due regard for the protection of victims and witnesses'. Article 22 of the ICTY Statute and Article 21 of the ICTR Statute then stipulate that their respective rules of procedure and evidence will provide for the protection of victims and witnesses with measures including the conduct of *in camera* proceedings and the protection of the victim's identity. In practice, Trial Chambers have extensive powers to determine the right balance between the rights of an accused and the rights of the victims or witnesses.

[56] Rule 85 (Definition of Victims) of the Rules of Procedure and Evidence.
[57] Rules 89–93 of the Rules of Procedure and Evidence.

In practice, protective measures include use of pseudonyms, non-disclosure of witness identities to the media and the public, giving evidence via video-conference link, accommodating witnesses during their presence at the seat of the international tribunal in safe houses where medical and psychiatric assistance is available, giving testimony in closed session, use of image-distortion, and redaction.[58] While the protection of victims and witnesses may be permitted to affect the public nature of the trial, it must not be allowed to affect the fairness of the trial.[59] For example, trial testimony of a victim may have to be disclosed to the Defence to the extent that it is relevant for the preparation of the Defence's case, but without thereby jeopardizing the safety of the victim.[60]

A five-pronged balancing test has been adopted by the ICTY to determine whether anonymity is to be granted to a witness. Firstly, there must be real fear for the safety of the witness or his family. Secondly, the evidence to be furnished by the witness must be sufficiently relevant and important to the Prosecutor's case. Thirdly, there must be a lack of *prima facie* evidence that the witness is untrustworthy. Fourthly, there must be a lack of a witness protection programme. Finally, any measure taken should be strictly necessary.[61] The Defence normally needs to know the identity of a witness so that investigation of evidence by the Defence can be made in advance of the cross-examination of the witness, and this would not be possible if the witness' identity is not known. The five-pronged test has been subject to criticism.[62] In the circumstances where crimes against humanity, genocide, or war crimes are widespread, most of the five conditions would be satisfied. This is despite the affirmation by the ICTY that protective measures are to be granted only in exceptional circumstances and on a case-by-case basis.[63] It is very difficult to persuade a witness to come forward. If one does come forward, there may not be *prima facie* evidence to indicate the untrustworthiness of the witness. An example is the case of 'Witness L' or Dragran Opacic, a star witness in *Tadic*, who testified that the accused committed murder and rape and that the witness was himself present when the accused killed the witness' father. His evidence was discredited only when his father turned up in court.[64]

In all, short of an effective witness protection programme that would permit the witness's identity to be known to the Defence prior to the disappearance of the

---

[58] See, e.g., *Furundzija*, paras. 16, 20, 28, 31; *Akayesu*, para. 143; *Tadic* Judgment, paras. 21, 29, 30–2.

[59] *Furundzija*, para. 93.

[60] Ibid., para. 31.

[61] *Prosecutor v. Dusko Tadic*, Case No. IT-94-I-T, Decision on the Prosecutor's Motion for Protective Measures for Victims and Witnesses, 10 Aug. 1995, paras. 62–6. Followed in *Prosecutor v. Tihomir Blaskic*, Case No. IT-95–14, ICTY T. Ch. I, Decision on the Application of the Prosecutor dated 17 Oct. 1996 requesting Protective Measures for Victims and Witnesses, 5 Nov. 1996, para. 41.

[62] See M. Leigh, 'The Yugoslav Tribunal: Use of Unnamed Witnesses Against Accused' (1996) **90** *AJIL* 235; C. M. Chinkin, 'Due Process and Witness Anonymity' (1997) **91** *AJIL* 75; M. Leigh, 'Witness Anonymity Is Inconsistent With Due Process', ibid., 80.

[63] *Prosecutor v. Anto Furundzija*, Case No. IT-95–17/1, Decision on Prosecutor's Motion requesting Protective Measures for Witnesses 'A' and 'D' at trial, 11 June 1998, paras. 7–8.

[64] See G. Robertson, *Crimes Against Humanity: The Struggle for Global Justice* (Penguin, 1999), 291–2.

witness and his or her family under the programme, the accused's right to a fair trial will continue to suffer in comparison to the right of the witness.

The ICC Statute attempts to pre-empt any potential imbalance between these two competing rights. Article 67(1)(e) of the Statute guarantees the right of the accused to examine, or have examined, the witnesses against him or her and to obtain the attendance and examination of witnesses on his behalf under the same conditions as witnesses against him. This replicates the provision of Article 21(4)(e) of the ICTY Statute, and Article 20(4)(e) of the ICTR Statute. Article 68 of the ICC Statute, on protection of victims and witnesses and their participation in the proceedings, is much more detailed than the comparable provisions of Article 22 of the ICTY Statute and Article 21 of the ICTR Statute. Article 68 of the Statute emphasizes repeatedly that the measures adopted under the Statute in this regard shall not be prejudicial to or inconsistent with the rights of the accused and a fair and impartial trial. The Rule, entitled 'Restrictions on disclosure', of the Rules of Procedure and Evidence of the ICC as adopted by the PCNICC authorizes the Chamber dealing with the matter to order the non-disclosure of the identity of the victims and witnesses and members of their family 'prior to the commencement of the trial'. Where material or information is in the possession or control of the Prosecutor which is withheld under Article 68 of the Statute, such material or information may not be introduced subsequently into evidence during the confirmation hearing or the trial without adequate prior disclosure to the accused.[65]

The ICC will have a Victims and Witnesses Unit within its Registry. The Unit will provide, in consultation with the Office of the Prosecutor, protective measures and security arrangements, counselling, and other appropriate assistance for witnesses, victims who appear before the ICC, and others who are at risk on account of such testimony given by such witnesses.[66] The Rule entitled 'Functions of the [Victims and Witnesses] Unit' provides, *inter alia*, that the Unit shall provide adequate protective and security measures and formulate long- and short-term plans for all witnesses, victims who appear before the ICC, and others who are at risk on account of testimony given by such witnesses, according to their particular needs and circumstances.[67]

The ICTY and the ICTR also have a Victims and Witnesses Unit set up under the authority of the Registrar. Rule 34 of the ICTY Rules of Procedure and Evidence, for example, provides that such Unit is to recommend protective measures in accordance with Article 22 of the ICTY Statute and provide counselling and support for victims and witnesses. The ICTR's Victims and Witness Support Unit is based in Arusha, Tanzania, and has a sub-office in Kigali, Rwanda. The Unit oversees the travel of the witnesses to and from their place of residence to Arusha and ensures their safety and

---

[65] Rule 81, Sub-Rules 4–5, of the Rules of Procedure and Evidence.

[66] Art. 43(6), ICC Statute.

[67] Rule 17, appearing under Chap. 2 (Composition and administration of the Court), Sect. III, Subsect. 2 of the Rules of Procedure and Evidence adopted by the PCNICC on 30 June 2000.

security during the 'testimony period'. After trial, the Unit regularly monitors and evaluates the security situation of each witness. Up to June 2000, the ICTR had prepared more than 250 witnesses from twenty States in Africa, Europe, and North America, with 223 of them having already appeared to testify before the ICTR Trial Chambers. The parties, including the accused and the judges, know the identity of the witnesses and can see them during the examination. Twenty witnesses have been relocated for their own personal safety.[68]

The problem, in practice, is the lack of witnesses relocation programmes whereby star witnesses in a criminal prosecution assume a new life and new identity under the protection of a Government that has sought their testimony. Such programmes are expensive to implement, and the ICTY and the ICTR do not have adequate resources to do it in every deserving case. It is hoped that things would be different with the ICC. States Parties to the ICC Statute willingly assume obligations under the Statute; they are not compelled to do so, as in the case of their obligations *vis-à-vis* the ICTY or the ICTR whose specific objectives and purposes they might not necessarily share. Therefore, States Parties to the ICC Statute and the ICC's Victims and Witnesses Unit should be able to cooperate in implementing witness relocation programmes or similarly effective programmes that will allow the Defence to know the identity of witnesses so that the accused's right to a fair trial can be preserved without jeopardizing the witnesses' safety.

CREDIBILITY

Courts are also sympathetic to survivors of traumatic experiences. Insofar as survivors or victims appear on cross-examination to be honest, any inconsistency in their testimony may be regarded as indicating truthfulness and the absence of witness interference.[69] In the case of the ICTR and the ICTY, there is no place for the Civil Law principle *unus testis, nullus testis* (one witness is no witness) whereby collaboration of evidence is required if it is to be admitted.[70] For instance, Rule 96(i) of the ICTY's and ICTR's Rules of Procedure and Evidence, which is the only provision that deals specifically with the issue of corroboration of testimony before these Tribunals, states that no corroboration shall be required in cases of testimony by victims of sexual assault. This sub-rule gives the testimony of a victim of sexual assault the same presumption of reliability as the testimony of victims of other crimes.[71] The fact that Rules provide that corroboration of the victims' testimony is not required for sexual crimes does not justify the inference that corroboration of witnesses' testimony is

---

[68] *An Overview of the Work of the International Criminal Tribunal for Rwanda: Judicial Developments*, submitted by the ICTR to the PCNICC on 12 June 2000, paras. 19–21.

[69] Ibid., paras. 108–9, 113, 115–6; *Akayesu*, paras. 142–3; *Prosecutor v. Alfred Musema*, Case No. ICTR-96–13-T, T. Ch. I of the ICTR, 27 Jan. 2000, paras. 100–1.

[70] *Akayesu*, paras. 132–7.

[71] *Tadic* Judgment, paras. 535–9. Cited with approval in *Akayesu*, para. 134.

required for other crimes.[72] On the contrary, the Trial Chamber is not bound by any rule of corroboration but must use its own assessment of the probative value of the evidence before it, and corroboration of testimonies does not in itself necessarily establish the credibility of these testimonies.[73]

TESTIMONY IN SEXUAL CRIMES

The rationale underlying the existence of a special provision for testimony in cases of sexual crimes under the ICTY's and the ICTR's Rules of Procedure and Evidence is the nature of the conflict during which the crimes were committed, with allegations of the systematic and mass rape of women.[74] Under Rule 96, in cases of sexual assault, no corroboration of the victim's testimony is required; and prior sexual conduct of the victim is not admitted in evidence. Consent is also not allowed as a defence if a victim has been subjected to or threatened with or has reason to fear violence, duress, detention, or psychological oppression, or reasonably believed that if the victim did not submit, another might be so subjected, threatened, or put in fear.

Rule 70, entitled 'Principles of evidence in cases of sexual violence', of the Rules of Procedure and Evidence of the ICC as adopted by the PCNICC provides, *inter alia*:

'Credibility, character or predisposition to sexual availability of a victim or witness cannot be inferred by reason of the sexual nature of the prior or subsequent conduct of a victim or witness.'

Rule 71, entitled 'Evidence of other sexual conduct', stipulates:

'In the light of the definition and nature of the crimes within the jurisdiction of the Court, and subject to article 69, paragraph 4, a Chamber shall not admit evidence of the prior or subsequent sexual conduct of a victim or witness.'

Article 69(4) of the Statute is of a general nature. It allows the ICC to rule on the relevance or admissibility of any evidence, taking into account, *inter alia*, the probative value of the evidence and any prejudice that such evidence may cause to a fair trial or a fair evaluation of a witness testimony.

These Rules were welcomed by general consensus of the delegations attending the Fourth Session of the PCNICC in March 2000. First of all, it was felt that the requisite element of a sexual crime is the use of physical force or coercion against the genuine consent of the victim, and the victim's prior or subsequent sexual conduct should not matter. Evidence of the victim's prior sexual conduct would be prejudicial rather than probative in value. This is especially so in the context of a widespread commission of sexual crimes of which the victim is just one among several victims. Introduction of

[72] *Rutaganda*, para. 18.
[73] *Musema*, paras. 45–6.
[74] *Prosecutor v. Zejnil Delalic et al.* ('*Celebici*' case), Case No. IT-96–21-T, ICTY T. Ch., Decision on the Prosecution's Motion for the Redaction of the Public Record, 5 June 1997, para. 44.

this type of evidence would deter victims from coming forward as they would be subject to further traumatization by the Defence.

The Rules as adopted by the PCNICC are influenced by the jurisprudence of the ICTY.[75] The Rules of Procedure and Evidence of the ICTY prohibit the introduction of evidence of prior sexual conduct between the victim in relation to the accused. In *Celebici*, Trial Chamber II of the ICTY refused to allow a waiver of the right not to have one's prior sexual conduct admitted as evidence.[76]

On the whole, reliability of witnesses must be determined on a case-by-case basis. As Trial Chamber II of the ICTY sums up succinctly in *Tadic*:

'The reliability of witnesses, including any motive they may have to give false testimony, is an estimation that must be made in the case of each individual witness. It is neither appropriate, nor correct, to conclude that a witness is deemed to be inherently unreliable solely because he was the victim of a crime committed by the person not of the same creed, ethnic group, armed force or any characteristic of the accused. That is not to say that ethnic hatred, even without the exacerbating influences of violent conflict between ethnic groups, can never be a ground for doubting the reliability of any particular witness. Such a conclusion can only be made, however, in the light of the circumstances of each individual witness, his individual testimony, and such concerns as [either party] may substantiate either in cross-examination or through its own evidence-in-chief.'[77]

11.4 APPEALS

International criminal tribunals set up to date are conducted without a jury. The judges are triers of both fact and law. The trial procedure of the ICTY and the ICTR reflects the adversarial nature of the Common Law procedure, with the accused pleading 'guilty' or 'not guilty' to the charge against him. Article 25 of the ICTY Statute and Article 24 of the ICTR Statute permit appeals from the convicted or from the Prosecutor on the grounds of an error of law invalidating the decision of the Trial Chamber, or an error of fact which has occasioned a miscarriage of justice. Both the ICTY and the ICTR have adopted the position that a party to the proceedings is not allowed, unless special circumstances can be shown, to raise issues on appeal that were not previously raised by counsel in the course of the trial only to return to the issues on appeal to seek a trial *de novo*.[78]

Part 8 of the ICC Statute governs appeals and revision. Article 81 provides for appeal against a decision of acquittal or conviction on the grounds of a procedural

---

[75] Cf. *Doc. PCNICC/ 2000/ WGRPE (6)/ INF/ 1*, submitted by the ICTY, which centres on Rule 96 of the ICTY and the decisions of the ICTY on this point in *Tadic* and *Celebici*.

[76] *Prosecutor v. Delalic et al.*, ICTY T. Ch. II, Decision on the Prosecutor's Motion for the Redaction of the Public Record.

[77] *Tadic* Judgment, para. 541.

[78] *Tadic* Appeals Judgment, para. 55; *Kambanda* Appeals Judgment, paras. 25–9.

error, an error of fact, an error of law, or any other ground that affects the fairness or reliability of the proceeding or decision. A sentence may be appealed on the ground of disproportion between the crime and the sentence. Article 82 governs appeal against other decisions, such as a decision regarding jurisdiction or admissibility.

The following analysis touches on important issues pertaining to appeals as encountered by international criminal tribunals.

ERROR OF FACT LEADING TO A MISCARRIAGE OF JUSTICE

The Appeals Chamber of the ICTY and the ICTR has held that in the case of an appeal alleging an error of fact, the Appellant must show that the Trial Chamber did indeed commit the error, and that the error resulted in a miscarriage of justice in the sense of a grossly unfair outcome in judicial proceedings, as when the accused is convicted despite a lack of evidence on an essential element of a crime.[79]

An appellate body must give a margin of deference to a finding of fact reached by a Trial Chamber, and it is only where the evidence relied on by the Trial Chamber could not reasonably have been accepted by any reasonable person that the appellate body can substitute its own finding for that of the Trial Chamber.[80] In other words, the standard of determining whether the Trial Chamber's factual finding should stand is the objective standard of unreasonableness; namely, a conclusion which no reasonable person could have reached. This is because two judges both acting reasonably can reach different conclusions on the basis of the same evidence.[81] Therefore, the Appeals Chamber in *Tadic* decided not to overturn the finding of the Trial Chamber accepting a witness's claim that the reason why the witness returned to the town where the paramilitary forces had been attacking, and from which he had escaped, was to feed his pet pigeons, during which time he saw the accused kill two policemen. The Appeals Chamber reasoned that it was conceivable that a person might take such an irrational risk, and since the Trial Chamber had seen the witness, heard his testimony, and observed him under cross-examination before deciding to accept his testimony as reliable evidence, the Appeals Chamber found no basis to consider the unreasonableness of the Trial Chamber's finding.[82]

PRESENTATION OF ADDITIONAL EVIDENCE AT THE APPELLATE STAGE

Pursuant to Rule 115 of the Rules of Procedure and Evidence of the ICTY and the ICTR, a party, including the accused, may seek leave from the Appeals Chamber to present additional documentary evidence not available to it at the trial, and the

[79] *Furundzija* (App. Ch.), para. 37, quoting the ICTR App. Ch. in *Prosecutor v. Serushago*, Case No. ICTR-98-39-A, 6 Apr. 2000.

[80] *Tadic* Appeals Judgment, para.64. Also Presiding Judge Shahabudeen's Separate Opinion, paras. 28–31.

[81] Ibid., para. 64. Followed in *Furundzija* (App. Ch. Judgment), para. 37.

[82] *Tadic* Appeals Judgment, para. 66.

Appeals Chamber shall authorize the presentation of such evidence if it considers that the interests of justice so require. In *Tadic,* the Defence requested a motion for review of the judgment of the ICTY Trial Chamber on the basis of a 'new fact'. The ICTY sets a high standard in these circumstances. There must be a reasonable explanation as to why the evidence was not available at trial. Such unavailability must not result from the lack of due diligence on the part of the party seeking to present additional documentary evidence.[83] As the Appeals Chamber of the ICTY remarks in *Erdemovic,* the appeal process of the ICTY is not designed for the purpose of allowing parties to rectify their own failure or oversights during trial or sentencing by a Trial Chamber.[84] In *Tadic* itself, the Appeals Chamber denied the Defence's motion on the grounds that the Defence had failed to satisfy the Appeals Chamber that the evidence was relevant to a material issue, that the evidence was credible, and that the evidence was such that it would probably show that the conviction was unsafe.[85]

MATTERS NOT SUBJECT TO APPEAL

If a point of law is a matter of general importance for an international tribunal's jurisprudence, an appellate body may consider it appropriate to set forth its view on the matter despite the fact that there is no appeal from a Trial Chamber on that point.[86] As the Appeals Chamber of the ICTY states in *Erdemovic,* the competence to raise issues *proprio motu* is inherent in the power pertaining to an appellate body, and it finds nothing in the Statute or Rules of Procedure and Evidence of the ICTY, practices of international institutions, or national judicial systems, which would confine its consideration of an appeal to the issues raised formally by the parties.[87]

NON-REMISSION OF THE CASE TO THE TRIAL CHAMBER

The ICTY Appeals Chamber in *Aleksovski* ruled that the Trial Chamber in that case applied the wrong tests and therefore its findings of the fact were made erroneously. Nevertheless, the Appeals Chamber found it would not serve a useful purpose to remit the case to the Trial Chamber for re-examination or to make its own determination of the facts. This was because the material acts of the Appellant underlying the charges were the same in respect of the two counts of grave breaches, for which the Trial Chamber applied the wrong tests and acquitted the Appellant, and in respect of the count of violations of the laws and customs of war, for which the Appellant had been convicted. The Appeals Chamber reasoned that, even if the verdict of acquittal were to be reversed by a finding of guilt on the former two counts, it would not be appropriate to increase the Appellant's sentence by virtue of the conviction on these two counts,

---

83 *Tadic* Appeals Judgment, para. 16.
84 *Prosecutor v. Drazen Erdemovic,* Case No. IT-96-22-A, ICTY App. Ch., 7 Oct. 1997, para. 15.
85 *Tadic* Appeals Judgment, para. 16.
86 Ibid., paras. 281, 316.
87 *Erdemovic,* para. 16. See also *Kambanda* Appeals Judgment, para. 98.

which sentence, moreover, would have to run concurrently with the sentence on the last count.[88]

11.5 REVIEW

National and international judicial bodies allow review of their decisions in certain circumstances. Article 26 of the ICTY Statute and Article 25 of the ICTR Statute provide with respect to the review proceedings as follows:

'When a new fact has been discovered which was not known at the time of the proceedings before the Trial Chambers or the Appeals Chambers and which could have been a decisive factor in reaching the decision, the convicted person or the Prosecutor may submit to the International Tribunal an application for review of the judgment.'

A distinction must be made between a fact and evidence of that fact. The mere subsequent discovery of evidence of a fact known at the previous proceedings is not itself a new fact. The reference to the 'Prosecutor' and the 'convicted person' indicates that each of the parties may seek review of a decision, not that the provision is to apply only after a conviction has been ordered. However, only a final judgment may be reviewed, and a final judgment is one which terminates the proceedings. If the new act is considered to be of sufficient strength that might reasonably affect the decision, it should not be excluded on the ground that reasonable diligence was not exercised to obtain it at the previous proceedings.[89]

Article 84 of the ICC Statute permits 'revision' of conviction or sentence on the grounds of new evidence of the nature and in the circumstances provided in the above provision of the ICTY and the ICTR Statutes; or on the grounds that decisive evidence has now been revealed to be false, forged, or falsified; or that one or more judges participating in conviction or confirmation of the charges has committed, in that case, an act of serious misconduct or serious breach of duty of sufficient gravity to justify the removal of that judge or those judges from office.

---

[88] *Aleksovski* (App. Ch.), paras. 153–4.

[89] *Barayagwiza*, Decision on the Prosecutor's Request for Review and Reconsideration, ICTR App. Ch., 31 Mar. 2000.

12

CUMULATIVE CHARGES, SENTENCING, AND COMPENSATION FOR VICTIMS

12.1 CUMULATIVE CHARGES[1]

The ICTR held in *Akayesu* that, on the basis of national and international law and jurisprudence, the accused may be convicted of two or more offences in relation to the same set of facts and against the same victim(s) in either one of the following three circumstances:[2]

(i) Where the offences have different elements. For example, war crimes may also constitute crimes against humanity; the same offences may amount to both types of crimes.[3]

(ii) Where the provisions creating the offences protect different interests. International crimes protect different interests. The concept of the crime of genocide protects certain groups from extermination or attempted extermination; that of crimes against humanity protects civilian populations from persecution, while the concept of war crimes protects non-combatants in armed conflicts.[4]

(iii) Where it is necessary to record a conviction for both offences in order to fully describe what crimes the accused committed.

Such accumulation of criminal charges does not offend against the principle of double jeopardy or *ne bis in idem* which prohibits judging an accused twice for the same offence. The accumulation of charges will only be pertinent at the time of the imposition of the penalty, and the penalty to punish proven criminal conduct does

---

[1] Also known as 'cumulation of offences' (*concursus delictorum*).

[2] *Prosecutor v. Jean-Paul Akayesu*, Case No. ICTR-96–4-T, ICTR T. Ch. I, 2 Sept. 1998, para. 468.

[3] *Prosecutor v. Dusko Tadic*, Case No. IT-94–1-T, ICTY T. Ch. II, 7 May 1997 (hereinafter '*Tadic* Judgment'), paras. 700–1.

[4] *Akayesu*, para. 469.

not depend on whether offences arising from the same conduct are alleged cumulatively or alternatively.[5] In *Tadic*, for instance, in relation to one particular beating, the accused received seven years' imprisonment for the beating as a crime against humanity, and a six-year concurrent sentence for the same beating as a violation of the laws or customs of war.[6]

However, it is not justifiable to convict an accused of two offences in relation to the same set of facts where (a) one offence is a lesser offence included in the greater offence—for example, murder and grievous bodily harm; robbery and theft; or rape and indecent assault; or (b) where one offence charges liability as an accomplice and the other offence charges liability as the principal, such as genocide and complicity in genocide.[7] Nevertheless, while genocide is the gravest crime, there is no justification for finding that crimes against humanity or war crimes are in all circumstances alternative charges or lesser included offences; these offences have different constituent elements.[8] This does not rule out a possibility that a crime against humanity or a war crime may be subsumed in a crime of genocide.

The issue is dealt with in greater depth by Trial Chamber II of the ICTY in *Kupreskic and Others*. It is considered relevant in two distinct but closely interrelated respects. Firstly, from the viewpoint of *substantive* international criminal law, the questions are whether and on what conditions the same act or transaction may infringe two or more rules of international criminal law, and how a double conviction for a single action should be reflected in sentencing. Secondly, from the viewpoint of *procedural* international criminal law, the questions are: (a) the occasion and the conditions that allow the Prosecutor to opt for cumulaltive charges for the same act or transaction; (b) the occasion when the Prosecutor should instead put forward the alternative charges; and (c) the powers of a Trial Chamber when faced with a charge that has been wrongly formulated by the Prosecutor.[9]

From the viewpoint of *substantive* law, there are two different legal situations. Firstly, various elements of a criminal act or transaction may infringe different provisions of a penal statute. For example, commission of the crime of enforced disappearance of persons includes within it kidnapping, prolonged deprivation of personal liberty, and execution without trial. Secondly, one and the same act or transaction may simultaneously breach two or more provisions of a penal statute.[10] For instance, the shelling of a religious group of enemy civilians by means of prohibited weapons is a war crime, but because it is coupled with the intent to destroy that religious group in whole or in part, it also constitutes genocide—both being crimes under the same criminal statute. There may be acts or transactions that are fully covered by the same

---

[5] *Prosecutor v. Dusko Tadic*, Case No. IT-94–1-T, ICTY T. Ch. II, Decision on Defence Motion on Form of the Indictment of 14 Nov. 1995, 10. Quoted with approval in *Akayesu*, para. 463.

[6] *Tadic*, Case No. IT-94–1-T, ICTY T. Ch. II, Sentencing Judgment of 14 July 1997. Cited with approval in *Akayesu*, para. 464.

[7] *Akayesu*, para. 468.

[8] Ibid, para. 470.

[9] *Prosecutor v. Kupreskic and Others*, Case No. IT-95–16-T, ICTY T. Ch. II, 14 Jan. 2000, para. 671.

[10] Ibid., paras. 679–80.

statutory provision, such as the systematic rape, by combatants, of enemy civilians in an occupied territory—which constitutes a war crime, a crime against humanity, and torture or cruel treatment under Article 3 common to the Geneva Conventions of 12 August 1949.

With regard to the first legal situation, some general principles of criminal law common to the major legal systems of the world can be deduced from a survey of national law and jurisprudence to determine whether there are two or more offences or only one. The test is whether each provision of the penal statute requires proof of an additional fact or element not required by the other; if it does, the criminal act that fulfils the extra requirements of each offence will constitute an offence under each provision. If the test is not met, one of the offences falls entirely within the scope of the other offences, and the choice between the two provisions is governed by the maxim *in toto iure generi per speciem derogatur* (or *lex specialis derogat generali*), whereby the more specific and less sweeping provision should be chosen because it is directed more specifically towards that action or transaction.[11] In other cases, although the provisions do not involve a *lex specialis-lex generalis* relationship, it would be unsound to apply both provisions but would be better to resort to the Common Law doctrine of the 'lesser included offence' or the principle of consumption under Civil Law. In this instance, when all the legal requirements for a lesser offence are met in the commission of a more serious offence, a conviction on the more serious offence fully covers the criminality of the act or transaction in question.[12]

With respect to the second legal situation, what is to be ascertained is whether the various provisions protect different values. If a single act or transaction simultaneously breaches two or more criminal provisions protecting different values, it may be held to infringe two or more criminal provisions and entail a double or more conviction.[13] For instance, the prohibition of murder as a crime against humanity and that of persecution or other inhumane acts as a crime against humanity aim to protect different values and interests and may be charged cumulatively.[14] However, in practice this test is hardly ever used except in conjunction with and in support of the other tests mentioned above.[15]

It is noted that each Article of the ICTY Statute is not confined to indicating a single category of well-defined acts but embraces broad clusters of offences sharing certain general ingredients. Moreover, some provisions have a scope so broad that they may overlap with each other; for example, some acts may be categorized as war crimes as well as crimes against humanity.[16] In these circumstances, specific offences rather than diverse sets of crimes must be considered.[17]

---

[11] Ibid., paras. 681–6.
[12] Ibid., paras. 687–9, and see the cases cited in paras. 690–2.
[13] Ibid., paras. 694–5.
[14] Ibid., para. 821.
[15] Ibid., para. 696.
[16] Ibid., paras. 698–9.
[17] Ibid., para. 700.

In the case of murder, murder as a crime against humanity must be committed as part of a widespread or systematic attack on a civilian population, therefore, murder as a crime against humanity is *lex specialis* in relation to murder as a war crime because the latter does not share the element of widespreadness or systematicity required in the former.[18] Besides, these crimes are designed to protect different values—a minimum humanitarian concern in the case of war crimes, and discouraging attacks on the civilian population and the persecution of identifiable groups of civilians in the case of crimes against humanity.[19] Thus, it would be permissible to record a double conviction in such a case.[20]

In the case of the crime against humanity of persecution and that of murder, persecution requires a discriminatory element which, under customary international law, murder as a crime against humanity does not.[21] In *Kupreskic and Others*, the accused were charged with murder as well as with persecution. The latter charge referred to killing as well as to 'the comprehensive destruction of Bosnian Muslim homes and property' and 'the organized detention and expulsion of the Bosnian Muslims from [a village] and its environs'; that is, 'ethnic cleansing'. It was held that if the accused were found guilty of persecution, *inter alia*, because of the commission of murders, they should be found guilty of persecution only. This was because the murders might be seen as either falling under *lex generalis* or a lesser included offence and there should be no additional conviction for these murders when there was already a conviction under *lex specialis* in the form of the more serious offence of persecutory murder; namely, murder forming part of persecution.[22] However, one single act or transaction of murder may infringe the prohibition against murder as a crime against humanity and that against persecution: (a) if murder as a form of persecution meets both the requirement of discriminatory intent and that of widespread or systematic persecution, and (b) if murder as a crime against humanity meets the requirement for the wilful taking of the lives of innocent civilians and that of a widespread or systematic practice of murder of civilians.[23] Furthermore, these crimes are intended to protect different values. Prohibition of murder serves to protect civilians from being eliminated on a large scale, while prohibition of persecution aims to safeguard civilians from severe forms of discrimination and ensure respect for equality.[24]

In the case of the relationship between 'inhumane acts' as a crime against humanity

---

[18] Ibid., para. 702.

[19] Ibid., para. 703.

[20] In the case of the ICTY Statute, the ICTY has jurisdiction over crimes against humanity only when committed during an armed conflict; hence, the 'inconsequential' or 'marginal' difference in values protected. Therefore, the accused may be convicted for murder as a crime against humanity only if the requirements of murder under both Art. 3 (war crimes) and Art. 5 (crimes against humanity) of the ICTY Statute are proved (*Kupreskic and Others*, paras. 704–5).

[21] Ibid., para. 707.

[22] Ibid., paras. 706, 708.

[23] Ibid., para. 709.

[24] Ibid., para. 710.

and 'cruel treatment' as a war crime under the ICTY Statute, they are alternatives to each other. Therefore, a conviction should only be recorded for one of them: inhumane acts if the prerequisite conditions of widespreadness and systematicity for crimes against humanity are met, and if they are not met, cruel treatment as a war crime.[25]

In *Kayishema and Ruzindana*, the Prosecution relied on the same culpable elements and culpable conduct to prove both a crime against humanity and an act of genocide, as a result of which Trial Chamber II of the ICTR held that the crime against humanity had to be subsumed in the crime of genocide and punished as such.[26] The Trial Chamber of the ICTR reached this decision on the grounds that all the elements including the *mens rea* element requisite to show genocide, extermination and murder in that case were the same, and the evidence relied on to prove the crimes were the same, and that therefore the Prosecutor should have charged the accused in the alternative. In its view, cumulative charges are acceptable only where the offences have differing elements or where the laws in question protect differing social interests.[27] However, subsequent cases prefer to adhere to the reasoning in *Akayesu*.[28] Trial Chamber I of the ICTR in *Rutaganda* and in *Musema* concurs with the dissenting opinion of Judge Tafazzal H. Khan in *Kayishema and Ruzindana* to the effect that where the culpable conduct amounts to two or more crimes the accused may be found guilty of more than one charge, whether or not the factual situation also satisfies the distinct elements of the two or more crimes in question. What is to be recorded in the conviction is the totality of the accused's culpable conduct that offends different values that the law seeks to protect.[29] Faced with these different approaches, the ICTY Appeals Chamber in *Celebici* has now settled once and for all that multiple convictions entered under different statutory provisions but based on the same conduct are permissible only if each statutory provision involved has a materially distinct element requiring proof of a fact not required in the other. Where this test is not met, the conviction under the more specific provision should be upheld.[30]

From the viewpoint of *procedural* law, the power of the Prosecutor to opt for cumulative or alternative charges is limited as follows. The Prosecution:

'(a) may make *cumulative* charges whenever it contends that the facts charged violate simultaneously two or more provisions of the Statute in accordance with the criteria discussed above;

(b) should charge *in the alternative* rather than cumulatively whenever an offence appears to be in breach of more than one provision, depending on the elements of the crime

---

[25] Ibid., para. 712.

[26] *Prosecutor v. Clément Kayishema and Obed Ruzindana*, Case No. ICTR-95–1-T, ICTR T. Ch. II, 21 May 1999, paras. 645–6, 650.

[27] Ibid., para. 627.

[28] E.g. *Prosecutor v. George Rutaganda*, Case No. ICTR-96–3, ICTR T. Ch., 6 Dec. 1999, para. 118; *Prosecutor v. Alfred Musema*, Case No. ICTR-96–13-T, ICTR T. Ch. I, 27 Jan. 2000, para. 299.

[29] *Rutaganda*, paras. 113–8; *Musema*, paras. 289–99.

[30] *Celebici*, App. Ch. Judgment, 20 Feb. 2001, paras. 412–3.

the Prosecution is able to prove. For instance, the Prosecution may characterize the same act as a crime against humanity and, in the alternative, as a war crime. Indeed, in case of doubt it is appropriate from a prosecutorial viewpoint to suggest that a certain act falls under a stricter and more serious provision of the Statute, adding however that if proof to this effect is not convincing, the act falls under a less serious provision. It may also prove appropriate to charge the indictee with a crime envisaged in a provision that is—at least in some respects—special *vis-à-vis* another (e.g. [genocide]) and, in the alternative, with a violation of a broader provision (e.g. [grave breaches or violation of the laws or customs of war]), so that if the evidence turns out to be insufficient with regard to the special provision (the *lex specialis*), it may still be found compelling with respect to a violation of the broader provision (the *lex generalis*). However, the Prosecution should make clear that these are alternative formulations by use of the word 'or' between the crimes against humanity and war crimes charges, for example, and refrain in these circumstances from using the word 'and', to make clear the disjunctive and alternative nature of the charges being brought;

(c) should *refrain* as much as possible from making charges based on the same facts but under *excessive multiple heads*, whenever it would not seem warranted to contend, in line with the principles set out above . . . that the same facts are simultaneously in breach of various provisions of the Statute.'[31]

There is no general principle of criminal law common to all major legal systems of the world to govern the situation when the Prosecutor decides to change the legal classification of facts in the course of trial. An international criminal court must therefore endeavour to look for a general principle of law consonant with the balance between safeguarding fully the rights of the accused and the discharge of its mission in the interests of justice. Such a balance can be achieved in the following manner:

(a) The Prosecutor must seek leave to amend the indictment to afford the Defence the opportunity to contest the charge where: (i) the Prosecutor discovers that he has not proved beyond reasonable doubt the commission of the crime charged, but that a *different offence*, not charged in the indictment, has been proved which has different objective or subjective elements, for example, where there is evidence of torture as a crime against humanity rather than rape as a crime against humanity; and (ii) where the Prosecutor concludes that *a more serious offence* than that charged in the indictment has been or may be proved.

(b) The Prosecutor need not request leave to amend the indictment where he concludes that a lesser included offence, not charged in the indictment, may be or has been proved in court; hence, the inapplicability of the *lex specialis* invoked by the Prosecutor but the applicability of the *lex generalis*. However, the Prosecutor is advised to give prompt notice to the Defence and the trial chamber of his intention to submit that the lesser but not the greater offence has been committed.[32]

---

[31] *Kupreskic and Others*, para. 728. Emphasis in original.
[32] Ibid., paras. 729–43. The summary is by this author.

For its part, the Trial Chamber has the power to depart from the classification of the offence suggested by the Prosecutor in the following ways:

(a) Where it concludes that the more serious offence has not been proved, it suffices to make this finding in its judgment without ordering the Prosecutor to amend the indictment. For instance, where the accused is charged with murder as a crime against humanity but it is conclusively proved that the murder was committed in the context of a war crime but not a crime against humanity, the Trial Chamber could convict the accused of murder as a war crime despite the fact that that crime has not been charged in the indictment.

(b) Where the facts proven by the Prosecutor show that the accused participated in the commission of an offence in a lesser role, for example, aiding and abetting instead of being the principal as charged, the Trial Chamber may classify the offence in a manner different from that suggested by the Prosecutor, without previously notifying the Defence of the change in the *nomen iuris*.

(c) Where the evidence conclusively shows that the accused has committed a more serious crime than the one charged, the Trial Chamber may call upon the Prosecutor to consider amending the indictment, or, alternatively, it may decide to convict the accused of the lesser offence charged. In the event the Prosecutor decides not to accede to the Trial Chamber's request that the indictment be amended, the Trial Chamber should convict the accused of the lesser offence charged.

(d) Where the Trial Chamber finds in the course of trial that only a different offence can be held to have been proved, the Trial Chamber should ask the Prosecutor to amend the indictment, and if the Prosecutor does not comply with that request, the Trial Chamber must dismiss the charge.[33]

12.2 SENTENCING

DETERMINATION OF SENTENCES

International law has not developed a sentencing pattern of its own and must rely on the experience of domestic jurisdictions for guidance.[34] In imposing criminal sentences, a court must take into account the goals of retribution, protection of society, rehabilitation of victims, deterrence, and the motives for the commission of

---

[33] Ibid., paras. 744–8. This is the author's summary.

[34] *Prosecutor v. Zejnil Delalic, Zravko Mucic, Hazim Delic, and Esad Landzo* ('*Celebici*' case), Case No. IT-96–21-T, ICTY T. Ch. II *quater*, 16 Nov. 1998, para. 1195; *Rutaganda*, para. 475; *Prosecutor v. Zlatko Aleksovski*, Case No. IT-95–14/1-A, ICTY App. Ch., 24 Mar. 2000 (hereinafter '*Aleksovski* (App. Ch.)'), para. 185.

offences.[35] As the ICTR puts it cogently in *Kambanda*, the penalties imposed must be directed, on the one hand, at retribution of the accused, who must see that their crimes are punished, and over and above that, on the other hand, at deterrence, namely dissuading forever those who will attempt in future to commit such crimes by showing them that the international community does not tolerate impunity for serious violations of international humanitarian law and human rights.[36] Retribution and deterrence serve as the primary purposes of sentence[37] in the practice of both the ICTY and the ICTR. The ICC will undoubtedly pursue this practice.

It is appropriate to distinguish between the particular circumstances concerning the commission of the crime in order to evaluate the gravity of the offence, on the one hand, and the particular personal circumstances of the accused in order to individualize the punishment to suit the accused and rehabilitate the accused, on the other.[38]

Article 24 of the ICTY Statute stipulates:

'1. The penalty imposed by the Trial Chamber shall be limited to imprisonment. In determining the terms of imprisonment, the Trial Chambers shall have recourse to the general practice regarding prison sentences in the courts of the former Yugoslavia.

2. In imposing the sentences, the Trial Chambers should take into account such factors as the gravity of the offence and the individual circumstances of the convicted person.'

Article 23(1) and (2) of the ICTR Statute copies the above provision verbatim, with the sole exception of the word 'Rwanda' replacing 'the former Yugoslavia'.

In practice, the Trial Chambers of the ICTY and the ICTR consider that the general practice in the courts of the former Yugoslavia or Rwanda, as the case may be, is merely indicative of the sentencing they should adopt in a particular case. The Trial Chambers have unfettered discretion to evaluate the facts and attendant circumstances to enable them to take into account any factor they deem pertinent to individualize penalties.[39] Generally, sentences should be imposed according to the gravity of the offence and degree of responsibility of the accused, and the existence of

---

[35] *Celebici*, paras. 1230–4; *Prosecutor v. Anto Furundzija*, Case No. IT-95–17/1-T, ICTY T. Ch. II, 10 Dec. 1998, paras. 288–91; *Kupreskic and Others*, paras. 838–9.

[36] *Prosecutor v. Jean Kambanda*, Case No. ICTR 97–23-S, ICTR T. Ch., 4 Sept. 1998, paras. 26–8.

[37] *Prosecutor v. Dusko Tadic*, Case No. IT-94–1-T *bis*, ICTY T. Ch. II, Sentencing Judgment of 11 Nov. 1999, paras. 7–9, citing *Celebici*, *Furundzija*, *Akayesu*, *Kayishema and Ruzindana*, *Kambanda*, and *Prosecutor v. Serushago*, Case No. ICTR-98–39-S, ICTR T. Ch., Sentencing Judgment of 5 Feb. 1999, para. 20.

[38] *Prosecutor v. Tihomir Blaskic*, Case No. IT-95–14-T, ICTY T. Ch. I, 3 Mar. 2000, para. 765.

[39] *Prosecutor v. Omar Serushago*, Case No. ICTR-98–39-A, ICTR App. Ch., 15 Feb. 2000; *Prosecutor v. Georges Ruggiu*, Case No. ICTR-97–32-I, ICTR T. Ch. I, 1 June 2000, para. 52. The ICTY Appeals Chamber in *Anto Furundzija*, Case No. IT-95–17/1-A, 21 July 2000 (hereinafter '*Furundzija* Appeals Judgment'), paras. 237–8, considers it premature to speak of an emerging 'penal regime' for the ICTY since the practice of the ICTY regarding sentencing is still in its early stage, and the three final sentencing judgments delivered to date (*Tadic*, *Aleksovski*, and *Erdemovic*) were revised on appeal.

aggravating and mitigating circumstances.[40] The discretion of a Trial Chamber in imposing a sentence is unlikely to be overturned on appeal[41] unless there is a manifest, or discernible, error in the exercise of such discretion. Such manifest error exists, for example, where a Trial Chamber recommends that a minimum sentence begins to run from the date of the final determination of any appeal, thereby discouraging appeals,[42] or where a Trial Chamber does not give the prisoner credit for time spent in detention in a State prior to the issuance of a request for deferral by the ICTY or the ICTR.[43]

By far the most important consideration is the gravity of the offence as determined by the effect on the victim or, at the most, on persons associated with the crime and nearest relations.[44] A sentence has to reflect the standard of proportionality between the gravity of the crime and the degree of responsibility of the offender in order to ensure respect for the law and the maintenance of a just, peaceful, and safe society.[45] However, as was pointed out in *Celebici*: 'Gravity is determined *in personam* and is not one of a universal effect; [w]hereas the guilt of the accused may be related to the specific and general harm of the victim and his relatives, it would be too remote to ascribe every woe of the surrounding neighbourhood to the guilty accused'.[46]

Examples of aggravating circumstances include premeditation by the accused, the physical or psychological consequences of the crime on the victim, the accused's willing participation in and enthusiastic support of the brutal commission of the crimes against helpless victims,[47] as well as the repulsive, bestial, and sadistic nature of his crime especially when committed in cold blood.[48] The motive for the commission of the crime can be an aggravating circumstance. The motives of persecution, vengeance, and sadism have been held to be aggravating circumstances in sentencing.[49]

---

[40] *Prosecutor v. Zlatko Aleksovski*, ICTY T. Ch. I, 25 June 1999 (hereinafter '*Aleksovski* Judgment'), paras. 242–3; *Kambanda*, paras. 11, 23, 30–1, 41; *Tadic*, Sentencing Judgment of 11 Nov. 1999, paras. 12–13; *Celebici*, paras. 1200–1; *Prosecutor v. Goran Jelisic*, Case No. IT-95–10-T, ICTY T. Ch. I, 14 Dec. 1999, paras. 114–16.

Rule 101(B) of the Rules of Procedure and Evidence of the ICTY merely mentions that in determining the sentence, the Trial Chamber shall take into account the factors mentioned in Art. 24(2) of the ICTY Statute as well as such factors as any aggravating circumstances; any mitigating circumstances including substantial cooperation with the Prosecutor by the convicted person; the general practice regarding prison sentences in the courts of the former Yugoslavia; and the extent to which any penalty imposed by a court of any State on the convicted person for the same act has already been served. In *Furundzija*, Trial Chamber II of the ICTY did take into account the relevant provisions of the law as well as the general practice of courts of the former Yugoslavia, but the Trial Chamber decided not to follow the law or the practice in the former Yugoslavia (*Furundzija*, paras. 285–6, 293–6). In *Tadic*, the Trial Chamber of the ICTY also imposed prison sentences exceeding the maximum sentence of twenty years in the general practice in the courts of the former Yugoslavia. See also *Prosecutor v. Dusko Tadic*, Case No. IT-94–1-A and IT-94–1-A *bis*, ICTY App. Ch., Judgment in Sentencing Appeals of 26 Jan. 2000, para. 21.

[41] See, e.g., *Tadic*, Judgment in Sentencing Appeals of 26 Jan. 2000, paras. 20, 22, 48, 59–64, 73.

[42] Ibid., paras. 31–3.

[43] Ibid., paras. 34–40, 75.

[44] *Celebici*, paras. 1225–6, 1260; *Jelisic*, para. 121.

[45] *Kambanda*, paras. 57–8.

[46] *Celebici*, para. 1226.

[47] *Tadic*, Sentencing Judgment of 11 Nov. 1999, paras. 19–20; *Blaskic*, paras. 787, 793.

[48] *Jelisic*, paras. 129–34; *Blaskic*, paras. 783–7.

[49] *Blaskic*, para. 785.

A superior's participation in the actual commission of a crime is an aggravating circumstance that attracts enhanced punishment of that superior.[50] So is abuse of positions of authority or trust that leads to the commission of a crime.[51]

There have been some *dicta* of international tribunals to the effect that, as a general rule, among the crimes listed in the ICTY Statute and the ICTR Statute, genocide is the gravest crime, followed by crimes against humanity short of genocide, and war crimes, in that order.[52] For example, in *Tadic*, the accused was sentenced by the Trial Chamber of the ICTY to twenty-four years' imprisonment for wilful killing as a grave breach, another twenty-four years' imprisonment for murder as a violation of the laws or customs of war, and twenty-five years for murder as a crime against humanity—all of these counts were based on the accused's active participation in the common criminal design to get rid of non-Serb population, as a result of which five men were killed in an attack.[53]

However, such an approach has been challenged. The Appeals Chamber in *Tadic* itself overturned the sentences against Tadic on this ground and substituted for the sentences imposed by the Trial Chamber that of twenty years' imprisonment for each of the aforesaid counts, holding that there is no basis in customary international law or in the ICTY Statute itself for a distinction between the seriousness of a crime against humanity and that of a war crime.[54] This was followed by the ICTY Appeals Chamber in *Furundzija*.[55] It is also doubtful whether the ICC would follow the *dicta* that uphold the relative gravity of crimes against humanity and war crimes for the purpose of sentencing where both crimes are constituted by the same acts or have precisely the same factual bases. Article 7 of the ICC Statute requires that crimes against humanity be committed 'as part of a widespread or systematic attack against any civilian population', while Article 8(1) of the ICC Statute confers jurisdiction on the ICC over war crimes 'in particular when committed as part of a plan or policy or as part of a large-scale commission of such crimes'. In the context of the ICC Statute,

---

[50] *Celebici*, paras. 1219, 1222–3; *Furundzija*, para. 283; *Kupreskic and Others*, para. 852; *Blaskic*, paras. 788–91. Trial Chamber I of the ICTR in *Ruggiu* (para. 77) cited the example of the accused in *Serushago* who was given fifteen years' imprisonment because his high political and military role was considered to be aggravating circumstances. He also killed Tutsi and ordered the killing of several others who were killed as a consequence of his order.

[51] *Kambanda*, para. 44. The ICTR found an aggravating factor in the fact that in personally participating in the genocide, Kambanda abused his position of Prime Minister of Rwanda and the trust of the civilian population in his government to maintain peace and security. In *Celebici*, the abuse of 'position and trust' by Hazim Delic, the deputy commander of the Celebici prison-camp, was found to be an aggravating factor in his sentencing (*Celebici*, para. 1268). See also *Rutaganda*, para. 488. In *Aleksovski*, the accused's superior responsibility as a warden of the prison camp where the victims were being detained seriously aggravated his offences (*Aleksovski* (App. Ch.), paras. 183, 187).

[52] *Kambanda*, paras. 14–17, 33, 42–3; *Tadic*, Sentencing Judgment of 11 Nov. 1999, paras. 28–9; *Akayesu*, Sentencing Judgment of 2 Oct. 1998, paras. 6–10; *Serushago* (5 Feb. 1999), paras. 13–14; *Kayishema and Ruzindana*, Sentencing Judgment of 21 May 1999, para. 9.

[53] *Tadic*, Sentencing Judgment of 11 Nov. 1999, para. 32E.

[54] *Tadic*, Judgment in Sentencing Appeals of 26 Jan. 2000, paras. 69, 76(3). Judge Cassese dissented on this point.

[55] *Furundzija* Appeals Judgment, para. 243.

there would seem to be no justification for imposing greater stigmatization on crimes against humanity than on war crimes. If one accepts the contention that crimes against humanity are crimes which offend 'humaneness' (that is, a certain quality of behaviour) rather than crimes against the human race or mankind as a whole,[56] then the relevant comparison for sentencing purposes should be between the specific acts that constitute the specific crimes, be they crimes against humanity or war crimes. For instance, the war crime of bombarding an undefended town that results in the death of hundreds of civilians should not be treated as less serious than the murder of ten men that falls within the definition of a crime against humanity.[57]

There has been some reluctance to rank crimes against humanity and genocide as one being the lesser of the other in terms of their respective gravity, although genocide has been considered the 'crime of crimes'.[58] After reviewing existing authorities on this point, Trial Chamber I of the ICTR in *Rutaganda* imposed a single sentence of life imprisonment for all the counts on which the accused was found guilty; namely, Count 1: Genocide; Count 2: Crime Against Humanity (Extermination); and Count 7: Crime Against Humanity (Murder). Likewise, in *Musema*, the same Trial Chamber imposed a single sentence of life imprisonment for all the counts on which the accused was found guilty; namely, Count 1: Genocide; Count 5: Crime Against Humanity (Extermination); and Count 7: Crime Against Humanity (Rape). In *Ruggiu*, Trial Chamber I of the ICTR imposed the same sentence on the accused for the charge of direct and public incitement to commit genocide and that of persecution as a crime against humanity.

Trial Chamber I of the ICTY in *Blaskic* adopts the combined objective-subjective method for assessing seriousness of a crime.[59] The objective method for assessing the seriousness of a crime (seriousness *per se*) is linked to the intrinsic seriousness of the crime's legal characterization as a crime of genocide, a crime against humanity, or a war crime. The subjective seriousness (seriousness *in personam*) of a crime is taken into account only in the phase of determining the sentence and thereby ensures that the circumstances of the case may be duly taken into account in setting the sentence. The scale of the sentence will follow from the relationship between, and the evaluation of, the objective seriousness, if relevant, and the subjective seriousness of a crime, on the understanding that the weight of the subjective seriousness should not, except in exceptional cases, cancel out the objective seriousness. Moreover and where necessary, the imposition of a minimum sentence to be served would give the

---

[56] E. Schwelb, 'Crimes Against Humanity', (1946) **23** *BYBIL* 178 at 195. This contention was adopted by Judge Li in paras. 18–26 of his Separate and Dissenting Opinion in *Prosecutor v. Drazen Erdemovic*, Case No. IT-96-22-A, ICTY App. Ch., 7 Oct. 1997, and by Judge Robinson in his Separate Opinion in *Tadic*, Sentencing Judgment of 11 Nov. 1999.

[57] Cf. Judge Robinson in *Tadic*, Sentencing Judgment of 11 Nov. 1999, following Judge Li in *Erdemovic*. Their views were endorsed by the majority of the Appeals Chamber in *Tadic*, Judgment in Sentencing Appeals of 26 Jan. 2000, especially by Presiding Judge Shahabudeen in his Separate Opinion.

[58] *Rutaganda*, paras. 469–70, 487, followed in *Musema*, Section 8: Sentencing, para. 8.2(4).

[59] *Blaskic*, paras. 797–804.

sentencing court some flexibility to fine-tune the sentence. The Chamber notes, however, that this notion is not universally recognized by the various legal systems.[60] It should be noted that the ICTY Appeals Chamber's judgment in *Furundzija*, rendered several months after the Trial Chamber's judgment in *Blaskic*, did not allude to *Blaskic* at all. The Appeals Chamber merely stated that it would 'follow its decision in the *Tadic* Sentencing Appeals Judgment on the question of relative gravity as between crimes against humanity and war crimes'.[61]

Mitigating circumstances include the accused's unwillingness in committing the crime, his young age at the time of the commission of his offence (hence, his impressionability and immaturity), particular personality traits and the effect that the armed conflict in the accused's locality had upon him,[62] family and background, character, timely admission of guilt, expression of remorse in open court with victims and witnesses present, conduct while in detention, and cooperation with the Prosecution before or after conviction.[63] It is the Trial Chamber, not the Prosecution, that determines whether an accused or convicted person has provided 'substantial cooperation' to warrant mitigation of sentence.[64] Generally, to be a mitigating factor, the cooperation must be serious, spontaneous, and gratuitous, with the information provided being of the quality and quantity useful to the Prosecution.[65] The sentencing tribunal will tread very carefully. In *Blaskic*, Trial Chamber I of the ICTY doubted the sincerity of the accused when he expressed his profound regrets and declared that he had done his best to ameliorate the situation. According to the Trial Chamber, the accused who had given orders leading to the commission of the crimes could not be believed to have attempted to limit the effects of his orders.[66] He was a man of duty who barely tolerated disobedience of his orders.[67]

The fact that the accused acted under a superior's order might be of little significance if the accused committed his crimes with cruelty.[68] Likewise, the fact that the accused is not charged with having committed the physical act constituting the basis

---

[60] Ibid., para. 804.

[61] *Furundzija* Appeals Judgment, para. 243. *Blaskic* was referred to only in the Declaration appended to the Judgment in that case by Judge Vohrah. He was a member of the ICTY Appeals Chamber in *Erdemovic* and part of the majority that agreed with the original Sentencing Judgment in *Tadic*. He has continued to subscribe to the view that all things being equal, crimes against humanity are intrinsically more serious than war crimes, and that this distinction should ordinarily be reflected in the sentencing. He merely quoted the following statement in *Blaskic* (paras. 801–2): '[I]t appears that the case-law of the Tribunal is not fixed. The Trial Chamber will therefore confine itself to assessing seriousness based on the circumstances of the case'.

[62] *Celebici*, paras. 1235, 1245, 1248, 1283–4; *Blaskic*, para. 778.

[63] *Prosecutor v. Drazen Erdemovic*, Case No. IT-96–22-T *bis*, ICTY T. Ch., Sentencing Judgment of 5 Mar. 1998, paras. 15–16, 20–1; *Kambanda*, paras. 11, 34–6, 46–54; *Tadic*, Sentencing Judgment of 11 Nov. 1999, paras. 23–4; *Celebici*, para. 1279.

[64] *Tadic*, Sentencing Judgment of 11 Nov. 1999, para. 22.

[65] *Blaskic*, para. 774.

[66] Ibid., para. 775.

[67] Ibid., para. 780.

[68] *Jelisic*, para. 126.

of any crimes in the indictment is not relevant as an attenuating factor if the accused is found responsible as a superior.[69]

Personal circumstances bear heavily on the issue of mitigation in accordance with the modern philosophy of penology that the punishment should fit the offender and not merely the crime.[70] Therefore, sentences need to reflect the relative importance of the role of the convicted in the broader context of the overall event. Thus, sentences for criminals who are small fry like Dusko Tadic, whose level in the command structure was low when compared to that of his superiors or the architects of the strategy of ethnic cleansing in the former Yugoslavia, ought to receive relatively lighter sentences than criminals in high command or masterminds of the atrocities, all things being equal.[71]

However, in principle, the reduction of the penalty stemming from the application of mitigating circumstances must not be considered in any way as diminishing the gravity of the offence; a finding of mitigating circumstances mitigates punishment, not the crime.[72] Therefore, in *Kambanda*, although the ICTR found numerous mitigating circumstances, including the guilty plea and cooperation by the accused, it nevertheless held that they were negated by the intrinsic gravity of the crimes of genocide and crimes against humanity knowingly committed by the accused who abused his position of Prime Minister of Rwanda and the trust of the civilian population in his office.[73] Kambanda was sentenced to life imprisonment, the highest sentence permissible by the ICTR Statute.

Rule 145, entitled 'Determination of sentence', under Chapter 7: Penalties, of the Rules of Procedure and Evidence of the ICC as adopted by the PCNICC, is rather lengthy, but broad at the same time. In determining the sentence, the ICC is obligated to bear in mind that the totality of any sentence of imprisonment and fine, as the case may be, must reflect the culpability of the convicted person, as well as to balance all relevant factors, including any mitigating and aggravating factors, and consider the circumstances both of the convicted person and of the crime. In addition to the gravity of the crime and the individual circumstances of the convicted person, the ICC shall consider, among other things, the extent of the damage caused, especially the harm suffered by the victims and their families, the nature of the unlawful behaviour and the means used to perpetrate the crime; the degree of participation of the convicted person; the degree of intent; the circumstances of manner, time, and location; and the age, education, social, and economic condition of the convicted

---

[69] *Blaskic*, paras. 768, 790–1. It was put succinctly that the position of a superior is more aggravating than a direct commission of the crime in question; however, while the direct participation of the superior is an aggravating circumstance, the absence of his direct participation cannot justify reduction of the punishment (ibid., para. 791).

[70] *Jelisic*, para. 25.

[71] *Tadic*, Judgment in Sentencing Appeals of 26 Jan. 2000, paras. 55–8.

[72] *Kambanda*, paras. 37, 56.

[73] Ibid., paras. 61–2. This fact was highlighted again in *Ruggiu*, para. 75. Kambanda's sentence was upheld by the ICTR Appeals Chamber. See *Jean Kambanda v. Prosecutor*, Case No. ICTR-97–23-A, 19 Oct. 2000 (hereinafter 'Kambanda Appeals Judgment'), paras. 114–26.

person. Mitigating circumstances include substantially diminished mental capacity or duress. Aggravating circumstances include abuse of power or official capacity, cruelty, multiplicity of victims, and discriminatory motives. Life imprisonment may be imposed only when justified by the extreme gravity of the crime and the individual circumstances of the convicted person, as evidenced by the existence of one or more aggravating circumstances. The ICC will undoubtedly refer to the jurisprudence of the ICTY and the ICTR in this matter for guidance.

Article 77 of the ICC Statute stipulates that in addition to imprisonment, the ICC may order a fine and a forfeiture of proceeds, property, and assets derived directly or indirectly from the crime, without prejudice to the rights of *bona fide* third parties. Pursuant to Rule 146, under the heading 'Imposition of fines under article 77', of the Rules of Procedure and Evidence adopted finally by the PCNICC, in determining whether to order a fine and in fixing the amount of the fine, the ICC shall determine whether imprisonment is a sufficient penalty, giving due consideration to the financial capacity of the convicted person, including any orders for forfeiture and reparation. The ICC shall also take into account whether and to what degree the crime was motivated by personal gain. These factors will figure in the ICC's calculation of the level of the fine, taking into consideration also the damage and injuries caused plus the proportionate gains derived by the perpetrator from the crime. However, the total amount of fine shall not exceed 75 per cent of the value of the convicted person's identifiable assets, liquidated or realizable, and property, after deducting an appropriate amount that would satisfy the financial needs of the convicted person and his dependants. The ICC may opt to calculate a fine according to a system of daily fines, with the minimum duration of three days and the maximum duration of five years. There may be imprisonment in lieu of paying a fine, but the term of imprisonment shall not be thereby extended to a total period of imprisonment in excess of thirty years.

MULTIPLE CONVICTIONS

In the case of multiple convictions, Rule 87(C) of the Rules of Procedure and Evidence of the ICTY and those of the ICTR stipulate that the Trial Chamber shall indicate whether multiple sentences shall be served consecutively or concurrently. In *Furundzija*, the ICTY notes that in numerous legal systems the penalty imposed in case of multiple conviction for offences committed by one single act, or by several acts which may be considered to form the same transaction, is limited to the punishment provided for the most serious offence.[74] So, the Trial Chamber in that case held that the sentence imposed for outrages on personal dignity including rape was to be served concurrently with the sentence imposed for torture which was the most serious offence of all.[75] In the other cases decided by the ICTY and in *Akayesu* and *Ruggiu*

---

[74] *Furundzija*, para. 294.   [75] Ibid., para. 295.

decided by the ICTR, the sentences were to be served 'concurrently'.[76] However, the ICTR in *Kambanda, Rutaganda, Musema,* and *Serushago,* and the ICTY in *Jelisic* and *Blaskic,* imposed 'a single sentence' for multiple convictions. The same approach had been taken by the Nuremberg and the Tokyo Tribunals. As explained by Trial Chamber I of the ICTY in *Jelisic* and *Blaskic,* this was because while the crimes of the accused had distinct qualities, they were part of the same criminal activities committed within such a short period of time or within a given geographical area and it was impossible to distinguish the intent and acts involved in one crime from those in the other crimes.[77] This approach has been endorsed by the ICTR Appeals Chamber in *Kambanda.* The Appeals Chamber finds the relevant provisions of the ICTR Statute, which are identical to the corresponding provisions of the ICTY Statute, sufficiently liberally worded to allow the Trial Chamber the discretion to impose either a single sentence or multiple sentences for convictions on multiple counts.[78] However, the Appeals Chamber gives the following guideline on the circumstances in which it is appropriate for the Trial Chamber to exercise its discretion to impose a single sentence:

'. . . [W]here the crimes ascribed to an accused, regardless of their characterization, form part of a single set of crimes committed in a given geographic region during a specific time period, it is appropriate for a single sentence to be imposed for all convictions, if the Trial Chamber so decides. . . .'[79]

The matter of sentencing in multiple convictions is discussed by Trial Chamber II of the ICTY in *Kupreskic and Others.* Where the accused is found guilty on two separate counts for a single act or omission, the sentences for the convictions for that same act shall be served concurrently, with the sentence for the more serious offence aggravated by the Trial Chamber if it considers that the less serious offence committed by that same conduct 'significantly adds to the *heinous nature* of the prevailing offence, for instance because the less serious offence is characterized by distinct, highly reprehensible elements of its own (e.g. the use of poisonous weapons in conjunction with the more serious crimes of genocide)'.[80] Of course, where the same act or omission is found to constitute just one offence, not two offences under two distinct provisions, only one sentence should be imposed.[81]

---

[76] *Akayesu,* paras. 464–6; *Celebici,* para. 1286; *Tadic,* Sentencing Judgment of 11 Nov. 1999, para. 32 G. The Trial Chamber in *Furundzija* itself stated that it was following the practice of the ICTY in *Tadic* and *Celebici* (*Furundzija,* para. 296). In *Ruggiu,* 'a single concurrent sentence' of twenty years was recommended by the Prosecutor (*Ruggiu,* para. 81). The Tribunal in that case imposed two twelve-year sentences to be served concurrently.

[77] *Jelisic,* paras. 136–7; *Blaskic,* para. 807. In *Blaskic* the charge of persecution covers the same set of facts as the other crimes with which the accused was charged, and the persecution in that case extended over a longer period than each of the other crimes charged. The accused was therefore given a single sentence of forty-five years' imprisonment, with all the aggravating and mitigating circumstances having been duly taken into account.

[78] *Kambanda* Appeals Judgment, paras. 102–9.

[79] Ibid., para. 111.

[80] *Kupreskic and Others,* para. 719. Emphasis in original.

[81] Ibid., para. 720.

Interestingly, the Trial Chamber in *Kupreskic and Others* observes that:

'[i]n practice there is no real difference in effect between the imposition of concurrent sentences for multiple sentences and one composite sentence for multiple offences. In the unlikely event of there being uncertainty about the length of the concurrent or consecutive sentences to be served, the State of imprisonment could approach the International Tribunal for clarification. Similarly, if a convicted person is eligible for pardon or commutation of sentences according to the law of the State of imprisonment, the State must inform the President of the Tribunal, who will determine whether pardon or commutation is appropriate. Further, in the event of a successful appeal on any count, there would be no problems with the sentences.'[82]

With respect to the ICC Statute, Article 78(3) stipulates that where a person has been convicted of more than one crime, the ICC shall pronounce a sentence for each crime and a joint sentence specifying the total period of imprisonment. This period of imprisonment shall not be less than the highest individual sentence pronounced and shall not exceed thirty years' imprisonment or a sentence of life imprisonment when justified by the extreme gravity of the crime and the individual circumstances of the convicted person.

12.3 COMPENSATION FOR VICTIMS

The ICTY and the ICTR do not award reparations to victims of crimes within their jurisdiction. Article 24(3) of the ICTY Statute and Article 23(3) of the ICTR Statute permit the Trial Chambers to order restitution of property and proceeds acquired by criminal conduct, including by means of duress, to their rightful owners after convicting the perpetrator of that criminal conduct. Rule 106 of the Rules of Procedure and Evidence governs compensation to victims. Under this Rule, the Registrar is to transmit to the competent authorities of the States concerned the judgment finding the accused guilty of a crime which has caused injury to a victim. The victim or persons claiming through that victim may then bring an action in a national court or other competent body to obtain compensation pursuant to the relevant national legislation. For the purposes of such a claim before the national court or other competent body, the judgments of the ICTY or ICTR, as the case may be, shall be final and binding as to the criminal responsibility of the convicted person for such injury.

The mechanism to provide remedies for victims under the ICC Statute is more direct in the sense that it does not require enforcement through a national court or other competent body.

Under Article 79 of the ICC Statute, the ICC may order money and other property collected through fines paid by a convicted person or forfeiture of that person's proceeds, property, and assets derived directly or indirectly from his crime, to be

---

[82] Ibid., para. 854.

transferred to the Trust Fund established for the benefits of victims of crimes within the ICC's jurisdiction and their families.

According to Rule 98, entitled 'Trust Fund', as adopted finally by the PCNICC, individual awards for reparations are made directly against a convicted person. However, the ICC may order that an award for reparations against a convicted person be deposited with the Trust Fund where at the time of the order it is impossible or impracticable to make individual awards directly to each victim. Such an award deposited in the Trust Fund is to be kept separate from other resources of the Trust Fund and is to be forwarded to each victim as soon as possible. Similarly, where the number of victims and the scope, forms and modalities of reparations make a collective award more appropriate, the ICC may order that an award for reparations against a convicted person be made through the Trust Fund. After consulting interested States and the Trust Fund, the ICC may order that an award for reparations be made through the Trust Fund to intergovernmental, international, or national organizations approved by the Trust Fund. Other resources of the Trust Fund may be used for the benefit of victims subject to the criteria determined by the Assembly of States Parties to the Statute.

In addition, Article 75 of the Statute provides that the ICC may make an order directly against a convicted person specifying appropriate reparations to, or in respect of, victims, including restitution, compensation, and rehabilitation. Where appropriate, the ICC may order that the award for reparations be made through the Trust Fund. The PCNICC has adopted Rule 97, entitled 'Assessment of reparations', under Chapter 4 (Provisions relating to various stages of the proceedings), Section III (Victims and witnesses), of the Rules of Procedure and Evidence of the ICC. This Rule was subject to lengthy debate in the PCNICC before its eventual adoption. As adopted, it provides in sub-rule 1:

'Taking into account the scope and extent of any damage, loss or injury, the Court may award reparations on an individualized basis or, where it deems it appropriate, on a collective basis or both.'

The rationale behind this sub-rule is as follows. As a general rule, damage should be given on an individualized basis. Nonetheless, in certain cases the number of victims may be so large that the convicted person does not have financial resources to compensate them all or adequately. In such situation, the ICC should be empowered to award reparations in the form of, for instance, a school, a hospital, or an orphanage. The ICC may also award reparations on both an individualized basis and a collective basis. Consider this hypothetical example. Where children orphaned by an international crime have left their national State to live abroad with their adopted parents, the collective reparation available to the other victims staying behind in their home State would not be available to these children. Reparations on an individualized basis may then be awarded to the children in that situation.[83]

---

[83] This discussion took place at the Informal Consultation on 21 March 2000, during the 4th sess. of the PCNICC. The views of Canada and Japan seemed to prevail eventually.

EPILOGUE

International criminal law has witnessed drastic developments and achievements in the past decade. The establishment of the ICTY and the ICTR has kept alive the momentum to have a permanent international criminal court. These *ad hoc* international criminal tribunals also serve as the testing ground. Their jurisprudence has influenced the ICC Statute as well as its accompanying Elements of Crimes and Rules of Procedure and Evidence.

The ICTY and the ICTR are proving gradually that international criminal justice can work, and is working.[1] The ICTY Prosecutor has been successful in building the groundwork to bring to justice top officials responsible for the atrocities committed in the territory of the former Yugoslavia. There is no place to hide for fugitives from justice. On 24 May 1999, Judge David Hunt confirmed the Indictment brought by the ICTY Prosecutor against the then President Slobodan Milosevic of the Federal Republic of Yugoslavia (FRY), President Milan Milutinovic of the Republic of Serbia, FRY Deputy Prime Minister Nikola Sainovic, Chief of the General Staff Dragoljub Ojdanic of the FRY Armed Forces, and Minister of Internal Affairs Vlajko Stojiljkovic of the Republic of Serbia. Each of them was charged with crimes against humanity, in accordance with Article 5 of the ICTY Statute, involving persecution, deportation of 740,000 Kosovo Albanians from Kosovo, and murder of over 340 identified Kosovo Albanians. Murder was also charged against each of them as a violation of the laws or customs of war, in accordance with Article 3 of the ICTY Statute, on the basis that murder is recognized as such by Common Article 3 of the four Geneva Conventions of 1949.[2] The five accused were alleged to have been criminally responsible upon two bases. Firstly, they were individually responsible for having planned, instigated, ordered, or otherwise aided and abetted the planning, preparation, or execution of these offences. Secondly, in relation to four of them (the accused Sainovic excepted), they were responsible as superiors, having known or had reason to know that their subordinates were about to commit such acts or had done so but having failed to take the necessary and reasonable measures to prevent such acts or to punish those subordinates who did these acts. Arrest warrants were issued against each of the accused,

---

[1] See, e.g., S. D. Murphy, 'Progress and Jurisprudence of the International Criminal Tribunal for the Former Yugoslavia' (1999) **93** *AJIL* 57.

[2] *Prosecutor v. Slobodan Milosevic, Milan Milutinovic, Nikola Sainovic, Dragoljub Ojdanic, and Vlajko Stojiljkovic*, Decision on Review of Indictment and Application for Consequential Orders, 24 May 1999.

and their assets frozen. Since the various accused were holding the highest positions of power within the FRY and the Republic of Serbia, the Indictment was kept secret until noon on 27 May 1999 so as to allow the Prosecutor to minimize risks of intimidation or reprisals against her staff and some other persons operating in the territories. The Prosecutor's statement on 27 May 1999 expressed her conviction that 'credible, lasting peace' cannot be built upon impunity and injustice, and that the evidence on which the Indictment was confirmed raised serious doubt about the accused's suitability to be the guarantors of any deal, let alone a peace agreement.[3]

The ICTR itself is convinced of the value of its contributions to international criminal justice. It believes that each of its judgments represents an important stepping-stone in the development of international criminal law, and that the judgments created legal precedence in one aspect or another.[4] With full cooperation of all States concerned, the ICTR expects to discharge its mandate by the deadline of May 2003.[5]

In sum, the two *ad hoc* Tribunals have advanced to the stage where they have taken the position that civilian, military, and paramilitary leaders should be tried before them in preference to minor actors.[6] After the general election in the Federal Republic of Yugoslavia that led to the end of the Milosevic regime, the UN Secretary-General has been requested to submit to the Security Council, as soon as possible, a report containing an assessment and proposals regarding the date ending the temporal jurisdiction of the ICTY.[7]

The ICC Statute embodies novel achievements and innovations. The acceptance of war crimes committed in internal conflicts as crimes falling within the ICC's jurisdiction make the ICC Statute reflect the reality that most of the present-day atrocities are ethnic conflicts committed within the territory of a single State. The active role played by women in the negotiations has ensured that the ICC Statute and the accompanying Elements of Crimes and Rules of Procedure and Evidence are gender-sensitive. The participation of individual victims in the proceedings before the ICC and their right to remedies awarded by an international criminal tribunal were unheard of in the history of international law.

Implementation of the obligations under the ICC Statute will also lead to unprecedented situations and national law will have to be enacted or amended to fulfil

---

[3] Statement by Justice Louise Arbour, ICTY Prosecutor, ICTY Press Release JL/ PIU/ 404-E, The Hague, 27 May 1999. For initial reaction in the media to the Indictment, see *Newsweek*, 7 June 1999, 23–31.

[4] An Overview of the Work of the International Criminal Tribunal for Rwanda: Judicial Developments, submitted by the ICTR to the PCNICC on 12 June 2000, paras. 5–6.

[5] *UN GA Doc. A/54/315/S/1999/943*. Agenda Item 51: Report of the International Criminal Tribunal for the Prosecution of Persons Responsible for Genocide and Other Serious Violations of International Humanitarian Law Committed in the Territory of Rwanda and Rwandan Citizens Responsible for Genocide and Other Such Violations Committed in the Territory of Neighbouring States between 1 January and 31 December 1994.

[6] UN Security Council Reso. 1329 (2000), 7th preambular paragraph (*UN Doc. S/RES/1329 (2000)*).

[7] Ibid., 6th operative paragraph.

international obligations.[8] For example, certain crimes within the ICC's jurisdiction are not crimes under domestic law. In Thailand, there is no offence of torture, and a perpetrator of 'torture' can only be prosecuted for the offences against the person, like assault. In Australia, genocide is not a crime under Australian law despite the fact that Australia has ratified the Genocide Convention.[9]

International cooperation in criminal matters will also enter into a new era. Besides the traditional extradition of an accused to another State, States will have to 'surrender' an accused to an international organization—the ICC. Since the ICTY and the ICTR are subsidiary organs of the UN Security Council, their requests for cooperation carry with them the authority of the UN Security Council, and States are bound to cooperate under the UN Charter. The case of the ICC is altogether different; it is a creature set up by the ICC Statute, which binds States Parties thereto. National law, or even national constitutions, will have to be changed to implement this development. Gone will be the troublesome political offence exception to the surrender of an accused to stand trial. This, in itself, is a quantum leap towards the end of impunity for perpetrators of crimes of serious concern to the international community as a whole.

The ICC's success or failure will be measured against the object and purpose of the ICC Statute. The pertinent parts of its preamble express the affirmation that the most serious crimes of concern to the international community as a whole must not go unpunished and their effective prosecution must be ensured, and resolve to guarantee lasting respect for international justice. The potential coming into existence of a permanent international criminal court in itself should serve as deterrence to future international criminals. The time-consuming and cumbersome process involved in setting up *ad hoc* tribunals will be averted.

The ICC Statute may not be perfect.[10] Its shortcomings are derived from a series of compromises in an attempt to satisfy, as far as practicable, the positions and demands of every State attending the Rome Conference. The reach of the ICC's jurisdiction may still be too narrow for some but too wide for others. The trigger mechanism may be balanced for some, but lopsided for others. A strange result reached in Rome appears in Article 12 of the Statute. Where an accused is in custody of a State, that

---

[8] Useful publications to guide States in enacting national legislation to implement the ICC Statute include: Bruce Broomhall, 'The International Criminal Court: A Checklist for National Implementation', in M. C. Bassiouni (ed.), *ICC Ratification and National Implementing Legislation* (Association Internationale de Droit Pénal, 1999), 113; and *International Criminal Court: Manual for the Ratification and Implementation of the Rome Statute* (International Centre for Criminal Law Reform and Criminal Justice Policy, in conjunction with Rights & Democracy, 2000).

[9] See further K. L. Doherty and T. L. H. McCormack, ' "Complementarity" as a catalyst for comprehensive domestic penal legislation' (1999) 5 *Univ. California, Davis J. Int'l L. & Policy* 196.

[10] For analyses of US criticisms of the ICC Statute, see B. Brown, 'US Objection to the Statute of the International Criminal Court: A Brief Response' (1999) 31 *New York Univ. J. Int'l L & Politics* 855; A. Frye (ed.), *Toward an International Criminal Court?* (Council on Foreign Relations, 1999); R. Wedgwood, 'The International Criminal Court: An American View' (1999) 10 *Euro. J. Int'l L.* 93; P. Malanczuk, 'The International Criminal Court and Landmines: What Are the Consequences of Leaving the US Behind?' (2000) 11 *Euro. J. Int'l L.* 77.

State cannot surrender him to the ICC, unless the State of nationality of the accused or the State where his conduct took place is a Party to the Statute or has accepted the jurisdiction of the ICC. It is also not relevant that the State of nationality of the victim of that conduct is a Party to the Statute or has accepted the ICC's jurisdiction.

The ICC's shortcomings and strengths will be known after it starts functioning. It is then up to the Assembly of States Parties to rectify the shortcomings and reinforce its strengths.

A lack of universality of States Parties to the ICC Statute is not fatal to the future of the ICC. What is vital is that a sufficient number of States 'whose interests are specially affected' accept the ICC. It is this category of States that creates customary rules of international law through their extensive and virtually uniform State practice even within a short time span.[11] It is also these States that will lobby for support in the UN Security Council and the UN General Assembly. They may not necessarily be one or more of the Permanent Members of the Council. For example, States neighbouring the State in whose territories atrocities are being committed or have been committed are 'specially affected' by the atrocities that force refugees to flee into their territories. Provided that such States accept the ICC, general or at least local customary international law may crystallize in trouble spots around the earth to help effectuate the administration of international criminal justice under the ICC Statute.[12] The fact that France, a Permanent Member of the Security Council, has ratified the Statute generates even more optimism for the prospect of a successful ICC.

For its part, the ICC needs to show that it upholds fairness and justice in proceedings before it. Once its credibility is established, the number of States Parties to the ICC Statute will increase naturally. So will the level of effective administration of international justice.

---

[11] *North Sea Continental Shelf Cases*, ICJ Rep. 1969, 3 at 42, para. 73.
[12] For the notion of local custom, see *Rights of Passage Case (Portugal v. India)*, ICJ Rep. 1960, 6.

APPENDIX 1: ICTY STATUTE

(Adopted 25 May 1993, as amended by Security Council Resolution 1166 (1998) of 13 May 1998 and Security Council Resolution 1329 (2000) of 30 November 2000)

Having been established by the Security Council acting under Chapter VII of the Charter of the United Nations, the International Tribunal for the Prosecution of Persons Responsible for Serious Violations of International Humanitarian Law Committed in the Territory of the Former Yugoslavia since 1991 (hereinafter referred to as 'the International Tribunal') shall function in accordance with the provisions of the present Statute.

ARTICLE 1

Competence of the International Tribunal

The International Tribunal shall have the power to prosecute persons responsible for serious violations of international humanitarian law committed in the territory of the former Yugoslavia since 1991 in accordance with the provisions of the present Statute.

ARTICLE 2

Grave breaches of the Geneva Conventions of 1949

The International Tribunal shall have the power to prosecute persons committing or ordering to be committed grave breaches of the Geneva Conventions of 12 August 1949, namely the following acts against persons or property protected under the provisions of the relevant Geneva Convention:

  (a) wilful killing;

  (b) torture or inhuman treatment, including biological experiments;

  (c) wilfully causing great suffering or serious injury to body or health;

  (d) extensive destruction and appropriation of property, not justified by military necessity and carried out unlawfully and wantonly;

  (e) compelling a prisoner of war or a civilian to serve in the forces of a hostile power;

  (f) wilfully depriving a prisoner of war or a civilian of the rights of fair and regular trial;

  (g) unlawful deportation or transfer or unlawful confinement of a civilian;

  (h) taking civilians as hostages.

ARTICLE 3

Violations of the laws or customs of war

The International Tribunal shall have the power to prosecute persons violating the laws or customs of war. Such violations shall include, but not be limited to:

(a) employment of poisonous weapons or other weapons calculated to cause unnecessary suffering;

(b) wanton destruction of cities, towns or villages, or devastation not justified by military necessity;

(c) attack, or bombardment, by whatever means, of undefended towns, villages, dwellings, or buildings;

(d) seizure of, destruction or wilful damage done to institutions dedicated to religion, charity and education, the arts and sciences, historic monuments and works of art and science;

(e) plunder of public or private property.

ARTICLE 4

Genocide

1. The International Tribunal shall have the power to prosecute persons committing genocide as defined in paragraph 2 of this Article or of committing any of the other acts enumerated in paragraph 3 of this Article.

2. Genocide means any of the following acts committed with intent to destroy, in whole or in part, a national, ethnical, racial or religious group, as such:

(a) killing members of the group;

(b) causing serious bodily or mental harm to members of the group;

(c) deliberately inflicting on the group conditions of life calculated to bring about its physical destruction in whole or in part;

(d) imposing measures intended to prevent births within the group;

(e) forcibly transferring children of the group to another group.

3. The following acts shall be punishable:

(a) genocide;

(b) conspiracy to commit genocide;

(c) direct and public incitement to commit genocide;

(d) attempt to commit genocide;

(e) complicity in genocide.

ARTICLE 5

Crimes against humanity

The International Tribunal shall have the power to prosecute persons responsible for the following crimes when committed in armed conflict, whether international or internal in character, and directed against any civilian population:

   (a) murder;

   (b) extermination;

   (c) enslavement;

   (d) deportation;

   (e) imprisonment;

   (f) torture;

   (g) rape;

   (h) persecutions on political, racial and religious grounds;

   (i) other inhumane acts.

ARTICLE 6

Personal jurisdiction

The International Tribunal shall have jurisdiction over natural persons pursuant to the provisions of the present Statute.

ARTICLE 7

Individual criminal responsibility

1. A person who planned, instigated, ordered, committed or otherwise aided and abetted in the planning, preparation or execution of a crime referred to in Articles 2 to 5 of the present Statute, shall be individually responsible for the crime.

2. The official position of any accused person, whether as Head of State or Government or as a responsible Government official, shall not relieve such person of criminal responsibility nor mitigate punishment.

3. The fact that any of the acts referred to in Articles 2 to 5 of the present Statute was committed by a subordinate does not relieve his superior of criminal responsibility if he knew or had reason to know that the subordinate was about to commit such acts or had done so and the superior failed to take the necessary and reasonable measures to prevent such acts or to punish the perpetrators thereof.

4. The fact that an accused person acted pursuant to an order of a Government or of a superior shall not relieve him of criminal responsibility, but may be considered in mitigation of punishment if the International Tribunal determines that justice so requires.

ARTICLE 8

Territorial and temporal jurisdiction

The territorial jurisdiction of the International Tribunal shall extend to the territory of the former Socialist Federal Republic of Yugoslavia, including its land surface, airspace and territorial waters. The temporal jurisdiction of the International Tribunal shall extend to a period beginning on 1 January 1991.

ARTICLE 9

Concurrent jurisdiction

1. The International Tribunal and national courts shall have concurrent jurisdiction to prosecute persons for serious violations of international humanitarian law committed in the territory of the former Yugoslavia since 1 January 1991.

2. The International Tribunal shall have primacy over national courts. At any stage of the procedure, the International Tribunal may formally request national courts to defer to the competence of the International Tribunal in accordance with the present Statute and the Rules of Procedure and Evidence of the International Tribunal.

ARTICLE 10

Non-bis-in-idem

1. No person shall be tried before a national court for acts constituting serious violations of international humanitarian law under the present Statute, for which he or she has already been tried by the International Tribunal.

2. A person who has been tried by a national court for acts constituting serious violations of international humanitarian law may be subsequently tried by the International Tribunal only if:

   (a) the act for which he or she was tried was characterized as an ordinary crime; or

   (b) the national court proceedings were not impartial or independent, were designed to shield the accused from international criminal responsibility, or the case was not diligently prosecuted.

3. In considering the penalty to be imposed on a person convicted of a crime under the present Statute, the International Tribunal shall take into account the extent to which any penalty imposed by a national court on the same person for the same act has already been served.

ARTICLE 11

Organization of the International Tribunal

The International Tribunal shall consist of the following organs:

(a) The Chambers, comprising three Trial Chambers and an Appeals Chamber,

(b) The Prosecutor, and

(c) A Registry, servicing both the Chambers and the Prosecutor.

ARTICLE 12

Composition of the Chambers

1. The Chambers shall be composed of sixteen permanent independent judges, no two of whom may be nationals of the same State, and a maximum at any one time of nine *ad litem* independent judges appointed in accordance with Article 12 *ter*, paragraph 2, of the Statute, no two of whom may be nationals of the same State.

2. Three permanent judges and a maximum at any one time of six *ad litem* judges shall be members of each Trial Chamber. Each Trial Chamber to which *ad litem* judges are assigned may be divided into sections of three judges each, composed of both permanent and *ad litem* judges. A section of a Trial Chamber shall have the same powers and responsibilities as a Trial Chamber under the Statute and shall render judgment in accordance with the same rules.

3. Seven of the permanent judges shall be members of the Appeals Chamber. The Appeals Chamber shall, for each appeal, be composed of five of its members.

ARTICLE 13

Qualifications of judges

The permanent and *ad litem* judges shall be persons of high moral character, impartiality and integrity who possess the qualifications required in their respective countries for appointment to the highest judicial offices. In the overall composition of the Chambers due account shall be taken of the experience of the judges in criminal law, international law, including international humanitarian law and human rights law.

ARTICLE 13 BIS

1. Fourteen of the permanent judges of the International Tribunal shall be elected by the General Assembly from a list submitted by the Security Council, in the following manner:

(a) The Secretary-General shall invite nominations for judges of the International Tribunal from States Members of the United Nations and non-member States maintaining permanent observer missions at United Nations Headquarters;

(b) Within sixty days of the date of the invitation of the Secretary-General, each State may nominate up to two candidates meeting the qualifications set out in paragraph 1 above, no two of whom shall be of the same nationality and neither of whom shall be of the same nationality as any judge who is a member of the Appeals Chamber and who was elected or appointed a judge of the International Criminal Tribunal for the Prosecution of Persons Responsible for Genocide and Other Serious Violations of International Humanitarian Law Committed in the Territory of Rwanda and Rwandan Citizens Responsible for Genocide and Other Such Violations Committed in the Territory of Neighbouring States, between 1 January 1994 and 31 December 1994 (hereinafter referred to as 'The International Tribunal for Rwanda') in accordance with Article 12 of the Statute of the Tribunal;

(c) The Secretary-General shall forward the nominations received to the Security Council. From the nominations received the Security Council shall establish a list of not less than twenty-eight and not more than forty-two candidates, taking due account of the adequate representation of the principal legal systems of the world;

(d) The President of the Security Council shall transmit the list of candidates to the President of the General Assembly. From that list the General Assembly shall elect the fourteen Judges of the International Tribunal. The candidates who receive an absolute majority of the votes of the States Members of the United Nations and of the non-member States maintaining permanent observer missions at United Nations Headquarters, shall be declared elected. Should two candidates of the same nationality obtain the required majority vote, the one who received the higher number of votes shall be considered elected.

2. In the event of a vacancy in the Chambers amongst the permanent judges elected or appointed in accordance with this Article, after consultation with the Presidents of the Security Council and of the General Assembly, the Secretary-General shall appoint a person meeting the qualifications of Article 13 of the Statute, for the remainder of the term of office concerned.

3. The permanent judges elected in accordance with this Article shall be elected for a term of four years. The terms and conditions of service shall be those of the judges of the International Court of Justice. They shall be eligible for re-election.

ARTICLE 13 TER

1. The *ad litem* judges of the International Tribunal shall be elected by the General Assembly from a list submitted by the Security Council, in the following manner:

(a) The Secretary-General shall invite nominations for *ad litem* judges of the International Tribunal from States members of the United Nations and non-member States maintaining permanent observer missions at United Nations Headquarters;

(b) Within sixty days of the date of the invitation of the Secretary-General, each State may nominate up to four candidates meeting the qualifications set out in Article 13 of the Statute, taking into account the importance of a fair representation of female and male candidates;

(c) The Secretary-General shall forward the nominations to the Security Council. From the nominations received the Security Council shall establish a list of no less than fifty-four candidates, taking due account of the adequate representation of the principal legal systems of the world and bearing in mind the importance of equitable geographical distribution;

(d) The President of the Security Council shall transmit the list of candidates to the President of the General Assembly. From that list the General Assembly shall elect the twenty-seven *ad litem* judges of the International Tribunal. The candidates who receive an absolute majority of the votes of the States Members of the United Nations and of the non-member States maintaining permanent observer missions at United Nations Headquarters shall be declared elected;

(e) The *ad litem* judges shall be elected for a term of four years. Thay shall not be eligible for re-election.

2. During their term, *ad litem* judges will be appointed by the Secretary-General, upon request of the President of the International Tribunal, to serve in the Trial Chambers for one or more trials, for a cumulative period of up to, but not including, three years. When requesting the appointment of any particular *ad litem* judge, the President of the International Tribunal shall bear in mind the criteria set out in Article 13 of the Statute regarding the composition of the Chambers and sections of the Trial Chambers, the considerations set out in paragraphs 1(b) and (c) above and the number of votes the *ad litem* judge received in the General Assembly.

ARTICLE 13 QUARTER

Status of *ad litem* judges

1. During the period in which they are appointed to serve the International Tribunal, *ad litem* judges shall:

(a) Benefit from the same terms and conditions of service *mutatis mutandis* as the permanent judges of the International Tribunal;

(b) Enjoy, subject to paragraph 2 below, the same powers as the permanent judges of the International Tribunal;

(c) Enjoy the privileges and immunities, exemptions and facilities of a judge of the International Tribunal.

2. During the period in which they are appointed to serve in the International Tribunal, *ad litem* judges shall not:

(a) Be eligible for election as, or to vote in the election of, the President of the Tribunal or the Presiding Judge of the Trial Chamber pursuant to Article 14 of the Statute;

(b) Have power:

    (i) To adopt rules of procedure and evidence pursuant to Article 15 of the Statute. They shall, however, be consulted before the adoption of those rules;

    (ii) To review an indictment pursuant to Article 19 of the Statute;

    (iii) To consult with the President in relation to the assignment of judges pursuant to Article 14 of the Statute or in relation to a pardon or commutation of sentence pursuant to Article 28 of the Statute;

(iv) To adjudicate in pre-trial proceedings.

ARTICLE 14

Officers and members of the Chambers

1. The permanent judges of the International Tribunal shall elect a President from amongst their number.

2. The President of the International Tribunal shall be a member of the Appeals Chamber and shall preside over its proceedings.

3. After consultation with the permanent judges of the International Tribunal, the President shall assign four of the permanent judges elected or appointed in accordance with Article 13 *bis* of the Statute to the Appeals Chamber and nine to the Trial Chambers.

4. Two of the judges elected or appointed in accordance with Article 12 of the Statute of the International Tribunal for Rwanda shall be assigned by the President of that Tribunal, in consultation with the President of the International Tribunal, to be members of the Appeals Chamber and permanent judges of the International Tribunal.

5. After consultation with the permanent judges of the International Tribunal, the President shall assign such *ad litem* judges as may from time to time be appointed to serve in the International Tribunal to the Trial Chambers.

6. A judge shall serve only in the Chamber to which he or she was assigned.

7. The permanent judges of each Trial Chamber shall elect a Presiding Judge from amongst their number, who shall oversee the work of the Trial Chamber as a whole.

ARTICLE 15

Rules of procedure and evidence

The judges of the International Tribunal shall adopt rules of procedure and evidence for the conduct of the pre-trial phase of the proceedings, trials and appeals, the admission of evidence, the protection of victims and witnesses and other appropriate matters.

ARTICLE 16

The Prosecutor

1. The Prosecutor shall be responsible for the investigation and prosecution of persons responsible for serious violations of international humanitarian law committed in the territory of the former Yugoslavia since 1 January 1991.

2. The Prosecutor shall act independently as a separate organ of the International Tribunal. He or she shall not seek or receive instructions from any Government or from any other source.

3. The Office of the Prosecutor shall be composed of a Prosecutor and such other qualified staff as may be required.

4. The Prosecutor shall be appointed by the Security Council on nomination by the Secretary-General. He or she shall be of high moral character and possess the highest level of competence and experience in the conduct of investigations and prosecutions of criminal cases. The Prosecutor shall serve for a four-year term and be eligible for reappointment. The terms and conditions of service of the Prosecutor shall be those of an Under-Secretary-General of the United Nations.

5. The staff of the Office of the Prosecutor shall be appointed by the Secretary-General on the recommendation of the Prosecutor.

ARTICLE 17

The Registry

1. The Registry shall be responsible for the administration and servicing of the International Tribunal.

2. The Registry shall consist of a Registrar and such other staff as may be required.

3. The Registrar shall be appointed by the Secretary-General after consultation with the President of the International Tribunal. He or she shall serve for a four-year term and be eligible for reappointment. The terms and conditions of service of the Registrar shall be those of an Assistant Secretary-General of the United Nations.

4. The staff of the Registry shall be appointed by the Secretary-General on the recommendation of the Registrar.

ARTICLE 18

Investigation and preparation of indictment

1. The Prosecutor shall initiate investigations *ex officio* or on the basis of information obtained from any source, particularly from Governments, United Nations organs, intergovernmental and non-governmental organizations. The Prosecutor shall assess the information received or obtained and decide whether there is sufficient basis to proceed.

2. The Prosecutor shall have the power to question suspects, victims and witnesses, to collect evidence and to conduct on-site investigations. In carrying out these tasks, the Prosecutor may, as appropriate, seek the assistance of the State authorities concerned.

3. If questioned, the suspect shall be entitled to be assisted by counsel of his own choice, including the right to have legal assistance assigned to him without payment by him in any such case if he does not have sufficient means to pay for it, as well as to necessary translation into and from a language he speaks and understands.

4. Upon a determination that a *prima facie* case exists, the Prosecutor shall prepare an indictment containing a concise statement of the facts and the crime or crimes with which the accused is charged under the Statute. The indictment shall be transmitted to a judge of the Trial Chamber.

ARTICLE 19

Review of the indictment

1. The judge of the Trial Chamber to whom the indictment has been transmitted shall review it. If satisfied that a *prima facie* case has been established by the Prosecutor, he shall confirm the indictment. If not so satisfied, the indictment shall be dismissed.

2. Upon confirmation of an indictment, the judge may, at the request of the Prosecutor, issue such orders and warrants for the arrest, detention, surrender or transfer of persons, and any other orders as may be required for the conduct of the trial.

ARTICLE 20

Commencement and conduct of trial proceedings

1. The Trial Chambers shall ensure that a trial is fair and expeditious and that proceedings are conducted in accordance with the rules of procedure and evidence, with full respect for the rights of the accused and due regard for the protection of victims and witnesses.

2. A person against whom an indictment has been confirmed shall, pursuant to an order or an arrest warrant of the International Tribunal, be taken into custody, immediately informed of the charges against him and transferred to the International Tribunal.

3. The Trial Chamber shall read the indictment, satisfy itself that the rights of the accused are respected, confirm that the accused understands the indictment, and instruct the accused to enter a plea. The Trial Chamber shall then set the date for trial.

4. The hearings shall be public unless the Trial Chamber decides to close the proceedings in accordance with its rules of procedure and evidence.

ARTICLE 21

Rights of the accused

1. All persons shall be equal before the International Tribunal.

2. In the determination of charges against him, the accused shall be entitled to a fair and public hearing, subject to Article 22 of the Statute.

3. The accused shall be presumed innocent until proved guilty according to the provisions of the present Statute.

4. In the determination of any charge against the accused pursuant to the present Statute, the accused shall be entitled to the following minimum guarantees, in full equality:

    (a) to be informed promptly and in detail in a language which he understands of the nature and cause of the charge against him;

    (b) to have adequate time and facilities for the preparation of his defence and to communicate with counsel of his own choosing;

    (c) to be tried without undue delay;

    (d) to be tried in his presence, and to defend himself in person or through legal assistance of his own choosing; to be informed, if he does not have legal assistance, of this right; and to have legal assistance assigned to him, in any case where the interests of justice so require, and without payment by him in any such case if he does not have sufficient means to pay for it;

(e) to examine, or have examined, the witnesses against him and to obtain the attendance and examination of witnesses on his behalf under the same conditions as witnesses against him;

(f) to have the free assistance of an interpreter if he cannot understand or speak the language used in the International Tribunal;

(g) not to be compelled to testify against himself or to confess guilt.

ARTICLE 22

Protection of victims and witnesses

The International Tribunal shall provide in its rules of procedure and evidence for the protection of victims and witnesses. Such protection measures shall include, but shall not be limited to, the conduct of *in camera* proceedings and the protection of the victim's identity.

ARTICLE 23

Judgment

1. The Trial Chambers shall pronounce judgments and impose sentences and penalties on persons convicted of serious violations of international humanitarian law.

2. The judgment shall be rendered by a majority of the judges of the Trial Chamber, and shall be delivered by the Trial Chamber in public. It shall be accompanied by a reasoned opinion in writing, to which separate or dissenting opinions may be appended.

ARTICLE 24

Penalties

1. The penalty imposed by the Trial Chamber shall be limited to imprisonment. In determining the terms of imprisonment, the Trial Chambers shall have recourse to the general practice regarding prison sentences in the courts of the former Yugoslavia.

2. In imposing the sentences, the Trial Chambers should take into account such factors as the gravity of the offence and the individual circumstances of the convicted person.

3. In addition to imprisonment, the Trial Chambers may order the return of any property and proceeds acquired by criminal conduct, including by means of duress, to their rightful owners.

ARTICLE 25

Appellate proceedings

1. The Appeals Chamber shall hear appeals from persons convicted by the Trial Chambers or from the Prosecutor on the following grounds:

(a) an error on a question of law invalidating the decision; or

(b) an error of fact which has occasioned a miscarriage of justice.

2. The Appeals Chamber may affirm, reverse or revise the decisions taken by the Trial Chambers.

ARTICLE 26

Review proceedings

Where a new fact has been discovered which was not known at the time of the proceedings before the Trial Chambers or the Appeals Chamber and which could have been a decisive factor in reaching the decision, the convicted person or the Prosecutor may submit to the International Tribunal an application for review of the judgment.

ARTICLE 27

Enforcement of sentences

Imprisonment shall be served in a State designated by the International Tribunal from a list of States which have indicated to the Security Council their willingness to accept convicted persons. Such imprisonment shall be in accordance with the applicable law of the State concerned, subject to the supervision of the International Tribunal.

ARTICLE 28

Pardon or commutation of sentences

If, pursuant to the applicable law of the State in which the convicted person is imprisoned, he or she is eligible for pardon or commutation of sentence, the State concerned shall notify the International Tribunal accordingly. The President of the International Tribunal, in consultation with the judges, shall decide the matter on the basis of the interests of justice and the general principles of law.

ARTICLE 29

Cooperation and judicial assistance

1. States shall cooperate with the International Tribunal in the investigation and prosecution of persons accused of committing serious violations of international humanitarian law.

2. States shall comply without undue delay with any request for assistance or an order issued by a Trial Chamber, including, but not limited to:

(a) the identification and location of persons;

(b) the taking of testimony and the production of evidence;

(c) the service of documents;

(d) the arrest or detention of persons;

(e) the surrender or the transfer of the accused to the International Tribunal.

ARTICLE 30

The status, privileges and immunities of the International Tribunal

1. The Convention on the Privileges and Immunities of the United Nations of 13 February 1946 shall apply to the International Tribunal, the judges, the Prosecutor and his staff, and the Registrar and his staff.

2. The judges, the Prosecutor and the Registrar shall enjoy the privileges and immunities, exemptions and facilities accorded to diplomatic envoys, in accordance with international law.

3. The staff of the Prosecutor and of the Registrar shall enjoy the privileges and immunities accorded to officials of the United Nations under Articles V and VII of the Convention referred to in paragraph 1 of this Article.

4. Other persons, including the accused, required at the seat of the International Tribunal shall be accorded such treatment as is necessary for the proper functioning of the International Tribunal.

ARTICLE 31

Seat of the International Tribunal

The International Tribunal shall have its seat at The Hague.

ARTICLE 32

Expenses of the International Tribunal

The expenses of the International Tribunal shall be borne by the regular budget of the United Nations in accordance with Article 17 of the Charter of the United Nations.

ARTICLE 33

Working languages

The working languages of the International Tribunal shall be English and French.

ARTICLE 34

Annual report

The President of the International Tribunal shall submit an annual report of the International Tribunal to the Security Council and to the General Assembly.

APPENDIX 2: ICTR STATUTE (EXCERPTS)

Having been established by the Security Council acting under Chapter VII of the Charter of the United Nations, the International Criminal Tribunal for the Prosecution of Persons Responsible for Genocide and Other Serious Violations of International Humanitarian Law Committed in the Territory of Rwanda and Rwandan Citizens responsible for genocide and other such violations committed in the territory of neighbouring States, between 1 January 1994 and 31 December 1994 (hereinafter referred to as 'The International Tribunal for Rwanda') shall function in accordance with the provisions of the present Statute.

ARTICLE 1

Competence of the International Tribunal for Rwanda

The International Tribunal for Rwanda shall have the power to prosecute persons responsible for serious violations of international humanitarian law committed in the territory of Rwanda and Rwandan citizens responsible for such violations committed in the territory of neighbouring States between 1 January 1994 and 31 December 1994, in accordance with the provisions of the present Statute.

ARTICLE 2

Genocide

1. The International Tribunal for Rwanda shall have the power to prosecute persons committing genocide as defined in paragraph 2 of this Article or of committing any of the other acts enumerated in paragraph 3 of this Article.

2. Genocide means any of the following acts committed with intent to destroy, in whole or in part, a national, ethnical, racial or religious group, as such:

(a) Killing members of the group;

(b) Causing serious bodily or mental harm to members of the group;

(c) Deliberately inflicting on the group conditions of life calculated to bring about its physical destruction in whole or in part;

(d) Imposing measures intended to prevent births within the group;

(e) Forcibly transferring children of the group to another group.

3. The following acts shall be punishable:

(a) Genocide;

(b) Conspiracy to commit genocide;

(c) Direct and public incitement to commit genocide;

(d) Attempt to commit genocide;

(e) Complicity in genocide.

ARTICLE 3

Crimes against Humanity

The International Tribunal for Rwanda shall have the power to prosecute persons responsible for the following crimes when committed as part of a widespread or systematic attack against any civilian population on national, political, ethnic, racial or religious grounds:

(a) Murder;

(b) Extermination;

(c) Enslavement;

(d) Deportation;

(e) Imprisonment;

(f) Torture;

(g) Rape;

(h) Persecutions on political, racial and religious grounds;

(i) Other inhumane acts.

ARTICLE 4

Violations of Article 3 common to the Geneva Conventions and of Additional Protocol II

The International Tribunal for Rwanda shall have the power to prosecute persons committing or ordering to be committed serious violations of Article 3 common to the Geneva Conventions of 12 August 1949 for the Protection of War Victims, and of Additional Protocol II thereto of 8 June 1977. These violations shall include, but shall not be limited to:

(a) Violence to life, health and physical or mental well-being of persons, in particular murder as well as cruel treatment such as torture, mutilation or any form of corporal punishment;

(b) Collective punishments;

(c) Taking of hostages;

(d) Acts of terrorism;

(e) Outrages upon personal dignity, in particular humiliating and degrading treatment, rape, enforced prostitution and any form of indecent assault;

(f) Pillage;

(g) The passing of sentences and the carrying out of executions without previous judgment pronounced by a regularly constituted court, affording all the judicial guarantees which are recognized as indispensable by civilized peoples;

(h) Threats to commit any of the foregoing acts.

ARTICLE 5

Personal jurisdiction

The International Tribunal for Rwanda shall have jurisdiction over natural persons pursuant to the provisions of the present Statute.

ARTICLE 6

Individual Criminal Responsibility

1. A person who planned, instigated, ordered, committed or otherwise aided and abetted in the planning, preparation or execution of a crime referred to in Articles 2 to 4 of the present Statute, shall be individually responsible for the crime.

2. The official position of any accused person, whether as Head of State or Government or as a responsible Government official, shall not relieve such person of criminal responsibility nor mitigate punishment.

3. The fact that any of the acts referred to in Articles 2 to 4 of the present Statute was committed by a subordinate does not relieve his or her superior of criminal responsibility if he or she knew or had reason to know that the subordinate was about to commit such acts or had done so and the superior failed to take the necessary and reasonable measures to prevent such acts or to punish the perpetrators thereof.

4. The fact that an accused person acted pursuant to an order of a Government or of a superior shall not relieve him or her of criminal responsibility, but may be considered in mitigation of punishment if the International Tribunal for Rwanda determines that justice so requires.

ARTICLE 7

Territorial and temporal jurisdiction

The territorial jurisdiction of the International Tribunal for Rwanda shall extend to the territory of Rwanda including its land surface and airspace as well as to the territory of neighbouring States in respect of serious violations of international humanitarian law committed by Rwandan citizens. The temporal jurisdiction of the International Tribunal for Rwanda shall extend to a period beginning on 1 January 1994 and ending on 31 December 1994.

ARTICLE 8

Concurrent jurisdiction

1. The International Tribunal for Rwanda and national courts shall have concurrent jurisdiction to prosecute persons for serious violations of international humanitarian law committed in the territory of Rwanda and Rwandan citizens for such violations committed

in the territory of the neighbouring States, between 1 January 1994 and 31 December 1994.

2. The International Tribunal for Rwanda shall have the primacy over the national courts of all States. At any stage of the procedure, the International Tribunal for Rwanda may formally request national courts to defer to its competence in accordance with the present Statute and the Rules of Procedure and Evidence of the International Tribunal for Rwanda.

ARTICLE 9

Non bis in idem

1. No person shall be tried before a national court for acts constituting serious violations of international humanitarian law under the present Statute, for which he or she has already been tried by the International Tribunal for Rwanda.

2. A person who has been tried before a national court for acts constituting serious violations of international humanitarian law may be subsequently tried by the International Tribunal for Rwanda only if:

   (a) The act for which he or she was tried was characterized as an ordinary crime; or

   (b) The national court proceedings were not impartial or independent, were designed to shield the accused from international criminal responsibility, or the case was not diligently prosecuted.

3. In considering the penalty to be imposed on a person convicted of a crime under the present Statute, the International Tribunal for Rwanda shall take into account the extent to which any penalty imposed by a national court on the same person for the same act has already been served.

ARTICLE 10

Organization of the International Tribunal for Rwanda

The International Tribunal for Rwanda shall consist of the following organs:

   (a) The Chambers, comprising three Trial Chambers and an Appeals Chamber;

   (b) The Prosecutor;

   (c) A Registry.

ARTICLE 11

Composition of the Chambers

The Chambers shall be composed of sixteen independent judges, no two of whom may be nationals of the same State, who shall serve as follows:

   (a) Three judges shall serve in each of the Trial Chambers;

(b) Seven judges shall be members of the Appeals Chamber. The Appeals Chamber shall, for each appeal, be composed of five of its members.

ARTICLE 12

Qualification and election of judges

1. The judges shall be persons of high moral character, impartiality and integrity who possess the qualifications required in their respective countries for appointment to the highest judicial offices. In the overall composition of the Chambers due account shall be taken of the experience of the judges in criminal law, international law, including international humanitarian law and human rights law.

2. Eleven of the judges of the International Tribunal for Rwanda shall be elected by the General Assembly from a list submitted by the Security Council, in the following manner:

(a) The Secretary-General shall invite nominations for judges of the Trial Chambers from States Members of the United Nations and non-member States maintaining permanent observer missions at United Nations Headquarters;

(b) Within sixty days of the date of the invitation of the Secretary-General, each State may nominate up to two candidates meeting the qualifications set out in paragraph 1 above, no two of whom shall be of the same nationality and neither of whom shall be of the same nationality as any judge who is a member of the Appeals Chamber and who was elected or appointed a permanent judge of the International Tribunal for the Prosecution of Persons Responsible for Serious Violations of International Humanitarian Law Committed in the Territory of the former Yugoslavia since 1991 (hereinafter referred to as 'the International Tribunal for the Former Yugoslavia') in accordance with Article 13 *bis* of the Statute of that Tribunal;

(c) The Secretary-General shall forward the nominations received to the Security Council. From the nominations received the Security Council shall establish a list of not less than twenty-two and not more than thirty-three candidates, taking due account of adequate representation on the International Tribunal for Rwanda of the principal legal systems of the world;

(d) The President of the Security Council shall transmit the list of candidates to the President of the General Assembly. From that list the General Assembly shall elect eleven judges of the International Tribunal for Rwanda. The candidates who receive an absolute majority of the votes of the States Members of the United Nations and of the non-member States maintaining permanent observer missions at United Nations Headquarters, shall be declared elected. Should two candidates of the same nationality obtain the required majority vote, the one who received the higher number of votes shall be considered elected.

3. In the event of a vacancy in the Chambers amongst the judges elected or appointed in accordance with this Article, after consultation with the Presidents of the Security Council and of the General Assembly, the Secretary-General shall appoint a person meeting the qualifications of paragraph 1 above, for the remainder of the term of office concerned.

4. The judges elected in accordance with this Article shall be elected for a term of four

years. The terms and conditions of service shall be those of the judges of the International Tribunal for the former Yugoslavia. They shall be eligible for re-election.

ARTICLE 13

Officers and members of the Chambers

1. The judges of the International Tribunal for Rwanda shall elect a President.

2. The President of the International Tribunal for Rwanda shall be a member of one of its own Trial Chambers.

3. After consultation with the judges of the International Tribunal for Rwanda, the President shall assign two of the judges elected or appointed in accordance with Article 12 of the present Statute to be members of the Appeals Chamber of the International Tribunal for the Former Yugoslavia and eight to the Trial Chambers of the International Tribunal for Rwanda. A judge shall serve only in the Chamber to which he or she was assigned.

4. The members of the Appeals Chamber of the International Tribunal for the Former Yugoslavia shall also serve as the members of the Appeals Chamber of the International Tribunal for Rwanda.

5. The judges of each Trial Chamber shall elect a Presiding Judge, who shall conduct all of the proceedings of that Trial Chamber as a whole.

ARTICLE 14

Rules of procedure and evidence

The judges of the International Tribunal for Rwanda shall adopt, for the purpose of proceedings before the International Tribunal for Rwanda, the rules of procedure and evidence for the conduct of the pre-trial phase of the proceedings, trials and appeals, the admission of evidence, the protection of victims and witnesses and other appropriate matters of the International Tribunal for the former Yugoslavia with such changes as they deem necessary.

ARTICLE 15

The Prosecutor

1. The Prosecutor shall be responsible for the investigation and prosecution of persons responsible for serious violations of international humanitarian law committed in the territory of Rwanda and Rwandan citizens responsible for such violations committed in the territory of neighbouring States, between 1 January 1994 and 31 December 1994.

2. The Prosecutor shall act independently as a separate organ of the International Tribunal for Rwanda. He or she shall not seek or receive instructions from any Government or from any other source.

3. The Prosecutor of the International Tribunal for the Former Yugoslavia shall also serve as the Prosecutor of the International Tribunal for Rwanda. He or she shall have additional staff, including an additional Deputy Prosecutor, to assist with prosecutions before the

International Tribunal for Rwanda. Such staff shall be appointed by the Secretary-General on the recommendation of the Prosecutor.

[*Author:* The rest of the provisions of the ICTR Statute are identical to those in the ICTY Statute, with the words 'the former Yugoslavia' in the relevant provisions of the ICTY Statute being replaced by 'Rwanda' in the ICTR Statute. However, Article 31 of the ICTY Statute is not replicated in the ICTR Statute.]

APPENDIX 3: ICC STATUTE*

[* as corrected by the *procés-verbaux* of 10 November 1998 and 12 July 1999]

PREAMBLE

The States Parties to this Statute,

Conscious that all peoples are united by common bonds, their cultures pieced together in a shared heritage, and concerned that this delicate mosaic may be shattered at any time,

Mindful that during this century millions of children, women and men have been victims of unimaginable atrocities that deeply shock the conscience of humanity,

Recognizing that such grave crimes threaten the peace, security and well-being of the world,

Affirming that the most serious crimes of concern to the international community as a whole must not go unpunished and that their effective prosecution must be ensured by taking measures at the national level and by enhancing international cooperation,

Determined to put an end to impunity for the perpetrators of these crimes and thus to contribute to the prevention of such crimes,

Recalling that it is the duty of every State to exercise its criminal jurisdiction over those responsible for international crimes,

Reaffirming the Purposes and Principles of the Charter of the United Nations, and in particular that all States shall refrain from the threat or use of force against the territorial integrity or political independence of any State, or in any other manner inconsistent with the Purposes of the United Nations,

Emphasizing in this connection that nothing in this Statute shall be taken as authorizing any State Party to intervene in an armed conflict or in the internal affairs of any State,

Determined to these ends and for the sake of present and future generations, to establish an independent permanent International Criminal Court in relationship with the United Nations system, with jurisdiction over the most serious crimes of concern to the international community as a whole,

Emphasizing that the International Criminal Court established under this Statute shall be complementary to national criminal jurisdictions,

Resolved to guarantee lasting respect for and the enforcement of international justice,

Have agreed as follows:

PART 1: ESTABLISHMENT OF THE COURT

ARTICLE 1

The Court

An International Criminal Court ('the Court') is hereby established. It shall be a permanent institution and shall have the power to exercise its jurisdiction over persons for the most

serious crimes of international concern, as referred to in this Statute, and shall be complementary to national criminal jurisdictions. The jurisdiction and functioning of the Court
shall be governed by the provisions of this Statute.

ARTICLE 2

Relationship of the Court with the United Nations

The Court shall be brought into relationship with the United Nations through an agreement
to be approved by the Assembly of States Parties to this Statute and thereafter concluded by
the President of the Court on its behalf.

ARTICLE 3

Seat of the Court

1. The seat of the Court shall be established at The Hague in the Netherlands ('the host
State').

2. The Court shall enter into a headquarters agreement with the host State, to be
approved by the Assembly of States Parties and thereafter concluded by the President of the
Court on its behalf.

3. The Court may sit elsewhere, whenever it considers it desirable, as provided in this
Statute.

ARTICLE 4

Legal status and powers of the Court

1. The Court shall have international legal personality. It shall also have such legal capacity
as may be necessary for the exercise of its functions and the fulfilment of its purposes.

2. The Court may exercise its functions and powers, as provided in this Statute, on the
territory of any State Party and, by special agreement, on the territory of any other State.

PART 2: JURISDICTION, ADMISSIBILITY AND APPLICABLE LAW

ARTICLE 5

Crimes within the jurisdiction of the Court

1. The jurisdiction of the Court shall be limited to the most serious crimes of concern to the
international community as a whole. The Court has jurisdiction in accordance with this
Statute with respect to the following crimes:

  (a) The crime of genocide;

(b) Crimes against humanity;

(c) War crimes;

(d) The crime of aggression.

2. The Court shall exercise jurisdiction over the crime of aggression once a provision is adopted in accordance with Articles 121 and 123 defining the crime and setting out the conditions under which the Court shall exercise jurisdiction with respect to this crime. Such a provision shall be consistent with the relevant provisions of the Charter of the United Nations.

ARTICLE 6

Genocide

For the purpose of this Statute, 'genocide' means any of the following acts committed with intent to destroy, in whole or in part, a national, ethnical, racial or religious group, as such:

(a) Killing members of the group;

(b) Causing serious bodily or mental harm to members of the group;

(c) Deliberately inflicting on the group conditions of life calculated to bring about its physical destruction in whole or in part;

(d) Imposing measures intended to prevent births within the group;

(e) Forcibly transferring children of the group to another group.

ARTICLE 7

Crimes against humanity

1. For the purpose of this Statute, 'crime against humanity' means any of the following acts when committed as part of a widespread or systematic attack directed against any civilian population, with knowledge of the attack:

(a) Murder;

(b) Extermination;

(c) Enslavement;

(d) Deportation or forcible transfer of population;

(e) Imprisonment or other severe deprivation of physical liberty in violation of funda-mental rules of international law;

(f) Torture;

(g) Rape, sexual slavery, enforced prostitution, forced pregnancy, enforced sterilization, or any other form of sexual violence of comparable gravity;

(h) Persecution against any identifiable group or collectivity on political, racial, national, ethnic, cultural, religious, gender as defined in paragraph 3, or other grounds that are universally recognized as impermissible under international law, in connection with any act referred to in this paragraph or any crime within the jurisdiction of the Court;

(i) Enforced disappearance of persons;

(j) The crime of apartheid;

(k) Other inhumane acts of a similar character intentionally causing great suffering, or serious injury to body or to mental or physical health.

2. For the purpose of paragraph 1:

(a) 'Attack directed against any civilian population' means a course of conduct involving the multiple commission of acts referred to in paragraph 1 against any civilian population, pursuant to or in furtherance of a State or organizational policy to commit such attack;

(b) 'Extermination' includes the intentional infliction of conditions of life, *inter alia*, the deprivation of access to food and medicine, calculated to bring about the destruction of part of a population;

(c) 'Enslavement' means the exercise of any or all of the powers attaching to the right of ownership over a person and includes the exercise of such power in the course of trafficking in persons, in particular women and children;

(d) 'Deportation or forcible transfer of population' means forced displacement of the persons concerned by expulsion or other coercive acts from the area in which they are lawfully present, without grounds permitted under international law;

(e) 'Torture' means the intentional infliction of severe pain or suffering, whether physical or mental, upon a person in the custody or under the control of the accused; except that torture shall not include pain or suffering arising only from, inherent in or incidental to, lawful sanctions;

(f) 'Forced pregnancy' means the unlawful confinement of a woman forcibly made pregnant, with the intent of affecting the ethnic composition of any population or carrying out other grave violations of international law. This definition shall not in any way be interpreted as affecting national laws relating to pregnancy;

(g) 'Persecution' means the intentional and severe deprivation of fundamental rights contrary to international law by reason of the identity of the group or collectivity;

(h) 'The crime of apartheid' means inhumane acts of a character similar to those referred to in paragraph 1, committed in the context of an institutionalized regime of systematic oppression and domination by one racial group over any other racial group or groups and committed with the intention of maintaining that regime;

(i) 'Enforced disappearance of persons' means the arrest, detention or abduction of persons by, or with the authorization, support or acquiescence of, a State or a political organization, followed by a refusal to acknowledge that deprivation of freedom or to give information on the fate or whereabouts of those persons, with the intention of removing them from the protection of the law for a prolonged period of time.

3. For the purpose of this Statute, it is understood that the term 'gender' refers to the two

sexes, male and female, within the context of society. The term 'gender' does not indicate any meaning different from the above.

ARTICLE 8

War crimes

1. The Court shall have jurisdiction in respect of war crimes in particular when committed as part of a plan or policy or as part of a large-scale commission of such crimes.

2. For the purpose of this Statute, 'war crimes' means:

(a) Grave breaches of the Geneva Conventions of 12 August 1949, namely, any of the following acts against persons or property protected under the provisions of the relevant Geneva Convention:

    (i)   Wilful killing;

    (ii)   Torture or inhuman treatment, including biological experiments;

    (iii)   Wilfully causing great suffering, or serious injury to body or health;

    (iv)   Extensive destruction and appropriation of property, not justified by military necessity and carried out unlawfully and wantonly;

    (v)   Compelling a prisoner of war or other protected person to serve in the forces of a hostile Power;

    (vi)   Wilfully depriving a prisoner of war or other protected person of the rights of fair and regular trial;

    (vii)   Unlawful deportation or transfer or unlawful confinement;

    (viii) Taking of hostages.

(b) Other serious violations of the laws and customs applicable in international armed conflict, within the established framework of international law, namely, any of the following acts:

    (i)   Intentionally directing attacks against the civilian population as such or against individual civilians not taking direct part in hostilities;

    (ii)   Intentionally directing attacks against civilian objects, that is, objects which are not military objectives;

    (iii)   Intentionally directing attacks against personnel, installations, material, units or vehicles involved in a humanitarian assistance or peacekeeping mission in accordance with the Charter of the United Nations, as long as they are entitled to the protection given to civilians or civilian objects under the international law of armed conflict;

    (iv)   Intentionally launching an attack in the knowledge that such attack will cause incidental loss of life or injury to civilians or damage to civilian objects or widespread, long-term and severe damage to the natural environment which would be clearly excessive in relation to the concrete and direct overall military advantage anticipated;

    (v)   Attacking or bombarding, by whatever means, towns, villages, dwellings or buildings which are undefended and which are not military objectives;

(vi)   Killing or wounding a combatant who, having laid down his arms or having no longer means of defence, has surrendered at discretion;

(vii)   Making improper use of a flag of truce, of the flag or of the military insignia and uniform of the enemy or of the United Nations, as well as of the distinctive emblems of the Geneva Conventions, resulting in death or serious personal injury;

(viii)   The transfer, directly or indirectly, by the Occupying Power of parts of its own civilian population into the territory it occupies, or the deportation or transfer of all or parts of the population of the occupied territory within or outside this territory;

(ix)   Intentionally directing attacks against buildings dedicated to religion, education, art, science or charitable purposes, historic monuments, hospitals and places where the sick and wounded are collected, provided they are not military objectives;

(x)   Subjecting persons who are in the power of an adverse party to physical mutilation or to medical or scientific experiments of any kind which are neither justified by the medical, dental or hospital treatment of the person concerned nor carried out in his or her interest, and which cause death to or seriously endanger the health of such person or persons;

(xi)   Killing or wounding treacherously individuals belonging to the hostile nation or army;

(xii)   Declaring that no quarter will be given;

(xiii)   Destroying or seizing the enemy's property unless such destruction or seizure be imperatively demanded by the necessities of war;

(xiv)   Declaring abolished, suspended or inadmissible in a court of law the rights and actions of the nationals of the hostile party;

(xv)   Compelling the nationals of the hostile party to take part in the operations of war directed against their own country, even if they were in the belligerent's service before the commencement of the war;

(xvi)   Pillaging a town or place, even when taken by assault;

(xvii)   Employing poison or poisoned weapons;

(xviii) Employing asphyxiating, poisonous or other gases, and all analogous liquids, materials or devices;

(xix)   Employing bullets which expand or flatten easily in the human body, such as bullets with a hard envelope which does not entirely cover the core or is pierced with incisions;

(xx)   Employing weapons, projectiles and material and methods of warfare which are of a nature to cause superfluous injury or unnecessary suffering or which are inherently indiscriminate in violation of the international law of armed conflict, provided that such weapons, projectiles and material and methods of warfare are the subject of a comprehensive prohibition and are included in an annex to this Statute, by an amendment in accordance with the relevant provisions set forth in Articles 121 and 123;

(xxi) Committing outrages upon personal dignity, in particular humiliating and degrading treatment;

(xxii) Committing rape, sexual slavery, enforced prostitution, forced pregnancy, as defined in Article 7, paragraph 2(f), enforced sterilization, or any other form of sexual violence also constituting a grave breach of the Geneva Conventions;

(xxiii) Utilizing the presence of a civilian or other protected person to render certain points, areas or military forces immune from military operations;

(xxiv) Intentionally directing attacks against buildings, material, medical units and transport, and personnel using the distinctive emblems of the Geneva Conventions in conformity with international law;

(xxv) Intentionally using starvation of civilians as a method of warfare by depriving them of objects indispensable to their survival, including wilfully impeding relief supplies as provided for under the Geneva Conventions;

(xxvi) Conscripting or enlisting children under the age of fifteen years into the national armed forces or using them to participate actively in hostilities.

(c) In the case of an armed conflict not of an international character, serious violations of Article 3 common to the four Geneva Conventions of 12 August 1949, namely, any of the following acts committed against persons taking no active part in the hostilities, including members of armed forces who have laid down their arms and those placed *hors de combat* by sickness, wounds, detention or any other cause:

(i) Violence to life and person, in particular murder of all kinds, mutilation, cruel treatment and torture;

(ii) Committing outrages upon personal dignity, in particular humiliating and degrading treatment;

(iii) Taking of hostages;

(iv) The passing of sentences and the carrying out of executions without previous judgment pronounced by a regularly constituted court, affording all judicial guarantees which are generally recognized as indispensable.

(d) Paragraph 2(c) applies to armed conflicts not of an international character and thus does not apply to situations of internal disturbances and tensions, such as riots, isolated and sporadic acts of violence or other acts of a similar nature.

(e) Other serious violations of the laws and customs applicable in armed conflicts not of an international character, within the established framework of international law, namely, any of the following acts:

(i) Intentionally directing attacks against the civilian population as such or against individual civilians not taking direct part in hostilities;

(ii) Intentionally directing attacks against buildings, material, medical units and transport, and personnel using the distinctive emblems of the Geneva Conventions in conformity with international law;

(iii) Intentionally directing attacks against personnel, installations, material, units or vehicles involved in a humanitarian assistance or peacekeeping mission in accordance with the Charter of the United Nations, as long as they are entitled to the protection given to civilians or civilian objects under the international law of armed conflict;

(iv)   Intentionally directing attacks against buildings dedicated to religion, education, art, science or charitable purposes, historic monuments, hospitals and places where the sick and wounded are collected, provided they are not military objectives;

(v)   Pillaging a town or place, even when taken by assault;

(vi)   Committing rape, sexual slavery, enforced prostitution, forced pregnancy, as defined in Article 7, paragraph 2(f), enforced sterilization, and any other form of sexual violence also constituting a serious violation of Article 3 common to the four Geneva Conventions;

(vii)   Conscripting or enlisting children under the age of fifteen years into armed forces or groups or using them to participate actively in hostilities;

(viii)   Ordering the displacement of the civilian population for reasons related to the conflict, unless the security of the civilians involved or imperative military reasons so demand;

(ix)   Killing or wounding treacherously a combatant adversary;

(x)   Declaring that no quarter will be given;

(xi)   Subjecting persons who are in the power of another party to the conflict to physical mutilation or to medical or scientific experiments of any kind which are neither justified by the medical, dental or hospital treatment of the person concerned nor carried out in his or her interest, and which cause death to or seriously endanger the health of such person or persons;

(xii)   Destroying or seizing the property of an adversary unless such destruction or seizure be imperatively demanded by the necessities of the conflict;

(f)   Paragraph 2(e) applies to armed conflicts not of an international character and thus does not apply to situations of internal disturbances and tensions, such as riots, isolated and sporadic acts of violence or other acts of a similar nature. It applies to armed conflicts that take place in the territory of a State when there is protracted armed conflict between governmental authorities and organized armed groups or between such groups.

3. Nothing in paragraph 2(c) and (e) shall affect the responsibility of a Government to maintain or re-establish law and order in the State or to defend the unity and territorial integrity of the State, by all legitimate means.

ARTICLE 9

Elements of Crimes

1. Elements of Crimes shall assist the Court in the interpretation and application of Articles 6, 7 and 8. They shall be adopted by a two-thirds majority of the members of the Assembly of States Parties.

2. Amendments to the Elements of Crimes may be proposed by:

(a) Any State Party;

(b) The judges acting by an absolute majority;

(c) The Prosecutor.

Such amendments shall be adopted by a two-thirds majority of the members of the Assembly of States Parties.

3. The Elements of Crimes and amendments thereto shall be consistent with this Statute.

ARTICLE 10

Nothing in this Part shall be interpreted as limiting or prejudicing in any way existing or developing rules of international law for purposes other than this Statute.

ARTICLE 11

Jurisdiction *ratione temporis*

1. The Court has jurisdiction only with respect to crimes committed after the entry into force of this Statute.

2. If a State becomes a Party to this Statute after its entry into force, the Court may exercise its jurisdiction only with respect to crimes committed after the entry into force of this Statute for that State, unless that State has made a declaration under Article 12, paragraph 3.

ARTICLE 12

Preconditions to the exercise of jurisdiction

1. A State which becomes a Party to this Statute thereby accepts the jurisdiction of the Court with respect to the crimes referred to in Article 5.

2. In the case of Article 13, paragraph (a) or (c), the Court may exercise its jurisdiction if one or more of the following States are Parties to this Statute or have accepted the jurisdiction of the Court in accordance with paragraph 3:

(a) The State on the territory of which the conduct in question occurred or, if the crime was committed on board a vessel or aircraft, the State of registration of that vessel or aircraft;

(b) The State of which the person accused of the crime is a national.

3. If the acceptance of a State which is not a Party to this Statute is required under paragraph 2, that State may, by declaration lodged with the Registrar, accept the exercise of jurisdiction by the Court with respect to the crime in question. The accepting State shall cooperate with the Court without any delay or exception in accordance with Part 9.

ARTICLE 13

Exercise of jurisdiction

The Court may exercise its jurisdiction with respect to a crime referred to in Article 5 in accordance with the provisions of this Statute if:

(a) A situation in which one or more of such crimes appears to have been committed is referred to the Prosecutor by a State Party in accordance with Article 14;

(b) A situation in which one or more of such crimes appears to have been committed is referred to the Prosecutor by the Security Council acting under Chapter VII of the Charter of the United Nations; or

(c) The Prosecutor has initiated an investigation in respect of such a crime in accordance with Article 15.

ARTICLE 14

Referral of a situation by a State Party

1. A State Party may refer to the Prosecutor a situation in which one or more crimes within the jurisdiction of the Court appear to have been committed requesting the Prosecutor to investigate the situation for the purpose of determining whether one or more specific persons should be charged with the commission of such crimes.

2. As far as possible, a referral shall specify the relevant circumstances and be accompanied by such supporting documentation as is available to the State referring the situation.

ARTICLE 15

Prosecutor

1. The Prosecutor may initiate investigations *proprio motu* on the basis of information on crimes within the jurisdiction of the Court.

2. The Prosecutor shall analyse the seriousness of the information received. For this purpose, he or she may seek additional information from States, organs of the United Nations, intergovernmental or non-governmental organizations, or other reliable sources that he or she deems appropriate, and may receive written or oral testimony at the seat of the Court.

3. If the Prosecutor concludes that there is a reasonable basis to proceed with an investigation, he or she shall submit to the Pre-Trial Chamber a request for authorization of an investigation, together with any supporting material collected. Victims may make representations to the Pre-Trial Chamber, in accordance with the Rules of Procedure and Evidence.

4. If the Pre-Trial Chamber, upon examination of the request and the supporting material, considers that there is a reasonable basis to proceed with an investigation, and that the case appears to fall within the jurisdiction of the Court, it shall authorize the commencement of the investigation, without prejudice to subsequent determinations by the Court with regard to the jurisdiction and admissibility of a case.

5. The refusal of the Pre-Trial Chamber to authorize the investigation shall not preclude the presentation of a subsequent request by the Prosecutor based on new facts or evidence regarding the same situation.

6. If, after the preliminary examination referred to in paragraphs 1 and 2, the Prosecutor concludes that the information provided does not constitute a reasonable basis for an investigation, he or she shall inform those who provided the information. This shall not preclude the Prosecutor from considering further information submitted to him or her regarding the same situation in the light of new facts or evidence.

ARTICLE 16

Deferral of investigation or prosecution

No investigation or prosecution may be commenced or proceeded with under this Statute for a period of 12 months after the Security Council, in a resolution adopted under Chapter VII of the Charter of the United Nations, has requested the Court to that effect; that request may be renewed by the Council under the same conditions.

ARTICLE 17

Issues of admissibility

1. Having regard to paragraph 10 of the Preamble and Article 1, the Court shall determine that a case is inadmissible where:

(a) The case is being investigated or prosecuted by a State which has jurisdiction over it, unless the State is unwilling or unable genuinely to carry out the investigation or prosecution;

(b) The case has been investigated by a State which has jurisdiction over it and the State has decided not to prosecute the person concerned, unless the decision resulted from the unwillingness or inability of the State genuinely to prosecute;

(c) The person concerned has already been tried for conduct which is the subject of the complaint, and a trial by the Court is not permitted under Article 20, paragraph 3;

(d) The case is not of sufficient gravity to justify further action by the Court.

2. In order to determine unwillingness in a particular case, the Court shall consider, having regard to the principles of due process recognized by international law, whether one or more of the following exist, as applicable:

(a) The proceedings were or are being undertaken or the national decision was made for the purpose of shielding the person concerned from criminal responsibility for crimes within the jurisdiction of the Court referred to in Article 5;

(b) There has been an unjustified delay in the proceedings which in the circumstances is inconsistent with an intent to bring the person concerned to justice;

(c) The proceedings were not or are not being conducted independently or impartially, and they were or are being conducted in a manner which, in the circumstances, is inconsistent with an intent to bring the person concerned to justice.

3. In order to determine inability in a particular case, the Court shall consider whether, due to a total or substantial collapse or unavailability of its national judicial system, the State is unable to obtain the accused or the necessary evidence and testimony or otherwise unable to carry out its proceedings.

ARTICLE 18

Preliminary rulings regarding admissibility

1. When a situation has been referred to the Court pursuant to Article 13(a) and the Prosecutor has determined that there would be a reasonable basis to commence an investigation, or the Prosecutor initiates an investigation pursuant to Articles 13(c) and 15, the Prosecutor shall notify all States Parties and those States which, taking into account the information available, would normally exercise jurisdiction over the crimes concerned. The Prosecutor may notify such States on a confidential basis and, where the Prosecutor believes it necessary to protect persons, prevent destruction of evidence or prevent the absconding of persons, may limit the scope of the information provided to States.

2. Within one month of receipt of that notification, a State may inform the Court that it is investigating or has investigated its nationals or others within its jurisdiction with respect to criminal acts which may constitute crimes referred to in Article 5 and which relate to the information provided in the notification to States. At the request of that State, the Prosecutor shall defer to the State's investigation of those persons unless the Pre-Trial Chamber, on the application of the Prosecutor, decides to authorize the investigation.

3. The Prosecutor's deferral to a State's investigation shall be open to review by the Prosecutor six months after the date of deferral or at any time when there has been a significant change of circumstances based on the State's unwillingness or inability genuinely to carry out the investigation.

4. The State concerned or the Prosecutor may appeal to the Appeals Chamber against a ruling of the Pre-Trial Chamber, in accordance with Article 82. The appeal may be heard on an expedited basis.

5. When the Prosecutor has deferred an investigation in accordance with paragraph 2, the Prosecutor may request that the State concerned periodically inform the Prosecutor of the progress of its investigations and any subsequent prosecutions. States Parties shall respond to such requests without undue delay.

6. Pending a ruling by the Pre-Trial Chamber, or at any time when the Prosecutor has deferred an investigation under this article, the Prosecutor may, on an exceptional basis, seek authority from the Pre-Trial Chamber to pursue necessary investigative steps for the purpose of preserving evidence where there is a unique opportunity to obtain important evidence or there is a significant risk that such evidence may not be subsequently available.

7. A State which has challenged a ruling of the Pre-Trial Chamber under this article may challenge the admissibility of a case under Article 19 on the grounds of additional significant facts or significant change of circumstances.

ARTICLE 19

Challenges to the jurisdiction of the Court or the admissibility of a case

1. The Court shall satisfy itself that it has jurisdiction in any case brought before it. The Court may, on its own motion, determine the admissibility of a case in accordance with Article 17.

2. Challenges to the admissibility of a case on the grounds referred to in Article 17 or challenges to the jurisdiction of the Court may be made by:

  (a) An accused or a person for whom a warrant of arrest or a summons to appear has been issued under Article 58;

  (b) A State which has jurisdiction over a case, on the ground that it is investigating or prosecuting the case or has investigated or prosecuted; or

  (c) A State from which acceptance of jurisdiction is required under Article 12.

3. The Prosecutor may seek a ruling from the Court regarding a question of jurisdiction or admissibility. In proceedings with respect to jurisdiction or admissibility, those who have referred the situation under Article 13, as well as victims, may also submit observations to the Court.

4. The admissibility of a case or the jurisdiction of the Court may be challenged only once by any person or State referred to in paragraph 2. The challenge shall take place prior to or at the commencement of the trial. In exceptional circumstances, the Court may grant leave for a challenge to be brought more than once or at a time later than the commencement of the trial. Challenges to the admissibility of a case, at the commencement of a trial, or subsequently with the leave of the Court, may be based only on Article 17, paragraph 1(c).

5. A State referred to in paragraph 2(b) and (c) shall make a challenge at the earliest opportunity.

6. Prior to the confirmation of the charges, challenges to the admissibility of a case or challenges to the jurisdiction of the Court shall be referred to the Pre-Trial Chamber. After confirmation of the charges, they shall be referred to the Trial Chamber. Decisions with respect to jurisdiction or admissibility may be appealed to the Appeals Chamber in accordance with Article 82.

7. If a challenge is made by a State referred to in paragraph 2(b) or (c), the Prosecutor shall suspend the investigation until such time as the Court makes a determination in accordance with Article 17.

8. Pending a ruling by the Court, the Prosecutor may seek authority from the Court:

  (a) To pursue necessary investigative steps of the kind referred to in Article 18, paragraph 6;

  (b) To take a statement or testimony from a witness or complete the collection and examination of evidence which had begun prior to the making of the challenge; and

  (c) In cooperation with the relevant States, to prevent the absconding of persons in respect of whom the Prosecutor has already requested a warrant of arrest under Article 58.

9. The making of a challenge shall not affect the validity of any act performed by the

Prosecutor or any order or warrant issued by the Court prior to the making of the challenge.

10. If the Court has decided that a case is inadmissible under Article 17, the Prosecutor may submit a request for a review of the decision when he or she is fully satisfied that new facts have arisen which negate the basis on which the case had previously been found inadmissible under Article 17.

11. If the Prosecutor, having regard to the matters referred to in Article 17, defers an investigation, the Prosecutor may request that the relevant State make available to the Prosecutor information on the proceedings. That information shall, at the request of the State concerned, be confidential. If the Prosecutor thereafter decides to proceed with an investigation, he or she shall notify the State to which deferral of the proceedings has taken place.

ARTICLE 20

Ne bis in idem

1. Except as provided in this Statute, no person shall be tried before the Court with respect to conduct which formed the basis of crimes for which the person has been convicted or acquitted by the Court.

2. No person shall be tried by another court for a crime referred to in Article 5 for which that person has already been convicted or acquitted by the Court.

3. No person who has been tried by another court for conduct also proscribed under Article 6, 7 or 8 shall be tried by the Court with respect to the same conduct unless the proceedings in the other court:

(a) Were for the purpose of shielding the person concerned from criminal responsibility for crimes within the jurisdiction of the Court; or

(b) Otherwise were not conducted independently or impartially in accordance with the norms of due process recognized by international law and were conducted in a manner which, in the circumstances, was inconsistent with an intent to bring the person concerned to justice.

ARTICLE 21

Applicable law

1. The Court shall apply:

(a) In the first place, this Statute, Elements of Crimes and its Rules of Procedure and Evidence;

(b) In the second place, where appropriate, applicable treaties and the principles and rules of international law, including the established principles of the international law of armed conflict;

(c) Failing that, general principles of law derived by the Court from national laws of legal systems of the world including, as appropriate, the national laws of States that would normally exercise jurisdiction over the crime, provided that those principles are not inconsistent with this Statute and with international law and internationally recognized norms and standards.

2. The Court may apply principles and rules of law as interpreted in its previous decisions.

3. The application and interpretation of law pursuant to this Article must be consistent with internationally recognized human rights, and be without any adverse distinction founded on grounds such as gender as defined in Article 7, paragraph 3, age, race, colour, language, religion or belief, political or other opinion, national, ethnic or social origin, wealth, birth or other status.

PART 3: GENERAL PRINCIPLES OF CRIMINAL LAW

ARTICLE 22

Nullum crimen sine lege

1. A person shall not be criminally responsible under this Statute unless the conduct in question constitutes, at the time it takes place, a crime within the jurisdiction of the Court.

2. The definition of a crime shall be strictly construed and shall not be extended by analogy. In case of ambiguity, the definition shall be interpreted in favour of the person being investigated, prosecuted or convicted.

3. This Article shall not affect the characterization of any conduct as criminal under international law independently of this Statute.

ARTICLE 23

Nulla poena sine lege

A person convicted by the Court may be punished only in accordance with this Statute.

ARTICLE 24

Non-retroactivity ratione personae

1. No person shall be criminally responsible under this Statute for conduct prior to the entry into force of the Statute.

2. In the event of a change in the law applicable to a given case prior to a final judgment, the law more favourable to the person being investigated, prosecuted or convicted shall apply.

ARTICLE 25

Individual criminal responsibility

1. The Court shall have jurisdiction over natural persons pursuant to this Statute.

2. A person who commits a crime within the jurisdiction of the Court shall be individually responsible and liable for punishment in accordance with this Statute.

3. In accordance with this Statute, a person shall be criminally responsible and liable for punishment for a crime within the jurisdiction of the Court if that person:

(a) Commits such a crime, whether as an individual, jointly with another or through another person, regardless of whether that other person is criminally responsible;

(b) Orders, solicits or induces the commission of such a crime which in fact occurs or is attempted;

(c) For the purpose of facilitating the commission of such a crime, aids, abets or otherwise assists in its commission or its attempted commission, including providing the means for its commission;

(d) In any other way contributes to the commission or attempted commission of such a crime by a group of persons acting with a common purpose. Such contribution shall be intentional and shall either:

   (i) Be made with the aim of furthering the criminal activity or criminal purpose of the group, where such activity or purpose involves the commission of a crime within the jurisdiction of the Court; or

   (ii) Be made in the knowledge of the intention of the group to commit the crime;

(e) In respect of the crime of genocide, directly and publicly incites others to commit genocide;

(f) Attempts to commit such a crime by taking action that commences its execution by means of a substantial step, but the crime does not occur because of circumstances independent of the person's intentions. However, a person who abandons the effort to commit the crime or otherwise prevents the completion of the crime shall not be liable for punishment under this Statute for the attempt to commit that crime if that person completely and voluntarily gave up the criminal purpose.

4. No provision in this Statute relating to individual criminal responsibility shall affect the responsibility of States under international law.

ARTICLE 26

Exclusion of jurisdiction over persons under eighteen

The Court shall have no jurisdiction over any person who was under the age of eighteen at the time of the alleged commission of a crime.

ARTICLE 27

Irrelevance of official capacity

1. This Statute shall apply equally to all persons without any distinction based on official capacity. In particular, official capacity as a Head of State or Government, a member of a Government or parliament, an elected representative or a government official shall in no case exempt a person from criminal responsibility under this Statute, nor shall it, in and of itself, constitute a ground for reduction of sentence.

2. Immunities or special procedural rules which may attach to the official capacity of a person, whether under national or international law, shall not bar the Court from exercising its jurisdiction over such a person.

ARTICLE 28

Responsibility of commanders and other superiors

In addition to other grounds of criminal responsibility under this Statute for crimes within the jurisdiction of the Court:

(a) A military commander or person effectively acting as a military commander shall be criminally responsible for crimes within the jurisdiction of the Court committed by forces under his or her effective command and control, or effective authority and control as the case may be, as a result of his or her failure to exercise control properly over such forces, where:

    (i) That military commander or person either knew or, owing to the circumstances at the time, should have known that the forces were committing or about to commit such crimes; and

    (ii) That military commander or person failed to take all necessary and reasonable measures within his or her power to prevent or repress their commission or to submit the matter to the competent authorities for investigation and prosecution.

(b) With respect to superior and subordinate relationships not described in paragraph (a), a superior shall be criminally responsible for crimes within the jurisdiction of the Court committed by subordinates under his or her effective authority and control, as a result of his or her failure to exercise control properly over such subordinates, where:

    (i) The superior either knew, or consciously disregarded information which clearly indicated, that the subordinates were committing or about to commit such crimes;

    (ii) The crimes concerned activities that were within the effective responsibility and control of the superior; and

    (iii) The superior failed to take all necessary and reasonable measures within his or her power to prevent or repress their commission or to submit the matter to the competent authorities for investigation and prosecution.

ARTICLE 29

Non-applicability of statute of limitations

The crimes within the jurisdiction of the Court shall not be subject to any statute of limitations.

ARTICLE 30

Mental element

1. Unless otherwise provided, a person shall be criminally responsible and liable for punishment for a crime within the jurisdiction of the Court only if the material elements are committed with intent and knowledge.
    2. For the purposes of this Article, a person has intent where:

(a) In relation to conduct, that person means to engage in the conduct;

(b) In relation to a consequence, that person means to cause that consequence or is aware that it will occur in the ordinary course of events.

3. For the purposes of this Article, 'knowledge' means awareness that a circumstance exists or a consequence will occur in the ordinary course of events. 'Know' and 'knowingly' shall be construed accordingly.

ARTICLE 31

Grounds for excluding criminal responsibility

1. In addition to other grounds for excluding criminal responsibility provided for in this Statute, a person shall not be criminally responsible if, at the time of that person's conduct:

(a) The person suffers from a mental disease or defect that destroys that person's capacity to appreciate the unlawfulness or nature of his or her conduct, or capacity to control his or her conduct to conform to the requirements of law;

(b) The person is in a state of intoxication that destroys that person's capacity to appreciate the unlawfulness or nature of his or her conduct, or capacity to control his or her conduct to conform to the requirements of law, unless the person has become voluntarily intoxicated under such circumstances that the person knew, or disregarded the risk, that, as a result of the intoxication, he or she was likely to engage in conduct constituting a crime within the jurisdiction of the Court;

(c) The person acts reasonably to defend himself or herself or another person or, in the case of war crimes, property which is essential for the survival of the person or another person or property which is essential for accomplishing a military mission, against an imminent and unlawful use of force in a manner proportionate to the degree of danger to the person or the other person or property protected. The fact that the person was involved in a defensive operation conducted by forces shall not in itself constitute a ground for excluding criminal responsibility under this subparagraph;

(d) The conduct which is alleged to constitute a crime within the jurisdiction of the Court has been caused by duress resulting from a threat of imminent death or of continuing or imminent serious bodily harm against that person or another person, and the person acts necessarily and reasonably to avoid this threat, provided that the person does not intend to cause a greater harm than the one sought to be avoided. Such a threat may either be:

   (i)   Made by other persons; or

   (ii) Constituted by other circumstances beyond that person's control.

2. The Court shall determine the applicability of the grounds for excluding criminal responsibility provided for in this Statute to the case before it.

3. At trial, the Court may consider a ground for excluding criminal responsibility other than those referred to in paragraph 1 where such a ground is derived from applicable law as set forth in Article 21. The procedures relating to the consideration of such a ground shall be provided for in the Rules of Procedure and Evidence.

ARTICLE 32

Mistake of fact or mistake of law

1. A mistake of fact shall be a ground for excluding criminal responsibility only if it negates the mental element required by the crime.

2. A mistake of law as to whether a particular type of conduct is a crime within the jurisdiction of the Court shall not be a ground for excluding criminal responsibility. A mistake of law may, however, be a ground for excluding criminal responsibility if it negates the mental element required by such a crime, or as provided for in Article 33.

ARTICLE 33

Superior orders and prescription of law

1. The fact that a crime within the jurisdiction of the Court has been committed by a person pursuant to an order of a Government or of a superior, whether military or civilian, shall not relieve that person of criminal responsibility unless:

(a) The person was under a legal obligation to obey orders of the Government or the superior in question;

(b) The person did not know that the order was unlawful; and

(c) The order was not manifestly unlawful.

2. For the purposes of this Article, orders to commit genocide or crimes against humanity are manifestly unlawful.

PART 4: COMPOSITION AND ADMINISTRATION OF THE COURT

ARTICLE 34

Organs of the Court

The Court shall be composed of the following organs:

- (a) The Presidency;
- (b) An Appeals Division, a Trial Division and a Pre-Trial Division;
- (c) The Office of the Prosecutor;
- (d) The Registry.

ARTICLE 35

Service of judges

1. All judges shall be elected as full-time members of the Court and shall be available to serve on that basis from the commencement of their terms of office.

2. The judges composing the Presidency shall serve on a full-time basis as soon as they are elected.

3. The Presidency may, on the basis of the workload of the Court and in consultation with its members, decide from time to time to what extent the remaining judges shall be required to serve on a full-time basis. Any such arrangement shall be without prejudice to the provisions of Article 40.

4. The financial arrangements for judges not required to serve on a full-time basis shall be made in accordance with Article 49.

ARTICLE 36

Qualifications, nomination and election of judges

1. Subject to the provisions of paragraph 2, there shall be eighteen judges of the Court.

2. (a) The Presidency, acting on behalf of the Court, may propose an increase in the number of judges specified in paragraph 1, indicating the reasons why this is considered necessary and appropriate. The Registrar shall promptly circulate any such proposal to all States Parties.

   (b) Any such proposal shall then be considered at a meeting of the Assembly of States Parties to be convened in accordance with Article 112. The proposal shall be considered adopted if approved at the meeting by a vote of two thirds of the members of the Assembly of States Parties and shall enter into force at such time as decided by the Assembly of States Parties.

   (c) (i)   Once a proposal for an increase in the number of judges has been adopted under subparagraph (b), the election of the additional judges shall take place at the next session of the Assembly of States Parties in accordance with paragraphs 3 to 8, and Article 37, paragraph 2;

(ii) Once a proposal for an increase in the number of judges has been adopted and brought into effect under subparagraphs (b) and (c)(i), it shall be open to the Presidency at any time thereafter, if the workload of the Court justifies it, to propose a reduction in the number of judges, provided that the number of judges shall not be reduced below that specified in paragraph 1. The proposal shall be dealt with in accordance with the procedure laid down in subparagraphs (a) and (b). In the event that the proposal is adopted, the number of judges shall be progressively decreased as the terms of office of serving judges expire, until the necessary number has been reached.

3. (a) The judges shall be chosen from among persons of high moral character, impartiality and integrity who possess the qualifications required in their respective States for appointment to the highest judicial offices.

(b) Every candidate for election to the Court shall:

(i) Have established competence in criminal law and procedure, and the necessary relevant experience, whether as judge, prosecutor, advocate or in other similar capacity, in criminal proceedings; or

(ii) Have established competence in relevant areas of international law such as international humanitarian law and the law of human rights, and extensive experience in a professional legal capacity which is of relevance to the judicial work of the Court;

(c) Every candidate for election to the Court shall have an excellent knowledge of and be fluent in at least one of the working languages of the Court.

4. (a) Nominations of candidates for election to the Court may be made by any State Party to this Statute, and shall be made either:

(i) By the procedure for the nomination of candidates for appointment to the highest judicial offices in the State in question; or

(ii) By the procedure provided for the nomination of candidates for the International Court of Justice in the Statute of that Court.

Nominations shall be accompanied by a statement in the necessary detail specifying how the candidate fulfils the requirements of paragraph 3.

(b) Each State Party may put forward one candidate for any given election who need not necessarily be a national of that State Party but shall in any case be a national of a State Party.

(c) The Assembly of States Parties may decide to establish, if appropriate, an Advisory Committee on nominations. In that event, the Committee's composition and mandate shall be established by the Assembly of States Parties.

5. For the purposes of the election, there shall be two lists of candidates:

List A containing the names of candidates with the qualifications specified in paragraph 3(b)(i); and

List B containing the names of candidates with the qualifications specified in paragraph 3(b)(ii).

A candidate with sufficient qualifications for both lists may choose on which list to appear. At the first election to the Court, at least nine judges shall be elected from list A and at least five judges from list B. Subsequent elections shall be so organized as to maintain the equivalent proportion on the Court of judges qualified on the two lists.

6. (a) The judges shall be elected by secret ballot at a meeting of the Assembly of States Parties convened for that purpose under Article 112. Subject to paragraph 7, the persons elected to the Court shall be the eighteen candidates who obtain the highest number of votes and a two-thirds majority of the States Parties present and voting.

   (b) In the event that a sufficient number of judges is not elected on the first ballot, successive ballots shall be held in accordance with the procedures laid down in subparagraph (a) until the remaining places have been filled.

7. No two judges may be nationals of the same State. A person who, for the purposes of membership of the Court, could be regarded as a national of more than one State shall be deemed to be a national of the State in which that person ordinarily exercises civil and political rights.

8. (a) The States Parties shall, in the selection of judges, take into account the need, within the membership of the Court, for:

   (i)   The representation of the principal legal systems of the world;

   (ii) Equitable geographical representation; and

   (iii) A fair representation of female and male judges.

   (b) States Parties shall also take into account the need to include judges with legal expertise on specific issues, including, but not limited to, violence against women or children.

9. (a) Subject to subparagraph (b), judges shall hold office for a term of nine years and, subject to subparagraph (c) and to Article 37, paragraph 2, shall not be eligible for re-election.

   (b) At the first election, one third of the judges elected shall be selected by lot to serve for a term of three years; one third of the judges elected shall be selected by lot to serve for a term of six years; and the remainder shall serve for a term of nine years.

   (c) A judge who is selected to serve for a term of three years under subparagraph (b) shall be eligible for re-election for a full term.

10. Notwithstanding paragraph 9, a judge assigned to a Trial or Appeals Chamber in accordance with Article 39 shall continue in office to complete any trial or appeal the hearing of which has already commenced before that Chamber.

ARTICLE 37

Judicial vacancies

1. In the event of a vacancy, an election shall be held in accordance with Article 36 to fill the vacancy.

2. A judge elected to fill a vacancy shall serve for the remainder of the predecessor's term and, if that period is three years or less, shall be eligible for re-election for a full term under Article 36.

ARTICLE 38

The Presidency

1. The President and the First and Second Vice-Presidents shall be elected by an absolute majority of the judges. They shall each serve for a term of three years or until the end of their respective terms of office as judges, whichever expires earlier. They shall be eligible for re-election once.

2. The First Vice-President shall act in place of the President in the event that the President is unavailable or disqualified. The Second Vice-President shall act in place of the President in the event that both the President and the First Vice-President are unavailable or disqualified.

3. The President, together with the First and Second Vice-Presidents, shall constitute the Presidency, which shall be responsible for:

(a) The proper administration of the Court, with the exception of the Office of the Prosecutor; and

(b) The other functions conferred upon it in accordance with this Statute.

4. In discharging its responsibility under paragraph 3(a), the Presidency shall coordinate with and seek the concurrence of the Prosecutor on all matters of mutual concern.

ARTICLE 39

Chambers

1. As soon as possible after the election of the judges, the Court shall organize itself into the divisions specified in Article 34, paragraph (b). The Appeals Division shall be composed of the President and four other judges, the Trial Division of not less than six judges and the Pre-Trial Division of not less than six judges. The assignment of judges to divisions shall be based on the nature of the functions to be performed by each division and the qualifications and experience of the judges elected to the Court, in such a way that each division shall contain an appropriate combination of expertise in criminal law and procedure and in international law. The Trial and Pre-Trial Divisions shall be composed predominantly of judges with criminal trial experience.

2. (a) The judicial functions of the Court shall be carried out in each division by Chambers.

(b) (i) The Appeals Chamber shall be composed of all the judges of the Appeals Division;

   (ii) The functions of the Trial Chamber shall be carried out by three judges of the Trial Division;

   (iii) The functions of the Pre-Trial Chamber shall be carried out either by three judges of the Pre-Trial Division or by a single judge of that division in accordance with this Statute and the Rules of Procedure and Evidence;

(c) Nothing in this paragraph shall preclude the simultaneous constitution of more than one Trial Chamber or Pre-Trial Chamber when the efficient management of the Court's workload so requires.

3. (a) Judges assigned to the Trial and Pre-Trial Divisions shall serve in those divisions for a period of three years, and thereafter until the completion of any case the hearing of which has already commenced in the division concerned.

(b) Judges assigned to the Appeals Division shall serve in that division for their entire term of office.

4. Judges assigned to the Appeals Division shall serve only in that division. Nothing in this Article shall, however, preclude the temporary attachment of judges from the Trial Division to the Pre-Trial Division or *vice versa*, if the Presidency considers that the efficient management of the Court's workload so requires, provided that under no circumstances shall a judge who has participated in the pre-trial phase of a case be eligible to sit on the Trial Chamber hearing that case.

ARTICLE 40

Independence of the judges

1. The judges shall be independent in the performance of their functions.

2. Judges shall not engage in any activity which is likely to interfere with their judicial functions or to affect confidence in their independence.

3. Judges required to serve on a full-time basis at the seat of the Court shall not engage in any other occupation of a professional nature.

4. Any question regarding the application of paragraphs 2 and 3 shall be decided by an absolute majority of the judges. Where any such question concerns an individual judge, that judge shall not take part in the decision.

ARTICLE 41

Excusing and disqualification of judges

1. The Presidency may, at the request of a judge, excuse that judge from the exercise of a function under this Statute, in accordance with the Rules of Procedure and Evidence.

2. (a) A judge shall not participate in any case in which his or her impartiality might reasonably be doubted on any ground. A judge shall be disqualified from a case in

accordance with this paragraph if, *inter alia*, that judge has previously been involved in any capacity in that case before the Court or in a related criminal case at the national level involving the person being investigated or prosecuted. A judge shall also be disqualified on such other grounds as may be provided for in the Rules of Procedure and Evidence.

(b) The Prosecutor or the person being investigated or prosecuted may request the disqualification of a judge under this paragraph.

(c) Any question as to the disqualification of a judge shall be decided by an absolute majority of the judges. The challenged judge shall be entitled to present his or her comments on the matter, but shall not take part in the decision.

ARTICLE 42

The Office of the Prosecutor

1. The Office of the Prosecutor shall act independently as a separate organ of the Court. It shall be responsible for receiving referrals and any substantiated information on crimes within the jurisdiction of the Court, for examining them and for conducting investigations and prosecutions before the Court. A member of the Office shall not seek or act on instructions from any external source.

2. The Office shall be headed by the Prosecutor. The Prosecutor shall have full authority over the management and administration of the Office, including the staff, facilities and other resources thereof. The Prosecutor shall be assisted by one or more Deputy Prosecutors, who shall be entitled to carry out any of the acts required of the Prosecutor under this Statute. The Prosecutor and the Deputy Prosecutors shall be of different nationalities. They shall serve on a full-time basis.

3. The Prosecutor and the Deputy Prosecutors shall be persons of high moral character, be highly competent in and have extensive practical experience in the prosecution or trial of criminal cases. They shall have an excellent knowledge of and be fluent in at least one of the working languages of the Court.

4. The Prosecutor shall be elected by secret ballot by an absolute majority of the members of the Assembly of States Parties. The Deputy Prosecutors shall be elected in the same way from a list of candidates provided by the Prosecutor. The Prosecutor shall nominate three candidates for each position of Deputy Prosecutor to be filled. Unless a shorter term is decided upon at the time of their election, the Prosecutor and the Deputy Prosecutors shall hold office for a term of nine years and shall not be eligible for re-election.

5. Neither the Prosecutor nor a Deputy Prosecutor shall engage in any activity which is likely to interfere with his or her prosecutorial functions or to affect confidence in his or her independence. They shall not engage in any other occupation of a professional nature.

6. The Presidency may excuse the Prosecutor or a Deputy Prosecutor, at his or her request, from acting in a particular case.

7. Neither the Prosecutor nor a Deputy Prosecutor shall participate in any matter in which their impartiality might reasonably be doubted on any ground. They shall be disqualified from a case in accordance with this paragraph if, *inter alia*, they have previously been involved in any capacity in that case before the Court or in a related criminal case at the national level involving the person being investigated or prosecuted.

8. Any question as to the disqualification of the Prosecutor or a Deputy Prosecutor shall be decided by the Appeals Chamber.

(a) The person being investigated or prosecuted may at any time request the disqualification of the Prosecutor or a Deputy Prosecutor on the grounds set out in this article;

(b) The Prosecutor or the Deputy Prosecutor, as appropriate, shall be entitled to present his or her comments on the matter;

9. The Prosecutor shall appoint advisers with legal expertise on specific issues, including, but not limited to, sexual and gender violence and violence against children.

ARTICLE 43

The Registry

1. The Registry shall be responsible for the non-judicial aspects of the administration and servicing of the Court, without prejudice to the functions and powers of the Prosecutor in accordance with Article 42.

2. The Registry shall be headed by the Registrar, who shall be the principal administrative officer of the Court. The Registrar shall exercise his or her functions under the authority of the President of the Court.

3. The Registrar and the Deputy Registrar shall be persons of high moral character, be highly competent and have an excellent knowledge of and be fluent in at least one of the working languages of the Court.

4. The judges shall elect the Registrar by an absolute majority by secret ballot, taking into account any recommendation by the Assembly of States Parties. If the need arises and upon the recommendation of the Registrar, the judges shall elect, in the same manner, a Deputy Registrar.

5. The Registrar shall hold office for a term of five years, shall be eligible for re-election once and shall serve on a full-time basis. The Deputy Registrar shall hold office for a term of five years or such shorter term as may be decided upon by an absolute majority of the judges, and may be elected on the basis that the Deputy Registrar shall be called upon to serve as required.

6. The Registrar shall set up a Victims and Witnesses Unit within the Registry. This Unit shall provide, in consultation with the Office of the Prosecutor, protective measures and security arrangements, counselling and other appropriate assistance for witnesses, victims who appear before the Court, and others who are at risk on account of testimony given by such witnesses. The Unit shall include staff with expertise in trauma, including trauma related to crimes of sexual violence.

ARTICLE 44

Staff

1. The Prosecutor and the Registrar shall appoint such qualified staff as may be required to

their respective offices. In the case of the Prosecutor, this shall include the appointment of investigators.

2. In the employment of staff, the Prosecutor and the Registrar shall ensure the highest standards of efficiency, competency and integrity, and shall have regard, *mutatis mutandis*, to the criteria set forth in Article 36, paragraph 8.

3. The Registrar, with the agreement of the Presidency and the Prosecutor, shall propose Staff Regulations which include the terms and conditions upon which the staff of the Court shall be appointed, remunerated and dismissed. The Staff Regulations shall be approved by the Assembly of States Parties.

4. The Court may, in exceptional circumstances, employ the expertise of *gratis* personnel offered by States Parties, intergovernmental organizations or non-governmental organizations to assist with the work of any of the organs of the Court. The Prosecutor may accept any such offer on behalf of the Office of the Prosecutor. Such *gratis* personnel shall be employed in accordance with guidelines to be established by the Assembly of States Parties.

ARTICLE 45

Solemn undertaking

Before taking up their respective duties under this Statute, the judges, the Prosecutor, the Deputy Prosecutors, the Registrar and the Deputy Registrar shall each make a solemn undertaking in open court to exercise his or her respective functions impartially and conscientiously.

ARTICLE 46

Removal from office

1. A judge, the Prosecutor, a Deputy Prosecutor, the Registrar or the Deputy Registrar shall be removed from office if a decision to this effect is made in accordance with paragraph 2, in cases where that person:

   (a) Is found to have committed serious misconduct or a serious breach of his or her duties under this Statute, as provided for in the Rules of Procedure and Evidence; or

   (b) Is unable to exercise the functions required by this Statute.

2. A decision as to the removal from office of a judge, the Prosecutor or a Deputy Prosecutor under paragraph 1 shall be made by the Assembly of States Parties, by secret ballot:

   (a) In the case of a judge, by a two-thirds majority of the States Parties upon a recommendation adopted by a two-thirds majority of the other judges;

   (b) In the case of the Prosecutor, by an absolute majority of the States Parties;

   (c) In the case of a Deputy Prosecutor, by an absolute majority of the States Parties upon the recommendation of the Prosecutor.

3. A decision as to the removal from office of the Registrar or Deputy Registrar shall be made by an absolute majority of the judges.

4. A judge, Prosecutor, Deputy Prosecutor, Registrar or Deputy Registrar whose conduct or ability to exercise the functions of the office as required by this Statute is challenged under this Article shall have full opportunity to present and receive evidence and to make submissions in accordance with the Rules of Procedure and Evidence. The person in question shall not otherwise participate in the consideration of the matter.

ARTICLE 47

Disciplinary measures

A judge, Prosecutor, Deputy Prosecutor, Registrar or Deputy Registrar who has committed misconduct of a less serious nature than that set out in Article 46, paragraph 1, shall be subject to disciplinary measures, in accordance with the Rules of Procedure and Evidence.

ARTICLE 48

Privileges and immunities

1. The Court shall enjoy in the territory of each State Party such privileges and immunities as are necessary for the fulfilment of its purposes.

2. The judges, the Prosecutor, the Deputy Prosecutors and the Registrar shall, when engaged on or with respect to the business of the Court, enjoy the same privileges and immunities as are accorded to heads of diplomatic missions and shall, after the expiry of their terms of office, continue to be accorded immunity from legal process of every kind in respect of words spoken or written and acts performed by them in their official capacity.

3. The Deputy Registrar, the staff of the Office of the Prosecutor and the staff of the Registry shall enjoy the privileges and immunities and facilities necessary for the performance of their functions, in accordance with the agreement on the privileges and immunities of the Court.

4. Counsel, experts, witnesses or any other person required to be present at the seat of the Court shall be accorded such treatment as is necessary for the proper functioning of the Court, in accordance with the agreement on the privileges and immunities of the Court.

5. The privileges and immunities of:

   (a) A judge or the Prosecutor may be waived by an absolute majority of the judges;

   (b) The Registrar may be waived by the Presidency;

   (c) The Deputy Prosecutors and staff of the Office of the Prosecutor may be waived by the Prosecutor;

   (d) The Deputy Registrar and staff of the Registry may be waived by the Registrar.

ARTICLE 49

Salaries, allowances and expenses

The judges, the Prosecutor, the Deputy Prosecutors, the Registrar and the Deputy Registrar shall receive such salaries, allowances and expenses as may be decided upon by the Assembly of States Parties. These salaries and allowances shall not be reduced during their terms of office.

ARTICLE 50

Official and working languages

1. The official languages of the Court shall be Arabic, Chinese, English, French, Russian and Spanish. The judgments of the Court, as well as other decisions resolving fundamental issues before the Court, shall be published in the official languages. The Presidency shall, in accordance with the criteria established by the Rules of Procedure and Evidence, determine which decisions may be considered as resolving fundamental issues for the purposes of this paragraph.

2. The working languages of the Court shall be English and French. The Rules of Procedure and Evidence shall determine the cases in which other official languages may be used as working languages.

3. At the request of any party to a proceeding or a State allowed to intervene in a proceeding, the Court shall authorize a language other than English or French to be used by such a party or State, provided that the Court considers such authorization to be adequately justified.

ARTICLE 51

Rules of Procedure and Evidence

1. The Rules of Procedure and Evidence shall enter into force upon adoption by a two-thirds majority of the members of the Assembly of States Parties.

2. Amendments to the Rules of Procedure and Evidence may be proposed by:

(a) Any State Party;

(b) The judges acting by an absolute majority; or

(c) The Prosecutor.

Such amendments shall enter into force upon adoption by a two-thirds majority of the members of the Assembly of States Parties.

3. After the adoption of the Rules of Procedure and Evidence, in urgent cases where the Rules do not provide for a specific situation before the Court, the judges may, by a two-thirds majority, draw up provisional Rules to be applied until adopted, amended or rejected at the next ordinary or special session of the Assembly of States Parties.

4. The Rules of Procedure and Evidence, amendments thereto and any provisional Rule shall be consistent with this Statute. Amendments to the Rules of Procedure and Evidence as well as provisional Rules shall not be applied retroactively to the detriment of the person who is being investigated or prosecuted or who has been convicted.

5. In the event of conflict between the Statute and the Rules of Procedure and Evidence, the Statute shall prevail.

ARTICLE 52

Regulations of the Court

1. The judges shall, in accordance with this Statute and the Rules of Procedure and Evidence, adopt, by an absolute majority, the Regulations of the Court necessary for its routine functioning.

2. The Prosecutor and the Registrar shall be consulted in the elaboration of the Regulations and any amendments thereto.

3. The Regulations and any amendments thereto shall take effect upon adoption unless otherwise decided by the judges. Immediately upon adoption, they shall be circulated to States Parties for comments. If within six months there are no objections from a majority of States Parties, they shall remain in force.

PART 5: INVESTIGATION AND PROSECUTION

ARTICLE 53

Initiation of an investigation

1. The Prosecutor shall, having evaluated the information made available to him or her, initiate an investigation unless he or she determines that there is no reasonable basis to proceed under this Statute. In deciding whether to initiate an investigation, the Prosecutor shall consider whether:

(a) The information available to the Prosecutor provides a reasonable basis to believe that a crime within the jurisdiction of the Court has been or is being committed;

(b) The case is or would be admissible under Article 17; and

(c) Taking into account the gravity of the crime and the interests of victims, there are nonetheless substantial reasons to believe that an investigation would not serve the interests of justice.

If the Prosecutor determines that there is no reasonable basis to proceed and his or her determination is based solely on subparagraph (c) above, he or she shall inform the Pre-Trial Chamber.

2. If, upon investigation, the Prosecutor concludes that there is not a sufficient basis for a prosecution because:

(a) There is not a sufficient legal or factual basis to seek a warrant or summons under Article 58;

(b) The case is inadmissible under Article 17; or

(c) A prosecution is not in the interests of justice, taking into account all the circumstances, including the gravity of the crime, the interests of victims and the age or infirmity of the alleged perpetrator, and his or her role in the alleged crime;

the Prosecutor shall inform the Pre-Trial Chamber and the State making a referral under

Article 14 or the Security Council in a case under Article 13, paragraph (b), of his or her conclusion and the reasons for the conclusion.

    3. (a) At the request of the State making a referral under Article 14 or the Security Council under Article 13, paragraph (b), the Pre-Trial Chamber may review a decision of the Prosecutor under paragraph 1 or 2 not to proceed and may request the Prosecutor to reconsider that decision.

    (b) In addition, the Pre-Trial Chamber may, on its own initiative, review a decision of the Prosecutor not to proceed if it is based solely on paragraph 1(c) or 2(c). In such a case, the decision of the Prosecutor shall be effective only if confirmed by the Pre-Trial Chamber.

4. The Prosecutor may, at any time, reconsider a decision whether to initiate an investigation or prosecution based on new facts or information.

ARTICLE 54

Duties and powers of the prosecutor with respect to investigations

1. The Prosecutor shall:

    (a) In order to establish the truth, extend the investigation to cover all facts and evidence relevant to an assessment of whether there is criminal responsibility under this Statute, and, in doing so, investigate incriminating and exonerating circumstances equally;

    (b) Take appropriate measures to ensure the effective investigation and prosecution of crimes within the jurisdiction of the Court, and in doing so, respect the interests and personal circumstances of victims and witnesses, including age, gender as defined in Article 7, paragraph 3, and health, and take into account the nature of the crime, in particular where it involves sexual violence, gender violence or violence against children; and

    (c) Fully respect the rights of persons arising under this Statute.

2. The Prosecutor may conduct investigations on the territory of a State:

    (a) In accordance with the provisions of Part 9; or

    (b) As authorized by the Pre-Trial Chamber under Article 57, paragraph 3(d).

3. The Prosecutor may:

    (a) Collect and examine evidence;

    (b) Request the presence of and question persons being investigated, victims and witnesses;

    (c) Seek the cooperation of any State or intergovernmental organization or arrangement in accordance with its respective competence and/or mandate;

    (d) Enter into such arrangements or agreements, not inconsistent with this Statute, as may be necessary to facilitate the cooperation of a State, intergovernmental organization or person;

(e) Agree not to disclose, at any stage of the proceedings, documents or information that the Prosecutor obtains on the condition of confidentiality and solely for the purpose of generating new evidence, unless the provider of the information consents; and

(f) Take necessary measures, or request that necessary measures be taken, to ensure the confidentiality of information, the protection of any person or the preservation of evidence.

ARTICLE 55

Rights of persons during an investigation

1. In respect of an investigation under this Statute, a person:

(a) Shall not be compelled to incriminate himself or herself or to confess guilt;

(b) Shall not be subjected to any form of coercion, duress or threat, to torture or to any other form of cruel, inhuman or degrading treatment or punishment;

(c) Shall, if questioned in a language other than a language the person fully understands and speaks, have, free of any cost, the assistance of a competent interpreter and such translations as are necessary to meet the requirements of fairness; and

(d) Shall not be subjected to arbitrary arrest or detention, and shall not be deprived of his or her liberty except on such grounds and in accordance with such procedures as are established in this Statute.

2. Where there are grounds to believe that a person has committed a crime within the jurisdiction of the Court and that person is about to be questioned either by the Prosecutor, or by national authorities pursuant to a request made under Part 9, that person shall also have the following rights of which he or she shall be informed prior to being questioned:

(a) To be informed, prior to being questioned, that there are grounds to believe that he or she has committed a crime within the jurisdiction of the Court;

(b) To remain silent, without such silence being a consideration in the determination of guilt or innocence;

(c) To have legal assistance of the person's choosing, or, if the person does not have legal assistance, to have legal assistance assigned to him or her, in any case where the interests of justice so require, and without payment by the person in any such case if the person does not have sufficient means to pay for it; and

(d) To be questioned in the presence of counsel unless the person has voluntarily waived his or her right to counsel.

ARTICLE 56

Role of the Pre-Trial Chamber in relation to a unique investigative opportunity

1. (a) Where the Prosecutor considers an investigation to present a unique opportunity to take testimony or a statement from a witness or to examine, collect or test evidence,

which may not be available subsequently for the purposes of a trial, the Prosecutor shall so inform the Pre-Trial Chamber.

(b) In that case, the Pre-Trial Chamber may, upon request of the Prosecutor, take such measures as may be necessary to ensure the efficiency and integrity of the proceedings and, in particular, to protect the rights of the defence.

(c) Unless the Pre-Trial Chamber orders otherwise, the Prosecutor shall provide the relevant information to the person who has been arrested or appeared in response to a summons in connection with the investigation referred to in subparagraph (a), in order that he or she may be heard on the matter.

2. The measures referred to in paragraph 1(b) may include:

(a) Making recommendations or orders regarding procedures to be followed;

(b) Directing that a record be made of the proceedings;

(c) Appointing an expert to assist;

(d) Authorizing counsel for a person who has been arrested, or appeared before the Court in response to a summons, to participate, or where there has not yet been such an arrest or appearance or counsel has not been designated, appointing another counsel to attend and represent the interests of the defence;

(e) Naming one of its members or, if necessary, another available judge of the Pre-Trial or Trial Division to observe and make recommendations or orders regarding the collection and preservation of evidence and the questioning of persons;

(f) Taking such other action as may be necessary to collect or preserve evidence.

3. (a) Where the Prosecutor has not sought measures pursuant to this article but the Pre-Trial Chamber considers that such measures are required to preserve evidence that it deems would be essential for the defence at trial, it shall consult with the Prosecutor as to whether there is good reason for the Prosecutor's failure to request the measures. If upon consultation, the Pre-Trial Chamber concludes that the Prosecutor's failure to request such measures is unjustified, the Pre-Trial Chamber may take such measures on its own initiative.

(b) A decision of the Pre-Trial Chamber to act on its own initiative under this paragraph may be appealed by the Prosecutor. The appeal shall be heard on an expedited basis.

4. The admissibility of evidence preserved or collected for trial pursuant to this article, or the record thereof, shall be governed at trial by Article 69, and given such weight as determined by the Trial Chamber.

ARTICLE 57

Functions and powers of the Pre-Trial Chamber

1. Unless otherwise provided in this Statute, the Pre-Trial Chamber shall exercise its functions in accordance with the provisions of this Article.

2. (a) Orders or rulings of the Pre-Trial Chamber issued under Articles 15, 18, 19, 54,

paragraph 2, 61, paragraph 7, and 72 must be concurred in by a majority of its judges.

(b) In all other cases, a single judge of the Pre-Trial Chamber may exercise the functions provided for in this Statute, unless otherwise provided for in the Rules of Procedure and Evidence or by a majority of the Pre-Trial Chamber.

3. In addition to its other functions under this Statute, the Pre-Trial Chamber may:

(a) At the request of the Prosecutor, issue such orders and warrants as may be required for the purposes of an investigation;

(b) Upon the request of a person who has been arrested or has appeared pursuant to a summons under Article 58, issue such orders, including measures such as those described in Article 56, or seek such cooperation pursuant to Part 9 as may be necessary to assist the person in the preparation of his or her defence;

(c) Where necessary, provide for the protection and privacy of victims and witnesses, the preservation of evidence, the protection of persons who have been arrested or appeared in response to a summons, and the protection of national security information;

(d) Authorize the Prosecutor to take specific investigative steps within the territory of a State Party without having secured the cooperation of that State under Part 9 if, whenever possible having regard to the views of the State concerned, the Pre-Trial Chamber has determined in that case that the State is clearly unable to execute a request for cooperation due to the unavailability of any authority or any component of its judicial system competent to execute the request for cooperation under Part 9.

(e) Where a warrant of arrest or a summons has been issued under Article 58, and having due regard to the strength of the evidence and the rights of the parties concerned, as provided for in this Statute and the Rules of Procedure and Evidence, seek the cooperation of States pursuant to Article 93, paragraph 1(k), to take protective measures for the purpose of forfeiture, in particular for the ultimate benefit of victims.

ARTICLE 58

Issuance by the Pre-Trial Chamber of a warrant of arrest or a summons to appear

1. At any time after the initiation of an investigation, the Pre-Trial Chamber shall, on the application of the Prosecutor, issue a warrant of arrest of a person if, having examined the application and the evidence or other information submitted by the Prosecutor, it is satisfied that:

(a) There are reasonable grounds to believe that the person has committed a crime within the jurisdiction of the Court; and

(b) The arrest of the person appears necessary:

    (i) To ensure the person's appearance at trial,

    (ii) To ensure that the person does not obstruct or endanger the investigation or the court proceedings, or

   (iii) Where applicable, to prevent the person from continuing with the commission
         of that crime or a related crime which is within the jurisdiction of the Court
         and which arises out of the same circumstances.

2. The application of the Prosecutor shall contain:

   (a) The name of the person and any other relevant identifying information;

   (b) A specific reference to the crimes within the jurisdiction of the Court which the
       person is alleged to have committed;

   (c) A concise statement of the facts which are alleged to constitute those crimes;

   (d) A summary of the evidence and any other information which establish reasonable
       grounds to believe that the person committed those crimes; and

   (e) The reason why the Prosecutor believes that the arrest of the person is necessary.

3. The warrant of arrest shall contain:

   (a) The name of the person and any other relevant identifying information;

   (b) A specific reference to the crimes within the jurisdiction of the Court for which the
       person's arrest is sought; and

   (c) A concise statement of the facts which are alleged to constitute those crimes.

4. The warrant of arrest shall remain in effect until otherwise ordered by the Court.

   5. On the basis of the warrant of arrest, the Court may request the provisional arrest or
the arrest and surrender of the person under Part 9.

   6. The Prosecutor may request the Pre-Trial Chamber to amend the warrant of arrest by
modifying or adding to the crimes specified therein. The Pre-Trial Chamber shall so amend
the warrant if it is satisfied that there are reasonable grounds to believe that the person
committed the modified or additional crimes.

   7. As an alternative to seeking a warrant of arrest, the Prosecutor may submit an application requesting that the Pre-Trial Chamber issue a summons for the person to appear. If the
Pre-Trial Chamber is satisfied that there are reasonable grounds to believe that the person
committed the crime alleged and that a summons is sufficient to ensure the person's
appearance, it shall issue the summons, with or without conditions restricting liberty (other
than detention) if provided for by national law, for the person to appear. The summons shall
contain:

   (a) The name of the person and any other relevant identifying information;

   (b) The specified date on which the person is to appear;

   (c) A specific reference to the crimes within the jurisdiction of the Court which the
       person is alleged to have committed; and

   (d) A concise statement of the facts which are alleged to constitute the crime.

The summons shall be served on the person.

ARTICLE 59

Arrest proceedings in the custodial State

1. A State Party which has received a request for provisional arrest or for arrest and sur-render shall immediately take steps to arrest the person in question in accordance with its laws and the provisions of Part 9.

2. A person arrested shall be brought promptly before the competent judicial authority in the custodial State which shall determine, in accordance with the law of that State, that:

(a) The warrant applies to that person;

(b) The person has been arrested in accordance with the proper process; and

(c) The person's rights have been respected.

3. The person arrested shall have the right to apply to the competent authority in the custodial State for interim release pending surrender.

4. In reaching a decision on any such application, the competent authority in the cus-todial State shall consider whether, given the gravity of the alleged crimes, there are urgent and exceptional circumstances to justify interim release and whether necessary safeguards exist to ensure that the custodial State can fulfil its duty to surrender the person to the Court. It shall not be open to the competent authority of the custodial State to consider whether the warrant of arrest was properly issued in accordance with Article 58, paragraph 1(a) and (b).

5. The Pre-Trial Chamber shall be notified of any request for interim release and shall make recommendations to the competent authority in the custodial State. The competent authority in the custodial State shall give full consideration to such recommendations, including any recommendations on measures to prevent the escape of the person, before rendering its decision.

6. If the person is granted interim release, the Pre-Trial Chamber may request periodic reports on the status of the interim release.

7. Once ordered to be surrendered by the custodial State, the person shall be delivered to the Court as soon as possible.

ARTICLE 60

Initial proceedings before the Court

1. Upon the surrender of the person to the Court, or the person's appearance before the Court voluntarily or pursuant to a summons, the Pre-Trial Chamber shall satisfy itself that the person has been informed of the crimes which he or she is alleged to have committed, and of his or her rights under this Statute, including the right to apply for interim release pending trial.

2. A person subject to a warrant of arrest may apply for interim release pending trial. If the Pre-Trial Chamber is satisfied that the conditions set forth in Article 58, paragraph 1, are met, the person shall continue to be detained. If it is not so satisfied, the Pre-Trial Chamber shall release the person, with or without conditions.

3. The Pre-Trial Chamber shall periodically review its ruling on the release or detention

of the person, and may do so at any time on the request of the Prosecutor or the person. Upon such review, it may modify its ruling as to detention, release or conditions of release, if it is satisfied that changed circumstances so require.

4. The Pre-Trial Chamber shall ensure that a person is not detained for an unreasonable period prior to trial due to inexcusable delay by the Prosecutor. If such delay occurs, the Court shall consider releasing the person, with or without conditions.

5. If necessary, the Pre-Trial Chamber may issue a warrant of arrest to secure the presence of a person who has been released.

ARTICLE 61

Confirmation of the charges before trial

1. Subject to the provisions of paragraph 2, within a reasonable time after the person's surrender or voluntary appearance before the Court, the Pre-Trial Chamber shall hold a hearing to confirm the charges on which the Prosecutor intends to seek trial. The hearing shall be held in the presence of the Prosecutor and the person charged, as well as his or her counsel.

2. The Pre-Trial Chamber may, upon request of the Prosecutor or on its own motion, hold a hearing in the absence of the person charged to confirm the charges on which the Prosecutor intends to seek trial when the person has:

(a) Waived his or her right to be present; or

(b) Fled or cannot be found and all reasonable steps have been taken to secure his or her appearance before the Court and to inform the person of the charges and that a hearing to confirm those charges will be held.

In that case, the person shall be represented by counsel where the Pre-Trial Chamber determines that it is in the interests of justice.

3. Within a reasonable time before the hearing, the person shall:

(a) Be provided with a copy of the document containing the charges on which the Prosecutor intends to bring the person to trial; and

(b) Be informed of the evidence on which the Prosecutor intends to rely at the hearing.

The Pre-Trial Chamber may issue orders regarding the disclosure of information for the purposes of the hearing.

4. Before the hearing, the Prosecutor may continue the investigation and may amend or withdraw any charges. The person shall be given reasonable notice before the hearing of any amendment to or withdrawal of charges. In case of a withdrawal of charges, the Prosecutor shall notify the Pre-Trial Chamber of the reasons for the withdrawal.

5. At the hearing, the Prosecutor shall support each charge with sufficient evidence to establish substantial grounds to believe that the person committed the crime charged. The Prosecutor may rely on documentary or summary evidence and need not call the witnesses expected to testify at the trial.

6. At the hearing, the person may:

(a) Object to the charges;

(b) Challenge the evidence presented by the Prosecutor; and

(c) Present evidence.

7. The Pre-Trial Chamber shall, on the basis of the hearing, determine whether there is sufficient evidence to establish substantial grounds to believe that the person committed each of the crimes charged. Based on its determination, the Pre-Trial Chamber shall:

(a) Confirm those charges in relation to which it has determined that there is sufficient evidence, and commit the person to a Trial Chamber for trial on the charges as confirmed;

(b) Decline to confirm those charges in relation to which it has determined that there is insufficient evidence;

(c) Adjourn the hearing and request the Prosecutor to consider:

(i) Providing further evidence or conducting further investigation with respect to a particular charge; or

(ii) Amending a charge because the evidence submitted appears to establish a different crime within the jurisdiction of the Court.

8. Where the Pre-Trial Chamber declines to confirm a charge, the Prosecutor shall not be precluded from subsequently requesting its confirmation if the request is supported by additional evidence.

9. After the charges are confirmed and before the trial has begun, the Prosecutor may, with the permission of the Pre-Trial Chamber and after notice to the accused, amend the charges. If the Prosecutor seeks to add additional charges or to substitute more serious charges, a hearing under this Article to confirm those charges must be held. After commencement of the trial, the Prosecutor may, with the permission of the Trial Chamber, withdraw the charges.

10. Any warrant previously issued shall cease to have effect with respect to any charges which have not been confirmed by the Pre-Trial Chamber or which have been withdrawn by the Prosecutor.

11. Once the charges have been confirmed in accordance with this article, the Presidency shall constitute a Trial Chamber which, subject to paragraph 9 and to Article 64, paragraph 4, shall be responsible for the conduct of subsequent proceedings and may exercise any function of the Pre-Trial Chamber that is relevant and capable of application in those proceedings.

PART 6: THE TRIAL

ARTICLE 62

Place of trial

Unless otherwise decided, the place of the trial shall be the seat of the Court.

ARTICLE 63

Trial in the presence of the accused

1. The accused shall be present during the trial.

2. If the accused, being present before the Court, continues to disrupt the trial, the Trial Chamber may remove the accused and shall make provision for him or her to observe the trial and instruct counsel from outside the courtroom, through the use of communications technology, if required. Such measures shall be taken only in exceptional circumstances after other reasonable alternatives have proved inadequate, and only for such duration as is strictly required.

ARTICLE 64

Functions and powers of the Trial Chamber

1. The functions and powers of the Trial Chamber set out in this Article shall be exercised in accordance with this Statute and the Rules of Procedure and Evidence.

2. The Trial Chamber shall ensure that a trial is fair and expeditious and is conducted with full respect for the rights of the accused and due regard for the protection of victims and witnesses.

3. Upon assignment of a case for trial in accordance with this Statute, the Trial Chamber assigned to deal with the case shall:

(a) Confer with the parties and adopt such procedures as are necessary to facilitate the fair and expeditious conduct of the proceedings;

(b) Determine the language or languages to be used at trial; and

(c) Subject to any other relevant provisions of this Statute, provide for disclosure of documents or information not previously disclosed, sufficiently in advance of the commencement of the trial to enable adequate preparation for trial.

4. The Trial Chamber may, if necessary for its effective and fair functioning, refer preliminary issues to the Pre-Trial Chamber or, if necessary, to another available judge of the Pre-Trial Division.

5. Upon notice to the parties, the Trial Chamber may, as appropriate, direct that there be joinder or severance in respect of charges against more than one accused.

6. In performing its functions prior to trial or during the course of a trial, the Trial Chamber may, as necessary:

(a) Exercise any functions of the Pre-Trial Chamber referred to in Article 61, paragraph 11;

(b) Require the attendance and testimony of witnesses and production of documents and other evidence by obtaining, if necessary, the assistance of States as provided in this Statute;

(c) Provide for the protection of confidential information;

(d) Order the production of evidence in addition to that already collected prior to the trial or presented during the trial by the parties;

(e) Provide for the protection of the accused, witnesses and victims; and

(f) Rule on any other relevant matters.

7. The trial shall be held in public. The Trial Chamber may, however, determine that special circumstances require that certain proceedings be in closed session for the purposes set forth in Article 68, or to protect confidential or sensitive information to be given in evidence.

8. (a) At the commencement of the trial, the Trial Chamber shall have read to the accused the charges previously confirmed by the Pre-Trial Chamber. The Trial Chamber shall satisfy itself that the accused understands the nature of the charges. It shall afford him or her the opportunity to make an admission of guilt in accordance with Article 65 or to plead not guilty.

(b) At the trial, the presiding judge may give directions for the conduct of proceedings, including to ensure that they are conducted in a fair and impartial manner. Subject to any directions of the presiding judge, the parties may submit evidence in accordance with the provisions of this Statute.

9. The Trial Chamber shall have, *inter alia*, the power on application of a party or on its own motion to:

(a) Rule on the admissibility or relevance of evidence; and

(b) Take all necessary steps to maintain order in the course of a hearing.

10. The Trial Chamber shall ensure that a complete record of the trial, which accurately reflects the proceedings, is made and that it is maintained and preserved by the Registrar.

ARTICLE 65

Proceedings on an admission of guilt

1. Where the accused makes an admission of guilt pursuant to Article 64, paragraph 8(a), the Trial Chamber shall determine whether:

(a) The accused understands the nature and consequences of the admission of guilt;

(b) The admission is voluntarily made by the accused after sufficient consultation with defence counsel; and

(c) The admission of guilt is supported by the facts of the case that are contained in:

(i) The charges brought by the Prosecutor and admitted by the accused;

(ii) Any materials presented by the Prosecutor which supplement the charges and which the accused accepts; and

(iii) Any other evidence, such as the testimony of witnesses, presented by the Prosecutor or the accused.

2. Where the Trial Chamber is satisfied that the matters referred to in paragraph 1 are established, it shall consider the admission of guilt, together with any additional evidence presented, as establishing all the essential facts that are required to prove the crime to which the admission of guilt relates, and may convict the accused of that crime.

3. Where the Trial Chamber is not satisfied that the matters referred to in paragraph 1 are

established, it shall consider the admission of guilt as not having been made, in which case it shall order that the trial be continued under the ordinary trial procedures provided by this Statute and may remit the case to another Trial Chamber.

4. Where the Trial Chamber is of the opinion that a more complete presentation of the facts of the case is required in the interests of justice, in particular the interests of the victims, the Trial Chamber may:

(a) Request the Prosecutor to present additional evidence, including the testimony of witnesses; or

(b) Order that the trial be continued under the ordinary trial procedures provided by this Statute, in which case it shall consider the admission of guilt as not having been made and may remit the case to another Trial Chamber.

5. Any discussions between the Prosecutor and the defence regarding modification of the charges, the admission of guilt or the penalty to be imposed shall not be binding on the Court.

ARTICLE 66

Presumption of innocence

1. Everyone shall be presumed innocent until proved guilty before the Court in accordance with the applicable law.

2. The onus is on the Prosecutor to prove the guilt of the accused.

3. In order to convict the accused, the Court must be convinced of the guilt of the accused beyond reasonable doubt.

ARTICLE 67

Rights of the accused

1. In the determination of any charge, the accused shall be entitled to a public hearing, having regard to the provisions of this Statute, to a fair hearing conducted impartially, and to the following minimum guarantees, in full equality:

(a) To be informed promptly and in detail of the nature, cause and content of the charge, in a language which the accused fully understands and speaks;

(b) To have adequate time and facilities for the preparation of the defence and to communicate freely with counsel of the accused's choosing in confidence;

(c) To be tried without undue delay;

(d) Subject to Article 63, paragraph 2, to be present at the trial, to conduct the defence in person or through legal assistance of the accused's choosing, to be informed, if the accused does not have legal assistance, of this right and to have legal assistance assigned by the Court in any case where the interests of justice so require, and without payment if the accused lacks sufficient means to pay for it;

(e) To examine, or have examined, the witnesses against him or her and to obtain the attendance and examination of witnesses on his or her behalf under the same conditions as witnesses against him or her. The accused shall also be entitled to raise defences and to present other evidence admissible under this Statute;

(f) To have, free of any cost, the assistance of a competent interpreter and such translations as are necessary to meet the requirements of fairness, if any of the proceedings of or documents presented to the Court are not in a language which the accused fully understands and speaks;

(g) Not to be compelled to testify or to confess guilt and to remain silent, without such silence being a consideration in the determination of guilt or innocence;

(h) To make an unsworn oral or written statement in his or her defence; and

(i) Not to have imposed on him or her any reversal of the burden of proof or any onus of rebuttal.

2. In addition to any other disclosure provided for in this Statute, the Prosecutor shall, as soon as practicable, disclose to the defence evidence in the Prosecutor's possession or control which he or she believes shows or tends to show the innocence of the accused, or to mitigate the guilt of the accused, or which may affect the credibility of prosecution evidence. In case of doubt as to the application of this paragraph, the Court shall decide.

ARTICLE 68

Protection of the victims and witnesses and their participation in the proceedings

1. The Court shall take appropriate measures to protect the safety, physical and psychological well-being, dignity and privacy of victims and witnesses. In so doing, the Court shall have regard to all relevant factors, including age, gender as defined in Article 7, paragraph 3, and health, and the nature of the crime, in particular, but not limited to, where the crime involves sexual or gender violence or violence against children. The Prosecutor shall take such measures particularly during the investigation and prosecution of such crimes. These measures shall not be prejudicial to or inconsistent with the rights of the accused and a fair and impartial trial.

2. As an exception to the principle of public hearings provided for in Article 67, the Chambers of the Court may, to protect victims and witnesses or an accused, conduct any part of the proceedings *in camera* or allow the presentation of evidence by electronic or other special means. In particular, such measures shall be implemented in the case of a victim of sexual violence or a child who is a victim or a witness, unless otherwise ordered by the Court, having regard to all the circumstances, particularly the views of the victim or witness.

3. Where the personal interests of the victims are affected, the Court shall permit their views and concerns to be presented and considered at stages of the proceedings determined to be appropriate by the Court and in a manner which is not prejudicial to or inconsistent with the rights of the accused and a fair and impartial trial. Such views and concerns may be presented by the legal representatives of the victims where the Court considers it appropriate, in accordance with the Rules of Procedure and Evidence.

4. The Victims and Witnesses Unit may advise the Prosecutor and the Court on appropriate protective measures, security arrangements, counselling and assistance as referred to in Article 43, paragraph 6.

5. Where the disclosure of evidence or information pursuant to this Statute may lead to the grave endangerment of the security of a witness or his or her family, the Prosecutor may, for the purposes of any proceedings conducted prior to the commencement of the trial, withhold such evidence or information and instead submit a summary thereof. Such measures shall be exercised in a manner which is not prejudicial to or inconsistent with the rights of the accused and a fair and impartial trial.

6. A State may make an application for necessary measures to be taken in respect of the protection of its servants or agents and the protection of confidential or sensitive information.

ARTICLE 69

Evidence

1. Before testifying, each witness shall, in accordance with the Rules of Procedure and Evidence, give an undertaking as to the truthfulness of the evidence to be given by that witness.

2. The testimony of a witness at trial shall be given in person, except to the extent provided by the measures set forth in Article 68 or in the Rules of Procedure and Evidence. The Court may also permit the giving of *viva voce* (oral) or recorded testimony of a witness by means of video or audio technology, as well as the introduction of documents or written transcripts, subject to this Statute and in accordance with the Rules of Procedure and Evidence. These measures shall not be prejudicial to or inconsistent with the rights of the accused.

3. The parties may submit evidence relevant to the case, in accordance with Article 64. The Court shall have the authority to request the submission of all evidence that it considers necessary for the determination of the truth.

4. The Court may rule on the relevance or admissibility of any evidence, taking into account, *inter alia*, the probative value of the evidence and any prejudice that such evidence may cause to a fair trial or to a fair evaluation of the testimony of a witness, in accordance with the Rules of Procedure and Evidence.

5. The Court shall respect and observe privileges on confidentiality as provided for in the Rules of Procedure and Evidence.

6. The Court shall not require proof of facts of common knowledge but may take judicial notice of them.

7. Evidence obtained by means of a violation of this Statute or internationally recognized human rights shall not be admissible if:

(a) The violation casts substantial doubt on the reliability of the evidence; or

(b) The admission of the evidence would be antithetical to and would seriously damage the integrity of the proceedings.

8. When deciding on the relevance or admissibility of evidence collected by a State, the Court shall not rule on the application of the State's national law.

ARTICLE 70

Offences against the administration of justice

1. The Court shall have jurisdiction over the following offences against its administration of justice when committed intentionally:

(a) Giving false testimony when under an obligation pursuant to Article 69, paragraph 1, to tell the truth;

(b) Presenting evidence that the party knows is false or forged;

(c) Corruptly influencing a witness, obstructing or interfering with the attendance or testimony of a witness, retaliating against a witness for giving testimony or destroying, tampering with or interfering with the collection of evidence;

(d) Impeding, intimidating or corruptly influencing an official of the Court for the purpose of forcing or persuading the official not to perform, or to perform improperly, his or her duties;

(e) Retaliating against an official of the Court on account of duties performed by that or another official;

(f) Soliciting or accepting a bribe as an official of the Court in connection with his or her official duties.

2. The principles and procedures governing the Court's exercise of jurisdiction over offences under this Article shall be those provided for in the Rules of Procedure and Evidence. The conditions for providing international cooperation to the Court with respect to its proceedings under this Article shall be governed by the domestic laws of the requested State.

3. In the event of conviction, the Court may impose a term of imprisonment not exceeding five years, or a fine in accordance with the Rules of Procedure and Evidence, or both.

4. (a) Each State Party shall extend its criminal laws penalizing offences against the integrity of its own investigative or judicial process to offences against the administration of justice referred to in this article, committed on its territory, or by one of its nationals;

(b) Upon request by the Court, whenever it deems it proper, the State Party shall submit the case to its competent authorities for the purpose of prosecution. Those authorities shall treat such cases with diligence and devote sufficient resources to enable them to be conducted effectively.

ARTICLE 71

Sanctions for misconduct before the Court

1. The Court may sanction persons present before it who commit misconduct, including disruption of its proceedings or deliberate refusal to comply with its directions, by administrative measures other than imprisonment, such as temporary or permanent removal from

the courtroom, a fine or other similar measures provided for in the Rules of Procedure and Evidence.

2. The procedures governing the imposition of the measures set forth in paragraph 1 shall be those provided for in the Rules of Procedure and Evidence.

ARTICLE 72

Protection of national security information

1. This Article applies in any case where the disclosure of the information or documents of a State would, in the opinion of that State, prejudice its national security interests. Such cases include those falling within the scope of Article 56, paragraphs 2 and 3, Article 61, paragraph 3, Article 64, paragraph 3, Article 67, paragraph 2, Article 68, paragraph 6, Article 87, paragraph 6 and Article 93, as well as cases arising at any other stage of the proceedings where such disclosure may be at issue.

2. This Article shall also apply when a person who has been requested to give information or evidence has refused to do so or has referred the matter to the State on the ground that disclosure would prejudice the national security interests of a State and the State concerned confirms that it is of the opinion that disclosure would prejudice its national security interests.

3. Nothing in this article shall prejudice the requirements of confidentiality applicable under Article 54, paragraph 3(e) and (f), or the application of Article 73.

4. If a State learns that information or documents of the State are being, or are likely to be, disclosed at any stage of the proceedings, and it is of the opinion that disclosure would prejudice its national security interests, that State shall have the right to intervene in order to obtain resolution of the issue in accordance with this Article.

5. If, in the opinion of a State, disclosure of information would prejudice its national security interests, all reasonable steps will be taken by the State, acting in conjunction with the Prosecutor, the defence or the Pre-Trial Chamber or Trial Chamber, as the case may be, to seek to resolve the matter by cooperative means. Such steps may include:

(a) Modification or clarification of the request;

(b) A determination by the Court regarding the relevance of the information or evidence sought, or a determination as to whether the evidence, though relevant, could be or has been obtained from a source other than the requested State;

(c) Obtaining the information or evidence from a different source or in a different form; or

(d) Agreement on conditions under which the assistance could be provided including, among other things, providing summaries or redactions, limitations on disclosure, use of *in camera* or *ex parte* proceedings, or other protective measures permissible under the Statute and the Rules of Procedure and Evidence.

6. Once all reasonable steps have been taken to resolve the matter through cooperative means, and if the State considers that there are no means or conditions under which the information or documents could be provided or disclosed without prejudice to its national security interests, it shall so notify the Prosecutor or the Court of the specific reasons for its

decision, unless a specific description of the reasons would itself necessarily result in such prejudice to the State's national security interests.

7. Thereafter, if the Court determines that the evidence is relevant and necessary for the establishment of the guilt or innocence of the accused, the Court may undertake the following actions:

(a) Where disclosure of the information or document is sought pursuant to a request for cooperation under Part 9 or the circumstances described in paragraph 2, and the State has invoked the ground for refusal referred to in Article 93, paragraph 4:

   (i) The Court may, before making any conclusion referred to in subparagraph 7(a)(ii), request further consultations for the purpose of considering the State's representations, which may include, as appropriate, hearings *in camera* and *ex parte*;

   (ii) If the Court concludes that, by invoking the ground for refusal under Article 93, paragraph 4, in the circumstances of the case, the requested State is not acting in accordance with its obligations under this Statute, the Court may refer the matter in accordance with Article 87, paragraph 7, specifying the reasons for its conclusion; and

   (iii) The Court may make such inference in the trial of the accused as to the existence or non-existence of a fact, as may be appropriate in the circumstances; or

(b) In all other circumstances:

   (i) Order disclosure; or

   (ii) To the extent it does not order disclosure, make such inference in the trial of the accused as to the existence or non-existence of a fact, as may be appropriate in the circumstances.

ARTICLE 73

Third-party information or documents

If a State Party is requested by the Court to provide a document or information in its custody, possession or control, which was disclosed to it in confidence by a State, intergovernmental organization or international organization, it shall seek the consent of the originator to disclose that document or information. If the originator is a State Party, it shall either consent to disclosure of the information or document or undertake to resolve the issue of disclosure with the Court, subject to the provisions of Article 72. If the originator is not a State Party and refuses to consent to disclosure, the requested State shall inform the Court that it is unable to provide the document or information because of a pre-existing obligation of confidentiality to the originator.

ARTICLE 74

Requirements for the decision

1. All the judges of the Trial Chamber shall be present at each stage of the trial and

throughout their deliberations. The Presidency may, on a case-by-case basis, designate, as available, one or more alternate judges to be present at each stage of the trial and to replace a member of the Trial Chamber if that member is unable to continue attending.

2. The Trial Chamber's decision shall be based on its evaluation of the evidence and the entire proceedings. The decision shall not exceed the facts and circumstances described in the charges and any amendments to the charges. The Court may base its decision only on evidence submitted and discussed before it at the trial.

3. The judges shall attempt to achieve unanimity in their decision, failing which the decision shall be taken by a majority of the judges.

4. The deliberations of the Trial Chamber shall remain secret.

5. The decision shall be in writing and shall contain a full and reasoned statement of the Trial Chamber's findings on the evidence and conclusions. The Trial Chamber shall issue one decision. When there is no unanimity, the Trial Chamber's decision shall contain the views of the majority and the minority. The decision or a summary thereof shall be delivered in open court.

ARTICLE 75

Reparations to victims

1. The Court shall establish principles relating to reparations to, or in respect of, victims, including restitution, compensation and rehabilitation. On this basis, in its decision the Court may, either upon request or on its own motion in exceptional circumstances, determine the scope and extent of any damage, loss and injury to, or in respect of, victims and will state the principles on which it is acting.

2. The Court may make an order directly against a convicted person specifying appropriate reparations to, or in respect of, victims, including restitution, compensation and rehabilitation.

Where appropriate, the Court may order that the award for reparations be made through the Trust Fund provided for in Article 79.

3. Before making an order under this article, the Court may invite and shall take account of representations from or on behalf of the convicted person, victims, other interested persons or interested States.

4. In exercising its power under this Article, the Court may, after a person is convicted of a crime within the jurisdiction of the Court, determine whether, in order to give effect to an order which it may make under this article, it is necessary to seek measures under Article 93, paragraph 1.

5. A State Party shall give effect to a decision under this Article as if the provisions of Article 109 were applicable to this article.

6. Nothing in this Article shall be interpreted as prejudicing the rights of victims under national or international law.

ARTICLE 76

Sentencing

1. In the event of a conviction, the Trial Chamber shall consider the appropriate sentence to be imposed and shall take into account the evidence presented and submissions made during the trial that are relevant to the sentence.

2. Except where Article 65 applies and before the completion of the trial, the Trial Chamber may on its own motion and shall, at the request of the Prosecutor or the accused, hold a further hearing to hear any additional evidence or submissions relevant to the sentence, in accordance with the Rules of Procedure and Evidence.

3. Where paragraph 2 applies, any representations under Article 75 shall be heard during the further hearing referred to in paragraph 2 and, if necessary, during any additional hearing.

4. The sentence shall be pronounced in public and, wherever possible, in the presence of the accused.

PART 7: PENALTIES

ARTICLE 77

Applicable penalties

1. Subject to Article 110, the Court may impose one of the following penalties on a person convicted of a crime referred to in Article 5 of this Statute:

   (a) Imprisonment for a specified number of years, which may not exceed a maximum of thirty years; or

   (b) A term of life imprisonment when justified by the extreme gravity of the crime and the individual circumstances of the convicted person.

2. In addition to imprisonment, the Court may order:

   (a) A fine under the criteria provided for in the Rules of Procedure and Evidence;

   (b) A forfeiture of proceeds, property and assets derived directly or indirectly from that crime, without prejudice to the rights of *bona fide* third parties.

ARTICLE 78

Determination of the sentence

1. In determining the sentence, the Court shall, in accordance with the Rules of Procedure and Evidence, take into account such factors as the gravity of the crime and the individual circumstances of the convicted person.

2. In imposing a sentence of imprisonment, the Court shall deduct the time, if any,

previously spent in detention in accordance with an order of the Court. The Court may deduct any time otherwise spent in detention in connection with conduct underlying the crime.

3. When a person has been convicted of more than one crime, the Court shall pronounce a sentence for each crime and a joint sentence specifying the total period of imprisonment. This period shall be no less than the highest individual sentence pronounced and shall not exceed thirty years imprisonment or a sentence of life imprisonment in conformity with Article 77, paragraph 1(b).

ARTICLE 79

Trust Fund

1. A Trust Fund shall be established by decision of the Assembly of States Parties for the benefit of victims of crimes within the jurisdiction of the Court, and of the families of such victims.

2. The Court may order money and other property collected through fines or forfeiture to be transferred, by order of the Court, to the Trust Fund.

3. The Trust Fund shall be managed according to criteria to be determined by the Assembly of States Parties.

ARTICLE 80

Non-prejudice to national application of penalties and national laws

Nothing in this Part affects the application by States of penalties prescribed by their national law, nor the law of States which do not provide for penalties prescribed in this Part.

PART 8: APPEAL AND REVISION

ARTICLE 81

Appeal against decision of acquittal or conviction or against sentence

1. A decision under Article 74 may be appealed in accordance with the Rules of Procedure and Evidence as follows:

(a) The Prosecutor may make an appeal on any of the following grounds:

   (i)   Procedural error,

   (ii) Error of fact, or

   (iii) Error of law;

(b) The convicted person, or the Prosecutor on that person's behalf, may make an appeal on any of the following grounds:

    (i)   Procedural error,

    (ii)   Error of fact,

    (iii) Error of law, or

    (iv) Any other ground that affects the fairness or reliability of the proceedings or decision.

2. (a) A sentence may be appealed, in accordance with the Rules of Procedure and Evidence, by the Prosecutor or the convicted person on the ground of disproportion between the crime and the sentence;

    (b) If on an appeal against sentence the Court considers that there are grounds on which the conviction might be set aside, wholly or in part, it may invite the Prosecutor and the convicted person to submit grounds under Article 81, paragraph 1(a) or (b), and may render a decision on conviction in accordance with Article 83;

    (c) The same procedure applies when the Court, on an appeal against conviction only, considers that there are grounds to reduce the sentence under paragraph 2(a).

3. (a) Unless the Trial Chamber orders otherwise, a convicted person shall remain in custody pending an appeal;

    (b) When a convicted person's time in custody exceeds the sentence of imprisonment imposed, that person shall be released, except that if the Prosecutor is also appealing, the release may be subject to the conditions under subparagraph (c) below;

    (c) In case of an acquittal, the accused shall be released immediately, subject to the following:

        (i)   Under exceptional circumstances, and having regard, *inter alia*, to the concrete risk of flight, the seriousness of the offence charged and the probability of success on appeal, the Trial Chamber, at the request of the Prosecutor, may maintain the detention of the person pending appeal;

        (ii) A decision by the Trial Chamber under subparagraph (c)(i) may be appealed in accordance with the Rules of Procedure and Evidence.

4. Subject to the provisions of paragraph 3(a) and (b), execution of the decision or sentence shall be suspended during the period allowed for appeal and for the duration of the appeal proceedings.

ARTICLE 82

Appeal against other decisions

1. Either party may appeal any of the following decisions in accordance with the Rules of Procedure and Evidence:

  (a) A decision with respect to jurisdiction or admissibility;

  (b) A decision granting or denying release of the person being investigated or prosecuted;

(c) A decision of the Pre-Trial Chamber to act on its own initiative under Article 56, paragraph 3;

(d) A decision that involves an issue that would significantly affect the fair and expeditious conduct of the proceedings or the outcome of the trial, and for which, in the opinion of the Pre-Trial or Trial Chamber, an immediate resolution by the Appeals Chamber may materially advance the proceedings.

2. A decision of the Pre-Trial Chamber under Article 57, paragraph 3(d), may be appealed against by the State concerned or by the Prosecutor, with the leave of the Pre-Trial Chamber. The appeal shall be heard on an expedited basis.

3. An appeal shall not of itself have suspensive effect unless the Appeals Chamber so orders, upon request, in accordance with the Rules of Procedure and Evidence.

4. A legal representative of the victims, the convicted person or a *bona fide* owner of property adversely affected by an order under Article 75 may appeal against the order for reparations, as provided in the Rules of Procedure and Evidence.

ARTICLE 83

Proceedings on appeal

1. For the purposes of proceedings under Article 81 and this Article, the Appeals Chamber shall have all the powers of the Trial Chamber.

2. If the Appeals Chamber finds that the proceedings appealed from were unfair in a way that affected the reliability of the decision or sentence, or that the decision or sentence appealed from was materially affected by error of fact or law or procedural error, it may:

(a) Reverse or amend the decision or sentence; or

(b) Order a new trial before a different Trial Chamber.

For these purposes, the Appeals Chamber may remand a factual issue to the original Trial Chamber for it to determine the issue and to report back accordingly, or may itself call evidence to determine the issue. When the decision or sentence has been appealed only by the person convicted, or the Prosecutor on that person's behalf, it cannot be amended to his or her detriment.

3. If in an appeal against sentence the Appeals Chamber finds that the sentence is disproportionate to the crime, it may vary the sentence in accordance with Part 7.

4. The judgment of the Appeals Chamber shall be taken by a majority of the judges and shall be delivered in open court. The judgment shall state the reasons on which it is based. When there is no unanimity, the judgment of the Appeals Chamber shall contain the views of the majority and the minority, but a judge may deliver a separate or dissenting opinion on a question of law.

5. The Appeals Chamber may deliver its judgment in the absence of the person acquitted or convicted.

ARTICLE 84

Revision of conviction or sentence

1. The convicted person or, after death, spouses, children, parents or one person alive at the time of the accused's death who has been given express written instructions from the accused to bring such a claim, or the Prosecutor on the person's behalf, may apply to the Appeals Chamber to revise the final judgment of conviction or sentence on the grounds that:

   (a) New evidence has been discovered that:

      (i) Was not available at the time of trial, and such unavailability was not wholly or partially attributable to the party making application; and

      (ii) Is sufficiently important that had it been proved at trial it would have been likely to have resulted in a different verdict;

   (b) It has been newly discovered that decisive evidence, taken into account at trial and upon which the conviction depends, was false, forged or falsified;

   (c) One or more of the judges who participated in conviction or confirmation of the charges has committed, in that case, an act of serious misconduct or serious breach of duty of sufficient gravity to justify the removal of that judge or those judges from office under Article 46.

2. The Appeals Chamber shall reject the application if it considers it to be unfounded. If it determines that the application is meritorious, it may, as appropriate:

   (a) Reconvene the original Trial Chamber;

   (b) Constitute a new Trial Chamber; or

   (c) Retain jurisdiction over the matter,

with a view to, after hearing the parties in the manner set forth in the Rules of Procedure and Evidence, arriving at a determination on whether the judgment should be revised.

ARTICLE 85

Compensation to an arrested or convicted person

1. Anyone who has been the victim of unlawful arrest or detention shall have an enforceable right to compensation.

2. When a person has by a final decision been convicted of a criminal offence, and when subsequently his or her conviction has been reversed on the ground that a new or newly discovered fact shows conclusively that there has been a miscarriage of justice, the person who has suffered punishment as a result of such conviction shall be compensated according to law, unless it is proved that the non-disclosure of the unknown fact in time is wholly or partly attributable to him or her.

3. In exceptional circumstances, where the Court finds conclusive facts showing that there has been a grave and manifest miscarriage of justice, it may in its discretion award compensation, according to the criteria provided in the Rules of Procedure and Evidence, to a person who has been released from detention following a final decision of acquittal or a termination of the proceedings for that reason.

PART 9: INTERNATIONAL COOPERATION AND JUDICIAL
ASSISTANCE

ARTICLE 86

General obligation to cooperate

States Parties shall, in accordance with the provisions of this Statute, cooperate fully with the
Court in its investigation and prosecution of crimes within the jurisdiction of the Court.

ARTICLE 87

Requests for cooperation: general provisions

1. (a) The Court shall have the authority to make requests to States Parties for cooperation. The requests shall be transmitted through the diplomatic channel or any
other appropriate channel as may be designated by each State Party upon ratification, acceptance, approval or accession.

    Subsequent changes to the designation shall be made by each State Party in
accordance with the Rules of Procedure and Evidence.

    (b) When appropriate, without prejudice to the provisions of subparagraph (a),
requests may also be transmitted through the International Criminal Police
Organization or any appropriate regional organization.

2. Requests for cooperation and any documents supporting the request shall either be in or
be accompanied by a translation into an official language of the requested State or one of the
working languages of the Court, in accordance with the choice made by that State upon
ratification, acceptance, approval or accession.

    Subsequent changes to this choice shall be made in accordance with the Rules of Pro-
cedure and Evidence.

3. The requested State shall keep confidential a request for cooperation and any documents supporting the request, except to the extent that the disclosure is necessary for
execution of the request.

4. In relation to any request for assistance presented under this Part, the Court may take
such measures, including measures related to the protection of information, as may be
necessary to ensure the safety or physical or psychological well-being of any victims, potential witnesses and their families. The Court may request that any information that is made
available under this Part shall be provided and handled in a manner that protects the safety
and physical or psychological well-being of any victims, potential witnesses and their
families.

5. (a) The Court may invite any State not party to this Statute to provide assistance
under this Part on the basis of an *ad hoc* arrangement, an agreement with such
State or any other appropriate basis.

    (b) Where a State not party to this Statute, which has entered into an *ad hoc* arrangement or an agreement with the Court, fails to cooperate with requests pursuant to any such arrangement or agreement, the Court may so inform the Assembly of States Parties or, where the Security Council referred the matter to the Court, the Security Council.

6. The Court may ask any intergovernmental organization to provide information or documents. The Court may also ask for other forms of cooperation and assistance which may be agreed upon with such an organization and which are in accordance with its competence or mandate.

7. Where a State Party fails to comply with a request to cooperate by the Court contrary to the provisions of this Statute, thereby preventing the Court from exercising its functions and powers under this Statute, the Court may make a finding to that effect and refer the matter to the Assembly of States Parties or, where the Security Council referred the matter to the Court, to the Security Council.

ARTICLE 88

Availability of procedures under national law

States Parties shall ensure that there are procedures available under their national law for all of the forms of cooperation which are specified under this Part.

ARTICLE 89

Surrender of persons to the Court

1. The Court may transmit a request for the arrest and surrender of a person, together with the material supporting the request outlined in Article 91, to any State on the territory of which that person may be found and shall request the cooperation of that State in the arrest and surrender of such a person. States Parties shall, in accordance with the provisions of this Part and the procedure under their national law, comply with requests for arrest and surrender.

2. Where the person sought for surrender brings a challenge before a national court on the basis of the principle of *ne bis in idem* as provided in Article 20, the requested State shall immediately consult with the Court to determine if there has been a relevant ruling on admissibility. If the case is admissible, the requested State shall proceed with the execution of the request. If an admissibility ruling is pending, the requested State may postpone the execution of the request for surrender of the person until the Court makes a determination on admissibility.

3. (a) A State Party shall authorize, in accordance with its national procedural law, transportation through its territory of a person being surrendered to the Court by another State, except where transit through that State would impede or delay the surrender.

   (b) A request by the Court for transit shall be transmitted in accordance with Article 87. The request for transit shall contain:

(i)   A description of the person being transported;

(ii)   A brief statement of the facts of the case and their legal characterization; and

(iii) The warrant for arrest and surrender;

(c) A person being transported shall be detained in custody during the period of transit;

(d) No authorization is required if the person is transported by air and no landing is scheduled on the territory of the transit State;

(e) If an unscheduled landing occurs on the territory of the transit State, that State may require a request for transit from the Court as provided for in subparagraph (b). The transit State shall detain the person being transported until the request for transit is received and the transit is effected, provided that detention for purposes of this subparagraph may not be extended beyond ninety-six hours from the unscheduled landing unless the request is received within that time.

4. If the person sought is being proceeded against or is serving a sentence in the requested State for a crime different from that for which surrender to the Court is sought, the requested State, after making its decision to grant the request, shall consult with the Court.

ARTICLE 90

Competing requests

1. A State Party which receives a request from the Court for the surrender of a person under Article 89 shall, if it also receives a request from any other State for the extradition of the same person for the same conduct which forms the basis of the crime for which the Court seeks the person's surrender, notify the Court and the requesting State of that fact.

2. Where the requesting State is a State Party, the requested State shall give priority to the request from the Court if:

(a) The Court has, pursuant to Article 18 or 19, made a determination that the case in respect of which surrender is sought is admissible and that determination takes into account the investigation or prosecution conducted by the requesting State in respect of its request for extradition; or

(b) The Court makes the determination described in subparagraph (a) pursuant to the requested State's notification under paragraph 1.

3. Where a determination under paragraph 2(a) has not been made, the requested State may, at its discretion, pending the determination of the Court under paragraph 2(b), proceed to deal with the request for extradition from the requesting State but shall not extradite the person until the Court has determined that the case is inadmissible. The Court's determination shall be made on an expedited basis.

4. If the requesting State is a State not Party to this Statute the requested State, if it is not under an international obligation to extradite the person to the requesting State, shall give priority to the request for surrender from the Court, if the Court has determined that the case is admissible.

5. Where a case under paragraph 4 has not been determined to be admissible by the Court, the requested State may, at its discretion, proceed to deal with the request for extradition from the requesting State.

6. In cases where paragraph 4 applies except that the requested State is under an existing international obligation to extradite the person to the requesting State not Party to this Statute, the requested State shall determine whether to surrender the person to the Court or extradite the person to the requesting State. In making its decision, the requested State shall consider all the relevant factors, including but not limited to:

(a) The respective dates of the requests;

(b) The interests of the requesting State including, where relevant, whether the crime was committed in its territory and the nationality of the victims and of the person sought; and

(c) The possibility of subsequent surrender between the Court and the requesting State.

7. Where a State Party which receives a request from the Court for the surrender of a person also receives a request from any State for the extradition of the same person for conduct other than that which constitutes the crime for which the Court seeks the person's surrender:

(a) The requested State shall, if it is not under an existing international obligation to extradite the person to the requesting State, give priority to the request from the Court;

(b) The requested State shall, if it is under an existing international obligation to extradite the person to the requesting State, determine whether to surrender the person to the Court or to extradite the person to the requesting State. In making its decision, the requested State shall consider all the relevant factors, including but not limited to those set out in paragraph 6, but shall give special consideration to the relative nature and gravity of the conduct in question.

8. Where pursuant to a notification under this article, the Court has determined a case to be inadmissible, and subsequently extradition to the requesting State is refused, the requested State shall notify the Court of this decision.

ARTICLE 91

Contents of request for arrest and surrender

1. A request for arrest and surrender shall be made in writing. In urgent cases, a request may be made by any medium capable of delivering a written record, provided that the request shall be confirmed through the channel provided for in Article 87, paragraph 1(a).

2. In the case of a request for the arrest and surrender of a person for whom a warrant of arrest has been issued by the Pre-Trial Chamber under Article 58, the request shall contain or be supported by:

(a) Information describing the person sought, sufficient to identify the person, and information as to that person's probable location;

(b) A copy of the warrant of arrest; and

(c) Such documents, statements or information as may be necessary to meet the requirements for the surrender process in the requested State, except that those requirements should not be more burdensome than those applicable to requests for extradition pursuant to treaties or arrangements between the requested State and other States and should, if possible, be less burdensome, taking into account the distinct nature of the Court.

3. In the case of a request for the arrest and surrender of a person already convicted, the request shall contain or be supported by:

(a) A copy of any warrant of arrest for that person;

(b) A copy of the judgment of conviction;

(c) Information to demonstrate that the person sought is the one referred to in the judgment of conviction; and

(d) If the person sought has been sentenced, a copy of the sentence imposed and, in the case of a sentence for imprisonment, a statement of any time already served and the time remaining to be served.

4. Upon the request of the Court, a State Party shall consult with the Court, either generally or with respect to a specific matter, regarding any requirements under its national law that may apply under paragraph 2(c). During the consultations, the State Party shall advise the Court of the specific requirements of its national law.

ARTICLE 92

Provisional arrest

1. In urgent cases, the Court may request the provisional arrest of the person sought, pending presentation of the request for surrender and the documents supporting the request as specified in Article 91.

2. The request for provisional arrest shall be made by any medium capable of delivering a written record and shall contain:

(a) Information describing the person sought, sufficient to identify the person, and information as to that person's probable location;

(b) A concise statement of the crimes for which the person's arrest is sought and of the facts which are alleged to constitute those crimes, including, where possible, the date and location of the crime;

(c) A statement of the existence of a warrant of arrest or a judgment of conviction against the person sought; and

(d) A statement that a request for surrender of the person sought will follow.

3. A person who is provisionally arrested may be released from custody if the requested State has not received the request for surrender and the documents supporting the request as specified in Article 91 within the time limits specified in the Rules of Procedure and

Evidence. However, the person may consent to surrender before the expiration of this period if permitted by the law of the requested State. In such a case, the requested State shall proceed to surrender the person to the Court as soon as possible.

4. The fact that the person sought has been released from custody pursuant to paragraph 3 shall not prejudice the subsequent arrest and surrender of that person if the request for surrender and the documents supporting the request are delivered at a later date.

ARTICLE 93

Other forms of cooperation

1. States Parties shall, in accordance with the provisions of this Part and under procedures of national law, comply with requests by the Court to provide the following assistance in relation to investigations or prosecutions:

(a) The identification and whereabouts of persons or the location of items;

(b) The taking of evidence, including testimony under oath, and the production of evidence, including expert opinions and reports necessary to the Court;

(c) The questioning of any person being investigated or prosecuted;

(d) The service of documents, including judicial documents;

(e) Facilitating the voluntary appearance of persons as witnesses or experts before the Court;

(f) The temporary transfer of persons as provided in paragraph 7;

(g) The examination of places or sites, including the exhumation and examination of grave sites;

(h) The execution of searches and seizures;

(i) The provision of records and documents, including official records and documents;

(j) The protection of victims and witnesses and the preservation of evidence;

(k) The identification, tracing and freezing or seizure of proceeds, property and assets and instrumentalities of crimes for the purpose of eventual forfeiture, without prejudice to the rights of *bona fide* third parties; and

(l) Any other type of assistance which is not prohibited by the law of the requested State, with a view to facilitating the investigation and prosecution of crimes within the jurisdiction of the Court.

2. The Court shall have the authority to provide an assurance to a witness or an expert appearing before the Court that he or she will not be prosecuted, detained or subjected to any restriction of personal freedom by the Court in respect of any act or omission that preceded the departure of that person from the requested State.

3. Where execution of a particular measure of assistance detailed in a request presented under paragraph 1, is prohibited in the requested State on the basis of an existing fundamental legal principle of general application, the requested State shall promptly consult with the Court to try to resolve the matter. In the consultations, consideration should be given to whether the assistance can be rendered in another manner or subject to conditions. If after

consultations the matter cannot be resolved, the Court shall modify the request as necessary.

4. In accordance with Article 72, a State Party may deny a request for assistance, in whole or in part, only if the request concerns the production of any documents or disclosure of evidence which relates to its national security.

5. Before denying a request for assistance under paragraph 1(1), the requested State shall consider whether the assistance can be provided subject to specified conditions, or whether the assistance can be provided at a later date or in an alternative manner, provided that if the Court or the Prosecutor accepts the assistance subject to conditions, the Court or the Prosecutor shall abide by them.

6. If a request for assistance is denied, the requested State Party shall promptly inform the Court or the Prosecutor of the reasons for such denial.

7. (a) The Court may request the temporary transfer of a person in custody for purposes of identification or for obtaining testimony or other assistance. The person may be transferred if the following conditions are fulfilled:

    (i)   The person freely gives his or her informed consent to the transfer; and

    (ii)   The requested State agrees to the transfer, subject to such conditions as that State and the Court may agree.

(b) The person being transferred shall remain in custody. When the purposes of the transfer have been fulfilled, the Court shall return the person without delay to the requested State.

8. (a) The Court shall ensure the confidentiality of documents and information, except as required for the investigation and proceedings described in the request.

(b) The requested State may, when necessary, transmit documents or information to the Prosecutor on a confidential basis. The Prosecutor may then use them solely for the purpose of generating new evidence.

(c) The requested State may, on its own motion or at the request of the Prosecutor, subsequently consent to the disclosure of such documents or information. They may then be used as evidence pursuant to the provisions of Parts 5 and 6 and in accordance with the Rules of Procedure and Evidence.

9. (a) (i)   In the event that a State Party receives competing requests, other than for surrender or extradition, from the Court and from another State pursuant to an international obligation, the State Party shall endeavour, in consultation with the Court and the other State, to meet both requests, if necessary by postponing or attaching conditions to one or the other request.

    (ii)   Failing that, competing requests shall be resolved in accordance with the principles established in Article 90.

(b) Where, however, the request from the Court concerns information, property or persons which are subject to the control of a third State or an international organization by virtue of an international agreement, the requested States shall so inform the Court and the Court shall direct its request to the third State or international organization.

10. (a) The Court may, upon request, cooperate with and provide assistance to a State Party conducting an investigation into or trial in respect of conduct which

constitutes a crime within the jurisdiction of the Court or which constitutes a serious crime under the national law of the requesting State.

(b) (i) The assistance provided under subparagraph (a) shall include, *inter alia*:

    a. The transmission of statements, documents or other types of evidence obtained in the course of an investigation or a trial conducted by the Court; and

    b. The questioning of any person detained by order of the Court;

(ii) In the case of assistance under subparagraph (b)(i) a:

    a. If the documents or other types of evidence have been obtained with the assistance of a State, such transmission shall require the consent of that State;

    b. If the statements, documents or other types of evidence have been provided by a witness or expert, such transmission shall be subject to the provisions of Article 68.

(c) The Court may, under the conditions set out in this paragraph, grant a request for assistance under this paragraph from a State which is not a Party to this Statute.

ARTICLE 94

Postponement of execution of a request in respect of ongoing investigation or prosecution

1. If the immediate execution of a request would interfere with an ongoing investigation or prosecution of a case different from that to which the request relates, the requested State may postpone the execution of the request for a period of time agreed upon with the Court. However, the postponement shall be no longer than is necessary to complete the relevant investigation or prosecution in the requested State. Before making a decision to postpone, the requested State should consider whether the assistance may be immediately provided subject to certain conditions.

2. If a decision to postpone is taken pursuant to paragraph 1, the Prosecutor may, however, seek measures to preserve evidence, pursuant to Article 93, paragraph 1(j).

ARTICLE 95

Postponement of execution of a request in respect of an admissibility challenge

Where there is an admissibility challenge under consideration by the Court pursuant to Article 18 or 19, the requested State may postpone the execution of a request under this Part pending a determination by the Court, unless the Court has specifically ordered that the Prosecutor may pursue the collection of such evidence pursuant to Article 18 or 19.

ARTICLE 96

Contents of request for other forms of assistance under Article 93

1. A request for other forms of assistance referred to in Article 93 shall be made in writing. In urgent cases, a request may be made by any medium capable of delivering a written record, provided that the request shall be confirmed through the channel provided for in Article 87, paragraph 1(a).

2. The request shall, as applicable, contain or be supported by the following:

(a) A concise statement of the purpose of the request and the assistance sought, including the legal basis and the grounds for the request;

(b) As much detailed information as possible about the location or identification of any person or place that must be found or identified in order for the assistance sought to be provided;

(c) A concise statement of the essential facts underlying the request;

(d) The reasons for and details of any procedure or requirement to be followed;

(e) Such information as may be required under the law of the requested State in order to execute the request; and

(f) Any other information relevant in order for the assistance sought to be provided.

3. Upon the request of the Court, a State Party shall consult with the Court, either generally or with respect to a specific matter, regarding any requirements under its national law that may apply under paragraph 2(e). During the consultations, the State Party shall advise the Court of the specific requirements of its national law.

4. The provisions of this article shall, where applicable, also apply in respect of a request for assistance made to the Court.

ARTICLE 97

Consultations

Where a State Party receives a request under this Part in relation to which it identifies problems which may impede or prevent the execution of the request, that State shall consult with the Court without delay in order to resolve the matter. Such problems may include, *inter alia*:

(a) Insufficient information to execute the request;

(b) In the case of a request for surrender, the fact that despite best efforts, the person sought cannot be located or that the investigation conducted has determined that the person in the requested State is clearly not the person named in the warrant; or

(c) The fact that execution of the request in its current form would require the requested State to breach a pre-existing treaty obligation undertaken with respect to another State.

ARTICLE 98

Cooperation with respect to waiver of immunity and consent to surrender

1. The Court may not proceed with a request for surrender or assistance which would require the requested State to act inconsistently with its obligations under international law with respect to the State or diplomatic immunity of a person or property of a third State, unless the Court can first obtain the cooperation of that third State for the waiver of the immunity.

2. The Court may not proceed with a request for surrender which would require the requested State to act inconsistently with its obligations under international agreements pursuant to which the consent of a sending State is required to surrender a person of that State to the Court, unless the Court can first obtain the cooperation of the sending State for the giving of consent for the surrender.

ARTICLE 99

Execution of requests under Articles 93 and 96

1. Requests for assistance shall be executed in accordance with the relevant procedure under the law of the requested State and, unless prohibited by such law, in the manner specified in the request, including following any procedure outlined therein or permitting persons specified in the request to be present at and assist in the execution process.

2. In the case of an urgent request, the documents or evidence produced in response shall, at the request of the Court, be sent urgently.

3. Replies from the requested State shall be transmitted in their original language and form.

4. Without prejudice to other Articles in this Part, where it is necessary for the successful execution of a request which can be executed without any compulsory measures, including specifically the interview of or taking evidence from a person on a voluntary basis, including doing so without the presence of the authorities of the requested State Party if it is essential for the request to be executed, and the examination without modification of a public site or other public place, the Prosecutor may execute such request directly on the territory of a State as follows:

(a) When the State Party requested is a State on the territory of which the crime is alleged to have been committed, and there has been a determination of admissibility pursuant to Article 18 or 19, the Prosecutor may directly execute such request following all possible consultations with the requested State Party;

(b) In other cases, the Prosecutor may execute such request following consultations with the requested State Party and subject to any reasonable conditions or concerns raised by that State Party. Where the requested State Party identifies problems with the execution of a request pursuant to this subparagraph it shall, without delay, consult with the Court to resolve the matter.

5. Provisions allowing a person heard or examined by the Court under Article 72 to invoke restrictions designed to prevent disclosure of confidential information connected with

national security shall also apply to the execution of requests for assistance under this article.

ARTICLE 100

Costs

1. The ordinary costs for execution of requests in the territory of the requested State shall be borne by that State, except for the following, which shall be borne by the Court:

    (a) Costs associated with the travel and security of witnesses and experts or the transfer under Article 93 of persons in custody;

    (b) Costs of translation, interpretation and transcription;

    (c) Travel and subsistence costs of the judges, the Prosecutor, the Deputy Prosecutors, the Registrar, the Deputy Registrar and staff of any organ of the Court;

    (d) Costs of any expert opinion or report requested by the Court;

    (e) Costs associated with the transport of a person being surrendered to the Court by a custodial State; and

    (f) Following consultations, any extraordinary costs that may result from the execution of a request.

2. The provisions of paragraph 1 shall, as appropriate, apply to requests from States Parties to the Court. In that case, the Court shall bear the ordinary costs of execution.

ARTICLE 101

Rule of speciality

1. A person surrendered to the Court under this Statute shall not be proceeded against, punished or detained for any conduct committed prior to surrender, other than the conduct or course of conduct which forms the basis of the crimes for which that person has been surrendered.

2. The Court may request a waiver of the requirements of paragraph 1 from the State which surrendered the person to the Court and, if necessary, the Court shall provide additional information in accordance with Article 91. States Parties shall have the authority to provide a waiver to the Court and should endeavour to do so.

ARTICLE 102

Use of terms

For the purposes of this Statute:

    (a) 'surrender' means the delivering up of a person by a State to the Court, pursuant to this Statute.

(b) 'extradition' means the delivering up of a person by one State to another as provided by treaty, convention or national legislation.

PART 10: ENFORCEMENT

ARTICLE 103

Role of States in enforcement of sentences of imprisonment

1. (a) A sentence of imprisonment shall be served in a State designated by the Court from a list of States which have indicated to the Court their willingness to accept sentenced persons.

   (b) At the time of declaring its willingness to accept sentenced persons, a State may attach conditions to its acceptance as agreed by the Court and in accordance with this Part.

   (c) A State designated in a particular case shall promptly inform the Court whether it accepts the Court's designation.

2. (a) The State of enforcement shall notify the Court of any circumstances, including the exercise of any conditions agreed under paragraph 1, which could materially affect the terms or extent of the imprisonment. The Court shall be given at least forty-five days' notice of any such known or foreseeable circumstances. During this period, the State of enforcement shall take no action that might prejudice its obligations under Article 110.

   (b) Where the Court cannot agree to the circumstances referred to in subparagraph (a), it shall notify the State of enforcement and proceed in accordance with Article 104, paragraph 1.

3. In exercising its discretion to make a designation under paragraph 1, the Court shall take into account the following:

   (a) The principle that States Parties should share the responsibility for enforcing sentences of imprisonment, in accordance with principles of equitable distribution, as provided in the Rules of Procedure and Evidence;

   (b) The application of widely accepted international treaty standards governing the treatment of prisoners;

   (c) The views of the sentenced person;

   (d) The nationality of the sentenced person;

   (e) Such other factors regarding the circumstances of the crime or the person sentenced, or the effective enforcement of the sentence, as may be appropriate in designating the State of enforcement.

4. If no State is designated under paragraph 1, the sentence of imprisonment shall be served in a prison facility made available by the host State, in accordance with the conditions set out in the headquarters agreement referred to in Article 3, paragraph 2. In such a case, the

costs arising out of the enforcement of a sentence of imprisonment shall be borne by the Court.

ARTICLE 104

Change in designation of State of enforcement

1. The Court may, at any time, decide to transfer a sentenced person to a prison of another State.

2. A sentenced person may, at any time, apply to the Court to be transferred from the State of enforcement.

ARTICLE 105

Enforcement of the sentence

1. Subject to conditions which a State may have specified in accordance with Article 103, paragraph 1(b), the sentence of imprisonment shall be binding on the States Parties, which shall in no case modify it.

2. The Court alone shall have the right to decide any application for appeal and revision. The State of enforcement shall not impede the making of any such application by a sentenced person.

ARTICLE 106

Supervision of enforcement of sentences and conditions of imprisonment

1. The enforcement of a sentence of imprisonment shall be subject to the supervision of the Court and shall be consistent with widely accepted international treaty standards governing treatment of prisoners.

2. The conditions of imprisonment shall be governed by the law of the State of enforcement and shall be consistent with widely accepted international treaty standards governing treatment of prisoners; in no case shall such conditions be more or less favourable than those available to prisoners convicted of similar offences in the State of enforcement.

3. Communications between a sentenced person and the Court shall be unimpeded and confidential.

ARTICLE 107

Transfer of the person upon completion of sentence

1. Following completion of the sentence, a person who is not a national of the State of enforcement may, in accordance with the law of the State of enforcement, be transferred to a State which is obliged to receive him or her, or to another State which agrees to receive him

or her, taking into account any wishes of the person to be transferred to that State, unless the State of enforcement authorizes the person to remain in its territory.

2. If no State bears the costs arising out of transferring the person to another State pursuant to paragraph 1, such costs shall be borne by the Court.

3. Subject to the provisions of Article 108, the State of enforcement may also, in accordance with its national law, extradite or otherwise surrender the person to a State which has requested the extradition or surrender of the person for purposes of trial or enforcement of a sentence.

ARTICLE 108

Limitation on the prosecution or punishment of other offences

1. A sentenced person in the custody of the State of enforcement shall not be subject to prosecution or punishment or to extradition to a third State for any conduct engaged in prior to that person's delivery to the State of enforcement, unless such prosecution, punishment or extradition has been approved by the Court at the request of the State of enforcement.

2. The Court shall decide the matter after having heard the views of the sentenced person.

3. Paragraph 1 shall cease to apply if the sentenced person remains voluntarily for more than thirty days in the territory of the State of enforcement after having served the full sentence imposed by the Court, or returns to the territory of that State after having left it.

ARTICLE 109

Enforcement of fines and forfeiture measures

1. States Parties shall give effect to fines or forfeitures ordered by the Court under Part 7, without prejudice to the rights of *bona fide* third parties, and in accordance with the procedure of their national law.

2. If a State Party is unable to give effect to an order for forfeiture, it shall take measures to recover the value of the proceeds, property or assets ordered by the Court to be forfeited, without prejudice to the rights of *bona fide* third parties.

3. Property, or the proceeds of the sale of real property or, where appropriate, the sale of other property, which is obtained by a State Party as a result of its enforcement of a judgment of the Court shall be transferred to the Court.

ARTICLE 110

Review by the Court concerning reduction of sentence

1. The State of enforcement shall not release the person before expiry of the sentence pronounced by the Court.

2. The Court alone shall have the right to decide any reduction of sentence, and shall rule on the matter after having heard the person.

3. When the person has served two thirds of the sentence, or twenty-five years in the case of life imprisonment, the Court shall review the sentence to determine whether it should be reduced. Such a review shall not be conducted before that time.

4. In its review under paragraph 3, the Court may reduce the sentence if it finds that one or more of the following factors are present:

(a) The early and continuing willingness of the person to cooperate with the Court in its investigations and prosecutions;

(b) The voluntary assistance of the person in enabling the enforcement of the judgments and orders of the Court in other cases, and in particular providing assistance in locating assets subject to orders of fine, forfeiture or reparation which may be used for the benefit of victims; or

(c) Other factors establishing a clear and significant change of circumstances sufficient to justify the reduction of sentence, as provided in the Rules of Procedure and Evidence.

5. If the Court determines in its initial review under paragraph 3 that it is not appropriate to reduce the sentence, it shall thereafter review the question of reduction of sentence at such intervals and applying such criteria as provided for in the Rules of Procedure and Evidence.

ARTICLE 111

Escape

If a convicted person escapes from custody and flees the State of enforcement, that State may, after consultation with the Court, request the person's surrender from the State in which the person is located pursuant to existing bilateral or multilateral arrangements, or may request that the Court seek the person's surrender, in accordance with Part 9. It may direct that the person be delivered to the State in which he or she was serving the sentence or to another State designated by the Court.

PART 11: ASSEMBLY OF STATE PARTIES

ARTICLE 112

Assembly of States Parties

1. An Assembly of States Parties to this Statute is hereby established. Each State Party shall have one representative in the Assembly who may be accompanied by alternates and advisers. Other States which have signed this Statute or the Final Act may be observers in the Assembly.

2. The Assembly shall:

(a) Consider and adopt, as appropriate, recommendations of the Preparatory Commission;

(b) Provide management oversight to the Presidency, the Prosecutor and the Registrar regarding the administration of the Court;

(c) Consider the reports and activities of the Bureau established under paragraph 3 and take appropriate action in regard thereto;

(d) Consider and decide the budget for the Court;

(e) Decide whether to alter, in accordance with Article 36, the number of judges;

(f) Consider pursuant to Article 87, paragraphs 5 and 7, any question relating to non-cooperation;

(g) Perform any other function consistent with this Statute or the Rules of Procedure and Evidence.

3. (a) The Assembly shall have a Bureau consisting of a President, two Vice-Presidents and eighteen members elected by the Assembly for three-year terms.

(b) The Bureau shall have a representative character, taking into account, in particular, equitable geographical distribution and the adequate representation of the principal legal systems of the world.

(c) The Bureau shall meet as often as necessary, but at least once a year. It shall assist the Assembly in the discharge of its responsibilities.

4. The Assembly may establish such subsidiary bodies as may be necessary, including an independent oversight mechanism for inspection, evaluation and investigation of the Court, in order to enhance its efficiency and economy.

5. The President of the Court, the Prosecutor and the Registrar or their representatives may participate, as appropriate, in meetings of the Assembly and of the Bureau.

6. The Assembly shall meet at the seat of the Court or at the Headquarters of the United Nations once a year and, when circumstances so require, hold special sessions. Except as otherwise specified in this Statute, special sessions shall be convened by the Bureau on its own initiative or at the request of one third of the States Parties.

7. Each State Party shall have one vote. Every effort shall be made to reach decisions by consensus in the Assembly and in the Bureau. If consensus cannot be reached, except as otherwise provided in the Statute:

(a) Decisions on matters of substance must be approved by a two-thirds majority of those present and voting provided that an absolute majority of States Parties constitutes the quorum for voting;

(b) Decisions on matters of procedure shall be taken by a simple majority of States Parties present and voting.

8. A State Party which is in arrears in the payment of its financial contributions towards the costs of the Court shall have no vote in the Assembly and in the Bureau if the amount of its arrears equals or exceeds the amount of the contributions due from it for the preceding two full years. The Assembly may, nevertheless, permit such a State Party to vote in the Assembly and in the Bureau if it is satisfied that the failure to pay is due to conditions beyond the control of the State Party.

9. The Assembly shall adopt its own rules of procedure.

10. The official and working languages of the Assembly shall be those of the General Assembly of the United Nations.

PART 12: FINANCING

ARTICLE 113

Financial Regulations

Except as otherwise specifically provided, all financial matters related to the Court and the meetings of the Assembly of States Parties, including its Bureau and subsidiary bodies, shall be governed by this Statute and the Financial Regulations and Rules adopted by the Assembly of States Parties.

ARTICLE 114

Payment of expenses

Expenses of the Court and the Assembly of States Parties, including its Bureau and subsidiary bodies, shall be paid from the funds of the Court.

ARTICLE 115

Funds of the Court and of the Assembly of States Parties

The expenses of the Court and the Assembly of States Parties, including its Bureau and subsidiary bodies, as provided for in the budget decided by the Assembly of States Parties, shall be provided by the following sources:

(a) Assessed contributions made by States Parties;

(b) Funds provided by the United Nations, subject to the approval of the General Assembly, in particular in relation to the expenses incurred due to referrals by the Security Council.

ARTICLE 116

Voluntary contributions

Without prejudice to Article 115, the Court may receive and utilize, as additional funds, voluntary contributions from Governments, international organizations, individuals, corporations and other entities, in accordance with relevant criteria adopted by the Assembly of States Parties.

ARTICLE 117

Assessment of contributions

The contributions of States Parties shall be assessed in accordance with an agreed scale of assessment, based on the scale adopted by the United Nations for its regular budget and adjusted in accordance with the principles on which that scale is based.

ARTICLE 118

Annual audit

The records, books and accounts of the Court, including its annual financial statements, shall be audited annually by an independent auditor.

PART 13: FINAL CLAUSES

ARTICLE 119

Settlement of disputes

1. Any dispute concerning the judicial functions of the Court shall be settled by the decision of the Court.

2. Any other dispute between two or more States Parties relating to the interpretation or application of this Statute which is not settled through negotiations within three months of their commencement shall be referred to the Assembly of States Parties. The Assembly may itself seek to settle the dispute or may make recommendations on further means of settlement of the dispute, including referral to the International Court of Justice in conformity with the Statute of that Court.

ARTICLE 120

Reservations

No reservations may be made to this Statute.

ARTICLE 121

Amendments

1. After the expiry of seven years from the entry into force of this Statute, any State Party may propose amendments thereto. The text of any proposed amendment shall be submitted to the Secretary-General of the United Nations, who shall promptly circulate it to all States Parties.

2. No sooner than three months from the date of notification, the Assembly of States Parties, at its next meeting, shall, by a majority of those present and voting, decide whether to take up the proposal. The Assembly may deal with the proposal directly or convene a Review Conference if the issue involved so warrants.

3. The adoption of an amendment at a meeting of the Assembly of States Parties or at a Review Conference on which consensus cannot be reached shall require a two-thirds majority of States Parties.

4. Except as provided in paragraph 5, an amendment shall enter into force for all States Parties one year after instruments of ratification or acceptance have been deposited with the Secretary-General of the United Nations by seven-eighths of them.

5. Any amendment to Articles 5, 6, 7 and 8 of this Statute shall enter into force for those States Parties which have accepted the amendment one year after the deposit of their instruments of ratification or acceptance. In respect of a State Party which has not accepted the amendment, the Court shall not exercise its jurisdiction regarding a crime covered by the amendment when committed by that State Party's nationals or on its territory.

6. If an amendment has been accepted by seven-eighths of States Parties in accordance with paragraph 4, any State Party which has not accepted the amendment may withdraw from this Statute with immediate effect, notwithstanding Article 127, paragraph 1, but subject to Article 127, paragraph 2, by giving notice no later than one year after the entry into force of such amendment.

7. The Secretary-General of the United Nations shall circulate to all States Parties any amendment adopted at a meeting of the Assembly of States Parties or at a Review Conference.

ARTICLE 122

Amendments to provisions of an institutional nature

1. Amendments to provisions of this Statute which are of an exclusively institutional nature, namely, Article 35, Article 36, paragraphs 8 and 9, Article 37, Article 38, Article 39, paragraphs 1 (first two sentences), 2 and 4, Article 42, paragraphs 4 to 9, Article 43, paragraphs 2 and 3, and Articles 44, 46, 47 and 49, may be proposed at any time, notwithstanding Article 121, paragraph 1, by any State Party. The text of any proposed amendment shall be submitted to the Secretary-General of the United Nations or such other person designated by the Assembly of States Parties who shall promptly circulate it to all States Parties and to others participating in the Assembly.

2. Amendments under this Article on which consensus cannot be reached shall be adopted by the Assembly of States Parties or by a Review Conference, by a two-thirds majority of States Parties. Such amendments shall enter into force for all States Parties six months after their adoption by the Assembly or, as the case may be, by the Conference.

ARTICLE 123

Review of the Statute

1. Seven years after the entry into force of this Statute the Secretary-General of the United

Nations shall convene a Review Conference to consider any amendments to this Statute. Such review may include, but is not limited to, the list of crimes contained in Article 5. The Conference shall be open to those participating in the Assembly of States Parties and on the same conditions.

2. At any time thereafter, at the request of a State Party and for the purposes set out in paragraph 1, the Secretary-General of the United Nations shall, upon approval by a majority of States Parties, convene a Review Conference.

3. The provisions of Article 121, paragraphs 3 to 7, shall apply to the adoption and entry into force of any amendment to the Statute considered at a Review Conference.

ARTICLE 124

Transitional Provision

Notwithstanding Article 12, paragraphs 1 and 2, a State, on becoming a party to this Statute, may declare that, for a period of seven years after the entry into force of this Statute for the State concerned, it does not accept the jurisdiction of the Court with respect to the category of crimes referred to in Article 8 when a crime is alleged to have been committed by its nationals or on its territory. A declaration under this Article may be withdrawn at any time. The provisions of this Article shall be reviewed at the Review Conference convened in accordance with Article 123, paragraph 1.

ARTICLE 125

Signature, ratification, acceptance, approval or accession

1. This Statute shall be open for signature by all States in Rome, at the headquarters of the Food and Agriculture Organization of the United Nations, on 17 July 1998. Thereafter, it shall remain open for signature in Rome at the Ministry of Foreign Affairs of Italy until 17 October 1998. After that date, the Statute shall remain open for signature in New York, at United Nations Headquarters, until 31 December 2000.

2. This Statute is subject to ratification, acceptance or approval by signatory States. Instruments of ratification, acceptance or approval shall be deposited with the Secretary-General of the United Nations.

3. This Statute shall be open to accession by all States. Instruments of accession shall be deposited with the Secretary-General of the United Nations.

ARTICLE 126

Entry into force

1. This Statute shall enter into force on the first day of the month after the 60th day following the date of the deposit of the 60th instrument of ratification, acceptance, approval or accession with the Secretary-General of the United Nations.

2. For each State ratifying, accepting, approving or acceding to this Statute after the

deposit of the 60th instrument of ratification, acceptance, approval or accession, the Statute shall enter into force on the first day of the month after the 60th day following the deposit by such State of its instrument of ratification, acceptance, approval or accession.

ARTICLE 127

Withdrawal

1. A State Party may, by written notification addressed to the Secretary-General of the United Nations, withdraw from this Statute. The withdrawal shall take effect one year after the date of receipt of the notification, unless the notification specifies a later date.

2. A State shall not be discharged, by reason of its withdrawal, from the obligations arising from this Statute while it was a Party to the Statute, including any financial obligations which may have accrued. Its withdrawal shall not affect any cooperation with the Court in connection with criminal investigations and proceedings in relation to which the withdrawing State had a duty to cooperate and which were commenced prior to the date on which the withdrawal became effective, nor shall it prejudice in any way the continued consideration of any matter which was already under consideration by the Court prior to the date on which the withdrawal became effective.

ARTICLE 128

Authentic texts

The original of this Statute, of which the Arabic, Chinese, English, French, Russian and Spanish texts are equally authentic, shall be deposited with the Secretary-General of the United Nations, who shall send certified copies thereof to all States.

IN WITNESS WHEREOF, the undersigned, being duly authorized thereto by their respective Governments, have signed this Statute.

DONE at Rome, this 17th day of July 1998.

APPENDIX 4: ELEMENTS OF CRIMES

General Introduction

1. Pursuant to Article 9, the following Elements of Crimes shall assist the Court in the interpretation and application of Articles 6, 7 and 8, consistent with the Statute. The provisions of the Statute, including Article 21, and the general principles set out in Part 3 are applicable to the Elements of Crimes.

2. As stated in Article 30, unless otherwise provided, a person shall be criminally responsible and liable for punishment for a crime within the jurisdiction of the Court only if the material elements are committed with intent and knowledge. Where no reference is made in the Elements of Crimes to a mental element for any particular conduct, consequence or circumstance listed, it is understood that the relevant mental element, i.e. intent, knowledge or both, set out in Article 30 applies. Exceptions to the Article 30 standard, based on the Statute, including applicable law under its relevant provisions, are indicated below.

3. Existence of intent and knowledge can be inferred from the relevant facts and circumstances.

4. With respect to mental elements associated with elements involving value judgment, such as those using the terms 'inhumane' or 'severe', it is not necessary that the perpetrator personally completed a particular value judgment, unless otherwise indicated.

5. Grounds for excluding criminal responsibility or the absence thereof are generally not specified in the elements of crimes listed under each crime.[1]

6. The requirement of 'unlawfulness' found in the Statute or in other parts of international law, in particular international humanitarian law, is generally not specified in the elements of crimes.

7. The elements of crimes are generally structured in accordance with the following principles:

— As the elements of crimes focus on the conduct, consequences and circumstances associated with each crime, they are generally listed in that order;

— When required, a particular mental element is listed after the affected conduct, consequence or circumstance;

— Contextual circumstances are listed last.

8. As used in these Elements of Crimes, the term 'perpetrator' is neutral as to guilt or innocence. The elements, including the appropriate mental elements, apply *mutatis mutandis*, to all those whose criminal responsibility may fall under Articles 25 and 28 of the Statute.

9. A particular conduct may constitute one or more crimes.

10. The use of short titles for the crimes has no legal effect.

---

[1] This paragraph is without prejudice to the obligation of the Prosecutor under Art. 54, paragraph 1, of the Statute.

ARTICLE 6

Genocide

Introduction
With respect to the last element listed for each crime:

— The term 'in the context of' would include the initial acts in an emerging pattern;

— The term 'manifest' is an objective qualification;

— Notwithstanding the normal requirement for a mental element provided for in Article 30, and recognizing that knowledge of the circumstances will usually be addressed in proving genocidal intent, the appropriate requirement, if any, for a mental element regarding this circumstance will need to be decided by the Court on a case-by-case basis.

ARTICLE 6(a)

Genocide by killing

Elements
1. The perpetrator killed[2] one or more persons.
2. Such person or persons belonged to a particular national, ethnical, racial, or religious group.
3. The perpetrator intended to destroy, in whole or in part, that national, ethnical, racial, or religious group, as such.
4. The conduct took place in the context of a manifest pattern of similar conduct directed against that group or was conduct that could itself effect such destruction.

ARTICLE 6(b)

Genocide by causing serious bodily or mental harm

Elements
1. The perpetrator caused serious bodily or mental harm to one or more persons.[3]
2. Such person or persons belonged to a particular national, ethnical, racial, or religious group.
3. The perpetrator intended to destroy, in whole or in part, that national, ethnical, racial, or religious group, as such.
4. The conduct took place in the context of a manifest pattern of similar conduct directed against that group or was conduct that could itself effect such destruction.

---

[2] The term 'killed' is interchangeable with the term 'caused death'.

[3] This conduct may include, but is not necessarily restricted to, acts of torture, rape, sexual violence, or inhuman or degrading treatment.

ARTICLE 6(c)

Genocide by deliberately inflicting conditions of life calculated to bring about physical destruction

Elements
1. The perpetrator inflicted certain conditions of life upon one or more persons.
2. Such person or persons belonged to a particular national, ethnical, racial, or religious group.
3. The perpetrator intended to destroy, in whole or in part, that national, ethnical, racial, or religious group, as such.
4. The conditions of life were calculated to bring about the physical destruction of that group, in whole or in part.[4]
5. The conduct took place in the context of a manifest pattern of similar conduct directed against that group or was conduct that could itself effect such destruction.

ARTICLE 6(d)

Genocide by imposing measures intended to prevent births

Elements
1. The perpetrator imposed certain measures upon one or more persons.
2. Such person or persons belonged to a particular national, ethnical, racial, or religious group.
3. The perpetrator intended to destroy, in whole or in part, that national, ethnical, racial, or religious group, as such.
4. The measures imposed were intended to prevent births within that group.
5. The conduct took place in the context of a manifest pattern of similar conduct directed against that group or was conduct that could itself effect such destruction.

ARTICLE 6(e)

Genocide by forcibly transferring children

Elements
1. The perpetrator forcibly transferred one or more persons.[5]
2. Such person or persons belonged to a particular national, ethnical, racial, or religious group.
3. The perpetrator intended to destroy, in whole or in part, that national, ethnical, racial, or religious group, as such.

---

[4] The term 'conditions of life' may include, but is not necessarily restricted to, deliberate deprivation of resources indispensable for survival, such as food or medical services, or systematic expulsion from homes.

[5] The term 'forcibly' is not restricted to physical force, but may include threat of force or coercion, such as that caused by fear of violence, duress, detention, psychological oppression or abuse of power, against such person or persons or another person, or by taking advantage of a coercive environment.

4. The transfer was from that group to another group.
5. The person or persons were under the age of 18 years.
6. The perpetrator knew, or should have known, that the person or persons were under the age of eighteen years.
7. The conduct took place in the context of a manifest pattern of similar conduct directed against that group or was conduct that could itself effect such destruction.

ARTICLE 7

Crimes against humanity

Introduction

1. Since Article 7 pertains to international criminal law, its provisions, consistent with Article 22, must be strictly construed, taking into account that crimes against humanity as defined in Article 7 are among the most serious crimes of concern to the international community as a whole, warrant and entail individual criminal responsibility, and require conduct which is impermissible under generally applicable international law, as recognized by the principal legal systems of the world.

2. The last two elements for each crime against humanity describe the context in which the conduct must take place. These elements clarify the requisite participation in and knowledge of a widespread or systematic attack against a civilian population. However, the last element should not be interpreted as requiring proof that the perpetrator had knowledge of all characteristics of the attack or the precise details of the plan or policy of that State or organization. In the case of an emerging widespread or systematic attack against a civilian population, the intent clause of the last element indicates that this mental element is satisfied if the perpetrator intended to further such an attack.

3. 'Attack directed against a civilian population' in these context elements is understood to mean a course of conduct involving the multiple commission of acts referred to in Article 7, paragraph 1, of the Statute against any civilian population, pursuant to or in furtherance of a State or organizational policy to commit such attack. The acts need not constitute a military attack. It is understood that 'policy to commit such attack' requires that the State or organization actively promote or encourage such an attack against a civilian population.[6]

ARTICLE 7(1)(a)

Crime against humanity of murder

1. The perpetrator killed[7] one or more persons.

---

[6] A policy which has a civilian population as the object of the attack would be implemented by State or organizational action. Such a policy may, in exceptional circumstances, be implemented by a deliberate failure to take action, which is consciously aimed at encouraging such attack. The existence of such a policy cannot be inferred solely from the absence of governmental or organizational action.

[7] The term 'killed' is interchangeable with the term 'caused death'. This footnote applies to all elements which use either of these concepts.

2. The conduct was committed as part of a widespread or systematic attack directed against a civilian population.
3. The perpetrator knew that the conduct was part of or intended the conduct to be part of a widespread or systematic attack against a civilian population.

ARTICLE 7(1)(b)

Crime against humanity of extermination

1. The perpetrator killed[8] one or more persons, including inflicting conditions of life calculated to bring about the destruction of part of a population.[9]
2. The conduct constituted, or took place as part of,[10] a mass killing of members of a civilian population.
3. The conduct was committed as part of a widespread or systematic attack directed against a civilian population.
4. The perpetrator knew that the conduct was part of or intended the conduct to be part of a widespread or systematic attack directed against a civilian population.

ARTICLE 7(1)(c)

Crime against humanity of enslavement

1. The perpetrator exercised any or all of the powers attaching to the right of ownership over one or more persons, such as by purchasing, selling, lending or bartering such a person or persons, or by imposing on them a similar deprivation of liberty.[11]
2. The conduct was committed as part of a widespread or systematic attack directed against a civilian population.
3. The perpetrator knew that the conduct was part of or intended the conduct to be part of a widespread or systematic attack directed against a civilian population.

ARTICLE 7(1)(d)

Crime against humanity of deportation or forcible transfer of population

1. The perpetrator deported or forcibly[12] transferred,[13] without grounds permitted under

---

[8] The conduct could be committed by different methods of killing, either directly or indirectly.

[9] The infliction of such conditions could include the deprivation of access to food and medicine.

[10] The term 'as part of' would include the initial conduct in a mass killing.

[11] It is understood that such deprivation of liberty may, in some circumstances, include exacting forced labour or otherwise reducing a person to a servile status as defined in the Supplementary Convention on the Abolition of Slavery, the Slave Trade, and Institutions and Practices Similar to Slavery of 1956. It is also understood that the conduct described in this element includes trafficking in persons, in particular women and children.

[12] The term 'forcibly' is not restricted to physical force, but may include threat of force or coercion, such as that caused by fear of violence, duress, detention, psychological oppression or abuse of power against such person or persons or another person, or by taking advantage of a coercive environment.

[13] 'Deported or forcibly transferred' is interchangeable with 'forcibly displaced'.

international law, one or more persons to another State or location, by expulsion or
other coercive acts.

2. Such person or persons were lawfully present in the area from which they were so
   deported or transferred.
3. The perpetrator was aware of the factual circumstances that established the lawfulness
   of such presence.
4. The conduct was committed as part of a widespread or systematic attack directed
   against a civilian population.
5. The perpetrator knew that the conduct was part of or intended the conduct to be part
   of a widespread or systematic attack directed against a civilian population.

ARTICLE 7(1)(e)

Crime against humanity of imprisonment or other severe deprivation of physical liberty

1. The perpetrator imprisoned one or more persons or otherwise severely deprived one
   or more persons of physical liberty.
2. The gravity of the conduct was such that it was in violation of fundamental rules of
   international law.
3. The perpetrator was aware of the factual circumstances that established the gravity of
   the conduct.
4. The conduct was committed as part of a widespread or systematic attack directed
   against a civilian population.
5. The perpetrator knew that the conduct was part of or intended the conduct to be part
   of a widespread or systematic attack directed against a civilian population.

ARTICLE 7(1)(f)

Crime against humanity of torture[14]

1. The perpetrator inflicted severe physical or mental pain or suffering upon one or more
   persons.
2. Such person or persons were in the custody or under the control of the perpetrator.
3. Such pain or suffering did not arise only from, and was not inherent in or identical to,
   lawful sanctions.
4. The conduct was committed as part of a widespread or systematic attack directed
   against a civilian population.
5. The perpetrator knew that the conduct was part of or intended the conduct to be part
   of a widespread or systematic attack directed against a civilian population.

---

[14] It is understood that no specific purpose needs to be proved for this crime.

ARTICLE 7(1)(g)–1

Crime against humanity of rape

1. The perpetrator invaded[15] the body of a person by conduct resulting in penetration, however slight, of any part of the body of the victim or of the perpetrator with a sexual organ, or of the anal or genital opening of the victim with any object or any other part of the body.
2. The invasion was committed by force, or by threat of force or coercion, such as that caused by fear of violence, duress, detention, psychological oppression or abuse of power, against such person or another person, or by taking advantage of a coercive environment, or the invasion was committed against a person incapable of giving genuine consent.[16]
3. The conduct was committed as part of a widespread or systematic attack directed against a civilian population.
4. The perpetrator knew that the conduct was part of or intended the conduct to be part of a widespread or systematic attack directed against a civilian population.

ARTICLE 7(1)(g)–2

Crime against humanity of sexual slavery[17]

1. The perpetrator exercised any or all of the powers attaching to the right of ownership over one or more persons, such as by purchasing, selling, lending or bartering such a person or persons, or by imposing on them a similar deprivation of liberty.[18]
2. The perpetrator caused such person or persons to engage in one or more acts of a sexual nature.
3. The conduct was committed as part of a widespread or systematic attack directed against a civilian population.
4. The perpetrator knew that the conduct was part of or intended the conduct to be part of a widespread or systematic attack directed against a civilian population.

ARTICLE 7(1)(g)–3

Crime against humanity of enforced prostitution

1. The perpetrator caused one or more persons to engage in one or more acts of a sexual

---

[15] The concept of 'invasion' is intended to be broad enough to be gender-neutral.

[16] It is understood that a person may be incapable of giving genuine consent if affected by natural, induced or age-related incapacity. This footnote also applies to the corresponding elements of Art. 7(1)(g)–3, 5 and 6.

[17] Given the complex nature of this crime, it is recognized that its commission could involve more than one perpetrator as a part of a common criminal purpose.

[18] It is understood that such deprivation of liberty may, in some circumstances, include exacting forced labour or otherwise reducing a person to a servile status as defined in the Supplementary Convention on the Abolition of Slavery, the Slave Trade, and Institutions and Practices Similar to Slavery of 1956. It is also understood that the conduct described in this element includes trafficking in persons, in particular women and children.

nature by force, or by threat of force or coercion, such as that caused by fear of violence, duress, detention, psychological oppression or abuse of power, against such person or persons or another person, or by taking advantage of a coercive environment or such person's or persons' incapacity to give genuine consent.

2. The perpetrator or another person obtained or expected to obtain pecuniary or other advantage in exchange for or in connection with the acts of a sexual nature.

3. The conduct was committed as part of a widespread or systematic attack directed against a civilian population.

4. The perpetrator knew that the conduct was part of or intended the conduct to be part of a widespread or systematic attack directed against a civilian population.

ARTICLE 7(1)(g)–4

Crime against humanity of forced pregnancy

1. The perpetrator confined one or more women forcibly made pregnant, with the intent of affecting the ethnic composition of any population or carrying out other grave violations of international law.

2. The conduct was committed as part of a widespread or systematic attack directed against a civilian population.

3. The perpetrator knew that the conduct was part of or intended the conduct to be part of a widespread or systematic attack directed against a civilian population.

ARTICLE 7(1)(g)–5

Crime against humanity of enforced sterilization

1. The perpetrator deprived one or more persons of biological reproductive capacity.[19]

2. The conduct was neither justified by the medical or hospital treatment of the person or persons concerned nor carried out with their genuine consent.[20]

3. The conduct was committed as part of a widespread or systematic attack directed against a civilian population.

4. The perpetrator knew that the conduct was part of or intended the conduct to be part of a widespread or systematic attack directed against a civilian population.

ARTICLE 7(1)(g)–6

Crime against humanity of sexual violence

1. The perpetrator committed an act of a sexual nature against one or more persons or caused such person or persons to engage in one or more acts of a sexual nature by

---

[19] The deprivation is not intended to include birth-control measures which have a non-permanent effect in practice.

[20] It is understood that 'genuine consent' does not include consent obtained through deception.

force, or by threat of force or coercion, such as that caused by fear of violence, duress, detention, psychological oppression or abuse of power, against such person or persons or another person, or by taking advantage of a coercive environment or such person's or persons' incapacity to give genuine consent.

2. Such conduct was of a gravity comparable to the other offences in Article 7, paragraph 1(g), of the Statute.
3. The perpetrator was aware of the factual circumstances that established the gravity of the conduct.
4. The conduct was committed as part of a widespread or systematic attack directed against a civilian population.
5. The perpetrator knew that the conduct was part of or intended the conduct to be part of a widespread or systematic attack directed against a civilian population.

ARTICLE 7(1)(h)

Crime against humanity of persecution

1. The perpetrator severely deprived, contrary to international law,[21] one or more persons of fundamental rights.
2. The perpetrator targeted such person or persons by reason of the identity of a group or collectivity or targeted the group or collectivity as such.
3. Such targeting was based on political, racial, national, ethnic, cultural, religious, gender as defined in Article 7, paragraph 3, of the Statute, or other grounds that are universally recognized as impermissible under international law.
4. The conduct was committed in connection with any act referred to in Article 7, paragraph 1, of the Statute or any crime within the jurisdiction of the Court.[22]
5. The conduct was committed as part of a widespread or systematic attack directed against a civilian population.
6. The perpetrator knew that the conduct was part of or intended the conduct to be part of a widespread or systematic attack directed against a civilian population.

ARTICLE 7(1)(i)

Crime against humanity of enforced disappearance of persons[23] [24]

1. The perpetrator:

---

[21] This requirement is without prejudice to paragraph 6 of the General Introduction to the Elements of Crimes.

[22] It is understood that no additional mental element is necessary for this element other than that inherent in Element 6.

[23] Given the complex nature of this crime, it is recognized that its commission will normally involve more than one perpetrator as a part of a common criminal purpose.

[24] This crime falls under the jurisdiction of the Court only if the attack referred to in Elements 7 and 8 occurs after the entry into force of the Statute.

    (a) Arrested, detained[25] [26] or abducted one or more persons; or

    (b) Refused to acknowledge the arrest, detention or abduction, or to give information on the fate or whereabouts of such person or persons.

2. (a)   Such arrest, detention or abduction was followed or accompanied by a refusal to acknowledge that deprivation of freedom or to give information on the fate or whereabouts of such person or persons; or

  (b)   Such refusal was preceded or accompanied by that deprivation of freedom.

3. The perpetrator was aware that:[27]

    (a) Such arrest, detention or abduction would be followed in the ordinary course of events by a refusal to acknowledge that deprivation of freedom or to give information on the fate or whereabouts of such person or persons;[28] or

    (b) Such refusal was preceded or accompanied by that deprivation of freedom.

4. Such arrest, detention or abduction was carried out by, or with the authorization, support, or acquiescence of, a State or a political organization.

5. Such refusal to acknowledge that deprivation of freedom or to give information on the fate or whereabouts of such person or persons was carried out by, or with the authorization or support of, such State or political organization.

6. The perpetrator intended to remove such person or persons from the protection of the law for a prolonged period of time.

7. The conduct was committed as part of a widespread or systematic attack directed against a civilian population.

8. The perpetrator knew that the conduct was part of or intended the conduct to be part of a widespread or systematic attack directed against a civilian population.

ARTICLE 7(1)(j)

Crime against humanity of apartheid

1. The perpetrator committed an inhumane act against one or more persons.

2. Such act was an act referred to in Article 7, paragraph 1, of the Statute, or was an act of a character similar to any of those acts.[29]

3. The perpetrator was aware of the factual circumstances that established the character of the act.

4. The conduct was committed in the context of an institutionalized regime of systematic oppression and domination by one racial group over any other racial group or groups.

5. The perpetrator intended to maintain such regime by that conduct.

---

[25] The word 'detained' would include a perpetrator who maintained an existing detention.

[26] It is understood that under certain circumstances an arrest or detention may have been lawful.

[27] This element, inserted because of the complexity of this crime, is without prejudice to the General Introduction to the Elements of Crimes.

[28] It is understood that in the case of a perpetrator who maintained an existing detention, this element would be satisfied if the perpetrator was aware that such a refusal had already taken place.

[29] It is understood that 'character' refers to the nature and gravity of the act.

6. The conduct was committed as part of a widespread or systematic attack directed against a civilian population.
7. The perpetrator knew that the conduct was part of or intended the conduct to be part of a widespread or systematic attack directed against a civilian population.

ARTICLE 7(1)(k)

Crime against humanity of other inhumane acts

1. The perpetrator inflicted great suffering, or serious injury to body or to mental or physical health, by means of an inhumane act.
2. Such act was of a character similar to any other act referred to in Article 7, paragraph 1, of the Statute.[30]
3. The perpetrator was aware of the factual circumstances that established the character of the act.
4. The conduct was committed as part of a widespread or systematic attack directed against a civilian population.
5. The perpetrator knew that the conduct was part of or intended the conduct to be part of a widespread or systematic attack directed against a civilian population.

ARTICLE 8: WAR CRIMES

Introduction

The elements for war crimes under Article 8, paragraph 2(c) and (e), are subject to the limitations addressed in Article 8, paragraph 2(d) and (f), which are not elements of crimes.

The elements for war crimes under Article 8, paragraph 2, of the Statute shall be interpreted within the established framework of the international law of armed conflict including, as appropriate, the international law of armed conflict applicable to armed conflict at sea.

With respect to the last two elements listed for each crime:

- There is no requirement for a legal evaluation by the perpetrator as to the existence of an armed conflict or its character as international or non-international;
- In that context there is no requirement for awareness by the perpetrator of the facts that established the character of the conflict as international or non-international;
- There is only a requirement for the awareness of the factual circumstances that established the existence of an armed conflict that is implicit in the terms 'took place in the context of and was associated with'.

---

[30] It is understood that 'character' refers to the nature and gravity of the act.

ARTICLE 8(2)(a)

ARTICLE 8(2)(a)(i)

War crime of wilful killing

Elements
1. The perpetrator killed one or more persons.[31]
2. Such person or persons were protected under one or more of the Geneva Conventions of 1949.
3. The perpetrator was aware of the factual circumstances that established that protected status.[32] [33]
4. The conduct took place in the context of and was associated with an international armed conflict.[34]
5. The perpetrator was aware of factual circumstances that established the existence of an armed conflict.

ARTICLE 8(2)(a)(ii)–1

War crime of torture

Elements[35]
1. The perpetrator inflicted severe physical or mental pain or suffering upon one or more persons.
2. The perpetrator inflicted the pain or suffering for such purposes as: obtaining information or a confession, punishment, intimidation or coercion or for any reason based on discrimination of any kind.
3. Such person or persons were protected under one or more of the Geneva Conventions of 1949.
4. The perpetrator was aware of the factual circumstances that established that protected status.
5. The conduct took place in the context of and was associated with an international armed conflict.

---

[31] The term 'killed' is interchangeable with the term 'caused death'. This footnote applies to all elements which use either of these concepts.

[32] This mental element recognizes the interplay between Arts. 30 and 32. This footnote also applies to the corresponding element in each crime under Art. 8(2)(a), and to the element in other crimes in Art. 8(2) concerning the awareness of factual circumstances that established the status of persons or property protected under the relevant international law of armed conflict.

[33] With respect to nationality, it is understood that the perpetrator needs only to know that the victim belonged to an adverse party to the conflict. This footnote also applies to the corresponding element in each crime under Art. 8(2)(a).

[34] The term 'international armed conflict' includes military occupation. This footnote also applies to corresponding element in each crime under Art. 8(2)(a).

[35] As Element 3 requires that all victims must be 'protected persons' under one or more of the Geneva Conventions of 1949, these elements do not include the custody or control requirement found in the elements of Art. 7(1)(e).

6. The perpetrator was aware of factual circumstances that established the existence of an armed conflict.

ARTICLE 8(2)(a)(ii)–2

War crime of inhuman treatment

Elements
1. The perpetrator inflicted severe physical or mental pain or suffering upon one or more persons.
2. Such person or persons were protected under one or more of the Geneva Conventions of 1949.
3. The perpetrator was aware of the factual circumstances that established that protected status.
4. The conduct took place in the context of and was associated with an international armed conflict.
5. The perpetrator was aware of factual circumstances that established the existence of an armed conflict.

ARTICLE 8(2)(a)(ii)–3

War crime of biological experiments

Elements
1. The perpetrator subjected one or more persons to a particular biological experiment.
2. The experiment seriously endangered the physical or mental health or integrity of such person or persons.
3. The intent of the experiment was non-therapeutic and it was neither justified by medical reasons nor carried out in such person's or persons' interest.
4. Such person or persons were protected under one or more of the Geneva Conventions of 1949.
5. The perpetrator was aware of the factual circumstances that established that protected status.
6. The conduct took place in the context of and was associated with an international armed conflict.
7. The perpetrator was aware of factual circumstances that established the existence of an armed conflict.

ARTICLE 8(2)(a)(iii)

War crime of wilfully causing great suffering

Elements
1. The perpetrator caused great physical or mental pain or suffering to, or serious injury to body or health of, one or more persons.

2. Such person or persons were protected under one or more of the Geneva Conventions of 1949.

3. The perpetrator was aware of the factual circumstances that established that protected status.

4. The conduct took place in the context of and was associated with an international armed conflict.

5. The perpetrator was aware of factual circumstances that established the existence of an armed conflict.

ARTICLE 8(2)(a)(iv)

War crime of destruction and appropriation of property

Elements

1. The perpetrator destroyed or appropriated certain property.

2. The destruction or appropriation was not justified by military necessity.

3. The destruction or appropriation was extensive and carried out wantonly.

4. Such property was protected under one or more of the Geneva Conventions of 1949.

5. The perpetrator was aware of the factual circumstances that established that protected status.

6. The conduct took place in the context of and was associated with an international armed conflict.

7. The perpetrator was aware of factual circumstances that established the existence of an armed conflict.

ARTICLE 8(2)(a)(v)

War crime of compelling service in hostile forces

Elements

1. The perpetrator coerced one or more persons, by act or threat, to take part in military operations against that person's own country or forces or otherwise serve in the forces of a hostile power.

2. Such person or persons were protected under one or more of the Geneva Conventions of 1949.

3. The perpetrator was aware of the factual circumstances that established that protected status.

4. The conduct took place in the context of and was associated with an international armed conflict.

5. The perpetrator was aware of factual circumstances that established the existence of an armed conflict.

ARTICLE 8(2)(a)(vi)

War crime of denying a fair trial

Elements
1. The perpetrator deprived one or more persons of a fair and regular trial by denying judicial guarantees as defined, in particular, in the third and the fourth Geneva Conventions of 1949.
2. Such person or persons were protected under one or more of the Geneva Conventions of 1949.
3. The perpetrator was aware of the factual circumstances that established that protected status.
4. The conduct took place in the context of and was associated with an international armed conflict.
5. The perpetrator was aware of factual circumstances that established the existence of an armed conflict.

ARTICLE 8(2)(a)(vii)–1

War crime of unlawful deportation and transfer

Elements
1. The perpetrator deported or transferred one or more persons to another State or to another location.
2. Such person or persons were protected under one or more of the Geneva Conventions of 1949.
3. The perpetrator was aware of the factual circumstances that established that protected status.
4. The conduct took place in the context of and was associated with an international armed conflict.
5. The perpetrator was aware of factual circumstances that established the existence of an armed conflict.

ARTICLE 8(2)(a)(vii)–2

War crime of unlawful confinement

Elements
1. The perpetrator confined or continued to confine one or more persons to a certain location.
2. Such person or persons were protected under one or more of the Geneva Conventions of 1949.
3. The perpetrator was aware of the factual circumstances that established that protected status.
4. The conduct took place in the context of and was associated with an international armed conflict.

5. The perpetrator was aware of factual circumstances that established the existence of an armed conflict.

ARTICLE 8(2)(a)(viii)

War crime of taking hostages

Elements
1. The perpetrator seized, detained, or otherwise held hostage one or more persons.
2. The perpetrator threatened to kill, injure, or continue to detain such person or persons.
3. The perpetrator intended to compel a State, an international organization, a natural or legal person or a group of persons to act or refrain from acting as an explicit or implicit condition for the safety or the release of such person or persons.
4. Such person or persons were protected under one or more of the Geneva Conventions of 1949.
5. The perpetrator was aware of the factual circumstances that established that protected status.
6. The conduct took place in the context of and was associated with an international armed conflict.
7. The perpetrator was aware of factual circumstances that established the existence of an armed conflict.

ARTICLE 8(2)(b)

ARTICLE 8(2)(b)(i)

War crime of attacking civilians

Elements
1. The perpetrator directed an attack.
2. The object of the attack was a civilian population as such or individual civilian not taking direct part in hostilities.
3. The perpetrator intended the civilian population as such or individual civilians not taking direct part in hostilities to be the object of the attack.
4. The conduct took place in the context of and was associated with an international armed conflict.
5. The perpetrator was aware of factual circumstances that established the existence of an armed conflict.

ARTICLE 8(2)(b)(ii)

War crime of attacking civilian objects

Elements

1. The perpetrator directed an attack.
2. The object of the attack was civilian objects, that is, objects which are not military objectives.
3. The perpetrator intended such civilian objects to be the object of the attack.
4. The conduct took place in the context of and was associated with an international armed conflict.
5. The perpetrator was aware of factual circumstances that established the existence of an armed conflict.

ARTICLE 8(2)(b)(iii)

War crime of attacking personnel or objects involved in a humanitarian assistance or peacekeeping mission

Elements

1. The perpetrator directed an attack.
2. The object of the attack was personnel, installations, material, units, or vehicles involved in a humanitarian assistance or peacekeeping mission in accordance with the Charter of the United Nations.
3. The perpetrator intended such personnel, installations, material, units, or vehicles so involved to be the object of the attack.
4. Such personnel, installations, material, units, or vehicles were entitled to that protection given to civilians or civilian objects under the international law of armed conflict.
5. The perpetrator was aware of the factual circumstances that established that protection.
6. The conduct took place in the context of and was associated with an international armed conflict.
7. The perpetrator was aware of factual circumstances that established the existence of an armed conflict.

ARTICLE 8(2)(b)(iv)

War crime of excessive incidental death, injury, or damage

Elements

1. The perpetrator launched an attack.
2. The attack was such that it would cause incidental death or injury to civilians or damage to civilian objects or widespread, long-term, and severe damage to the natural environment and that such death, injury, or damage would be of such an extent as to

be clearly excessive in relation to the concrete and direct overall military advantage anticipated.[36]

3. The perpetrator knew that the attack would cause incidental death or injury to civilians or damage to civilian objects or widespread, long-term, and severe damage to the natural environment and that such death, injury, or damage would be of such an extent as to be clearly excessive in relation to the concrete and direct overall military advantage anticipated.[37]

4. The conduct took place in the context of and was associated with an international armed conflict.

5. The perpetrator was aware of factual circumstances that established the existence of an armed conflict.

ARTICLE 8(2)(b)(v)

War crime of attacking undefended places[38]

Elements

1. The perpetrator attacked one or more towns, villages, dwellings, or buildings.
2. Such towns, villages, dwellings, or buildings were open for unresisted occupation.
3. Such towns, villages, dwellings, or buildings did not constitute military objectives.
4. The conduct took place in the context of and was associated with an international armed conflict.
5. The perpetrator was aware of factual circumstances that established the existence of an armed conflict.

ARTICLE 8(2)(b)(vi)

War crime of killing or wounding a person *hors de combat*

Elements

1. The perpetrator killed or injured one or more persons.
2. Such person or persons were *hors de combat*.
3. The perpetrator was aware of the factual circumstances that established this status.

---

[36] The expression 'concrete and direct overall military advantage' refers to a military advantage that is foreseeable by the perpetrator at the relevant time. Such advantage may or may not be temporally or geographically related to the object of the attack. The fact that this crime admits the possibility of lawful incidental injury and collateral damage does not in any way justify any violation of the law applicable in armed conflict. It does not address justifications for war or other rules related to *jus ad bellum*. It reflects the proportionality requirement inherent in determining the legality of any military activity undertaken in the context of an armed conflict.

[37] As opposed to the general rule set forth in paragraph 4 of the General Introduction, this knowledge element requires that the perpetrator make the value judgment as described therein. An evaluation of that value judgment must be based on the requisite information available to the perpetrator at the time.

[38] The presence in the locality of persons specially protected under the Geneva Conventions of 1949 or of police forces retained for the sole purpose of maintaining law and order does not by itself render the locality a military objective.

4. The conduct took place in the context of and was associated with an international armed conflict.
5. The perpetrator was aware of factual circumstances that established the existence of an armed conflict.

ARTICLE 8(2)(b)(vii)–1

War crime of improper use of a flag of truce

Elements
1. The perpetrator used a flag of truce.
2. The perpetrator made such use in order to feign an intention to negotiate when there was no such intention on the part of the perpetrator.
3. The perpetrator knew or should have known of the prohibited nature of such use.[39]
4. The conduct resulted in death or serious personal injury.
5. The perpetrator knew that the conduct could result in death or serious personal injury.
6. The conduct took place in the context of and was associated with an international armed conflict.
7. The perpetrator was aware of factual circumstances that established the existence of an armed conflict.

ARTICLE 8(2)(b)(vii)–2

War crime of improper use of a flag, insignia, or uniform of the hostile party

Elements
1. The perpetrator used a flag, insignia, or uniform of the hostile party.
2. The perpetrator made such use in a manner prohibited under international law of armed conflict while engaged in an attack.
3. The perpetrator knew or should have known of the prohibited nature of such use.[40]
4. The conduct resulted in death or serious personal injury.
5. The perpetrator knew that the conduct could result in death or serious personal injury.
6. The conduct took place in the context of and was associated with an international armed conflict.
7. The perpetrator was aware of factual circumstances that established the existence of an armed conflict.

---

[39] This mental element recognizes the interplay between Art. 30 and Art. 32. The term 'prohibited nature' denotes illegality.

[40] This mental element recognizes the interplay between Art. 30 and Art. 32. The term 'prohibited nature' denotes illegality.

ARTICLE 8(2)(b)(vii)–3

War crime of improper use of a flag, insignia, or uniform of the United Nations

Elements
1. The perpetrator used a flag, insignia, or uniform of the United Nations.
2. The perpetrator made such use in a manner prohibited under the international law of armed conflict.
3. The perpetrator knew of the prohibited nature of such use.[41]
4. The conduct resulted in death or serious personal injury.
5. The perpetrator knew that the conduct could result in death or serious personal injury.
6. The conduct took place in the context of and was associated with an international armed conflict.
7. The perpetrator was aware of factual circumstances that established the existence of an armed conflict.

ARTICLE 8(2)(b)(vii)–4

War crime of improper use of the distinctive emblems of the Geneva Conventions

Elements
1. The perpetrator used the distinctive emblems of the Geneva Conventions.
2. The perpetrator made such use for combatant purposes[42] in a manner prohibited under the international law of armed conflict.
3. The perpetrator knew or should have known of the prohibited nature of such use.[43]
4. The conduct resulted in death or serious personal injury.
5. The perpetrator knew that the conduct could result in death or serious personal injury.
6. The conduct took place in the context of and was associated with an international armed conflict.
7. The perpetrator was aware of factual circumstances that established the existence of an armed conflict.

ARTICLE 8(2)(b)(viii)

The transfer, directly or indirectly, by the Occupying Power of parts of its own civilian population into the territory it occupies, or the deportation or transfer of all or parts of the population of the occupied territory within or outside this territory

Elements
1. The perpetrator:

---

[41] This mental element recognizes the interplay between Art. 30 and Art. 32. The 'should have known' test required in the other offences found in Art. 8(2)(b)(vii) is not applicable here because of the variable and regulatory nature of the relevant prohibitions.

[42] 'Combatant purposes' in these circumstances means purposes directly related to hostilities and not including medical, religious, or similar activities.

[43] This mental element recognizes the interplay between Art. 30 and Art. 32. The term 'prohibited nature' denotes illegality.

(a) Transferred,[44] directly or indirectly, parts of its own population into the territory it occupies; or

(b) Deported or transferred all or parts of the population of the occupied territory within or outside this territory.

2. The conduct took place in the context of and was associated with an international armed conflict.

3. The perpetrator was aware of factual circumstances that established the existence of an armed conflict.

ARTICLE 8(2)(b)(ix)

War crime of attacking protected objects[45]

Elements

1. The perpetrator directed an attack.

2. The object of the attack was one or more buildings dedicated to religion, education, art, science or charitable purposes, historic monuments, hospitals, or places where the sick and wounded are collected, which were not military objectives.

3. The perpetrator intended such building or buildings dedicated to religion, education, art, science or charitable purposes, historic monuments, hospitals, or places where the sick and wounded are collected, which were not military objectives, to be the object of the attack.

4. The conduct took place in the context of and was associated with an international armed conflict.

5. The perpetrator was aware of factual circumstances that established the existence of an armed conflict.

ARTICLE 8(2)(b)(x)–1

War crime of mutilation

Elements

1. The perpetrator subjected one or more persons to mutilation, in particular by permanently disfiguring the persons, or by permanently disabling or removing an organ or appendage.

2. The conduct caused death or seriously endangered the physical or mental health of such persons or persons.

3. The conduct was neither justified by the medical, dental, or hospital treatment of

---

[44] The term 'transfer' needs to be interpreted in accordance with the relevant provisions of international humanitarian law.

[45] The presence in the locality of persons specially protected under the Geneva Conventions of 1949 or of police forces retained for the sole purpose of maintaining law and order does not by itself render the locality a military objective.

the person or persons concerned nor carried out in such person's or persons' interest.[46]

4. Such person or persons were in the power of an adverse party.
5. The conduct took place in the context of or was associated with an international armed conflict.
6. The perpetrator was aware of factual circumstances that established the existence of an armed conflict.

ARTICLE 8(2)(b)(x)–2

War crime of medical or scientific experiments

Elements
1. The perpetrator subjected one or more persons to a medical or scientific experiment.
2. The conduct caused death or seriously endangered the physical or mental health or integrity of such person or persons.
3. The conduct was neither justified by the medical, dental, or hospital treatment of the person or persons concerned nor carried out in such person's or persons' interest.
4. Such person or persons were in the power of an adverse party.
5. The conduct took place in the context of or was associated with an international armed conflict.
6. The perpetrator was aware of factual circumstances that established the existence of an armed conflict.

ARTICLE 8(2)(b)(xi)

War crime of treacherously killing or wounding

Elements
1. The perpetrator invited the confidence or belief of one or more persons that they were entitled to, or were obliged to accord, protection under rules of international law applicable in armed conflict.
2. The perpetrator intended to betray that confidence or belief.
3. The perpetrator killed or injured such person or persons.
4. The perpetrator made use of that confidence or belief in killing or injuring such person or persons.
5. Such person or persons belonged to an adverse party.
6. The conduct took place in the context of and was associated with an international armed conflict.
7. The perpetrator was aware of factual circumstances that established the existence of an armed conflict.

---

[46] Consent is not a defence to this crime. The crime prohibits any medical procedure which is not indicated by the state or health of the person concerned and which is not consistent with generally accepted medical standards which would be applied under similar medical circumstances to persons who are nationals of the party conducting the procedure and who are in no way deprived of liberty. This footnote also applies to the same element for Art. 8(2)(b)(x)–2.

ARTICLE 8(2)(b)(xii)

War crime of denying quarter

Elements
1. The perpetrator declared or ordered that there shall be no survivors.
2. Such declaration or order was given in order to threaten an adversary or to conduct hostilities on the basis that there shall be no survivor.
3. The perpetrator was in a position of effective command or control over the subordinate forces to which the declaration or order was directed.
4. The conduct took place in the context of and was associated with an international armed conflict.
5. The perpetrator was aware of factual circumstances that established the existence of an armed conflict.

ARTICLE 8(2)(b)(xiii)

War crime of destroying or seizing the enemy's property

Elements
1. The perpetrator destroyed or seized certain property.
2. Such property was property of a hostile party.
3. Such property was protected from that destruction or seizure under the international law of armed conflict.
4. The perpetrator was aware of the factual circumstances that established the status of the property.
5. The destruction or seizure was not justified by military necessity.
6. The conduct took place in the context of and was associated with an international armed conflict.
7. The perpetrator was aware of factual circumstances that established the existence of an armed conflict.

ARTICLE 8(2)(b)(xiv)

War crime of depriving the nationals of the hostile power of rights or actions

Elements
1. The perpetrator effected the abolition, suspension, or termination of admissibility in a court of law of certain rights or actions.
2. The abolition, suspension, or termination was directed at the nationals of a hostile party.
3. The perpetrator intended the abolition, suspension, or termination to be directed at the nationals of a hostile party.
4. The conduct took place in the context of and was associated with an international armed conflict.
5. The perpetrator was aware of factual circumstances that established the existence of an armed conflict.

ARTICLE 8(2)(b)(xv)

War crime of compelling participation in military operations

Elements
1. The perpetrator coerced one or more persons by act or threat to take part in military operations against that person's own country or forces.
2. Such person or persons were nationals of a hostile party.
3. The conduct took place in the context of and was associated with an international armed conflict.
4. The perpetrator was aware of factual circumstances that established the existence of an armed conflict.

ARTICLE 8(2)(b)(xvi)

War crime of pillaging

Elements
1. The perpetrator appropriated certain property.
2. The perpetrator intended to deprive the owner of the property and to appropriate it for private or personal use.[47]
3. The appropriation was without the consent of the owner.
4. The conduct took place in the context of and was associated with an international armed conflict.
5. The perpetrator was aware of factual circumstances that established the existence of an armed conflict.

ARTICLE 8(2)(b)(xvii)

War crime of employing poison or poisoned weapons

Elements
1. The perpetrator employed a substance or a weapon that releases a substance as a result of its employment.
2. The substance was such that it causes death or serious damage to health in the ordinary course of events, through its toxic properties.
3. The conduct took place in the context of and was associated with an international armed conflict.
4. The perpetrator was aware of factual circumstances that established the existence of an armed conflict.

---

[47] As indicated by the use of term 'private or personal use', appropriations justified by military necessity cannot constitute the crime of pillaging.

ARTICLE 8(2)(b)(xviii)

War crime of employing prohibited gases, liquids, materials or devices

Elements
1. The perpetrator employed a gas or other analogous substance or device.
2. The gas, substance, or device was such that it causes death or serious damage to health in the ordinary course of events, through its asphyxiating or toxic properties.[48]
3. The conduct took place in the context of and was associated with an international armed conflict.
4. The perpetrator was aware of factual circumstances that established the existence of an armed conflict.

ARTICLE 8(2)(b)(xix)

War crime of employing prohibited bullets

Elements
1. The perpetrator employed certain bullets.
2. The bullets were such that their use violates the international law of armed conflict because they expand or flatten easily in the human body.
3. The perpetrator was aware that the nature of the bullets was such that their employment would uselessly aggravate suffering or the wounding effect.
4. The conduct took place in the context of and was associated with an international armed conflict.
5. The perpetrator was aware of factual circumstances that established the existence of an armed conflict.

ARTICLE 8(2)(b)(xx)

War crime of employing weapons, projectiles and material and methods of warfare listed in the annex to the Statute

Elements
[Elements will have to be drafted once such weapons, projectiles, or material or methods of warfare have been included in an annex to the Statute.]

---

[48] Nothing in this element shall be interpreted as limiting or prejudicing in any way existing or developing rules of international law with respect to development, production, stockpiling, and use of chemical weapons.

ARTICLE 8(2)(b)(xxi)

War crime of outrages upon personal dignity

Elements

1. The perpetrator humiliated, degraded, or otherwise violated the dignity of one or more persons.[49]
2. The severity of the humiliation, degradation, or other violation was of such degree as to be generally recognized as an outrage upon personal dignity.
3. The conduct took place in the context of and was associated with an international armed conflict.
4. The perpetrator was aware of factual circumstances that established the existence of an armed conflict.

ARTICLE 8(2)(b)(xxii)–1

War crime of rape

Elements

1. The perpetrator invaded[50] the body of a person by conduct resulting in penetration, however slight, of any part of the body of the victim or of the perpetrator with a sexual organ, or of the anal or genital opening of the victim with any object or any other part of the body.
2. The invasion was committed by force, or by threat of force or coercion, such as that caused by fear of violence, duress, detention, psychological oppression or abuse of power, against such person or another person, or by taking advantage of a coercive environment, or the invasion was committed against a person incapable of giving genuine consent.[51]
3. The conduct took place in the context of and was associated with an international armed conflict.
4. The perpetrator was aware of factual circumstances that established the existence of an armed conflict.

[49] For this crime, 'persons' can include dead persons. The victim need not personally be aware of the existence of the humiliation or degradation, or other violation. This element takes into account relevant aspects of the cultural background of the victim.

[50] The concept of 'invasion' is intended to be broad enough to be gender-neutral.

[51] It is understood that a person may be incapable of giving genuine consent if affected by natural, induced or age-related incapacity. This footnote also applies to the corresponding elements of Art. 8(2)(b)(xxii)–3, 5 and 6.

ARTICLE 8(2)(b)(xxii)–2

War crime of sexual slavery[52]

Elements
1. The perpetrator exercised any or all of the powers attaching to the right of ownership over one or more persons, such as by purchasing, selling, lending, or bartering such a person or persons, or by imposing on them a similar deprivation of liberty.[53]
2. The perpetrator caused such person or persons to engage in one or more acts of a sexual nature.
3. The conduct took place in the context of and was associated with an international armed conflict.
4. The perpetrator was aware of factual circumstances that established the existence of an armed conflict.

ARTICLE 8(2)(b)(xxii)–3

War crime of enforced prostitution

Elements
1. The perpetrator caused one or more persons to engage in one or more acts of a sexual nature by force, or by threat of force or coercion, such as that caused by fear of violence, duress, detention, psychological oppression or abuse of power, against such person or persons or another person, or by taking advantage of a coercive environment or such person's or persons' incapacity to give genuine consent.
2. The perpetrator or another person obtained or expected to obtain pecuniary or other advantage in exchange for or in connection with the acts of a sexual nature.
3. The conduct took place in the context of and was associated with an international armed conflict.
4. The perpetrator was aware of factual circumstances that established the existence of an armed conflict.

ARTICLE 8(2)(b)(xxii)–4

War crime of forced pregnancy

Elements
1. The perpetrator confined one or more women forcibly made pregnant, with the intent of affecting the ethnic composition of any population or carrying out other grave violations of international law.

[52] Given the complex nature of this crime, it is recognized that its commission could involve more than one perpetrator as a part of a common criminal purpose.

[53] It is understood that such deprivation of liberty may, in some circumstances, include exacting forced labour or otherwise reducing a person to servile status as defined in the Supplementary Convention on the Abolition of Slavery, the Slave Trade, and Institutions and Practices Similar to Slavery of 1956. It is also understood that the conduct described in this element includes trafficking in persons, in particular women and children.

2. The conduct took place in the context of and was associated with an international armed conflict.

3. The perpetrator was aware of factual circumstances that established the existence of an armed conflict.

ARTICLE 8(2)(b)(xxii)–5

War crime of enforced sterilization

Elements
1. The perpetrator deprived one or more persons of biological reproductive capacity.[54]
2. The conduct was neither justified by the medical or hospital treatment of the person or persons concerned nor carried out with their genuine consent.[55]
3. The conduct took place in the context of and was associated with an international armed conflict.
4. The perpetrator was aware of factual circumstances that established the existence of an armed conflict.

ARTICLE 8(2)(b)(xxii)–6

War crime of sexual violence

Elements
1. The perpetrator committed an act of a sexual nature against one or more persons or caused such person or persons to engage in an act of a sexual nature by force, or by threat of force or coercion, such as that caused by fear of violence, duress, detention, psychological oppression or abuse of power, against such person or persons or another person, or by taking advantage of a coercive environment or such person's or persons' incapacity to give genuine consent.
2. The conduct was of a gravity comparable to that of a grave breach of the Geneva Conventions.
3. The perpetrator was aware of the factual circumstances that established the gravity of the conduct.
4. The conduct took place in the context of and was associated with an international armed conflict.
5. The perpetrator was aware of factual circumstances that established the existence of an armed conflict.

---

[54] The deprivation is not intended to include birth-control measures which have a non-permanent effect in practice.
[55] It is understood that 'genuine consent' does not include consent obtained through deception.

ARTICLE 8(2)(b)(xxiii)

War crime of using protected persons as shields

Elements
1. The perpetrator moved or otherwise took advantage of the location of one or more civilians or other persons protected under the international law of armed conflict.
2. The perpetrator intended to shield a military objective from attack or shield, favour or impede military operations.
3. The conduct took place in the context of and was associated with an international armed conflict.
4. The perpetrator was aware of factual circumstances that established the existence of an armed conflict.

ARTICLE 8(2)(b)(xxiv)

War crime of attacking objects or persons using the distinctive emblems of the Geneva Conventions

Elements
1. The perpetrator attacked one or more persons, buildings, medical units, or transports or other objects using, in conformity with international law, a distinctive emblem or other method of identification indicating protection under the Geneva Conventions.
2. The perpetrator intended such persons, building, units, or transports or other objects so using such identification to be the object of the attack.
3. The conduct took place in the context of and was associated with an international armed conflict.
4. The perpetrator was aware of factual circumstances that established the existence of an armed conflict.

ARTICLE 8(2)(b)(xxv)

War crime of starvation as a method of warfare

Elements
1. The perpetrator deprived civilians of objects indispensable to their survival.
2. The perpetrator intended to starve civilians as a method of warfare.
3. The conduct took place in the context of and was associated with an international armed conflict.
4. The perpetrator was aware of factual circumstances that established the existence of an armed conflict.

ARTICLE 8(2)(b)(xxvi)

War crime of using, conscripting or enlisting children

Elements

1. The perpetrator conscripted or enlisted one or more persons into the national armed forces or used one or more persons to participate actively in hostilities.
2. Such person or persons were under the age of fifteen years.
3. The perpetrator knew or should have known that such person or persons were under the age of fifteen years.
4. The conduct took place in the context of and was associated with an international armed conflict.
5. The perpetrator was aware of factual circumstances that established the existence of an armed conflict.

ARTICLE 8(2)(c)

ARTICLE 8(2)(c)(i)–1

War crime of murder

Elements

1. The perpetrator killed one or more persons.
2. Such person or persons were either *hors de combat*, or were civilians, medical personnel, or religious personnel[56] taking no active part in the hostilities.
3. The perpetrator was aware of the factual circumstances that established this status.
4. The conduct took place in the context of and was associated with an armed conflict not of an international character.
5. The perpetrator was aware of factual circumstances that established the existence of an armed conflict.

ARTICLE 8(2)(c)(i)–2

War crime of mutilation

Elements

1. The perpetrator subjected one or more persons to mutilation, in particular by permanently disfiguring the person or persons, or by permanently disabling or removing an organ or appendage.
2. The conduct was neither justified by the medical, dental, or hospital treatment of the person or persons concerned nor carried out in such person's or persons' interests.
3. Such person or persons were either *hors de combat*, or were civilians, medical personnel, or religious personnel taking no active part in the hostilities.

---

[56] The term 'religious personnel' includes those non-confessional non-combatant military personnel carrying out a similar function.

4. The perpetrator was aware of the factual circumstances that established this status.
5. The conduct took place in the context of and was associated with an armed conflict not of an international character.
6. The perpetrator was aware of factual circumstances that established the existence of an armed conflict.

ARTICLE 8(2)(c)(i)–3

War crime of cruel treatment

Elements
1. The perpetrator inflicted severe physical or mental pain or suffering upon one or more persons.
2. Such person or persons were either *hors de combat*, or were civilians, medical personnel or religious personnel taking no active part in the hostilities.
3. The perpetrator was aware of the factual circumstances that established this status.
4. The conduct took place in the context of and was associated with an armed conflict not of an international character.
5. The perpetrator was aware of factual circumstances that established the existence of an armed conflict.

ARTICLE 8(2)(c)(i)–4

War crime of torture

Elements
1. The perpetrator inflicted severe physical or mental pain or suffering upon one or more persons.
2. The perpetrator inflicted the pain or suffering for such purposes as: obtaining information or a confession, punishment, intimidation or coercion or for any reason based on discrimination of any crime.
3. Such person or persons were either *hors de combat*, or were civilians, medical personnel or religious personnel taking no active part in the hostilities.
4. The perpetrator was aware of the factual circumstances that established this status.
5. The conduct took place in the context of and was associated with an armed conflict not of an international character.
6. The perpetrator was aware of factual circumstances that established the existence of an armed conflict.

ARTICLE 8(2)(c)(ii)

War crime of outrages upon personal dignity

Elements

1. The perpetrator humiliated, degraded, or otherwise violated the dignity of one or more persons.[57]
2. The severity of the humiliation, degradation, or other violation was of such degree as to be generally recognized as an outrage upon personal dignity.
3. Such person or persons were either *hors de combat*, or were civilians, medical personnel or religious personnel taking no active part in the hostilities.
4. The perpetrator was aware of the factual circumstances that established this status.
5. The conduct took place in the context of and was associated with an armed conflict not of an international character.
6. The perpetrator was aware of factual circumstances that established the existence of an armed conflict.

ARTICLE 8(2)(c)(iii)

War crime of taking hostages

Elements

1. The perpetrator seized, detained, or otherwise held hostage one or more persons.
2. The perpetrator threatened to kill, injure, or continue to detain such person or persons.
3. The perpetrator intended to compel a State, an international organization, a natural or legal person or a group of persons to act or refrain from acting as an explicit or implicit condition for the safety or the release of such person or persons.
4. Such person or persons were either *hors de combat*, or were civilians, medical personnel or religious personnel taking no active part in the hostilities.
5. The perpetrator was aware of the factual circumstances that established this status.
6. The conduct took place in the context of and was associated with an armed conflict not of an international character.
7. The perpetrator was aware of factual circumstances that established the existence of an armed conflict.

ARTICLE 8(2)(c)(iv)

War crime of sentencing or execution without due process

Elements

1. The perpetrator passed sentence or executed one or more persons.[58]

---

[57] For this crime, 'persons' can include dead persons. It is understood that the victim need not personally be aware of the existence of the humiliation or degradation, or other violation. This element takes into account relevant aspects of the cultural background of the victim.

[58] The elements laid down in these documents do not address the different forms of individual criminal responsibility, as enunciated in Arts. 25 and 28 of the Statute.

2. Such person or persons were either *hors de combat*, or were civilians, medical personnel, or religious personnel taking no active part in the hostilities.
3. The perpetrator was aware of the factual circumstances that established this status.
4. There was no previous judgment pronounced by a court, or the court that rendered judgment was not 'regularly constituted', that is, it did not afford the essential guarantees of independence and impartiality, or the court that rendered judgment did not afford all other judicial guarantees generally recognized as indispensable under international law.[59]
5. The perpetrator was aware of the absence of a previous judgment or of the denial of relevant guarantees and the fact that they are essential or indispensable to a fair trial.
6. The conduct took place in the context of and was associated with an armed conflict not of an international character.
7. The perpetrator was aware of factual circumstances that established the existence of an armed conflict.

ARTICLE 8(2)(e)

ARTICLE 8(2)(e)(i)

War crime of attacking civilians

Elements
1. The perpetrator directed an attack.
2. The object of the attack was a civilian population as such or individual civilians not taking direct part in hostilities.
3. The perpetrator intended the civilian population as such or individual civilians not taking direct part in hostilities to be the object of the attack.
4. The conduct took place in the context of and was associated with an armed conflict not of an international character.
5. The perpetrator was aware of factual circumstances that established the existence of an armed conflict.

ARTICLE 8(2)(e)(ii)

War crime of attacking objects or persons using the distinctive emblems of the Geneva Conventions

Elements
1. The perpetrator attacked one or more persons, buildings, medical units, or transports

---

[59] With respect to Elements 4 and 5, the Court should consider whether, in light of all relevant circumstances, the cumulative effect of factors with respect to guarantees deprived the person or persons of a fair trial.

or other objects using, in conformity with international law, a distinctive emblem or other method of identification indicating protection under the Geneva Conventions.

2. The perpetrator intended such persons, building, units, or transports or other objects so using such identification to be the object of the attack.

3. The conduct took place in the context of and was associated with an armed conflict not of an international character.

4. The perpetrator was aware of factual circumstances that established the existence of an armed conflict.

ARTICLE 8(2)(e)(iii)

War crime of attacking personnel or objects involved in a humanitarian assistance or peacekeeping mission

Elements

1. The perpetrator directed an attack.

2. The object of the attack was personnel, installations, material, units, or vehicles involved in a humanitarian assistance or peacekeeping mission in accordance with the Charter of the United Nations.

3. The perpetrator intended such personnel, installations, material, units, or vehicles so involved to be the object of the attack.

4. Such personnel, installations, material, units, or vehicles were entitled to that protection given to civilians or civilian objects under the international law of armed conflict.

5. The perpetrator was aware of the factual circumstances that established that protection.

6. The conduct took place in the context of and was associated with an armed conflict not of an international character.

7. The perpetrator was aware of factual circumstances that established the existence of an armed conflict.

ARTICLE 8(2)(e)(iv)

War crime of attacking protected objects[60]

Elements

1. The perpetrator directed an attack.

2. The object of the attack was one or more buildings dedicated to religion, education, art, science or charitable purposes, historic monuments, hospitals, or places where the sick and wounded are collected, which were not military objectives.

3. The perpetrator intended such buildings dedicated to religion, education, art, science or charitable purposes, historic monuments, hospitals, or places where the sick and

---

[60] The presence in the locality of persons specially protected under the Geneva Conventions of 1949 or of police forces retained for the sole purpose of maintaining law and order does not by itself render the locality a military objective.

wounded are collected, which were not military objectives, to be the object of the attack.

4. The conduct took place in the context of and was associated with an armed conflict not of an international character.

5. The perpetrator was aware of factual circumstances that established the existence of an armed conflict.

ARTICLE 8(2)(e)(v)

War crime of pillaging

Elements

1. The perpetrator appropriated certain property.
2. The perpetrator intended to deprive the owner of the property and to appropriate it for private or personal use.[61]
3. The appropriation was without the consent of the owner.
4. The conduct took place in the context of and was associated with an armed conflict not of an international character.
5. The perpetrator was aware of factual circumstances that established the existence of an armed conflict.

ARTICLE 8(2)(e)(vi)–1

War crime of rape

Elements

1. The perpetrator invaded[62] the body of a person by conduct resulting in penetration, however slight, of any part of the body of the victim or of the perpetrator with a sexual organ, or of the anal or genital opening of the victim with any object or any other part of the body.
2. The invasion was committed by force, or by threat of force or coercion, such as that caused by fear of violence, duress, detention, psychological oppression or abuse of power, against such person or another person, or by taking advantage of a coercive environment, or the invasion was committed against a person incapable of giving genuine consent.[63]
3. The conduct took place in the context of and was associated with an armed conflict not of an international character.
4. The perpetrator was aware of factual circumstances that established the existence of an armed conflict.

---

[61] As indicated by the use of term 'private or personal use', appropriations justified by military necessity cannot constitute the crime of pillaging.

[62] The concept of 'invasion' is intended to be broad enough to be gender-neutral.

[63] It is understood that a person may be incapable of giving genuine consent if affected by natural, induced or age-related incapacity. This footnote also applies to the corresponding elements of Art. 8(2)(e)(vi)–3, 5 and 6.

ARTICLE 8(2)(e)(vi)–2

War crime of sexual slavery[64]

Elements

1. The perpetrator exercised any or all of the powers attaching to the right of ownership over one or more persons, such as by purchasing, selling, lending, or bartering such a person or persons, or by imposing on them a similar deprivation of liberty.[65]
2. The perpetrator caused such person or persons to engage in one or more acts of a sexual nature.
3. The conduct took place in the context of and was associated with an armed conflict not of an international character.
4. The perpetrator was aware of factual circumstances that established the existence of an armed conflict.

ARTICLE 8(2)(e)(vi)–3

War crime of enforced prostitution

Elements

1. The perpetrator caused one or more persons to engage in one or more acts of a sexual nature by force, or by threat of force or coercion, such as that caused by fear of violence, duress, detention, psychological oppression or abuse of power, against such person or persons or another person, or by taking advantage of a coercive environment or such person's or persons' incapacity to give genuine consent.
2. The perpetrator or another person obtained or expected to obtain pecuniary or other advantage in exchange for or in connection with the acts of a sexual nature.
3. The conduct took place in the context of and was associated with an armed conflict not of an international character.
4. The perpetrator was aware of factual circumstances that established the existence of an armed conflict.

ARTICLE 8(2)(e)(vi)–4

War crime of forced pregnancy

Elements

1. The perpetrator confined one or more women forcibly made pregnant, with the intent of affecting the ethnic composition of any population or carrying out other grave violations of international law.

---

[64] Given the complex nature of this crime, it is recognized that its commission could involve more than one perpetrator as a part of a common criminal purpose.

[65] It is understood that such deprivation of liberty may, in some circumstances, include exacting forced labour or otherwise reducing a person to servile status as defined in the Supplementary Convention on the Abolition of Slavery, the Slave Trade, and Institutions and Practices Similar to Slavery of 1956. It is also understood that the conduct described in this element includes trafficking in persons, in particular women and children.

2. The conduct took place in the context of and was associated with an armed conflict not of an international character.
3. The perpetrator was aware of factual circumstances that established the existence of an armed conflict.

ARTICLE 8(2)(e)(vi)–5

War crime of enforced sterilization

Elements
1. The perpetrator deprived one or more persons of biological reproductive capacity.[66]
2. The conduct was neither justified by the medical or hospital treatment of the person or persons concerned nor carried out with their genuine consent.[67]
3. The conduct took place in the context of and was associated with an armed conflict not of an international character.
4. The perpetrator was aware of factual circumstances that established the existence of an armed conflict.

ARTICLE 8(2)(e)(vi)–6

War crime of sexual violence

Elements
1. The perpetrator committed an act of a sexual nature against one or more persons or caused such person or persons to engage in an act of a sexual nature by force, or by threat of force or coercion, such as that caused by fear of violence, duress, detention, psychological oppression or abuse of power, against such person or persons or another person, or by taking advantage of a coercive environment or such person's or persons' incapacity to give genuine consent.
2. The conduct was of a gravity comparable to that of a serious violation of Article 3 common to the four Geneva Conventions.
3. The perpetrator was aware of the factual circumstances that established the gravity of the conduct.
4. The conduct took place in the context of and was associated with an armed conflict not of an international character.
5. The perpetrator was aware of factual circumstances that established the existence of an armed conflict.

---

[66] The deprivation is not intended to include birth-control measures which have a non-permanent effect in practice.

[67] It is understood that 'genuine consent' does not include consent obtained through deception.

ARTICLE 8 (2)(e)(vii)

War crime of using, conscripting and enlisting children

Elements
1. The perpetrator conscripted or enlisted one or more persons into an armed force or group or used one or more persons to participate actively in hostilities.
2. Such person or persons were under the age of fifteen years.
3. The perpetrator knew or should have known that such person or persons were under the age of fifteen years.
4. The conduct took place in the context of and was associated with an armed conflict not of an international character.
5. The perpetrator was aware of factual circumstances that established the existence of an armed conflict.

ARTICLE 8(2)(e)(viii)

War crime of displacing civilians

Elements
1. The perpetrator ordered a displacement of a civilian population.
2. Such order was not justified by the security of the civilians involved or by military necessity.
3. The perpetrator was in a position to effect such displacement by giving such order.
4. The conduct took place in the context of and was associated with an armed conflict not of an international character.
5. The perpetrator was aware of factual circumstances that established the existence of an armed conflict.

ARTICLE 8(2)(e)(ix)

War crime of treacherously killing or wounding

Elements
1. The perpetrator invited the confidence or belief of one or more combatant adversaries that they were entitled to, or were obliged to accord, protection under rules of international law applicable in armed conflict.
2. The perpetrator intended to betray that confidence or belief.
3. The perpetrator killed or injured such person or persons.
4. The perpetrator made use of that confidence or belief in killing or injuring such person or persons.
5. Such person or persons belonged to an adverse party.
6. The conduct took place in the context of and was associated with an armed conflict not of an international character.
7. The perpetrator was aware of factual circumstances that established the existence of an armed conflict.

ARTICLE 8(2)(e)(x)

War crime of denying quarter

Elements

1. The perpetrator declared or ordered that there shall be no survivors.
2. Such declaration or order was given in order to threaten an adversary or to conduct hostilities on the basis that there shall be no survivor.
3. The perpetrator was in a position of effective command or control over the subordinate forces to which the declaration or order was directed.
4. The conduct took place in the context of and was associated with an armed conflict not of an international character.
5. The perpetrator was aware of factual circumstances that established the existence of an armed conflict.

ARTICLE 8(2)(e)(xi)–1

War crime of mutilation

Elements

1. The perpetrator subjected one or more persons to mutilation, in particular by permanently disfiguring the person or persons, or by permanently disabling or removing an organ or appendage.
2. The conduct caused death or seriously endangered the physical or mental health of such persons or persons.
3. The conduct was neither justified by the medical, dental, or hospital treatment of the person or persons concerned nor carried out in such person's or persons' interest.[68]
4. Such person or persons were in the power of another party to the conflict.
5. The conduct took place in the context of or was associated with an armed conflict not of an international character.
6. The perpetrator was aware of factual circumstances that established the existence of an armed conflict.

ARTICLE 8(2)(e)(xi)–2

War crime of medical or scientific experiments

Elements

1. The perpetrator subjected one or more persons to a medical or scientific experiment.
2. The conduct caused the death or seriously endangered the physical or mental health of such persons or persons.

---

[68] Consent is not a defence to this crime. The crime prohibits any medical procedure which is not indicated by the state or health of the person concerned and which is not consistent with generally accepted medical standards which would be applied under similar medical circumstances to persons who are nationals of the party conducting the procedure and who are in no way deprived of liberty. This footnote also applies to the similar element in Art. 8(2)(e)(xi)–2.

3. The conduct was neither justified by the medical, dental, or hospital treatment of the person or persons concerned nor carried out in such person's or persons' interest.
4. Such person or persons were in the power of another party to the conflict.
5. The conduct took place in the context of or was associated with an armed conflict not of an international character.
6. The perpetrator was aware of factual circumstances that established the existence of an armed conflict.

ARTICLE 8(2)(e)(xii)

War crime of destroying or seizing the enemy's property

Elements
1. The perpetrator destroyed or seized certain property.
2. Such property was property of an adversary.
3. Such property was protected from that destruction or seizure under the international law of armed conflict.
4. The perpetrator was aware of the factual circumstances that established the status of the property.
5. The destruction or seizure was not justified by military necessity.
6. The conduct took place in the context of and was associated with an armed conflict not of an international character.
7. The perpetrator was aware of factual circumstances that established the existence of an armed conflict.

BIBLIOGRAPHY

ABIEW, F. K., *The Evolution of the Doctrine and Practice of Humanitarian Intervention* (Kluwer, 1999).

ACKERMAN, J. E., and O'SULLIVAN, E., *Practice and Procedure of the International Criminal Tribunal for the Former Yugoslavia* (Kluwer, 2000).

AFFOLDER, N. A., '*Tadic*, the Anonymous Witness and the Sources of International Procedural Law' (1998) **19** *Michigan J. Int'l L.* 445.

ALDRICH, G. H., 'Jurisdiction of the International Criminal Tribunal for the Former Yugoslavia' (1996) **90** *AJIL* 64.

ALLAIN, J., and JONES, J. A., 'A Patchwork of Norms: A Commentary on the 1996 Draft Code of Crimes Against the Peace and Security of Mankind' (1997) **8** *Euro. J. Int'l L.* 100.

AMBOS, K., 'The Role of the Prosecutor of an International Criminal Court from a Comparative Perspective' (1997) **58–59** *Int'l Comm'n Jurists Rev.* 45.

ANAYA, S. J., *Indigenous Peoples in International Law* (Oxford University Press, 1996).

ANDERSON, D. L. (ed.), *Facing My Lai: Moving Beyond the Massacre* (University Press of Kansas, 1998).

ANDREOPOLOUS, G. J. (ed.), *Genocide: Conceptual and Historical Dimensions* (University of Pennsylvania Press, 1994).

ANDREWS, L. W., 'Sailing Around the Flat Earth: The International Criminal Tribunal for the Former Yugoslavia as a Failure of Jurisprudential Theory' (1997) **11** *Emory Int'l L. Rev.* 471.

ANNAN, K., 'Advocating for an International Criminal Court' (1997) **21** *Fordham Int'l L. J.* 363.

AOLAIN, F. N., 'Racial Rules: The Effects of Evidential and Procedural Rules on the Regulation of Sexual Violence in War' (1997) **60** *Albany L. Rev.* 883.

ARBOUR, L., 'The Need for an Independent and Effective Prosecutor in the Permanent International Criminal Court' (1999) **17** *Windsor Yearbook of Access to Justice* 207.

AREND, A. C., and BECK, R. J., *International Law and the Use of Force: Beyond the UN Charter Paradigm* (Routledge, 1993).

ARMSTRONG, A., 'Evidence in Rape Cases in Four Southern African Countries' (1989) **33** *J. African L.* 172.

ARSANJANI, M. H., 'The Rome Statute of the International Criminal Court' (1999) **33** *AJIL* 22.

ASKIN, K. D., *War Crimes Against Women: Prosecution in International War Crimes Tribunals* (Martinus Nijhoff, 1997).

—— 'Sexual Violence in Decisions and Indictments of the Yugoslav and Rwandan Tribunals: Current Status' (1999) **93** *AJIL* 97.

ATKINS, R. D. (ed.), *The Alleged Transnational Criminal* (Martinus Nijhoff and International Bar Association, 1995).

AUBERT, M., 'The question of superior orders and the responsibility of Commanding Officers in the Protocols additional to the Geneva Conventions of 12 August 1949 and relating to the protection of victims of international armed conflicts (Protocol I) of 8 June 1977' (1988) **263** *Int'l Rev. Red Cross* 105.

BACHRACH, M. 'The Protection of Rights of

Victims Under International Criminal Law' (2000) **34** *International Lawyer* 7.

BAKKER, J. L., 'The Defence of Obedience to Superior Orders: The *Mens Rea* Requirement' (1989) **17** *American J. Crim. L.* 55.

BALIANT, J. L., 'Accountability for International Crime and Serious Violations of Fundamental Human Rights: The Place of Law in Addressing International Regime Conflicts' (1996) **59** *Law & Contemporary Problems* 103.

BALL, H., *Prosecuting War Crimes and Genocide: the Twentieth-Century Experience* (University of Kansas, 1999).

BASSIOUNI, M. C., *Legal Responses to International Terrorism* (Martinus Nijhoff, 1988).

—— 'Human Rights in the Context of Criminal Justice: Identifying International Procedural Protections and Equivalent Protections in National Constitutions' (1993) **3** *Duke J. Comp. & Int'l L.* 235.

—— *Crimes against Humanity in International Criminal Law*, 2nd ed. (Martinus Nijhoff, 1999).

—— 'The United Nations Commission of Experts Established Pursuant to Security Council Resolution 780' (1994) **88** *AJIL* 784.

—— (ed.), *The Protection of Human Rights in the Administration of Criminal Justice: A Compendium of United Nations Norms and Standards* (Transnational Publishers, 1994).

—— (comp.), *The Statute of the International Criminal Court: A Documentary History* (Transnational Publishers, 1998).

—— (ed.) *ICC Ratification and National Implementing Legislation* (Assoc. de Droit Pénal, 1999).

—— and MANIKAS, P., *The Law of the International Criminal Tribunal for the Former Yugoslavia* (Transnational Publishers, 1996).

BEIGBEDER, Y., *The Role and Status of International Humanitarian Volunteers and Organizations: The Right and Duty to Humanitarian Assistance* (Martinus Nijhoff, 1991).

—— *Judging War Criminals: the Politics of International Justice* (Macmillan/St. Martin's Press, 1999).

BELL-FIALKOFF, A., 'A Brief History of Ethnic Cleansing', *Foreign Affairs* (Summer 1993), 110.

BENNETT, T. W., 'A Linguistic Perspective of the Definition of Aggression' (1988) **31** *German YB Int'l L.* 48.

BENTON, W. E., and GRIMM, G. (eds.), *Nuremberg: German Views of the War Crimes Trials* (Southern Methodist University Press, 1955).

BILDER, R. B., 'Judicial Procedures Relating to the Use of Force' (1991) **31** *Virginia J. Int'l L.* 249.

BLAKESLEY, C., 'Finding Harmony Amidst Disagreement over Extradition, Jurisdiction, the Role of Human Rights and Issues of Extraterritoriality under International Criminal Law' (1991) **24** *Vanderbilt J. Transnat'l L.* 1.

BOISSON DE CHAZOURNES, L., and SANDS, P. (eds.), *International Law, the International Court of Justice and Nuclear Weapons* (Cambridge University Press, 1999).

BOISTER, N., and BURCHILL, R., 'The Pinochet Precedent: Don't Leave Home Without It' (1999) **10** *Crim. L. Forum* 405.

BOVAY, N., 'The Russian Armed Intervention in Chechnya and Its Human Rights Implications' (1995) **54** *Int'l Comm'n Jurists Rev.* 29.

BRACKMAN, A. C., *The Other Nuremberg: The Untold Story of the Tokyo War Crimes Trials* (Quill/Morrow, 1988).

BRAND, R. A., 'External Sovereignty and International Law' (1995) **18** *Fordham Int'l L. J.* 1685.

BRIERLY, J. L., *The Law of Nations: An Introduction to the International Law of Peace*, 6th ed. C. H. M. Waldock (Clarendon Press, 1963).

BROWN, B. S., 'Primacy or Complementarity; Reconciling the Jurisdiction of National Courts and International Criminal Tribunals' (1998) **23** *Yale J. Int'l L.* 383.

—— 'U.S. Objections to the Statute of the International Criminal Court: A Brief Response' (1999) **31** *New York Univ. J. Int'l L. & Politics* 855.

BROWNLIE, I., *International Law and the Use of Force by States* (Clarendon Press, 1963).

—— *Principles of Public International Law*, 5th ed. (Oxford University Press, 1999).

BURGER, J., and HUNT, P., 'Towards the International Protection of Indigenous Peoples' Rights' (1994) **4** *Netherlands Q. Human Rights* 409.

BURROUGHS, J., *The Legality of Threat or Use of Nuclear Weapons: A Guide to the Historic Opinion of the International Court of Justice* (LIT Verlag, 1997).

BUSS, D. E., 'Women at the Borders: Rape and Nationalism in International Law' (1998) **6** *Feminist Legal Stud.* 171.

BUTLER, A. H., 'Universal Jurisdiction' (2000, forthcoming) **11** *Crim. L. Forum.*

BYERS, M., 'Conceptualizing the Relationship between *Jus Cogens* and *Erga Omnes*' (1997) **66** *Nordic J. Int'l L.* 211.

—— 'The Law and Politics of the *Pinochet* Case' (2000) **10** *Duke J. of Comp. & Int'l L.* 415.

CAREY, J., and PRITCHARD, R. J. (eds.), *International Humanitarian Law: Origins, Challenges and Prospects* (Edwin Mellen Press, 2000).

CARNAHAN, B. M., 'Lincoln, Lieber and the Laws of War: The Origins and Limits of the Principle of Military Necessity' (1998) **92** *AJIL* 213.

CARPENTER, A. C., 'The International Criminal Court and the Crime of Aggression' (1995) **64** *Nordic J. Int'l L.* 223.

CASSESE, A., '*Ex iniuria ius oritur*: Are We Moving towards International Legitimation of Forcible Humanitarian Countermeasures in the World Community?' (1999) **10** *Euro. J. Int'l L.* 23.

—— 'The Statute of the International Criminal Court: Some Preliminary Reflections', ibid., 144.

—— 'A Follow-Up: Forcible Humanitarian Countermeasures and *Opinio Necessitatis*', ibid., 791.

CASSESE, A., ESER, A., and GAJA, G. (eds.), *The Rome Statute for an International Criminal Court: A Commentary* (Oxford University Press, 2001).

CHADWICK, E., *Self-Determination, Terrorism and the International Humanitarian Law of Armed Conflict* (Martinus Nijhoff, 1996).

CHANDLER, D. P., KIERNAN, B., and BOUA, C., *Pol Pot Plans the Future: Confidential Leadership Documents from Democratic Kampuchea, 1976–1977* (Yale University Southeast Asia Studies, 1988).

CHARNEY, J. I., 'The Persistent Objector Rule and the Development of Customary International Law' (1985) **56** *BYBIL* 1.

—— 'Progress in International Criminal Law' (1999) **93** *AJIL* 452.

CHESTERMAN, S., 'Never Again . . . and Again: Law, Order and the Gender of War Crimes in Bosnia and Beyond' (1997) **22** *Yale J. Int'l L.* 299.

—— 'An Altogether Different Order: Defining the Elements of Crimes Against

Humanity' (2000) **10** *Duke J. of Comp. & Int'l L.* 307.

CHINKIN, C. M., '*Amicus Curiae* Brief on Protective Measures for Victims and Witnesses' (1996) 7 *Crim. L. Forum* 179.

—— 'Due Process and Witness Anonymity' (1997) **91** *AJIL* 75.

CLARK, R. S., 'The Development of International Criminal Law', Paper presented at the Conference: 'Just Peace? Peace Making and Peace Building for the New Millennium', Massey University, Auckland, New Zealand, 24–28 Apr. 2000.

—— and SANN, M. (eds.), *The Prosecution of International Crimes* (Transaction Publishers, 1996).

COHN, I., and GOODWIN-GILL, G., *Child Soldiers: The Role of Children in Armed Conflict* (Clarendon Press, 1994).

COLES, S., 'The Proposed International Criminal Court: Experiences of Human Rights Jurisprudence at the International Criminal Tribunal for Former Yugoslavia' (1998) 6 *Proc. Australia-NZ Soc. Int'l L. Annual Conf.* 65.

CORREA, J., 'Dealing with Past Human Rights Violations: The Chilean Case after Dictatorship' (1992) **67** *Notre Dame L. Rev.* 1455.

COUSSELL, D., 'Lessons from the Americas: Guidelines for International Responses to Amnesties for Atrocities' (1996) **59** *L. & Contemp. Probs.* 197.

CRETA, V. M., 'The Search for Justice in the Former Yugoslavia and Beyond: Analyzing the Rights of the Accused under the Statute and the Rules of Procedure and Evidence of the International Criminal Tribunal for the Former Yugoslavia' (1998) **20** *Houston J. Int'l L.* 381.

DAES, E-I. A., *Status of the Individual and Contemporary International Law: Promotion, Protection and Restoration of Human Rights at National, Regional and International Levels* (United Nations, 1992).

DAMROSCH, L. F. (ed.), *Enforcing Restraint: Collective Intervention in Internal Conflicts* (West View Press, 1995).

DAVIDSON, E., *The Nuremberg Fallacy* (University of Missouri Press, 1973 and 1998).

DE HOOGH, A., *Obligations* Erga Omnes *and International Crimes: A Theoretical Inquiry into the Implementation and Enforcement of International Responsibility of States* (Kluwer, 1996).

—— 'Australia and East Timor: Rights *Erga Omnes,* Complicity and Non-Recognition' (1999) *Australia Int'l L. J.* 63.

DINSTEIN, Y., *The Defence of 'Obedience of Superior Orders' in International Law* (Sijthoff, 1965).

—— *War, Aggression and Self-Defence,* 2nd ed., (Grotius Publications, 1994).

—— and TABORY, M. (eds.), *War Crimes in International Law* (Martinus Nijhoff, 1996).

DIXON, R., 'Developing International Rules of Evidence for the Yugoslavia and Rwanda Tribunals' (1997) 7 *Transnat'l L. & Contemp. Probs.* 81.

DODD, C. J., 'The Legacy of Nuremberg' (1997) **12** *Connecticut J. Int'l L.* 199.

DOHERTY, K. L., and McCORMACK, T. L. H., '"Complementarity" As a Catalyst for Comprehensive Domestic Penal Legislation' (1999) 5 *Univ. Cal., Davis J. Int'l L. & Policy* 196.

DRAPER, G. I. A. D., 'The Geneva Conventions of 1949' (1965) **114** *Hague Recueil* 63.

DUBOIS, O., 'Rwanda's National Criminal Courts and the International Tribunal' (1997) **321** *Int'l Rev. Red Cross* 717.

DUGARD, J., and VAN DEN WYNGAERT (eds.), *International Criminal Law and Procedure* (Dartmouth, 1996).

DURHAM, H., and McCORMACK, T. L. H.

(eds.), *The Changing Face of Conflict and the Efficacy of International Humanitarian Law* (Martinus Nijhoff, 1999).

Editorial Comments, 'NATO's Kosovo Intervention: Kosovo and the Law of "Humanitarian Intervention"' (1999) **93** *AJIL* 824.

FALK, R. A., 'Nuclear Weapons, International Law and the World Court: A Historic Encounter' (1997) **91** *AJIL* 64.

FATIĆ, A., *Reconciliation via the War Crimes Tribunal?* (Ashgate, 2000).

FEDER, N. M., 'Reading the UN Charter Connotatively: Toward a New Definition of Armed Attack' (1987) **19** *Int'l L. & Politics* 395.

FEIN, H. (ed.), *Genocide Watch* (Yale University Press, 1992).

FENRICK, W., 'International Humanitarian Law and Criminal Trials' (1997) **7** *Transnat'l L. & Contemp. Probs.* 23.

FERENCZ, B., 'The Nuremberg Precedent and the Prosecution of State-Sponsored Murder' (1990) **11** *New York L. Sch. J. Int'l & Comp. L.* 325.

—— *An International Criminal Court: A Step Toward World Peace—A Documentary History and Analysis* (Harvard University Press, 1992).

—— 'Can Aggression be Deterred by Law?' (1999) **11** *Pace Int'l L.Rev.* 304.

FLECK, D. (ed.), *The Handbook of Humanitarian Law in Armed Conflicts* (Oxford University Press, 1995).

FLYNN, M., 'Genocide: It's a Crime Everywhere, But not in Australia' (2000) **29** *Univ. W. Australia L. Rev.* 59.

FOX, H., 'The Objections to the Transfer of Criminal Jurisdiction to the UN Tribunal' (1997) **46** *Int'l & Comp. L. Q.* 434.

FRANCK, T. M., *Fairness in International Law and Institutions* (Clarendon Press, 1995).

FRYE, A. (ed.), *Toward an International Criminal Court?* (Council on Foreign Relations, 1999).

GAETA, P., 'The Defence of Superior Orders: The Statute of the International Criminal Court *versus* Customary International Law' (1999) **10** *Euro. J. Int'l L.* 172.

GALLANT, K. S., 'The Role and Powers of Defense Counsel in the Rome Statute of the International Criminal Court' (2000) **34** *International Lawyer* 21.

GARVEY, J. I., 'The UN Definition of Aggression: Law and Illusion in the Context of Collective Security' (1997) **17** *Virginia J. Int'l L.* 177.

GINSBURG, G., *Moscow's Road to Nuremberg: The Soviet Background to the Trial* (Martinus Nijhoff, 1996).

—— and KUDRIAVTSEV, V. N. (eds.), *The Nuremberg Trial and International Law* (Martinus Nijhoff, 1990).

GLUECK, S., *The Nuremberg Trial and Aggressive War* (Knopf, 1946).

GOLDSTONE, R., 'The United Nations' War Crimes Tribunals: An Assessment' (1997) **12** *Connecticut J. Int'l L.* 227.

GOODE, M., 'The Tortured Tale of Criminal Jurisdiction' (1997) **21** *Melbourne Univ. L. Rev.* 411.

GRAYSON, J., 'The Defence of Superior Orders in the International Criminal Court' (1995) **64** *Nordic J. Int'l L.* 243.

GREEN, L. C., *Superior Orders in National and International Law* (Sijthoff, 1976).

—— *The Contemporary Law of Armed Conflict* (Manchester University Press, 1993).

—— 'The Defence of Superior Order in the Modern Law of Armed Conflict' (1993) **31** *Alberta L. Rev.* 320.

GREENWOOD, C., 'Is there a right of humanitarian intervention?', *The World Today* (Feb. 1993), 34.

—— 'International Humanitarian Law and the *Tadic* Case' (1996) **7** *Euro. J. Int'l L.* 265.

GROSS, L., 'The Peace of Westphalia, 1648–1948', (1948) 42 *AJIL* 20.

GROSS, O., 'The Grave Breaches System and the Armed Conflict in the Former Yugoslavia' (1994–95) 16 *Michigan J. Int'l L.* 783.

GUFFEY-LANDERS, N. E., 'Establishing an International Criminal Court: Will It Do Justice?' (1996) 20 *Maryland J. Int'l L. & Trade* 199.

GUTMAN, R., and REIFF, D. (eds.), *Crimes of War: What the Public Should Know* (W. W. Norton & Co., 1999).

HAMPSON, F. J., 'The International Criminal Tribunal for the Former Yugoslavia and the Reluctant Witness' (1998) 47 *Int'l & Comp. L. Q.* 50.

HARHOFF, F., 'Consonance or Rivalry? Calibrating the Efforts to Prosecute War Crimes in National and International Tribunals' (1995) 64 *Duke J. Comp. & Int'l L.* 683.

HENKIN, L., 'Conceptualizing Violence: Present and Future Developments in International Law' (1997) 60 *Albany L. Rev.* 571.

HOGAN-DORAN, J., and VAN GINKEL, B., 'Aggression as a Crime under International Law and the Prosecution of Individuals by the Proposed International Criminal Court' (1996) 43 *Netherlands Int'l L. Rev.* 321.

HORTATOS, C. P., *International Law and the Crimes of Terrorism against the Peace and Security of Mankind* (Ant. N. Sakkoulas, 1993).

HOSOYA, C., ANDO, N., ONUMA, Y., and MINEAR, R. (eds.), *The Tokyo War Crimes Trial: An International Symposium* (Kodansha, 1986).

HSIAO, A., 'Is China's Policy to Use Force against Taiwan a Violation of the Principle of Non-Use of Force under International Law' (1998) 32 *New England L. Rev.* 715.

Human Rights Watch, *Justice in the Balance: Recommendations for an Independent and Effective International Criminal Court* (Human Rights Watch, 1998).

HWANG, P., 'Defining Crimes against Humanity in the Rome Statute of the International Criminal Court' (1998) 22 *Fordham Int'l L. J.* 457.

ICRC, *Basic Rules of the Geneva Conventions and Their Additional Protocols* (ICRC, 1987).

INGRAM, P. G., 'Self-Defence as a Justification for War' (1994) 7 *Canadian J. of L. & Jurisprudence* 283.

IRELAND, G., '*Ex Post Facto* Law from Rome to Tokyo' (1947) 21 *Temple L. Q.* 27.

ISENBERG, B. A., 'Genocide, Rape, and Crimes against Humanity: An Affirmation of Individual Accountability in the Former Yugoslavia in the Karadzic Actions' (1997) 60 *Albany L. Rev.* 1051.

JARASCH, F., 'Establishing, Organizing and Financing the International Criminal Court (Parts I, IV, XI-XIII)' (1998) 6 *Euro. J. Crime, Crim. L. & Crim. Justice* 9.

JENNINGS, R., and WATTS, A. (eds.), *Oppenheim's International Law*, 9th ed., i. (Longman, 1992).

JOHNSON, D. H. N., 'The Defence of Superior Orders' (1985) 9 *Australia Y. B. Int'l L.* 301.

JONES, R. W. D., *The Practice of the International Criminal Tribunals for the Former Yugoslavia and Rwanda*, 2nd ed. (Transnational Publishers, 2000).

JOYNER, C. C., 'Arresting Impunity: The Case for Universal Jurisdiction in Bringing War Criminals to Accountability' (1996) 59 *L. & Contemp. Probs.* 153.

KARHILO, J., 'The Establishment of the International Tribunal for Rwanda' (1995) 64 *Nordic J. Int'l L.* 699.

KAUL, H.-P., 'Special Note: The Struggle for

the International Criminal Court's Jurisdiction' (1998) **6** *Euro. J. Crime, Crim. L. & Crim. Justice* 364.

—— 'Breakthrough in Rome: The Statute of the International Criminal Court' (1999) **59/60** *Law and State* 114.

KEITH, K. J., 'The Proposed International Criminal Court: Over What Crimes Should It Have Jurisdiction?' (1998) **6** *Proc. Aust.-NZ Soc. Int'l L. Annual Conf.* 69.

KIERNAN, B., *The Pol Pot Regime: Race Power and Genocide in Cambodia under the Khmer Rouge, 1975–79* (Yale University Press, 1996).

KING, F. P., 'Public Disclosure in Rule 61 Proceedings before the International Criminal Tribunal for the Former Yugoslavia' (1997) **29** *New York Univ. J. Int'l L. & Pol.* 523.

KIRSCH, P., and HOLMES, J. T., 'The Rome Conference on an International Criminal Court: The Negotiating Process' (1999) **93** *AJIL* 2.

KITTICHAISAREE, K., 'Practical Difficulties for the International Criminal Court to Overcome' (1998) **6** *Proc. Aust.-NZ Soc. Int'l L. Annual Conf.* 79.

—— 'The International Criminal Court and Its Potential Impact on Future Military Actions of NATO' (2000, forthcoming) **4** *Singapore J. Int'l & Comp. L.*

KLIP, A., 'Enforcement of Sanctions Imposed by the International Criminal Tribunals for Rwanda and the Former Yugoslavia' (1997) **5** *Euro. J. Crime, Crim. L. & Crim. Justice* 144.

—— and SLUITER, G. (eds.), *Annotated Leading Cases of International Criminal Tribunals*, i: The International Criminal Tribunal for the Former Yugoslavia 1993–1998 (Intersentia—Hart—Verlag Osterreich, 1999).

KLOTZ, A., *Norms in International Relations: The Struggle against Apartheid* (Cornell Studies in Political Economy, 1996).

KOHN, E. A., 'Rape as a Weapon of War: Women's Human Rights During the Dissolution of Yugoslavia' (1995) **24** *Golden Gate Univ. L. Rev.* 203.

KOCHAVI, A. J., *Prelude to Nuremberg: Allied War Crimes Policy and the Question of Punishment* (University of North Carolina Press, 1998).

KREß, C., and LATTANZI, F. (eds.), *The Rome Statute and Domestic Legal Orders*, i: General Aspects and Constitutional Issues (Nomos, 2000).

KUPER, J., *International Law Concerning Child Civilians in Armed Conflict* (Oxford University Press, 1997).

KUPER, L., *The Prevention of Genocide* (Yale University Press, 1985).

KUSHEN, R., and HARRIS, K. J., 'Surrender of Fugitives by the United States to the War Crimes Tribunals for Yugoslavia and Rwanda' (1996) **90** *AJIL* 510.

LAGOS, R., and MUNOZ, H., 'The Pinochet Dilemma', *Foreign Policy* (Spring 1999), 26.

LA HAYE, E., 'The Jurisdiction of the International Criminal Court: Controversies over the Preconditions for Exercising Its Jurisdiction' (1999) **46** *Netherlands Int'l L. Rev.* 1.

LAKATOS, A. C., 'Evaluating the Rules of Procedure and Evidence for the International Tribunal in the Former Yugoslavia: Balancing Witnesses' Needs against Defendants' Rights' (1995) **46** *Hastings L. J.* 909.

LAURENTI, S., 'The Crime of Aggression', Discussion Paper submitted by the Lelio Basso International Foundation to the PCNICC (26 July–13 Aug. 1999).

LATTANZI, F., and SCHABAS, W. A. (eds.),

Essays on the Rome Statute of the International Criminal Court, i (il Sirente, 1999).

LAUTERPACHT, H., 'The Law of Nations and the Punishment of War Crimes' (1944) 21 *BYBIL* 58.

LEE, R. S., 'The Rwanda Tribunal' (1996) 9 *Leiden J. Int'l L.* 42.

—— (ed.), *The International Criminal Court: The Making of the Rome Statute—Issues—Negotiations—Results* (Kluwer, 1999).

LEIGH, M., 'The Yugoslav Tribunal: Use of Unnamed Witness Anonymity against the Accused' (1996) 90 *AJIL* 235.

—— 'Witness Anonymity is Inconsistent with Due Process' (1997) 91 *AJIL* 80.

LEMKIN, R., *Axis Rule in Occupied Europe* (Carnegie Endowment, 1944).

—— 'Genocide as a Crime Under International Law' (1947) 41 *AJIL* 145.

LESCURE, K., and TRINTINGNAC, F., *International Justice for Former Yugoslavia: The Working of the International Criminal Tribunal of The Hague* (Kluwer, 1996).

LEVIE, H. S., *The Code of International Armed Conflict* (Oceana, 1986).

—— (ed.), *The Law of Non-International Armed Conflict: Protocol II to the 1949 Geneva Conventions* (Martinus Nijhoff, 1987).

—— 'The Statute of the International Tribunal for the Former Yugoslavia: A Comparison with the Past and a Look at the Future' (1995) 21 *Syracuse J. Int'l L. & Com.* 1.

LIETZAU, W. K., 'Checks and Balances and Elements of Proof: Structural Pillars for the International Criminal Court' (1999) 32 *Cornell Int'l L. J.* 477.

LIN, C. T.-H., 'The International Criminal Court: Taiwan's Last Hope?' (1997) 6 *Pacific Rim L. & Policy Assoc.* 755.

LIPPMAN, M., 'The Drafting of the 1948 Convention on the Prevention and Punishment of the Crime of Genocide' (1985) 3 *Boston Univ. Int'l L. J.* 1.

—— 'The 1948 Convention on the Prevention and Punishment of the Crime of Genocide: Forty-Five Years Later' (1994) 8 *Temple Int'l & Comp. L. J.* 1.

LOFGREN, N., and KILDUFF, P., 'Genocide and Australian Law' (1994) 3 *Aboriginal L. Bull.* 6.

MARKS, S. P., 'Elusive Justice for the Victims of the Khmer Rouge' (1999) 52 *J. Int'l Affairs* 691.

MACK, K., 'Continuing Barriers to Women's Credibility: A Feminist Perspective on the Proof Process' (1993) 5 *Crim. L. Forum* 327.

MAGNARELLA, P. J., *Justice in Africa: Rwanda's Genocide, Its Courts and the UN Criminal Tribunal* (Ashgate, 2000).

MALANCZUK, P., 'The International Criminal Court and Landmines: What Are the Consequences of Leaving the US Behind?' (2000) 11 *Euro. J. Int'l L.* 77.

MALEKIAN, F., *The Concept of Islamic International Criminal Law: A Comparative Study* (Graham & Trotman/Martinus Nijhoff, 1994).

MANSFIELD, L., 'Crimes against Humanity: Reflections on the Fiftieth Anniversary of Nuremberg and a Forgotten Legacy' (1995) 64 *Nordic J. Int'l L.* 293.

MARRUS, M. R. (ed.), *The Nuremberg War Crimes Tribunal 1945–1946: A Documentary History* (St. Martin's Press, 1997).

MAYK, J. E., 'Crimes against Peace: An Analysis of the Nuremberg Prohibition on Planning and Waging Aggressive War and its Applicability to the Gulf War' (1992) 24 *Rutgers L. J.* 253.

McCORMACK, T. H. L., and SIMPSON, G. J.

(eds.), *The Law of War Crimes: National and International Approaches* (Kluwer, 1997).

McCoubrey, H., *International Humanitarian Law: The Regulation of Armed Conflicts* (Dartmouth, 1990).

—— and White, N. D., *International Law and Armed Conflicts* (Dartmouth, 1992).

McDonald, G. K., 'The Eleventh Annual Waldemar A. Solf Lecture: The Changing Nature of the Laws of War' (1998) **135** *Military L. Rev.* 30.

—— and Swaak-Goldman, O. (eds.), *Substantive and Procedural Aspects of International Criminal Law*, 3 vols. (Kluwer, 2000).

McRae, H., Nettheim, G., and Beacroft, L., *Indigenous Legal Issues*, 2nd ed. (LBC, 1997).

Meindersma, C., 'Violations of Common Article 3 of the Geneva Conventions as Violations of the Laws or Customs of War under Article 3 of the Statute of the International Criminal Tribunal for the Former Yugoslavia' (1995) **42** *Netherlands Int'l L. Rev.* 375.

Metzl, J. F., 'The UN Commission on Human Rights and Cambodia, 1975–1980' (1996) **3** *Buffalo J. Int'l L.* 691.

Meron, T., *Bloody Constraints: War and Chivalry in Shakespeare* (Oxford University Press, 1998).

—— *War Crimes Law Comes of Age: Essays* (Clarendon Press, 1998).

Millar, M. S., *State of the Peoples: A Global Human Rights Report on Societies in Danger* (Beacon Press, 1993).

Minow, M., *Between Vengeance and Forgiveness: Facing History after Genocide and Mass Violence* (Beacon Press, 1998).

Momeni, M., 'Balancing the Procedural Rights of the Accused against a Mandate to Protect Victims and Witnesses: An Examination of the Anonymity Rules of the International Criminal Tribunal for the Former Yugoslavia' (1997) **41** *Harvard L. J.* 155.

Moore, J. N. (ed.), *Law and Civil War in the Modern World* (Johns Hopkins University Press, 1974).

Morosin, M. N., 'Double Jeopardy and International Law: Obstacles to Formulating a General Principle' (1995) **64** *Nordic J. Int'l L.* 261.

Morris, M., 'The Trials of Concurrent Jurisdiction: The Case of Rwanda' (1997) **7** *Duke J. Comp. & Int'l L.* 349.

Morris, S. J., *Why Vietnam Invaded Cambodia: Political Culture and the Causes of War* (Stanford University Press, 1999).

Morris, V., and Scharf, M. P., *An Insider's Guide to the International Criminal Tribunal for the Former Yugoslavia* (Transnational Publishers, 1995).

—— *An Insider's Guide to the International Criminal Tribunal for Rwanda* (Transnational Publishers, 1997).

Mullerson, R., and Scheffer, D. J., 'Legal Regulation of the Use of Force', in Damrosch, L. F., Danilenko, G. M., and Mullerson, R. (eds.), *Beyond Confrontation: International Law for the Post-Cold War Era* (Westview Press, 1995), 93.

Murphy, J. F., 'The Quivering Gulliver: US Views on a Permanent International Criminal Court' (2000) **34** *International Lawyer* 45.

Murphy, S. D., *Humanitarian Intervention: The United Nations in an Evolving World Order* (University of Pennsylvania Press, 1996).

—— 'Progress and Jurisprudence of the International Criminal Tribunal for the Former Yugoslavia' (1999) **93** *AJIL* 57.

Nanda, V. P. and Krieger, D., *Nuclear Weapons and the World Court* (Transnational Publishers, 1998).

NAHAPETIAN, K., 'Selective Justice: Prosecuting Rape in the International Criminal Tribunals for the Former Yugoslavia and Rwanda' (1999) 14 *Berkeley Women's L. J.* 126.

NEIER, A., *War Crimes: Brutality, Genocide, Terror, and the Struggle for Justice* (Random House/Times Books, 1998).

NSEREKO, D., 'Rules of Procedure and Evidence of the International Tribunal for the Former Yugoslavia' (1994) 5 *Crim. L. Forum* 507.

OPPENHEIM, J., and VAN DER WOLF, W. (eds.), *Global War Crimes Tribunal Collection* (Global Law Assoc., 1997–).

ORENTLICHER, D. F., 'Politics by Other Means: the Law of the International Criminal Court' (1999) 32 *Cornell Int'l L. J.* 489.

ORFORD, A., 'Locating the International: Military and Monetary Interventions after the Cold War' (1997) 38 *Harvard Int'l L. J.* 443.

O'SHEA, S., 'Interaction between International Criminal Tribunals and National Legal Systems' (1995–96) 28 *New York Univ. J. Int'l L. & Pol.* 367.

PAUST, J. J., 'It's No Defense: *Nullum Crimen*, International Crime and the Gingerbread Man' (1997) 60 *Albany L. Rev.* 657.

—— BASSIOUNI, M. C., WILLIAMS, S., SCHARF, M., GARULÉ, J., and ZUGARIS, B. (eds.), *International Criminal Law: Cases and Materials* (Carolina Press, 1996).

PEJIC, J., 'The ICC Statute: An Appraisal of the Rome Package' (2000) 34 *International Lawyer* 65.

PETERS, S., 'The Genocide Case: *Nulyarimma v. Thompson*' (1999) *Aust. Int'l L. J.* 233.

PICTET, J. (ed.), *Commentary: I Geneva Convention for the Amelioration of the Condition of the Wounded and Sick in Armed Forces in the Field* (ICRC, 1958).

—— (ed.), *Commentary: II Geneva Convention for the Amelioration of the Condition of Wounded, Sick and Shipwrecked Members of the Armed Forces at Sea* (ICRC, 1958).

—— (ed.), *Commentary: III Geneva Convention Relative to the Treatment of Prisoners of War* (ICRC, 1958).

—— (ed.), *Commentary: IV Geneva Convention Relative to the Protection of Civilian Persons in Time of War* (ICRC, 1958).

—— *Development and Principles of International Humanitarian Law* (Kluwer, 1985).

PILLOUD, C., SANDOZ, Y., SWINARSKI, C., and ZIMMERMANN, B. (eds.), *Commentary on the Additional Protocols of 8 June 1977 to the Geneva Conventions of 12 August 1949* (Kluwer, 1987).

PRITCHARD, R. J. (ed.), *The Tokyo Major War Crimes Trial*, 124 vols. (Edwin Mellen Press, 1998).

PRITCHARD, S. (ed.), *Indigenous Peoples, the United Nations and Human Rights* (Zed Books, 1998).

Proceedings, *Establishment of the International Criminal Court*, Seminar held in Helsinki, 23 Feb. 2000 (Ministry of Foreign Affairs of Finland, 2000).

RAILSBACK, K., 'A Genocide Convention Action Against the Khmer Rouge: Preventing a Resurgence of the Killing Fields' (1990) 5 *Connecticut J. Int'l L.* 457.

RAMUSSEN, M. A., 'Rules of Evidence for the International Criminal Court' (1995) 64 *Nordic J. Int'l L.* 275.

RANDALL, K. C., 'Universal Jurisdiction under International Law' (1988) 66 *Texas L. Rev.* 785.

RATNER, S. R., 'The United Nations Group

of Experts for Cambodia' (1999) **93** *AJIL* 948.

—— and ABRAMS, J. S., *Accountability for Human Rights Atrocities in International Law* (Clarendon, 1997).

RAYFUSE, R., and CODY, C., 'Genocide in Rwanda: Legal Responses of International Community and Rwandan Government' (1997) **6** *Human Rights Defender* 11.

REISMAN, W. M., and ANTONIOU, C. T. (eds.), *The Laws of War: A Comprehensive Collection of Primary Documents on International Laws Governing Armed Conflict* (Vintage Books, 1994).

REYDAMS, L., 'Universal jurisdiction over atrocities in Rwanda: Theory and practice' (1996) **1** *Euro. J. Crime, Crim. L. & Crim. Justice* 18.

RIFAAT, A., *International Aggression—A Study of the Legal Concept: Its Development and Definition in International Law* (Humanities Press, 1979).

ROBERGE, M-C., 'Jurisdiction of the *Ad Hoc* Tribunals for the Former Yugoslavia and Rwanda over Crimes against Humanity and Genocide' (1977) **37** *Int'l Rev. Red Cross* 651.

ROBERTS, A., and GUELFF, R. (eds.), *Documents on the Law of War*, 3rd ed. (Oxford University Press, 1999).

ROBERTSON, G., *Crimes Against Humanity: The Struggle for Global Justice* (Penguin, 1999).

ROBINSON, D., 'Defining "Crimes against Humanity" at the Rome Conference' (1999) **93** *AJIL* 43.

ROBINSON, M., 'Genocide, War Crimes, and Crimes Against Humanity' (1999) **23** *Fordham Int'l L. J.* 275.

ROBINSON, N., *The Genocide Convention: A Commentary* (Institute of Jewish Affairs (New York), 1960).

ROGERS, A. P. V., *Law on the Battlefield* (Manchester University Press, 1995).

ROGERS, G. C., 'Argentina's Obligation to Prosecute Military Officials for Torture' (1989) **20** *Columbia L. Rev.* 259.

ROHT-ARRAIZA, N., 'State Responsibility to Investigate and Prosecute Grave Human Rights Violations in International Law' (1990) **78** *California L. Rev.* 451.

—— *Impunity and Human Rights in International Law and Practice* (Oxford University Press, 1995).

—— 'Combating Impunity: Some Thoughts on the Way Forward' (1996) **59** *L. & Contemp. Probs.* 93.

RÖLING, B. V. A., *The Tokyo Trial and Beyond: Reflections of a Peacemonger* (Polity Press, 1993).

—— and RÜTER, C. F. (eds.), *The Tokyo Judgement: The International Military Tribunal for the Far East (I.M.T.F.E.), 29 April 1946–12 November 1948*, i (APA–University Press Amsterdam BV, 1977).

ROSENNE, S., *The World Court: What It Is and How It Works*, 5th ed. (Martinus Nijhoff, 1995), chap. 5.

ROSTOW, N., 'The Use of Force after the Cold War' (1991) **32** *Harvard Int'l L. J.* 411.

ROWE, P. J., *Defence: The Legal Implications—Military Law and the Laws of War* (Brassey's Defence Publishers, 1987).

—— 'The International Criminal Tribunal for Yugoslavia: the Decision of the Appeals Chamber on the Interlocutory Appeal on Jurisdiction in the *Tadic* Case' (1996) **45** *Int'l & Comp. L. Q.* 699.

SAUL, B., 'The International Crime of Genocide in Australian Law' (2000) **22** *Sydney Law Rev.* 527.

SCHABAS, W. A., 'Justice, Democracy and Impunity in Post Genocide Rwanda: Searching for Solutions to Impossible Problems' (1996) **7** *Crim. L. Forum* 523.

SCHABAS, W. A., 'Sentencing by International Tribunals: A Human Rights Approach' (1997) 7 *Duke J. Comp. & Int'l L.* 461.

—— *Genocide in International Law: the Crimes of Crimes* (Cambridge University Press, 2000).

SCHARF, M. P., *Balkan Justice: the Story behind the First International War Crimes Trial since Nuremberg* (Carolina Academic Press, 1997).

—— 'A Critique of the Yugoslavia War Crimes Tribunal' (1997) 25 *Denver J. Int'l L. & Policy* 305.

SCHEFFER, D. J., 'The United States and the International Criminal Court' (1999) 93 *AJIL* 12.

—— 'U.S. Policy and the International Criminal Court' (1999) 32 *Cornell Int'l L. J.* 529.

SCHELTEMA, C., and VAN DER WOLF, W., *The International Tribunal for Rwanda: Facts, Cases, Documents* (Global Law Association, 1999).

SCHWEBEL, S. M., 'Aggression, Intervention and Self-Defence in Modern International Law' (1972-II) 136 *Hague Recueil* 413.

—— 'The Role of the Security Council and the International Court of Justice in the Application of International Humanitarian Law' (1995) 27 *Int'l L. & Politics* 731.

SCHWELB, E., 'Crimes Against Humanity' (1946) 23 *BYBIL* 178.

SEWALL, S. B., AND KAYSEN, C. (eds.), *The United States and the International Criminal Court: National Security and International Law* (Rowman & Littlefield, 2000).

SHARP, Sr., W. G., 'International Obligations to Search for and Arrest War Criminals: Government Failure in the Former Yugoslavia?' (1997) 7 *Duke J. Comp. & Int'l L.* 411.

SHRAGA, D., and ZACKLIN, R., 'The International Criminal Tribunal for the Former Yugoslavia' (1994) 5 *Euro. J. Int'l L.* 367.

SIMONOVIC, I., 'The Role of the ICTY in the Development of International Criminal Adjudication' (1999) 23 *Fordham Int'l L. J.* 440.

SLAUGHTER, A.-M., 'The Long Arm of the Law', *Foreign Policy* (Spring, 1999), 34.

SMOLIN, D. M., 'The Future of Genocide: A Spectacle for the New Millennium?' (1999) 23 *Fordham Int'l L. J.* 460.

SORENSEN, C. E., 'Drug Trafficking on the High Seas: A Move Towards Universal Jurisdiction under International Law' (1990) 4 *Emory Int'l L. Rev.* 207.

SPRECHER, D. A., *Inside the Nuremberg Trial: A Prosecutor's Comprehensive Accounts*, 2 vols. (University Press of Americas, 1999).

STAPLETON, 'Ensuring a Fair Trial in the International Criminal Court: Statutory Interpretation and the Impermissibility of Derogation' (1999) 31 *New York Univ. J. Int'l L. & Pol.* 543.

STEINER, G. J., and ALSTON, P., *International Human Rights in Context: Law, Politics, Morals—Text and Materials* (Clarendon Press, 1996).

STEPHEN, N., *War Crimes Trials and the Future* (Centre for Int'l & Pub. L., Aust. Nat'l Univ., L. & Pol. Paper No. 10, 1998).

STERN, B., 'La compétence universelle en France: le cas des crimes commis en ex-Yougoslavie et au Rwanda' (1997) 40 *German. Y. B. Int'l L.* 280.

STONE, J., 'Hopes and Loopholes in the 1974 Definition of Aggression' (1997) 71 *AJIL* 224.

STOREY, M., '*Kruger v. Commonwealth*: Does Genocide Require Malice?' (1998) 21 *Univ. New South Wales L. J.* 224.

SUIKKARI, S., 'Debate in the United Nations on the International Law Commission's

Draft Statute for an International Criminal Court' (1995) **64** *Nordic J. Int'l L.* 205.

SUNGA, L. S., *Individual Responsibility in International Law for Serious Human Rights Violations* (Martinus Nijhoff, 1992).

—— *The Emerging System of International Criminal Law: Developments in Codification and Implementation* (Kluwer, 1997).

SWISS, S., and GILLER, J. E., 'Rape as a Crime of War: A Medical Perspective' (1993) **270** *J. American Medical Assoc.* 612.

Symposium, 'Toward an International Criminal Court? A Debate' (2000) **14** *Emory Int'l L. Rev.* 159.

TANAKA, T., 'Implementation of International Criminal Law: Reconsideration from the Perspective of Japanese Law' (1995) **38** *Japanese Annual Int'l L.* 65.

TATZ, C. (ed.), *Genocide Perspectives—Essays in Comparative Genocide* (Centre for Comparative Genocide Studies, Macquarie University, 1997).

—— *Genocide in Australia* (Research Discussion Paper No. 8, Australian Institute of Aboriginal and Torres Strait Islander Studies, 1999).

TAULBEE, J. L., 'A Call to Arms Declined: The United States and the International Criminal Court' (2000) **14** *Emory Int'l L. Rev.* 105.

TAVERNIER, P., 'The Experience of the International Criminal Tribunals for the Former Yugoslavia and for Rwanda' (1997) **321** *Int'l Rev. Red Cross* 605.

TEBBS, J., *Rwanda, War and Peace?!* (Global Law Association, 1999).

TENNANT, C. C., and TURPEL, M. E., 'A Case Study of Indigenous Peoples: Genocide, Ethnocide and Self-Determination' (1990) **59** *Nordic J. Int'l L.* 287.

THIEROFF, M., and AMLEY, Jr., E. A., 'Proceeding to Justice and Accountability in the Balkans: The International Criminal Tribunal for the Former Yugoslavia and Rule 61' (1998) **23** *Yale J. Int'l L.* 231.

TOMUSCHAT, C., 'Obligations for States without or against Their Will' (1993-IV) **241** *Hague Recueil* 195.

TRIFFTERER, O. (ed.), *Commentary on the Rome Statute of the International Criminal Court: Observers' Notes, Article by Article* (Nomos, 1999).

TUCK, R., *The Rights of War and Peace: Political Thought and the International Order from Grotius to Kant* (Oxford University Press, 1999).

TURNS, D., 'The International Criminal Tribunal for the Former Yugoslavia: The *Erdemovic* Case' (1998) **47** *Int'l & Comp. L. Q.* 461.

TZARTZOURAS, M. E., 'The Law of Humanitarian Intervention after Somalia' (1993) **46** *Revue Héllénique de Droit Int'l* 197.

UN Secretary-General, *Historical Survey of the Question of International Criminal Jurisdiction: Memorandum submitted by the Secretary-General* (United Nations, 1949).

US General Accounting Office, *Former Yugoslavia: War Crimes Tribunal's Workload Exceed Capacity* (US Govt. Doc. GAO/NSIAD-98–134, 1998).

VAN DEN WIJNGAERT, C., *The Political Offence Exception to Extradition: The delicate problem of balancing the rights of the individual and the international public order* (Kluwer, 1980).

VAN DER VYVER, J. D., 'Prosecution and Punishment of the Crime of Genocide' (1999) **23** *Fordham Int'l L. J.* 286.

—— 'Personal and Territorial Jurisdiction of the International Criminal Court' (2000) **14** *Emory Int'l L. Rev.* 1.

VAN SCHAACK, B., 'The Crime of Political Genocide: Repairing the Geneva Convention's Blind Spot' (1997) **106** *Yale L. J.* 2259.

VAN SCHAACK, B., 'The Definition of Crimes Against Humanity: Resolving the Incoherence' (1999) 37 *Columbia J. Transnat'l L.* 787.

VERDIRAME, G., 'The Genocide Definition in the Jurisprudence of the *Ad Hoc* Tribunals' (2000) 49 *Int'l & Comp. L. Q.* 578.

VETTER, G. R., 'Command Responsibility of Non-Military Superiors in International Criminal Court (ICC)' (2000) 25 *Yale J. Int'l L.* 89.

VILLALPANDO, S., 'L'affaire Pinochet: beaucoup de bruit pour rien? L'apport au droit international de la décision de la chambre des Lords du 24 mars 1999' (2000) 104 *Revue Générale de Droit Int'l Public* 393.

VON HEBEL, H. A. M., LAMMERS, J. G., and SCHUKKING, J. (eds.), *Reflections on the International Criminal Court: Essays in Honour of Adriaan Bos* (Kluwer, 1999).

VON STERNBERG, M. R., 'A Comparison of the Yugoslav and Rwandan War Crimes Tribunals: Universal Jurisdiction and the "Elementary Dictates of Humanity"' (1996) 22 *Brooklyn J. Int'l L.* 111.

WALDOCK, C. H. M., 'The Regulation of the Use of Force by Individual States in International Law' (1952-II) 81 *Hague Recueil* 467.

WARBRICK, C., 'Co-operation with the International Criminal Tribunal for Yugoslavia' (1996) 45 *Int'l & Comp. L. Q.* 947.

WATTS, A., 'Legal Position in International Law of Heads of States, Heads of Government and Foreign Ministers' (1994) 247 *Hague Recueil* 1.

WEDGWOOD, R., 'The International Criminal Court: An American View' (1999) 10 *Euro. J. Int'l L.* 93.

—— 'The United States and the International Criminal Court: Achieving a Wider Consensus Through the "Ithaca Package"' (1999) 32 *Cornell Int'l L. J.* 535.

—— 'International Criminal Law and Augusto Pinochet' (2000) 40 *Virginia J. Int'l L.* 829.

WEISBURD, A. M., *Use of Force: The Practice of States Since World War II* (Pennsylvania State University Press, 1997).

WEXLER, L. S., 'The Interpretation of the Nuremberg Principles by the French Court of Cassation: From *Touvier* to *Barbie* and Back Again' (1994) 32 *Columbia J. Transnat'l L.* 289.

WEILER, J. H. H., CASSESE, A., and SPINEDI, M. (eds.), *International Crimes of State* (De Gruyter, 1989).

WHITEMAN, M. M. (ed.), *Digest of International Law*, x & xi (US Govt. Printing Office, 1968).

WIPPMAN, D., 'Atrocities, Deterrence, and the Limits of International Justice' (1999) 23 *Fordham Int'l L. J.* 473.

WOETZEL, R. K., *The Nuremberg Trials in International Law* (Stevens & Sons, 1962).

YEO, S., 'Mistakenly Obeying Unlawful Superior Orders' (1993) 5 *Bond L. Rev.* 1.

GENERAL INDEX